THE

EDGAR CAYCE

COMPANION

A comprehensive treatise of the Edgar Cayce readings
compiled and published by B. Ernest Frejer

11th Printing, July 2011

To LISA ANNE and SAMANTHA JADE

A.R.E. Press
215 67th Street
Virginia Beach, VA 23451-2061

Library of Congress Cataloging-in-Publication Data
Cayce, Edgar 1877-1945
    The Edgar Cayce companion : a comprehensive treatise of the Edgar Cayce readings / compiled by B. Ernest Frejer.
        p.   cm.
    Includes index.
    ISBN 13: 978-0-87604-357-8
    1. Parapsychology. 2. Occultism. 3. Spiritual Life. I. Frejer, B. Ernest, 1937- . II. Cayce, Edgar, 1877-1945. Edgar Cayce readings. III. Title
BF1031.C456   1995
133.8'092—dc20   95-44660

The study from the human standpoint, of subconscious, subliminal, psychic, soul forces, is and should be the great study for the human family, for through self man will understand its Maker when it understands its relation to its Maker, and it will only understand that through itself, and that understanding is the knowledge as is given here in this state.   3744-4

Think on these things. For here ye may find not only the key to thine nature but that which may unlock the...mysteries of life itself in relationship to thy dealing with thy fellow man.   954-1

A SEEKER'S PRAYER

Give me the eyes to see the truth,
Give me the heart to feel the truth,
And the courage to follow its light.
Let my search for truth and knowledge
Lead to the wisdom of love,
The desire to be helpful to others.

WHO WAS EDGAR CAYCE?

The only son in a family of five children, Edgar Cayce was born on a farm near Hopkinsville, Kentucky, on March 18, 1877.

Signs of his psychic sensitivities were evident as a child. He often reported seeing and conversing with his deceased grandfather and invisible playmates. Later he described some of these early experiences: "When I was possibly eighteen or twenty months old, I had a playhouse in the back of an old garden, among the honeysuckle and other flowers. One afternoon my mother came down the garden walk calling me. My playmate (who appeared to me to be about the same size as myself) was with me. It never occurred to me that he was not real, or that he wasn't one of the neighbors' children, until my mother spoke and asked me my playmate's name. I turned to ask him but he disappeared.

"A few years afterward (when I had grown to be six or seven years old) our home was in a little wood. Here I learned to talk with the trees or it appeared that they talked with me. It was there that I read the Bible through the first time, that I learned to pray, that I had many visions and experiences; not only of visioning the elves but what seemed to me to be the hosts that must have appeared to the people of old, as recorded in Genesis particularly. To describe these elves of the trees, the fairies of the woods, or--to me--the angels or hosts, with all their beautiful and glorious surroundings would be almost a sacrilege."

It was also there in the woods that he visioned an angelic lady, who asked him what he would like most of all, and his reply was, "To be helpful to others, and especially to children when they are sick." Using an unusual gift that he was soon to discover, Edgar Cayce devoted most of his life to the fulfillment of this childhood desire.

In school he was a poor student, until one evening, after wrestling with a spelling lesson and receiving many rebuffs from his father for stupidity, he got the idea that a short sleep would be helpful. After his father consented to this unexpected request, he said, "I closed the book, and leaning on the back of the chair went to sleep. At the end of five minutes I handed my father the book. I not only knew my lesson, but I could then spell any word in the book; not only spell the words but could tell on what page and what line the word would be found. From that day on I had little trouble in school, for I would read my lesson, sleep on it a few minutes, and then be able to repeat every word of it."

However, it was not until 1901, when Edgar Cayce was twenty-four that his fuller psychic potential was discovered. For no apparent reason he had lost his voice and could scarcely speak above a whisper for at least one year. Even attempts to obtain a cure through hypnosis failed because he would not respond to post-hypnotic suggestion. Edgar felt the same condition taking place when hypnotized as he did when putting himself to sleep, so a noted New York hypnotist suggested that maybe Edgar could talk about his own case while asleep.

So, on March 31, 1901, Edgar Cayce, in a self-induced state of unconsciousness was given a suggestion, by a local hypnotist, to see his body and describe the trouble in his throat. His response was, "Yes, we see the body. In the normal physical state this body is unable to speak, due to a partial paralysis of the inferior muscles of the vocal cords, produced by nerve strain. This is a psychological condition producing a physical effect. This may be removed by increasing the circulation to the affected parts by suggestion while in this unconscious state."

The indicated suggestion was given, and blood could be seen rushing to his throat. When awake, his voice had returned. This unconscious diagnosis was Cayce's very first reading. The very next day, using the hypnotist as a test case, Cayce demonstrated that he could also correctly diagnose other people.

Cayce had previously chosen photography as a vocation because it seemed compatible with his vocal handicap. In 1935, he recalled, "I finally selected photography as a life work and gave only my spare time and evenings to the increasing number of requests for readings. It was only when I began to come in contact with those who received help from following the suggestions given in the readings that I began to realize the true nature of the work which lay before me."

However, it was not until the readings saved his wife's life and his son's eyesight that he decided to use his gift full-time to diagnose illnesses. Treatments, usually involving diet, eliminations and exercise, were given to improve the over-all health of the patient, although sometimes the instructions were as surprising as the cure was dramatic.

He was initially fearful that these 'physical' readings might prove harmful, so the policy of recording all the readings for the benefit of the patient and the attending physician was initiated.

In 1923, a wealthy printer from Ohio eagerly suggested that the sleeping Cayce expand his readings to include virtually any topic, such as, the meaning and purpose of life, philosophy, psychic phenomena, astrology, and Biblical history. Intrigued by the prospect of answering questions on such universal topics, Cayce agreed to try.

The experiment was a surprising success, although the sleeping Cayce introduced subjects that were completely alien to his fundamentalist Christian beliefs. However, in time, even the theory of reincarnation became an integral part of his own thinking. In his own words, "I certainly believe that the information contained in hundreds of readings in our files helps clarify and explain the Bible for me."

Where did the unconscious Cayce get his information? He suggested that, "There would seem to be not only one, but several sources of information that I tap when in this sleeping condition.

"One source is, apparently, the record that an individual or entity makes in all its expressions through what we call time. The sum-total of that soul is written, so to speak in the subconscious of the individual as well as in what is known as the Akashic records. Anyone may read these records if they can attune themselves properly.

"Some people think the information coming through me is given by some departed personality who wants to communicate with them, or some benevolent spirit or physician from the other side. This may sometimes be the case, though in general I am not a medium in that sense of the term. However, if a person comes seeking that kind of contact and information, I believe he receives it."

In a lecture given by Cayce in 1933, he alludes to the Book of Life, or the Akashic Record, as the readings call it. "I would like to give an experience which I have had at infrequent intervals for many years, during the time when I am in the unconscious (so-called) or super-conscious state. The experience has come eight or ten times while giving life readings for individuals. I remember nothing of the reading, but have a very vivid impression of the following. This may help you to understand your own experiences.

"I knew my spirit, mind or soul was separated from my body and that it was seeking information for another. I passed into outer darkness, so dark that it actually hurt--yet there was a stream of light that I knew I must follow, and nothing on either side of the light must detract from my purpose to receive for that other what it was seeking in the way of aid for itself.

"As I passed along the line of light I became conscious of forms of movement crowding toward the light. Coming to the next plane (if we choose to call it such), I realized that the forms of movement or figures were taking shape as humans...rather the exaggeration of human desires. Passing a little farther, these forms were gradually lost; still I had the consciousness that they were seeking the light--or more light. Then the figures gradually took form, continually coming toward the light.

"Finally I passed through a place where individuals appeared much as they do today--men and women--but satisfied with their position. The number of individuals in this state of satisfaction continued to grow, and then there were homes and cities where they were content to continue as they were.

"Still following the light, which grew stronger and stronger, I heard music in the beyond. Then there came a space where all was spring-time, all was a-blossom, all was summer. Some were happy, some desired to remain, but many were pressing on and on to the place where there might be greater understanding, more light, more to be gained. Then I reached a place where I was seeking the records of the lives of people that lived in the earth.

"Don't ever think that your life isn't written in the Book of Life! I found it! I have seen it! It is being written; YOU are the writer!"

The readings typically describe the source of information as: "In this state the conscious mind becomes subjugated to the subconscious, superconscious or soul mind; and may and does communicate with like minds, and the subconscious or soul becomes universal. From any subconscious mind information may be obtained."

In his global predictions, Cayce foresaw the end of Russian Communism as we knew it. In 1932, he stated that "changes are coming, this may be sure--an evolution, or revolution, in the ideas of religious thought. The basis of it for the world will eventually come out of Russia; not Communism, no!--but rather that which is the basis of same, as Christ taught--His kind of Communism."

In 1943, Cayce predicted that serious international disputes, due to religious and economic differences, would eventually arise. Apparently, the increased economic interdependence, that is taking place, will be aggravated by the lack of a stable international currency, to such a degree, that "there may indeed be another war over just such conditions."

Frequently while in trance, Cayce spoke in other languages, and on one occasion a Greek scholar asked him to speak in Greek; he broke out in Homeric Greek, as if he were living in that period.

Even in the waking state, there seemed to be no limit to his clairvoyant and psychic powers. His ability to see and read auras made him keenly aware of people's emotional state and health.

On more than one occasion, he reluctantly used his telepathic powers to demonstrate the awesome potential power of the mind to direct and influence the actions of other people without their knowledge. He didn't continue such mental exercises because he thought it was wrong and dangerous.

His clairvoyance interfered with his total enjoyment of card games. If he made a concentrated effort, no card in the deck was hidden from him. Asleep or awake, very little seemed hidden from him, as he demonstrated by reading someone else's mail while asleep, or by writing down the correct combination to a bank safe in the presence of the stunned banker.

Many humorous incidents and spectacular cures are contained in several fascinating biographies of his life; in fact, the University of Chicago accepted a Ph.D thesis based on his life and work.

His life was not easy; there were times when he was faced with the laughter of ignorant crowds, the scorn of tabloid headlines, the cold smirks of self-satisfied intellectuals, the anger of accusing doctors, and the indifference of greedy businessmen who wanted to exploit the readings.

Cayce charged very little for his readings because of his sincere desire to help the needy and the suffering. Consequently, the Cayces were desperately poor at times, but this did not sway him to accept offers of fame and fortune, by those who wanted to commercialize the readings.

In most cases Cayce never met the recipients of readings who were usually hundreds of miles away. His wife, Gertrude, would suggest to the sleeping Cayce to direct his mind to the recipient of the reading and after he replied "Yes, we have the body," she would ask the questions. Cayce's delivery seemed effortless even though trance readings are energy depleting. His lifelong secretary, Gladys Davis Turner, recorded everything in shorthand.

By 1943 the demand for readings was mounting so he unselfishly gave four to six readings a day, instead of the usual two. In August, 1944, suffering from over exertion and edema of the lungs, he collapsed, and the following month had a stroke. His last reading given for himself, was not followed by the doctors in charge and so on January 3, 1945, Edgar Cayce's soul was freed to continue its celestial journey.

INTRODUCTION

The transcripts of more than 14,000 readings given by Edgar Cayce between 1901 and 1945 are available for examination and study in the library of the Edgar Cayce Foundation, Virginia Beach, Virginia.

A break-down of these readings indicates that: 68% are Physical Readings concerned with the diagnosis and treatment of physical ailments; 14% are Life Readings on past and present incarnations; 5% involve business inquiries; 4% give dream interpretations; 3% answer questions related to the nature of the mind and soul, and the remaining 6% are readings containing miscellaneous topics.

Each reading was given a number. A number such as 3744-2 indicates the second reading for entity 3744.

In 1931 the Association for Research and Enlightenment, Inc. (A.R.E.), was established as a non-profit, open-membership, educational organization, concerned with the presentation and publication of the readings.

This book is a comprehensive compendium of the Edgar Cayce readings, all under a single cover. The intention was to organize the readings so that the main ideas and principles involved would usually be reasonably transparent to the student, without the author interjecting additional explanatory comments. In order to make the manuscript easy to study from and to add continuity to such a diverse collection of material, the following guidelines were adopted.

Similar topics within each of the ten chapters are adjacent to each other. Similar readings within each topic are also adjacently placed. The meticulously selected readings and titles for the 264 topics generally emphasize a recurring theme or key principle. The index's extensive synthesis and cross-referencing of similar or connected ideas should also be helpful in unifying ideas and in suggesting new ones.

Topics that are historical in nature are arranged chronologically, resulting in a continuous story and not just a compilation of distinct readings. The life of Jesus in chapter six and Atlantean and Egyptian history in chapter ten are examples of this.

It should be kept in mind, that each reading was given to a specific entity, with unique psychological and physical needs and desires. However, the readings selected usually contain a guiding principle, common to many readings, that probably has universal application.

Hopefully this organization of the readings will provide insights into the more cryptic readings and into the mysteries of life itself. This compilation should nicely complement the CD-ROM disc containing all of the readings.

Regarding the literal interpretation of things and dates, prophetic or otherwise, the following personal viewpoint may be helpful. The readings and the Bible agree that "As was given of Him, not given to man to know the time or period of the end (364-8)," and regarding future earth upheavals, "As to specific date or time at present this may not be given (270-32)." This suggests that if seers divulge specific dates, of significant global events, their literal or common interpretation may be incorrect.

Three different dates were given for Jesus' birth and the explanation was that different time points of reference were used. In general, uncertainty in a time reference point could leave the year, century, and even the millennium of a given date in doubt. In addition to the unknown reference point, the symbolism or numerological implication of number dates must also be considered when we are confronted with dates such as 36 (world catastrophe), 69 (rising of Atlantis) and 98 (end of an age). For example, the Bible uses the number 40 years to represent a testing period and I believe the 40 year period 58 to 98 is what Cayce referred to when he said we are "entering the testing period (5749-2)." Such Biblical similarities should not be surprising because the readings do have a Biblical flavor, and reading 1770-2 states that most numerology "may be gained from the ONE BOOK--the Bible!" For any number, in any context, there is always the possibility of a symbolic or esoteric interpretation.

More generally, the readings state, "There is that as may be said to be the literal and the spiritual and the metaphysical interpretation of almost all portions of the Scripture...Yet all of these to be true, to be practical, to be applicable in the experiences of individuals, must coordinate; or be as one, even as the Father, the Son and the Holy Spirit." The three-fold nature of life and consciousness is a central unifying principle of the readings. Typical statements are: "The basis, the beginning of law carries all the way through. And that which comes or begins first is conceived in spirit, grows in the mental, manifests in the material (2072-10)," or, "That we find in the spirit taketh form in the mind. Mind becomes the builder. The physical body is the result (3359-1)," or, "There is the pattern in the material or physical plane of every condition as exists in the cosmic or spiritual plane (5756-4)." This reminds us of the Hermetic idiom, 'as above so below'. Emanual Swedenborg makes exhaustive use of this 'Law of Correspondence' to unlock many secrets hidden in the Bible. According to him, a knowledge of correspondence was the foremost knowledge of the ancient people. To further emphasize this correspondence, note, "The fourth dimension then being that condition as is reached wherein physical objects are spiritually understood, spiritual objects are physically understood (900-66)."

This correspondence and the three-fold nature of life are often abstractly couched in phrases such as "purposes, hopes, desires (1747-5)," or, "cause, effect, and purpose...time, space and patience (3412-2)." Reading 5749-7 states that the three Wise Men as well as the three countries, Egypt, Persia and India, "represent in the metaphysical sense the three phases of man's experience...body, mind, soul." Concerning the Book of Revelation the readings state, "all places--as Egypt or Sodom or the Crucifixion, or the Lord--are conditions, circumstances, experiences, as well as individual places (281-33)." Similarly, in the readings Zu, Og and On sometimes name a person and sometimes a place.

Sometimes, instead of identifying one's past life with a specific exalted entity such as Hermes, Noah or Iltar, etc., it makes more sense to regard these names as classifications of archetypical spiritual or mental lineages that we may have been, or are associated with, for, "The law of environment, relativity, heredity, is the same in the spiritual activity as in material earthly--**matter** conditions (683-1)."

The readings consistently identify Spirit with Power (1472-1) or the Motivative Influence (262-123). It is crucial to remember, that "Mind is indeed the Builder...what is held in the act of mental vision becomes a reality in the material experience (906-3)," and "We are gradually builded to that image created within our own mental being (270-17)." The Mind is also often referred to as the Way (1348-1) which "leads to the Christ (281-63)," and in (254-92) Christ Jesus is referred to as a Guide. Using these descriptions of Mind and Spirit, consider the following event in the readings, in which an allegorical interpretation, as well as a literal one, seems quite natural.

The readings say that the Great Pyramid was constructed under the authority and direction of Ra Ta the Priest, and with Hermes as the guide or construction architect, and with Isis as the advisor (294-151). Legend associates Hermes with learning, knowledge, or the mind. In terms of a trinity, the above readings corroborate the following correspondences. The Priest clearly represents spirit, power and the motivative influence. Hermes, the construction architect and guide, represents the mind that builds, and that leads the way, and the result is a manifestation in mother earth represented by Isis.

Again, regarding the literal interpretation of numbers, is it merely a coincidence that in a sequence of readings the similar numbers 10,500 (5748-5) and 10,500,000 (5748-2) were used to date a period or periods in prehistoric Egypt? The history of the Great Pyramid is interwoven with this period which is so incredibly remote that the geographical and anthropological state of the world was astonishingly different than now. Throughout history we see new cities, temples, and pyramids built on or near the disintegrating rubble of more ancient ones (5748-6, 195-14). The original structure of the Great Pyramid may also have disintegrated eons ago, as was the case with its contemporary the Temple Beautiful (281-25). In which case the Great Pyramid could have been suitably modified or reconstructed several times, permitting the latter date of 10,500,000 years ago to be applicable also! This latter date is a little more consistent with science's growing knowledge of the kind of global changes the readings espouse, including the sinking and shifting of continents and the resulting disappearance of advanced ancient civilizations. It behooves us to keep an open mind and give science a chance to find the truth, for, "Do **not**...make claims that are not able to be verified, from **every** angle (254-88)," and "It is not meant that information given through this channel should be interpreted as being infallible (1472-14)."

Phrases such as "Before the Prince of Peace came," are also often used in the readings as a point of reference. However, Jesus had many incarnations, one of which was Melchizedek, also referred to as a prince of peace (2072-4). In this connection note, "There has never been an experience when His Christ-mass, His death, His birth, wasn't an experience of the age (281-33)."

A book could be written to further illustrate the need to exercise caution when attempting to peek behind the veil of time and space. Truth is a growing thing (1554-6), consciousness evolves and uses matter as a vehicle for its expression, and unanswered questions will, and must, always remain. In our search for answers, let us not lose sight of the readings' central message of love and service.

I suggest that most prophetic dates of global significance, which don't have a symbolic intention, are primarily given for the benefit of future generations that will witness the fulfilling of prophecy and will therefore be in a better position to decipher and appreciate the original intended meaning of certain dates. This hindsight of global predictability could leave a profound impression that everything is according to natural law (1885-2, 3902-2), a divine pattern. As a consequence, many peoples' faith and courage, perhaps during chaotic and trying times, would probably be strengthened.

Free will and the law of averages make the individual, groups and classes, less predictable than the general mass of people. However, precise foreknowledge of global events is not for us to know. Every entity is guided from within, in a manner consistent with its karmic pattern. Global catastrophe to the individual may just be a cleansing action from a more universal perspective, for, "What is God? Law and Love (3574-2)," and Love and Law bring order out of chaos.

To include such a large number of topics in one book of reasonable size, it was usually necessary and desirable, that portions of readings that do not focus one's attention on the main idea presented, be omitted. A portion omitted is indicated by the usual three dots. In a few readings (e.g. 2109-2, page 228) one word or phrase was inserted in brackets, in order to make sense out of a fragmented reading. Biblical references were also inserted in brackets, wherever such quotes exist.

Where applicable a question **Q-** answer **A-** format is in place. **Q-** indicates the original question asked, or information requested. In a few cases only part of a long and possibly awkward question was included, in order to save space. In "Massage and Oil Rub Therapy," and in "Castor Oil Pack Therapy," I simply listed, under **Q-**, many of the ailments associated with this treatment and then gave a 'typical' answer under **A-**.

The words or phrases in bold type indicate ideas that were stressed by the inflection of Cayce's voice during a reading.

Occasionally the exact word listed in the index does not appear on the required page, but the same 'idea' does.

I don't believe these few editorial aids will in any way misrepresent or bias the essential message of any particular topic. With the exception of these editorial aids, every possible effort has been made to keep the text consistent with the original transcripts of the readings.

B. Ernest Frejer
Guelph, Ontario

CONTENTS

CONTENTS

PART V
EVOLUTION OF MIND AND MATTER

PART VI
RELIGION, THE BIBLE AND JESUS THE CHRIST

PART VII
THE CARE AND FUNCTION OF THE BODY

PART VIII
SELECTING AND PREPARING FOODS

PART IX
ATTITUDES AND EMOTIONS

PART X
PAST AND FUTURE WORLD CONDITIONS

THE

EDGAR CAYCE

COMPANION

PART I

SPIRITUAL ASSOCIATIONS AND THE TRINITY

THE AKASHIC RECORD AND ITS INTERPRETATION

Q-The Book of Life is?
A-The record that the individual entity itself writes upon the skein of time and space, through patience--and is opened when self has attuned to the infinite, and may be read by those attuning to that consciousness.
Q-The Book of God Remembrances is?
A-This is the Book of Life.
Q-The Akashic Records are?
A-Those made by the individual, as just indicated.   2533-8

Q-Akashic Records are recorded on the ether. Then, cannot an instrument be invented to induct ether and thus tap in on the Akashic Records?
A-...This may be done--eventually will be!   443-5

All force, all matter, is motivative by force known as spiritual. While the body is made up of elements that are atomic, super atomic, gas, influences that combine, all give off their radiation, both as to the mental reaction and what the body-mind does about that reaction of that phase or manifestation in which the entity is conscious at such a period. And it is recorded upon that known or experienced by the conscious mind as time and space. And it may be read even as the records of a printed page. Hence that which has been the thought, the activity of the entity throughout its experience in matter, in gaseous forces, in the atomic influences, is part and parcel of the entity's being. Thus we are, then, the sum, the substance, of that we do, we have, or may think and do. For each entity has that imprint of the Creative Energies or Force that makes of it an influence that is seen, known, felt, throughout the universe.   833-1

The Akashic Records are as these:
Activity of **any** nature, as of the voice, as of a light made, produced in the natural forces those of a motion--which pass on, or are upon, the record of that as time. As may be illustrated in the atomic vibration as set in motion for those in that called audition, or the radio in its

activity. It passes even faster than time itself. Hence **light** forces pass much faster, but the records are upon the esoteric, or etheric, or Akashic forces, as they go along upon the wheels of time, the wings of time, or in **whatever** dimension we may signify as a matter of its momentum or movement. Hence, as the forces that are attuned to those various incidents, periods, times, places, may be accorded to the record, the **contact** as of the needle upon the record, how perfect an attunement of the instrument used as the reproducer of same is attuned to those **keepers**--as may be termed--**of** those records. What would be indicated by the keepers? That as just given, that they are the records upon the wings or the wheel of time itself. Time, as that as of space--as inter-between. That inter-between, that which is, that of which, that from one object to another when in matter is of the same nature, or what that is is what the other is, only changed in its vibration to produce that element, or that force, as is termed in man's terminology as **dimensions** of space, or **dimensions** that give it, what-ever may be the solid, gas, or what **its form** or dimension.   364-6

The record as is builded by an entity is to the mental world as the cinema is to the physical world, as pictured in its activity. So, in the direction to an entity and its entrance into the material plane in a given period, time, place--which indicate the relative universal sources--then one only turns, as it were, to those **records** in the akashian forms to read that period of that builded or that lost during **that** experience.   275-19

This film (between time and space) is the difference between the movement **of** the atomic force about its center and the impression that is made **upon** those passing **between** light and heat, not darkness, for darkness may not exist where light has found its way. Though you may not be conscious or aware of its existence, its rays from the very records of time and space turn their emanations to give to a finite mind the dimensions themselves.   490-1

These records are **not** as pictures on a screen, not as written words, but are as active forces in the life of an entity, and are **often**--as may be surmised--**in**describable in words...The **attempt** is made, which makes often an inadequate way of expressing or signifying that that is **intended to** be transmitted to the entity or individual **seeking** such information. Nevertheless, it be **correct**--but do not make the mistake, as has often been given through these channels, of attempting to discern **spiritual** interpretations with a **material** mind, nor **material** interpretations with the spiritual mind, **unless** same is signified by that of the incident, accident, or state of being is **emblematical**, or of any activity that is of the nature that **represents** a condition--see? 288-27

How well the record may be given depends upon how well that which has been made may be interpreted by one who may read such records. As to how true the interpretation is depends upon how strong the desire of such a soul is, or how well those responsible for such an activity of a soul may be in accord or attuned to those realms of experience.   559-7

The light moves on in time, in space, and upon that skein between same are the records written by each soul in its activity through eternity; through its awareness...not only in matter but in thought.   815-2

That done and that thought, becomes as a living record...in whatever sphere of consciousness this activity may be.   1292-1

The purposes for each soul's experience in materiality are that the Book of Remembrance may be opened that the soul may know its relationship to its Maker.   1215-4

The Akashic Record may be said to be Destiny in the entrance of a soul into materiality.   903-23

The records made by...the activity of **energy** expended leave its imprint upon the etheric wave that records between time and space that **desired** to be put, as to that impelling or producing...
Then, this body through whom the information comes being in accord or attune, by the subjugation of consciousness into materiality, becomes the channel through which such records may be read.
The interpretation of the records, then, depends upon how good a reader the body is, or how well in accord with the varied experiences through which the entity seeking has passed--or the records that have been made by that soul. Hence there may be much more of a detailed record read of an experience through which both souls passed, then of environs that were not a portion of that soul so interpreting the activities.   416-2

Interpretations of these (records) may vary somewhat, dependent upon what phases the approach is made. In the same manner that in material experiences entities, viewing an event or happening, are prompted to give **their** version according to the reaction upon their ideal--and upon those promptings of the purpose of the individual so viewing same. 1448-2

In giving the interpretations of the records of this entity, much appears upon the record in symbol.   2498-1

All bodies radiate those vibrations with which it, the body, controls itself in mental, in physical, and such radiation is called the aura. The mediums, or a psychic in certain phases of psychic phenomena, gain their impressions from such radiation...

As related to the psychic work of Edgar Cayce, this we find quite a different radiation. One (mediums, as given) working from without, as the psychic forces manifested in Edgar Cayce radiating from within. The radiation from an individual may be wholly the soul and spirit radiation, as from mental. The radiation may be material, from debased thoughts, or from animal portions as radiate through the individuals manifesting such radiation; hence the variation in the interpretation of radiation by a medium. Some gaining then, as we see, the purely soul and spirit relations of the individual, others gaining those of the material nature. The development, the ability of the medium in such conditions, then tempering the messages as obtained and radiated, or tempered again by the ability in mental forces of such medium to express same to the individual from which such message is obtained.   5756-1

Q-Explain from what sources this information may be obtained?

A-Conditions, thoughts, activities of men in **every** clime are things; as thoughts are things. They make their impressions upon the skein of time and space...They become as records that may be read by those in accord or **attuned** to such a condition.   3976-16

Whether the messages presented through such a channel as this are worthy of consideration--and by what standard ye shall judge.

For what was the judgment, what **is** the judgment, what will ever be the judgment? They that deny that He hath come in the flesh are not worthy of acceptation. They that give thee that which is not helpful, hopeful, and patient and humble, and not condemning any, are not worthy.

Q-Is the source of this information a group source, an individual source, or a recorded source?

A-As has so often been given, this is rather of the universal. That which is recorded may be read. That which is written may be interpreted. That which is individual may be had. But it is also a constructive source, so only gives that which is helpful if it will be applied.

When an individual seeks for personal or bodily aid, it is part and parcel of that individual and is read by and through the real desire of the seeker. When it is the Life Source, it is recorded upon space and time...Hence **all** may be touched, **all** may be drawn upon.   254-95

Many an one may question you as to the sources, as to the channel through which such information that may be given you at this time has come. Know it has reached that which is as high for each of you in your respective development as you have merited, and do merit...

Not only then must the information be instructive enlightening: yet it must also be given that it may be a **practical** thing in the experience of thine own self.   3976-15

In this (trance) state the conscious mind is under subjugation of the subconscious or soul mind. The information...is obtained through the power of mind over mind, or power of mind over matter, or obtained by the suggestion as given to the active part of the subconscious mind. It obtains its information from that which it has gathered, either from other subconscious minds--put in touch with the power of the suggestion of the mind controlling and speaking faculties of this body, or from minds that have passed into the Beyond, which leave their impressions and are brought in touch by the power of the suggestion. What is known to one subconscious mind or soul is known to another.

Q-Is this information always correct?

A-Correct in so far as the suggestion is in the proper channel or in accord with the action of the subconscious or soul matter.   254-2

In this state the conscious mind becomes subjugated to the subconscious, superconscious or soul mind; and may and does communicate with like minds, and the subconscious or soul force becomes universal. From any subconscious mind information may be obtained, either from this plane or from impressions as left by individuals that have gone before. 3744-2

It is not meant that information given through this channel should be interpreted as being infallible.   1472-14

In seeking information there are certain factors in the experience of the seeker and in the channel through which such information might come. Desire on the part of the seeker to be shown. And, as an honest seeker, such will not be too gullible; neither will such be so encased in prejudices as to doubt that which is applicable in the experience of such seeker. Hence the information must not only be practical, but it must be rather in accord with the desires of the seeker also...

On the part of the channel through whom such information may come, there must be the unselfish desire to be of aid to a fellow man. Not as for self-exaltation because of being a channel...

What prevents the information from always being accurate, or being wholly of unquestionable nature? The fact that such information must be interpreted in material things. And that then depends upon how well the training of the physical-mental self is in picturizing, visualizing and wording that which takes place in such a communion.   531-2

When the body, Edgar Cayce, is in the psychic or subconscious condition, he is able then to reach all the subconscious minds, when directed to such subconscious minds by suggestion, whether in the material world or in the spiritual world, provided the spiritual entity has not passed entirely into that condition where the radiation, or the relative forces, are superseded by other radiations. Then we only reach those radiations left in earth's plane that are taken again when entering in earth's plane, whether entity is conscious of same or not. The consciousness of reaching that condition wherein the physical body may take up that truth known, must be reached by all.   900-22

Edgar Cayce's mind is amenable to suggestion, the same as all other subconscious minds, but in addition thereto it has the power to interpret to the objective mind of others what it acquires from the subconscious mind of other individuals of the same kind. The subconscious mind forgets nothing. The conscious mind receives the impression from without and transfers all thought to the subconscious, where it remains even though the conscious be destroyed. The subconscious mind of Edgar Cayce is in direct communication with all other subconscious minds, and is capable of interpreting through his objective mind and imparting impressions received to other objective minds, gathering in this way all knowledge possessed by millions of other subconscious minds.   294-1

How (some would ask) did the body, Edgar Cayce, or soul, attune self at that particular period (deceased entities were speaking through him) and yet not remember in the physical consciousness that conversation?...
If the body, from its material and mental development, were to be wholly conscious of that through which it passes in its **soul's** activity in such realms, the strain would be so great...as to become demented in its relationship. And he is thought crazy enough anyway! 5756-14

Q-If Edgar Cayce goes into trance without any control, could he not in a waking state get inspiration direct?
A-Not until there has been a more perfect cleansing of the carnal influences in the experiences of the soul, as has been indicated. With the regeneration that should come into the experience of the entity, this then may be the manner, the channel, the way through which much of constructive forces may be given.
Q-What entity is giving this information?
A-Being directed...from the records through Halaliel.   507-1

Mental or material consciousness is laid aside through the subjugation of that consciousness. Thus there is brought into the material plane that view or manifested force of the subconscious mind, which is a portion, if you please, of the mind of the universal forces--that has been builded, made, or that has come into existence through an individual's experience in the material or earth's plane. As this mind is subjugated (the physical of an individual), and the subconscious comes into action through suggestion (for, as is seen, suggestion is another name for thought or idea), that thought or idea is being expressed then by one who is speaking to such a mind, or such a manifestation, directing then the conditions through which the trend of that experience is to travel, or to direct same in its travel, or in its giving the information through its experience with those ideas, those suggestions, as are made toward mind.

Then, as is seen, there is the necessity of that mind so directing to be **absolutely** negative, should the positive of the subconscious (which is **altogether** positive) operate with same in giving the condition, or the instruction necessary concerning that desired to be known. Should the question, should the mind, should the person of such a directing be in that of a wishy-washy, willy-nilly, **inconceivable** way of direction, the same may be expected of that information as is taken. For, remember, the directing of the suggestion may come back from the positive to the negative in that same direction from which it has been given. For, laws concerning reflex, as would be seen in light, in sound, in any of the other laws, must be carried out in that same way and manner. These being directed in a negative manner towards a positive answer will **obtain** that as is desired. And that to which such mind is directed must be in that state of negative, that the positive of the subconscious force, so directed, may obtain the information necessary to be returned, as it were, to those sources so directing. Or, as may be classified in the material: A positive and a negative are necessary to obtain any direct connection in any form. Or, as may be classified from the spiritual: The **desire** of the mind must be toward that which is **wished** for (get the difference between wish and desire!), that the information may be obtained through those same sources or channels.   195-31

As to the attitude of the individual through which the questioning is...passive. that of the individual through whom the information may come--active: the desire--**sincere** desire--to be of help.   254-63

Q-What was the cause of not being able to obtain 335's Life Reading?
A-...That which wavers or hinders or repels or blocks the activity through this channel when in such a state may be from these causes; namely: The unwillingness of the body-consciousness to submit to the suggestion as pertaining to information desired at that particular time. Or the activity of the physical in such a manner as to require the influence or supervision of the superconsciousness in the body, or ill health, at such a period. Or the mental attitude of those about the body that are not in accord with the type, class or character of information sought at that particular time. Or there may be many variations of the combination of these, influencing one to another, as to the type, class or real activity of the entity or soul that seeks the information.   254-67

With the bringing into creation the manifested forms, there came that which has been, is, and ever will be, the spirit realm and its attributes--designated as angels and archangels. They are the spiritual manifestations in the spirit world of those attributes that the developing forces accredit to the One Source, that may be seen in material planes through the influences that may aid in development of the mental and spiritual forces through an experience--or in the acquiring of knowledge that may aid in the intercourse one with another.

Then, how do they aid? Under what law do they operate?

The divine, in its intercourse, influences and manifestation with that which partakes of the same forces as they manifest.

Q-Are angels and archangels synonymous with that which we call laws of the universe; if so, explain and give an example.

A-They are as the laws of the universe; as is Michael the lord of the Way, **not** the Way but lord of the Way, hence disputed with the influence of evil as to the way of the spirit of the teacher or director in his entrance through the outer door. (See Jude 1:9)   5749-3

Q-What is the relationship between Michael the lord of the Way, and the Christ the Way?

A-Michael is an archangel that stands before the Throne of the Father. The Christ is the Son, the Way **to** the Father, and one that came into the earth as man, the Son of man, that man might have the access to the Father; hence the Way. Michael is the lord or the guard of the change that comes in every soul that seeks the Way, even as in those periods when His manifestations came in the earth.   262-28

For, the lord of the Way is as but a growing in understanding and comprehension of those things, conditions and elements that would make for finding contentment in the service of Truth.

Then, the message that would be given by him, the lord of the Way: BOW THINE HEADS, O YE CHILDREN OF MEN. FOR THE DAY OF THE LORD IS NIGH AT HAND. MAKE THINE OWN PATHS STRAIGHT, IN THAT YE WALK CIRCUMSPECTLY BEFORE THINE BROTHER, THAT YE PLACE NOT STUMBLING-BLOCKS IN HIS WAY NOR CAUSE HIM TO ERR IN THAT HE IS SEEKING TO FIND HIS WAY. LET THE LIGHT THOU HAST SHINE IN A MORE PERFECT WAY: FOR AS THE DAY DRAWS NEAR WHEN ALL MUST BE TRIED SO AS BY FIRE, FIND SELF ON THAT SIDE WHEREIN THINE BROTHER HAS BEEN AIDED. 254-66

Hark! Ye children of men bow thine head, for Michael the lord of the Way would show **thee** thine way--Who is able to stand in the day of the Lord? He that has purified his heart in the ways that make for the sons of men to know the Lord of Hosts **would** approach to thine own throne; for **who** is this Lord? He that is **holy** in His name! Amen.   3976-7

Gabriel is, to be sure, the announcer.   5277-1

Q-Who is Halaliel, the one who gave us a message on October 15th?
A-One in and with whose courts Ariel fought when there was a rebellion in heaven.

Now, where is Heaven? Where is Ariel, and who was he? A companion of Lucifer or Satan, and one that made for the disputing of the influences in the experiences of Adam in the Garden.   262-57

To each entity, each soul, there is ever the ministering angel before the Throne of Grace, the Throne of God. The ministering angel is the purposefulness, the spirit with which ye would do anything in relationship to others.   3357-2

Each soul in its walks in the earth has its angel, its gnome, its face before the Throne of that which is the First Cause, the Creative Influence, God. And these are always ready to guide, to guard, if the soul will but put itself in the position in material things to be guided by spiritual truths.   531-2

The guardian angel--that is the companion of each soul as it enters into a material experience--is ever an influence for the keeping of that attunement between the creative energies or forces of the soul-entity **and** health, life, light and immortality...
Mind is the Builder; Mind is the Way--as the Christ-Consciousness. As it is directed then through the influences of the bodily functions it becomes aware of its oneness, and thus is the guardian force made to be at-one with the whole of the purposes and desires, and the will of the individual...
Then as the guardian influence or angel is ever before the face of the Father, through same may that influence ever speak--but only by the command of or attunement to that which is thy ideal.
What then is thy ideal? In **whom** have ye believed, as well as in what have ye believed? Is that in which thou hast believed able to keep ever before thee that thou committest unto Him?
Yes--through thy angel, through thy **self** that **is** the angel--does the self speak with thy Ideal?   1646-1

It is true that there is a guide or guard for each and every entity or soul, or a developing influence that may be from the entity's own activities as a new star in the universe.   1695-1

For, ye find thyself body, mind, soul. These three bear witness in the earth. And the Christ-Consciousness, the Holy Spirit **and** thy guardian angel bear witness in the spirit.   2246-1

We--from the source of all knowledge that is promised in Him--salute thee, and give that which will be helpful to those who seek to be in the ministry of those influences and forces that make for more and more awareness of the divine in each and every soul...Then, from the heights of those experiences, those hierarchies in the earth and in the air, we come as messengers of truth to those who will hear, and question.

Q-For the better and more rational presentation of the work of Edgar Cayce to the world, will you, if you consider same in order, kindly inform us of thine Identity and the source or sources from which you bring us the information. Is it from the Astral--

A-(interrupting) From the Universal Forces that are acceptable and accessible to those who in earnestness open their minds, their souls, to the wonderful words of truth and light.

Q-Who are the Masters directly in charge? Is Saint Germain--

A-(interrupting) Those that are directed by the Lord of lords, the King of kings, Him that came that ye might be one with the Father.

Q-Is Saint Germain among them? Who is Halaliel?

A-These are all but messengers of the Most High. Halaliel is that one who from the beginning has been as a leader of the heavenly host, who has defied Ariel, who has made the ways that have been heavy-- but as a means for the **understanding**.

Q-Is Saint Germain among them?

A-When needed.

Q-Please give us Thine Identity.

A-He that seeks that has not gained the control seeks damnation to his own soul. Control thine inner self that ye may know the true life and light. For he that would name the Name must become perfect in himself.

Q-If Mr. Cayce is a member and a messenger of the Great White Brotherhood, how do the Masters wish him to proceed and should not his activities henceforth be presented as Their Work?

A-As the work of the **Master** of masters, that may be presented when in those lines, those accords necessary through the White Brotherhood. This--this--**this**, my friends, even but **limits**; while in Him is the Whole. Would thou make of thyself, of thyselves, a limited means of activity? Would thou seek to be hindered by those things that have made of many contending forces that continue to war one with another even in the air, even in the elemental forces? For He, thy Lord, thy God, hath called thee by name, even as He has given, "Whosoever will drink the cup, even as of my blood, he may indeed be free." While ye labor, let **Him** that is the author, that is the finisher, that **is** the Life, that is the bread of life, that is the blood of life, let **Him** alone be thy guide. Dost He call any soul into service, **then** by name will He--does He--designate, and to whom it becomes a charge to keep--even as he has walked with Him, this body that ye use as a channel of approach to the Throne; make of same oft as a laughingstock to thy very soul through thine own selfishness. Let the light of Him, thy Christ, thy God, **in,** that it may cleanse thy body, that it may lighten thy soul, that it may purge thy mind, that ye will only be just gentle, just kind; not finding fault with any, for with faults ye build **barriers** to thine own soul's enlightenment. "I, thy God, thy Christ, beseech thee!"   254-83

Q-Is it likely that I will meet any of the brothers (White Brotherhood) in the flesh, as Mr. Cayce has done, in this incarnation?
A-Ye may meet many. Oft doth man entertain angels unawares.   3011-3

(May) the sons of light as from the holy mount guide thee in thy walks and thy meditations, for thou **art** of that Brotherhood.   812-1

Thou wert of the Great White Brotherhood thine self in Ohum and Og.845-1

SPIRITUAL FORCES WITHIN AND WITHOUT

There are those consciousnesses or awarenesses that have not participated in nor been a part of earth's **physical** consciousness; as the angels, the archangels, the masters to whom there has been attainment, and to those influences that have prepared the way.   5755-2

Man was made a little lower than the angels, yet with that power to become one with God, while the angel remains the angel.   900-16

As to the mental forces of body, these, as we have given, are above ordinary, though not super-normal. Above normal as to the spiritual forces, for we find that the body has an earthly as well as a spiritual guide; that is, one who has passed into the Beyond, is a guide for the spiritual forces of this entity, of which this spirit and soul force is a part.   2801-1

There are forces outside of self, there are forces and influences within self. The true God Forces meet within, not without self. For when there are altars builded outside, which individuals approach for the interpretation of law, whether it be physical, mental, or spiritual, these are temptations...And the first command is, "Thou shalt have no other gods before me" (Exodus 20:3).   3548-1

There is that within self that is creative; and it, that creative force, coordinating, cooperating with the divine without, will make for the choice of that which **is** life in the experience of each entity. 1580-1

Each and every soul has its guide that may be designated by the desires of the inmost self. In the realm of spirit many may seek to give that which may be of interest, and at times of aid, to individuals seeking from such realms; yet--as the promise has been unto the sons of men--He, the Lord is sufficient unto thee. Then, that which may be the greater, the better guide to each and every soul, is that of self through its associations--its own associations--in the spirit realm.

Hence, to the body, there may be given from time to time that--through channels or from sources--which may verify or correlate that which may be gained through self's own seeking in the quietness of self; yet that which may be the greater aid is in the mental developments, the mental expansions in self from such meditations, such intuitive forces that may be aroused in and from activity of the soul in its passage through the various experiences of development in the spheres of reality.   423-2

We all have a guide, either dead or living. Some are guided by dead, and some by living spirits. This man's guide is his mother. There is a warring of spirits mental and metaphysically, all three within the same body as is in every man or woman...All guides whether spiritual or material have the power to direct and influence their subjects.   4348-1

There be many phases, many characters of the psychic forces in the material world. There are influences from without the veil that seek-- seek--that they may find an expression, that they may still be a portion of this evolution in the earth, not considering their present estate. And these bring turmoil, strife.   1135-2

The sojourn of a soul-entity other than in materiality often influences or bears weight with individuals within the material plane--as an odor, a scent, an emotion, a wave, a wind upon the activities.

Such are termed or called by some guardian angels, or influences that would promote activities for weal or for woe.   538-59

Angels of light only use material things for emblems, while angels of death use these as to lures that may carry men's souls away.   1159-1

For there has been the continued battle with those forces as Michael fought **with** over the body of Moses. He that leads, or **would** direct, is continually beset by the forces that **would** undermine.   2897-4

When thou hast shown in thine heart thy willingness to be guided and directed by **His** force, He gives His angels charge concerning thee.   423-3

In the material plane the raising of the mental consciousness to the various spheres of attunement is accomplished only in concentrating and in attuning self to those forces as are without. The body-consciousness is made up, as has been given, of more than one consciousness...As one develops, or as one opens self to those various spheres of understanding, one attains or gains an access, a vision, an insight, a hearing, a feeling, into these various planes. By the use of that in hand does one attain the next plane.   5472-1

For, in that creation in which souls of men were given the opportunity to become aware of those forces without themselves, when time and space began, there was given that incentive for each entity, each soul, in whatever environment it might be, to make a manifestation of its awareness of its relationships to the Creative Forces, or God.2173-1

Reason in the physical from this premise: God **Is**. Man is. Man is an enigma to himself, unless there be an influence from without that may work within.
The body of the individual soul, then, is the temple of the living God. God is God of the living, **not** of the dead.   2677-1

Q-On March 2nd, whose voice did I hear speak to me?
A-...It is the awakening within of the abilities to so associate and so connect and communicate with those influences from without. 262-40

For, He came into the earth that through Him man might have access again to the grace and mercy of those spiritual forces that are the directing ideals of each soul-entity.   3132-1

Q-How can I discern the helpful entities or forces from those forces that would do me harm?
A-In each experience ask that they acknowledge the life, the death, the resurrection of the Jesus, the Christ. They that answer only as in the affirmative; otherwise, "Get thee behind me, I will have no part with thee. Through His name only **will I, accept** direction."   422-1

Q-What is meant by the gods of the universe in the readings?
A-Just as in this. All force has its incentive, the directing or creating of that force. That force to the human mind apparent, as different conditions, or relations, as referred to as the God, or the ruling force, of that individual force, as is giving the expression, and is referred to as the God, as of War, as of Peace, as of Water, as of the elements under the Sea. As of those above, as the God of High Heaven, the ruler over all, the one in all and the all in one...
It has been said correctly that the Creator, the gods and the God of the Universe speak to man through this (his) individual self. 3744-4

In the attaining of development, through the mental, the soul forces, in the earths plane, there have been set bounds about every force as manifested in the material, the mental, the soul, the spiritual planes. These bounds are the gods, or guards, of such attainment.   900-17

We all--and ye are as others--are gods in the making; not **The** God, but gods in the making! For He would have thee be one with Him.   877-21

Ye **are** gods! But you are becoming devils or real gods!   281-30

Q-What is meant by the term 'brownies'?
A-The manner in which those of the elementals--entities who have not entered into materiality--have manifested and do at times manifest themselves before or to the entity.
Brownies, pixies, fairies, gnomes are not elementals but are elements that are as definite **entities** as man materialized, see?   1265-3

(To) call upon the Infinite is much greater, much more satisfying, much more worthwhile in the experience of an individual soul than being guided or directed merely by an entity outside of self that--**as** self--**is** being in a state of transition or development...
Should the Maker use a gnome, a fairy, an angel, a developing entity for a guide, all right--for a specific direction; for He hath given His angels charge concerning thee; and **thy** god, thy face, is ever before the Throne of the Infinite.   338-3

SPIRIT COMMUNICATION

What is ordinarily termed spirit communication--should be...**soul** communication.   5756-14

There are ever about those in the flesh in the earth's plane those desiring to communicate with those in the earth plane; being attracted by the act, the intent and purport of the individual--or by the act, intent and purport of that entity in the spirit plane...
Those intents, those purports, as were once set forth by Saul of Tarsus (epistle to the Corinthians) are as near the correct interpretation of spirit communication as may be studied in any literature or writings that may be obtained at the present period.   900-330

If there is desire on the part of those in the spirit or fourth dimensional plane to be communicated with, and the same element of desire is attuned from another plane, stratum, sphere or condition, then such may be done; hence, it truly may be said that **all** factors have their influence, desire the ruling one; and the desire must be attuned to the same vibration of the one in another plane, as the radio.

Q-Does communication further or retard, or not affect, the spiritual progression of those in spirit life?

A-It does all!   5756-8

A union of force makes for strength and power. Thus, the communion of saints means that all who have one purpose, whose thoughts and motivative forces are one, may communicate; whether those in the material plane, in the borderland, or those that may be upon the shores of the other side of life.   262-87

Q-His (deceased) subconsciousness and my subconsciousness meet as a vibration force meets a radio machine and causes a sound when tuned in?

A-...This is the illustration, see? Both must be in that attunement and separated from the physical forces to become conscious.   140-10

The spirits of all that have passed from the physical plane remain about the plane until their developments carry them onward, or they are in the plane of communication, or remain with this sphere, any may be communicated with. There are thousands about us here at present. 3744-2

Pray for the dead. For they only sleep, as the Lord indicated. And if we are able to attune to such, there we may help. Though we may not call back to life as the Son, we can point the way.   3657-1

Those who have passed on need the prayers of those who live aright. For the prayers of those who would be righteous in spirit may save many who have erred, even in the flesh.   3416-1

Q-Does he (deceased) know of my prayers?

A-Do you wish him to? Do you wish to call him back to those disturbing forces, or do you wish the self to be poured out for him that he may be happy? Which is it you desire,--to satisfy self that you are communicating, or that you are holding him in such a way as to retard?   1786-2

When the body (material) attunes self to that plane wherein the sensuous consciousness is in obeisance to the laws of physical or material, and the spiritual or astral laws are effective, those of the astral plane may communicate, in thought, in power, in form. What form, then, do such bodies assume? The desired form as is built and made by that individual in its experience through the material plane...

Is such information always true? Always true, so far as the individual has brought self into that attunement as is necessary for the perfect understanding of same. Do not attempt to govern information, or judge information, by the incorrect law, see? When force is taken, what is the impelling force such as is seen in the movement of material objects?...

Such impelling forces, we find, are the combination of that in the individual receiving and in the abilities of the individual so communicating--that is, we find that in the various experiences of individuals, levitation, or objects that are of material nature, are moved about by the active principle of the **individual through whom such manifestations are being made**, and not by spirit action, or soul action. Yet **controlled** by that cosmic consciousness. Don't leave that out, see? Controlled--for, as given, the body must be subjugated that such force may manifest. Then we see undue strength, undue power, is seen exercised at such periods. True--for things are controlled by spirit alone are of a great deal greater active force than of the sensuous mind, as a trained mind is more active than one untrained.

Q-What physical thing may an individual do to be able to communicate with those that have passed into the spirit plane?

A-Lay aside the carnal or sensuous mind and desire that those who would use that mentality, that soul, for its vehicle of expression, do so in the manner chosen by that soul; for some communicate in act, in sight, in movement, in voice, in writing, in drawing, in speaking, and in the various forces as are manifest--for force is **one** force.   5756-4

Q-One recent morning. Saw my mother (in a dream). She told me that I should warn my Aunt Helen against an accident. Helen seemed to get into an accident, get badly hurt, and my mother took sick form it.

A-This, is presented, is an accident regarding getting injured in an automobile and street car accident. Be warned, then, and warn the body as regarding same, see? and when the body keeps in that way of being warned, or keeps from the car, then this may not be expected to happen, for here we have as it were, the direct communication of the entity in the spirit plane with the entity in the material plane, the attunement being reached when the entity is the body-conscious mind being subjugated and an at-onement with the universal forces. This also shows the entity how that the entity in the spirit plane, or spirit entity is mindful of conditions which transpire, exist, in the material plane, see?   136-48

Q-What form do spirits have?

A-That within the mental capacities of the medium obtaining such vibration from an aura to create; or to give, such manifestations a form: it assuming then that form...

Not that we would belittle such manifestations, but let them be rather the silent voice from within communicating with the individuals themselves, rather than manifesting through other individuals who give them shape, form, and words of their individual development and of their individual environment.   5756-1

Spirit is the First Cause, the primary beginning, the motivative influence--as God is Spirit.   262-123

Spirit is the impelling influence of infinity, or the one creative source, force, that is manifest. Hence we find that in the physical plane we seek soul manifestation as the spirit moves same in activity. 5749-3

Spirit is that portion of the First Cause which finds expression in all that is everlasting in the consciousness of mind **or** matter.   2533-1

Spirit **is** the association or the life itself of the soul, whether in man, in a nation, in a city, in a group, or what.   476-1

There is a vast difference between spiritual and soul forces, for, as given, about each force there has been set guards or bounds. Spirit forces are the animation of **all life** giving life-producing forces in animate or inanimate forces. Spiritual elements become corporeal when we speak of the spiritual body in a spiritual entity; then composed of spirit, soul and superconsciousness...
Spiritual forces being the life, the reproductive principle, the soul, the development principle...The active principle is the spirit. 900-17

The spirit is the whole. The soul is the individual.   3357-2

Give self the **opportunity** to function normally, mentally, physically, spiritually. The **spirit** will act, irrespective of what a body does with its physical or mental body--and it may make a very warped thing if you keep it under cover or expose it too much!   564-1

In the physical forces, keep fit--keep the **mental** attuned properly, and the **spiritual** life **will** guide in all things!   4405-1

All force, all manifestations in materiality are the expressions of spirit, and are **prompted** by same.   816-3

The basis of the individuality of an entity must come from its ideal spiritually. For all is born first in spirit, then in mind, then it may become manifested in the material plane. For God moved and the heavens and the earth came into being. God is Spirit. Man with his soul, that may be a companion to the Creative Forces, is of that same source. Thus to grow in grace and knowledge, one applies, one has, one uses one's spiritual self. And with what spirit we apply, we grow also in mind and in body.   3424-1

Know that all that materializes must first happen in the spirit, and the law of cause and effect ever remains. Hence in spirit it is purpose and ideal.   3412-2

The soul is **all** of that the entity is, has been or may be.   2475-1

Man in his former state, or natural state, or permanent consciousness **Is** soul.   262-89

Know that ye **are** a soul, and do not merely attain to one.   2283-1

The soul is an individual, individuality, that may grow to be one with, or separate from, the whole.   5749-3

Spirit being its portion of the Creator, its soul that of its entity itself, making itself individual, separate entity, that may be one **with** the Creative Force from which it comes--or which it is, of which it is made up, in its atomic forces, or in its very essence itself.   364-10

Only in man is there the existence of the soul that is not just universal, but individual; capable of becoming as a god, as one with the Creative Forces.   1587-1

Though there may be worlds, many universes, even much as to solar systems, greater than our own that we enjoy in the present...Yet the soul of man, thy soul encompasses **all** in this solar system or in others...
Canst thou conceive the requirements of influence to meet all the idiosyncrasies of a **single** soul? How many systems would it require? 5755-2

The soul of man is a mere speck in space, yet the soul--though indefinite--is that vital force or activity which is everlasting. Though the earth, though the stars, may pass away; though there may be changes in the universe as to the relative position, these are brought about by those combinations of that speck of human activity as relative **to** the soul's expression in any sphere of experience.   1297-1

The soul is the real self, the continuous self. The mind is the builder, continuous to the extent that it is constructive...and that which is constructive and good is continuous.   1620-1

The soul **is,** and lives on; making its record in the building influence, or that stream in the experience of the body, the mind, the soul, called the mental life of an entity.
Entity, then, is the soul in its spiritual form, the mental body in or of its mental form, the physical that is the material manifestation of the two in the earth experiences.   954-1

No limitation of the soul or mind in spirituality but in materiality they reach limitations because of lack of means of expression.   5367-1

The soul is the **Entity**! The entity is the soul and the mind and the body of same, see?   1494-1

Q-Please expand on what the readings mean by entity.

A-As given in the information, the entity is that combination of the physical body throughout all its experiences in or through the earth, in or through the universe, and the reactions that have been builded by those various or varied experiences, or the spiritual body of an individual. That that **is** individual; that that is the sum total of all experience. Then for the **entity** to create, or give, or be life, it must be a living, acting example of that it is, and not as something separated, inactive, inanimate, not giving but gradually deteriorating. There is the variation that may be seen in the material world as an example: As long as life is in whatever may be a manifestation in the material plane, it **is a growth**. As soon as it becomes an inanimate object (though it may be serving a purpose), it **immediately begins** to deteriorate, disintegrate. **Be** an entity! **Be a living** entity! See?   262-10

The soul is the God-part in thee, the **living** God.   262-77

(The soul) was made in the image of thy Maker--not thy body, no-- not thy mind, but thy **soul** was in the image of thy Creator.   281-41

For while the body changes, for it--too--must be purified, the **soul** remains ever as one. For it is in the image of the Creator and has its birthright in Him.   1243-1

An entity, or soul, is a spark--or a portion--of the Whole, the First Cause: or Purpose.   2079-1

When the body-physical lays aside the material body, that in the physical called soul becomes the body of the entity.   900-304

The soul is the **body** of, or the spiritual essence of, an entity manifested **in** this material plane.   5754-2

When the soul departs from a body--(this is not being spoken of the Christ)--it has all the form of the body from which it has passed--yet it is not visible to the carnal mind, unless that mind has been and is, attuned to the infinite. Then it appears, in the infinite, as that which may be handled, with all the attributes of the physical being; with the appetites, until these have been accorded to a unit of activity with the Universal Consciousness.   2533-8

The soul looks through the eyes of the body--it handles with the emotions of the sense of touch--it may be aware through the factors in every sense.   487-17

Q-Does the soul ever die?
A-May be banished from the Maker, not death.   3744-2

The basis, the beginning of law carries all the way through. And that which comes or begins first is conceived in spirit, grows in the mental, manifests in the material.   2072-10

That which has been, which is, which may be,--these are still founded in that summed up in , "The Lord thy God is One" (Mark 12:29).
Father-God is as the body, or the whole. Mind is as the Christ, which is the Way. The Holy Spirit is as the soul, or--in material interpretation--purposes, hopes, desires.   1747-5

Mind is represented in the Godhead as the Christ, the Son, the Way. The Father is represented in the earth as the body. The soul is all of those attributes that manifest in the body.   4083-1

The individual entity finds itself body, mind, soul, so are the manifestations in a three-dimensional plane. Hence the concept of the finite is in the realm of cause, effect, and purpose, as in the infinite there is the Father, Son, Holy Spirit. The attaining from the mind to the infinite is through time, space, and patience. All of these phases of a human experience in mind and in materiality should be considered.   3412-2

Man's concept of the Godhead is three-dimensional--Father, Son and Holy Spirit. The communication or the activity or the motivating force we find is three-dimensional--time, space and patience.   4035-1

The body, the mind, the soul are one in whatsoever realm it manifests, that the other portion of this triune is in subjugation during the sojourn of the soul either in the spiritual world or the soul and spirit while sojourning in the material world--yet they are one.   609-1

The body is made up of the physical, the mental, the spiritual. Each have their laws, which work one with another, and the whole is the physical man; yet do not treat physical conditions wholly through spiritual or mental laws and expect same to respond as one. Neither treat spiritual or mental conditions as material; for **Mind** is the builder, and through the mind **application** of the laws pertaining to physical, mental, and spiritual, one is made **One** with the whole.   4580-1

The body-physical with the emotions of same is physical and spiritual: the body-mental with its desires is both carnal and very spiritual. The **spirit** is willing. The spirit desires, the spirit seeks the greater understanding, the greater knowledge of thy relationships to the Creative Forces or God.   1754-1

For as life is continuous, then the soul finds itself both in eternity and in spirit; in mind, yet in materiality.   1353-1

As the mental and the spiritual become more and more expressive, or controlling through the experience in the earth, the entity becomes, aware of other dimensions in its material sojourn...While the body is subject to all the influences of materiality, it may be controlled--emotions thereof--by the mind. And the mind may be directed by spirit.   2533-1

Spirituality, mentality, and the physical being are all one, yet may indeed separate and function one without the other--and one at the expense of the other. Make them cooperative, make them one in their purpose--and we will have a greater activity.   307-10

While the body is made up of the three divisions; mind and body, and spirit--they are one. Yet each interpretation and each application of self, of the entity, of the mental and soul mind, to its experience in the earth, are **just** as separate or distinct as may be the application of the **body** to the elements in the earth. **Earth, air, fire, water**--these are one, in their **varied** aspect, to human or bodily existence.   601-11

There is the body with its attributes, its weaknesses, its strength, its inclinations, its tendencies. From whence arise these tendencies. They arise from both the mental and spiritual manifestation in a causation world.
Then there is the mind, that is a body-mind; both spiritual **and** material. From whence arise the emotions, the attributes, the activity of such? From its environ to the influences from the physical in all of its consciousnesses, as well as the spiritual--the First Cause.
Also we find the body-spiritual.
They are one; as the Father, the Son and the Holy Spirit are one. God as the Father, Creator, Maker; the Son as the Way, the Mind, the Activity, the Preserver; the Holy Spirit as the motivative force--or the destroyer or the maker alive, dependent upon the manners in which the individual entity, or these influences are used by, whether there are or have been retardments or advancements towards--what? That we may be one with Him, know ourselves to **be** ourselves, yet one in creative purpose and in activity in this material world.   2420-1

The body is the manifestation of the individual entity, the mind is the manifestation of the Son--both as an earthly experience and as an at-onement with the Father, the Whole.
So the soul is that which is eternal.
Thus does there come in the experience of each soul those problems in a material world of the constant warring of the material or changing things, or earthly experience, with mental and spiritual or soul forces.   2600-2

There are attributes of the physical body that may or may not be controlled by mental forces and influences. There is the soul-body that may not be controlled by, or may be controlled by, the good or the bad influence of spirit. These are as the shadows which were indicated in the mount by the outer court (the body), the inner court (the mind), and the still more holy of holies (the soul). These are but shadows, and yet indicate the trend of development.   2067-1

There is the physical body, there is the mental body, there is the soul body. They are One, as the Trinity; yet these may find a manner of expression that is individual unto themselves. The body itself finds its **own** development.   281-24

Know that there is the physical body, the mental body, the soul body. These are one. In the material manifestation one becomes aware of the material, the mental; and the hope or desire for the knowledge, the awareness of the soul body. They each are dependent upon the other in material manifestation. Consider them as one, yet know that they may be separated. For instance, the body-physical in repose is not aware of a physical consciousness. The mind at rest is aware only of the spiritual and the physical import, as in deep meditation or prayer. The soul body or mind body absent from the physical is in the presence of the Lord.

Ask self, then, who and what is the Lord thy God. Is it the gratifying of selfish desires, the gaining of fame or fortune, or to be wellspoken of, or to be considered this or that in the material sense? All of these change. For the body is temporal. The mind is both temporal and carnal--hence is the builder. The soul is eternal, for it is of God.   2540-1

For, every force which may not be separated, produced, given, shown growth of, by man, that force is of God and of the Universal Forces, which when speaking of man's relation to same meaning, coming in contact with those three forces in man:

Spiritual--of God.

Cosmic--made forces of the man.

The Subconscious--that which connects each and becomes the condition of mental--mind in a spiritual, see?   900-147

Q-Let the light represent the Spiritual, the film the physical faculties of the senses (mind), and the moving picture on the screen this physical life--talking, feeling, tasting, thinking, emotion, etc., and one has a good comparison. Changing pictures, but One Fixed Light.

A-Correct.   900-156

Q-Describe Edgar Cayce and his ability to give readings.

A-Application of the harmonious triune...

It is the harmony of the triune--of body, mind, and soul--towards the purpose of being a help, an assistance, an aid to others.   254-108

The study from the human standpoint, of subconscious, subliminal, psychic, soul forces, is and should be the great study for the human family, for through self man will understand its Maker when it understands its relation to its Maker, and it will only understand that through itself, and that understanding is the knowledge as is given here in this state.   3744-4

Each of these terms--mystic, psychic, occult--represent phases of experience in the human experience acting through the mental body, the spiritual body, the physical body. While each of these are one, as the Father, the Son, the Holy Spirit--the body, the mind, the soul-- mystic is as the spirit or the **activity**, while the psychic is the soul, the occult is the mind. Do not confuse; for each in their respective sphere --if and when taken alone--becomes confusing.   1265-3

We find all psychic phenomena or force, presented through one of the acknowledged five senses of the physical or material body--these being used as the mode of manifesting to individuals. Hence we would have in the truest sense, **psychic**, meaning the expression to the material world of the latent, or hidden sense of the soul and spirit forces, whether manifested from behind, or in and through the material plane.

Q-How many kinds of psychic phenomena are known to mankind at present?

A-Almost as many as there are individuals, each entity being a force, or world within itself. Those of the unseen forces become then the knowledge of the individual, the power of expression, or of giving the knowledge obtained, being of an individual matter.

Q-Why do women usually show more interest in psychic matters than men?

A-For their minds, women are filled, or left vacant for the study of spiritual forces more than men, for the same reason as we have given. What their minds fill or feed upon for development toward psychic force comes from the subconscious or the spirit and soul minds...

The only real life being that which in the material or physical plane is called psychic.

Without the psychic force in the world the physical would be in that condition of 'hit or miss', or that as a ship without a rudder or pilot, for that element that is the guiding force in each and every condition is the spirit or soul of that condition which is the psychic or occult force.

Q-What period in the world's history were psychic readings given?

A-That as given among the Chaldeans was first used as the means of assistance to the physical bodies. Not as applied in the present day usage of such force or phenomena, but that as the natural means of expression of that unseen force of the soul and spirit...nearly four thousand years before the Prince of Peace came.   3744-1

There is both mental phenomena, the soul phenomena, the spiritual phenomena. All psychic phenomena, for psychic means of the mind, in the accepted term. Then, as we see manifestations of any of the conditions that relate to the physical mind the portion of soul entity belonging to physical, the portion of the spiritual belonging to physical, we see the phenomena, or the psychic phenomena, manifested in a material world, whether projected from the world into mental space, or from spirit world into the mental or material world. Keep each separate...there is no condition existing in a world as the earth plane but what there is the phenomena in every action of psychic forces manifesting.   900-19

Listen to the birds. Watch the blush of the rose...These serve their Maker. Through what? That psychic force, that **is** Life itself.   364-10

We are conscious of the action of psychic...forces in the same manner in which we are conscious of the action of electrical forces.   254-32

No greater psychic lived than Jesus of Nazareth.   2630-1

Q-What must she do that she may develop her psychic abilities?
A-Psychic is of the soul; the abilities to reason **by** the faculties or by the mind of the soul. And when this is done, enter into the inner self, opening self through the ideals of the meditation...and surrounding self with the consciousness of the Christ that He may guide.   513-1

Q-What is the highest possible psychic realization?
A-That God, the Father, speaks directly to the sons of men.   440-4

Q-What is the difference between psychic forces and occult forces?
A-...One is the study of the other. One is the essence of the sources, and the other the channels through which, of which, the study.   262-20

Q-Explain the difference between occult and mystic forces.
A-Occult, rather those that are of the ability of personal application; while the mysterious, the necessity of certain activities or feelings to be aroused before there may be expression.   491-1

(Occult forces are) the application of unseen or unfelt laws to the physical or material life...There is a pattern in the material for all things in the spiritual realm.   4185-2

Know Self if ye would know the occult.   3344-1

When there is the same interest or study given to things or phases of mental and spiritual phenomena as has been and is given to the materialized or material phenomena, then it will become just as practical, as measurable, as, meter-able, as any other phase of human experience.   2012-1

O, that all men would know, "Know, O ye children of men, the Lord thy God is **One**." Each spirit, each manifestation of **Life** is **One**, and a manifestation either in this, that or the other sphere, or scope, or space of development **towards** the knowledge, the understanding, the conception of that **One--Him--I Am--Jehovah--Yah--All One!** 262-32

The basis, then: "Know, O Israel, (Know, O People) the Lord thy God is One" (Mark 12:29).

From this premise we would reason, that: In the manifestation of all power, force, motion, vibration, that which impels, that which detracts, is in its essence of **One** Force, One source, in its elemental form. As to what has been done or accomplished by or through the activity of entities that have been delegated powers in activity is another story.

As to the One Source or One Force, then, are the questions presented in the present.

God, the First Cause, the First Principle, the First Movement, **IS!** That's the beginning. That is, that was, that ever shall be.

The following of those sources, forces, activities that are in accord with the Creative Force or First Cause--Its laws, then--is to be one with the source, or equal with yet separate from that First Cause.

When, then, may man--as an element, an entity, a separate being manifested in material life and form--be aware or conscious of the moving of that First Cause within his own environ?

Or, taking man in his present position or consciousness, how or when may he be aware of that First Cause moving within his realm of consciousness?

In the beginning there was the force of attraction and the force that repelled. Hence, in man's consciousness he becomes aware of what is known as the atomic or cellular form of movement about which there becomes nebulous activity. And this is the lowest form (as man would designate) that's in active forces in his experience. Yet this very movement that separates the forces in atomic influence is the First Cause, or the manifestation of that called God in the material plane.

Then, as it gathers of positive-negative forces in their activity, whether it be of one element or realm or another, it becomes magnified in its force or sources through the universe.

Hence we find worlds, suns, stars, nebulae, and whole solar systems **moving** from a first cause. When this first cause comes into man's experience in the present realm he becomes confused, in that he appears to have an influence upon this force or power in directing same. Certainly! Much, though, in the manner as the reflection of light in a mirror. For, it is only reflected force that man may have upon those forces that show themselves in the activities, in whatever realm into which man may be delving in the moment--whether of the nebulae, the gaseous, or the elements that have gathered together in their activity throughout that man has chosen to call time or space. And becomes, in its very movement, or that of which the First Cause takes thought in a finite existence or consciousness.

Hence, as man applies himself--or uses that of which he becomes conscious in the realm of activity, and gives or places the credit (as would be called) in man's consciousness in the correct sphere or realm he becomes conscious of that union of force with the infinite with the finite force. Hence, in the fruits of that--as is given oft, as the fruits of the spirit--does man become aware of the infinite penetrating, or interpenetrating the activities of all forces of matter, or that which is a manifestation of the realm of the infinite into the finite--and the finite becomes conscious of same...

So does life in all its force begin in the earth. The moving of the infinite upon the negative of the finite in the material, or to become manifested force.   262-52

The Lord thy God is **ONE**. Would that all souls could, would, comprehend that great sentence,--which has been, is, the motivating force in **all** who seek. Not in all who impel, but in all who **seek** to live, who **seek** to manifest, who **seek** to give expression of God's force or power.   2067-1

Man is ever in that field of being a channel, an emissary, for that he worships as his god. May that god ever be the Lord, God of Hosts--His name is **ONE**.   442-1

Know in self all that has happened, all that may happen in thy experience in the earth is as an opportunity that ye may know the Lord thy God is one Lord.   3581-1

The first lesson for **six months** should be **ONE**--One-One--**One**; Oneness of God, oneness of man's relation, oneness of force, oneness of time, oneness of purpose, **oneness** in every effort--Oneness--Oneness.900-429

In the First Cause, or Principle, all is Perfect.   900-10

The **spirit** of numbers is as **one**, from which each and every other ratio **must** be measured; for in the **beginning** was the Word, and the Word **was** God. The same in the beginning was one, and all that **was** made was of the Word. The same dwelt among men, and men knew it not--for being blinded to the light, only those that chose to make themselves one with the whole, are given the introspective influence in their material phases...In thine self alone little may be gained, yet in the oneness of the whole all may be attained, **all** may be gained. 1716-1

As in numbers one builds upon the other (as units) and all are formations or divisions or multiples or units of one, so the universe and the expressions of all natures within same are the manifestations of the One Force, One Power, One Spirit, One Energy known as or called a Universal Force, Creative Energy, or God.   1462-1

The Life, or manifestation of that which is in motion, is receiving its impulses from a first cause.

What is the first cause?

That which has brought, is bringing, all life into being; or animation or force, or power, or movement, or consciousness, as to either the material plane, the mental plane, the spiritual plane.

Hence it is the force that is called Lord, God, Jehovah, Yah, Ohum (Ohm?), Abba and the like. Hence the activity that is seen of any element in the material plane is a manifestation of that first cause. One Force...For, the movement itself (to make applicable another law) **draws** about a nucleus the positive and negative forces as to bring into visibility from one sphere or realm to another that force or power...

Negative being error, positive being right--good.   254-67

For know, the greater lesson the world has ever known and may ever learn is, "Know, O ye peoples, the Lord thy God is **One---One.**"

This is thy message, this is thy purpose. Proclaim and sow that seed of unity of purpose, that may be found **within**. And **that** is thy mission through these experiences.   1770-2

First the continuity of life. There is no time; it is one time; there is no space; it is one space; there is no force; it is one force. 4341-1

No man, no physical matter, has ever seen **God** at any time; only the **manifestations** of Him.   707-1

Know that the Creative Energy called God may be as personal as an individual will allow same to be; for the Spirit is in the image of the Creative Forces and seeks manifestation. It may take that personality, that personal activity that will be allowed by the individual itself; for we are co-laborers, co-creators with that Energy we call God, that Energy we call Universal Forces. While this may appear to be the Whole, if we will understand that "The Lord thy God is **ONE**" (Mark 12:29) and all power, all force emanates from that One Source, we will get an understanding of ourselves and our abilities. **Know Self!** Be **true to Self** and ye will not be false to anyone!   391-4

The living force or Creative Energy (are) known as the guards, or God, in the universal influence.   708-1

Q-Is it correct when praying to think of God as an impersonal force or energy, everywhere present; or as an intelligent listening mind, which is aware of every individual on earth and who intimately knows everyone's needs and how to meet them?
A-Both. For He is also the energies in the finite moving in material manifestation. He is also the Infinite, with the awareness. And thus as ye attune thy own consciousness, thy own awareness, the unfoldment of the presence within beareth witness with the presence without. 1158-14

Each individual is, in reality, that manifestation of the individual's conception of the impelling force from within, whether it be termed or called God, Nature, Universal Forces, natural powers or what not. 900-234

Life is creative, and is the manifestation of that energy, that oneness, which may never be **wholly** discerned or discovered in materiality, --and yet is the basis of all motivative forces and influences in the experiences of an individual. 2012-1

For the **soul** was made in the image of the Creator, to be a companion with that influence which is constructive, which is creative. And in materiality...it carries with it that natural import of, "As ye do it unto the least of thy brethren, of thy fellow man, ye do it unto **thy** God, thy **source** of power, thy **source** of supply" (Matthew 25:40). 1232-1

And as the electrical vibrations are given, know that Life itself--to be sure--is the Creative Force or God, yet its manifestations in man are electrical--or vibratory.
Know then that the force in nature that is called electrical or electricity is that same force ye worship as Creative or God in action. 1299-1

Electricity or vibration is that same energy, same power, ye call God. Not that God is an electric light or an electric machine, but vibration that is creative is of the same energy as life itself. 2828-4

All energy is electrical in its activity in a manifested form. 735-1

All power, all force, is a manifestation of that which is termed the God-consciousness. 601-11

Life, as a whole, is a continuous thing; emanating from power, energy, God-consciousness, ever. 1472-1

God seeks all to be one with Him. And as all things were made by Him, that which is the creative influence in every herb, every mineral, every vegetable, every individual activity, **is** that same force ye call God--and **seeks** expression! Even as when God said: "Let there be light," and there was light. For, this is law; this is love. 294-202

What, then is life? God; in power, in might, in the awareness of the strength needed to meet every problem day by day.   3161-1

Know that the **living** forces of thy God are **active**!   1257-1

The vibratory force is the active principle all radiates from.   195-54

Spiritual Forces being the Life, the reproductive principle, the soul, the development principle...The active principle is the spirit.   900-17

Life is, in all its manifestations in every animate force, Creative Force in action; and is the love of expression--or expressing that life; truth becoming a result of life's love expressed. For, these are but names--unless experienced in the consciousness of each soul.   262-46

That of life vibratory force in electrical vibration is of the **lowest** electrical vibration, that that builds for active forces or principles with that that is of the highest known vibration in a human body.   2155-1

Life in its manifestations is vibration. Electricity is vibration.   1861-16

And what is life? God manifested in the material plane. For it is still in Him that we live and move and have our being (Acts 17:28). Thus life as a material manifestation is the expression of that Universal Force or Energy we call God.   3590-1

Life is real, Life is earnest, Life is everlasting. For life **is** the manifestation of that which is worshiped, that which is sought by each soul; God, in movement, in manifestation!   1300-1

Truth is life, life is light; and He **is** light, He **is** the Creative Force in thine experience.   412-9

For man **is** flesh, as man is of Divine origin. And the mind of man, though it may--through the prunings, the trainings, the guidings in that direction for ages upon ages--become somewhat purified, only that portion of the mind that **is** divine can know, does know, that Life **is** the manifestation of God in motion.   1298-1

He is an ever active force...that brought the Pleiades into being, or set the bands of Orion (Job 38:31) or the waters of the deep that are cast upon the land, or brings breath in the life of all His creatures and supplies the union with those Creative Forces that makes for the songs of the spheres--the Lord is His name.   262-23

In each atom, in each corpuscle, is life. Life is that ye worship as God.   2968-1

What is life? **GOD**!--in action with thy fellowman!   793-2

What is Truth? Law. What is Law? Love. What is Love? God. What is God? Law and Love. These are as the cycle of truth itself.   3574-2

Q-What is the law of love?

A-Giving. As is given in this injunction, "Love thy Neighbor as Thyself"..."Love the Lord Thy God with all Thine Heart, Thine Soul and Thine Body." In this, as in many, we see upon the physical or earth or material plane the manifestations of the law, without the law itself...**That Is The Law Of Love**. Giving in action, without the force felt, expressed, manifested, shown, desired or reward from that given. Not that the law of love does away with other laws, but makes **The Law Of Recompense, The Law Of Faith, The Law Of Divine, With The Law Of Earth Forces**, if you please, of effect, not defective, but effect.

So we have **Love** is **Law, Law Is Love. God Is Love, Love Is God** ...Now, if we, as individuals, upon the earth plane, have all of the other elementary forces that make to the bettering of life, and have not love we are as nothing--nothing.   3744-4

God is Love. The influence or force that motivates the life of each soul is love. But it may be love of self, of fame, of fortune, of glory, of beauty, or of self-indulgence, self-aggrandizement.   1579-1

What is Love Divine? That the Father and the Son and the Holy Spirit may direct thee, does direct thee, **will** direct thee, in every thought, in every act.   262-104

Love, then, Divine; as was manifested in Jesus of Nazareth, must be the rule--yea, the measuring stick--the rod, by which ye shall judge thy motives, thy impulses, thy associations.   1497-1

The First Cause, the First Principle, Love. For God so loved the world that He gave His own Son that ye, as an individual, might have access to the Father.   4083-1

Not as Moses painted a God of wrath; not as David painted a God that would fight thine enemies; but as the Christ--(who presented Him as) the Father of love, of mercy, of justice.   262-100

All good, all hope, all mercy, all purpose of **divine** flows from Love itself; that He would have man in his former estate, knowing himself to be one with Him yet individual, capable of making those influences upon, those influences roundabout, that make known the joy of **love**-- that law is love, love is law to all, as it expresses itself.   1157-1

God is Love; hence occupies a space, place, condition, and is the Force that permeates all activity.   5749-4

There must be a law to **everything**--spirit, mental, material. To be sure, there **is**: but it is guided, guarded, and kept in accord with that which is the principle, the spirit, the **soul** of the First Cause. 1885-2

Know in self that there are immutable laws, and that as the universe visioned about self is directed by laws set in motion from the beginning, so in man's relationship to same under the law. 2449-1

The law of the Lord is perfect and it is as applicable in man as in the universe, as in nature, as in the realms of spirit itself. For the first principle is that the Lord, the God of the universe is One. 4035-1

There are divine or universal laws, as there are nature's laws and their application change according to circumstance, or manner of application through understanding. 2615-1

All manifestation of life is spirit. Hence matter, materiality, should be nothing. But when spirit is manifesting in a three-dimensional world of matter, form **and** spirit, it becomes subject to the laws of materiality--which in themselves are temporal, and thus subject to decay. 1678-1

Natural laws are God's laws. Everything in the earth is ruled by law. He said, "Let there be light" (Genesis 1:3), and there was light--by law.
What law? Of the spirit of truth, of light itself moving into activity thus becoming creative by law. 3902-2

"Like begets like. As he sows, so shall he reap. As a man thinketh in the heart, so is he." These are all but trite sayings to most of us, even the thinking man; but should the mind of an individual (the finite mind) turn within his own being for the law pertaining to these trite sayings, until the understanding arises, then there is the consciousness in the finite of the infinite moving upon and in the inner self. 262-52

That ye dwell upon, that ye become;--just as that ye hate suddenly befalls thee. This is natural law. 2034-1

Remember, Love is Law and Law is Love, and with the measure that same is meted the same is meted to self. Through every channel does this law hold good, whether of the mental, the spiritual or the physical being of man. 270-15

Man's development, as given, is of man's understanding and applying the laws of the Universe. And as man applies these, man develops, man brings up the whole generation of man. Individuals, we find, carry out certain elements and laws, and gradually man becomes capable of applying and using these in the everyday life of man. This, whether applied in medical science, in anatomical science, in mechanical science. 900-70

Universal forces...become manifest in the material world as the mentality of man develops and gains the knowledge of the laws of the universe...Jesus, who only used the universal law, and in the deflection of same, through the life lived, made same manifest in the world, in the last overcoming even the disintegration of the spirit and soul from the physical or corporeal body, and able to force all law to become subjugated to the body, or, as we see, manifest in the electrical forces.   900-17

As Jesus, the man, that is in relationship to thyself,--as He applied the law. He made himself equal with the law, by becoming the law. No doubt, no fear, no animosity, no self--but selfless in God's purpose. This overcomes the law as related to all phases of materiality, including gravity.   2533-7

For, there has not been the full concept as to the meaning of the blood as shed for the eternal sacrifice, or the law being of none effect in the law itself; that as individuals, in body, in mind, in spirit **become** the law, it is then as void in **their** experience--for they **are** the law! And the law is love, the law is God.   2067-2

"I came not to take away the law, but to fulfill same" (Matt. 5:17). 1541-11

Then **know**, this is the whole law--to love God, eschew evil, and love thy neighbor as thyself!   1603-1

Until individuals are in their thought, purpose and intent **the** law-- that is constructive--they are subject to same.
Hence those injunctions that have been so oft given "When ye know the truth, the truth shall indeed set you free" (John 8:32). Free from what? That of **Self.**   1538-1

Practice...charity to all, love to all; finding fault with none; being patient with all, showing brotherly love and brotherly kindness. Against these there **is** no law. And...by the application of them...ye become free of the laws that are of body or of mind; for ye are then conscious of being one **with** the Creative Forces.   1620-1

Man by **his** compliance with divine law bring **order** out of chaos; or, by his **disregard** of the associations and laws of divine influence, bring chaos and **destructive** forces into his experience.   416-7

And if thy life is disturbed, if thy heart is sad, if thy body is racked with pain, it is thine bungling of the laws that are as Universal as Life itself.   281-27

Don't think that the body is a haphazard machine, or that the things which happen to individuals are chance. It is all law!   2067-1

First, let it be understood there is the pattern in the material or physical plane of every condition as exists in the cosmic or spiritual plane, for things spiritual and things material are but those same conditions raised to a different condition of the same element--for all force is as of one force. 5756-4

For to begin from the first, we have in the material plane the counterpart, pattern or model through which all may be understood in the etheric or in the celestial, terrestrial plane--if we choose to use such terms. 900-348

The basis, the beginning of law carries all the way through. And that which comes or begins first is conceived in spirit, grows in the mental, manifests in the material. 2072-10

All one sees manifest in a material world is but a reflection or shadow of the real or spiritual life. Brotherhood, then, is an expression of the fellowship that exists in the **spiritual** life. 262-23

The law of environment, relativity, heredity, is the same in the spiritual activity as in material earthly--**matter** conditions. 683-1

In whatever position self occupies, force self to be **content** but **not** satisfied, knowing that the application of the spiritual, mental, and physical laws are but the pattern one of another. 349-6

The fourth dimension then being that condition as is reached wherein physical objects are spiritually understood, spiritual objects are physically understood. 900-66

There is no difference between the unseen world and that which is visible; save that in the unseen, so much greater expanse or space may be covered. 5754-3

Whatever there may be conceived by the mind of a body, it finds **its** replica in a material experience; for with the body, mind and spirit does one present itself **wholly** acceptable **unto** the divine, **whatever** that may be made in the terms of worshipfulness; for **in** the spiritual one lives, moves, and has one's being--and the spirit is willing, the flesh will follow, will the mental build in that direction that they are kept in accord one with another. 454-1

We have the first three laws in the activity of spirit in matter in the earth.
Preservation of self; perseverance in perpetuation of self, by impregnation of matter to become a reproduction of itself; and--the like begets like. 5756-11

He who understands nature walks close with God.   1904-2

In **all nature** the Spirit of Creation is **emanating**, and one that attunes self in **mind** or mental forces towards **beings** of emanation, gains knowledge in an **inestimable** manner, that becomes the soul, the personality, the **being** of the individual.   345-2

Listen to the birds. Watch the blush of the rose. Listen to the life rising in the tree. These serve their Maker. Through what? That psychic force, that **is** Life itself...Learn, O Man, from that about thee.   364-10

Think not that the snail or the dragon fly, as he crawls from his slime, does not glorify his Maker. And as he mounts on his wings of gossamer, he fills that place for which he has been--in his realm of activity--designated; in his field, his manner of showing forth his love as manifested from the Creator in the materialized world.   254-68

Go to the ant, thou sluggard--understand his ways and be wise!...They choose by their instinct. Ye learn by application of choice.   1965-1

(In the Garden of Eden) the fruit, the leaves, trees, had their spiritual meaning in peoples' lives.   5373-1

THE LAW OF RELATIVITY

Q-Explain in detail the law of relativity.

A-This law of relativity we find, as has been given, relates to the law as was set in motion in the beginning, when the universe as a whole came into existence.

As related to the mind, and to the earth conditions, we find first beginning with the earth in its position, with the other elements about same. Those became the law of the relative position regarding the spheres, and as there begun the lowest form of the animal and mineral, and vegetable, forces in the earth, we begun with all relative condition regarding those conditions from other spheres, and their relations to same.

In the mind, then and the soul forces as given in man, in his creation, it bears its relation then to all other forces in the universe, and as man's mind developed in the earth's forces, the seeking to find those relations still remaining that relative force as exercised in the earth plane; each bearing its relation to the other. Just as the planetary system is to earth and its relation to each and every kingdom as presented itself in its relation to the earth condition, and to those of the Creator and the created...Then, in the soul's development to reach that plane wherein the whole entity may become one with creative forces, that creative energy, that oneness with God, this we find needs then that development through all the planes in the universal forces, or throughout the universe. Hence the necessity of developing in that plane. All bearing, then, the relative condition, position, action, state of being, to that creative force, and that created...

As is shown in the earth's plane from the elements about the earth, all combination in chemical form begins a form of condition with force, less the creative plasm of the entity, the being, to give reproduction in itself, that energy, that first force, that spirit agent; in such being the relative force to all life giving forces. Hence, in its development, each bearing its relation, and its relative relation, to those conditions upon which the existence of such force depends.   900-24

Q-Explain how the law of relativity applies to man's evolution?

A-As each and every atom in the universe has its relative relation with every other atom, then man's development lies in the relativity of all forces, whether applied in the physical world as existent today, or that existent in man' earthly existence before, for the relativity of one force applies to another. Hence all relative forces apply to man's development, whether mental, physical or spiritual.   900-70

All life **is** one, all conditions then are relative as one to another... For what is **was**, and ever will be; so far as the spirit, the life, the soul is concerned--even of things.   1402-1

All **force** all **power** is of one source, as is life--but the **associations** of each are individual, and should be classified so **by** the entity in its **study** of the relationships of animal matter, celestial matter, material matter. In **spirit** one, but all flesh is not of one flesh--as some are given a cosmic influence only and others the ability to become one with the Creative Energy itself, in its **cleansing** of itself to be one in its relationships.   1910-1

Q-Does the incoming soul take on some of the parents' karma?

A-Because of its relative relationship to same, yes. Otherwise, no.

Q-Does the soul itself have an earthly pattern which fits back into the one created by the parents?

A-Just as indicated, it is relative--as one related to another; and because of the union of activities they are brought in the pattern. For in such there is the explanation of universal or Divine laws, which are ever one and the same; as indicated in the expression that God moved within Himself and then He didn't change, though did bring to Himself that of His own being made crucified even in the flesh.   5749-14

Elements have their attraction and detraction, or those of **animosity** and those of gathering together. This we see throughout all of the kingdoms, as may be termed, whether we speak of the heavenly hosts or of those of the stars, or of the planets, or of the various forces within any or all of same, they have their attraction and detraction. The attraction increases that as gives an impulse, that that becomes the aid, the stimuli, for an impulse to create. Hence, as may be seen--or may be brought to man's own--that of attraction one for another gives that **stimuli**, that **impulse**, to be the criterion of, or the gratification of, those influences in the experience of individuals or entities. To smother same oft becomes deteriorations for each other, as may come about in any form, way or manner. Accidents happen in creation, as well as in individual's lives! Peculiar statement here, but true! 364-6

Those (people) to whom you're drawn may be your weakness or may be your strength, depends upon that to which they respond.   5259-1

Souls in their varied experiences...are again and again **drawn** together by the natural law of attractive forces for the activity towards what? The **development** of the soul to the **ONE** purpose, the **One Cause**--to be companionate with the **First Cause**!
Then as the entity here contacts in materiality those of its own body, those of its own sympathetic condition, it is for the development of each in its associations one to another toward that First Cause.   903-23

The law that is ever present: like attracts like; like begets like. 541-1

In astrological aspects...the natural attraction, law of attraction, or law of repulsion, becomes manifest. For separated from the body, the mind and the soul are drawn to that influence manifested; just as in the material world those that are thinking alone the same lines or who are desirous of individual achievement, are drawn to those sources from which help or stimulating influences may be had.   2410-1

There are about us many, **many, many**, soul bodies; those upon whom the thought of an individual, the whole being of an individual is attracted to, by that element of thought--just the same as the action in the material body--for remember, we are patterned, see? one as of another. 5756-4

Q-Will you explain the laws of attraction and repulsion.
A-There are atomic vibrations, and as there is the breaking up of each element in its forces and forms, there is produced the attraction or repulsion...All of uranium elements are an attractive force for those influences that produce same, you see--platinum and all mercury products are attracted by uranium.   2431-1

The individuality is that with which ye live yourself, your inner self. And this is deep, far-reaching...

Know that in patience ye become aware of thy soul. And thy body and thy mind, and thy soul, are one. They live together.

Your personality, then, is the material expression; and your individuality is the personality of the soul.   2995-1

Personalities in the material plane arise from the application of the entity's urges in earthly sojourns. Individualities arise from what an entity would or does about the entity's ideal in a material experience...

While individuality and personality here may war at times one with another, when the individual makes the personality of the Divine manifested in the personality of the entity, and the individuality of the entity becomes one with the personality of God, we will find the attaining to that same experience as attained in the Holy Land. 3211-2

The gift of God to man is an **individual** soul that may be one **with** Him, and that may know itself to be one with Him and yet individual in itself, with the attributes **of** the whole, yet **not** the whole.   262-11

Personality is that seen by others. Individuality is that which shines out from within, separating one from another. Though one may be but a dot, that dot remains ever individual. Though it may be in line with many lines, yet it, the individual entity--the gift of the Creative Energy, that would have emanations to be within self. Yet a portion of the whole. The nearer one becomes to that which will give its **individuality**-- yet losing itself in the whole--the **more** individuality one attains.

Q-In painting, what is most to be desired?

A-Soul! Soul! That is, that which gives an atmosphere, that makes for that called individuality.   345-2

Personality is that ye wish others to think and see. Individuality is that your soul prays, your soul hopes for, desires. They need not necessarily be one. But their purpose must be one, even as the Father, the Son and the Holy Spirit are one; so must body, mind and soul be one in purpose and aim; and as ye ask, believing, so is it done unto thee.   5246-1

The individuality is the motive forces of **innate** desires, while secular forces are the motive more in the personality.   1914-1

The individuality of a soul must be lost in the personality of the Christ--in God. These become unified, then in their activities. 3343-1

For the purpose of an entity's entrance into the earth (and this might apply to all) is to manifest the personality of God in the own individuality and personality.   3351-1

Know, no urge surpasses the individual will of an entity, that birth-right of each soul, that gift of the Creative Forces that makes or causes the individuality in an entity, the ability to know itself to be itself and yet one with the Creative Forces.   2629-1

As those influences or forces entered that took man away **from** Him, then it was from that consciousness or spirit that the individuality has its source, its essence, its influence that might be made a personality in its activity.   262-119

This may be termed as a **true** definition of the two: Personality leadeth. **Individuality** commandeth; not as men call command, "obey" and he obeyeth, through fear--but commandeth and commendeth being nearer of the same term.   1720-1

In Saturn we find the changes, the weaknesses as indicated in both the mental forces and the application at times. For, with its powerful, magnetic personality, the weakness of the entity is to forget that it isn't personality that is spiritual but the individuality--that is the personality of God, or the Son in activity...
In **individuality** you may give the expression of the Father, the Son, and the Holy Spirit, **without** the destruction of the personality.   2420-1

That which a conscious mind does with pleasure becomes a part of the entity's personality...The understanding of a body in the material environs as to the laws of a particular experience, making for that termed as sincerity of the entity, of the soul, pertaining to the law that is known, is the soul's personality. Think on that.   378-14

The entity is an individual, individual in itself; that is, its person-ality and its individuality are nearer one and the same than you will find in one out of a million...
Ye have practiced peace first within self.   5125-1

(Astrological influences) are but the mental urges that arise, and become as the individuality of an entity in expression in the material world; while the appearances in the earth...are as but the personality in the entity's experience--and are as the urges from the emotions that have been created.   633-2

As spirit he (man) pushed his individuality into matter and began to express or manifest **personal** influence--for self, for ease, for comfort, for those things that would enable the individual entity to in matter lord over others.   1448-2

That which one would pretend to be and isn't is indeed sin! 826-6

God meant man to be free and thus gave man will, a will even to defy God. 3976-29

To be free is to gain the knowledge necessary to loose the bonds that bind one, whether they be mental, physical, or spiritual. 1215-8

"When ye know the truth, the truth, shall indeed set you free" (John 8:32). From what? That of **Self**. 1538-1

For hath not God given freedom of choice to every soul? and it is the heritage of every man, every soul--**Freedom**! 1129-2

One may be free indeed in thought, though the body may be bound in chains; and be much more free than those who are chained by their own consciousnesses. 1669-1

By sin came death; by the shedding of blood came freedom--freedom from a consciousness, into a greater consciousness. 276-7

Jesus, the Christ...has set the example--of freedom of speech, freedom of activity; yet bound within that which is ever constructive. He has not given freedom that is licentious, or freedom that is self-indulgent, or freedom that does not consider...others. 1352-4

Every form of manifestation, of expression of the spirit of a time, of a place, of a condition, of an individual, of a group, of a country, of a nation, **is** the attempt of that individual, group or nation to give expression of self or its God. 2279-1

The creative influence in every herb, mineral, vegetable or individual activity **is** that same force ye call God--and **seeks** expression! 294-202

Life is, in all its manifestations in every animate force, Creative Force in action; and is the love of expression--or expressing that life; truth becoming a result of life's love expressed. For, these are but names--unless experienced in the consciousness of each soul. 262-46

In the beginning, all souls that were as portions of the thought of God were given the opportunity for expression, as to be companions for that Creative Force--or God. 2420-1

See in the raindrop, the storm, all nature, and even in those ugly things in people's lives, the desire for expression rather than the hate and turmoil and the disorders. For, **all** are seeking expression. 410-2

The soul enters in, to make manifest **its** concept of, **its own** concept of, the first cause...To make manifest **itself**, or--as it were--it has flown out from its source to try **its** wings. 311-2

Know that the birthright of every soul is choice, or will.   2329-1

Choice is made by the will, guided by the mental according to that which in the consciousness of self is an entity's ideal.   1885-1

Each individual has the choice, which no one has the **right** to supersede--even God does not!   254-102

If our will were broken, if we were commanded to do this or that, or to become as an automaton, our individuality then would be lost and we would only be as in Him without conscience--**conscience**--consciousness of being one with Him; with the abilities to choose for self.   1567-2

As from the beginning, choice is that which separated the entity from the Creative Forces or makes for its being one with same.   1470-2

We have continually the conflicting influences, or good and bad constantly before an entity for choice...
For with free-will we become as the children of the Father. Without free-will we become as automatons, or as nature in its beauty--but ever **just that** expression; while the soul of man may grow to be equal with, one with, the Creative Forces.   1435-1

Will, that companion of the consciousness to which one must become conscious before the application of will becomes a factor. One may not, then, will to do thus or so without the consciousness of a choice existent. When this is not **in** action, then the environmental sphere has its sway.   900-357

There is no urge in the astrological, in the vocational, in the hereditary or the environmental which surpasses the will or determination.   5023-2

Know that it is this will--the birthright of each soul--that makes for growth or retardment in any given experience or activity...
Forms, shadows, colors, numbers,--even as to astrological aspects,-- have their place. But know that they are but as lessons, as signposts along the way. They indicate, as the weather vane, from what direction the impulse may arise,--the easier way of any activity; and are not, thus, the thing nor the power itself.   1992-1

So soon as man contemplates his free will he thinks of it as a means of doing the opposite of God's will, though he finds that only by doing God's will does he find happiness. Yet the notion of serving doesn't sit well with him, for he sees it as a sacrifice of his will.
Only in disillusion and suffering, in time, space, and patience, does he come to the wisdom that his real will is the will of God, and its practice is happiness and heaven.   2537-1

Will is given to man over and above all creation: **that** force which may separate itself from its Maker, for with **will** man may either adhere or contradict the Divine law--those immutable laws which are set between the Creator and the created.   3744-4

What is **will**? That which makes for the dividing line between the finite and the infinite, the divine and the wholly human, the carnal and the spiritual. For the **will** may be made one with Him, or for self alone. With the will, then, does man destine in the activities of a material experience how he shall make for the relationships with Truth262-81

For what ye sow, ye must reap. And remember, **every** experience is a conditional one. For, choice must be made daily.   2034-1

Ye have been chosen; each one that **chooses** to **do** His biddings.   262-57

Will is the factor in the experience of each soul making it separate or individual. It is the individuality of a soul.   3351-1

For the will of each entity, of each soul, is that which individualizes it, makes it aware of itself.   853-9

The will of the soul attuned to God may change the circumstances or the environment...in fact, all the forces even in nature itself.   3374-1

First there is the spirit, then soul (man we are speaking of), then mind with its various modifications and with its various incentives, with its various ramifications, if you please, and the will the balance in the forces that may make all or lose all.
In the developing, then, that the man may be one with the Father, necessary that the soul pass, with its companion the will, through all the stages of development, until the will is lost in Him and he becomes one with the Father.
The illustration of this we find in the man called Jesus. This man, as man, makes the will the will of the Father, then becoming one with the Father and the model for man.   900-10

As to whether circumstances or environ is to rule an entity's being or experience, or **will**, depends then--the most--upon what the entity or soul sets as its standard of qualifications to meet or measure up to, within its **own** self; or as to how well self may be guided by its standard in making decisions in those directions.   590-1

Each entity is endowed with its choice. And the choice is the result of the application of self in relationships to that which is its ideal-- and finds manifestation in what individuals call habit, or subconscious activity. Yet it has its inception in that of choice.   830-2

Q-Is the body aware of the destiny of the physical body at birth?
A-God Himself knows not what man will destine to do with himself, else would He have repented that He had made man. He has given man free will. **Man** destines the body.   262-86

(God) did not prevent (the fall of man), once having given free will. For, He made the individual entities or souls in the beginning. For, the beginnings of sin, of course, were in seeking expression of themselves outside of the plan or the way in which God had expressed same. Thus it was the individual, see?
Having given free will, then,--though having the foreknowledge, though being omnipotent and omnipresent--it is only when the soul that is a portion of God **chooses** that God knows the end thereof.   5749-14

There is that within self that is creative; and it, that creative force, cooperating with the Divine without, will lead to the choice of that which is life. And when the choice is made, then there may be a vision, astrologically and otherwise, of what the end thereof is. But each soul is given the birthright of the ability to choose--under any environment, any circumstance, any experience.   1580-1

Q-Is it the destiny of every spiritual entity to eventually become one with God?
A-Unless the entity wills its banishment...Yet God has not **willed** that **any** soul should perish.   900-20

Q-If the soul fails to improve itself, what becomes of it?
A-...Can the will of man continue to defy its Maker.   826-8

The soul, then, must return--**will** return--to its Maker. It is a portion of the Creative Force, which is energized into activity even in materiality, in the flesh.   272-9

Each soul is destined to become a portion again of the First Cause, or back to its Maker.   987-2

Doth the time of birth, the place of environment, make or have a part in destiny? Do the days or the years, or the numbers, all have their part? Yea, more than that! Yet, as has been given, all these are but signs along the way; they are but omens; they are but the marks that have indicated--for, as given, He has set His mark, and these are **signs,** not the destinies. For the destiny of the mind, of the body, or the soul, is with Him.   262-75

Destiny is within, or is as of faith, or is as the gift of the Creative Forces. Karmic influence is, then, rebellious influence against such.

When opportunities are presented, it is the entity's own **will** force that must be exercised...Hence as for the entity's fulfilling, it is **ever** on the road.   903-23

The entity was ever a part of the Universal Consciousness, but was given the will...that it might be individual, knowing itself to be itself and yet one with the Creative Forces.   2524-1

No urge--whether of the material sojourns or of the astrological aspects--surpasses the mental and spiritual abilities of a soul to choose its course that it, the soul and mind, may take.   2533-1

Mind is, as has been given, both spiritual and physical. In the material world, where we find expressions of the physical and of the spiritual, we find Mind. Yet what is known as the Group Mind--or that of the plant kingdom, the mineral kingdom and the animal kingdom or group--returns (as its Destiny) to the Creative Force which is its author, its maker. Man-- the free will agent; man made to become a companion to the Creator through the purification, by manifestation of the love of God as may be manifested in the earth--makes his Destiny as to whether his Mind (that accompanies his soul) is one with or in opposition to the Creative Forces. For he, for weal or for woe, gives expression of same in his activity. And his Destiny--Mind's Destiny--is in Him if he, man, will but make the Mind one with that which is creative in its essence, in its activity, in its flow. For Mind is the dividing line between that which is human, that which is man, and that which is animal--or of that division of a group soul or consciousness. Hence the variation in that He taught as He gave to Nicodemus, "Know ye not ye must be born again" (John 3:3)? Born of water and of blood; that is, of the spirit--yet the spirit making manifest in the flesh the last command, the whole command as He gave, "A new commandment I give, that ye love one another"--that ye be of one mind of one purpose, or one aim, of one desire. That each must approach from his or her own vision, his or her own status of development, does not alter that as has been spoken, "as the man thinketh in his heart, so is he" (Proverbs 23:7). So does the Mind bring health, wealth, happiness; in that it is made **one with** Constructive Force, one with the Creator; and thus fulfil its Destiny--to become One in Him, One with the Father.   262-80

Though the heavens fall, though the earth may pass away, in His own time He will draw thee--wilt thou but show thy **willingness** to be drawn; but not against thine better or thine inner self.   366-5

Man alone is given...free will. He alone may defy his God. 5757-1

Will...designates...man from the rest of the animal world.   3340-1

For while a very material-minded individual might say that "bad luck" had come to the body, we find nothing happens by chance.   3684-1

There is nothing by chance. Friendships are only the **renewing** of former purposes, ideals. For, as the preacher gave, "There is nothing new under the sun" (Ecclesiastes 1:9). For, in the beginning all was made that was made, and as it unfolds from what man terms time to time, period to period, there is only the renewing of the First Cause. Isn't the last apple also that portion of the first one created? 2946-2

No association or experience is by chance, but is the outgrowth of a law, spiritual, mental, or material.   2753-2

It is never by chance but as with all things in this material world, there are causes, there are effects. To be sure, at time there may be what might be called accidents. But these, too, in a causation world, have their cause and effect.   2927-1

Little happens by chance. True, there may be errors--which is indicated oft in the experience of the mental, the spiritual and material activities of an entity. These may be called accidents at times. 2881-1

Know there is little or naught which happens by chance save accidents. These appear even in creation.   5106-1

Each nation, each individual head of a nation, is not in the position it occupies merely by a 'happen chance' but by the grace of God. 5142-1

Nothing is by chance, but is...a pattern of...the choices made by the entity in its relationships to things, conditions, and...entities.   1825-1

Each individual constantly meets self. There are no coincidences, or accidents, that arise in the meeting of people or individuals. 2074-1

It is never by chance that a soul enters any material experience; rather by choice. For, the will is the birthright, the manifested right of every soul. It is the gift of the Creator, yet it is the price one pays for material expression.   2464-2

No one enters an experience by chance, but that all may come to know their relationships to the Creative Force.   2891-1

Each entity enters a material experience for a purpose; not accidentally, not by chance. But life and its expressions are purposeful.   1792-2

We meet few people by chance, but all are opportunities in one experience or another. We are due them or they are due us certain considerations.   3246-1

O that all would realize, come to the consciousness that what we are--in any given experience, or time--is the combined result of what we have done about the ideals that we have set. 1549-1

The most important experience of this or any individual entity is to first know what **is** the ideal--spiritually. 357-13

An ideal, then, **cannot, should** not, **will** not, be that that is manmade, but must be of the spiritual nature--that has its foundation in Truth, in God, in the Godhead, that there may be the continual reaching out of an individual, whether applied to the physical life, the mental life, or the spiritual life; knowing that **first** principle, that the gift of God to man is an **individual** soul that may be one **with** Him, and that may know itself to be one with Him and yet individual in itself, with the attributes **of** the whole, yet **not** the whole. Such must be the concept, must be the ideal, whether of the imaginative, the mental, the physical, or the spiritual body of man. All may **attain** to such an ideal, yet never become the ideal--but **one with** the ideal, and such an one is set in Him. 262-11

One of the influences that must first be builded, then, is to first know thy ideals--spiritually, mentally, materially. And in the spiritual --know that the ideal must be that which is able to keep whatever may be committed unto it against **any** experience. In the mental, it must be ever constructive, creative in its influence, in its activity...
Then, what thy destiny is depends upon what ye will do with thyself in relationship to thy ideal. 2021-1

Confusion is often caused, then, and is ever caused unless there is an ideal drawn or accepted by which all of these conditions, all of these experiences--whether physical, mental or spiritual--may be judged or from which conclusions may be drawn.
Otherwise we are measuring ourselves **by** ourselves, and this becomes unwise. For it again leaves confusions as to what is another's standard...
But who may answer but thyself, thy Lord, thy ideal?
Then in Him, and in self, seek, seek to know; using that thou hast-- not unto the satisfying of any phase of thy own personality but to the glory of thy divinity, and to the **individuality** of thy Ideal. 954-5

Study, then, to show thyself approved unto an ideal. What is an ideal? This ye must first determine in thine self...
Choose that most in keeping with thy purposes, thy aims, thy desires. Are thy desires and thy purposes ideal, in thine own consciousness? What is thy ideal, spiritually?
Then from that may be gained the ideal mentally.
And the material is the outgrowth of those two. 2981-1

Q-What is judgement?

A-With what judgement shall ye be judged? Law is Love; Love is Law. Judgement is weighing love, law, according to the intent, the purpose of the activity in its relationships to thyself and to the force that impelled same.   262-81

God looketh upon the heart and He judgeth rather the purposes, the desires, the intents.   987-4

First, one finds self in a three-dimensional plane of consciousness; all that may be known materially is subject to that dimension.

That as may be comprehended in the mental may reach into a fourth-dimensional plane, as the variation between a book with its dimensions and the contents of same, which may be of a mental reaction entirely.

Yet the spiritual import is the premise, as to what is the ideal, purpose and intent of same--as to the effect the contents of such a book would have upon an individual entity.

Or, one in the material phases of his experience draws mentally upon comparisons of things, conditions, experiences, through the mental faculties of the body; and his reaction is still dependent upon the ideal he holds.   1861-4

The law of cause and effect ever remains. Hence in spirit it is purpose and ideal.   3412-2

There is one ideal--that which manifests in the earth in the Christ-Jesus. **That** should be every entity's ideal--physically, mentally, materially...For, He **Is** the **light**, He **Is** the **way**, He **Is** the **truth.**   2533-7

Ideals are principles acted upon **by** your mind.   2533-6

Who is to say as to whether any individual is great? He that fulfills to the fullest his ideals in relationship to his fellow man. For, as one does to others is the measure of greatness or goodness towards the Creative Forces.   1100-31

As has been so well pointed out in Holy Writ, if the ideal of the individual is lost, then the abilities to contact the spiritual forces are gradually lost, or barriers are builded that prevent the individual from sensing his nearness to a spiritual development.   5754-3

Man may not have the same **idea.** Man--**all** men--may have the **same Ideal** not the one **idea,** but "Thou shalt love the Lord Thy God with all thine heart, thy neighbor **as** thyself." This (is) the whole law.   3976-8

Without the ability to constantly hold before self the ideal as is attempted to be accomplished, man becomes as one adrift.   239-1

Know the ideal. Measure the moral life, the social life, the material life, the spiritual life, by that standard. Lose not sight of that thou believest. 488-6

Not that these (ideals) will ever be reached, but an ideal must be set towards which it is able to keep working or to answer what ever questionable experiences may arise in the experience of the entity. 5040-1

Will the body set some condition in the mental as an ideal, and labor or work towards that end, rather than being pulled or allowed to be influenced from day to day in so **uncertain** ways as to approach that point where the body does not know itself **what** it desires to do, except for the moment! 1000-10

Study to show thyself approved unto God, the Ideal. 2283-1

He without an ideal is sorry indeed; he with an ideal and lacking courage to live it is sorrier still. Know that. 1402-1

TRUTH IS A GROWING THING

Q-What is truth?
A-That which makes aware of the Divine within each and every activity: that is of the mental, the material, the spiritual self--and is a growth in each and every soul...What is Truth? That which makes aware to the inmost self or the soul the Divine and its purposes with that soul. 262-81

If there be any virtue or truth in those things given in the spiritual or Christian or Jehovah-God faith, His laws are immutable. What laws are immutable, if truth and God Himself is a growing thing--yet ever changeable, and yet "ever the same, yesterday and today and forever?"
These things, these words, to many minds become contradictory but they are in their inception **not** contradictory; for Truth, Life, Light, Immortality, are only words that give expression to or convey a concept of one and the same thing. 276-7

Truth is a growing thing, as infinity, as Creative Force. 1554-6

Then truth, then life, to the human experience, is a growth. You grow in grace, in knowledge, in understanding of the Lord and His ways. 1387-1

Truth is a growth. For what is truth today may be tomorrow only partially so, to a developing soul! 1297-1

No finite mind has **all** the truth! For **truth** is a **growing** thing! 282-4

Truth is a growth, and hence, an **earning**, a yearning, a growing, and is **earned** by he or she that applies that known in the manner that **is** in keeping with His Will.   262-19

Truth is the unalterable, unchangeable law, ever. What is truth? Law! What is Law? Love! What is Love? God! What is God? Law and Love. These are as the cycle of truth itself...He is the same yesterday, today and forever--unalterable...**I Am That I Am.** That is true.   3574-2

Truth, while a growth, is indeed ever the same; and is the stepping-stone to material, mental and spiritual success.   1538-1

If the ideal is prompted by Truth, no matter what may be the outward appearance, the assurance of filling and fulfilling the purpose for which the entity seeks expression in this experience in every **phase** of its consciousness, it will bring contentment, peace, harmony.   1470-2

To know the truth is to make you free (John 8:32)! Truth is as Life, a **growing** consciousness in self.   323-2

(Truth) must find a response within self, else to the individual it is a theory or an idea.   4047-2

It is needful for man to interpret in his own experience "The Lord thy God is One " (Mark 12:29). Each and every individual are attempting to give **their** interpretation, and you may be sure that each is just as sincere as the other. That they each have found something which does not answer to that something within the other is not evidence that either is wrong, or that either is right. The answer is according to that each one is doing about that which answers to the first and the last command to man: **"Thou shalt love the Lord thy God with all thy heart, thy mind, thy body: thy neighbor as thyself."** Those who conform the nearer to that are correct. Yet, do any? Do you? Does your neighbor? 5142-1

Know what ye believe and know who is the author of thy beliefs; not just because you have been taught this or that by any man. They can only bring to your mind that already contained and all those influences which may add to or take from, according to what spirit or truth ye entertain. For truth maketh thee not afraid. Truth is truth everywhere the same, under every circumstance. It is creative. For light, the Christ, Jesus is the truth, is the perfect way. They who climb up some other way are thieves and robbers to their own better selves.   5030-1

The spirit of light, of hope, of desire to know truth, must be greater than that man has called scientific proof, and yet it is the science of light, of truth, of love, of hope, of desire, of God.   5023-2

PART II

VIBRATION AND SYMBOLOGY

LIFE IN ITS MANIFESTATIONS IS VIBRATION

Everything in motion, everything that has taken on materiality as to become expressive in any kingdom in the material world, is **by** the **vibrations** that are the motions, or those positive and negative influences that make for that differentiation that man has called matter in its various stages of evolution into material things. For it enters and it passes through. For, as is the better understood, and as will be proclaimed, all vibration must eventually, as it materializes into matter, pass through a stage of evolution and out. For it rises in its emanations and descends also. Hence the cycle, or circle, or arc, that is as a description of all influence in the experience of man. And very few do they come at angles!   699-1

Life in its manifestations is vibration. electricity is vibration. But vibration that is creative is one thing. Vibration that is destructive is another. Yet they may be from the same source. As in the electrical forces in the form or nature prepared even for use in the body.
Q-What is my ray?
A-Depends on what you are thinking. Remember life is vibration. So is mind. So is matter. As to the ray, this changes. Don't think you sit on a ray and it carries you along. You make the ray.   1861-16

Electricity or vibration is that same energy, same power, ye call God. Not that God is an electric light or an electric machine, but vibration that is creative is of the same energy as life itself.   2828-4

The lowest form of vibration electrically gives creative forces, rather than the highest. It is the high vibration that destroys.   933-3

The lowest form of electrical vibration **is** the basis of life.   444-2

For they (periods of history) will be seen to come in cycles...for, as in energy, there is seen the relativity of space and force as is begun, and as same continues to vibrate, that one law remains. Whenever it vibrates in the same vibration, it shows as the same thing.   254-47

All force is vibration, as all come from one central vibration and its activity into, out from, and its own creative forces, as given, within that of the divine as manifested in man, is same vibration, taking different form. Here, we may give a dissertation, in a manner, as to what Creative Energy is, as related to man and his activity, and as the forces as are seen in and about man. True it was said, "Come let us make man in our image," in His own image created God, or created by God, was man. Then containing all of the vibrations that were without, were given into that whole being of man, which in **its** vibration gave man the soul. **Above** all else created, see? Then we see how the evolution of force in vibration brought up to the point wherein man becomes one **with** the Creative Energy, or the Godhead, **with** the ability to become that that he is **not** at the beginning, by making himself from the will of the Creator or Creative Energy. How? In that the ability to create mentally, and with the hand **makes** that which **is** the created force of that mind, and with that may make destructive forces for self. Hence man becomes one **with** the Creative Energy, or away **from** that Creative Energy. When man makes himself one **with,** then all things were created by Him, without Him there was nothing created, or made--and are then **his** by rightful heir, even as shown in His Son, wherein man (is) shown the way, or the access to this all Creative Energy.   900-422

For returning to first principle, as there are those forces that move one within another to bring harmony, as for light, or color, or sound, or motion, all of these are but variations of movement, vibration.   2012-1

Moving of the spirit brought materiality into existence as a **thing** as a condition, for the souls and spirits and minds of men!   1947-1

The thing may be one thing standing still and an entirely different thing in vibratory forces in motion.   195-54

Q-The one substance vibrates in different dynamic degrees, and sound, heat, light, electricity, are the effections of the one substance by specific degrees of the One Energy, and there is no difference between anything such as electricity and, say iron, save in rate of effection. Is this correctly stated?
A-Correctly stated.
Q-It is more than probable that at the sun's surface there are many higher degrees of vibrations than are known or understood on this planet. Is this correct?
A-Correct.   195-70

For, without passing through each and every stage of development, there is not the correct vibration to become one with the Creator.   900-16

All force in nature, all matter, is a form of vibration, and the vibratory force determines as to what its nature **is**--that given by the cell itself, from which it produces, as is seen in all matter.   900-448

When matter comes into being, what has taken place? The Spirit ye worship as God has **moved** in space and in time to make for that which gives its expression; perhaps as wheat, as corn, as flesh, as whatever may be the movement in that ye call time and space.   281-24

Matter moved upon--or matter in motion in materiality--**becomes** the motivative force we know as the evolutionary influence in a material world. An entity or soul is a portion of the First Cause, or God, or Creative Energy; or the terms that may be had for the **movement** that brings matter into activity or being.   903-23

The **movement** of spirit upon things that do not appear has brought into being the things that **do** appear; not of things that do appear.   1486-1

Matter is an expression of spirit in motion...
In the beginning God created the heavens and the earth. How? The **Mind** of God **moved**, and matter, form, came into being.   262-78

Vibration is movement. Movement is activity of a positive and negative force.   281-29

Q-How can an article by mechanical means be charged with positive electricity continuously and economically?
A-It may not--without having its counterpart in the negative.
For in manifestations, this is the basis of materiality. Only when they become spiritual are they **only** positive.
For materiality **is**--or matter **is**--that demonstration and manifestation of the units of positive and negative energy, or electricity, or God.   412-9

Each atomic force of a physical body is made up of its units of positive and negative forces, that brings it into a **material** plane. These are of the ether, of atomic forces, being electrical in nature as they enter into a material basis, or become **matter** in its ability to take on or throw off. So, as a **group** may raise the atomic vibrations that make for those positive forces as bring Divine Force in actions into a material plane, those that are destructive are broken down by the raising of that vibration. That's **material**, see? This is **done** through **Creative** Forces, which are God in manifestation.   281-3

Each atom of the body-physical is an expression of a spiritual import. That is how matter comes into being.   264-45

Q-What are positive vibrations? How would they be explained?

A-How would one explain the differentiation between time in night and in day? How would one explain the differentiation in the activity of forces when there is a vibratory force set in a cellular force, and one is set in an oval or oblong force--which perpetrates, or penetrated, that force which produces or generates force as in its activity. In a negative force, as is seen in what has ordinarily or commonly in alchemy been called nightside. That as is of positive force is that as of the active force in its action, see?...A balance is a negative force--as you would see from a scale--weigh so much--balance, see? Now in this we have the activity of gravitation, added to that force which keeps this in action, see? This constant action of gravitation, which is a portion **of** the force as of universal forces, which keeps all in its balance. See, it applies right there, **everywhere**--in space, out of space, carries through in every form...

In gravitation--**commonly** known--is that everything sinks to a common center, or is **drawn** to a common center; while that as is expanded is the positive energy in opposite relation to that force drawing...

When we begin to understand these, then we begin to see how the vibratory force is the active principle all radiates from. What is gravitation? the centralization of vibratory force, ready to be changed in power by non-activity, see?   195-54

Q-Are radial forces negative forces?

A-Not always are radial forces negative forces. Only when they become passive, or of being acted upon as gravitation, do they become negative forces--while they are emanating from the positive; else they would not be drawn to the earth's force, in **its** emanation with the positive rays--and they are positive rays. From the sun's emanation does it produce the heat, see? This is seen in a better application, in that the deflection from--and the direct rays of--the sun's emanation **to** the earth, **through** the various stages of its activity, brings summer, or the heat wave, or the moving **of** the various forms; for these--acting upon--become negative, and then are positive in their action, though at times these, to be sure, become negative in their action; for each has its radial activity and is throwing **off**, as well as drawing **to**. Hence the various positions or conditions as is seen in the sun, through the activity of the various forms of gas or metal, or those various conditions that seem to cause the various eruptions as apparent within the sun itself. It receives as well as throws off, is positive as well as negative--see? and only until it becomes in such a force that it is altogether negative, as the gravitation that hold in place--for when each are lost in their relative position, these then are thrown off, as was the moon from the earth, or as is the various satellites of the various planets, as **well** as the various effects out in space.

Q-What argument would be most conclusive to prove that the sun is not hot at the surface?

A-The breaking up of the rays, just as has been described, in that it takes **back** as well as gives off, being both positive and negative. 195-70

Each atomic force has its energy, as is seen in that of the variation of the force as would be by the fall of an apple or that of an orange from the same distance. Or, to put it in a **different** degree, would be as is seen in the **ability** of force to cast off a **metal**--or to cast off a wooden ball. Each weighing the same, the metal can be cast off farther on account of the variation in atomic energy, as is exercised through that of the force itself. 195-57

In the fall of the apple there was little other then may be experienced in any individuals' life. Only Newton first saw that it applied to his relation with the universe and how it held the whole in the oneness one with another. 900-429

Q-Give the atomic structure of metal which will prevent the gravitational pull.

A-It is a long way to these--and there must be determined for what purpose these are to be used before ye may be given how, in what manner. For, **these** take hold upon Creative Forces. 412-9

These may be well illustrated by that same condition as exists in natural law as to why the needle points toward north. In the radial force of the axis of the earth there is seen that the force from which this planet is kept in motion is radiated through, or from, that directive force. Hence the constant draw, pull, in that direction. Just as is seen in gravitational in **its** active law in drawing all to the earth according to its capacity of displacement as relative to the elements that go to make up the density of the object; yet each are relativity of forces one with another, employing all of the elements in their various octave of density to combine in their active principle of weight; yet each of these same laws are in the same relative position to that law of the needle point, and that of gravitation to the radius about which the object is radiating or being drawn to the radial center...

So, as was given, that compass point has much to do in the active force, as a **relativity**; not as to whether it turns north, east, south or west--for, as gravitation--whether north, east, south or west--acts in the same capacity; so as in gravitation active forces, as that of the needle, compass, always in its relative position or condition, for or through the radial forces of its active principle. 4665-13

There is an (astrological) influence from without self of a nature that self may be in accord with or in opposition to; for all entities realize they in themselves are both positive and negative influences, and the First Cause--or the Spirit--must of necessity within itself be likewise, yet more positive than negative, for it attracts with attraction and repels with rebellion of that same activity of which every entity is a part. Hence the realizing of self's dependence upon that influence is that which makes for the change in the experience of the entity, in becoming conscious--through the mental--spiritual forces in self--of the willingness to be led rather than leading or demanding other than, "Thy will be done in me."   264-31

In the analyzing of principles that go to make up things, in their relationships one to another, there are principles that are assumed or declared as being the positive and negative forces in such. So in thy spiritual relationship and thought, know: They that would know spirit must believe it is, and as they seek for same, in the same way and manner there is sought the positive and negative forces in matter, it may be found--**just** as positive and **just** as negative as all that becomes manifested in this material world.   2012-1

Q-"The positive may be considered as the active forces in their activity and the negative as those tending to keep the balance." Please expand on this and give a better explanation of positive and negative force.
A-This (is) as **good** an explanation as may be given, other than illustrating same; for it **is** a positive or a **plain statement** as to the conditions as regarding relativity of force; for **positive** is the active and negative is passive...The statement we would **not** expand upon in this instance, for it (the statement) must react with the individual **development** of each individual who takes the time to become positive **or** negative to the statement, and as one responds to same may the activity of the statement be seen.   195-70

In the first premise--know what was the cause of indifference, or sin, entering material manifestations. Was it the purpose by God that such should be, or by the Godhead? or was it that this force or power seeking expression found--with the expression--that there came the forces of positive and negative? And with same the awareness of one influence or force, taking certain courses or directions, became negative. The others became the greater positive.

Thus in the experience of souls through their evolution in the material things of the earth, there has been brought just that same effect in the material affairs of the souls active in expressing or manifesting at this particular period or sphere of development.

Much of just this comprehending is indicated in some of those records that are now becoming more and more a part of man's experience, or awareness; in that the cosmic or universal or spiritual laws are bringing same into that category or phases of experience where they become a part of individual experience.

This may be indicated from the records in the rocks; it may be indicated in the pyramids--man's attempts to leave a sign to those who, in the spiritual comprehension of material associations in spirit, would interpret that which had been, that which is, and that which was to be.

Hence it is seen that there are interpretations that become a matter of the consciousness of the individual so making same.

Or, to return to the first premise, it depends upon which line is taken by such an individual making such interpretation; whether a pessimistic or an optimistic, or a positive or a negative; or (by negative we mean) one that sees the world, as related to the earth and its position in the universe, being damned irrespective of what souls do about same--taking little or no account of the words, the promises, yea the activities of Him.   1602-5

Q-"Ether may be defined as the combination of a higher plane, leading us to metaphysics, to where every consideration of the atom finally leads one." Is this statement concerning ether correct?

A-There's no **better** definition. This is correct--for, same as the statement of positive and negative forces as relating to gravitation, they act upon the individual's **development**...there are...certain **characters** of disease that accentuate mental forces, or the metaphysical activity of a human body. There are others that so dull the senses that they become one-sided, or only passive not positive; yet a **normal**, perfectly well and normal mind may be so active as to be considered by others as of being unbalanced, but only is it considered **peculiar**.   195-70

Unless a helpful experience may be presented in an individual's activity as a parallel, as a complement, as a positive and negative force that may be united in one effort, it does not run true. For **opposites** create disturbances, dissensions, disruptions, devilment. A union of force makes for strength and power.   262-87

As we find the entity is very positive--and often tends to become argumentive with those who disagree.   1669-1

The life or spiritual or creative forces are positive, **and** the body-forces in material manifestation negative. To reach that as to where they will not be as combative forces is to unify the purposes, the energies, the activities.   1822-1

Each state, country or town makes its own vibrations by or through the activities of those that comprise same; hence creates for itself a realm in which the activities of each city, town, state...bring the associations through relativity of influence in the material plane. Hence why astrological influences, and why in the various activities or centers may there be born or brought into the earth the various influences, even though their realm or place of activity may be very foreign to that place wherein they entered. Those activities make for such an impression upon the realm of data, or between time and space, as to make for what men have called Destiny in the material affairs of individuals.   262-66

(The entity should live) across waters--over waters, on waters, near waters, the larger the better...To live under any environ is to be aided by those surrounding conditions, see? or, mathematically speaking...to grasp the problem one must at least attune self to the fundamentals of that relating to **numbers** and **their** relation one to another. So, in an entity's development, when the environs are in keeping with the **entity's universal** development, the attunement is much easier. Now study that.   256-2

These (creative urges)...will find their greater expression near bodies of water, and near those environs where the entity's activities in the earth's plane have been a portion of the entity's experience.   649-1

Much might be pointed out as to how the environs of a place, house, room or surroundings are changed or produced by the dwelling there of an individual that radiates even distressed conditions from itself.   664-1

Each entity, each atom of the entity radiates that vibration to which it attunes itself.   2842-2

How few realize the vibratory forces as create influences from even one individual to another, when they are even in the same vibratory forces or influence. And yet ye ask what will the Aquarian age bring. 602-3

Remember, all are attuned to their own vibrations in the same manner as has been given that the variations are as that builded in the entity through which such may manifest. That is hard to be understood. Let us illustrate. We have a body, one capable of attuning even to the masters of the holy place, or holy mount; such an one may gain for self an experience that is beyond description in words, only feeling may express same. The same with other vibrations would change same even as that and current of, electronic force may be altered by being sent through copper, or through nickel, see? Now you are catching the idea. Study that.   136-83

Quite an interesting fact about people born here...Something in the soil; get it between your toes and you'll never commit suicide. 5125-1

What is Light? That from which, through which, in which may be found all things, out of which all things come. Thus the first of everything which may be visible in earth, in heaven and in space is of that Light, **is** that Light.   2533-8

God moved, the spirit came into activity. In the moving it brought light, and then chaos. In this light came creation of that which in the earth came to be matter; in the spheres about the earth, space and time; and in patience it has evolved through those activities until there are the heavens and all constellations, the stars, the universe. 3508-1

Vibration whether electronic or of light only are electronic in action, but the word itself does **not** indicate the variation. Yet their variations are entirely different...and it may be thoroughly demonstrated--or experimentation may be made:
A plant treated by a low form of electrical vibration will--kept from light, but given moisture and air--will extenuate itself to a greater extent than when allowed light--but **will not be able to reproduce itself**, see? What's cut off in same! While the same, without electrical vibration--save as **light** itself, **with** the other forms with same, are able to bring that which reproduces itself.   900-448

Q-How do light rays affect health?
A-Well--this you might write nineteen books on and then not have finished the subject; yet it may be answered in such a way and manner as to understand. What is the necessity of light as related to the functioning of the sensory system? Get **that!** There is not functioning of any portion of the system which functions through the nervous system not affected by rays of light, or, in other words, life itself in manifested form is vibration, of which light is a part. Now **get that!**   165-8

Q-What light should be used (Mastoiditis)?
A-Any penetrating light. That of the dry heat, or that that acts the quickest with the blood stream, see?...
All bacilli or all germs are afraid, as it were, of light--or light is destructive to all. Some, as is seen accumulate in heat that is not penetrating. Hence the variation in the quartz, the ultra-violet light, the blue light, the red light--each one taking out that that filters through the system. Hence for this, that one most penetrating without being destructive to the tissue proper.   140-21

A light--as the sun--gives off rays that respond to those elements seen and unseen in the earth.
Thus the heat, the radial activity is given off in the earth, and brings a universal consciousness to what is called nature.   2823-1

Fire, earth, air, water. These are the **natural** elements in the physical plane, and--as the forces of these have the influence--as the **spirit** of the air...The **spirit** of each! see?   288-27

That (burial) that would be **ideal** is that it may be hermetically sealed, or by fire, or by the separation of the atmosphere from the body.
    Q-What is the best disposition of a body, for the sake of all?
    A-By fire!   275-29

There are only four elements in your body,--water, salt, soda, and iodine. These are the basic elements, they make all the rest.   2533-6

(Regeneration) is a growth in the energies of the body and thus necessitates there being kept a normal balance in the chemistry of the body-force itself. For it is either from potash, iodine, soda or fats, that each of these in their various combinations and multiple activities supply all the other forces of the body-energies. Yet in each body there is born or projected that something of the soul-self also.   3124-1

Q-Please explain "The Kingdom of the Father."
A-...**How** does water, then, supply that which nourishes in this material plane? Being made up of elements in itself that are the essence of that which may truly be called spiritual itself, it gives that association or connection between the spiritual forces acting in the material elements of the earth, or material forces; hence entering into the Kingdom of the Father is knowing and following and **being** those elements that supply the needs of that which builds in the material plane towards the continuity of the spiritual forces manifesting in the earth.   262-28

There are elements in the earth from which, to which, every atom of the body responds...Silver and gold are those necessary elements that are needed in body when mind has been attuned to Creative Forces.   3491-1

Those elements of gold and silver were lacking (Parkinson's Disease) in those periods of gestation, which produces in the first cycle of activity the inability of the glands to create.   3100-1

The entity will gain most through sojourn near, or passing over, large bodies of water, and **salt** water is preferable; for...fresh hasn't **always** meant for living water.   243-10

Q-Why do all my big experiences begin near the water or on the water?
A-Is it not because water is the mother, the life of all material experiences? Is it not a natural law? Is it not as He, the great teacher gave? that we are born of the spirit and of water (John 3:5)?...
Water--the most flexible, the most solid; the most destructive yet the

most necessary. Three-fourths of the universe, three-fourths of the human body, three-fourths of all that is--contained in water. 1554-6

Pure water, the mother of creation is the beginning through which all matter...one day, some day, somewhere has passed. 5148-2

Have you not read of: "Know ye not, that ye must be born of water and of the Spirit?" The water in material the Mother of life; the Spirit, the Father, or the moving to bring life. Is it possible, then, that a man when he is old, shall again enter his Mother's womb and be born again? Ye must be born of water and of blood. Blood, a manifestation of force that through which life manifests in its various forms. Water, the cleansing force as one moves from experience to experience. 136-83

Water, as manifest, (is) the **beginning** of life. Over large bodies of water, then, do many men of many lands learn that (which) is hard to be understood by those on land...Hence, many are given to dwell near large bodies of water, where sands and sea, where much comes that may not be touched by hands, may not be seen with the human eye, but is felt in the heart and trains the soul. 900-465

GEMS AND STONES

Vibrations of numbers, of metals of stones, these are merely to become the necessary influence to make thee in attune, one with the Creative Forces. 707-2

The very **nature** of the thing (stone) makes it effective with any--**any**--human body, you see; but the more effective with one that is more in accord, or whose positive and negative vibrations are according with the stone itself, see. For it throws off as well as draws in, you see, through the positive--negative vibration...As the stone in its vibration is then in sympathy with a body that is also sympathetic--or may be said to be **sensitive**--it assists in 'stepping up' the sensitiveness. 440-18

There being, then, individuals who when wearing a fire opal would be hard individuals to deal with when it came to sex...The same individuals wearing or having in the apparel the moonstone might find that it would bring peace, harmony and those tendencies towards spiritual things. There are those to whom the bloodstone brings harmony, and less of the tendencies for anger; and so with each...

The auras as compared to the stones, these should work in ninety-nine percent of the conditions where these are considered as those things that work with, not against, the colors seen in the auras; that is, those which indicate the fire signs in the aura of such should never wear opals, and they will even fade flowers when worn.   5294-1

Each entity, has within its inner being the sum of what it has done, is doing, about its relationships to the whole. And this is the stone (bloodstone) to which the entity vibrates. Thus it is a helpful force physically, an encouragement to the mental, and vibrates upon the real or inner self.   2163-1

Well that the entity have the stones or minerals about self when in periods of meditation.   688-2

The pearl is a natural consequence of irritation--and it will bring either peace or irritation to the wearer as will the diamond.   3657-1

Its (pearl) vibrations are healing, as well as creative.   951-4

Expose (pearl) necklace to the ultraviolet ray for one-tenth of a second, or as a flash. This will demagnetize it and set it for better body vibration for this body.   951-6

The light or reflection from the ruby, worn on hand or body, will enable the body to concentrate in its mental application the greater...
How? Each element, each stone, each variation of stone, has its own atomic movement, held together by the units of energy that in the universe are concentrated in that particular activity. Hence they come under varied activities according to their color, vibration or emanation...
Hence (for **this** soul) it is an aid, a crutch to lean upon.   531-3

If the ruby is kept close to the body it will bring strength, power and might in a manner to the purposes set by the entity.   2571-1

Not that these should be merely considered as good luck stones that the entity should wear about self often, or most always--but the lapis ligurius would bring much that will act in that manner as would be termed a **protective** influence, if kept about the entity. This is the green stone, you see--the crystallization of copper and those influences that are creative within themselves...
The radial activity of radium, as well as the strengthening influences of gold, the stabilizing influence of silver, are all a part of those elements that make for the transmission through the activity of the very vibratory forces themselves, and become to **this** body of a great influence; for this entity is not only destined but rather prone to be thrown **into** those channels where all of such are necessary for usage in either the protection or destruction of mankind himself.   1931-1

To approach the subject from the viewpoint as to make same worthwhile in the lives of individuals is the **purpose** of this discourse.

Then, as there is the necessity then of looking at the matter from more of a statistical or scientific standpoint, then let each apply same according to the dictates of their individual consciences or developments.

As may be surmised from the fact that the ancients in all lands have and did place the interest in numbers, these indicate that individuals under different circumstances gave to numbers certain valuations, principally according to the **influences** same were **supposed** to have upon the ritual or the form of individual worship in some manner or another. Hence we see that under varying circumstances there were attributed certain powers to certain numbers, according to the form or ritual of that individual group. As to whether these actually exist or not depended much upon the confidence or faith of the subjects in that ritual, that rite, the belief; yet when one looks about them they may see that in a scientific manner there are numbers that break or form combinations in nature itself, or that in man's response to the conditions **in** nature there are the recurrent conditions or circumstances in certain numbers. As we find in music, that the scale itself is composed of so many tones, tone values, and that those numbers that are half pitch or half tones are those that in most of the formulas given are the breaking points or divisions in numbers. The same may be seen in color combinations, that when certain tones or the valuation of tone in color, that in the combination of certain numbers these begin to alter or change much in the same manner or way as they do in tones in music. The same may also be illustrated in the elements themselves, when there is the division of those elements these same numbers, same conditions, are seen in the elements in their variations themselves. Then, is it any wonder that the ancients--or even the students of the mystic, of the mental or occult forces of today give credence or valuation to numerology, or numbers?

Then, what form, what force, has given the most perfect illustration of **how** numbers, either in individual life or individuals' experiences in life, affect individuals; or the numbers themselves, and as individuals, or 1, 2, 3, 4, 5, 6, 7, 8, 9, 10, 11, 12, **or** whatnot--how do the **numbers themselves** value? Possibly the best authority on such is that of the Talismanic, or that obtained from the Talmud--which is a combination of the ancient Persian or Chaldean, Egyptian, Indian, Indo-China, and such.

One is the beginning, to be sure. Before **One** is nothing. After **One** is nothing, if all be **in One**--as **One** God, **One** Son, **One** Spirit. This, then, the **essence** of **all** force, **all** manners of energies. All activities **emanate** from the **One**.

Two--the **combination**, and begins a division of the Whole, or the One. While **Two** makes for strength, it **also** makes for weakness. This is **illustrated** in that of your music, of your paintings, of you metals, of **whatever** element we may consider.

Three--again a combination of One and Two; this making for strength, making for--in division--that ability of Two **against** One, or One against Two. In **this** strength is seen, as in the Godhead, and is as a greater strength in the whole of combinations.

Again, in **Four** we find that of a division--and while a beauty in strength, in the divisions also makes for the greater weakness--as may be illustrated as in the combinations seen in metal, or numbers, or music, or color.

Five--as seen, a change--as may be seen in a comparison of any of the forces outlined.

Six--again makes for the **beauty** and the symmetrical forces of **all numbers**, making for strength;

As does **Seven** signify the **spiritual** forces, as are seen in all the ritualistic orders of any nature; as seen in the dividing up of conditions, whether they be of the forces in nature or those that react to the sensual forces of man in any character.

Eight--again showing that combination in strength, also a combination in weakness.

Nine making for the **completeness** in numbers; yet showing not the strength as of Ten, nor yet the weakness as of Eight, yet making for that termination in the **forces** in natural **order** of things that come as a change imminent in the life.

In **Ten** we have those of the completeness as of numbers, and a strength as is found in **few**; yet these are as a combination in the force as are manifest.

In **Eleven** is again seen those of the **beauty** of numbers, yet that weakness as was signified by those of the betrayal in the numbers.

Twelve--as a **finished** product, as is given in all forces in nature; as was given in all forces as combined to those of the ritualistic forms, those of the mystic forces, those of the numbers as related to those of a combination; for as of the voices of **Twelve** requiring twenty to even drown same, or to overcome same. The same as may be seen in all of the forces in nature. **Twelve** combined forces brought those strengths into the world as (were) necessary for a replenishing of same.

Now, how may we apply same to our daily lives? How--or what is **my** number? How do numbers affect me?

Numerology, or numbers, may be termed as one of the **non**-essentials to those who feel or know that same cannot affect them, unless they allow same to affect them. Just so with any other forces as in nature, will there be set within self that which is as to be combative against every other force **that** may affect little or none at all, dependent upon the activities of that being guarded against or guarded with. So, in approaching or reaching the effect of numbers:

The period of the year--dependent, of course, upon that point reasoned from. The numbers, or the name--these give the significance to the numbers of the individual. These may be reached either by adding the numbers as applied **to** each individual letter in the name. These will give the sum total of that which applied to the individual.

How do they affect the individual? It will be found that one, then, that is of a given number--from the name given--is under those influences that have been indicated by the influences of numbers in the forces, or among the forces, in nature itself. These may be reached by the various forces or various manners in which individuals have **classified** same.

In applying same, use them for **benefits**--and not for the destructive forces. We are through. 5751-1

Numbers as a whole only give that as is the relative activity of the **mind** of man concerning same, and it is **not** infallible. For **man** may change his **mind** as respecting **any** condition, and may therefore upset **any** factor as would be the criterion of the dates, month, or year, as taken as respecting any individual stock. But each number, then, has its **own** vibration. All emanating from one...

Always, in the division, the even numbers--as two, four, six, eight-- are the weaker, while the odd numbers are the strength...

Five always active--and double the two, and one--or three and two, which it is the sum of. Hence, as is questioned here, no factor is more active than would be that of a five--fifth division--or five-eighth division, or five-sixth division, or five **any** division--in any activity. Five being the **active** number. 137-119

One who has given time and patience and long thought upon mathematical problems sees, experiences every phase of human experiences as a mathematical ratio. As one experiences one activity relative one to another but as mathematical in its essence. 1152-4

As indicated from information respecting numerological aspects, these represent what may be said to be the power of concentration of power or ability of application, the power or the abilities of centralizing self in a given direction. 338-2

Q-What numbers vibrate best for me?
A-Thine own birth date, which is the highest that may be! 2533-146

One--the all power. Two--divided. Three--the strength of One and weakness of Two. Four--the greater weakness in all its associations and powers. Five--a change imminent, ever, in the activities of whatever influence with which it may be associated. Six--the strength of a Three, with a helpful influence. Seven--the spiritual forces that are activative or will be the activative influences in the associations of such an influence. Eight--a money number. Nine--the change. Ten--back to one.   261-14

For, as we see in numbers, or numerology:

One, indicates **strength**, power, influence; yet has all the weaknesses of all other influences that may be brought to bear upon any given activity in which same may be indicated. But it is **known** as strength and power; even as the **union** of self with the Creative Forces that express themselves in the activity of matter, in **any** form, is power.

Two makes for a division; yet in the multiple of same, in four, it makes for the greater weaknesses in the divisions. In six and eight it makes for the same characterizations, yet **termed** more in these that one is power, two is weakness, three is the strength of one with the weakness of two; four being more of a division and weakness; six being the changes that have been made in the **double** strength of three. Seven is the spiritual number. Eight indicates the commercial change. Nine indicates strength and power, with a change.

These, then, are as **indications**; and **not** other than the **signs** of things, that may be altered ever by the force or factor from which they emanate.

Hence, **intuitive** force is the better, for in this there may come more of the union of the spirit of truth with Creative Energy.

(Individuals) vibrate to certain numbers according to their name, their birth date, their relationships to various activities. Then when these appear, they become either as strengths or as losses or as helps or as change, or as the spiritual forces. But, as indicated, they are rather as signs, as the omens; and may be given as warnings, may be given as helps, may be given in any manner that they may be constructive in the experience of the individual.   261-15

Desire, first, creates certain forces about which there is a physical nucleus that is the pattern of the Universe; with a number. Thence it is given by some sages that each entity, each expression in a material experience has its number. Yet the more often there is the 'guess' or mistake as to what physically caused there to be a number for an individual entity. There may be all the variations possible represented in the digits from one to nine. This means the variations of the positive and negative influences of the neurones or electrons, or forces that form that vibration upon which the individual entity **will** or **does** vibrate at its period or source or conception. And each relationship of its vibration to the universe is relative, according to its number.   281-46

As in numbers one builds upon the other (as units) and all are formations or divisions or multiples of units of one, so the universe and the expressions of all natures within same are the manifestations of that force, one power, one spirit, one energy known as or called a Universal Force, Creative Energy, or God.

Hence there is a purposefulness in every experience; and this may be worked out, just as mathematically as any problem of such nature.

That there are those relative relationships through influences through which an entity or soul as a unit passes becomes then natural; or a natural consequence just as conscience **Is**, Life **Is**, God **Is**...

For the mathematics of music, the mathematics of **every** activity bespeaks for the entity its real worth in the experiences of all.   1462-1

Numbers and numerology in its **deeper** sense...may be worked out with mathematical precision in **many** individuals...

The entity was among those who were of the Wise Men coming into Jerusalem and to Bethlehem when the Master came into the earth...The entity gained through this period in pointing out that through the various forces as were added in the experiences of man with that creation of forces necessary to keep the balance in the universal forces, the earth must bring forth that that would make man's balance of force with the Creative Energy as one, and the Son of Man appeared. The entity brought the frankincense and gave same to the Master at that period...

The entity builded in that of setting up the first study of how that the square of the one equal in the square of the others, as related to numbers and the **positions** of numbers as related to the stars in the universe, and the relation of one to another. The entity will **easily** understand Einstein's theory. Few would!   256-1

Q-Why has mathematics a special attraction for the entity?

A-The **analytical**, or the seeking for first causes--as has been the oft experience of the entity in its sojourn through the earth's experience. The **elements** and their component factors have a particular **influence**, too, upon the entity. They may be divided, as is seen--while air and water has its particular **beauties** for the entity, the earth and fire (one positive and one negative--which keeps for well balance) are particularly of interest as to **their influence**.   488-6

Q-What is my soul number?

A-You set that yourself...Some days you are a four, other days maybe you are a one or an eleven.   1861-18

When...numbers used by the runners conform, you can bet on the horse. Five times out of eight it will win; the other three it won't.   417-6

Q-What is my soul number? Explain the significance of it.
A-Seven is the soul number. The significance is the blessedness of the unity in activity.   2072-4

Q-What is my Cosmic Number?
A-Numbers, as indicated, are arrived at the better either by the numerology of the name, of the birth, or the general number for the sex and the date itself that may be arrived at by the astrological aspects of the date. As a general, or a combination of them.   275-37

(**Most** all numerology) may be gained from the **One Book**–the Bible! 1770-2

The nine the sufficient, the ending, the whole, as it were, of all forces as combined in the unit of numbers.   136-27

Thirteen numerologically becomes very much in the same position as Saturn does astrologically--or Uranus. These become either very good or very bad...Thirteen indicates that such and such changes are ever within reach of the entity, or that opportunities are constantly presenting themselves; and they must be weighed in the balance of that which is set within the mental self as a standard--from the moral, the mental and the spiritual aspects of the entity's activities.   416-8

Twenty--for in this we find in keeping with those numbers as are set in purpose; for two and naught is as an initial entrance into that of the days as are set for man's existence in an experience...In this number there is that which prevents the ones who through that of purely the seeker for only personal interests would be loath to part, and he who is able to contribute little may not be hindered by same. 254-35

In the lower portion (of the aura chart), in the center, put an altar. This should be indicated as one built of stones. There should be at least in that portion showing, twenty-two stones; indicating the fulfilling of a purpose in the experience of the entity...The fire, of course, would be indicated as of twelve sticks--by fire on same; this indicating the twelve centers of the body to be purified.   585-10

Twenty-two to be sure, being the infinite, or infinity in number. 1152-14

The male, the twenty-three. The female, the twenty eight.   443-6

(Twenty-three means) a body balanced mentally, physically, spiritually; for it is as the prefect odd number, divisible by nothing; hence perfect in its ratio to one.   440-3

Do learn music. It is part of the beauty of the spirit. For remember, music alone may span that space between the finite and the infinite. In harmony of sound, harmony of color, even in harmony of motion itself, its beauty is akin to that expression of the soul-self, in harmony of the mind, if used properly in relationship to the body. Not that music is to be made the greater portion of thy life, but let much of thy life be controlled by the same harmony that is in the best music, yea and the worst also; for it, too, has its place. But cling to that which may be experienced by listening to a mother sing the lullaby of Brahms...Catch something of the note that is indicated in the love and emotion of the mother as she sings the "Songs my mother sang to me." 3659-1

The entity's music may be the means of arousing and awakening the best of hope the best in the heart and soul of those who will and do listen. Is not music the universal language, both for those who would give praise and those who are sorry in their hearts and souls? Is it not a means, a manner of universal expression? 2156-1

Music itself is a means or a manner of expressing the harmonies of the mental self in relationship to spiritual ideals and spiritual concepts. Hence, as is the very nature of rhythm or harmony in the expression of tone or sound--it is to arouse, does arouse the natures of the hearers to activity, either for uplifting the soul or the mind to activity or otherwise, in the directions that are indicated by the harmony itself. 949-13

If you learn music, you'll learn history. If you learn music you'll learn mathematics. If you learn music, you'll learn most all there is to learn, unless it's something bad. 3053-3

Music is of the soul, and one may become mind and soul-sick for music, or soul and mind-sick from certain kinds of music. 5401-1

Sounds, music and color may have much to do with creating the proper vibrations about individuals that are mentally unbalanced, physically deficient or ill in body and mind. 1334-1

The entity developed that which later became the chant which to many would drive away what was called the evil eye, the evil influence. And, with their variations, many of those incantations of the savages of today, many of the beautiful martial pieces of music, many of the beautiful waltzes that give the rhythm to the body, many of the various characters of music used today have arisen from the efforts of **this** entity. Yet many, of course, were added to, many were defamed. 949-12

Music is...that which may arouse violent passion, which may soothe the beast of passion, may make for thoughts of home, of heaven. 5253-1

Music arouses emotions in the body to an unusual degree, well that there be choices made regarding what emotions are aroused and by the character of music.   1406-1

The lute, as well as the stringed instruments, become those that act more as the soothing influence, as well as those in which the entity may in its dance interpret the better; rather than brass instruments.   2700-1

Keep about the body the colors of purple and lavender, and all things bright; music that is of harmony--as of the Spring Song, the Blue Danube and that character of music, with either the stringed instruments or the organ. These are the vibrations that will set again near normalcy--yea, normalcy, mentally and physically.   2712-1

The Prince of Peace was a harpist Himself.   275-35

Music should be a part of each souls development.   2780-3

There **is** music in jazz, but is there perfect harmony in same? 2072-10

Music, color, vibration are all a part of the planets, just as the planets are a part--and a pattern--of the universe.   5755-1

The viola tuned to the vibrations of the fire of nature may be destructive or smothering or aflaming same.   275-43

There are forces or pitches above and below the scale, as are applied in the human voice. There are colors above and below the spectrum, as applied by man in a nominal manner. There are the same octaves of force seen or applied in the various elements as go to make up the forces as applicable to elements in any generative force.   4665-8

Nickname the entity Franz, for it will be in keeping with the entity (who was once Franz Lizt) and is that it will be inclined to call itself when it begins to lisp or think...

In the musical abilities should the entity be trained from the beginning. There is the natural intent and interest toward things of the artistic nature and temperament...

The entity was in the earth during those periods of the preparation and the accomplishing of the setting up of the music in the temple that was planned by David and completed by Solomon.

The entity was an associate then of both David and Solomon, being among the chief musicians for setting the psalms to the order of preparation for the various instruments upon which there would be the music for services in the temples. And the psalms of David as well as the songs of Solomon were a part of the entity's experience...

The entity was among those (Atlanteans in Egypt) who first set the chants of the various peoples to any form of music. This made for that establishing in the Temple of Sacrifice of the chants...that aided in healing--and in bringing the mental attributes of those who had determined to become as channels through which there might be the spiritual expression in the Temple Beautiful.   2584-1

The entity was during those periods when the great artist, the great musician, the great scientist was attempting to make the first experiments with lighter than air machines, or painting the pictures that have become as the mystery of the smile of that particular one.

The entity then, in the name Gurialeldio, was that one who aided Da Vinci when much experimentation was made, and much that has been accredited to the scientist Da Vinci in the experimentations made may rather have been accredited to this entity.   490-1

COLOR AND THE AURA

Color itself is vibration, just as much vibration as--or even more than music.   3637-1

Each body, each activity, each soul-entity vibrates better to this, that or the other color.   288-38

You will rarely find individuals being intolerant with others with something intrinsically carved being worn; or never very, very mad with blue being worn.   578-2

Q-What is the best color for health room walls.
A-Between green and blue.   165-17

Q-What color scheme would you suggest for cartons, labels and advertising?
A-...The blue package with the white lettering would, then, make a preferable type. For, as the psychology of a sales proposition: that which catches the eye the quicker, people will ask about--even if it is sitting on the shelf of a drug store!
Yellow partakes of those things that are contagious. Red, of those things warned of or against. Black, that which is of death itself. 1800-20

Q-What is the meaning of the white lightning I have seen?
A-That awakening that is coming. More and more as the white light comes to thee, more and more will there be the awakening. For as the lights are in the colors: In the green, healing; in the blue, trust; in the

purple, strength; in the white, the light of the throne of mercy itself. Ye may never see these save ye have withheld judgment or shown mercy. 987-4

Blue, turning to shades of green--which shows a high mental, tending towards spiritual development.   276-4

Q-What would be a good symbol in the form of colors, of our ideal?
A-These are **many**--in the **various** phases of expression. Those of purple and gold present the highest of that as attained in **color** vibration.   2087-3

Each city has its own color.   1456-1

Q-Discuss the relation of colors to the seven glandular centers.
A-...Vibration is the essence or the basis of color. As color and vibration then become to the consciousness along the various centers in an individual's experience in meditation made aware, they come to mean definite experiences. Just as anger is red, or as something depressing is blue...Rosy to most souls means delight and joy--yet to others, as they are formed in their transmission from center to center, come to mean or to express what **manner** of joy; whether that as would arise from a material, a mental or a spiritual experience.
Q-Give color for: (1) Gonads (2) Lyden (3) Solar Plexus (4) Thymus (5) Thyroid (6) Pineal (7) Pituitary.
A-These come from the leaden, going on through to the highest--to that as is the halo. To each they become the various forces as active throughout, and will go in the regular order of the prism.   281-30

Know as to what colors mean. For the entity is not only able and capable to receive the vibrations of individuals about the entity as to their colors, but as to their vibrations. And these then make for a sensitiveness that is often disturbing to the entity.
This may be developed or it may be passed over. But those that are as symbols or signs or conditions that may be used constructively, use same; do not abuse same. For that which is good, to be sure, may be used to one's own undoing.
Know that when there is felt, seen or experienced those vibrations of low, leaden or dark red, these are as dangers; not only for self but self's associations with individuals...
When there is felt that glow of orange, and the violet hues with the orange, know that these bespeak of sentimentality in the experience and are not always good; yet these in their proper relationships should be a portion of the experiences...in which one may know what such vibrations and such colors mean--that the individuals may be trusted.
When these reach those stages as to where there is felt the lighter red, and those that turn to shades of green with the influences that

make for shadings into white, then these trust, these hold to; for such individuals, such associations, may bring in the experience of the entity that which will make for spiritual enlightenment, a mental understanding, and...bring helpful influences in every experience...

It would be impossible for the entity to go even among a group of a thousand and not all be conscious that the entity had entered. Why?

As the colors, as the vibrations are a portion of the entity, they also radiate from the entity. Hence many, many, **many** are influenced by the entity.   1406-1

All bodies radiate those vibrations with which the body controls itself in mental, in physical and such radiation is called the aura.   5756-1

The body in action--or a live body--emanates from same the vibrations to which it as a body is vibrating, both physical and spiritual. Just as there is an aura when a string of a musical instrument is vibrated...In the body the tone is given off rather in the higher vibration, or color ...Only three colors are necessary to make, for the perfecting of the various shades or tones that may be had in **any** vibration.   440-6

Auras are twofold. That which indicates the physical emanations, and that which indicates the spiritual development...

In this entity in the present there is signified a blue and a purple, or a bluish purple; indicating the spirituality, the spiritual seeking. 319-2

Q-Give scale of auras, and what development of the soul each one means.

A-These vibrations (that are emanations from the activity of an entity and its individuality) run in the same ratio as do the colors, that are known as primary colors, and their shades; running from the low red or orange **through all of the colors** to the higher reds, these being at the extremes. Each indicates the step of development, whether (as the first) toward the purely carnal, material or earth forces, or to the mental proclivities, or to the higher forces, in the greens and reds that indicate the spiritual developments.   275-30

Each entity **radiates** that tone, that reflection of the concept of its creative force. Each entity--each atom of the entity radiates that vibration to which it attunes itself.   2842-2

Aura changes, to be sure, to the **temperament**.   282-4

(The aura of this body) is that of the high orange, which is the intellectual--but the seeker.   452-7

White for purity, the blue for purpose, red for strength needed.   2378-1

Purple, high mental abilities; the blue, the sincerity.   2425-1

Q-What is the sign of His presence?
A-The circle with the Cross.   423-3

The circle--this is a figure, a symbol of completeness; as indicated by the words, "The Lord thy God is One" (Mark 12:29).   2174-2

Q-Why do I see a cross so often in meditation?
A-...The Cross leads the way, **ever!**   307-15

Q-What were the symbols of the seven stages of man's development?
A-The world as the beetle. Birth as the cockerel. The mind as the serpent. Wisdom as the hawk.   281-25

As has always been given the eye is as the singleness of purpose; or the oneness of the love of the Father to the sons of men.   281-18

Fish representing the water from which all were drawn out. 5748-2

The very shape (a harp) of the (akashic) record itself.   1473-1

Beautiful (akashic) record--all white, with knowledge.   1837-1

A Maltese cross of teakwood should be worn by the entity at all times, next to the skin, about the neck or waist...This would have a helpful influence by creating a **vibration.** Not that it would within itself have an influence, but the associations of same would become as helpful influences--just as that you think gradually grows to become **you**--as you digest its influence or force.   2029-1

. The star with the rose upon same should be the emblem worn ever by the entity about its body, for it will to the entity bring strength and light and hopefulness...
One is the light that will guide thee. The other is the symbol of life that is ever as a sweet essence or incense before Him, guiding, unfolding in the service that thou dost give to thy fellow man.   695-1

Q-You will give in detail the symbols, colors, and the stages in the development as signified in a complete spiritual aura of the entity, so that it may be depicted in a drawing to be used as a helpful influence.
A-(In an undertone Cayce said), you will give an aura chart of the entity, indicating the symbols, colors, and the meaning of each, that they may be made into a drawing that would be of help to the entity. 288-50

An aura chart is the attempt to interpret the material experiences of individuals in their journeys through the earth; indicating, pictorially, as to that place in the earth of the individual activity, and--upon either the right or the left--the sources from which the entity came into activity in the earthly or material consciousness. About same is symbolized, in the signs of the Zodiac, as to that portion of the body which was stressed through that particular period of activity.

By color certain activities are also symbolized--for instance, black indicates the whole combination of all. For, to material interpretation, white is the absence of color, black is the combination of them all.

The dark blue indicates awakening; purple, healing; white, purity; gold, attaining. All of these and their varied shades indicate the activity; this applying to the stars as well as the sun or moon.

The sun indicates strength and life, while the moon indicates change-- and in one direction indicating the singleness of that activity through an individual experience--the variations being indicated by the variations in the color.

Star--the white, purity, the five-pointed, the whole senses of man indicated as attained to activity--the colors showing the variation; the forms of sex, seven or eight-pointed indicating the attainment--as do the seven stars in a figure indicate the attaining to the seven particular centers in the body.

As for the whole chart--the interpretation is more up to the artist--as to its beauty.   5746-1

In giving an aura chart (symbolic picture)--this we would indicate as to the high points in the experiences of the entity in the earth, having to do with the manner in which the entity has conducted or is conducting itself in the present for the greater unfoldment--spiritually, mentally and materially. One should not be stressed more than the other...

The picturizations are attainments, the symbols of the Universal Consciousness or astrological aspects are the manners, and the symbols about same indicate that portion of the body represented in same; signifying the manner or stress put by the entity. For instance, Aries indicated the mind--or use of the head; while Libra indicated the balance kept in body, mind and purpose in such an experience. 533-20

Q-You will have before you the entity Edgar Cayce, born March 18, 1877, in Christian County, near Hopkinsville, Kentucky. You will give an aura chart of the entity, indicating the symbols, colors, and the meaning of each, that they may be made into a drawing that would be of help to the entity.

A-Yes. In giving the signs, the symbols, as may indicate activities which may be picturized into an aura chart--much depends upon the concept of the artist in making such a drawing a thing of beauty, or a helpful experience for an entity.

In giving the interpretations of same, the influences or activities during the period of the experience of such an entity may be indicated the better, possibly, in picturizations of a place; while the manners in which such an activity was applied may be given in the signs or symbols to which the entity was attracted from such an activity in that particular sphere of consciousness.

Then, for this entity, we would begin first by picturizing that to illustrate the period when the morning stars sang together and the sons of God came together announcing the advent of man into material consciousness.

Thus, across the lower portion, extending almost the whole width of the design--begin in the right-hand side by putting the crescent, with the seven stars; the one closer to the crescent the brighter. These, the stars, would be five-pointed--in gold and in silver. This portion of such a drawing should be rather with the background the blue canopy of the heaven; dark, while toward the left side would come the shading to the light, lighter, lightest--with just the very tip of the sun arising--over the expanse as of water; with heavy vegetation and growth. The animals all would be indicated as in a state of expectancy towards the light, or the sun; from the serpent to the fowls of the air; indicating especially the raven and the doves in the fowls of the air, and the serpent upon one of the trees or shrubs indicated, and the ox, the camel. These especially would be indicated in such a drawing.

Upon the left, in the lower portion, put the symbol of the sun. Upon the right put the symbol of the earth. Each of these would be in white and green; even the sun would be in the light green with the white and gold center.

Above this indicate a mountain, and the symbol or sign that is the symbol of Gemini--or the two-bodied figure, or united bodies as a figure (small), on the edge of this mountain. The vegetation here would be very verdant, in the central portion; this shading off to the left in that as of the temple--or the crystal, or an obelisk with the crystal in the top. This, to be sure, would not be too large a figure; with many figures at worship about the light that comes from this obelisk.

On the right side would be the fields with laborers in chains or bonds.

This, to be sure, would indicate the period in Atlantis when there was the separation of the sexes indicated among things, or the thought-figures or bodies; those that had caught the vision and those still kept in bondage.

Upon the left put the symbol of Mercury--this in gold and green. About same would be the sign or symbol of Aries--or the ram--four in number; small, and black.

Upon the right side put the symbol of Jupiter--in purple and coral; while about same would be four symbols of Scorpio.

These indicate the place, the activities, and the manner in which these were applied in the experience.

Above this, extending almost across the whole of the drawing (which should be in vignette, and not encircled as the first), indicate--in the left--the trek of a group or body of people, with a leader--with a staff in hand--leading peoples; with a few beasts of burden--as the ass, the camel, and also elephants, but few in number of each of these--rather distributed through the group and not as the mere leaders or in the front of the caravan. Then the pyramid would be indicated in the central portion, in sand, with the top not complete; for over this would be the light as of a flame. In the right portion put the facade of the Temple of Sacrifice, indicating within at least three crude rock-built altars. Upon same would be the fires builded, but not a sacrifice on any of these. Also a little farther to the right of this figure would be the Temple Beautiful...and upon the columns would be the stars-- seven, indicated by a facade of many columns, the central bearing the larger star--the higher in color as well as in size. And the entrance to same would be indicated by the white and green light that would appear from same.

In the sides from this indicate the heart on the left and the cross on the right. No characters, no symbols would be about either of these. This would rather be indicated in the activities as experienced by the entity through that Egyptian sojourn; indicating the entrance, the activity, and that attainment in the sacrifice and in the temple service...

Above this the central figure, also a vignette, would be a series, first, of terraces of rock--and the lame man upon same, with the light as from heaven above shining upon the figure; with the raven upon one ledge of the rock and two doves together upon another. This should be as a central or larger figure, the center the rock and the man, though the small-sized figure of the man, but indicating the lameness.

Upon the left put the sign or symbol of Venus, with Pisces--four, black-faced, about same.

Upon the right side put Uranus; part gold, part green, the gold the upper portion. About same would be the symbol of Libra, four in number.

These would indicate the place of activity, and the manner in which there was the activity in the experience.

Above this, in the central portion to the left side put a ship or boat, with a very small mast; with at least three people in same--one a man of middle age, one a younger man, and a girl. Indicate them, by their dress, as orientals. Upon the right side of this, in the center, put the anchor--this not too large yet balancing with the figure of the ship, and the cross--still to the left. The cross would be in gold, while the would be in steel-gray edged with the lighter gray; with sufficient rope or cord to same to make a balanced figure.

This would indicate a period of the entity's activity, and of being anchored in the cross, through that period in Laodicea.

In the left-hand put the symbol of Mercury, and about same the symbols of Leo.

In the right-hand put the symbol of Mars, and about same the symbols of Aries.

The figure above this would be a small ship, rowboat. This, however, would be upon the right side. The central figure would be a brothel, or as a counter over which drink is dispensed, and the crowd about same--the dancing girl also indicated in the central figure. And to the left would be indicated the river in which there is the destruction of the raft when crossing is attempted.

Upon the left side here put Neptune as the symbol, with the symbols of Gemini about the same.

Upon the right put the earth sign, with the symbols about same of Libra. All these symbols would be in black, but small.

As to the attaining of the entity: In the top put the all-seeing eye-- the singleness--the eye; this rather large but balanced with the rest of the design or chart. The clouds would be about same in pink or purple, the blue and green--all indicated in the lights as from the cloud; with the cross, and this leaning just a bit towards the right. Here, under same put the small white star. In the edge of the clouds, extending below the eye, put the gold eight-pointed star.

These are the symbols, this is the aura chart, of this entity Edgar Cayce.   294-206

SYMBOLS AND THE LIFE SEAL AS REMINDERS

As has been given through these channels, oft individuals are given life seals. These vary quite a bit from even the figures in an aura chart. And at times they conform. But one is made for that as a study by the individual of those things wherein it failed or developed, and are to be as lessons--and that is why it has ben given. This may become a helpful influence to the individual; while a plaque is usually as the reminder of some individual fact or act to be attained or discarded.   5746-1

In analyzing the urges which are latent and manifested for this body, as we find, an emblem might prove very helpful and very significant for this body, as a constant reminder to the entity not to allow itself to become a sponge absorbing all the worries and troubles of others. For very easily the entity becomes a confidante, and while it is well to be able to counsel with and help others, yet this may be carried so far as to make that tendencies for morbidity...

These, as we find, would be the pattern which may be seen as a part of the experience of the entity through the sojourns which may be indicated in the earth. This we would put on at least a fourteen-inch square white card. Make a circle at least thirteen inches in diameter. Then, we would put in the center of this a crab with a sponge in its claws. This should be in the colors, green, yellow and gray, and then about it put the Cross in the upper left-hand corner and an open book. These figures should be small. In the upper right-hand corner, put the tree of life with all manners of fruits and the leaves, as aspen leaf in shape; this green but the fruit golden.

And in the lower left-hand or inside the circle, of course, would be the lily, this with three flowers on one stalk. This represents three graces, or the three phases of experience. This would be in color also.

These will signify to the entity, first, a reminding of the Cross, which should be in gold and square in shape, a reminding of the source which is fully indicated in the open book of knowledge.

While that in the lower left indicates the beauty, grace, loveliness of the individual itself; its patience, its affections, its beauty, while that in the lower right represents that which may be attained, not only the tree of abundant supply and with the manner of fruits but the leaves as healings to the peoples with whom the entity may come in contact...

Know, then, as indicated in the seal (symbolic picture), the sources of supply and put not only thy burdens upon Him but point the more often to others that their burdens, too, must be placed with Him, who is capable and able to bear them, as He did the burdens, the sorrows, the sins of the whole world, upon His shoulders. For He first spiritualized life and then through life lived in the earth by the patience, as attained and gained, spiritualized body and mind.   5373-1

In interpreting the records, these are unusual--in that there is a seal, or the activities of the entity are indicated in a symbol with the record here: A moon, a star; the cross, the shepherd and the staff, but with a circle of light.

These might be arranged in a symbol to mean much to the entity. 2880-1

If the life reading (2880-1 above) is interpreted, it will be seen the activities in the experience are represented in the seal by the symbols. The interpretation is that these symbols should enable the entity to visualize the proper interpretation of problems in the lives of others.

It is **not** as a motive for meditation, but the symbols are signs--just as given in the beginning, that the sun, the moon, the stars are given as signs, as symbols; and these should allow--in periods of meditation--the questions and answers to others, as well as enabling self to be made aware of--or given, we might say--the cue, or the key, or a prompting.   2880-2

Q-Please explain to me my seal and its meaning.

A-As we find, this would be as the fern leaf and the activities of the stones as from the pyramid and the raising of the sun upon same; giving in its expression the life as the growth from the base to the height, carrying with same the emanations from the rays of the sun in its expression upon material or matter.   562-3

Q-Please give my seal and its interpretation.

A-Not exactly the holy mount or the pyramid should be in the center, but Mt. Horeb--which would rise as a triangle in the center but reaching the apex only from one side; and the rose on the cross on the side of the same. The interpretation: The way through the Cross is the **beauty**, even in the **strength** of the Mount and the **beauty** as received through same.   603-2

PALMISTRY

Use the hands, the lines, the fingers and formations merely as signs or symbols, not as a prompting of self...

Use as the model, as the symbol, the line of the hand, to interpret for individuals their idiosyncrasies, their shortcomings, their abilities and such, but do **not** prognosticate.   5259-1

The very emotions may be expressed in lines of the hand, feet or face. For, remember the law--all carry the mark in their body.   2067-1

Q-To what extent can palmistry be relied upon?

A-As we have given in regard to any and every omen, it is an indication--yes. As to whether or not it will come to pass depends upon what the body, the mind of such an one does about that it knows in relationship to itself. It may be depended upon, then, about twenty percent as being absolute--and about eighty percent 'chance' or what a body does with its opportunities. The same as may be said about an individual that has prepared himself to be a medium through which there may be expressed an excellent executive. How much does the preparation have to do with the body being an excellent executive? About twenty percent, and the application is the rest. It is so with all activities.   416-2

PART III

MEDITATION AND THE MIND

MIND IS THE ACTIVE PRINCIPLE THAT GOVERNS MAN

Q-Definition of the word **Mind**.

A-That which is the active force in an animate object; that is the spark, or image of the Maker. Mind is the factor that is in direct opposition of will. Mind being that control of, or being the spark of the Maker, the **Will**, the individual when we reach the plane of man. Mind being and is the factor governing the contention, or the inter-laying space, if you please, between the physical to the soul, and the soul to the spirit forces within the individual or animate forces. We have the manifestation of this within the lowest order of animal creation. These are developed as the mind is developed, both by the action of all of the senses of the body, as we have them developed in man. **Mind** is **that** that reasons the impressions from the senses, as they manifest before the individual.

The Active Principle That Governs Man. Mind a factor, as the senses are of the mind, and as the soul and spirit are factors of the entity, one in all, all in one. We are speaking from the normal plane, of course. As the impressions are reached to the storehouse of the body, the mind is that factor, that principle, that portion that either surrogates, correlates or divides the impression to the portion needed, to develop the entity or physical force toward the spark or infinite force, giving the life force to the body. The mind may be classified into the two forces--that between the physical and soul, and that between the soul and the spirit force. We see the manifestations of this, rather than the object of the mind itself. We find this always manifested through one of the senses, the same as we find the psychic force a manifestation of the soul and spirit; the **Mind** a manifestation of the physical.

With the division of the mind force as given, we see why in the physical plane individuals become misunderstood or misrepresented. They do not reach the same manifestations from other individuals. Hence the expression, "They are all of one mind." "To **do good,** they become of one mind, **to do evil** they are many." The nearer approach the mind comes to the divide, between the soul and spirit forces, the nearer we become to that infinite force that guides when it is allowed to the individual's actions day by day.

Definition of the words 'conscious mind':

The **conscious** means **that** that is able to be manifested in the physical plane through one of the senses.

Definition of the words 'sub-conscious mind':

That lying between the soul and spirit forces within the entity, and is reached more thoroughly when the conscious mind is under subjugation of the soul forces of the individual or physical body. We may see manifestation in those of the so-called spiritual-minded people. The manifestation of the subconscious in their action. That portion of the body better known as the one that propagates or takes care of the body-physical, mental, moral or whatnot, when it is not able to take care of itself.

Sub-conscious is Unconscious force. This may be seen in every nerve end, in every muscular force. Subconscious action may be brought into manifestation by the continual doing of certain acts in the physical plane, so the body becomes unconscious of doing the acts.   3744-1

The subconscious mind is both consciousness and thought or spirit-consciousness. Hence may be best classified, in the physical sense, as a habit.   266-10

In the consciousness of earthy or material forces there enters all the attributes of the physical, fleshly body. In the subconscious there enters the attributes of soul forces, and of the conscious forces. In the superconscious there enters the subconscious forces, and spiritual discernment and development.   900-16

Q-Explain and illustrate the difference in the faculties of Mind, Subconscious and Superconscious.

A-The superconscious mind being that of the spiritual entity, and in action only when the subconscious is become the conscious mind. The subconscious being the superconscious of the **physical** entity, partaking then of the soul forces, and of the material plane, as acted upon through and by mental mind. Hence the developing in the physical plane through environment being that as is given to the soul forces in subconscious mind to live upon.

Illustrated, as has been given, in the light as came to Saul on the way to Damascus. The superconsciousness of Jesus came to the subconsciousness of Saul, yet he could not retain in conscious that necessary for him to do. The superconscious came to that of him directed to act in the conscious manner, or Saul, as he continued in the subconscious, seeking for the light of that he could not make clear to his consciousness.

Q-Is the superconsciousness the mind or supreme controlling force of the Universal Forces?

A-As pertaining to an individual, yes. As pertaining to Universal Forces, in the larger sense, no, but through the superconscious the Universal Forces are made active in subconsciousness. As is illustrated in the work as done through the body, Edgar Cayce...The superconsciousness (is) a portion of the great Universal Forces.

Q-Do animals have the faculty of mind known as subconscious?

A-No. The mind of the animal is as pertaining to the conditions that would bring the continuation of species and of foods, and in that manner all in the animal kingdom; pertaining then, Mind and Spirit; man reaching that development where the soul becomes the individual that may become the companion, and One with the Creator.

Q-Explain the difference between experience as in an animal and experiences as in man, as related to Mind.

A-In the animal is that as appertains to the consciousness of the animal mind, with spirit. As in man, that is of consciousness co-related with man's development, or the higher elements of mind and of matter. Hence man developed, becomes lord and master over the animal kingdom. Man degraded becomes the companion, the equal with the beast, or the beastly man. Then we would find this illustrated as in this: Experience to man gives the understanding through the subconscious obtaining the remembrance. The animal only the animal forces, as would be found in this: Fire to man is ever dread, to an animal only by sense of smell does it know the difference. The experience does not lead it away.   900-31

The time has arisen in the earth when men--everywhere--seek to know more of the **mysteries** of the mind, the soul, the **soul's** mind which man recognizes as existent, yet has seen little of the **abilities** of same. 254-52

Q-Explain "mind is a factor as senses are of the mind, and as the soul and spirit are factors of the entity, one in all, all in one."

A-As has been given, these conditions, mind of the soul, mind of the physical body, mind of the spiritual entity, are separated, that one may gain the knowledge of its action. As we have then in the mind of the spiritual entity, that mind wherein the entity (spiritual entity we are speaking of) manifests in the spiritual plane; the mind in the physical body (is) the subconscious, the conscious through which the entity manifests in the physical world; one in all, all in one. In one, in the spiritual mind, acted upon by their attributes, principally will, for it is the factor in the physical world, in the spiritual world, for the action being that through which the manifestations of any factor are known. As we would have in this: Knowledge comes through the senses in the physical body to the conscious mind. The subconscious has the storing of the given condition; when the consciousness receives through the sense that knowledge, the will is the action against the incentives set forth.

Q-Explain what the divide between the soul and spiritual forces is?

A-This is of the spiritual entity in its entirety. The superconscious is the divide, that oneness lying between the soul and the spirit force, within the spiritual entity. Not of earth forces at all, only awakened with the spiritual indwelling and acquired individually.   900-21

In the spiritual that is known in the physical as the superconscious becomes the subconscious.   900-23

When the body-physical lays aside the material body, that in the physical called soul becomes the body of the entity, and that called the superconscious the consciousness of the entity, as the subconscious is to the physical body. The subconscious (becomes) the mind or intellect of the body.   900-304

The subconscious mind may only be fully understood when viewed from the spiritual viewpoint or aspect. The conscious mind rarely gains the entrance to truth in the subconscious, save in rest, sleep, or when such consciousnesses are subjugated through the act of the individual, as in the case of Edgar Cayce.   900-59

Q-Explain that barrier between conscious and subconscious mind. How may we eliminate it to allow the subconscious to direct?

A-As would best be illustrated in this: We (individuals) find in the earth's plane those mental conditions wherein the conscious and subconscious would manifest by some given suggestion. The entity, through will, reasons with the condition. Hence the barrier as created...

To overcome such conditions, bring about consciousness, the oneness of mind, soul and body, that when such submerged conditions are enacted, we find the subconscious takes the direction in the physical plane. Then such an entity is given, as spiritual minded, subconscious minded, subconscious directed, spiritual directed individuals. The more this becomes manifested, the more the entity may gain the impressions, the actual conditions of the subconscious forces, those ever directing, that give light and development to the soul's forces from the physical plane.   900-25

In the words of the Master Himself, "In my Father's house are many mansions" (John 14:2), many consciousnesses, many stages of enfoldment, of unfoldment, of blessings, of sources.   2879-1

The ability to be conscious of a thing--**mentally**--is the only manner through which **anyone** experiences anything!   272-4

Mind is an effect, or an active force that partakes of spiritual as well as material import. Mind is an essence or a flow between spirit and that which is made manifest materially. 262-123

Mind as a stream, not mind as purely physical or as wholly spiritual, but is that which shapes, which forms, which controls, which directs, which builds, which acts upon. 4083-1

For, that we find in the spirit taketh form in the mind. Mind becomes the builder. The physical body is the result. 3359-1

For, ever in the flesh and in the spirit, **Mind** is the builder. 3333-1

Know that the mental **is** the builder, in character, in nature, in characteristics, in spirituality, in morality, and all influences that direct. For it, the mind, is both physical **and** spiritual. 759-12

Mind is the Builder, and--if there will be kept a balance--the physical mind **and** the spiritual mind should cooperate, coordinate. 1593-1

THOUGHTS ARE DEEDS

Thoughts are deeds, and are children of the relation reached between the mental and the soul, and has its relation to spirit and soul's plane of existence, as they do in the physical or earth plane. What one thinks continually, they become, what one cherishes in their heart and mind they make a part of the pulsation of their heart, through their own blood cells, and build in their own physical, that which its spirit and soul must feed upon, and that with which it will be possessed. 3744-4

Thoughts become as deeds, or deeds are the father of thoughts. 136-63

"He that hateth his brother has committed as great a sin as he that slayeth a man" (1 John 3:15), for the deed is as of an accomplishment in the mental being, which is the builder for every entity. 243-10

That builded by thought and deed becomes the active particles, atoms, that make up that soul body, see? 5756-4

As a man thinketh **in his heart, so IS he** (Proverbs 23:7)! Not what **man** says, nor what man even makes **out** like he does. For we are gradually builded to that image created within our own mental being; for, as has been given, the Spirit is the life, the Mind is the active force that, coordinated with the spirit that is of the creative energy, or of God, gives the physical result that is effective in every sense. Get that! 270-17

If the Mind dwells upon the spiritual things, then it follows that it becomes what it has dwelt upon, what it has lived upon, what it has made itself a portion of. But if the Mind dwells upon self-indulgences, self-aggrandizement, self-exaltation, selfishness in any of its forms, in any of its variations, then it has set itself at variance to that First Cause; and we have that entered in as from the beginning, that of making will--through the Mind--at variance to Creative Forces before it has come into the movements of matter that we know as physical, material.   262-78

That which the mind of a soul--a soul--dwells upon, it becomes, for mind is the builder. And if the mind is in attune with the law of the force that brought the soul into being, it becomes spiritualized in the activity. If the mind is dwelling upon or directed in that desire towards the activities of the carnal influences, then it becomes destructive.   262-63

Mind is indeed the builder, it will see that what is held in the act of mental vision becomes a reality in the material experience.

Mind is the builder and that which we think upon may become crimes or miracles. For thoughts are things and as their currents run through the environs of an entity's experience these become barriers or stepping stones, dependent upon the manner in which these are laid as it were. For **as** the mental dwells upon these thoughts, so does it give strength, power to things that do not appear. And thus does indeed there become that as is so oft given, that faith **is** evidence of things not seen.   906-3

Well that the entity, or all, know that the law of love, or love as law, is cause and effect; or each impulse has its own corresponding reaction in thought, life, mental, physical and material. Not understood by some! **This:** "As ye sow, so shall ye reap" (Galatians 6:7).

Each thought, as things, has its seed, and if planted, or when sown in one or another ground, brings its own fruit; for thoughts **are** things, and as their currents run must bring their own seed. 288-29

For thoughts are things; just as the Mind is as concrete as a post or tree or that which has been molded into things of any form.   1581-1

Each entity makes a record upon time and space, through the very activities of that stylus, the mind.   1885-1

The beginning of all great institutions, of all great things, is first in the mind of individuals who are in touch with infinite forces.   254-31

The constant thought of hate, malice, jealousy...results...(in) warring conditions of nations...(and) physical disturbances in a body.   3246-2

What we think and eat combined together **make** what we **are.** 288-38

The visualizing of any desire as may be held by an individual **will** come to pass, with the individual **acting** in the manner as the desire is held. 311-6

Q-Is it more difficult to visualize things than to feel them?

A-More difficult to visualize than feel, but they become one and a part of the same--as felt, **then** visualized, see? Here:

In the activities of the mind of man, visualization is a portion of a **material** experience, no matter whether in the present experience or a combination and correlation of many experiences. While that **felt** is the sum total of **all** experiences, correlated with the superconscious, or the life itself, provided the purport or the **individual** is in keeping **with** the purport of life, or truth, see? Then we find when one--as the body here, my servant (137)--visualizes this the sum of the experience. When **felt**, the sum of not **only** experience, but of the Divine--hence, as has oft been said, those that would guide the body--mentally, physically and spiritually--are **above** the normal or ordinary, or the regular--or the even higher forces in cosmic influence. Hence harder to visualize until felt. When felt, the visualization is a portion of the activity set out. 900-422

Be **oft** in prayer, oft in meditation, **seeing** self gaining the proper nourishment, proper resuscitation forces from those elements being given to the system for its resuscitation. 2097-1

Well that there be kept that continued attitude of **seeing** the body replenished, rebuilded, in a mental, a spiritual, and a material way and manner. This held by the body-consciousness as seeing these things accomplished, will aid **also** in the correcting in the physical forces. 4482-1

The body is able within itself to see those activities taking place, will there be given or known that which is being **desired** to be **accomplished** in the body--see? Get that! **That's** the differentiation able to be seen and known by the body-functioning and body-activities itself. 1742-3

Q-To bring a desired **thing** or **condition** into manifestation, is it advisable to visualize it by making a **picture** or just to hold to the idea in prayer and let God produce it in His own way without out making a pattern?

A-The pattern is given thee in the mount. The **mount** is within thine inner self. To visualize by picturizing is to **become** idol worshippers. Is this pleasing, with thy conception of thy God that has given, "Have no other gods before me" (Exodus 20:3)? The god in self, the God of the universe, then meets thee in thine inner self. Be patient, and leave it with Him. He knoweth what thou hast need of before ye ask. Visualizing is telling Him how it must look when you have received it. Is that thy conception of an All-Wise, All-Merciful Creator? 705-2

Q-How may I project a counterpart of my conscious awareness to any given place desired, and comprehend or even take part in events there?

A-Read what we have just been given. This is an explanation of how. For it takes first spirit and mind form; and may be aware of the elements in space. For time and space are the elements of man's own concept of the infinite and are not realities as would be any bodily element in the earth--as a tree, a rose, a bird, an animal, as even a fellow being.

Yet, just as a body may in its own material mind visualize, draw a concept of an incident that has happened in time, so may the body in spirit and in spiritual mind project itself, be conscious of elements, be conscious of form, by and through spirit mind--as patterned in a conscious mind.

Mind, then, becomes as a stream, with its upper and lower stratum, with that which moves swiftly or that which is resting upon either spirit or physical being.

These come, then, as flashes to a conscious mind. They may be gradually sustained; just as mind may be projected.

Here we will have an illustration: In a camp near here, near this particular spot a place ye occupy, there has been a gift taken by someone else. There will be a projection of the thought, "This **must be returned**!" and it will be. For here we have the parties to this physical condition existent--right and wrong, good and bad, spirit, mind, body. They are parts of this happening, and it is now being returned.   2533-8

Q-Explain, "All the elements that go to make up the expressions reached to the mental forces of an individual, are actions of the psychic forces from another individual, and are the collaboration of truth as found in the individual, or entity, expressing or manifesting itself, one with the other."

A-In this, we find that as giving how that each entity gains the impressions through the transmission of impressions, one toward another, and when the elements in the entity are such that the mental forces (speaking of physical, see?) allow the suggestions from such entity, the collaboration, the mental impressions, depressions, the mental forces, give then that expression to the individual and find the lodgement in which the mental will build, as we would find illustrated in this: Though an entity in the earth plane may be adverse to conditions, a mental mind of another individual may so picture conditions of that directly opposed to the mental development of the other individual that those collaborations may become such as to be wavered, as to be given the truth, or be given the untruth, for we are giving then of physical conditions alone, and not seeking the collaboration through the spiritual or the subconscious forces. And we find through such chasms, through such elements, comes the mental development, the soul development, the ability of each entity to take that necessary for that soul's development, and in this manner do we find collaboration of truths, collaboration of every thought coming to each and every entity, for "Thoughts are Deeds," and carry that impression that acts through the individual entity. 900-25

When the thought of many individuals is directed to one focusing point, the condition becomes accentuated by force--see? of thought manifested...

As thoughts are directed, the transmission of thought waves gradually becomes the reality--just as light and heat waves in the material world are now used by man. Just so in the spiritual planes the elements of thought transmission, or transference, may become real. Be sure of this fact, and assured of same.

Thought transference occurs when both bodies, or entities, are in the subconscious condition--whether for a moment or whether for ages. For time in spiritual forces is not as it is in material forces.   900-23

Q-In the physical plane, do the thoughts of another person affect a person either mentally or physically?

A-Depending upon the development of the individual to whom the thought may be directed...Individuals of this plane will and are developing this (thought transference) as the senses were and are developed. 3744-2

(The entity was in Atlantis during) the higher state of civilization (and) was the teacher in the psychological thought and study, especially as that of the transmission of thought through ether.   187-1

Q-Explain the statement "Etheronic energy **is** mental control."

A-A thesis of 184 pages may be written, my son, on this. But etheronic energy is the emanation from the spirit force through the active force of that which makes for matter being held in its positive position, or in its space of activity. Hence thought as a body, whether of an animal or plant, is shown as of plant receiving in its freshness of vigor influences that come from or through the etheronic energy.   440-13

Thoughts are things, and they have their effect upon individuals, especially those that become supersensitive to outside influences. These are just as physical as sticking a pin in the hand.   386-2

Q-During meditation I have experienced a strong vibration. Have I been able to direct this current to those we are trying to aid?

A-As the vibrations are raised within self through this very visualization...The body--as everyone--is able to send, or direct, or create an environ--to such an one to whom the thought is directed--that is helpful, hopeful, beneficial in every way.   281-15

Fear, with a mental aberration, always creates activity in the minds of those feared.   290-1

Disincarnate entities (that may be earth-bound, or that may be heaven-bound) may influence the thought of an entity or a mind...
When an entity, a body, fills its mind (mentally, materially) with... carnal forces...the mental mind, or physical mind, becomes carnally directed...As individuals become abased, or possessed, are their thoughts guided by those in the borderland? Certainly! If allowed to be!   5753-1

Q-Please explain what took place while asleep I visited and talked with an old neighbor. Later this neighbor told others that she had seen me. Should I attempt to develop this type of projection?
A-This should be a result and not an attempt; unless ye know for what purpose ye are using same.   853-9

Q-Give the principle and technique of conscious telepathy.
A-The consciousness of His abiding presence. For, He is all power, all thought, the answer to every question...
First, begin between selves. Set a definite time, and each at that moment put down what the other is doing. Do this for twenty days. And ye will find ye have the key to telepathy.   2533-7

No one can tell another exactly what he thinks, though certain vibrations may be felt.   5118-1

HYPNOTHERAPY AND SUGGESTION

Begin with the study of self, which may be best done by suggestive forces to the body through hypnosis.   3483-1

(This sleeping sickness) can only be removed...through the suppression of the normal mind of this body by that of a stronger mind--or an equal mind...In other words, put the body under what is commonly called hypnotic influence...Go through some three to four months of treatment.
Q-Who shall put this body under hypnotic treatment?
A-One of the people that has a clean mind themselves. The body is good to look at, and it would not be well to put under the influence of one with ulterior motives or desires.   4506-1

It is also dangerous to submit to submerging of self through hypnosis, unless the body-mind of such an operator is in accord with **constructive,** forces in a body.   458-1

All bodies are amenable to suggestion, through the abnormal mind, or through the subconscious mind, or through sympathetic nerve system.   4648-1

The **Mind** acts upon the resuscitating forces of the physical being, by and through suggestion. Just so there may be the realization that spiritual forces are a part of the whole physical being. For, the **real** being is the spiritual import, intent and purpose, see?

Thus a meditation, a centralizing, a localizing of the mind upon those portions of the system affected.   1992-3

Q-What is the best method to be used in curing children of injurious habits already formed?

A-In using that of suggestion to the subconscious or soul mind of the body as it loses itself in normal sleep, and praying with and for the body. In that state when the body loses consciousness in sleep, the soul mind (not the unconscious, but the subconscious proper, or superconscious) may be impressed by suggestion that will be retroactive in the waking, or in the physical normal body. In these manners may the better results be obtained in a developing body, for it becomes then retentive and will retain same as the ideas and ideals of every element of the body's activities; for they become as the virtues of the body-mind.   5747-1

Always (use) constructive, never negative suggestions.   1163-2

(Overcoming bed-wetting) may be accomplished best by making the suggestion...when the body is almost asleep, by the one who makes the application of the massage and rubs. **Positive** suggestion! Not that she **won't** do, but that she **will** do this or that, see? (Suggest) that when the desire is for the activity, the body will arouse and attend to same. 308-2

As the daughter (who is afraid of water) turns to sleep, **make** the suggestion as for the usefulness of water in the experience.   2428-1

(Biting fingernails) is a natural expression of the body. But it should be overcome merely by suggestion and not by aggravating.   415-8

Q-Mr. Cayce, what do you mean by suggestion and who should do this?

A-All force controlling any individual body...is reached to all the forces of the physical, soul or spiritual forces by suggestion, see?

(By) suggestion we mean, say a thing is black, it is black, say a thing is white, it is white, say a thing is wet, it is wet, etc...

(Remove the headaches) through the suggestion as has been outlined here: "The body will become normal when in its wakening state, the circulation will so be equalized as to remove all strain from any and every portion of the body," see? You say "you are not going to have any headache and you wake up," you don't mean anything.   294-4

Q-What causes the tingling in the sole of my foot all the time?

A-Because of the connections along the nerve centers, and these will be parts of the suggestions made under the hypnosis; that there will be the perfect coordination through the centers of the body-- between sympathetic and cerebrospinal system.   3125-1

Q-Could hypnotism be used in his case (deaf-mutism, epilepsy)?

A-It might be used, but be **mindful** of who would use same!

Q-Would auto-suggestion be helpful?

A-Most beneficial. This can be given best by the mother.

Q-Please give form of suggestion.

A-...As the body sinks into slumber: May the self, the ego, awaken to its possibilities, its **responsibilities**, that, as I speak to you, in the normal waking state you will respond in that same loving, careful manner this is given to you. See?   146-3

The suggestions (dementia praecox) that we would make when the body is sleeping, resting...(is) "There will be, in the whole of the physical and mental body, that response to that creative energy which is being carried into the system. Perfect coordination will come to the body. There will be reactions in every way and manner through the creative forces of divine love that is manifest in the hearts and minds of those about the body." This should be repeated three to four times, until it has gradually reached the subconscious, or the unconscious, or the consciousness of the **living** forces that are impelling activity in a distorted condition, as to the balance in the mental forces.   271-5

Q-What can we do to stop crying?

A-...These depressions arise from the inability of coordinating the physical with the mental forces of the body, see?...This may be accomplished more by suggestions than by other treatments.   1553-26

If it is deemed wise or necessary to overcome it (smoking), then have the suggestions made to the body, as it is going to sleep by one who is in sympathy with the body's desire to change--that it will produce nausea, or that there will be the lack of desire for it.   263-11

Use the radio active appliance daily to put the body (retarded child) to sleep. Then as it is going to sleep, let the parents--the father, the mother--together, not separately...make suggestions to the body. 5022-1

If you desire a strong, robust, healthy body, then think health and bring it. Should you weaken within yourself and feel that the physical is below normal, then you become oppressed by it. The mere suggestion causes the condition to become active within the body.   902-54

Q-In certain types of insanity, is there an etheric body involved?

A-Possession. Let's for the moment use examples that may show what has oft been expressed from here: There is the physical body, there is the mental body, there is the soul body. They are One, as the Trinity; yet these may find a manner of expression that is individual unto themselves. The body itself finds its own level in its **own** development. The mind, through anger, may make the body do that which is contrary to the better influences of same; it may make for a change in its environ, its surrounding, contrary to the laws of environment or hereditary forces that are a portion of the 'elan vitale' of each manifested body, with the spirit or the soul of the individual.

Then, through pressure upon some portion of the anatomical structure that would make for the disengaging of the natural flow of the mental body through the physical in its relationships to the soul influence, one may be dispossessed of the mind; thus ye say rightly, he is "**out of his mind**."

Or, where there are certain types or characters of disease found in various portions of the body, there is the lack of the necessary **vital** for the resuscitating of the energies that carry on through brain structural forces of a given body. Thus disintegration is produced, and ye call it dementia praecox--by the very smoothing of the indentations necessary for the rotary influence or vital force of the spirit within same to find expression. Thus derangements come.

Such, then, become possessed as of hearing voices, these are termed deranged when they may have more of a closeness to the universal than one who may be standing nearby and commenting; yet they are awry when it comes to being normally balanced or healthy for their activity in a material world.   281-24

Q-What causes him to lose control of himself?

A-Possession!

Q-Does (possession) mean by other entities, while under the influence of liquor?

A-By others while under the influence (of liquor) that causes those reactions and makes for the antagonism.   1183-3

There are those (alcoholic cases) that are of the sympathetic nature, or where there has been the possession by the very activity of same; but gold will destroy desire in any of them!   606-1

There are those who are geniuses and yet are so very close to the border that an emotional shock may make a demon of a genius. There are those activities in which a spiritualized cell, by environment, may make of the demon a saint.   281-63

The body is a supersensitive individual entity who has allowed itself through study, through opening the centers of the body, to become possessed with reflexes and activities outside of itself.

Q-What is it exactly that assails me?

A-Outside influences. Disincarnate entities.   5221-1

Q-Please explain how to heal an epileptic, and are they possessed by an unclean spirit? If so, should we command it to leave in the name of Jesus Christ, and to no more enter?

A-There are various characterizations in those that are termed epileptics. Some arise from one condition, some from another. Some are indeed possessed with an uncleanness from those of the moral life itself, and then become epileptics, **meeting** in self those very conditions that have been as omissions in its experiences in the earth; bringing then that necessity that others in aiding **command**, demand, in the Name, that these be cast out. Too, there are those that need the body vibrations each day, that these may be made whole by the laying on of hands, which will require some two, three to four weeks, that will bring an understanding and a change in the body, or bodies, that will make for wholeness of purpose.

Q-How may epileptics possessed by an unclean spirit be designated or be known?

A-As to whether there be consciousness or not through the falling, or spell. Those that are unconscious are possessed, or are possessed during that unconsciousness--see? Such need, then, the raising of daily vibration. This may be accomplished by placing the left hand over the abdominal region and the right hand over the 9th and 10th dorsal or solar plexus ganglia, and so held for half to three-quarters of an hour each day. It will leave.   281-4

Q-Why should those entities return to this body after our prayers?

A-They are as material as individuals, why doesn't an entity return home? They are seeking a home.   281-6

(Dual personality) is the personality--at times giving expression to being influenced by sojourns in the material plane, and at other times the individuality of the entity giving expression to the urges from the experiences during the interims between the earthly sojourns.2175-1

There has already been departure of the soul, which only waits here. No physical help (dementia praecox), as we find, may be administered. 5344-1

Q-What caused this condition (insanity)?

A-Mental worry, and--as given--poison accumulation in the system both from toxics and uremia. Neglect of self!   387-1

Q-Why is it difficult for me to remember?

A-It isn't difficult! It's rather trained in self to **forget**! See the differentiation between forgetting and remembering is--**memory** is the exercising of the inner self as related to thought. To acknowledge that the memory is poor, is to say you don't think much. The forgetting is to say that the thought becomes self-centered, for memory is thought--even as thought is memory, brought to the forefront by the association of ideas. 69-2

Mostly when individuals forget it is because something within themselves, all their inner consciousness, has rebelled--and they prepare to forget. 5022-1

We find in Mercury the high influences, as manifested in the abilities of the entity to **remember** as well as to forget. For, the faculty of being able in manifestation to forget is as much of a virtue as the ability to remember. 2443-1

Remember the soul never forgets. For it is eternal. 2425-1

Q-Is memory thought, or thought memory?

A-With the evolving of the individual, the thought becomes a part of the memory...Physically, memory and thought are not synonymous, neither are they of the same beginning in physical forces. In that of the soul and spirit force, they become one and the same in evolution. 3744-2

Q-Make clear what is meant by "in that of the spirit and soul forces thought and memory are as the entity."

A-...A material entity may wonder whether thought is memory, or memory thought, for we find that the indwelling of the subconscious forces, in the spiritual entity, entering the material planes, bringing gradually the thought of the development necessary for the entity's development towards the higher realm. Hence where will again enters into the condition of being the opposition of the soul and spirit forces. For we find, when thought would take the possession of the inmost soul or being of an entity, this is as of memory necessary for development of the entity; when such conditions are willfully banished for the lighter conditions, that would remove the necessary environment, the body is exercising thought and memory by will's forces. Not that any entity should enter into any condition that would so unbalance the mind (conscious, we are speaking of), as to bring upon itself condemnation, but rather that, that will make the balanced mind, for the bringing of condemnation from other minds becomes environment in the mind itself. Separate these. Correlate these as truths given here, for this the basis of heredity and environment. 900-23

Q-How can I attain a better memory?

A-...As ye apply, as ye ask, as ye manifest, as ye recall--more and more is recalled to thee. This is memory. For, know the basic principle comes in Him as He has given, "I will bring **all** things to thy memory from the foundation of the world" (Isaiah 40:21).

Do not think, then, that the mind of any active individual may ever be such as to be overburdened with memories, but make them ever a helpful influence.   1206-13

Do not study or ponder--what may be termed--hard, or too long. Rather study, ponder same, and let the physical body immediately rest. Then the mental self has the opportunity to assimilate same.   416-10

Q-How can the body improve memory and the power of concentration?

A-By acting in that manner in which self is lost in that being done. This is the **best** manner to lose self-consciousness, and to become in the way of power in personality, and in being **just** one's self.   5420-1

Q-How can I improve memory and concentration?

A-Study well that which has been given through these sources on meditation. Through meditation may the greater help be gained. 987-2

SLEEP AND THE SIXTH SENSE

Q-You will please outline clearly and comprehensively the material which should be presented to the general public in explaining just what occurs in the conscious, subconscious and spiritual forces of an entity while in the state known as sleep.

A-...first, we would say, sleep is a shadow of, that intermission in earth's experience of, that called death; for the physical consciousness becomes unaware of existent conditions, save as are determined by the attributes of the physical that partake of the attributes of the imaginative or the subconscious and unconscious forces of that same body; that is, in a normal sleep (from the physical standpoint we are reasoning now) the **senses** are on guard, as it were, so that the auditory forces are those that are the more sensitive. The auditory sense being of the attributes or senses that are more universal in aspect, when matter in its evolution has become aware of itself being capable of taking from that about itself in its present state. That is as of the lowest to the highest of animate objects or beings...

(During sleep) the organs that are of that portion known as the inactive, or not necessary for conscious movement, keep right on with their functioning--as the pulsations, the heart beat, the assimilating and excretory system keep right on functioning; yet there are periods during such a rest when the heart, the circulation, may be said to be at rest. What, then, **is** that that is not in action during such period? That known as the sense of perception as related to the physical brain. Hence it may be truly said, by the analogy of that given, that the auditory sense is sub-divided, and there is the act of hearing by feeling, the act of hearing by the sense of smell, the act of hearing by **all** the senses that are independent of the brain centers themselves, but are rather of the lymph centers--or throughout the entire sympathetic system is such an accord as to be more **aware, more** acute, even though the body-physical and brain-physical **is** at repose, or **un**aware...

These, then--or this, then--the sixth sense, as it may be termed for consideration here, partakes of the **accompanying** entity that is ever on guard before the throne of the Creator itself, and is that that may be trained or submerged, or left to its **own** initiative until it makes either war **with** the self in some manner of expression--which must show itself in a material world as in dis-ease, or disease, or temper, or that we call the blues, or the grouches, or any form that may receive either in the waking state or in the sleep state, that has **enabled** the brain in its activity to become so changed or altered as to respond much in the manner as does a string tuned that vibrates to certain sounds in the manner in which it is strung or played upon.

Then we find, this sense that governs such is that as may be known as the other self of the entity, or individual. Hence we find there must be some definite line that may be taken by that other self, and much that has been accorded--or recorded--as to that which may produce certain given effects in the minds or bodies (not the minds, to be sure, for its active forces are upon that outside of that which the mind, as ordinarily known, or the brain centers themselves, functions), but--as may be seen by all such experimentation, these may be produced--the same effect--upon the same individual, but they do not produce the same effect upon a different individual in the same environment or under the same circumstance. Then, this should lead one to know, to understand, that there is a **definite** connection between that we have chosen to term the sixth sense, or acting through the auditory forces of the body-physical, and the other self within self.

In purely physical...the same body fed upon **meats**, and for a period-- then the same body fed upon only herbs and fruits--would **not** have the same character or activity of the other self in its relationship to that as would be experienced by the other self in its activity through that called the dream self.   5754-1

What relation has this sixth sense (as has been termed in this presented) with this **soul** body, this cosmic consciousness? What relation has it with the faculties and functionings of the normal physical mind? Which must be trained? The sixth sense? Or must the body be trained in its other functionings to the dictates of the sixth sense?...

This sixth sense activity, is the activating power or force of the other self. What other self? That which has been builded by the entity or body, or soul, through its experience as a whole in the material and cosmic world, see? Or is as a faculty of the soul-body itself. Hence, as the illustration given, does the subconscious make aware to this active force when the body is at rest, or this sixth sense, some action on the part of self or another that is in disagreement with that which has been builded by that other self, then **this** is the warring of conditions or emotions within an individual. Hence we may find that an individual may from sorrow **sleep** and wake with a feeling of elation. What has taken place? We possible may then understand what we are speaking of. There has been, and ever when the physical consciousness is at rest, the other self communes with the **soul** of the body, see? Or it goes **out** into that realm of experience in the relationships of all experiences of that entity that may have been throughout the **eons** of time, or in correlating **with** that as it, that entity, **has** accepted as its criterion or standard of judgments, or justice, within its sphere of activity.

Hence through such an association in sleep there may have come that peace, that understanding, that is accorded by that which has been correlated through that passage of the selves of a body in sleep. Hence we find the more spiritual-minded individuals are the more easily pacified, at peace, harmony, in normal active state as well as in sleep. Why? They have set before themselves (now we are speaking of one individual!) that that **is** a criterion that may be wholly relied upon, for that from which an entity or soul sprang is its **concept**, its awareness of, the divine or creative forces within their experience. Hence they that have named the Name of the Son have put their trust in Him. He is their standard, their model, their hope, their activity. Hence we see how that the action through such sleep, or such quieting as to enter the silence--what do we mean by entering the silence? Entering the presence of that which is the criterion of the selves of an entity!

On the other hand oft we find one may retire with a feeling of elation, or peace, and awaken with a feeling of depression, of aloofness, of being without hope, or of fear entering, and the **body-physical** awakes with that depression that manifests itself as of low spirits, as is termed, or of coldness, gooseflesh over the body, in expressions of the forces. What has taken place?...The physical self being unawares of those comparisons between the soul and its experiences of that period with the experiences of itself throughout the ages, and the experience may not have been remembered as a dream--but it lives **on**--and on...

Sleep--that period when the soul takes stock of that it **has** acted upon during one rest period to another...In sleep all things become possible, as one finds self flying through space, lifting, or being chased, or what not, by those very things that make for a comparison of that which has been builded by the very soul of the body itself.

What, then, is the sixth sense? Not the soul, not the conscious mind, not the subconscious mind, not intuition alone, not any of those cosmic forces--but the very force or activity of the soul in its experience through **whatever** has been the experience of that soul itself. See? The same as we would say, is the mind of the body the body? No! Is the sixth sense, then, the soul? No? No more than the mind is the body! For the soul is the **body** of, or the spiritual essence of, an entity manifested in this material plane.   5754-2

Q-How may one train the sixth sense?

A-This has just been given; that which is constantly associated in the mental visioning in the imaginative forces, that which is constantly associated with the senses of the body, that will it develop toward.

Q-How may one be constantly guided by the accompanying entity on guard at the throne?

A-It is there! It's as to whether they desire or not! It doesn't leave but is the active force?...This sense is that ability of the entity to associate its physical, mental or spiritual self to the realm that it, the entity, or the mind of the soul, seeks for its association during such periods--see? This might confuse some, for--as has ben given--the subconscious and the abnormal, or the unconscious conscious, is the mind of the soul; that is, the sense that this is used, as being that subconscious or subliminal self that is on guard ever with the Throne itself; for has it not been said, "He has given his angels charge concerning thee, lest at any time thou dashest thy foot against a stone?" Have you heeded? Then He is near. Have you disregarded? He has withdrawn to thine own self, see? That self that has been builded, that that is as the companion, that must be presented--that **is** presented--**is** before the Throne itself! **Consciousness**--(physical) consciousness--see--man seeks this for his **own** diversion. In sleep it (the soul) seeks the **real** diversion, or the **real** activity of self.

Q-What governs the experiences of the astral body while in the fourth dimensional plane during sleep?

A-This is, as has been given, that upon which it has fed. That which it has builded; that which it seeks; that which the mental mind, the subconscious mind, the subliminal mind, **seeks**! Then we come to an understanding of that, "He that would find must seek" (Luke 11:9). In the physical or material this we understand. That is a pattern of the subliminal or the spiritual self.

Q-What connection is there between the physical or conscious mind and the spiritual body during sleep or during an astral experience?

A-It's as has been given, that **sensing**! With what? That separate sense, or the ability of sleep, that makes for acuteness with those forces in the physical being that are manifest in everything animate. As the unfolding of the rose, the quickening in the womb, of the grain as it buds forth, the awakening in all nature of that which has been set by the divine forces, to make the awareness of its presence in **matter**.   5754-3

Q-Why am I so dependent upon sleep, and what do I do during sleep?

A-Sleep is a **sense**...and is that needed for the physical body to recuperate, or to draw from the mental and spiritual powers or forces that are held as ideals of the body...

What happens to a body in sleep? Dependent upon what it has thought, what it has set as its ideal...

There are individuals who in their sleep gain strength, power, might --because of their thoughts, their manner of living. There are others who find that when any harm, any illness, any dejection comes to them, it is following sleep!...

(Sleep) **is** the exercising of a faculty, a condition that is meant to be a part of the experience of each soul. It is as but the shadow of life, or lives, or experiences, as each day of an experience is a part of the whole that is being builded by an entity, a soul. And each night is but a period of putting away, storing up into the superconscious or the unconsciousness of the soul itself.

Q-What is the best way for me to get to sleep?

A-Labor sufficiently of a physical nature to tire the body; not mentally, but physically.   2067-3

Each and every soul leaves the body as it rests in sleep.   853-8

Q-Why does she walk and talk so much in her sleep?

A-Close to the music that spans the distance between the finite and the infinite.   3621-1

Q-What are the best hours for sleep?

A-When the body is physically tired, whether at noon or twelve o'clock at night.   440-2

Q-How much sleep does this body need?

A-Seven and a half to eight hours should be for **most** bodies. 816-1

In dreams, those forces of the subconscious, when correlated into forms that relate to the various phases of the individual, give to that individual the better understanding of self, when correctly interpreted.

Forget not that it has been said correctly that the Creator; the gods and the God of the Universe; speaks to man through this individual self.

Man approaches the nearer condition to that field when the normal is at rest; in sleep or slumber. And when more of the forces are taken into consideration, and are studied by the individual, (not by someone else), it is the individual's job, each individual's condition, each individual's relation, each individual's manifestation, each individual's receiving the message from the higher forces themselves.

Q-What is a dream?

A-...When those forces through which the spirit and soul have manifested themselves are re-enacted by this same soul and spirit force (in such a manner) as to convey or bring back impressions to the conscious mind in the earth plane; it is termed a dream.

This may well be caused by those forces that are taken into the system. The action of digestion that takes place under the guidance of subconscious forces becomes a part of that plane through which the spirit and soul of the entity pass at such time. Such manifestations are termed or called nightmares, or the abnormal manifestations on the physical plane of these forces.

In the normal force of dreams, those forces are enacted that may be the **foreshadows** of a condition, when the soul and spirit force compares the conditions in various spheres through which (the soul and spirit of) a given entity has passed in its evolution to its present sphere.

In this age at present, 1923, there is not sufficient credence given dreams; for the best development of the human family is to give the greater increase in the knowledge of the subconscious soul or spirit world. This is a **dream**.

Q-How should dreams be interpreted?

A-Depending upon the physical condition of the entity, and that which produces or brings the dream to that body's forces. The better definition is this: correlate those truths that are enacted in each and every dream that becomes a part of the entity of the individual and use such (for the purpose of) better development; ever remembering that "develop" means going **toward** the higher forces, or the Creator. 3744-4

Those who are nearer the spiritual realm, their visions, dreams, and the like, are more often--and are more often retained by the individual; for as is seen as a first law, it is self-preservation. Then self rarely desires to condemn self, save when the selves are warring one with another, as are the elements within a body when eating of that which produces what is termed a nightmare--they are warring with the senses of the body, and partake either of those things that make afraid, or produce visions of the nature as partaking of the elements that are taken within the system, and active within same itself...

For such experiences as dreams, visions and the like, are but the **activities** in the unseen world of the real self of an entity.

Q-What state or trend of development is indicated if an individual does not remember dreams?

A-The negligence of its associations, both physical, mental and spiritual. Indicates a very negligible personage!

Q-Does one dream continually but simply fail to remember consciously?

A-Continues an association or withdraws from that which is its right, or its ability to associate. There is no difference in the unseen world to that that is visible, save in the unseen so much greater expanse or space may be covered! Does one always desire to associate itself with others? So individuals always seek companionship in this or that period of their experiences in each day? Do they withdraw themselves from? That desire lies or carries on! See? It's a **natural** experience! It's **not** an unnatural! Don't seek for unnatural or supernatural! It is the natural--it is nature--it is God's activity. His associations with man. His **desire** to make for man a way for an understanding.

Q-Is it possible for a conscious mind to dream while the astral or spirit body is absent?

A-There may be dreams--(this is a division here)--a conscious mind, while the body is absent, is as one's ability to divide self and do two things at once, as is seen by the activities of the mental mind.

The ability to read music and play is using different faculties of the same mind. Different portions of the same consciousness. Then, for one faculty to function while another is functioning in a different direction is not only possible but probable, dependent upon the ability of the individual to concentrate, or to centralize in their various places those functionings that are manifest of the spiritual forces in the material plane. **Beautiful**, isn't it?   5754-3

There are those (dreams) that are of the purely physical nature--the reaction of properties taken in the system when digestion is not in keeping with assimilations, and then one experiences those conditions that may be called nightmares.

Then there is the mental condition of the body wherein worry, trouble, or any unusual action of the mind--mentally--physically--causes seeking for the way and manner of understanding. This may bring either the action of the subconscious with the mental abilities of the body, or it may bring wholly correlations of material sensuous conditions. These may appear in the form of visions that are in a manner the key to the situations, or they may appear in conditions as warnings, taking on conditions that are as illustrations or experiences.

Then there is the action of the purely subconscious forces, giving lessons to the body out of its own experiences. 4167-1

Dreams are the correlation of various phases of the mentality of the individual, see?...There may be taken into the body-physical that of elements that...produces hallucinations, nightmares, or abortions to the mental forces of an individual...There may be conditions from the mental mind of an entity, by deep study or thought, wherein the experiences of the individual entity are correlated through the subconscious forces, the latent forces of the entity--the hidden forces of the entity--and correlating same in a vision or dream. Often these are as symbolic conditions, each representing a various phase to the mental development of the entity.

Others there are, a correlation between mentalities or subconscious entities, wherein there has been attained, physically or mentally, a correlation of individual ideas or mental expressions that bring from one subconscious to another those of actual existent conditions, either direct or indirect, to be acted upon or that are ever present, see?

Hence we find visions of the past, visions of the present, visions of the future. For to the subconscious there is no past or future--all present. This would be well to remember. 136-54

Dreams and visions...are of various classes and groups, and are the emanations from the conscious, subconscious, or superconscious, or the combination and correlation of each depending upon the individual and the personal development of the individual, and are to be used in the lives of such for the betterment of such an individual. 39-3

In visions there is oft the **inter-between** giving expressions that make for an awakening between the mental consciousness, or that that has been turned over and over in the physical consciousness and mind being weighed with that the self holds as its ideal. In visions where spiritual awakenings, these most often are seen in symbols or signs, to the entity; for as the training of self's consciousness in a manner of interpreting the visions would be in expressions of eye, hand, mouth, posture or the like, these are **interpreted** in thine own language. When these are, then, in symbols of such, know the awakening is at hand. 262-9

Have ye not wondered why in the sacred writings it is said that God no longer spoke to man in visions or dreams? It is because man fed not his soul, his mind, upon things spiritual; thus closing the avenue or channel through which God might speak with the children of men. 1904-2

The conscious forces feed the subconscious, and for the better indwelling of the subconscious, good and **only** good thoughts should be projected into the subconscious, for developments come through such ...For dreams are that of which the subconscious is made, for any condition ever becoming reality is first dreamed.   136-7

A dream may be either in toto to that which is to happen, is happening or may be only presented in some form that is emblematical. 5754-1

The entity should keep a record of its dreams...enabling the entity to warn others as well as self.   2346-1

Dreams...should be made record of, else the physical in gaining its equilibrium often loses much that may be worthwhile.   294-46

Interpret them (dreams) in thyself. Not by dream book, not by what others say, but dreams are presented in symbols, in signs.   1968-10

The **body** may analyze same (dreams), interpret same, **better**; for it can do it better for its own activity than were it done by the most wonderful of all interpreters. And so may it be given to all. 257-138

In visions there is given the correlation of the mental mind with the subconscious forces of the entity, and as the conscious mind only reasons by comparisons, and the subconscious by inductive reasoning, then the correlation of these are presented in the manner that is often emblematical, often in a way of direct comparison.   137-60

In dreams, visions and experiences each individual soul passes through or reviews or sees from a different attitude those experiences of its own activities.   257-136

(Through dreams) the entity may gain the more perfect understanding of the relationships between God and man, and the way in which He, God, manifests himself through mankind.   900-143

As the consciousness of the **entity** becomes nearer to that one consciousness--that is, as the body-conscious, the physical or sensuous consciousness, and the subconsciousness, becomes nearer in one, or nearer in accord with each, the visions, the dreams, as are seen, are more profound in their presentation.   900-240

Q-Dreamed I died.
A-This is the manifestation of the birth of thought and mental development awakening in the individual, as mental forces and physical forces develop. This, then, is the awakening of the subconscious, as is manifested in death in physical forces, being the birth in the mental. 136-6

What **is** Meditation?

It is not musing, not daydreaming; but as ye find your bodies made up of the physical, mental and spiritual, it is the attuning of the mental body and the physical body to its spiritual source...

It is the attuning of thy physical and mental attributes seeking to know the relationships to the Maker. **That** is true meditation...

Ye must learn to meditate--just as ye have learned to walk, to talk...

There are physical contacts which the anatomist finds not, or those who would look for imaginations or the minds. Yet it is found that within the body there are channels, there are ducts, there are glands, there are activities that perform no one knows what! in a living, **moving**, thinking being. In many individuals such become dormant. Many have become atrophied. Why? Non-usage, non-activity...

In thine own body there are the means for the approach--through the desire first to know Him; putting that desire into activity by purging the body, the mind of those things that ye know or even conceive of as being hindrances--not what someone else says! It isn't what you want someone else to give! As Moses gave of old, it isn't who will descend from heaven to bring you a message, nor who would come from over the seas, but lo, ye find Him within thine own heart, within thine own consciousness! If ye will **meditate**, open thy heart, thy mind! Let thy body and mind be channels that **ye** may **do** the things ye ask God to do for you! Thus ye come to know Him.   281-41

Meditation, then, is prayer, but is prayer from **within** the **inner** self, and partakes not only of the physical inner man but the soul that is aroused by the spirit of man from within.

Well, that we consider this from **individual** interpretation, as well as from group interpretation; or individual meditation and group meditation.

As has been given, there are **definite** conditions that arise from within the inner man when an individual enters into true or deep meditation. A physical condition happens, a physical activity takes place! Acting through what? Through that man has chosen to call the imaginative or the impulsive, and the sources of impulse are aroused by the shutting out of thought pertaining to activities or attributes of the carnal forces of man. That is true whether we are considering it from the group standpoint or individual. Then, changes naturally take place when there is the arousing of that stimuli **within** the individual that has within it the seat of the soul's dwelling, within the individual body of the entity or man, and then this partakes of the individuality rather than the personality.

If there has been set the mark (mark meaning here the image that is raised by the individual in its imaginative and impulse force) such that it takes the form of the ideal the individual is holding as its standard to be raised to, within the individual as well as to all forces and powers that are magnified or to be magnified in the world from without, **then** the individual (or the image) bears the mark of the Lamb, or the Christ, or the Holy One, or the Son, or any of the names we may have given to that which enables the individual to enter **through it** into the very presence of that which is the creative force from within itself--See?

Some have so overshadowed themselves by abuses of the mental attributes of the body as to make scars, rather than the mark, so that only an imperfect image may be raised within themselves that may rise no higher than the arousing of the carnal desires within the individual body. We are speaking individually, of course; we haven't raised it to where it may be disseminated, for remember it rises from the glands known in the body as the lyden, or to the lyden (Leydig) and through the reproductive forces themselves, which are the very essence of Life itself within an individual--see? for these functionings never reach that position or place that they do not continue to secrete that which makes for virility to an individual physical body. Now we are speaking of conditions from without and from within!

The spirit and the soul is within its encasement, or its temple within the body of the individual--see? With the arousing then of this image, it rises along that which is known as the Appian Way, or the pineal center, to the base of the **brain**, that it may be disseminated to those centers that give activity to the whole of the mental and physical being. It rises then to the hidden eye in the center of the brain system, or is felt in the forefront of head, or in the place just above the real face-- or bridge of nose, see?

Do not be confused by the terms that we are necessarily using to give the exact location of the activities of these conditions within the individuals, that we may make this clarified for individuals.

When an individual then enters into deep meditation:

It has been found throughout the ages (individuals have found) that self-preparation (to **them**) is necessary. To some it is necessary that the body be cleansed with pure water, that certain types of breathing are taken, that there may be an even balance in the whole of the respiratory system, that the circulation becomes normal in its flow through the body, that certain or definite odors produce those condi- tions (or are conducive to producing of conditions) that allay or stimulate the activity of portions of the system, that the more carnal or more material sources are laid aside, or the whole of the body is **purified** so that the purity of thought as it rises has less to work against in its dissemination of that it brings to the whole of the system, in its rising through the whole of these centers, stations or places along the body. To be sure, these are conducive, as are also certain incantations, as a drone of certain sounds, as the tolling of certain tones, bells, cymbals, drums, or various kinds of skins...

So, to **all** there may be given:

Find that which is to **yourself** the more certain way to your consciousness of **purifying** body and minds, before ye attempt to enter into the meditation as to raise the image of that through which ye are seeking to know the will or the activity of the Creative Forces; for ye are **raising** in meditation actual **creation** taking place within the inner self!

When one has found that which to self cleanses the body, whether from the keeping away from certain foods or from certain associations (either man or woman), or from those thoughts and activities that would hinder that which is to be raised from **finding** its full measure of expression in the **inner** man (**inner** man, or inner individual, man or woman, meaning in this sense those radial senses from which, or centers from which all the physical organs, the mental organs, receive their stimuli for activity), we readily see how, then, **in** meditation (when one has so purified self) that **healing** of **every** kind and nature may be disseminated on the wings of thought...

It is **without** the cleansing that entering into such finds **any** type or any form of disaster, or of pain, or of any dis-ease of any nature. It is when the thoughts, then, or when the cleansings of **group** meditations are conflicting that such meditations call on the higher forces raised within self for manifestations and bring those conditions that either draw one closer to another or make for that which shadows (shatter?) much in the experiences of others; hence short group meditations with a **central** thought around some individual idea, or either in words, incantations, or by following the speech of one sincere in abilities, efforts or desires to raise a cooperative activity **in** the minds, would be better.

Then, as one formula--not the only one, to be sure--for an individual that would enter into meditation for self, for others:

Cleanse the body with pure water. Sit or lie in an easy position, without binding garments about the body. Breathe in through the right nostril three times, and exhale through the mouth. Breathe in three times through the left nostril and exhale through the right. Then either with the aid of low music, or the incantating of that which carries self deeper--deeper--to the seeing, feeling, experiencing of that image in the creative forces of love, enter into the Holy of Holies. As self feels or experiences the raising of this, see it disseminated through the **inner** eye (not the carnal eye) to that which will bring the greater understanding in meeting every condition in the experience of the body. Then listen to the music that is made as each center of thine body responds to that new creative force that is being, and that is disseminated through its own channel; and we will find that little by little this entering in will enable self to renew all that is necessary--in Him.

First, **cleanse** the room; cleanse the body; cleanse the surroundings, in thought, in act! Approach not the inner man, or the inner self, with a grudge or an unkind thought held against **any** man! or do so to thine own undoing sooner or later!

Prayer and meditation: Prayer is the concerted effort of the physical consciousness to become attune to the consciousness of the Creator, either collectively or individually. **Meditation** is **emptying** self of all that hinders the creative forces from rising along the natural channels of the physical man to be disseminated through those centers and sources that create the activities of the physical, the mental, the spiritual man; properly done must make one **stronger** mentally, physically, for has it not been given He went in the strength of that meat received for many days? was it not given by Him who has shown us the Way, "I have had meat that ye know not of" (John 4:32)? As we give out, so does the **whole** of man--physically and mentally-- become depleted, yet in entering into the silence, entering into the silence in meditation, with a clean hand, a clean body, a clean mind, we may receive that strength and power that fits each individual, each soul, for a greater activity in this material world.

"Be not afraid, it is I" (Mark 6:50). Be sure it is Him we worship that we raise in our inner selves for the dissemination; for, as He gave, "Ye must eat of my **body**; ye must drink of **my** blood" (I Corinthians 11:24-25). Raising then in the inner self that image of the Christ, love of the God-consciousness, is **making** the body so cleansed as to be barred against all powers that would in any manner hinder.

Be thou **clean**, in Him.   281-13

Q-Please explain the steps I should take in meditation.

A-In whatever manner that to thine own consciousness is a cleansing of the body and of the mind...Whether washing of the body with water, purging same with oils, or surrounding same with music or incense. But **do that thy consciousness** directs thee...Then, meditating upon that which is the highest ideal within thyself, raise the vibrations from thy lower consciousness through the centers of thy body to the temple of thy mind, thy brain, the eye that is single in purpose; or to the glandular forces of the body as the Single Eye. Then listen--listen. 826-11

(Circular vibrations experienced during meditation) **spiritualized**, are the emanations that may be sent out as thought waves, as a force in the activity of universal or cosmic influence, and thus have their effect upon those to whom by suggestive force they are directed...

(In meditation) when one is able to so raise within themselves such vibrations, as to pass through the whole course of the attributes of physical attunements, to the disseminating force or center, or the Eye, then the body of the individual becomes a magnet that may (if properly used) bring healing to others with the laying of hands.

Q-Should one allow unconsciousness to follow?

A-Unconsciousness is a physical-natural consequence, unless there is the radiation passed off into some other force for raising same, or aiding same.

Q-How can one direct the vibration culminating in the head to the one they would aid?

A-By **thought**. (Now we are speaking of a purely mechanical, meta-physical--spiritual activity that would take place.)   281-14

Q-Why don't I have more success with meditation?

A-Oft we find individual activity becomes so personal in even the meditations that there is sought that this or that, which may have been reported to have happened to another, **must** be the manner of happening to self. And in this manner there is cut away, there is built the barrier which prevents the real inner self from **experiencing**.   705-2

(In meditation) never open self, my friend, without surrounding self with the spirit of the Christ, that ye may ever be guarded.   440-8

(The crystal ball is) a means of concentration for those that allow themselves either to be possessed or to centralize their own spiritual activity through the raising of those activative forces in the physical body known as the centers through which concentration and meditation is accentuated by the concentrated effort on **anything** that will **crystallize** same into activity. A means for some. rather, as has been given, let the proof come from that as may be visioned in the self.   254-71

Q-What is my best time for meditation?

A-As would be for all, two to three o'clock in the morning.   462-8

Q-(What is the best polarity for this body) as it meditates?

A-Facing the East, to be sure.   2072-12

For this body--not for everybody--odors would have much to do with the ability of the entity to meditate...Let the mind become, as it were, attuned to such (oriental incense) by the humming; producing those sounds of o-o-o-ah-ah-o-o-o; not as to become monotonous, but 'feel' the essence of the incense through the body forces in its motion of body. This will open the kundaline forces of the body.   2823-3

For prayer is supplication for direction, for understanding. Meditation is listening to the Divine within.   1861-19

For the prayer is as a supplication or a plea to thy superior; yet thy meditation is that thou art meeting on **common** ground.   281-28

He that would know the way must be oft in prayer, joyous prayer, **knowing** He giveth life to as many as seek in sincerity to be a channel of blessing to someone.   281-12

Prayer is the concerted effort of the physical consciousness to become attuned to the consciousness of the Creator, either collectively or individually.   281-13

All prayer is answered. Don't tell God how to answer it.   4028-1

Why worry, when ye may pray? Know that the power of thyself is very limited. The power of Creative Force is unlimited.   2981-1

The prayers of ten may save a city; the prayers of twenty-five may save a nation--as the prayers and activities of **one** may! but in union there is strength.   1598-2

The body mental and spiritual needs spiritual food--prayer, meditation, thinking upon spiritual things.   4008-1

Pray at two o'clock in the morning...facing east.   3509-1

ATTUNING TO THE GOD WITHIN

For, as was given of old--say not as to who will descend from heaven that ye may have a message, for lo, it is in thine own heart. For, thy body is indeed the temple of the living God. There He--as all knowledge, all undertakings, all wisdom, all understanding--may commune with thee...by attuning, turning thy thought, thy purpose, thy desire to be at an at-onement with Him.   2533-4

Let the strength of self not be wavered by advice of the many; but turn to the within, knowing that the **power** lieth there. For when ye enter into the holy of holies, in thine own self, there ye may find **strength** that is beyond compare of man's physical abilities.   1752-1

The time and times and half times shall pass, and **then** shall man come to know that in the temple, in the tabernacle of his **own** temple will he meet his God face to face!   257-201

Each material manifestation is an undertaking by an entity in its attempts to become more attuned to a consciousness of God. 2533-1

Gifted meaning then **innately** developed by the use of those faculties of the Mind to attune themselves to the Infinite.   792-2

In the use of the Radio-Active Appliance...as the vibrations of the body are brought into coordination so that the mental, the physical and the spiritual attribute of the physical forces of the body are in attune or coordinant, the experiences of the mental forces are keen, active, positive; thus periods come when any experience sought may find in itself its answer.   920-9

Q-Is it possible to meditate and obtain needed information?
A-On any subject! whether you are going digging for fishing worms or playing a concerto!   1861-12

Vibrations of numbers, of metals, of stones, these are merely to become the necessary influence to make thee in attune, one with the Creative Forces; just as the pitch of a song of praise is not the song nor the message therein...So, use them to attune self. How, ye ask? as ye apply, ye are given the next step.   707-2

Attunements on any of the radios may be **somewhere near** the same point, but no two will **ever** be in exact same ratio. For their **positions** alter that, even when sitting side by side. In like manner, individuals attuning their soul-consciousness to the Divine within must attune according to their **own** development.   281-3

We recognise the vibratory forces in electricity; they are weighed and measured. In radio we have the magnifying of electrical vibration. It is the same in spirit or psychic, or mind vibration. There is the magnifying, by the action on those in attunement with that vibration.   254-32

All force and power as is applied through psychic forces comes from a universal energy, that is directed by individual application. As the entity studies, develops, and seeks, such application may be gained or attained by those forces through which attunement is gained. As is seen in all of the forms of vibration, whether in the mineral, in the vegetable, in the animal, in music, in those of chemics or chemicals, or those of spiritual vibrations...If the body is made animal by the excess of the gratification of animal desires, they become of the lower vibration. If that is made of an attunement with the bodies celestial, bodies terrestrial, or of whatever form--these develop through that same vibration; for that as is meted is measured again. To that vibration one attunes self, that response is back. See? 256-2

In the deeper meditations...those influences may arise when the spirit of the Creative Force, the universality of soul, of mind...not **in** time and space but **of** time and space--may become lost in the Whole...

It has been given by Him that is Life, that the kingdom of God, the kingdom of heaven, is within and...thy body is the temple of the living God; a tabernacle, yea, for thy soul. And in the holy of holies within thine own consciousness He may walk and talk with thee. How? How?

Is it the bringing of sacrifice? Is it the burning of incense? Is it the making of thyself of no estate?

Rather is it that ye **purpose.** For the try, the purpose of thine inner self, to **Him** is the righteousness. For He hath known all the vicissitudes of the earthly experience...And until ye show forth in His love that patience, ye cannot become aware of thy relationship with Him.

Q-What is the meaning of the white light I have see?

A-That awakening that is coming. More and more as the white light comes to thee, more and more will there be an awakening...

For He is the light, and the life eternal.   987-4

As the Master, thy Lord, thy Christ has given, "I stand at the door and knock, and if ye will open I will enter and abide with thee--I and the Father" (Revelation 3:20). This as ye conceive, this as ye understand, is the highest source of understanding, of knowledge.   1581-2

As ye raise the consciousness to that within self, He meeteth thee in thine own tabernacle, in the holy of holies; in the third eye.   1782-1

When ye call on the Lord, **He will** hear; for He has promised to meet thee in thine own temple, in **His** temple, in His holy of holies! 991-1

Faith and hope and brotherly love and kindness...applied in one's daily life may lead to an opening of the veil which enters into the holy of holies,--even as that veil which was rent when His Spirit cried unto His God. Then, make that God--His God--thy God.   2067-1

Seeking Him first is the whole duty of an entity.   2549-1

Do not trust in forces other than those that are within self. 3384-1

Enter into the holy of holies within thine own consciousness; turn within; see what has prompted thee. And He has promised to meet thee there. And there **shall** it be **told** thee from within the steps thou shalt take day by day, step by step. Not that some great exploit, some great manner of change should come within thine body, thine mind, but line upon line, precept upon precept, here a little, there a little. For it is, as He has given, not the knowledge alone but the practical application in thine daily experience with thy fellow man that counts.   922-1

(There is) the sounding of what we call in the present the vowels in such a manner that they proclaimed--or aroused to the physical organism the associations of the centers through which there is the connection of the spiritual forces.   949-12

In all of thy meditation, Ohm--O-h-m-mmmmm has ever been, is ever a portion of that which raises self to the highest influence and the highest vibrations throughout its whole being that may be experienced. 1286-1

As ye begin with the incantation of the Ar-ar-r-r-r--the e-e-e, the o-o-o, the m-m-m, **raise** these in thyself; and ye become close in the presence of thy Maker--as is **shown** in thyself! They that do such for selfish motives do so to their own undoing.   281-28

The entity will find that there are the combinations of that ye call the scale--or those harmonies set to the Ar-ar-r-r--e-e-e--o-o-o--mmm ...that awaken within self the abilities of drawing that love of the Father as shown to the children of men.   1158-10

It is well with this entity that in the sounding of the name, in the writing of same, it always all be included. The vibration, the harmonious effect of same becomes almost as a shield in the entity's experience; as well as in the numerological effects and their vibration upon those the entity may approach...
Sound within self, -O-oooo-ah--m-mmm-u-uuu-r-rrr-n-nn. These as they...rise along the center from the bodily forces to unite the activities--the entity may bring greater harmony within the experience.1770-2

In that period (Mu) He was called Zu-u-u-u-u; in the next Ohm-Oh-u-m; in the next (Egypt) with Ra Ta, He was called **God**--g-o-r-r-d! 436-2

Q-What is the note of the musical scale to which I vibrate?
A-As we have indicated, Ah--this is not R, but Ah--aum, see? These are the sounds. Those that respond to the centers of the body, in opening the centers so that the kundaline forces arise...
As to the note of thy body,--is there always the response to just one? Yes. As we have indicated oft, for this entity as well as others, there are certain notes to which there is a response, but is it always the same? No more than thy moods or thy tendencies, **unless** ye have arisen to the understanding of perfect attunement.   2072-10

Follow that known in thine own present as i-e-o-u-i-o-umh...for the raising of that from within of the Creative Forces, as it arises along that which is set within the inner man as that cord of life that once severed may separate, does separate, that balance between the mind, the body, the soul.   275-43

The answer to every problem, the answer to know His way, is ever within--the answering within to that real desire, that real purpose which motivates activity in the individual. These appear at times to become contradictory, of course; but know attunement, atonement and at-onement are **One**; just as the inner self is that portion of the infinite, while the self-will or personality is ever at war with the infinite within--for lack of what may be called stamina, faith, patience or what not. Yet each entity, each soul, knows within when it is in an at-onement.   2174-3

Q-What will help me most in coming to right decisions as to my life?
A-Prayer and meditation, to be sure. For, as He has given, "Behold I stand at the door and knock. If ye will open I will enter in" (Revelation 3:20). Then, in thine own mind, decide as to whether this or that direction is right. Then pray on it, and leave it alone. Then suddenly ye will have the answer, yes or no. Then, with that yes or no, take it again to Him in prayer, "Show me the way." And yes or no will again direct thee from deep within. **That** is practical direction.   3250-1

Q-When confronted with difficult situations, how can I be sure the decision I reach is from the Light and not my own thinking?
A-...Ask the question in self in the physical mind so that it may be answered yes or no, and in meditation get the answer. Then closing self to physical consciousness, through the meditation, ask the same question. If these agree, go ahead. If these disagree, analyze thy own self and see the problem that lies in the way.   5091-2

Hence seek in self the more, and that which is answered first in self on any subject, where material or mental aid is sought, **answer** the problem in the consciousness of self. **Then** seek a verification in the period of meditation. And **this** aid will be the greater.   423-2

Q-Discuss plan and operation to cover next two years to guide me.
A-We would'nt cover two days. These will have to be worked out by self and not from here. For remember what you do **today** reflects in what may happen tomorrow and to be sure bears fruit in its regular season.   257-234

That choices are made by counsel here or counsel there only makes for confusion with self, oft. Rather meet within thine own self thy Maker, and let the guide come **there** as to what ye shall do.   333-6

Q-Will it be the proper time to go now?
A-...Such decisions are to be directed by that within self that answers to the influences or forces from without--but the answers and directions must come from within; rather than by any helping hand.
Rememberest thou all that has been given as to the manner in which

the individual finds self? Did Moses receive direction save by the period in the mount? Did Samuel receive rather than by meditating within his own closet? Did David not find more in the meditating within the valley and the cave? Did not the Master in the mount and in the Garden receive the answers of those directing forces.   707-6

Q-Please analyze my relationship with (1210) and give me directions for its continuance if it should continue.
A-...Know that until the answer is within thine own conscience as pertaining to thy relationships mental, physical **or** spiritual--to any soul or entity--until the answer is thine, it can only be confusion...
Who may answer but thyself, thy Lord, thy ideal?...
Whatever may be the problem, take it to Him!
These are questions not to be answered through mortal, nor disincarnate spirits, but **thyself** and with **Him**...Listen to that voice, that answer that comes within, and ye will know and realize that this can **only--only--**be answered in thine own conscience.   954-5

HEAVEN AND HELL ARE STATES OF CONSCIOUSNESS

Heaven is that place, that awareness where the soul--with all its attributes, its mind, its body--becomes aware of being in the presence of the Creative Forces, or one with same. That is heaven.   262-88

You grow to heaven, you don't go to heaven.   3409-1

The will **must** be made one with the Father, that we may enter into that realm of the blessed, for, as has been given, only the true, the perfect, may see God, and we **must** be one with Him.   294-15

The kingdom of the Father or the kingdom of Heaven is within. Why? because our mind, the Son, is within us.   1567-2

It is **within** that there is the kingdom of heaven! The kingdom of **God** is without.   877-27

All ye may know of heaven or hell is within your own self. 4035-1

Thy mind that is both spiritual and material, that partakes of heaven --yea, and of hell also.   922-1

To live in life with a conscience that is continually dogging thee, continually warning against thine own better self in the desire to do good, is to indeed live in a hellfire itself.   417-8

For as given of old, there is each day set before us life and death, good and evil. We choose because of our natures. If our will were broken, if we were commanded to do this or that, or to become as an automaton, our individuality then would be lost and we would only be as in Him without conscience--**conscience**--consciousness of being one with Him; with the abilities to choose for self!   1567-2

The judge shall be thine **own** conscience; for conscience **is** that which awakens the mind of the soul; the **Soul** that of thine self that is the nearest portion of the dwelling place **of** the Holy of Holies Himself--the **Spirit** of the Master.   254-54

Each soul (is) accountable unto its own conscience.   1767-2

The time cometh when ye must stand before the judgment bar of thine own conscience, as must each soul.   5195-1

Ye **cannot** go against thine own conscience and be at peace with thyself, thy home, thy neighbor, thy God!   1901-1

These doubts, these fears that come in thine experience are but thine own conscience--or the mind of thy subconscious self--**smiting** thee.   784-1

How are ye to know when ye are on the straight and narrow way?
My Spirit beareth witness with thy spirit (Romans 8:16)...How? Thy God-consciousness, thy soul, either condemns, rejects, or falters before conditions that exist in the experience of the mental and material self.1436-1

Act as thy conscience and thy heart dictate.   254-87

INTUITION

Q-Give detailed directions for developing the intuitive sense.
A-Trust more and more upon that which may be from within. Or, this is a very common--but very definite--manner to develop: On any question that arises, ask the mental self--get the answer, yes or no. Rest on that. Do not act immediately (if you would develop the intuitive influences). Then, in meditation or prayer, when looking within self, ask--is this yes or no? The answer is intuitive development.   282-4

Intuitive forces are developed more by the introspective activities of a conscious mind...Hence the **ability** of those of **any** cult, or any group of people who by constant introspection through entering into the silence, are **able to bring** to the surface the activities of the entity as a whole.

Hence they are called sages, lamas, or such. These, when they are **made** to be what is **commonly** termed **practical**, yet remaining spiritual in aspect (that is, sticking to the truth), they become masters...Know the **basis** of introspection, which is--in that termed **Christian** religion --prayer, while that termed in many a cult as introspection, meditation, or mysticism, or occult influences brought in. They are one and the **same** in their essence, but **know** they are all of one source.   282-3

The more and more each is impelled by that which is intuitive, or the relying upon the soul force within, the greater, the farther, the deeper, the broader, the more constructive may be the result. 292-2

Anyone with great imagination, of course, is intuitive.   1744-1

How received woman her awareness? Through the sleep of the man! Hence **intuition** is an attribute of that made aware through the suppression of those forces from that from which it sprang, yet endowed **with** all of those abilities and forces of its Maker.   5754-2

The entity is one **very** intuitive; easily separating self from itself-- which so few may do; or, as it were, the ability to stand aside and watch self pass by.   2464-1

AUTOMATIC WRITING

Q-Please tell me how I may develop automatic handwriting?
A-By practice. Sit alone with pencil and paper, and let that guide that may be sought--or may come in--direct. It will come. Anyone may do this--but is it the better way? It may oft be questioned.   262-25

Q-What is the source of the automatic writing I have received? Should I develop this? Please explain.
A-...Those influences that are about thee are good, but rather **ever** let that which thou would gain through thy writing be inspired by the best in self as magnified through the Christ, than **any entity** or spirit or soul! While these seek for expression ever, they be seekers as thyself...Be thou led rather by that which comes from thine own soul, which thou meetest in the temple of the body, thy God in thee. And if He uses other influences, He will **direct** same.   792-1

Q-Should I develop automatic handwritings?
A-We would not advise it. Too easily it is misleading; especially when there are so many flashes about. Rather use the intuitive force.   281-4

The records each entity makes are written or impressed upon time and space; and through patience one may attain to the awareness or consciousness of same in one's own experience. Thus may the relationships of the entity and the Universal Consciousness, or God, become more and more a conscious reality. Not that it may be even describable in words. For, words are merely a means of communicating ideas to one individual from another, while Universal Consciousness with Creative Forces is rather the awareness that bespeaks of Life itself...

For, as the spirit of the Christ is one, and the individual entity in its manifestations of thought, purpose and desire makes its awareness one with that consciousness, so may that soul awareness come.   2246-1

For **as** one uses that one knows, the awareness of its source, of its ability, of its end, is more and more a part of the entity, of the soul...Then the next step that should be for the self is given through that of meeting oft with thy god-self from within. For the growth, as He gave, the knowledge of God and his righteousness is a growth from within...So the awareness of the kingdom, of being at-one, of having the Christ Consciousness as thy companion, as at-oneness with thee, is **doing**, being--not by faith or by works alone, but by **being**, by doing--that which is as the promptings of the desire of the heart, that has met and does meet in the secret chambers of the mind, of thy heart.   264-45

What is necessary will be given thee--of thy past, of thy present, of thy future. Are they not one in Him. He **is** from the foundations of the world. He IS! And as He has given, "Come and know ye me, and I will give thee that knowledge that thou hadst with me since the foundations of the world" (Isaiah 40:21).   922-1

When the purposes of an entity or soul are the more and more in accord with that for which the entity has entered, then the soul-entity may take **hold** upon that which may bring to its remembrance that it was, where, when and how. Thinkest thou that the grain of corn has forgotten what manner of expression it has given?...Only man forgets. And it is only in His mercy that such was brought about. For what was the first cause? Knowledge--knowledge! What then is that cut off in the beginnings of the Sons of God becoming entangled with the daughters of men, and the Daughters of God becoming entangled with the sons of men? As in Adam they forgot what manner of men they were. Only when he lives, he manifests that life that **is** the expression of the divine, may man **begin** to know **who**, where, what and when he was.   294-189

As ye **use** that as is **known**, there is given the more and more light to know from whence ye came and whither ye go.   364-4

The gift of God to man is an **individual** soul that may be one **with** Him, and that may know itself to be one with Him and yet individual in itself, with the attributes **of** the whole, yet **not** the whole.   262-11

For he, man, has been made just a little lower than the angels; with all the abilities to become **one with Him**! not the whole, nor yet lost in the individuality of the whole, but becoming more and more personal in **all** of its consciousness of the application of the individuality of Creative Forces, thus more and more at-onement with **Him**, --yet conscious of being himself.   2172-1

In keeping with the precepts of Jesus, "I and the Father are one" (John 10:30); not individually, but in the personal applications of the tenets, commandments, being one in purpose, one in application.   2067-11

Remember, it has been given that the purpose of the heart is to know **yourself** to **be** yourself and yet one with God even as Jesus, even as is represented in God the Father, Christ the Son, and the Holy Spirit; each knowing themselves to be themselves yet **One**!   281-37

What, then, is the First Cause of man's expression? That he may know himself to be himself and yet one with the Father; separate, yet as Father, Son and Holy Spirit are one, so the body, the mind, the soul of an entity may also be at-one with the First Cause.   815-7

No urge exceeds the will of the individual entity, that gift from and of the Creative Forces that separates man, even the son of man, from the rest of creation. Thus it is made to be ever as one with the Father, knowing itself to be itself and yet one with the Father, never, losing its identity. For, to lose its identity is death indeed,--death indeed--separation from the Creative Force. The soul may never be lost, for it returns to the One Force, but knows not itself to be itself any more.   3357-1

All moves and has its being in Him (Acts 17:28). So it is in self. Life itself is the consciousness, the awareness of that oneness of that Universal Consciousness in the earth.   2828-2

Seek, to know, to experience its (soul's) relationships to its Creator, its mate, its part of itself. For the Creative Forces are more even than companionship; for the heritage of each soul is to know itself to be itself yet one with the Creative Force.   1210-1

The first law of knowing self, of understanding self, is to become more and more sincere with that thou doest in the relationships one to another. For the proof of same is the fruit thereof. And when thou hast found the way, thou showest the way to thy brother.   262-15

There is no short cut to a consciousness of the God-Force. It is part of your own consciousness, but it cannot be realized by the simple desire to do so. Too often there is a tendency to want it and expect it without applying spiritual truth through the medium of mental processes. This is the only way to reach the gate. There are no shortcuts in metaphysics, no matter what is said by those who see visions, interpret numbers, or read the stars. These may find urges, but they do not rule the will. Life is learned within self. You don't profess it; you learn it. 5392-1

The coming into the earth has been and is, for the evolution or the evolving of the soul unto its awareness.   5749-5

Know thyself and thy relationships to Creative Forces. For the relationship of man and woman to God should be no different from the relationship to the fellow man.   1224-1

The greater the awareness (of that relationship to the Creative Forces), the more easily is the will made one with the purposes of the Creative Forces.   2109-2

(At-onement) is making self's will one with the Creative Forces.   262-45

Without the gift of free will to the soul, how **could** it become aware of the presence of the All-Abiding Creative Force?   945-1

Know that the Lord thy God is One Lord. That is of soul, of mind and of body. Then when the soul, the image of the Creator, is attuned to the divine, you are on the road to meeting thy own self.   3174-1

The **real** being is the spiritual import, intent and purpose.   1992-3

The understanding of the relationships with that Creative Force which is as the longing for the soul.   1458-1

In the fruits of that--as is given oft, as the fruits of the spirit-- does man become aware of the infinite penetrating, or interpenetrating the activities of all forces of matter, or that which is a manifestation of the realm of the infinite into the finite--and the finite becomes conscious of same.   262-52

"In all thy getting, my son, get understanding" (Proverbs 4:7). That of Self. When one understands self, and self's relation to its Maker, the duty to its neighbor, its own duty to self, it cannot, it will not be false to man or to its Maker.   3744-4

In patience we become aware of our souls, of our identity, of our being each a corpuscle, as it were, in the great body, in the heart of our God. And He has not willed otherwise.   262-114

The purposes for which an entity enters a material experience:

As indicated, the entity comes from without--or from an unknown quantity--into, first, that of desire, association, and conceptive activity with mental and physical growth, developing into a channel through which the spiritual import manifests.

Then its purpose is that such an entity, as this, may make manifest the spiritual influence in a material world. Each soul was in its first division from the Godhead to be a companion with that force, that influence, that purpose. Hence the purpose is to grow in grace, knowledge, understanding, for the indwelling in that **presence.** Hence all that manifests in the material world is a shadow of that which is of mental or spiritual import. And as to whether or not each division in mind, matter, becomes sufficient to be indwelling, or an at-onement with the Creative Force, is dependent upon the application of the purposes and desires of such force in...materiality.   1861-4

There is the physical body, there is the mental body, there is the spiritual body. They are one. They each have their attributes. They each have their weaknesses. They each have their associations. Yet they must be all coordinated.

The spirit is the life. Then each phase of the experience of the entity must be of the spiritual import in its very nature, if it is to live, to be the fulfilling of its purpose--to bring peace and harmony, for which purpose it **is** in existence. It must be constructive in the very nature and the very desires, without thought of self being the one glorified in or by same. Rather the **glory** is to the influence of force that **prompts** same.   1579-1

The whole of the experience of an individual entity in a material plane is the coordinating and cooperation of Creative Forces from without to the divine within, as to keeping an activity that may bring into manifestations health and happiness.   1158-8

What then ye may ask, **are** the purposes for a soul manifesting in flesh in **any** individual entity?

In the beginning, all souls that were as portions of the thought of God were given the opportunity for expression, as to be companions for the creative Force--or God.   2420-1

The purposes for each soul's experience in materiality are that the Book of Remembrance may be opened that the soul may know its relationship to its Maker.   1215-4

Each soul (and ye especially) has a definite job to do. But ye alone may find and do that job.   2823-1

What, then, is the purpose of the entity's activity in the consciousness of mind, matter, spirit in the present? That it, the entity, may **know** itself to **be** itself and part of the Whole; not the Whole; not the Whole but one **with** the Whole; and thus retaining its individuality, knowing itself to be itself, yet one with the purposes of the First Cause that called it, the entity, into **being** into the awareness, into the consciousness of itself. That is the purpose, that is the cause of **being**. 826-11

The purposes for which each soul enters materiality are that it may become aware of its relationship to the Creative Forces or God; by the material manifestation of the things thought, said, **done**, in relation to its fellow man!   1567-2

Little by little does **one** come to the understanding of the **purpose** for which they came into the earth. Purpose is of the **makings** of the individual, **plus** that **given** in the beginning, and as souls seek the Father, in that companionship that one may have through communion with Him--and communion with Him means **doing**; not shutting self away from thine brother, from thine neighbor, even from thine self--rather **applying** self to duties material, mental **and** spiritual, as **is** known. 99-8

Opportunity is a material manifestation of a spiritual ideal. Through a physical body the soul has an opportunity to express the attainments developed in other spheres of consciousness. Life in the earth becomes an opportunity for paralleling, correlating, cooperating, bringing into existence the effects of using all experience presented for the development of the soul. Hence, opportunity, primarily, is material manifestation of spiritual actions in conscious forces of the material plane.   262-50

Each sojourn or indwelling may be compared to that as ye have in your mental experience as a lesson, as a schooling for the purposes for which each soul-entity enters in earth experience; and why an entity under such environments came into that experience. Each study of each lesson then adds some phase of development for the soul.   1158-5

The entering of **every** soul is that it, the soul, may become more aware or conscious of the Divine within, that the soul-body may be purged that it may be a fit companion for the **glory** of the Creative Forces.   518-2

The purposes, the import of the earthly sojourn...is to meet self, to overcome those weaknesses in self, and become more and more adaptable to the spiritual truths that are a part of each and every entity.   1362-1

Remember, ye are as corpuscles in the body of God. Each with a duty, a function to perform if the world would be better for thou having lived in it, and this is thy purpose in the earth.   3481-2

PART IV

REINCARNATION, KARMA AND ASTROLOGY

REINCARNATION

That phase of Christian experience (reincarnation) is questioned by many, yet there is this period when the fact needs stressing to answer many questions.   1152-12

Life and its expressions are one. Each soul or entity will and does return, or cycle, as does nature in its manifestations about man; thus leaving, making or presenting--as it were--those infallible, indelible truths that it--Life--is continuous. And though there may be a few short years in this or that experience, they are one; the soul, the inner self being purified, being lifted up, that it may be one with that First Cause, that first purpose for its coming into existence.

And though there may be those experiences here and there, each has its relationships with that which has gone before, that is to come. 938-1

Q-What is the strongest argument against reincarnation?
A-That there is the law of cause and effect in **material** things. But the strongest argument against reincarnation is also, turned over, the strongest argument for it; as in **any** principle, when reduced to its essence. For the **law** is set--and it happens! though a soul may will itself **never** to reincarnate, but must burn and burn and burn--or suffer and suffer and suffer! For, the heaven and hell is built by the soul! The companionship in God is being one with Him; and the gift of God is being conscious of being one with Him, yet apart from Him--or one with, yet apart form the Whole.   5753-1

That that one meets must be met again. That (which) one applies will be applied again and again until that oneness, time, space, force, or the own individual is one with the Whole.   4341-1

When an individual incarnated in the earth, he has **possibly** passed through all the various spheres, either once, twice, **many** times--yet the changes bring those same conditions about for an understanding of each relationship in its **magnified** sphere. In the earth alone do we find them **all** in **one!** For man has taken on a bodily **form** in matter, or in nature. In the others we find in the **varied** forms, dependent upon that to which it has builded for **its** sojourn--see?...(Incarnations) **do not** come at **regular, given,** periods--but more as cycles, dependent upon what the individual, the entity, **has** done, or **has** accomplished through **its** cycle of the earth's passage **through this** solar system.   311-2

Ye, as a soul-entity, in the beginning sought companionship with God; losing that companionship by choice of that which would satisfy or gratify a material desire only. Thus, ye as the Master, enter again and again, ye come to fulfill the law, the law that brought thy soul into being to be one with Him.   3645-1

The Father has not willed that any soul should perish, and is thus mindful that each soul has again--and yet again--the opportunity for making its paths straight.   2021-1

Q-Must each soul continue to be reincarnated in the earth until it reaches perfection, or are some souls lost?
A-Can God lose itself, if God be God--or is it submerged, or is it as has been given, carried into the Universal Soul or Consciousness? The **soul** is not lost; the **individuality** of the soul that separated itself is lost. The reincarnation or the opportunities are continuous until the soul has of itself become an **entity** in its whole or has submerged itself.
Q-If a soul fails to improve itself, what becomes of it?
A-That's why the reincarnation, why it reincarnates; that it **may** have the opportunity. Can the will of man continue to defy its Maker? 826-8

To find that ye only lived, died and were buried under the cherry tree...does not make thee one whit better neighbor, citizen, mother or father. But to know ye spoke unkindly and suffered for it, and in the present may correct it by being righteous--**that** is worth while.5753-2

Why does one not recall more often those (past life) experiences? The same may be asked as to why there is not the remembering of the time when two and two to the entity became four, or when C A T spelled cat.
It always did! You only became aware of this as it became necessary for you to make practical application in your experience.   2301-4

(Many incarnations) are not well even to be known by self, thus have they been blotted from the book of thy remembrance--even as He blots them from the book of God's remembrance--if ye love one another.   5231-1

Q-Does spirit action ever change the sex of an entity from one incarnation to another?
A-At times.   136-27

For what is builded from any experience in the earth is as a habit in the present. 3395-2

As to race, color, or sex--this depends upon that experience necessary for the completion, for the building up of the purposes for which each and every soul manifests in the material experience. For as is generally accepted, and is in greater part true, the experiences of a soul-entity in materiality...are as lessons or studies in that particular phase of the entity's or soul's development...

As to when--it may be perhaps a hundred, two hundred, three hundred, a thousand years--as you may count time in the present. This may not be given. For how gave He? The day no man knoweth, **only** the Father in heaven knoweth it. 294-189

Q-Should it be said that the pattern (made by parents at conception) attracts a certain soul because it approximates conditions which that soul wishes to work with?

A-It approximates conditions. It does not set. For, the individual entity or soul, given the opportunity, has its own free will to work in or out of those problems as presented by that very union.

Q-Does the incoming soul take on some of the parents' karma?

A-Because of its relative relationship to same, yes. Otherwise, no.

Q-Are there several patterns which a soul might take on, depending on what phase of development it wished to work on?

A-Correct.

Q-What action of the early church, or council, can be mentioned as that which ruled (out) reincarnation from Christian theology?

A-Just as indicated,--the attempts of individuals to accept or take advantage of, because of this knowledge, see? 5749-14

Q-What part of the New Testament definitely teaches reincarnation?

A-John, six to eight; third to fifth. Then the rest as a whole. 452-6

Did not John come as the voice of one crying in the wilderness and in the spirit of Elijah? Yet he **was** Elijah! 1158-6

Q-What will convince me of reincarnation?

A-An experience. 956-1

This entity was among those who persecuted the church and fiddled while Rome burned. That's the reason this entity in body has been disfigured...Yet...it has advanced from a low degree to that which may not even necessitate a reincarnation in the earth. Not that it has reached perfection but there are realms for instruction if the entity will hold to the ideal of those whom it once scoffed. 5366-1

Q-When an entity has completed its development, such that it no longer needs to manifest on earth's plane, how far then is it along towards its complete development toward God?

A-Not to be given. Reach that plane, and develop in Him, for in Him the will then becomes manifest.   900-20

Perfection is not possible in a material body until you have at least entered some 30 times.   2982-2

Oft, the longer the periods between the earthly sojourns the greater has been--or may be--the development of the soul entity to that which **each** soul **is** to attain through its appearances among men.   1486-1

Q-About how much time have I spent in reincarnation up to the present?

A-Almost in all the cycles that have had the incoming from period to period has thou dwelt. Thine first incoming in the earth was during those periods of the Atlanteans that made for the divisions. Hence, counting in time, some twenty thousand years.   707-1

The entity's departure and entrance in the present covered an earthly cycle, according to that accounted by those of Holy Writ. The entity departed on the 24th of August, 1876. It entered again the 24th of August, 1910. Thus a cycle...In this particular sojourn in the present,-- that at the same age in years (earthly) there was that consideration for the same experience as **had** been gained or had before. For, as is and was understood by the preacher (Solomon--Ecclesiastes), "What **is** has been, and will be again" (Ecclesiastes 3:15).   2390-2

Though few (incarnations) in number, old indeed in earth's experience **is** the entity or soul.   276-2

All souls are from one. It is the application that has grown to be that which is termed old or young soul. For all souls were created in the one. The entity has applied self...hence an 'old' soul in service.   1770-2

Q-Were my parents selected by me before my present incarnation? Is such a choice usually accidental--or deliberate?

A-A whole dissertation might be given on this subject...

There is the law of cause and effect. There is the law of attraction. These are not **just** the same, though they join one to another. Hence the individual entity, of self, **chose**--partially--because of there being created the channel through which expression might be found.   2170-1

Q-From what side of my family do I inherit most?

A-You inherit most from yourself, not from family! The family is only a river through which it (the entity's soul) flows.   797-1

Q-Does the soul enter at conception or birth or in between?
A-It may at the first moment of breath; it may some hours before birth; it may many hours after birth.   457-10

The spiritual and physical birth varied little, there was the **physical** under one sign and the **spiritual** under another. Hence the doubts that often arise, from an astrological view.   488-6

In entering the present experience we find coming in the early afternoon, or just after the forenoon; while the spiritual entrance was in the late evening. Hence the entity may test this within self. When there are the activities with material things, the mornings are the periods when greater changes may be wrought. But in dealing with those in the mental, and when reason may be brought to bear, the shades of evening are the periods when the entity may reason and may work the better with those influences that abide in each soul in its relationships to mental and spiritual forces.   1397-1

Q-What keeps the physical body living until the soul enters?
A-Spirit! For, the spirit of matter--its source is life, or God. 2390-2

Q-Give exact time of physical and soul birth.
A-With **this** particular entity, we find there was...a period of four to four and a half hours difference...The soul, is that which would use, or be the companion of, that life-physical through any given period of existence in an earth's appearance. As the variations come, there are brought by the activities of those who through their own desire attract or detract those that would manifest in a particular body. See?...
The **interim** between that is as of **that** period when the decision is being made by **that** soul that would occupy **that** individual body. 276-3

Many souls are seeking to enter, but not all are attracted. Some may be repelled. Some are attracted and then suddenly repelled, so that the life in the earth is only a few days.   281-53

Q-What makes the difference between physical birth and soul birth?
A-One is earthy, the other is truth--or spiritual. Not that the spirit isn't--for Life is of the Creator! That which is **given to** be the Creator's activity enters in, even as "He breathed into him the breath of life and he became a living soul" (Genesis 2:7). As the sleep fell upon him, and the soul separated--through the taking of man's portion --and He becoming a portion of man. That the division. Hence when the culmination, or combination as comes through those relationships as made, they are **man** made, or is as of the offspring. Then that which comes in is from outside--see? Hence the variation.   282-3

It is not all of life to live, nor all of death to die; for one is the birth of the other when viewed from the whole or the center, and is but the experience of an entity in its transitions to and from that universal center from which **all** radiation is given.   369-3

It is not all of life to live, nor yet all of death to die. For life and death are one, and only those who will consider the experience as one may come to understand or comprehend what peace indeed means.   1977-1

With error entered that as called **death**, which is only a transition--or through God's other door...
In the comprehension of no time, no space, no beginning, no end, there may be the glimpse of what simple transition or birth into the material is; as passing through the other door into another consciousness.
Q-Describe some of the planes into which entities pass on experiencing the change called death.
A-Passing from the material consciousness to a spiritual or cosmic, or outer consciousness, oft does an entity or being not become conscious of that about it; much in the same manner as an entity born into the material plane only becomes conscious gradually of that designated as time and space for the material third dimensional plane...
For, as we have given, that we see manifested in the material plane is but a shadow of that in the spiritual plane.   5749-3

Q-Does death instantly end all feeling in the physical body? If not, how long can it feel?
A-...Death--as commonly spoken of--is only passing through God's other door. That there is continued consciousness is evidenced, ever, by the associations of influences, the abilities of entities to project or to make those impressions upon the consciousness of sensitives or the like.
As to how long--many an individual has remained in that called death for what ye call **years** without realizing it was dead!
The feelings, the desires for what ye call appetites are changed, or not aware at all. The ability to communicate is that which usually disturbs or worries others...
As to how long it requires to lose physical consciousness depends upon how great are the **appetites** and desires of a physical body. 1472-2

Cosmic consciousness, or elemental consciousness, after death projects from one to the other, see?   140-10

There are those various realms about the solar system in which each entity may find itself when absent from the body, it takes on in those other realms not an earthly form but a pattern--conforming to the same dimensional elements of that individual planet or space.   2533-8

Q-Where do entities recede to after leaving earth's plane?

A-As was given, in that "Touch not, for I have not yet ascended unto my father" (John 20:17). In the separation of the soul and spirit from an earthly abode, each enter the spirit realm. When the entity has fully completed its separation, it goes to that through which the entity merits in the action upon the earth's plane, and in the various spheres, or in the various elements, as has been prepared for its development, so the sojourn is taken, until the entity is ready for again manifesting through the flesh that development attained in the spiritual entity.   294-15

Q-(Is it true) that the memory reveals itself some time after death to a spiritual-minded person, not only as related to the earthly life, or the remaining earthly thoughts of earthly life, but **also** reveals itself as a self-unfoldment of **all** past experiences?

A-Correct. For life, in its continuity, is that experience of the soul or entity--including its soul, its spirit, its superconsciousness, its subconscious, its physical consciousness, or its **material** consciousness, in that as its **development** goes through the various experiences takes on more and more that ability of knowing itself to be itself, yet a portion of the Great Whole, or the One Creative Energy.   900-426

Life is continuous, and is Infinite.   1554-2

Q-What is meant by paradise as referred to by Jesus in speaking to the thief on the Cross?

A-The inter-between; the awareness of being in that state of transition between the material and the spiritual phases of consciousness of the soul...The awareness that there is the companionship of entities or souls, or separate forces in those stages of the development.   262-92

Some call this (psychic reading) going into the unknown. **Some** call this spiritual, or spirit, communication. Some call it the ability to gain the force of the activities of the fourth dimension--which is nearer correct than any explanation that may be given. For it is the plane that is of the inter-between, or that of the borderland--which all individuals occupy through that period of gaining consciousness of that sphere they themselves occupy, until such a period or such a time that there is that joining together of such forces as may again bring that individual entity into the realm of physical experience or being.   538-28

Death is but the beginning of another form of phenomenized force in the earth's plane, and may not be understood by the third dimensional mind from third dimensional analysis, but must be seen from the fourth dimensional force as may be experienced by an entity gaining --the insight and concept of such phenomenized conditions, see? 136-18

Q-Are the desires of the earth's plane carried over into the spiritual plane?

A-When those desires have fastened such hold upon the inner being as to become a portion of the subconsciousness, those desires pass on. Such as one may have in gluttonousness, or in any condition that benumbs the mental forces of the entity. For the subconscious, as given, is the storehouse of every act, thought, or deed. Hence, as we have been given, all are weighed in the balance...Hence the condition as is seen about such entity having passed into the spirit plane; it seeks the gratification of such through the low minded individuals in an earth plane. For..."thoughts are deeds" and live as such...

When an entity, in the earth plane, desires will manifested to do an error, assisted by error in spirit, as well as in earth plane, as such desire to do that that would assist, they receive hindrances, again they receive the assistance of all good in spirit plane, governed by the law. For law is love, love is law, God is love.   900-20

When the soul departs from the body--(this is not being spoken of the Christ)--it has all the form of the body from which it has passed-- yet it is not visible to the carnal mind, unless that mind has been, and is, attuned to the infinite. Then it appears, in the infinite, as that which may be handled, with all the attributes of the physical being; with the appetites, until these have been accorded to a unit of activity with the Universal Consciousness.   2533-8

Remember, there are material urges and there are materials in other consciousnesses not three dimensions alone.   5366-1

Q-At the change called death is the entity free of a material body?

A-Free of the material body but not free of matter; only changed in the form as to matter; and is just as acute to the realms of consciousness as in the physical or material or carnal body, or more so.   262-86

The spirits of all that have passed from the physical plane remain about the plane until their developments carry them onward. 3744-2

Now, this is very interesting, to know that the entity known as (3817) (that died some eight to ten years previous) has just come to the realization of being in the Borderland.   3817-1

Q-What form of consciousness does the spirit entity assume?

A-That of the subconscious consciousness, as known in the material plane, or the acts and deeds, and thoughts, done in the body, are ever present before that being. Then consider what hell digged by some, and what haven and heaven builded by many.

Q-What are the powers of the spirit entity?

A-...As **varying** as individual's power or ability to manifest, or to exercise that manifestation, in the material. We have not changed...

Many carnal minds have passed from the body for days before they realized they were passed. Sensuousness! 5756-4

Q-In regard to my first projection of myself into the astral plane, about two weeks ago: Some of the people were animated and some seemed like waxen images of themselves. What made the difference?

A-Some--those that appear as images--are the expressions or shells or the body of an individual that has been left when its soul self has projected on, and has not been as yet dissolved--as it were--to the realm of that activity.

Q-Why did I see my father and his two brothers as young men, although, I knew them when they were white-haired?

A-They are growing, as it were, upon the eternal plane. For, as may be experienced in every entity, a death is a birth. 516-4

Mama and Dr. House and uncle Porter and the baby (all deceased) --we are all here. Grandpa (deceased) has built the home here, and it's **nice**! And we are all waiting until you (Mrs. Cayce) come...for we have reached together where we see the light and know the pathway to the Savior is along the narrow way that leads to **His** throne. We are on that plane where you have heard it spoken of that the body, the mind, are one with those things we have builded. Yes, I still play baseball, and Charlie has recently joined my club and I am still Captain to many of 'em. Well, we will be waiting for you! 5756-13

The last to be overcome is death, and the knowledge of life is the knowledge of death. 254-17

It is the **fear** of the unknown that first makes fear. Death is separation and thus man hath dreaded same; yet when it has lain aside its phase that maketh afraid, it is but the birth of **opportunities.** 1776-1

Death...the pangs of the loss of self. 3188-1

(Jesus') real test was in the garden in the realization that he had met every test and yet must know the pang of death. 5277-1

Learn to **live**! Then there **is** no death, save the transition, when desired. See?...**Many** live who have never died as yet! 900-465

That each entity must and will some day attain to the ability to be conscious of physical death without the physical suffering is true, but the day--to most--is far, too far away. 993-7

Q-Have I karma from any previous existence that should be overcome?
A-Well that karma be understood, and how it is to be met. For, in various thought--whether considered philosophy or religion or whether from the scientific manner of cause and effect--karma is all of these and more. Rather it may be likened unto a piece of food, whether fish or bread, taken into the system; it is assimilated by the organs of digestion, and then those elements that are gathered from same are made into the forces that flow through the body, giving the strength and vitality to an animate object, or being, or body. So, in experiences of a soul, in a body, in an experience in the earth. Its thoughts make for that upon which the soul feeds, as do the activities that are carried on from the thought of the period make for the ability of retaining or maintaining the active force or active principle of the thought **through** the experience. Then the soul reentering into a body under a different environ either makes for the expending of that it has made through the experience in the sojourn in a form that is called in some religions as destiny of the soul, in another philosophy that which has been builded must be met in some way or manner, or in the more scientific manner that a certain cause produces a certain effect. Hence we see that karma is **all** of these and more. What more? Ever since the entering of spirit and soul into matter there has been a way of redemption for the soul, to make an association and a connection with the Creator, **through** the love **for** the Creator that is in its experience. Hence **this**, too, must be taken into consideration; that karma may mean the development **for self**--and must be met in that way and manner; or it may mean that which has been acted upon by the cleansing influences of the way and manner through which the soul, the mind-soul, or the soul-mind is purified, or to be purified, or purifies itself and hence these changes come about--and some people term it "Lady Luck" or "The body is born under a luck star." It's what the soul-mind has done **about** the source of redemption of the soul! Or it may be yet that of cause and effect, as related to the soul, the mind, the spirit, the body.   440-5

Destiny is: "As ye sow, so shall ye reap" (Galatians 6:7). And like begets like. And the first law of nature, which is the material manifestation of spiritual law in a physical world, is self-propagation--which means that it seeks self-preservation and the activity of the same law that brought the thought of man (or the spirit of man) into existence--companionship...
    Then, that which is cosmic--or destiny, or karma--depends upon what the soul has done about that it has become aware of.   267-7

Thy Father-God is within self and without. Then as ye treat thy fellow man, ye are treating thy Maker. These are immutable, unchangeable laws of divine origin--not of man's concept. What ye sow in body, in mind, in purpose, ye must one day in the physical being, reap. That, too, is immutable, unchangeable. Thus what ye do to others, ye are doing to thyself, whether it is in abuse of privileges, abuse of body, abuse of mind, or just the opposite in adding to the abilities in any direction.   3198-3

Cause and effect to many are the same as karma.
Karma is that brought over, while cause and effect may exist in the one material experience only.   2981-21

Karma influences are more of the spiritual than of an earth's exper-ience, for what we create in the earth we meet in the earth--and what we create in the realm through spiritual forces we meet there! And getting outside of the realm of the material does not mean necessarily angelic, or angelic influence.   314-1

Q-Is there some karmic debt to be worked out with either or both and should I stay with them until I have made them feel more kindly toward me?
A-These--What **is** karmic debt?...It is merely self being **met** in rela-tionships to that they **themselves** are working out and not a karmic debt **between** but a **karmic** debt of **self** that may be worked out **between** the associations that exist in the present!...
For He stands in thy stead, before that **willingness** of thy inner self, thy soul, to do good unto others.   1436-3

As individuals in their material or mental experience in the material world find that they are in the activity of being mistreated, as from their angle, from their own angle have they mistreated.   262-81

Every harsh word...every unkind thing, no matter what others have done, that an individual says about or of another individual, **must** be met by self. For, only self can actually defame self.   257-122

Offences must come...but woe to him that bringeth same to pass.   272-9

Karma is, then, that that has been in the past builded as indifference to that known to be right. Taking chances, as it were--"Will do better tomorrow--this suits my purpose today--I'll do better tomorrow." 257-78

What is karma but giving way to impulse?   622-6

While a man may defy the laws of nature, defy even the laws of his Creator, he must pay and **pay** and **pay!**   830-2

Live with this in mind (and every soul may take heed): Ye shall pay every whit, that ye break of the law of the Lord. For the law of the Lord is perfect, it converteth the soul.   3559-1

Whatsoever an entity, an individual, sows, that must he also reap. That as law cannot be changed. As to whether one meets it in the letter of the law or in mercy, in grace, becomes the choice of the entity. If one would have mercy, grace, love, friend, one must show self in such a manner to those whom one becomes associated. For like begets like.   5001-1

Karmic influences must ever be met, but He has prepared a way that takes them upon Himself, and as ye trust in Him He shows thee the way to meet the hindrances or conditions that would disturb thee in any phase of thine experience. For, karmic forces are: What is meted must be met. If they are met in Him that is the Maker, the Creator of all that exists in manifestation, as He has promised, then not in blind faith is it met--but by the deeds and the thoughts and the acts of the body, that through Him the conditions may be met day by day. Thus He bought every soul that would trust in Him. For, since the foundations of the world He has paved the ways, here and there entering into the experience of man's existence that He may know every temptation that might beset man in all of his ways. Then in that as the Christ He came into the earth, fulfilling then that which makes Him that channel, that we making ourselves a channel through Him may--with the boldness of the Son--approach the Throne of mercy and grace and pardon. 442-3

In sacrifice there is penance, but grace doth more greatly abound to him who sheds the love of the Father upon those that the body may contact from day to day.   99-8

It is only as ye forgive that even the Savior, the Christ, is able to forgive thee.   3124-2

For it is line upon line, precept upon precept. We grow in grace, in knowledge, in understanding.   349-12

There has not been the full concept as to the meaning of the blood as shed for the eternal sacrifice, or the law being of none effect in the law itself; that as individuals, in body, in mind, in spirit **become** the law, it is then as void in **their** experience--for they **are** the law! And the law is love, the law is God, the law **is** circumstance...
He **alone** is each soul pattern! **He** is the **karma**, if ye put thy trust **wholly** in Him. See? Not that every soul shall not give account for the deeds done in the body, and in the body meet them! but in each meeting, in **each** activity, let the pattern--not in self, not in mind alone, but in Him--be the guide.   2067-2

(Karma) can be met most in Him who, taking away the law of cause and effect by fulfilling the law, establishes the law of grace.   2828-4

The answer to know His way, is ever within...(and) know that attunement, atonement and at-onenent are **one**.   2174-3

At-onement is making self's will one with the Creative Forces that
may become the impelling influence in thought, in mind, that is the
builder to every act of a physical, mental or material body...
The shedding of the blood in the **man** Jesus made for the atoning
for **all** men, through making Himself in at-onement with the law and
with love. For, through **love** was brought the desire to make self and
His brother in at-onement. Hence in the atoning or shedding of the
blood comes the redemption to man, through that which may make
for **his**--man's--at-onement with Him.   262-45

Q-Explain how the "Atonement of Christ" and the "At-onement with
Christ" are in harmony.
A-The atonement and at-onement is one in the faith that He, the Christ,
presented to man that manner of life, that manner of activity...that
leaves easy the spiritual self in at-one-ment for that which has been
met in the experience of the entity, or self--and hence becomes the
oneness through atonement, **with** the Creative Forces--which is God.
Hence the **oneness** of Christ-life...brings those that trust in Him--and
act that way--to the consciousness of that at-onement in Him.
Q-Explain the harmony between "Atonement of Christ" and reincarnation.
A-That as is the experience must be met in the activity of that soul,
that is an **individuality**, that may be one **with** God yet **not** God--yet
one with Him in its individuality. Hence, as the Son of man--made in
the flesh--Adam brought sin, or separation from God--in the last
Adam, the Christ, brought that **at-onement with** God. So does this,
then, make the at-one-ment with those that, as He, make themselves--
through Him--in the same activity, the same at-onement, **with** Him. 452-3

For, He has given, no sacrifice is acceptable save as of the **desires**
of self to be one with Him.   531-5

Repentance, then, is, "Not my will but Thine, O Lord, be done in
me, through me, day by day."   2533-7

All can be holy; that is, dedicating body, mind and purpose. That is
being holy.   3621-1

In Him, by faith and works, are ye made every whit whole. 3395-2

By sin came death; by the shedding of blood came freedom--freedom
from a consciousness, into a greater consciousness.   276-7

Each soul pays for his **own** shortcomings, not someone else's. 1056-2

All illness is sin; not necessarily of the moment, as man counts time, but as a part of the whole experience.   3395-2

Here we find conditions advanced in multiple sclerosis, so called, or the inability of the digestive forces and the glands in the liver (in the right lobe) to supply those tendencies needed, or energies needed, to supply the return force in nerve energy...Thus we find what is commonly called the law of cause and effect, or karmic conditions being met by an individual entity. For, as given of old, each soul shall give an account of every idle word spoken. It shall pay every whit. And this is as self-evident as the statement, "In the day ye eat thereof ye shall surely die" (Genesis 2:17). It is as demonstrative as, "Be ye fruitful, multiply, **subdue** the earth" (Genesis 1:28).

The entity, then, is still at war with itself, but all hate, all malice, all that would make man afraid, must be eliminated, first from the mind of the individual entity.   3124-1

It is not always the sin of the parents that such (child physically and mentally incapacitated) be their measure of responsibility, but oft it is as here--rather that the soul-consciousness of this entity may become aware of what true abiding love leads individuals to do concerning those who are wholly dependent upon others for every care...

Thus we find here an entity who...in many of these sojourns was well acquainted with--those who did minister to the need of those who were without hope, who were disturbed in body and in mind as to which way to turn and as to what course to pursue. Yet the entity turned away from same, that there might be the joys of the material nature, the enjoying of appetites in self for a season.   2319-1

Here we have an entity meeting its own self (mongoloidism)...

Much may be the contribution for this entity in the present in kindness, patience, love. All of these are needed in the body. These will aid the soul. For, remember, the soul never forgets...

Here we find an individual entity born not only to be charged to the parents but it is needed for the parents as well as needed by the entity. Don't put the body away, it needs the love, the attention.   5335-1

The condition (speech defect) is karmic...The body is meeting itself; but so must those responsible for this entity meet themselves. 4013-1

(Muscular dystrophy) is karma for both the parents and the body. 5078-1

In another experience we find that the entity was a chemist, and she used many of those various things for the producing of itching in others. She finds it (allergies) in herself in the present!   3125-2

Here (asthma) we have truly a pathological condition but a psychological as well as the physiological, and it extends to karmic reactions also. For one doesn't press the life out of others without at times seeming to have same pressed out of self.   3906-1

The entity overcame that ruler (in a Peruvian experience) who lost self in aggrandizement of selfish desires as respecting the fair sex; becoming the ruler, yet much **blood** was shed. Thence anemia.   4248-1

Q-Why was I so fearful in childhood, especially of animals, spiders, and sharp knives--and still dislike to use or to see used a sharp knife?
A-Because of those experiences when thou wert bound about, in those periods in France, when thine associates bound thee for thine virtue, and those activities in the knives, the racks of torture.   823-1

Q-What influence causes me to be afraid of darkness?
A-...The experiences in the dungeon in which thou wert plunged.   852-12

The entity made light of same (suffering in the Roman arena). Hence the entity sees suffering in self (paralysis) in the present, and must again make light of same--but for a different purpose.   1215-4

The entity **laughed** at those who were crippled by such activities (Roman arena) and lo, they return again to thee (poliomyelitis). How blest then art thou, that there are those close to thee that ye once laughed at; that are patient, that are kind, that are gentle with thee.   1504-1

The entity was in the land of the present nativity, among the earlier settlers who brought consternation, hate, temperaments that wrecked the mental forces in the experience of others...which in the present are finding expression in the madness within self (mental imbalance).   1969-2

Q-What is the cause of the body's dislike for eating fish, fowl, game and certain meats?
A-From the condition as existed in that as a Norseman, when he lived on these.   5162-1

Q-Is there a reason for the previous lives that creates the physical condition (eczema) today?
A-Resentments in regard to those not thinking as self.   2872-3

Beware, ever, of two influences in the life from that experience--in this sojourn: Nicotine in any form, and alcohol, in its hard forms. These will become stumbling experiences if there are indulgences in those directions such that they become habitual in the inclinations of the influences that arise not only as appetites but as the emotions or sensory forces of the body; for these will be easily influenced by such. 1417-1

Ye are sensitive to things about you (hypertension); because ye have lived not only in this experience but in many others a very **extravagant** life in **every** phase of your associations with your fellow man!   1537-1

Oft did the entity laugh at those less nimble of activity, owing to their heaviness in body.

Hence we find the entity not only meeting same in the present from a physical angle (obesity) but there are the **necessities** of it being worked out by diet as **well** as outdoor activity.   1339-2

The basic reactions of these (deafness) are somewhat of the karmic nature...Then, do not close the ears, the mind or the heart again to those who plead for aid.   3526-1

Q-How did the entity's inferiority complex originate?
A-From the fear and dislike of men. You cannot be one who took the vows and kept them and then lightly turn around and try to gratify the appetites of those who are not easily satisfied.   4082-1

These (homosexuality) are the effects of karmic influences...Thus there is brought not merely a physical or purely pathological condition, but a physiological and psychological disturbance to the body. 3364-1

Here we have a quick return--from fear, to fear through fear. And these bring, with those experiences of the entity, that which will require special influences to be put into the experiences of this mind; that it may be kept away from fear, away from loud noises, darkness, the scream of sirens, the shouts of individuals of fear to the entity.

For, the entity was only just coming to that awareness of the beauty of associations, of friendships, of the beautiful outdoors, nature, flowers, birds, and of God's manifestations to man of the beauty, of the oneness of purpose with individual activities in nature itself; and then the tramping of feet the shouts of arms, brought destructive forces. The entity then was only a year to two years older than in the present experience (1943), that finds the world in such a turmoil for the entity in its dreams, its visions, its experiences in those periods when the body-mind is active again to those fears about it.

The entity then, in the name Theresa Schwalendal, was on the coasts of Lorraine. The entity only passed out and then in less than nine months again entered a material world.

Be patient. Do not scold. Do not speak harshly. Do not fret nor condemn the body-mind. But do tell it daily of love that Jesus had for little children, of peace and harmony; never those stories such of the witch, never those as of fearfulness of any great punishment; but love patience.   3162-1

Q-Please give a definition of the word astrology.

A-That position in space about our own earth that is under the control of the forces that are within the sphere of that control, and all other spheres without that control. That is astrology, the study of those conditions.

In the beginning, our own plane, the Earth, was set in motion. The planning of other planets began the ruling of the destiny of all matters as created, just as the division of waters was ruled and is ruled by the Moon in its path about the earth; just so as the higher creation as it begun is ruled by its action in conjunction with the planets about the earth. The strongest force used in the destiny of man is the Sun first, then the closer planets to the earth, or those that are coming to ascension at the time of the birth of the individual, **but let it be understood here, no action of any planet or the phases of the Sun, the Moon or any of the heavenly bodies surpass the rule of man's will power, the** power given by the Creator of man, in the beginning, when he became a living soul, with the power of choosing for himself. The inclinations of man are ruled by the planets under which he is born, for the destiny of man lies within the sphere or scope of the planets...

In the sphere of many of the planets within the same solar system, we find they are banished to certain conditions in developing about the spheres from which they pass, and again and again and again return from one to another until they are prepared to meet the everlasting Creator of our entire Universe, of which our system is only a very small part...

Though one may pass from one plane to another without going through all stages of the condition, for only upon the earth plane at present do we find man is flesh and blood, but upon others do we find those of his own making in the preparation of his own development.

Q-Give the names of the principal planets, and the influence on the lives of people.

A-Mercury, Mars, Jupiter, Venus, Saturn, Neptune, Uranus, Septimus.

Q-Are any of the planets, other than the earth, inhabited by human beings or animal life of any kind?

A-No

Q-Is it proper for us to study the effects of the planets on our lives in order to better understand our tendencies and inclinations, as influenced by the planets?

A-When studied aright, very, very, very much so. How aright then? In that influence as is seen in the influence of the knowledge already obtained by mortal man. Give more of that into the lives, giving the understanding **that the will must be the ever guiding factor to lead man on, ever upward.**

Q-Who were the first people in the world to use astrology, and what time in history was it first used?

A-Many, many thousands, thousands of years ago. The first record as is given is as that recorded in Job, who lived before Moses was.

Q-Are the tendencies of an individual influenced most by the planets nearer the earth at the time of the individual's birth?

A-At, or from that one which is at the zenith when the individual is in its place or sphere, or as is seen from that sphere or plane the soul and spirit took its flight in coming to the earth plane. For each plane, in its relation to the other, is just outside, just outside, relativity of force, as we gather them together.   3744-3

It is not so much that an entity is influenced because the Moon is in Aquarius or the Sun in Capricorn or Venus or Mercury in that or the other house, sign, or the Moon and Sun sign, in that one of the planets is in this or that position in the heavens; but rather because those positions in the heavens are from the **entity** having been in that sojourn as a soul. This is how the planets have the greater influence in the earth, see? For the application of an experience is what makes for the development of a body, a mind, **or** a soul...

There's life there (Jupiter) (not as known in earth), as there is in Saturn, Sun, Moon, Venus, Mercury, Uranus, Neptune, Mars; all have their form--as about the earth, the inhabitants of the air, fire, water-- in and out of the earth. The elements about same are inhabited, if you choose, by those of their own peculiar environment.   630-2

Q-Would it be well for me to make a study of astrology?

A-Well for everyone to make a study of astrology! for, as indicated, while many individuals have set about to prove the astrological aspects and astrological survey enable one to determine future as well as the past conditions, these are well to the point where the individual under-stands that these act upon individuals because of their sojourn or correlation of their associations with the environs through which these are shown, see? Rather than the star directing the life, the life of the individual directs the courses of the stars, see? for was it not given when His star appeared? Is it not shown in all the studies of the positions that the earth occupies in its course through the spheres that every condition is as cause and effect? but that the scale has gradually been on the increase or the **individuals** as they passed **through** their various experiences in the cycles of position? This is not intended to indicate that (as some astrological reports have been made) there is a definite period when **individuals** enter a cycle, or that every two thousand or one thousand, or five hundred or twenty-four hundred years an individual re-enters the earth: but as a race, as a **whole** does the twenty-four hundred year period hold good, see? for in each period does the earth, do the planets, do all of those about space again revert to that it would begin over again. The **individual** activity is a thing of itself, see? or, as may be illustrated in **Life**--as of an individual: It may be said that the line of thought in the present is towards a change in the Aries age from the Pisces, or from the Aquarius, or **to** those various activities, see? but it doesn't mean that every individual changes, for each individual has its own development. As we look about us we see the various spheroids, spheres, planets or solar systems, and they have their individual activity. Look at the soul of man and know it may be equal to, or greater; for it must be man's ability to control one of such! Vast study, yes!

Q-Who is giving this information?

A-Zorain. Student with Zoroaster, yes.   311-10

The sun, the moon, the stars, the position in the heavens or in all of the hosts of the solar systems...have their influence (upon the entity) in the same manner (this is very crude illustration, but very demonstrative) that the effect of a large amount of any element would attract a compass. Drawn to! Why? Because of the influence of which the mind element of a soul, an entity, has become conscious.   5753-1

There are sojourns in other realms of the solar system which represent certain attributes. Not that ye maintain a physical earth-body in Mercury, Venus, Jupiter, Uranus or Saturn; but there is an awareness or a consciousness in those realms when absent from the body, and the response to the position those planets occupy in this solar system.   2823-1

Rather, then, than the stars **ruling** the life, the life should rule the stars. For man was created a little bit higher than all the rest of the whole universe, and is capable of harnessing, directing, enforcing the laws of the universe.   5-2

It is not that certain influences are existent because of...the astrological aspects, at...birth; but rather...(planets) are in their **positions** because of the **entity's** influences upon the universe.   2113-1

Remember, all of these planets, stars, universes, were made for the **entity** and its associates to rule, and not to be ruled by them, save as an individual entity gives itself to their influence.   2830-2

Each planetary influence vibrates at a different rate of vibration. An entity entering that influence enters that vibration; not necessary that he change, but it is the grace of God that he may.   281-55

Each of the environs about this present solar system has its part in the abilities or the awareness of each entity, as it enters same, or as it passes through,--in the same manner as each entity passing through a grade in school is subject to the lessons the mental self retains or uses, or applies, in whatever may be the problem in its relationship to other things, other conditions, or other souls. 3037-1

For this, as is seen, will be proven--that, as the scientific change has been found by the observation into the terrestrial forces and into those places and conditions about the earth's plane, there is missing some one of the earth's companions or planets; and the combustion or destruction of same caused much change. 195-43

Q-Does the soul choose the planet to which it goes after each incarnation? If not, what force does?
A-In the Creation we find all force relative one with the other, and in the earth's plane that of the flesh. In the developing from plane to plane becomes the ramification, or the condition of the will merited in its existence finding itself through eons of time.
The illustration, or manifestation in this, we find again in the man called Jesus:
When the soul reached that development in which it reached earth's plane, it became in the flesh the model, as it had reached through the developments in those spheres, or planets, known in the earth's plane, obtaining then One in All.
As in Mercury pertaining of Mind.
In Mars of Madness.
In Earth as of Flesh.
In Venus as Love.
In Jupiter as Strength.
In Saturn as the beginning of earthly woes, that to which all insufficient matter is cast for the beginning.
In Uranus as of the Psychic.
In that of Neptune as of Mystic.
In Septimus as of Consciousness.
In Arcturus as of the Developing. 900-10

Each of those companions that are about the solar system represents as it were one of the phases of our conscience--the elements of our understanding--or our senses; then they each in their place, in their plane, bear a relationship to us...
Hence they bear witness by being **in** certain positions--because of our activity, our sojourn in those environs, in relationships to the universal forces of activity. 1567-2

Analyze the astrological aspects, the interims between earthly incarnations, as being the hereditary part of the entity from a mental standpoint. The appearances or the sojourns in the earth we would analyze as the emotional forces of the entity, or the basis from which the emotions arise. Rather than these becoming then for the entity that which supersedes, they become rather as a part of the environment of an entity.   1743-1

The urges that arise from astrological aspects--that is, from the sojourns of the entity in the environs about the earth--that become as the individuality; or that innate in the experience. Thus the expression of same is found in the intuition or the mental, or the deeper meditation, or the arousing of the inner or super or soul consciousness...

Yet these are only as indications or signs. For, to be sure, the will... makes individuality of the soul...surpassing any urge.   1373-2

Astrological aspects are represented as stages of consciousness; given names that represent planets or centers or crystallized activity.

Not that flesh and blood, as known in the earth, dwells therein; but in the consciousness, with the form and manner as befits the environ.   1650-1

The sojourns of souls in the environs about the earth that made--and make--for the mental urges in the souls of man.   256-5

The law of environment, relativity, heredity, is the same in the spiritual activity as in material earthly--**matter** conditions.   683-1

What one is today is because of what one (the individual soul) **has done about** that the soul knows **of** the Creative Forces or God **in** its experience, in **whatever** environ or consciousness it may manifest.

The environs then in the earth, in any given experience, are those things that make for the emotional body in that experience.

That which is innate, or that (which) finds expression when the individual soul turns to the Creative Force or God within, arises from the **soul's** experience in those environs **about** the earth.

Study these, and it--the study--will make for a great interest, or greater interest, in the **causes** of relationships in the earth; or in that which is termed the genealogy of ideas, of individuals, of nations, of those things that go to make up **why** individuals are born in this or that environment. For **that** is true genealogy!   852-12

The sojourn of a soul in its environ about the earth, or in this solar system, gives the factors that are often found in individuals in the earth that are of the same parentage, in the same environ; yet one might be a genius and the other a fool; one might be a moral degenerate and the other a high, upright, upstanding individual.   541-1

Q-What is a horoscope?

A-That in which the planets and their relative forces (have) to do with the planets that control the actions without respect of will, or without respect of the earthly existence through which the body has passed?

Q-Do horoscope readings include former appearances in the earth plane?

A-Not at all. The former appearances and the relation of the solar forces in the universe have their relations to what might be termed life readings, or experiences. For, as has been shown and given, horoscope, the science of the solar system...is only the mathematical calculation of earth's position in the universe at any given time, while in the life reading would be the correlation of the individual with a given time and place, with its relative force as applied and received through other spheres and manifested in earth's sphere in the flesh, and the development being the extenuation of the soul's development manifested in the earth plane through subconscious forces of a body or entity. 254-21

The astrological aspects may give a tendency, an inclination; and a systematic, scientific study of same would indicate the vocation. And about eighty percent of the individuals would be in the position of being influenced by such astrological aspects; or would be in the position for their abilities to be indicated from same.

But the other twenty percent would not be in that position, due to the influences from activity or the use of their abilities in material experience. Hence in these it would be not only necessary that their material sojourn be given, but as to what had been accomplished through same, and that to be met in the present experience. 5753-3

Q-Should an astrological horoscope be based on the time of physical birth or the time of soul birth?

A-On time of physical birth; for these are merely **inclinations**, and because of inclinations are not the influence of will. **Will** is that factor of the spiritual forces or the gift, as it were, **to** man, hu-man, as he came into material form, with which choice is made, see?...

There are two, yea three phases or schools through which such information, such charts, such characters have been carried--the Egyptian, the Persian, the Indian. The Persian is a combination and the **older** of all of these, and these are as logos (?), or as charts that have been set. That they have become as experiences in the activities of individuals, to be sure, is not disputed; but the world does not govern **man, Man** governs the world! And the inclinations astrologically show whether man has not applied will! 826-8

If the entity would study astrology, do not put the signs in the Egyptian calendar but in the Persian, for the Persian interpretations are more proficient than the Egyptian. This is not belittling the efforts of the entity nor of the Egyptians in those periods, but the variations in time have been corrected by the Persians and not by the Egyptians. The Egyptian calculations are thirty degrees off (one sign).   2011-3

Q-What is the correct system to use in astrology--the heliocentric or geocentric system?
A-The Persian--or the geocentric--is the nearer correct.   933-3

Pisces, ye say. Yet astrologically from the records, these are some two signs off in thy reckoning.   5755-1

Q-Regarding my daughter's Life Reading, did difference of three days in statement of birth date make any difference in the information given?
A-Had the information been given from a purely astrological aspect, a minute or half an hour--yes ten minutes at least, might make a difference in the report. But this is read from the records of the entity, and **not** from the exact birth date as related to the astrological inclinations-- for these were taken from the records themselves.   1947-4

FOUR AND MORE DIMENSIONS

Learn the lesson of the interpreting of the dimensions of the earth, or that the three dimensions in the mind may be seven, and in spirit eleven and twelve and twenty two. These, then, are encompassed in the knowledge, and the understanding; the Lord thy God is one Lord. 5149-1

That which is known in the earth as a three dimensional phase of existence with a five-consciousness of its existence.   5756-11

There are those various realms about the solar system in which each entity may find itself when absent from the body, it takes on in those other realms not an earthly form but a pattern--conforming to the same dimensional elements of that individual planet or space.   2533-8

We find in the earth plane the three dimensions, in Venus the four, in Jupiter the five, in Uranus the seven--all of these; not as of planes, as sometimes spoken, but consciousnesses--the ability to reason from certain activities.   3006-1

There may be as seven, in Mercury--or four, in Venus--or five, as in Jupiter. There may be only one as in Mars. There may be many more as in those of Neptune, or they may become even as nil--until purified in Saturn's fires.   311-2

In Venus the body-form is near to that in the three dimensional plane. For it is what may be said to be **all**-inclusive.   5755-1

How many dimensions are in this solar system? Eight! What positions do others occupy? That relative relationship one to another. 5755-2

For this entity,--Mercury, Venus, Jupiter, Saturn and Uranus all become a part of the consciousness or awareness, or the manner which this entity thinks or reacts. For, as the earth is a three dimensional awareness or consciousness,--indicated by body, mind, soul,--so is the Universal Consciousness manifested or expressed in the three dimensional as Father, Son, Holy Spirit; while it might be manifested or indicated in many more in Jupiter, Venus, Mercury or Uranus. For, each has its consciousness, just as each entity has its abilities, its activities.3037-1

Truly is there found that the desire must precede the action and that directed thought become action in the concrete manner, through each force that the spiritual elements manifest through. And there then becomes the three manifestations in the three manners, in the three ways, all projections from a fourth dimensional condition into a third dimensional mind.   106-9

First--one finds self in a three-dimensional plane of consciousness; all that may be known materially is subject to that dimension.
That as may be comprehended in the mental may reach into a four-dimensional plane--as the variation between a book with its dimension and the contents of same, which may be of a mental reaction entirely.   1861-4

Four dimension then being that condition as is reached wherein physical objects are spiritually understood, spiritual objects are physically understood, and able of experience (and experienced?). These become hard questions to the single track mind, or two track mind, but to the full rounded out individual become understanding conditions, to the mental processes of the well rounded mind. In this condition then does the individual reach its abilities of development in the planes as experienced in the advances from the earth's plane, coming then in that position of being able to have height, breadth, depth, thickness, and all without space.   900-66

The fourth dimensional mind gaining the privilege of seeing all in one.   900-113

Best definition that ever may be given of fourth dimension is an idea! Where will it project? Anywhere! Where does it arise from? Who knows! Where will it end? Who can tell! It is all inclusive. It has both length, breadth, height, depth--is without beginning and is without ending. 364-10

No two (solar systems) have the same awareness, neither are they parallel...There are centers through which those of one solar system may pass to another.   5755-2

Q-It was given through this source that the entity Edgar Cayce went to the system of Arcturus, and then returned to earth. Does this indicate a usual or an unusual step in soul evolution?

A-As indicated, or as has been indicated in other sources besides this one as respecting this very problem, Arcturus is that which may be called the center of this universe, through which individuals pass and at which period there comes the choice of the individual as to whether it is to return to complete there--that is, in this planetary system, our sun, the earth sun and its planetary system, or to pass on to others. This was an unusual step, and yet a usual one.   5749-14

Not that the sun that is the center of this solar system is all there is. For the entity has attained to that realm even of Arcturus, or that center from which there may be the entrance into other realms of consciousness. And the entity has chosen in itself to return to the earth for a definite mission.   2823-1

As long as an entity is within the confines of that termed the earth's and the sons of the earth's solar system, the developments are within the sojourns of the entity from sphere to sphere; and when completed it begins--throughout the music of the sphere with Arcturus, Polaris, and through those sojourns to the outer sphere.   441-1

The entity passes from (earth's) solar system, or sphere, through Arcturus or (from) Septimus as we see...And as such development reaches that plane, wherein the development may pass into other spheres and systems, of which our solar system is only a small part; in this then, is meant the entity must develop in that sphere until it has reached that stage wherein it may manifest through the spiritual planes, as would be called from the relation to physical or fleshly plane. 900-25

An entity passes on, as has been given, from this present--or **this** solar system, **this** sun, **these** forces, it passes through the various spheres--leading first into that central force, through which--known as Arcturus--nearer the Pleiades, in this passage about the various spheres --on and **on**--through the **eons** of time, as called--or space--which is **One** in the various spheres of its activity; even passing into the inner forces, **inner** sense, may they again--after a period of nearly ten **thousand** years--may an entity enter into the earth to make manifest those forces gained in **its** passage. In entering it takes on those forms that may be known in the dimensions of that plane which it occupies.   311-2

Arcturus comes in this entity's chart, or as a central force from which the entity came again into the earth-material sojourns. For, this is the way, the door out of this system. Yet purposefully did the entity return in this experience.   2454-3

Arcturus is that junction between the spheres of activity as related to cosmic force, and is that about which this particular environ or sphere of activity rotates, or is a relative source of activity.   263-15

The entity (Uhjltd in Persia) came from those centers about which thine own solar system moves--in Arcturus.   5755-1

The Sun and Arcturus, the Greater Sun, giving of the strength in mental and spiritual elements toward developing of soul and of the attributes toward the better forces in earth's spheres.   137-4

In Arcturus' forces, these become all magnified in will's force, and the conquering of self is truly greater than were one to conquer **many** worlds, and **is** conquering those of **our**, or of our **sun's** own attributes.   115-1

In form, in mind, in manifestations of its, the entity's personality-- and, most of all, the individuality--shines through in that influence gained in Arcturus, the power and influence over many.   2686-1

In the entity's dwellings in the hills and plains of Persia, also in Egypt, the beauties and music of the spheres sang and brought into the experience of the entity its studies of the light by day, the joy of the voices of the night, and the star that led the entity--that source from which and to which it may gain so much of its strength in the present, **Arcturus** the wonderful, the beautiful. As the bright and **glorious** light from same set afire, as it were, its meditations in the plains, so may the illuminations do the same in the lives of those the entity contacts through its gentleness and kindness and service.   827-1

Sojourns in Uranus and Arcturus being those interests in the mental expressions in a varied line of endeavor...Things that are hidden to many become a portion of the entity's activity...Relationships that deal with mystical subjects--not only of gases, chemistry, the elementals of the earth, the elements of space, of the universe, those sojournings into such fields of activity--make for particular interest in the mental sojourn...Also the delving into the realm of the questionable scientific subjects, whether it be in regard to explorations in the material far corners of the earth or the sojourning or delving into the ether.   757-8

Beginning with Mercury, the entity has run the gamut even unto Neptune and Arcturus, and then returned to earth.   3637-1

When the heavens and the earth came into being, this meant the universe as the inhabitants of the earth know same; yet there are many suns in the universe, those even about our sun, our earth, revolves; and all are moving toward some place, yet space and time appear to be incomplete...Astronomy is considered a science and astrology as foolishness. Who is correct? One holds that because of the position of the earth, the sun, the planets, they are balanced one with another in some manner, some form; yet that they have nothing to do with man's life or the expanse of life, or the emotions of the physical being in the earth.

Then, why and how do the effects of the sun **so** influence other life in the earth and not affect **man's** life, man's emotions?...

Then, what are the sun spots? A natural consequence of that turmoil which the sons of God in the earth reflect upon same. Thus they oft bring confusion to those who become aware of same.   5757-1

(Regarding weather) the greatest degree of heat in given places has been and may be reported when the larger sun spots show, or are in good position of being observed from the earth's aspect or view. 195-29

Q-The heart in the human body may be compared to the sun of a solar system. Then by analogy the sun is the center of forces of the solar system. Similarly to the blood flowing from the heart through the arterial system, Force emerges from the sun drawn to the opposite polarity of the planets and in this outgoing flow it would be possible to develop magnetism, electricity, light , color, heat, sound, and lastly matter, in the order of lessening dynamic degrees of vibration. Matter then would be the offspring of energy and not the parent, as is often thought. Is this correctly stated?
A-Correctly stated, and just what happens in the human organism.
Q-Is there a solar power reservoir corresponding to the lungs?
A-Solar power corresponding.   195-70

Other environs are manifestations of the influence that controls centers in the human body--as the brain the sun--sex, the moon. 2608-1

(The earth) is slowly receding or gathering closer to the sun, from which it receives its impetus for the awakening of the elements that give life itself, by radiation of like elements from that which it receives from the sun. Hence that of one type, that has been through the ages, of mind--that gives the **sun** as the father **of** light in the earth.   364-6

The entrance into the Ra Ta experience (in ancient Egypt)...was from the infinity forces, or from the sun...Is it any wonder that in the ignorance of the earth the activities of that entity were turned into the influence called the sun worshippers?   5755-1

The sun indicates strength and life, the moon indicates change. 5746-1

(These tendencies toward insanity are) **governed** considerably by the amount of anxiety that is around in the surroundings for the body at periods when there is the change in the moon.
These are not then purely mental aberrations but physical also.
We find that the castor oil packs over the abdomen and right side would be well occasionally for the lack of eliminations...
We find that the suggestive treatments will be more quieting to the body if they are continued in the present, especially during those periods when it is the **increase** of the moon and the full activity, or during the light of the moon period. 1553-7

The sympathetic (nervous) system has much to do with the changes, of the lunar conditions, see? 2501-7

Not on the increase of the moon have the tonsils taken care of. 2963-2

The oil massages...should be given...about three days in succession, at those periods when the moon changes--or the new moon, see? 3375-1

The osteopathic adjustments should be taken periodically three to four treatments right along together each month. For this body, if they are taken at the first quarter of the moon, it would be preferable. 3211-3

The moon's elements...bring the forces in love affairs. 900-6

Being under the influences of moon and sun also, we find in the sun the strength and in the moon, the weakness. 2990-2

The division of waters was and is ruled by the moon. 254-2

When troubles, consternation or distresses arise **in the day,** they may be easily understood or analyzed in the moonlight; when troubles arise in the **evening,** these may only be analyzed or understood when the entity **studies** same in the day--and among the crowd; yet those in the evening must be alone. 99-6

The moonstone or the agate should be as an amulet, either about the neck or as a ring, or worn upon the person.
From the astrological aspect there was a sojourn upon the moon.
Hence the moon is an active influence for the entity, and do not ever sleep with the moon shining upon the face. In the sunshine, much; for the moon and the sun are the ruling of the emotions. 1401-1

On dark days with little sunshine there is an appreciable manifestation of fear and dread. And especially does this occur when the moon by its position is on the opposite side of the orb of the earth. 264-31

From Mercury we find the high mental abilities, and yet these may at times cause rather harsh judgments.   958-3

Mercury--high minded; a thinker; deep.   2823-1

From Mercury we find...the necessity for reasoning things out--within thy own mind, that of reaching conclusions by the entity.   2144-1

In Jupiter's forces we find those great ennobling (elements), those conditions that would bring the monies and forces of good in the life.
In Neptune, those of the mysticism, mystery, spiritual insight...
The Mercury influence of mental understanding of each.
Then, with the mental insight into the operative elements of ennobling, of virtues, of good, of beautiful, with the mysteries of the universal forces, given understanding, brings the development to the soul's forces. For the soul feeds upon that environment to which the mental guides and directs, and the expectancy is that soul development that each entity must exercise through will.   900-14

In Mercury, there is the influence of a keenness of perception in mental things; adaptable easily to some forms of mathematical problems, and for order or symmetrical activity in association with those in the activities of self; prompt in keeping the appointments to self, to others; slothful in forgiving those that would in any manner **willfully** attempt to deceive; especially interested in the minds of the young in their response to the association of things or numbers, as to their development. 553-1

In Mercury...a memory that if kept in a developing way and manner becomes rather unusual--as to data, as to facts or figures, as to statistical developments in any field in which it may be applied.   1252-1

Mercury gives the abilities of the entity to consider the problems as a whole. This tends to make for the optimistic outlook...The entity sees problems, conditions or activities, as a finished product rather than the detail necessary for the completing of same.   2460-1

The influences from Mercury, with Uranus, make for the high mental abilities...(to) read character easily...one who may direct the activities of others...especially as to such things as **collecting**--whether money or things...As insurance, banking, or the like.   630-2

The entity is among those who have entered the earth during those years when there was the great entrance of those who have risen high in their abilities; and...there must be application of the will, else the very abilities that have maintained in the sun and mercurian influences will become as stumbling blocks.   633-2

In Venus the body-form is near to that in the three-dimensional plane. For it is what may be said to be rather **all**-inclusive. For it is that ye would call love--which, to be sure, may be licentious, selfish; which also may be so large, so inclusive as to take on the less of self and more of the ideal, more of that which is **giving!**

What is love? Then what is Venus? It is beauty, love, hope, charity-- yet all of these have their extremes. But these extremes are not in the expressive nature or manner as may be found in the tone or attune- ment of Uranus; for they (in Venus) are more in the order that they blend as one with another. 　　　　　5755-1

In Venus we find the lovely becoming the expressions in activities in which there is the beauty seen in love, in companionship, in asso- ciation, in music, in art, in **all** the things that bespeak of the **loveli- ness** even of nature and the material things, rather than the expression of same in the earthly form or manner. 　　　　　949-13

From sojourns in the Venus environs, the entity is a lover of beauty...
All things that have to do with phases of man's ability of expression in beautiful ways and manners will be of interest to the entity--whether pertaining to nature, to voice or song, or even to art subjects. 　　1990-3

We find in Venus the appreciation of beauty, of nature, or nature's storehouse, those products of the soil; those that combine good, beauty **and** its effect **from** nature in the activity of the mental forces of the associates. 　　　　　2627-1

We find in Venus both the benevolent and rather the extravagant appreciation of finer things. 　　　　　2460-1

The Uranian influence with that of Venus brings the pure love of all forces that are of the scientific turn, as well as all occult influence upon the life. 　　　　　105-2

Venus is manifested in the beauty, the joy, the ability to write. 2992-1

Those influences in Venus make for an open, frank, loving disposition; making for friends in most any walk or every walk of life. 　　1442-1

Venus makes for an easy disposition, very easily imposed upon.1206-3

One of a tender, loving disposition; that may be ruled or reasoned with through love, obedience or duty; yet may not be driven to do any of these through sheer force or fear of corporal punishment. 　309-1

We find in Venus that unusual attraction that the opposite sex will have for the entity, and the entity for the opposite sex. 　　2890-2

In the many stages of development, throughout the universal, or in the great system of the universal forces, and each stage of development (is) made manifest through flesh, which is the testing portion of the universal vibration. In this manner then, and for this reason, all made manifest in flesh, and development through the eons of time, space, and **called** eternity. 900-16

Q-Do souls become entangled in other systems as they did in this one?
A-In other systems that represent the same as the earth does in this system, yes. 5749-14

Q-Do other solar systems have a planet, like earth, which is a focal point for the material expression of its forces and principles?
A-Relatively so. 5755-2

One enters for a specific activity in Mars, Mercury or Venus, and in Saturn for that cleansing that must come to all that have departed from the earth and have not kept the ways clean. But in the earth we find **all** rolled into one, with a body and a body-mind for self-expression. 442-3

Ye are **relatively** related to all that ye have contacted in materiality, mentality, spirituality. All of these are a portion of thyself in the material plane. In taking form they become a mental body with its longings for its home, with right and righteousness. 5755-1

In earth--we have that position in which matter takes all its various forms of presentation of a given energy, **or** force, as radiated from the various effects of this solar aspect, and take on **bodily** form, occupying a position of, as it were, three in one--or all force in **this** sphere taking on that appearance of that known as threefold, or the aspects of a threefold nature. 311-2

As to the appearances or sojourns in the earth--these we find expressed or manifested in the material body through the senses. Do understand and do interpret the differences between the emotions that arise from the sensory system and those that arise from the **glandular** system alone. True, physically those interchange; yet one (glandular) represents the **whole** of the development, the other (sensory) represents the step-by-step activity by an entity in...the material world. 2620-2

As the mind of the soul is under that urge of the emotional forces from earthly sojourns, it becomes much in the same manner as may be indicated in the study of language. For, whether it be in that direction of a musical or vocal of whatever nature, in that environ there is the crystallization of ideas, intents and purposes. Thus does an entity become under the influence of that in which it has **manifested** a consciousness. 2113-1

From Mars we find a tendency for the body-mind at times to be easily aroused to anger. Anger is correct, provided it is **governed**. For it is as material things in the earth that are not governed. There is **power** even in anger. He that is angry and sinneth not controls self. 361-4

In Mars we find anger, animosity, covetousness becoming the influence or force for detrimental activity in the experience.   1797-1

Mars indicates the abilities to hate as well as to love.   2902-1

In Mars and Vulcan--beware of fire, and especially of firearms, or explosives...Beware of wrath in self, and in grudges as may be builded through wrath's influence in the relationships of the fellow man. 1735-2

Mercury and Mars bring...mental abilities...quick judgments. 2051-5

JUPITER AS BROADMINDEDNESS

Jupiter brings the bigness of vision, the nobleness of purpose, the patience with self as well as with others.   428-4

In Jupiter--taking on those ennobling forces, whether they may be from earth, from Venus, from Mars, they are **broadened**, they are **changed** in their aspects, in their forms.   311-2

In Jupiter we find the great ennobling influences, the broadmindedness, the ability to consider others, the Universal Consciousness that are a part of the entity's unfoldment.   2890-2

We find in Jupiter that Universal Consciousness, that longing for the knowledge of something outside of self...The universal desire or the desire to be of help to many irrespective of the cost to self. 3184-1

From Jupiter the abilities are...as an instructor, a teacher, or preferable in alleviating sufferings--or in a political field, as one controlling some great movement...or as an active practitioner in the alleviating of physical ills.   309-1

In Jupiter we find abilities in a helpful, universal way and manner. Hence the entity is given to verboseness, as well as abilities to depict situations, to analyze people and places, things and conditions. Thus may the entity be gifted in writing, lecturing, and in group direction. 3299-1

In Jupiter we find the broad vision of the entity, as well as the mighty force, power or influence as may be wielded by the entity.   2067-1

In Saturn we find the sudden or violent changes--those influences and environs that do not grow, as it were, but are sudden by that of change of circumstances materially, or by activities apparently upon the part of others become a part of self in the very associations. And yet these are testing periods of thy endurance, of thy patience. 1981-1

From Saturn we find the tendency for the starting of new experiences, the starting of new associations in the activities; and unless these are tempered with the mental influences they are rarely carried to their full termination. This again should be as a warning to the entity. When thou hast chosen that direction, that activity thou would take, know that thou are kept in the balance that is of material, mental and spiritual influences near to right. Then lay it not aside until it, the activity, has borne fruit in thine mental and material experience. 361-4

In Saturn as the beginning of earthly woes, that to which all insufficient matter is cast for the beginning.   900-10

In Saturn for that cleansing that must come to all that have departed from the earth and have not kept the ways clean.   442-3

Q-What is meant by banishment of a soul from its Maker?
A-Of the will as given in the beginning to choose for self as in the earthly plane, all insufficient matter is cast unto Saturn. To work out his own salvation as would be termed in the word, the entity or individual banishes itself, or its soul.   3744-2

Saturn (is) that condition in the earth's solar system to which all insufficient matter is cast for the remolding, as it were.   900-25

The earth and Saturn are opposites, as it were; for to Saturn go those that would renew or begin again.   945-1

In Saturn we find the inclinations for changes as to this, that or the other, and to muddle a great many things together.   1426-1

Saturn would make for the entity having **many** homes, or many marriages--and these are **not** well in the experience if there are to be developments.   1431-1

We find in Saturn the influences that to man, and oft to self, become stumbling stones or blockings of ways in which all the beautiful thoughts, all the good intentions come tumbling because of material or social hindrances.   2823-1

From Saturn we find the influences from which there is the new beginning--ever the constant wanting to rub out and begin again. 949-13

In Uranus we find the extremes. Thus the entity in spiritual, in mental and in material things finds periods when it is as to the mountain tops and again in the depths of despair.   3706-2

From the Uranian influences we find the extremist, and these tendencies we find will develop especially through the early teenage years, when there will be moods and the tendency for wonderments...These (influences) make for also the intuitive influences and the abilities for the development in the very psychic forces of the entity.   1206-3

(The entity) is not only a Uranian but an Atlantean, and the combination will be something to **deal with!** as to temper, as to having its own way; for it **will** have its way, irrespective, for the first fourteen years...As for the aspects in the Uranian influence, we find the extremes. The entity will be at times very beautiful in character--at other (times) very ugly; very beautiful in body and mind--at others the other extreme...**Do not** break the will of the body in correcting same,--rather give the lesson by precept and example.   1958-1

The tendencies from Uranus towards the occult and the mystic forces; as visions, hearing, seeing and knowing without having the physical contact with experiences in the **mental** body.   361-4

Those of exceptional abilities with Uranian influence may be **well** said also to mean exceptional abilities to err, or to be led astray in the direction not best for self or self's development.   38-1

In the Uranian influence we find the interest in the spiritual things, as well as the awareness of that which is sordid. The extremes, ye know, meet only in the Christ, who came unto His own and they received Him not. So in thy extreme, when ye become discouraged, disconsolate, when ye become in such an attitude as to wonder what is the way know that He **is** listening--listening! As ye **call**, He hath said, "I will hear and will answer speedily" (Isaiah 30:19).   1968-1

Uranus is the greater influence...Hence we will find an individual that will oft be called an extremist; either very active or very dull or lazy; inclining to be in the position of over enthusiasm about any association or activity, or not caring or paying much attention to same...
There will also be made experiences or periods when the entity would be called lucky at any game of chance, yet there will be also periods when--from the influence--it would be practically impossible for the entity to gain through games of chance.   406-1

In Uranus we find the extremes, and the interest in the occult or the mystical. This is well if it is balanced in the spiritual nature.   2571-1

From Neptune we find that being close to waters, on waters, or about waters, is very well for the entity and this also gives those abilities as the mystic--the interest in the unusual, as in the abilities of seeing, feeling, experiencing that which to most would be the unseen forces about the entity. 2308-1

In Neptune, those of the mysticism, mystery, spiritual insight. 900-14

In those influences through Neptune with Arcturus, the entity has swung far from the earth's influence and at times--with these visions of the inner self, or the dreams--as they may be termed--lost, as it were, the import of the material activity or the material upon the activities of a soul; yea, of a body, in its expressions in materiality. Hence at times do those about the entity call the entity the dreamer, the visioner of dreams. 764-1

In the influences which arise innately and manifestedly from Neptune, we find the forces or powers of the earthly mother--water--as an influence; coming more in the form of the warning regarding the occult or mystic powers. These are children of doubt and fear,--yea, they are also children of light. But know their import. Know that their manifestations have oft sought personal manifestation, as in the spirits of those who sought in the beginnings for personal gratification--when the very evolution of materiality presented an opportunity. Thus they brought to themselves confusion, as well as the necessity of man's own materiality by encasement in matter. 2067-1

The soul and spirit took its flight from the far-away force as exercised in Neptune. Hence we have an entity that...will be peculiar to other people, rarely ever being understood; yet one with spiritual insight of the developing in (the) earth plane. 2553-8

We find in Neptune the power of water, or of the influences about same; the creative expression, the ability to aid in reviving or in giving life to things. And most anything that would be planted in the earth by the entity would live. And flowers and those things that are cut from nature blossom or give off **better** perfume by being about or on the body of the entity (and there are few of which this could be said). 2641-1

Never on or very **close** to waters does the entity experience that of hate, yet inland, on mountain, this would be a different experience. 99-6

Keep away from large bodies of water. These are opposite from much of that accredited as an influence from the astrological aspects of Neptune; though those things that come **from** and **over** large bodies of water, places and surroundings of such nature, will be of great interest. 2005-1

Q-What are the effects of Pluto, in conjunction with one's ascendant?
A-This, as we find, is entirely amiss from what we might call a physical expression--but, as we find indicated, these (influences) are a development that is occurring in the universe, or environs about the earth--Pluto. Not, as some have indicated, that it is gradually being dissipated. It is gradually **growing** and thus is one of those influences that are to be as a demonstrative activity in the future affairs or developments of man towards the spiritual-minded influences, or those influences, outside of himself.

These (individuals) in the present, as might be said, are merely becoming **aware** of same. Rather, within the next hundred to two hundred years there may be a great deal of influence (of Pluto) upon the ascendancy of man, for it's closest of those to the activities of the earth, to be sure, and is a **developing** influence, and not one already established. 1100-27

Pluto and Vulcan are one and the same.   826-8

These (Dog Star and Vulcan) make for that influence as has been of sudden changes in the social affairs...yet these **adversities** may be used, or applied in the experience of the entity as stepping stones for (the) soul's development...for in adversities **most** conditions grow, provided same is not of a nature to break the **will,** or to make for those conditions in which an entity reaches that position wherein it pities or belittles its own responsibilities, or its own individuality in the experiences through which it may pass.   1727-1

Sudden changes are indicated in Saturn; high mental ability and capabilities in Mercury; **self-centeredness** in Pluto...
In Mars a high, exalted opinion of self; which is well, but abused--as it may be in Pluto, or in Mercury--may become a stumbling stone. 3126-1

In the influences that bring for warnings, as seen in Mars and Vulcan--beware of fire, and especially of firearms, or explosives... Beware of wrath in self, and in grudges as may be builded through wrath's influences...Keep self attuned to the love force, even as in the occult influences. Beware of those that are of the forces as make through chance...as of cabalistic or paleozoistic influences.   1735-2

Be wary of that influence of Septimus and the conjunction that will be within the next six months, else...accident either through self or from the conditions of the trunk or the torso of the body.   583-1

The afflictions of the body come under those with the constellation of the Twins, or of Gemini, and that of the Great Bear. They will have to do with those of the digestion as afflicted by Septimus. 487-1

The **solar** system is also passing through its various spheres, that are being acted upon by the forces from without, or that as is ordinarily known-or has been **determined** and named, though not rightly, or wholly rightly in their aspects--as those forms in the various **months**. 311-2

The study of the meaning of Aries, Sagittarius, Pisces, Libra, or any or all of such phases, would indicate the activity of the individual. For, remember, it is body manifestation--some the feet, some the head, some the thigh, some the groin, some the bowels, some the breast,--some one and some another, see? these indicating the **activity** of the individual. 5746-1

As each of the twelve Apostles represented major centers or regions or realms through which consciousness became aware in the body of the earth itself, so did He find--as in thine own self ye find--those twelve stumbling stones, those twelve things that oft not only disgust but disappoint thee--as to the reaction and way people and things react. These are the price of flesh, of material consciousness, and are only passing. 2823-1

Q-What is meant by the twelve gates (Revelation 21)?
A-The twelve manners, the twelve ways, the twelve openings, the twelve experiences of the physical to all, and those that have all been purified in purpose for the activities with same.
Q-Please explain the twelve names which represent the twelve tribes of the children of Israel.
A-The same as the twelve gates, the twelve angels, the twelve ways, the twelve understandings; or the approach to **Israel** the seeker--all seeking not then as the expression of self but as **one** in the Holy One! 281-37

It may be said that the line of thought in the present is towards a change in the Aries age from the Pisces, or from the Aquarius, or **to** those various activities, see? but it doesn't mean that every individual changes, for each individual has its own development. 311-10

Q-You will have before you the inquiring mind of (1602), present in this room, who seeks guidance--impersonal guidance and light regarding the teachings of Jacob Boehme, the German philosopher and mystic of the 17th century who used the corresponding Principles of Nature--of the entire Astral, with man, as the true Spiritual approach to the Primal Light beyond the Circuit of Reincarnation.
A-Yes, we have the inquiring mind, and those tenets and teachings and illustrations as presented by Jacob Boehme; as respecting the relationships of man in his search for the Creative Forces or God.
In giving first those approaches as we find of same, much of that presented by Boehme, in illustrating the activities, the various phases of consciousness or awareness, the effect of the astral, the cosmic

consciousness of same in its relationships to the emotions and activities of which the body is conscious in its various stages of development,-- we find these are identical with those presented by John in Patmos.

And as the individual analyzes or studies the bodily forces and emotions as arise through the activities in a material sphere in relationship to the influences arising from without, these come to be the representations and interpretations of that presented by John in Patmos.

Here, though, we will find these are variations in some of those things presented. For here we find with Boehme more of the consciousness through which man has passed in his study and his search for that as might be used as an illustration of same, as related to what has been termed by some as the consciousness related to the seasons and the changes and the zodiac, as well as the planetary forces and the activities of same.

All of these, as we have indicated through these channels from time to time, are relative as one to another...

For as an individual entity or soul becomes aware of the full consciousness of being aware of its relationship or its position, it **is** part of the law itself, it **is** the law of that relationship, by the full awareness of it, and not merely an outlet, not merely a channel through which an activity or awareness or consciousness may be made as a manner or way...

(The constellation Perseus is) only as a station along the way, a consciousness of, a place through which as each individual entity passes is illustrated in the manner in which their approaches come-- they are then as aware **of** that position or place. The name is the consciousness, not the name the way, see?   1602-3

The entity coming under the influence of Jupiter, Venus, Mercury, and of Ox-ides--or the relative force of Pleiades, in that of Orion, with the effect in the Ox-Orion--Y--E--S--unusual.   2886-1

Through Aries associations, there are the abilities of a high **mental** development; yet there are rather those warnings for this entity regarding accidents to the head.   406-1

The entity under Aries makes for one headstrong, headwilled.   517-1

For while in Gemini children there are those influences that make for the double-mindedness, in this entity it finds expression in its inclinations at times to change and to become speculative.   962-1

Failures in the sojourns in the earth have brought--as for all of Gemini children--the experience of becoming morose, melancholy; speaking quick without taking thought of other than to give vent to self's own spleen. In same patience must be manifested.   815-2

Coming under the astrological influences when Gemini becomes very close to its activities, we find the entity often wondering within self if there is not a double personality within self. 1107-1

Astrologically we find urges, not because the Moon or the Sun or Leo or Pisces may have been in this or that position when the entity was born. But the entity as a consciousness experienced those activities or awarenesses in those environs. Thus become part of the soul experience. As will be found, Leo--or the consciousness of that mind--will be a part of the entity's awareness. Thus at times the entity will appear headstrong, willful. 2905-3

For remember, the soul is co-creator with God and Leo demands, and if you keep demanding you will keep on having to face the truth.5259-1

Leo gives the quick change in the...attitude towards conditions. 4840-1

As to the physical, as created in the present plane, its weaknesses being indigestion, and in the circulation, overtaxed through Scorpio, which is as the seat of the central portion of the body, see? 2895-1

We find the afflictions come in that of Sagittarius, Saturn afar off, and the Moon in the wane. Hence the afflictions have been to the body of the digestion and the thighs. 4219-3

Just as those experiences upon the doorways to the greater consciousness of a soul. For here, too, hath the entity had those experiences upon the fixed stars, as upon Capricornus, as upon the influences of that great entrance into the holy of holies. And as the entity upon the mornings of its visions hath caught here and there the beauties of the glorious life, glorious expressions of the Son of man. 774-5

Remember thou art in the same signs, omens, as the mother of Him; that gave to the earth the physical man, Jesus--Aquarius in its **perception,** perfection. 1222-1

Q-What will the Aquarian Age mean to mankind as regards physical, mental and spiritual development?
A-Think ye this might be answered in a word? These are as growths. What meant that awareness as just indicated? In the Piscean age, in the center of same, we had the entrance of Emmanuel or God among men, see? What did that mean? The same will be meant by the full consciousness of the ability to communicate with or to be aware of the relationships to the Creative Forces and the uses of same in material environs. This awareness during the era or age in the age of Atlantis and Lemuria or Mu brought What? Destruction to man, and his

beginning of the needs of the journey up through that of selfishness.

Then, as to what will these be--**only** those who accept same will even become aware of what's going on about them.

Q-Can a date be given to indicate the beginning of the Aquarian Age?

A-...It laps over from one to another...we will begin to understand fully in '98.   1602-3

In the abilities as come through the influence in Aquarius, we find the entity could, or would be able to apply self in...mathematical calculations, especially regarding aeronautics or boat building. The entity may become an architect beyond compare, provided these have to do with those elements that have to do with water or air.   256-1

(The entity) coming under those influences of Pisces; so that water and religion or spiritual imports have an untold influence.   816-3

Of the Piscean (influence) that make for the mystic, for the leadership, for love and beauty, for the abilities to direct; especially when self has been conquered.   1346-1

The Piscean influences...(are) the **tendency** for security, the **tendency** for companionship of others, the tendency for an interest in those things that are mysteries and that are of a mysterious nature--or that arise from out of the metaphysical or psychical force.   1232-1

Pisces making for a very intuitive force.   2082-1

In entering the present experience (born March 29, 1907) we find the entity is indeed one that may be said to be in the influence of-- in the astrological understanding--the cusps...We find that those who are near to the rising of one influence and the submerging--as it were --of another--are oft in those experiences where, from the mental abilities or mental developments, they are in a strait, as it were, as to what should be the activity. For there are the tendencies for such individuals to reason through the influence of those urges that arise from Leo or of the head, or Pisces as of the spiritual import. Hence to such individuals we find these influences of virtue, morality, activities of individuals as related to these mean much more--or their import are of a great deal more influence in the experience of such an entity than much said by this, that or the other person. Such individuals, then, have within themselves that innate ability to become **really** a judge of human nature; and such individuals in such capacities in any activity or experience in the earth may make for themselves and for others a teacher, instructor, detective, or one of such natures or such fields of activity that are beyond most individuals.   801-1

PART V

EVOLUTION OF MIND AND MATTER

CYCLES OF UNFOLDMENT

There is nothing by chance...for, in the beginning all was made that was made, and as it unfolds from what man terms time to time, period to period, there is only the renewing of the First Cause.　　2946-2

Even as He said, "There is nothing new under the sun" (Ecclesiastes 1:9). What is has been, and will be again (Ecclesiastes 3:15). 3976-27

The purpose for each soul's entrance is to complete a cycle, to get closer to the Infinite.　　3131-1

Q-What is meant by "the cycle of things"?
A-That to which an attunement turns in its orbit about an influence; for, as is seen, in **any** cycle--cycle means, as is seen, in the **beginning** is the end; for when there is the beginning it means only a change. A cycle is the change, or the using up of the force, energy, to where the change may be **definitely** set **as** change. That is a cycle, whether of the life in a manifested form--in body, mind, in stars, in the whole of **any**--as a change, a cycle.　　256-2

For that which is, **was** and will be. Only the mortal or material, or matter, changeth; but the expressions of same prompted by the Spirit of truth live on.　　1448-2

Only the soul lives on. That which had a beginning has an end. Thy soul is a part of the beginning and the end.　　1641-2

Each entity is a part of the universal whole. All knowledge, all understanding that has been a part of the entity's consciousness, then, is a part of the entity's experience. Thus the unfoldment in the present is merely becoming aware of the experience through which the entity, either in body or in mind, has passed in a consciousness.　　2823-1

The birth of the entity into Uranus was not from the earth into Uranus, but from those stages of consciousness through which each entity or soul passes into oblivion as it were, save for understanding, there have been failures and there are needs for help. Then help **consciously** is sought. Hence the entity passes along those stages that some have seen as planes, some have seen as steps, some have seen as cycles, and some have experienced as places.

How far? How far is tomorrow to any soul? How far is yesterday from thy consciousness? You are **in** same (that is, all time is one time), yet becoming gradually aware of it; passing through, then, as it were, God's record or book of consciousness or of remembrance; for meeting, being measured out as it were to that to which thou hast attained.   5755-1

Oft, ones that enter an experience as a complete cycle; that is...under the same astrological experiences as in the sojourn just before (that is, being born upon the same day of the month--though time may have been altered) find periods of activity that will be very much the same as ...in the previous sojourn, in the unfoldment and in the urges. 2814-1

Each body has its individual cycle and vibration.   3329-1

Those entering the material plane in '43, '44, '45, and '46 are purposeful individual entities, and much will depend upon these souls as to what manner of activity there will be in the world a score years hence.5306-1

In those cycles especially of '9, '10, and '11, many, many Atlanteans were incarnated into the earth experience.   1776-1

For they (periods of history) will be seen to come in cycles. 254-47

The period (Grecians and Trojans), as man would count time, was eleven fifty-eight to ten twelve B.C.; at a period when many of those who had been in the activities of the Atlantean, Lemurian and Og age were entering, at that period or cycle in the affairs of man. For there has ever been during a period of fifty-eight a cycle, unit, age, year, period or era when there has been the breeding, as it were, of strife.   294-183

In Carmel--the original place where the school of prophets was established during Elijah's time, Samuel--these were called then Essenes; and those that were students of what ye would call astrology, numerology, phrenology, and those phases of that study of the return of individuals--or incarnation.

These were then the reasons that there had been a proclaiming that certain periods were a cycle; and these had been the studies then of Aristotle, Enos, Mathesa, Judas, and those that were in the care of supervision of the school--as you would term.

These having been persecuted by those of the leaders, this first caused that as ye have an interpretation of the Sadducees, or "there is no resurrection" (Matthew 22:23), or there is no incarnation, which is what resurrection meant in those periods.

In the lead of these, with those changes that had been as the promptings from the positions of the stars--that stand as it were in the dividing of the ways between the universal, that is the common vision of the solar system of the sun, and those from without the spheres--or as the common name, the North Star, as its variation made for those cycles that would be incoordinate with those changes that had been determined by some--this began the preparation--for the three hundred years, as has been given, in this period...

In these signs then was the new cycle, that as was then--as we have in the astrological--the beginning of the Piscean age, or that position of the Polar Star or North Star as related to the southern clouds. These made for the signs, these made for the symbols, as would be the sign used, the manner of the sign's approach and the like.

These then were the beginnings and these were those that were made a part of the studies during that period. 5749-8

Q-Is it necessary to finish the solar system cycle before going to other systems?

A-Necessary to finish the solar cycle.

Q-Can oneness be attained--or the finish of evolution reached--on any system, or must it be in a particular one?

A-Depending upon what system the entity has entered, to be sure. It may be completed in any of the many systems.

Q-Must the solar system be finished on earth, or can it be completed on another planet, or does each planet have a cycle of its own which must be finished?

A-If it is begun on the earth it must be finished on the earth. The solar system of which the earth is a part is only a portion of the whole. For, as indicated in the number of planets about the earth, they are of one and the same--and they are relative one to another. It is the cycle of the whole system that is finished, see? 5749-14

A cycle is seven years, known or called in the earth, and information may be given or records read as to the varying appearances or activities that may change in that period. 487-17

The body renews itself, every atom, in seven years. How have ye lived for the last seven? And then the seven before? 3684-1

It is not (if the student is interested in these phases) merely coincidental that there are seven days to the week; but the seven centers and the seven phases of experience and of reactions of sojourns of the entity in environs produce what may be termed a cycle of urge or experience. 2594-1

These (7th and 14th year) are as cycles of impressions and changes; and activities in the developing of the body, the mind, the soul. 1788-3

As we find from the records here...the greater influence will during its 7th to 14th or 15th year be changed--as when it is 21 and 28; and **then** it will be determined as to whether it is to be the material or the mental and spiritual success...in the present sojourn.   1332-1

As there was in the entering of the entity's inner forces into this physical body, the first (change) will come at the age of 7, then at 14, at 22--these will be decided changes, or will so lap over the other...for there was some lapse of time (as time is counted from the material) between the physical birth and the spiritual birth.   566-1

Each organ has its own cycle.   47-1

The **digestive** forces of the body; the lungs, the liver, the heart, the digestive system, the pancreas, the spleen...change the more often, so that when it is ordinarily termed that the body has changed each atom in seven years, these organs have changed almost **seven times** during those seven years.   796-2

SOUL'S SEPARATION AND RETURN TO ITS SOURCE

Because an atom, a matter, a form, is changed, does not mean that the essence, the source or the spirit of it has changed; only in its form of manifestations, and **not** in its relation with the first cause. That man reaches that consciousness in the material plane of being aware of what he does about or with the consciousness of the knowledge, the intelligence, the first cause, makes or produces that which is known as the entering into the first cause, principles, basis, or the essence...

Then, this is the principle: Like begets like. Those things that are positive and negative forces combine to form in a different source, or different manifestation, the combinations of which each element, each first principle manifested, has gained from its associations...

Hence man, the crowning of all manifestations in a material world--a causation world, finds self as the cause and the product of that he, with those abilities given, has been able to produce, or demonstrate, or manifest from that he has gained, does gain, in the transition, the change, the going toward that (and being of that) from which he came...

Hence, in man's analysis and understanding of himself, it is as well to know from whence he came as to know whither he is going. 5753-1

As to the appearances in the earth, all will not be indicated but these that ye may know from whence ye came and whither ye go. For thy pattern is set and ye are a free-willed soul. 4047-2

For, life is of the Creator--and it may only be changed, it **cannot** be ended or destroyed. It can **only** return from whence it came. 497-1

All souls were created in the beginning, and are finding their way back to whence they came. 3744-4

For man may separate himself from God--the Spirit--but the spirit does not separate from man. 589-1

Among those spirits that include all that ever was, that ever will be, were those that in spirit rebelled against that law of love; hence turned in self upon self hence separating self from that first companionship.

Hence that all in this form might return, or that there might not be continual warfare in this realm of peace, happiness, glory...that there might be the return of every soul bearing the imprint of his image in Spirit (and body), there came first those in the earth as thought forms that were able to partake of that about them; and so absorb them, much as we see in the lower forms of material manifestations in life, and **moved** by the spirit to become that they found or absorbed in their being. Hence we see how that the entering of the spirit into matter in the earth was both good and bad. And we find that, as given in the records, each soul became conscious of a relationship to an outside influence or spirit as it, individually, personally, applied those influences in the activities that were about it. How could there become, then, other than sun worshippers? But rather some became worshippers of that sun produced, rather than of that which produces the sun! There's a difference. **That's** the difference between Spiritualism and Spiritism; Spirit-u-u-u-al-ism, and Spiritism. Spiritism, then, is that which acknowledges, that acts, that comprehends, the source of activity. Spiritualism is that which comprehends rather only the result, than the source. 5756-11

Reaching to the core, becoming a portion of the center, and yet this being an **individual** in itself, yet conscious of being the center, yet able to act independent **of** the center, yet wholly the center and acting only with the center, see? This then the final end of each individual soul or being in its evolution to that from which it (the soul) radiated in the beginning, for through the various phases as have been given we find each building, little by little, line upon line, precept upon precept, becoming one **with** the whole, yet not the whole within itself, but within itself wholly within the whole...Yet each being aware of that **it** is and its relation to the whole...for this grows on and on. 900-348

All is of a one source in its power, and that changed or altered from the purpose is only the change in activity of that force that may be manifested in man. Yet with the setting of those alterations there came good and that opposite from good (to know good) into the material manifestations. And man, through the will, makes for his development or redardment through what he does about that he sees manifested in the material world. This is a law that is applicable, whether we are speaking of purely material, mental or spiritual things...

By becoming aware in a material world is--or was--the only manner or way through which spiritual forces might become aware of their separation from the spiritual atmosphere...

All souls in the beginning were one with the Father. The separation or turning away brought evil.   262-56

Error or separation began before there appeared what we know as the earth, the heavens; or before space was manifested.   262-115

In the beginning, as matter was impregnated with spirit of the creative influence, there came into being Man...

That matter became impregnated with spirit arose from the very fact that spirit (separated) had erred, and only through the environ of matter (or flesh) might the attributes of the source of good be manifested.

For, the spirit of evil has not, did not, become manifested in matter; only has it moved by or upon or through matter...

What separated spirit from its first cause, or causes good and evil? Desire! **Desire!**

Hence Desire is the opposite of Will. Will and Desire, one with the Creative Forces of Good, brings all its influence in the realm of activity that makes for that which is constructive in the experience of the soul, the mind, the body, one with the spirit of truth.   5752-3

Sin--the separation--that as caused the separation of souls from the universal consciousness--came not in the sphere of materiality first, but in that of spirit...

Hence the awareness of the soul as to its separateness, or its being separated, only comes through the manifestations of the principles of that cosmic consciousness in materiality.

Hence it is as evolution in a part of the development of the whole of the universe; not this consciousness of our own solar system, but of that about all solar force, of which our own system is only a mere part of the whole consciousness.   1602-3

The beginnings of sin, of course, were seeking expression of themselves outside of the plan or way in which God had expressed same. 5749-14

If the soul were at all periods, all manifestation, to keep in that perfect accord, or law, with the Over-soul, or the First Cause, or the Soul from which it comes, then there would be only a continuous at-onement with the First Cause.

But when an entity, a soul, uses a period of manifestation--in whatever realm of consciousness--to its **own indulgencies** then there is need for the lesson, or for the soul understanding or interpreting, or to become aware of the error of its way.

What, then, was the first cause of this awareness?

It was the eating, the partaking, of knowledge; knowledge without wisdom--or that as might bring pleasure, satisfaction, gratifying--not of the soul but of the phases of expression in that realm in which the manifestation was given.

Thus in the three-dimensional phases of consciousness such manifestations become as pleasing to the eye, pleasant to the body appetites. Thus the interpretation of the experience, or of that first awareness of deviation from the divine law, is given in the form as of eating of the tree of knowledge.

Who, what influence, caused this ye ask?

It was that influence which had, or would, set itself in opposition to the souls remaining, or the entity remaining in that state of at-onement.   815-7

Self-glory, self-exaltation, self-indulgence becometh those influences that become as abominations to the Divinity in each soul; and separate them from a knowledge of Him.   1293-1

Know, self is the only excuse. Self is the only sin; that is, selfishness--and all the others are just a modification of that expression of the ego.   1362-1

What caused the first influences in the earth that brought selfishness? The desire to be as gods, in that rebellion became the order of the mental forces in the soul; and sin entered.   5753-1

Sin...is not of **God**--save through His sons that brought error, through selfishness, into the experience of the souls of men, the body by which angels and archangels are separate from the fullness of the Father.   479-1

How far is ungodliness from godliness? Just under, that's all.   254-68

Only good, or purposefulness, lives on; for it is a part of the eternal oneness--or at-onement with the purposes of Creative Energies.   1007-3

For only that which is good, that which is constructive, that which is true, that which is spiritual, **can** live--**does** live **on** an **On!**   1691-1

Death is separation, lost opportunity in some sphere of activity. 3343-1

Q-Please tell us how we should define Virtue.

A-...In the daily life of individuals as respecting the cooperation, self, the ideal, and the faith, to each it is given...but to **each** in their **own** approach. Not that God is many, but the attributes **of** the Creative Forces **respond** according to the development **of** that entity. 262-18

What may be good for one may be questionable for another. But the Lord knoweth His own and calleth them by name. 3976-27

Q-Define sin and original sin, or what was original sin?

A-It may be defined in one word,--disobedience. In the beginning, the perfect man was given all the attributes of the Father-God, in ideal environments prepared by God for man's material manifestation. Let's draw the comparison of man made perfect through experience, and man **willfully** being disobedient.

In the first we find man listening to those influences which were at variance to God's way. Then in the temple even at twelve, we find the perfect man seeking, asking, and answering questions as to man's relationship to God. 262-125

Q-Explain how so called good and evil forces are one.

A-...When there is delegated power a body that has separated itself from the spirit...as to how far it may go afield, depends upon how high it has attained in its ability to throw off both negative and positive forces...

Then, that which has been separated into the influence to become a body, whether celestial, terrestrial, or plain clay manifested into activity as man, becomes good or bad. The results to the body so acting are dependent and independent (inter-between, see) upon what he does with the knowledge of--or that source of--activity.

Q-In relation to the Oneness of all force, explain the popular concept of the Devil, seemingly substantiated in the Bible.

A-In the beginning, celestial beings. We have first the Son, then the other sons or celestial beings that are given their force and power.

Hence that force which rebelled in the unseen forces (or in spirit), that came into activity, was that influence which has been called Satan, the Devil, the Serpent; they are One. That of **rebellion!** 262-52

The prince of this world, Satan, Lucifer, The Devil--as a soul--made those necessities, as it were, of the consciousness in materiality; that man might--or that the soul might--become aware of its separation from the God-force. Hence the continued warring that is ever present in materiality or in the flesh, or the warring--as is termed--between those influences of good and evil. 262-89

Each soul enters each experience for development, that it may be prepared to dwell with that which it seeks as its goal. Hence the necessity for each entity to set its ideal in each experience.

Hence we find that the developments throughout the entity's activities, either in a material sojourn or through an astrological experience are but an evolution--or a making-practical. For it is not what an individual entity may proclaim that counts; but what each soul--does about what it has set as its ideal, in relationship to other individuals.   1235-1

As man applies the laws of which he becomes conscious, the development of man brings forth those results merited by that knowledge... This we find, then, is evolution. Man's development through man's acquiring, man's understanding of spiritual laws, of earthly laws, of God's laws, and applying same.   900-70

The attributes of the soul and spirit are as many--and as many more! --as the attributes of the physical or mental mind. Each, in the beginning, endowed with that same condition--position. Each, in itself, building to itself, by means of its development through the ages as they manifest upon the earth...

'Develop' means going toward the higher forces, or Creator. 3744-4

What the entity is today is the **result** of what it has been in days and experiences and ages and eons past. For, life is continuous; and whether it is manifested in materiality or in the realm of an individual alone, it is one and the same.   2051-5

The self is constantly meeting self. And as ye may learn to stand aside and watch self pass, there may come more and more the knowledge and the comprehension that it is earnest, it is real; and that the real is rather the unseen than that which is so material as to cause disappointments, fears, and those things that make the mind of man afraid.

There may be circles at times, but **no** standing still for the development of a soul. For it is in movement, in change, that we find awarenesses have and do come, and ever will be. For it is the divine law. 1771-2

Life and truth and understanding, and happiness, in its greater sense, are but a growth. For ye grow in grace, in knowledge, in understanding.   1301-1

In the growth of every force we find the multiple of itself by its activity upon itself constitutes growth; whether this is in the mental self, the spiritual self or the physical world. It is the multiple of itself upon itself; not **for** itself but **of** itself. As it gives out then, it grows. So does the entity, using that in hand day by day.   416-10

Life is continuous! The soul moves on, gaining by each experience that necessary for its comprehending of its kinship...to the Divine. 1004-2

(Soul growth) may be not felt in the consciousness of materialization. It is experienced by the consciousness of the soul.   254-68

Q-Discuss the various phases of spiritual development before and after reincarnation in the earth.

A-...When there was in the beginning a man's advent in the plane known as earth, and it became a living soul, amenable to the laws that govern the plane itself as presented, the Son of Man entered the earth as the first man. Hence the Son of Man, the Son of God, the Son of the First Cause, making manifest in a material body.

This was not the first spiritual influence, spiritual body, spiritual manifestation in the earth but the first man--flesh and blood; the first carnal house, the first body amenable to the laws of the plane in its position in the universe.

For, the earth is only an atom in the universe of worlds.

And man's development began through the laws of the generations in the earth; thus the development, retardment, or the alterations in those positions in a material plane...

Hence, as there came the development of that first entity of flesh and blood through the earth plane, he became **indeed** the Son--through the things which He experienced in the varied planes, as the development came to the oneness with the position in that which man terms the Triune...

In materiality we find some advance faster, some grow stronger, some become weaklings. Until there is redemption through the acceptance of the law (or love of God, as manifested through the Channel or the Way), there can be little or no development in a material or spiritual plane. 5749-3

Q-As created by God in the first, are souls perfect, and if so, why any need of development?

A-In this we find only the answer in this; the evolution of life as may be understood by the finite mind. In the first cause, or principle, all is perfect. In the creation of soul, we find the portion may become a living soul and equal with the Creator. To reach that position, when separated, must pass through all stages of development, that it may be one with the Creator...

The illustration of this we find in the man called Jesus. This man, as man, makes the will the will of the Father, then becoming one with the Father and the model for man...

(In) Jesus we find an Oneness with the Father, the Creator, passing through all the various stages of development; in mental perfect, in wrath perfect in flesh made perfect, in love become perfect, in death become perfect, in psychic become perfect, in mystic become perfect, in consciousness become perfect, in the greater ruling forces becoming perfect. Thus He is as the model, and through the compliance with such laws made perfect, destiny, the predestined, the forethought, the will, made perfect, the condition made perfect, He is an example for man, and only as a man, for He lived only as man, He died as man. 900-10

Q-From a study of these (readings) it seems that there is a trend downward, from early incarnations, toward greater earthliness and less mentality. Then there is a swing upward , accompanied by suffering, patience, and understanding. Is this the normal pattern, which results in virtue and oneness with God obtained by free will and mind?
A-This is correct. It is the pattern as it is set in Him.
Q-Is the average fulfillment of the soul's expectation more or less than fifty percent?
A-It's a continuous advancement, so it is more than fifty percent.
Q-Are heredity, environment and will equal factors in aiding or retarding the entity's development?
A-Will is the greater factor, for it may overcome any or all of the others, provided that will is made one with the pattern, see?
Q-(Concerning) the factors of soul evolution. Should mind, the builder, be described as the last development because it should unfold until it has a firm foundation of emotional virtues?
A-This might be answered Yes and No, both. But if it is presented in that there is kept, willfully, see, that desire to be in at-one-ment, then it is necessary for that attainment before it recognizes mind as the way. 5749-14

As the development of the earth as a sphere **became** a dwelling place, capable of caring for the conditions to which an entity might assume its abode in any form, the entity was among those **souls** given to such entities to **manifest** that divine in the earth's plane, and chose of itself to enter, that it might--of itself--become a portion of same, to show forth that held **innate and** manifested within self of the divine itself...
As the entity goes on and on, and passes through these spheres--the sun, the planets, the earth--it develops **towards**--taking all, being a portion of all, **manifesting** all--to carry that back to that source from whence it came. 413-1

Q-When an entity has completed its development, such that it no longer needs to manifest on earth's plane, how far then is it along towards its complete development towards God?
A-Not to be given. Reach that plane, and develop in Him, for in Him the will then becomes manifest. 900-20

Not so much self-development, but rather developing the Christ Consciousness in self, being selfless, that He may have His way with thee, that He--the Christ--may direct thy ways, that He will guide thee in the things thou doest, thou sayest.   281-20

That which is so hard to be understood in the minds or the experiences of many is that the activities of a soul are for self-development, yet must be **selfless** in its activity for it, the soul, to develop.   275-39

In the earth, one only meets self. Learn, then, to stand oft aside and watch self pass by--even in those influences that at times are torments to thy mind.   3292-1

Q-What was the purpose of my entering the earth's plane at this time?
A-To complete self's finding self.   3407-1

THERE IS A NAME TO EACH SOUL

There is a Name to each soul. For He hath called His own **by name!** What name? All the names that may have been as a material experience through the experience of an entity in that environ or those relative associations of Venus, Mars, Jupiter, Uranus, Saturn, Sun, Moon, or what. Or a Name that is above **every** name...
Every influence--you see--is **relative!** Hence the name is relative to that which is accomplished by the soul in its sojourn throughout its whole experience...Was one named John by chance? was one named Joe or Llewellyn by chance? No; they are relative!...and in the end the name is the sum total of what the soul-entity in all of its vibratory forces has borne toward the Creative Force itself.   281-30

Names have their meaning, and these depend upon the purposes when such are bestowed upon an individual entity entering the earth's plane.
Have ye not understood how that in various experiences individuals, as their purposes or attitudes or desires were indicated, had their names henceforth called a complete or full name meaning or indicating the purpose to which the individual entity or soul had been called?
Q-When would it be best to choose a name for the child?
A-When ye have determined as to the purpose to which ye hope, and which ye will, which ye are willing to dedicate same.   457-10

Names have their vibration, to be sure, names have their element of influences or force, by the very activity of the name.   934-7

Q-How would entity benefit by changing his name from (452) to John?
A-How did Abraham benefit by the changing of the name from Abram to Abraham? How did Paul gain by the change from Saul to Paul? How was there difference in the names of the Hebrew children in their varied surroundings? There is builded about each name that which carries its own meaning or significance, that gives rather the impelling of, and the lifting up to, meeting such conditions. So does the changing or the altering of a name set about varied environs or vibrations, that makes for the conduciveness of changed surroundings.   452-6

It is given in thy writings of Scripture, although in a hidden manner, ye may observe if ye will look, how Adam named those that were brought before him in creation. Their **name** indicates to the carnal mind their relationships in the sex condition or question. 5747-3

Each animal, each bird, each fowl, has been so named for some peculiarity of that individual beast, bird or fowl, and in this manner represents some particular phase of man's development in the earth's plane, or that consciousness of some particular element or personality that is manifested in man.   294-87

In all of the animals...in their **natural** state these are in the forms as their **names** indicate. And from these man may learn many lessons; which **was** attempted in the beginning.   826-6

Who, having named the name of the Christ, has become conscious of that He represented or presented in the world? As the records have been handed down that Abraham represents the faithful, Moses meekness, David the warrior yet humility, so the Christ represents Love.   262-56

When each entity, each soul has so manifested, so acted in its relationships as to become then as the new name; white, clear, known only to him that hath overcome. Overcome what? The world, even as He...
As has been indicated in another portion of Revelation, all those that bear the mark, those that have the name, those that have the stone...they **have** overcome, they **have** the new name, they **have** the manna, they **have** the understanding.   281-31

As to times, as to seasons, as to places, **alone** is it given to those who have named the name and who bear the mark of those of His calling and His election in their bodies. To them it shall be given. 3976-15

Ye shall know Him even as He knows thee; for He calls thee by name.   281-10

Hence they that have the Name of the Son have put their trust in Him. He is their standard, their model, their hope, their activity.   5754-2

There is the evolution of the soul, evolution of the mind, but not evolution of matter--save **through** mind, and that which builds same. 262-56

Every individual should recognize and understand that Life from its every element or essence is a growth.   349-12

The destiny of the soul--as of all creation--is to be one with Him; continually growing, growing, for that association.   262-88

Q-What is meant by "eternal life"?
A-Life in its oneness is a continual growth, whether in the material, astral, or spiritual realm.   900-387

That as would be manifested must first be in spirit, then in mind, then in material activity. For, this is the evolution of the earth, the evolution of things, the evolution of ideas and of ideals.   3132-1

Spirit **moving** in space becomes matter, that in time and in evolution becomes aware of its oneness with the source of its energy and activity.   873-1

Spirit is the life-giving force in every condition, whether of mental or material action. Whatever force is acted upon has its attributes, the same as we find in all life-producing element. Whenever the element reaches that stage where it, the element, is able to give or reproduce self, we see the manifestation of the spirit force, modified by that element's own attributes, even from the lowest form of life to the highest. When we have the physical body of the lord of creation, man, we find all such conditions manifest through that body; the mind being that element that directs and makes the master of the condition, situation, or creation. The soul is the element, that given to man that man may be one with the Creator. Hence the developing of that portion that becomes the spiritual element, that it may be made one with the Creator. Hence we see from the lowest to the highest the manifestations of psychic phenomena in the material world. Hence we have the psychic phenomena of the lower animal kingdom, of the mineral kingdom, of the plant kingdom, of the animal kingdom as advanced, and as then becomes the man's condition, position. Hence we find the evolution of the soul, as has been given, and as is manifest in the material world, took place before man's appearance, the evolution of the soul in the mind of the Creator, not in the material world.   900-19

Q-When did I first exist as a separate entity?
A-Would this add to thy knowledge? The first existence, of course, was in the **mind** of the Creator, as all souls became a part of the creation. As to time this would be in the beginning. When was the beginning? First consciousness!   2925-1

Q-Please explain "For the soul had understanding before he partook of the flesh in which the choice was to be made." Why (if the soul had understanding) the necessity to take flesh in order to make the choice?

A-Considereth thou that Spirit hath its manifestations, or does it **use** manifestations for its activity? The Spirit of God is aware through activity, and we see it in those things celestial, terrestrial, of the air, of all forms. And **all** of these are merely manifestations. The knowledge, the understanding, the comprehending, then necessitated the entering in because it partook of that which **was** in manifestation; and thus the **perfect** body, the celestial body, became as earthly body and thus put on flesh. (The explanation to some becomes worse than the first! This then:)...

When the earth became a dwelling place for matter, when gases formed into those things that man sees in nature and in activity about him, then matter began its ascent in the various forms of physical evolution...in the **mind** of God! The spirit chose to enter (celestial, not an earth spirit--he hadn't come into the earth yet!), chose to put on, to become apart of that which was as a command not to be done.

Then those so entering must continue through the earth until the body-mind is made perfect for the soul, or the body-celestial again.   262-99

The earth and the universe, as related to man, came into being through the **Mind--Mind**--of the Maker, and, as such, has its same being much as each atomic force multiplies in itself, or, as worlds are seen and being made in the present period, and as same became (earth we are speaking of) an abode for man, man entered as man, through the **Mind** of the Maker, see? in the form of flesh **man**; that which carnally might die, decay, become dust, entering into material conditions.   900-227

As this evolution began in the mind of the Creator, there then came the point, the place, the beginning, when that as created was **given** that necessary to make its development by applying these same forces **One** with the Creative Energy. Hence the next creation...

As the worlds were created--and are still in creation in this heterogeneous mass as is called the outer sphere, or those portions as man looks up to in space, the mists that are gathering--what's the beginning of this? In this same beginning, so began the earth's sphere. The earth's sphere, with the first creation in the mind of the Creator, has kept its same Creative Energy, for God is the same yesterday, to-day and forever, and the same in one creation creates that same in the other creation. One keeps right on through with the other, see? Now, as this mass has pushed up into that wherein it reverses itself, as it were making then its own environmental condition, and the survival of the stronger of these came to that as the animal kingdom, see? Now, as this came into the animal kingdom, then correct is that as is said, "God said, we will make man." Then man--the creation in itself, that combining all of the forms of the creation so far created, that that same force might understand by having passed through that same creation as was necessary to bring up that dividing point between man and animal and plant, and mineral kingdom--was **given** then the will, and the soul, that it might make itself One with that Creation. Now, that will, then, is heredity. That environment is the evolution. There you have reincarnation, there you have evolution, there you have the mineral kingdom, the plant kingdom, the animal kingdom, each developing towards its own source, yet all belonging and becoming one in that force as it develops itself to become one with the Creative Energy, and One with God. The one then surviving in the earth, through mineral, through plant kingdom, through the vegetable kingdom, through the animal kingdom, each as the geological survey shows held its sway in the earth, passing from one into the other; yet man was given that to be lord over all, and the **only** survivor of that creation.   900-340

God moved, the spirit came into activity. In the moving it brought light, and then chaos. In this light came creation of that which in the earth came to be matter; in the spheres about the earth, space and time; and in patience it has evolved through those activities until there are the heavens and all the constellations, stars, the universe as is known--or sought to be known by individual soul-entities in the material plane.

Then came into the earth materiality, through the spirit pushing itself into matter. Spirit was individualized, and then became what we recognize in one another as individual entities.   3508-1

In the beginning God created the heavens and the earth. How? The **Mind** of God **moved**, and matter, form, came into being.   262-78

Q-Please explain the statement given in Genesis, "In six days God made the heaven and the earth and **rested the seventh day.**"

A-...This was colored by the writers desire to express to the people the power of the Living God--rather than a statement of six days as man comprehends days in the present. Not that such was an impossibility. 262-57

Q-Have the lower forms of creation, such as animals, souls or do they have any life in the spirit plane?

A-All have the spirit force. The man, as made, carrying the soul force, that made equal with the Creator in the beginning, in that of relative production in its (man's) plane of existence. Hence the necessity of developing of that soul energy. Only when reached in that of the man, do we find both the spirit entity and the physical entity.   900-24

Q-Define the word evolution with reference to the human family.

A-Evolution with reference to the human family is, as commonly understood by the human family, relative. Upon this subject of evolution there has been much discussion by many peoples, and the question has become one that involves many different phases and meanings to many peoples. In reference to the human family, evolution means rather resuscitation of those forces that have gradually brought man to understand the law of self from within, and by understanding such law brought the better force in man to bring about the gradual change that has come to man, known through all the ages.

Man was made as man. As given, there were, there are, as we find, only three creations: matter, force, and mind. In each we find the forces developed into the conditions as we find at the present time. All flesh is not of one flesh, but the developing of one has always, remained in the same; it has only been to meet the needs of man, for there was made all that was made, and man's evolving--or evolution--has only been that of the gradual growth upward to the mind of the Maker.

Q-Is the Darwinian theory of evolution of man right or wrong? Give such an answer as will enlighten the people on this subject of evolution.

A-Man was made in the beginning, as the ruler over those elements that were prepared in the earth plane for his needs. When the plane became such that man was capable of being sustained by the forces and conditions which were upon the face of the earth plane, man appeared--not from that already created by as the Lord over all that was created. In man there is found--in the living man--that, all of that, which may be found without, in the whole or earth plane; and **other** than (in addition to) that, the **soul of man** is that making him above all animal, vegetable, mineral kingdom of the earth plane.

Man **did not** descend from the monkey, but man has evolved--resuscitation, you see--from time to time, time to time, here a little, there a little, line upon line, and line and line upon line.

In all ages we find this has been the developing--day by day, day by day; or the evolution as we see from those forces as may be manifested by that which man has made himself--the gradual improvement upon the things made by man, yet made to suffice the needs of certain functioning portions of man's will force, as may be manifested by man, but ever remaining that element to supply that need, whether of sustenance or other functions of man's individual needs, as created by man. This becomes then the exponent of the force as his Creator made him, for the world and the needs and conditions. Man's compliance nearer with those laws brings him gradually to that development necessary to meet the needs of the conditions, place or sphere in which the individual is placed. As in this:

The needs of those in the North Country are not the same as those in the Torrid Region. Hence development comes to meet the needs in the various conditions under which man is placed. He only uses those laws that are ever and ever in existence in the plane, as given in that of relativity, according to the needs from one relation to another.

The theory is, man evolved--or evolution--from first cause in creation, and brings forth to meet the needs of the man. The preparation for the needs of man has gone down many, many thousands and millions of years, as known in this plane, for the needs of man in the hundreds and thousands of years to come...

(The body) becomes a living soul, provided it has reached that developing in the creation where the soul may enter and find the lodging place.

All souls were created in the beginning, and are finding their way back to whence they came.

Q-Where does the soul go when fully developed?
A-To its Maker.   3744-4

The physical world, and the cosmic world, or the astral world, are one-- for the consciousness, the sensuous consciousness, is as the growth from the subconsciousness into the material world. The growth in the astral world is the growth, or the digesting and the building of that same oneness in the spirit, the conscious, the subconscious, the cosmic, or the astral world. We find, from one to another, individuals--individuals-- retained in that oneness, until each is made one in the Great Whole.5756-4

Creative forces **grow**, while destructive forces deteriorate.   1431-1

For only that which is continuous in its creative influence--as Life itself--is everlasting. For that which is **was** and ever will be (Ecclesiates 3:15). Only the mortal or material, or matter, changeth; but the expressions of same prompted by the Spirit of truth live on.   1448-2

The earth and its manifestations were only the expression of God and not necessarily as a place of tenancy for the souls of man, until man was created--to meet the needs of existing conditions.   5749-14

The **earth** was peopled by **animals** before peopled by man! First that of a mass, about which there arose the mist, and then the rising of same with light breaking **over** that as it **settled** itself, as a companion of those in the universe, as it began its **natural** (or now natural) rotations, with the varied effects **upon** the various portions of same, as it slowly-- and is slowly--receding or gathering closer to the sun, from which it receives its impetus for the awakening of the elements that give life itself, by radiation of like elements from that which it receives.   364-6

The evolution of man in spiritual plane being one, the evolution of man in flesh being another. Hence, as has been given, it is hard to understand conditions in one plane when viewed from another plane, without the realization of having experienced that plane...As man applies the laws of which he (man) becomes conscious, the development of man brings forth those results merited by that knowledge. As man passes into the spiritual plane from earthly existence, the development in the spiritual plane becoming the same evolution in spiritual planes as is acquired in the physical plane...This we find, then, is evolution. Man's development through man's acquiring man's understanding of spiritual laws, of earthly laws, of God's laws, and applying same...

Physical, mental and spiritual forces manifest in man, taken in this conception as was given from the beginning. As the earth plane became in that state wherein man might find residence, the spirit forces (which were developing through the spiritual forces to make oneness with the Father) were given the soul of man to make manifest in the flesh. All souls were created in the beginning, all spirit is of one spirit. The Spirit of God is that spirit manifest in flesh, that spirit manifest in all creation, whether of earthly or universal forces--all spirit being one spirit. All flesh is not of one flesh--flesh being that it has merited by its development in its plane of existence...

Many times has the evolution of the earth reached the stage of development as it has today and then sank again, to rise again in the next development. Some along one line, some along others. For often we find the higher branches of so-called learning destroys itself in the seed it produces in man's development... 900-70

What created the first energy, or what **is** the Creative Energy, or God?

Then, we do not set that energy as a super man, more than the energy of heat, rather than that of animal or of tissue, or of any element, is able to create or propagate itself, for each has **innate** within, from the first concept, that ability of creative forces, see?

Q-Then, the intellect, as Bergsen says, must do a hand-spring and transcend itself to find the essence of its own self.

A-Must turn itself inside out, as it were, see? for it must become introspective, rather than outro (outer?) or extrospective (extroversive).

Q-But this principle, in the first two degrees--matter and animal--is constantly repeating its integrating and disintegrating process. In man similarly, yet how does this process prove exceptional to that phase of man, or that entity of creative force that does **not** repeat this activity?

A-For man was given that ability, with will, to become one with the Creative Energy, made a little higher than the other energies, yet combining all, see? 900-274

Q-May we assume that the term "entangle" means a soul's participation and immersion in a form or system of creative expression which was not necessarily intended for such participation and immersion, as the earth?

A-To be sure, there are those consciousnesses or awarenesses that have not participated in nor been a part of earth's **physical** consciousness; as the angels, the archangels, the masters to whom there has been attainment, and to those influences that have prepared the way.

Remember, as given, the earth is that speck, that part in creation where souls projected themselves into matter, and thus brought that conscious awareness of themselves entertaining the ability of creating without those forces of the spirit of truth.

Hence that which has been indicated--that serpent, that satan, that power manifested by entities that, created as the cooperative influence, through will separated themselves.

As this came about, it was necessary for their own awareness in the **spheres** of activity. Thus realms of systems came into being; as vast as the power of thought in attempting to understand infinity, or to comprehend that there is no space or time.

Yet in time **and** space, in patience, you may comprehend.

Q-In systems where conditions for expression parallel those in the solar system, is entanglement a parallel experience to entanglement in this system, so that a soul is apt only to become immersed in one of these systems, and after working out of it, be immune to the attractions of others?

A-No. No two leaves of a tree are the same. No two blades of grass are the same. No two systems have the same awareness, neither are they parallel.

There **are** those awarenesses that are relative relationships, yes. But hast thou conceived--or canst thou conceive--the requirements of the influence to meet all the idiosyncrasies of a **single** soul? How many systems would it require?   5755-2

There lived in this land of Atlantis one Amilius, who had first noted that of the separations of the beings as inhabited that portion of the earth's sphere or plane of those peoples into male and female as separate entities, or individuals. As to their forms in the physical sense, these were much rather of the nature of thought forms, or able to push out of themselves in that direction in which its development took shape in thought--much in the way and manner as the amoeba would in the waters of a stagnant bay, or lake, in the present. As these took form, by the gratifying of their own desire for that as builded or added to the material conditions, they became hardened or set--much in the form of the existent human body of the day, with that of color as partook of its surroundings much in the manner as the chameleon in the present. 364-3

The entity was in the Atlantean land and in those periods before Adam was in the earth. The entity was among those who were then 'thought projections', and the physical being had the union of sex in one body, and yet a real musician on pipes or reed instruments. 5056-1

Individuals in the beginning were more of thought forms than individual entities with personalities as seen in the present, and their projections into the realm of fields of thought that pertain to a developing or evolving world of matter...became manifest. Hence we find occult or psychic science, as would be called at the present, was rather the natural state of man in the beginning. Very much as (in illustration) when a baby, or babe, is born into the world and its appetite is first satisfied, and it lies sleeping. Of what is its dreams? That it expects to be, or that it had been? Of what are thoughts? That which is to be, or that which has been or that which is? Now remember we are speaking--these were thought forms...

The mind constantly trained makes for itself **mental** pictures, or makes for that as is reasoned with from its own present dimensional viewpoints-- but the babe, from whence its reasoning? From whence its dream? From that that has been taken in, or that that has been its experience from whence it came? Oft has it been said, and rightly, with a babe's smile 'Dreaming of angels', and close in touch with them--but what has **produced** that dream? The contact with that upon which **it** fed! Don't forget our premise now from which we are reasoning! and we will find that we will have the premise from which those individuals, or the entities, reasoned within the beginning in this land. (We are speaking of Atlanteans, when they became as thought forces). From whence did **they** reason? From the Creative Force from which they had received their impetus, but acted upon by the thought **forms** as were in **material** forms about them, and given that power (will) to be one with that from what it sprang or was given its impetus, or force, yet with the ability to use that in the way that seemed, or seemeth, good or well, or pleasing, unto itself...

With those so endowed with that as may be called an insight into psychic sources there may be visioned about a body its astral (if chosen to be termed), rather its **thought** body, as is projected...in much the way and manner as individuals in the Atlantean period of psychic and occult development brought about in their experience. Through such projections there came about that first necessity of the division of the body, to conform to those necessities of that as seen in its own mental vision as builded (**Mental** now--don't confuse these terms, or else you will become **very** confused in what is being given!)...

The greater development of that called occult, or psychic forces, during the Atlantean period--and the use of same, and the abuse of same was during its first thousand years...(and) those that partook of carnal to the gratification of that that brought about its continual **hardening** and less ability to harken back through that from **which** it came, and partaking more and more **of** that upon which it became an eater of...

To what uses, then, did these people in this particular period give their efforts, and in what directions were they active? As many almost as there were individuals! for, as we find from the records as are made, to some there was given the power to become the sons of God; others were workers in brass, in iron, in silver, in gold; others were made in music, and the instruments of music. These, then, we find in the world today (today, now--we are reasoning from today). Those that are especially gifted in art--in various forms; and a real artist (as the world looks at it) isn't very much fit for anything else! yet it is-- What? An expression of its concept **of** that from **which** it, that entity, sprang--through the various stages of its evolution (if you choose to call it such) in a material world, or that which it fed its soul or its mental being for its development through its varied experiences **in** a material world. These, then, are but manifestation (occult forces) in individuals who are called geniuses, or gifted in certain directions.

These, then, are the manners in which the **entities**, those **beings**, those **souls**, in the beginning partook of, or developed. Some brought about monstrosities, as of its (that entity's) association by its projection with its association with beasts of various characters. Hence those of the Styx, satyr, and the like; those of the sea, or mermaid; those of the unicorn...those that sought forms in minerals--and being able to be that the mineral was.   364-10

The land (Gobi) was among those in which there was the first appearance of those that were as separate entities or souls disentangling themselves from material or that we know as animal associations. For the projections of these had come from those influences that were termed Lemure, Lemurian, or the land of Mu. These then we find as the period when there was the choice of that soul that became in its final earthly experience the Savior, the Son in the earth dwellings, or of those as man sees or comprehends as the children of men.   877-10

The entity was in the Egyptian land when there were those preparations for purifying the body and those activities that enabled men to put away appendages, that man...inherited through the pushing of spirit into matter to become materially expressive and thus brought the necessity of man being materialized in the earth as the perfect body in Adam. 3333-1

All thought forms in matter were put away--through the experience of Noah.   257-201

Q-Explain the "Sons of God--Daughters of Men--Sons of Man."

A-...The influences of those souls that sought material expression pushed themselves into thought forms in the earth...

Then, as those expressed they were called the Sons of the Earth or the Sons of Man.

When the Creative Forces, God, made then the first man--or Godman-- he was the beginning of the Sons of God.

Then those souls who entered through a channel made by God--not by thought, not by desire, not by lust, not by things that separated con-tinually--were the Sons of God, the Daughters of God.

The Daughters of Men were those who became channels the through which lust knew its activity; and it was in this manner then that the conditions were expressed as given of old, that the Sons of God looked upon the Daughters of Men and saw that they were fair, and **lusted.**   262-119

In the Atlantean land when there were divisions between those of the Law of One and the Sons of Belial, and the offspring of what was the pure race and those that had projected themselves into creatures that became as the sons of man (as the terminology would be) rather than the creatures of God.   1416-1

The **entity** was among the children of the Law of One; those that were the sons of men, yet of the daughters of the Lord--or those who had become purified of those entanglements in the animal forces.   1066-1

The entity was among the children of the Law of One that succumbed to the wiles--and it may be **well** interpreted in that answer recorded in Holy Writ--"Ye shall not **surely** die (Genesis 3:4), but it is pleasant for the moment, and for satisfying the longings within." Thus did the entity begin to use spiritual forces for the satisfying of material appetites. 2850-1

These were the offspring of the mixtures of the children of the Law of One and those that had been entangled in matter, with those various defects in the bodies. these gradually grew to be defects, as might be said; in the characteristics...for, the entity was among those people that were the offspring of the native Egyptians and the 'things' that had appendages. These especially at that time were exhibited as feathers on the limbs of the native Egyptians, and then those peoples where there were the attempts for the purification not only of color but of character. These had been purified in the temple through operative measures. 585-12

When the first of life in flesh form appeared in the earth's plane, this entity was among those making the first appearance in the form of man, or when the development reached such that the universal forces then created the soul man. The entity was among the firstborn of the sons of men.4609-1

(In Atlantis) during those periods when the first of the sons of men coming for their expression into matter...there were again and again the expressions of the Sons of God coming into their manifestations in the earth through taking on of the form of flesh in that experience.   866-1

Just previous to the...first destruction (of Atlantis)...were the periods as termed in thy Scripture when, "The Sons of God looked upon the daughters of men, and saw them as being fair" (Genesis 6:2). 1406-1

When there was the second coming of souls into the earth's plane, the entity was...of giant stature, and was of those who were called Sons of the Highest...This was before the day of the Flood.   2802-1

Where the Red Sea, the Dead Sea **now** occupy--was the entity's dwelling land...The entity was an associate and a companion of one Tubal-Cain (Genesis 4:22), the first of the sons that had been made perfect. 1179-2

In the Atlantean land during those periods between second and last upheaval when there was great antagonism between the Sons of Belial and the Sons of the Law of One--a priestess to the laboring ones, made overtures to the people for the acknowledging of the laborers to make their experience easier. These laborers were considered by many as 'things' rather than individual souls.   1744-1

Q-What is meant by automatons who labored in that experience? Were they individual souls developing, or was it spiritual evolution?
A-Both, and neither. They were the offspring of the sons of God with daughters of men, or vice versa.
Q-What was the character of the Atlantean teachings, that the Priest (Ra Ta) was called back (from banishment) to counteract?
A-That all those who were without sufficient of the purposes to seek the whole light, because of the very influence of the appendages and conditions which had been manifested in materiality such as to make them 'things', were to be kept submerged to be used by those with greater abilities. The Priest held that these were one, and that such conditions offered, the possibilities through which each soul might find a way of escape,--by and through the purifying of the body. 281-44

In the Atlantean land the entity was the time keeper for those who were called things, or the servants, or the workers of the peoples, and the entity felt latent and manifest, as in the present, the wanting to reform, to change things, so that every individual soul had the right to freedom of speech, freedom of thought, freedom of activity...
The entity felt the need of God's hand in what evil, or Satan, had brought in the earth (for this was before Adam).   5249-1

Q-Explain the information given regarding Amilius, who first noted the separation of the peoples into male and female, as it relates to the story in the bible of Adam and Eve in the Garden of Eden, giving the meaning of the symbols Adam, Eve, the apple, and the serpent.

A-...This Amilius--Adam, as given--first discerned that from himself, not of the beasts about him, could be drawn--**was** drawn--that which made for the propagation **of** beings **in** the flesh, that made for that companionship as seen by creation in the material worlds about same. The story, the tale (if chosen to be called such), is one and the same. The apple, as 'apple of the eye,' the desire of that companionship innate in that created, as innate in the Creator, that brought companionship into creation itself. Get that one!   364-5

Q-How is the legend of Lilith connected with the period of Amilius?

A-In the beginning, as was outlined, there was presented that that became as the Sons of god, in that male and female were as in one, with those abilities for those changes as were able or capable of being brought about. In the changes that came from those **things**, as were of the projections of the abilities of those entities to project, this as a being came as the companion; and when there was that turning to the within, through the sources of creation, as to make for the helpmeet of that as created by the first cause, or of the Creative Forces that brought into being that as was made, **then**--from out of self--was brought that as was to be the helpmeet, **not** just companion, of the body. Hence the legend of the association of the body during that period before there was brought into being the last of the creations, which was not of that that was **not** made, but the first of that that **was** made, and a helpmeet to the body, that there might be no change in the relationship of the **Sons** of God **with** those relationships of the sons and daughters of men.

In this, also comes that as is held by many who have reached especially to that understanding of how **necessary**, then, becomes the **proper** mating of those souls that may be the **answers** one to another of that that may bring, through that association, that companionship, into being that that may be the more helpful, more sustaining, more well-**rounded** life or experience of those that are a **portion** one of another. Do not misinterpret, but knowing that all are **of** one--yet there are those divisions that make for a **closer** union, when there are the proper relationships brought about. As an illustration, in this:

In the material world we find there is in the mineral kingdom those elements that are of the nature as to form a closer union one with another, and make as for compounds as make for elements that act more in unison with, or against, other forms of activity in the experience in the earth's environ, or the earth's force, as makes for those active forces in the elements that are about the earth. Such as we find in those that made for the active forces in that of uranium, and that of ultramarine, and these make then for an element that becomes the more active forces as with the abilities for the rates of emanation as may be thrown off from same. So, as illustrated in the union, then, of--in the **physical** compounds--that as may vibrated, or make for emanations in the activities of their mental and spiritual, and material, or physical forces, as may make for a **greater** activity in this earth environ. Then, there may be seen that as is in an elemental, or compound, that makes for that as is seen in the material experience as to become an antipathy for other elements that are as equally necessary in the experience of man's environ as in combination of gases as may produce whenever combined that called water, and its antipathy for the elements in combustion is easily seen or known in man's experience. So in those unions of that in the elemental forces of creative energies that take on the form of man, either in that of man or woman, with its **natural** or **elemental**, see? **elemental** forces of its vibration, with the union of two that vibrate or respond to those vibrations in self, create for that ideal that become as that, in that created, in the form--as is known as radium, with its fast emittal vibrations, that brings for active forces, principles, that makes for such atomic forces within the active principles of all nature in its active force, as to be one of the elemental bases from which life in its essence, as an active principle in a material world, has its sources, give off that which is **ever** good--unless abused, see? So in that may there be basis for **those** forces, as **has** been, as **is** sought, thought, or **attained by** those who have through the abilities of the vibrations, to make for a continued force in self as to meet, know, see, feel, understand, those sources from which such begets that of its kind, or as those that become as an antipathy for another, or as makes for those that make for the variations in the tempering of the various elements, compounds, or the like; so, as is seen **these**--then--the **basis** for those things as has been given here, there, in their various ways and manners, as to the companion of, that that first able--through its projection of itself and its abilities in the creation--to bring about that that was either of its **own** making, or creation, or that given in the beginning to **be** the force **through** which there might **be** that that would bring ever blessings, good, right, and love, in even the physical or material world. See?

Q-How long did it take for the division into male and female?

A-That depends upon which, branch or **line** is considered. When there was brought into being that as of the projection of that created **by** that created, this took a period of evolutionary--or, as would be in the present year, fourscore and six years. That as brought into being was of the creating **of** that that became a portion, **of** that that was already created by the **Creator, that** brought into being as **were** those of the forces in nature itself. God said, "Let there be light!" and there was light! God said, "Let there be life!" and there **was** life!

Q-Were the thought forms that were able to push themselves out of themselves inhabited by souls, or were they of the animal kingdom?

A-That as created by that **created,** of the animal kingdom. That created by the Creator, with the soul.

Q-What was meant by the Sons of the Highest in Atlantis and the second coming of souls to the earth, as mentioned in a life reading given through this channel?

A-In this period or age, as was seen--there is fault of words here to **project** that as actually **occurs** in the formations of that as comes about! There was, with the **will** of that as came into being through the correct channels of that as created by the Creator, that of the **continuing** of the souls in its projection, see? while in that as was **of** the offspring, of that as pushed itself **into** form to **satisfy, gratify,** that of the desire of that known as carnal forces of the **senses,** of those created, there continued to be the war one with another, and there were then--**from** the other **sources** (worlds) the continuing entering of those that **would** make for the keeping of the balance, as of the first purpose of the Creative Forces, as it magnifies itself in that given sphere of activity, of that that had been **given** the **ability** to **create** with its **own** activity-- see? and hence the second, or the **continued** entering of souls into that known as the earth's plane during this period, for that activity as was brought. Let's **remember** that as was given, in the second, third from Adam, or fourth, or from Amilius, there was "In that day did they **call upon** the **name** of the Lord" (Genesis 4:26)--is right! and ever, when the elements that make for littleness, uncleanness, are crucified in the body, the **Spirit** of the Lord, of God, is present! When these are over- balanced, so that the body (physical), the mental man, the imagination of its heart, is evil, or his purpose is evil, then is that war continuing --as from the beginning. Just the continued warring of those things within self as from the beginning; for with these changes as brought **sin** into the world, with same came the **fruits** of same, or the seed as of sin, which we see in the material world as those things that corrupt good ground, those that corrupt the elements that are of the compounds of those of the first causes, or elements, and pests are seen, and the like, see? So does it follow throughout all creative forces, that the fruits of that as is active brings that seed that makes for the corruption of, or the clearing of, in the activative forces of, that **being** acted upon. 364-7

When the earth brought forth the seed in her season, and man came in the earth plane as the lord of that sphere, man appeared in five places then at once--the five senses, the five reasons, the five spheres, the five developments, the five nations.   5748-1

Q-Was Atlantis one of the five points at which man appeared in the beginning, being the home of the red race?

A-One of the five points. As has been given, in what is known as Gobi, India, in Carpathia (?), or in that known as the Andes, and that known as in the western plain of what is now called America--the five places. In their presentation, as we find, these--in the five places, as **man** (Let's get the difference in that as first appeared (as thought forms) in what is known as Atlantis, and that as **man** appearing from those projections in the five places--and, as has been given, from their environ took on that as became necessary for the meeting of those varying conditions under which their individualities and personalities began to put on form)--one in the white, another in the brown, another in the black, another in the red. These, as we find, taking that form--Would snow be the place for the black? or the sun the place for the white? or the desert and the hills for the white or the black? as were partakers of those things that brought about those variations in that which enters, or becomes as the outer presentation, or the skin, or the pigment that is presented in same.

Q-The center or beginning of these projections was in Atlantis?

A-Was in Atlantis. Hence we have, as from the second incarnation there--or the story as is given in Judaism doesn't vary a great deal from that of the Chaldean; neither does it vary at all from that that will be discovered in Yucatan; nor does it vary a great deal from that as from the **older** ones of the Indian (East Indian, of course--as it is from the present).   364-9

Those in the Gobi, the yellow. The white...in the Carpathians...The red, of course, in the Atlantean and in the American. The brown in the Andean. The black in the plain and the Sudan, or in African.

Q-Where was the Carpathian region?

A-Aarat.

Q-Where is the location? Is it on the map today?

A-Southern part of Europe and Russia, and Persia and the land. Caucasian mountains.

Q-Why was the number five selected for the projection of the five races?

A-This, as we find, is that element which represents man in his physical form, and the attributes to which he may become conscious **from** the elemental or spiritual to the physical consciousness. As the senses; as the sensing **of** the various forces that bring to man the activities in the sphere in which he finds himself.

This, to be sure, may be expanded upon. This must bear in the same relation to that as did exist, to the promise that He will come again. Does any individual group think of themselves so exalted as the only to one peoples will He appear? As in the beginning, so shall it ever be, that man's indwelling must recognize that not only must his desires carnally be crucified, but all elements that make for the awareness **of** the spiritual manifestations in the material plane!

Q-Did the appearance of the five races occur simultaneously?

A-Occurred at once.

Q-Describe the earth's surface at the period of the five projections?

A-This has been given. In the first, or that known as the beginning, or in the Caucasian and Carpathian, or the Garden of Eden, in that land which lies now much in the desert, yet much in mountain and much in rolling lands there. The extreme northern portions were then the southern portions, or the polar regions were then turned to where they occupied more of the tropical and semi-tropical regions; hence it would be hard to discern or discriminate the change. The Nile entered into the Atlantic Ocean. What is now the Sahara was an inhabited land and very fertile. What is now the central portion of this country, or the Mississippi basin, was then all in the ocean; only the plateau was existent, or the regions that are now portions of Nevada, Utah and Arizona formed the greater part of what we know as the United States. That along the Atlantic board formed the outer portion then, or the lowlands of Atlantis. The Andean, or the Pacific coast of South America, occupied then the extreme western portion of Lemuria. The Urals and the northern regions of same were turned into a tropical land. The desert in the Mongolian land was then the fertile portion. This may enable you to form **some** concept of the status of the earth's representation at that time! The oceans were then turned about; they no longer bear their names, yet from whence obtained they their names? What is the legend, even as to their names?

Q-Are the following the correct places? Atlantean, the red?

A-Atlantean and American, the red race.

Q-Upper Africa for the black?

A-Or what would be known now as the more **western** portion of upper Egypt for the black. You see, with the changes--when there came the uprisings in the Atlantean land, and the sojourning south-ward--with the turning of the axis--the white and yellow races came into that portion of Egypt, India, Persia and Arabia.

Q-There was no original projection in upper India?

A-This was a portion rather of the white and the yellow as represented.

Let these represent the attributes of the physical, or the senses and what forms they take, rather than calling them white, black, yellow, red and green, etc. What do they signify in the **sensing**? Sight, vision--white. Feeling--red. Black--gratifying of appetites in the senses. Yellow--mingling in the hearing. What is the law of the peoples that these represent? Their basic thoughts run to those elements!   364-13

The entity was in the Egyptian land, the Indian land, the lands from which most of those came for one of the branches of the first appearances of the Adamic influence that came as five at once into the expressions in the earth, or the expression in that now known as the Gobi land.

The entity then was among those who assisted in bringing an interpretation to the peoples in the Indian land now called, and the Egyptian land, when there were the undertakings for a correlating again of the troublesome forces that had separated, had caused those periods of destructive forces in the activities of man his brother's keeper, man as expressing himself in flesh in the earth.

The activities of the entity then brought about the correlating of Saneid, Og, Ra Ta, Zu and those of the Pyrenees as well as the Nordic from the upper portions of what is now Norway (though quite a different looking Norway!).

In that experience the entity made for advancement. For not differences were sought but rather a unification of that which was for the moral, the mental, the material uplift of those that united not by body but in oneness of purpose for the protection against those forces and influences that man had projected himself into that had become as monstrosities in the earth, and those periods when there were sought from the Atlantean experience for the destructive forces for the creatures that overran the land.

The entity aided in bringing about the counsel to the five nations, or the five centers in the experience...The knowledge, not without but from within, is the real source. That without as the sign, as the guide, so long as it is along the way--but **only** the way.   1210-1

Then as we become more and more aware within ourselves of the answering of the experiences, we become aware of what He gave to those that were the first of **God's** projection--not man's but God's projection--into the earth; Adam and Eve.   262-115

Man, in Adam (as a group; not as an individual), entered into the world (for he entered in five places at once, we see--called Adam in one, see?).   900-227

He hath made of one blood the nations of the earth.   3976-24

PART VI

RELIGION, THE BIBLE AND JESUS THE CHRIST

RELIGIOUS DIFFERENCES

More wars, more bloodshed have been shed over the racial and religious differences than over any other problem. These, too, must go the way of all others; and man must learn--if he will know the peace as promised by Him--that God loveth those who love Him, whether they be called of this or that sect or schism or ism or cult, the Lord is **One**.   3976-27

But remember, truth is truth in any language, in any clime and that to which man needs to subscribe is, namely; "Thou shalt love the Lord thy God, with all thy mind, thy body, thy soul, and thy neighbor as thyself (Luke 10:27)." The rest of philosophy, the rest of theology is only the explaining of that in individuals' lives.   5037-2

No matter what ye say, the manner in which ye treat thy fellowman is the answer to what ye really believe. The manner in which ye treat thy neighbor is the manner in which ye are treating thy Maker.   3684-1

Q-Which person, or group, today, has the nearest to the correct teachings of Jesus?
A-This would depend upon who is the judge. The teaching, the consciousness of the Christ-life is a **personal** thing. And hence they that are aware of His abiding presence are the nearer.
Who? They that walk with Him and do not, **cannot, will** not force themselves on others--even as He.   1703-36

Looking for rather that in which thoughts agree, than their difference, may there be brought peace and harmony and greater understanding to self. Look not for the differences in either the religious thought, the political conditions, the economic influences, but how that their union of purposes in one may become helpful to the greater number.   1226-1

It is indeed not strange there are even in the protestant churches, Methodist, Christian, Baptist, Congregational or the what, but it is to meet the needs. What is God? All things to all men that all might know Him. Not that one is better than the other.   2072-15

As He has given, it will ever be found that Truth--whether in this or that schism or ism or cult--is of the One source. Are there not trees of oak, of ash, of pine? There are the needs of these for meeting this or that experience.   254-87

All religious faiths have their element of truth.   900-59

Aid others to walk circumspectly, and not to confuse or disturb any in that which they are satisfied, or in that which for **them** constitutes righteousness **or** sin.   262-124

Q-Is faith of man in Buddha or Mohammed equal in the effect on his soul to the faith in Jesus Christ?
A-...Each in their respective spheres are but stepping stones to that that may awaken in the individual the knowledge of the Son in their lives.   262-14

One's religion, one's love of the fellow man, one's love of the Creator is a **living** thing--and **not** just form only!   1564-1

The purpose, yea, the intent of religion is that peace may be to body and mind of those who embrace same.
Then the fewer definitions there be of that to which an individual is to subscribe, the greater may be the peace and the harmony in the experience of every soul.   1467-3

In God, in the Son, in the Holy Spirit, there is **no** creed; for creeds are only man-made. And remember that creeds are like those things that are done as in rote. However, to some rote becomes necessary. 2420-1

The church is within yourself and not in any pope or preacher, or in any building but in self! For thy body is indeed the temple of the living God, and the Christ becomes a personal companion in mind and body; dependent upon the personality and individuality of the entity as it makes practical application of the tenets and truths that are expressed. 5125-1

Q-Is Gnosticism the closest type of Christianity to that which is given through this source?
A-This is a parallel, and was the commonly accepted one until there began to be set rules in which there were attempts to take short cuts. And there are none in Christianity!   5749-14

A particular church organization is well. For it centers the mind. But don't get the idea you have the whole cheese.   3350-1

Science and religion are one when their purposes are one. 5023-2

O what crimes have been committed in the name of religion! 3344-1

Q-What present printed version of the Bible gives the nearest to the true meaning of both the New and Old Testaments?

A-The nearest true version for the entity is that ye apply of whatever version ye read, in your life. It isn't that ye learn from anyone. Ye only may have the direction. The learning, the teaching is within self. For where hath He promised to meet thee? Within the temple! Where is the temple? Where is heaven on earth? Within!...

There have been many versions of that which was purposed to have been written, and has been changed from all of those versions, but remember that the whole gospel of Jesus Christ is; "Thou shalt love the Lord thy God with all thy mind, thy heart, thy body, and thy neighbor as thyself." Do this and thou shalt have eternal life. The rest of the book is trying to describe that. It is the same in any language, any version. 2072-14

Q-In canonizing the Bible, why was the life of Zan (Zend) left out?

A-Called in other names...The Bible has passed through many hands. Many that would turn that which was written into the meanings that would suit their own purposes, as **ye** yourselves oft do. But if ye will get the spirit of that written there ye may find it will lead thee to the gates of heaven...Read it to be wise. Study it to understand. Live it to know that the Christ walks through same with thee.   262-60

The mysteries of the gospels of Christ are as great a mystery as life itself.   5149-1

Study and know thy relationship to the Creator. No better hand-book may be used than the Scripture itself.   1966-1

There is that as may be said to be the literal and the spiritual and the metaphysical interpretation of almost all portions of the Scripture, and especially of the Revelation as given by John.

Yet all of these to be true, to be practical, to be applicable in the experiences of individuals, must coordinate; or be as one, even as the Father, the Son and the Holy Spirit.   281-31

Q-How can I get well-educated, kind and refined associations?

A-Read the Book, if you would get educated. If you would be refined, live it! If you would be beautiful, practice it in thy daily life! 3647-1

Read them (Scriptures) not as history, read them not as axioms or as dogmas, but as of thine own being. For in the study of these ye will find that ye draw unto that force from which the writers of same gained their strength, their patience...

Q-What passages especially should be read in the Bible?

A-The admonition of Moses, the creation of man in the first three chapters, the admonition of Joshua, the 1st Psalm, the 2nd and 4th Psalm, the 22nd, 23d and 24th Psalm, the 91st Psalm, the 12th of Romans, the 14th, 15th, 16th, 17th of John, 13th of 2nd Corinthians (13th of 1st Corinthians?) and the Book of Revelation.

And in the Revelation study as this: Know, as there is given each emblem, each condition, it is representing or presenting to self a study of thine own body, with **all** of its emotions, all of its faculties. All of its physical centers represent experiences through which thine own mental and spiritual and physical being pass. For it is indeed the revelation of self.   1173-8

Begin to analyze self and the relationship the entity bears with the universe and its Maker. Begin first by reading something from the Book itself. It would be well to read first the first five to six verses of the first chapter of Genesis, and in the third verse understand what it means--that knowledge is within thine own self, the light necessary for you to be one of the best men God ever created. For He has promised to be with you, as an individual, if you will be with Him.

Then turn to Exodus 19:5. This is not merely talking to Jews or Hebrews or Israelites--it is talking to (you).

Then read the 30th chapter of Deuteronomy. Again it is to you, an individual.

Read then the promises in the 14th, 15th, 16th, and 17th of John. They are not foolishness, my friend! It's the law of the Lord! and you must one day face it.   3432-1

Not merely read to know them (Exodus 19:5, 30th of Deuteronomy, Story of Ruth), but get the meaning of universal love, not attempting to make it personal but universal. For God is Love.   5124-1

Q-What books should I read to bring out the Divine within me?
A-None more beautiful than that found in the Scriptures, especially the latter portion of Genesis and the 14th, 15th, 16th, 17th chapter in that recorded by John in the Gospels, or those by the second John in his epistles; first, second and third John.   505-4

Do study scripture. Do analyze it. Begin with definite portions, as: Exodus 19:5. Then study thoroughly the whole of Exodus 20, then Deuteronomy 30. Then make the pattern of thy life the 23rd Psalm, and then the first ten verses of the first chapter of John. And then the 14th, 15th, 16th, 17th of John. And then the 13th of 1st Corinthians.   2969-2

For the **general** development in the mental attributes or the spiritual forces, nothing is better than the Psalms, John (especially the 14th, 15th, 16th and 17th chapters), and the letters of John--James. 275-30

From the very first of the Old Testament to the very last even of Revelation, He is not merely the subject of the book, He (Jesus the Christ) is the author of the greater part, having given to man the mind and the purpose for its having been put in print. 5322-1

The sons of God came together to reason, as recorded in the book of Job. **Who** recorded same? The son of Man, Melchizedek wrote Job. 262-55

Do learn the promises of the Christ, the Savior; especially those given to man after He arose from the grave. For these are quite different from those given in the hour before His trial and crucifixion. 3694-1

Q-Would the history of the Jewish race from Abraham to Jesus parallel the development of the embryo from conception to birth?
A-Rather would the history of man from Noah to Abraham; while that from Abraham to Christ would be the mental unfoldment of the body. For, that which leads to the Christ is the mind. And the mind's unfoldment may be indicated from Abraham to the Christ. 281-63

THE WORD

Who is the Word? He that made himself manifest in the flesh! Who is the beginning and the end? Even Jesus, the Christ! 5755-2

In the beginning was the Word, and that Spirit, that Christ Spirit **was** the Word. That Word was made flesh, even as each soul...in the earth is made flesh. That soul, that spirit, **dwelt** among men, and that soul made itself of no estate; yet Creator, the Maker, the giver of life. 524-2

In the beginning was the Word. The Word was God. The Word was with God. He **moved**...(and) souls--portions of Himself--came into being...
Of the dust of the earth was the body-physical created. But the **Word** the **Mind**, is the controlling factor of its shape, its activity, from the source, the spiritual--entity. 262-13

He is the Word; He **is** that which may not be divided--but **divined** in each word that makes for the correlating, the coordinating, the understanding of those motivative forces of thy activities in the earth. 1089-3

"All things will be brought to remembrance that I have given thee since the foundations of the world, for thou wert with me in the beginning (Isaiah 40:21) and thou may abide with me in that day when the earth will be rolled as the scroll (Revelation 6:14); for the heavens and the earth will pass away but my word shall **not** pass away (Matt. 24:35)."262-28

Q-Who wrote the Four Gospels?

A-These, we find, may **best** be determined by investigations of the records as related to same...in the Vatican's own libraries.

Mark was first dictated, greatly by Peter--and this in those periods just before Peter was carried to Rome.

The next was **Matthew** written by the one whose name it bears. **As** for the **specific** reasons--to those who were scattered into the upper portions of Palestine and through Laodicea. This was written something like thirty-three to four years later than **Mark** and while this body that wrote same was in exile.

Luke was written by Lucius, rather than Luke, though a companion with Luke during those activities of Paul--and written, of course, unto those of the faith under the Roman **influence.** Not to the Roman peoples, but to the provinces ruled **by** the Romans. And it was from these sources that the very changes were made as to the differences in that given by **Mark** and **Matthew.**

John was written by several; not by the John who was the beloved, but the John who **represented** or was the scribe for, John the beloved--and, as much of same, was written much later. Portions of it were written at different times and combined some fifty years after the Crucifixion. 1598-2

ISRAEL MEANS SEEKER

Q-What should be understood by the statement (Genesis 49:10), "The scepter has not departed from Israel"?

A-Israel is the chosen of the Lord, and that His promise, His care, His love has not departed from those that seek to know His way, that seek to see His face, that would draw nigh unto Him. **This** is the meaning, this should be the understanding to all. Those that seek are Israel. So Abraham means call; so Israel means those who seek. How obtained the supplanter the name Israel? For he wrestled with the angel, and he was face to face with the seeking to know His way.   262-28

For those who seek are indeed Israel, and Israel indeed is **all** who seek; meaning not those as of the children of Abraham, but of every nation, every tribe, every tongue--Israel of the Lord! That is the full meaning of Israel.   2772-1

Let there be the study, the closer study of the promises which are made in the book, yes, the history of the Jew; yet these having failed, who is Israel? Not the Jew, but Israel is the seeker after truth. 5377-1

(Genesis) is the presentation of a teacher of a peoples that separated for that definite purpose of keeping alive in the minds, the hearts, the **soul**-minds of entities, that there may be seen their closer relationships to the divine influences of Creative Forces, that brought into being all that appertains to man's indwelling as man in the form of flesh.   364-5

A peculiar people, set aside for a purpose--as a channel through which there might be the discerning of the spirit made manifest in flesh.   2879-1

Q-Who are the "Chosen"?

A-This applies to these as we have shown, that the first laws set forth to the people of the earth were seen in the experience in the Temple, the reconstruction of the Jewish law to the Jewish people in their promised land. In the present it is seen that the study of the first laws, and the application of the laws as reconstructed, come to the Jews and to those who love the Lord.   142-1

Q-You will give at this time information which may stimulate in the hearts and minds of those gathered here a greater appreciation of the true spirit of Thanksgiving.

A-It is well that ye be reminded how in those periods when there were the preparations in the lives and experiences of a peculiar people under unusual circumstances, in extraordinary environments--they were reminded, not in the days when each day they were given only sufficient for that day, that periods were to be, set aside when thanksgiving was to be a part of their activity,--their remembrances for all the joys, the sorrows, the disappointments, the hopes that were and might be theirs if--**if** they would but hold to those promises; relying,--as it was necessary in those days, those hours, for a complete dependence,--upon the bounty of a merciful Father, who had a purpose in the bringing out, in the edifying, in the directing.

And today, as ye look back upon those experiences, ye--**too**--find thyselves chosen. Have ye chosen Him?

For as was given, "If ye will be my people, I will be thy God." 3976-21

We find (the entity) in that land when there was the return from the wanderings, and the walls of the temple were rebuilt...the entity was among those that made for the **betterment** of the understanding influences of the peoples as a chosen peoples, as a people with a definite mission, a definite purpose, called of the Divine to establish the name in a given place, a given purpose, to a **waiting** world. 454-2

Those peoples though they **were** called--have wandered far afield, and their rebelliousness and their seeking into the affairs of **others** has rather brought **them** into **their** present (1933) position.

Read they not that which has been given? "When ye forsake my ways ye shall be scattered, ye shall be without those things that would bring ye into the knowledge--until that time is fulfilled."   3976-13

The entity was in the English land, but during the early periods of those journeyings of the peoples of Hezekiah's rein--during the time when the children of promise were carried into captivity...In the experience the entity gained, for it was the seeking for freedom as well as for the preservation of those tenets and truths which brought the entity's desire to seek out other lands, and the putting of same into activity and the setting up of the stones in the forms of circles for altars. 2205-1

The entity was in the English land in the early settlings of the children of Israel who were foregathered with the daughters of Hezekiah in what is now Somerland, Somerhill, or Somerset. There the entity saw group organizations for the preservation of tenets and the truths of the Living God.   5384-1

The entity was in the Holy Land when there were those breakings up in the periods when the land was being sacked by the Chaldeans and Persians. The entity was among those groups who escaped in the ships that settled in portions of the English land near what is now Salisbury, and there builded those altars that were to represent the dedications of individuals to a service of a Living God.   3645-1

There was the founding of those activities in the English land in and about those places where the stones were set up as the altars. These were to represent the tabernacle...Thus all forms of mysticism, all forms of occult science, occult influences were a portion of the activity; as the holy of holies, the ephod, Urim and Thummim...
The entity guided the interpreting of the worship in the forms which set up discarding blood sacrifice for those as of fruits.   5259-1

The entity was of the daughters of Zedekiah, and among those who-- through the activities of some of the children of Benjamin, Juda and Dan--came to the Isles, and began the establishing of an understanding that the mysteries of the ages that had been handed down to the priests --in the judgment of the records given by the prophets and sages of old --could or might be established in such a form, such a manner as to ever present--to the peoples who looked upon same--a reminder of the promises of Divinity to the children of men--even in their weakness.
Then the entity was in the name Zeurah, and a prophetess--yea, as one given in the understanding of the influences of the seasons, of the years, of the signs as set in what ye call the zodiac, in what ye call the various phases of man's experience.

Hence the entity gained, yet set--as it were--a temptation in the way of others; in that the **symbol** became to mean more than that for which it stood.   1580-1

The entity...escaped from the activities under Nebuchadnezzar's forces and took ship for that now known as Ireland.   2005-1

The entity was again in the land of the present nativity during those periods when activities were set up or established in the Southwest, by those who had journeyed from other lands when the ten tribes were carried away. The entity was among those children born in the land, now a portion of Arizona and New Mexico.   3513-1

The entity was in the own land of nativity during the early settlings, not America as is known in history, but when there were the activities of those peoples that were dispersed by the carrying away of the children of promise into captivity. The entity was among those born to those who escaped across the water into what is now the south-western portion of the entity's present native land (America).
There the entity came in contact with those who were a part of the Atlantean civilization before it was broken up, and the entity was made a priestess--as in keeping with a combination of the old Mosaic teachings and those of Ax-tell and the Children of the Law of One. 2540-1

During that period as would be called 3,000 years before the Prince of Peace came, those peoples that were of the Lost Tribes, a portion came into the land; infusing their activities upon the peoples from Mu in the southernmost portion of that called America or United States, and then moved on to the activities in Mexico, Yucatan, centralizing that now about the spots where the central of Mexico now stands, or Mexico city.
Q-How did the Lost Tribe reach this country?
A-In boats.   5750-1

The entity was in the land of the present nativity, during those periods when there were the spreadings of those teachings that had come from the lands from which those peoples came that were known as the Lost Tribes, as well as from Atlantis, Yucatan, the Inca and the land of On.
They were portions of the entity's people then, in that part of the land now known as the central portion of Ohio, during the early period of the Mound Builders.   1286-1

(In Peru) the entity was a priestess in those interpretations of what later became known as the Incals, the Lost Tribes, the people from the Atlantean land, the peoples who came west from the activities in the Lemurian land.   1159-1

The entity was again in the activities of the builder, when there was the second and third return of the people of promise from the lands where they had been in exile for so long. There we find the entity was the leader, the lawyer, the soldier, the director--Nehemiah.   1767-2

The entity was in the land or isle of Samoa, during those periods in the latter portion of the fifteen century, when there were settlings and the first combinations of the natives that were the descendants of those peoples who had lost their way from the others--or those called the Lost Tribes, or the peoples of Naphtali. The entity's forefathers then were in that line. The entity was a combination then in that experience between the peoples of the Mediterranean and the natives.   1258-1

BIBLICAL CHARACTERS

Melchizedek, a prince of peace, one seeking ever to be able to bless those in their judgments who have sought to become channels for a helpful influence without any seeking for material gain or mental, or mental or material glory.   2072-4

The life of the man Abraham was not beautiful, yet that faith which motivated same is beautiful.   4035-1

Though he walked in many ways contrary to God's edicts and laws, Abram's try was counted to him for righteousness.   3129-1

Q-Please explain what is meant by "Look not back; remember Lot's wife"?
A-Looking to the front ever, for as one looks towards the light, the shadows fall behind and do not become stumbling blocks to individual development...Even as Lot's wife looked upon that left as longing for those satisfying elements that made for the carnal, rather than the spiritual life.   262-28

Moses after he had finished all of his own egotism had come to realize that there was not to be the experience in self for the enjoying of that which had been builded, owing to that weakness of selfishness. 262-100

(Joshua) was oft a lonely, lonely man--as man.   3188-1

The patient Joshua was the one who followed closely in the way that would give to the individual (who would study) the life and interpretation of the Son of man. These (Joshua and Jesus) in the earth activity were much alike not as combative, as in the warrings, but in spirit and in purpose, in ideals, these were one.   3409-1

David the king worshipped God in a manner such that it was given, "a man after mine own heart." Not that he failed not, but not guilty of the same offense twice, and gave credit ever to God--not to self; the **glory** to God, the weakness acknowledged in self, but the glory to Him.   2796-1

The seal should be worn at most times about the body; the king's (David) seal. The cup with king's crown upon same. Either in the form of cameo or other stones. Any stone in which it may be; not as a charm, but rather as that which comes with the lineal activity or descendant, and the influences that come about; for the soul--or entity--was indeed the king's daughter.   601-1

The seal that the entity wore then, as the gift from the king, should ever be about the body. This we would give in some detail:
A cross; each prong being the same length, you see. Cut as a shadow box in its making. On the cross, the rosette of the king. In the center of the rosette a raised figure; or **plane**, and **on** this plane **this** figure; Draw a seven. draw it! In the front **raise** the upper line of the seven, see? In front of this line draw a mark slanting towards the right; **heavy**, and slanting almost straight down. On the back side of the seven a line leaning towards the seven, you see, just a little space from same. This, of course, represents the Hebraic characters of the cabalistic intent or import; meaning El Yah (?)--(God Preserves!)...
It will **one** day be uncovered in Jerusalem.   601-5

The entity (sister of Solomon) was among those that were favored, not only of the people but of those that came for counsel--as the people of many nations--to receive...counsel from the--preacher or the teacher in Solomon, and those **greater** in the Psalms of David. 601-2

Those were the periods when there was the great amount of what today would be called notoriety, or during those periods when the Queen of Sheba visited Solomon, the entity was chosen as the one to make music for Solomon to make love by, to the Queen.   5056-1

(Samson had) unusual strength and power, the ability to cope with exterior forces and influences that were beyond the understanding and comprehension of his associates. Yet his ability to say no to the opposite sex was nil--his ability not to be influenced by the opposite sex was nil --because of the desire for the gratification of those activities which were of a glandular nature within the body.   281-49

The entity appeared in the Holy Land during...that period of what is oft spoken of as Jephthah's rash vow. The entity was a close friend of Jephthah's daughter offered as a human sacrifice.   3653-1

What indeed is thy tabernacle? It is thy body, thy mind, thy soul. 877-22

Q-Is the temple here (Revelation chapter eleven) the physical body?

A-Rather the **mental** in which is the pattern as of the tabernacle; or the holy mount--or that as set by a **unified** service of the body-mind, the body-physical, (as was the tabernacle as a pattern), not bound together, yet a covering, a place, an understanding for a unified activity with Creative Forces, or the power of God. The veil without, the holy within, and the holy of holies--knowing that there must be the cleansing, there must be the purifying, there must be the consecration. All of these are as patterns, they are as conditions, they are as experiences for each and every soul.   281-32

In the expressions as shown in the tabernacle, in the orders as given for its construction--the size, the shape, the measurements, the figures above the holy of holies, the directions of the colors as indicated for the hangings, the manner in which each board was to be set, the manner in which each skin was to be used or dyed--these were not only for the physical protection but for the expressions that would come in the experience of individuals that took the service of worship there as being a thing within themselves. Hence became material, emblematical. 338-4

Q-Who were the persons that appeared to me (in this dream)?

A-Meeting in the inner self the triune of the body, the mind and the soul; these three ye met in the inner court, as represented in the figures and in the numbers; for the body is ever that triune--body, mind, soul. Soul, of the Maker. The mind, the Christ. The **body**--or the individual entity.   338-3

The entity then was among the daughters of Levi, and those chosen to make the vestment of the priest. And to the entity, because of its own abilities, there was given the preparation of the settings of the breastplate and the putting of the stones thereon, and the preparation of the Urim and Thummim for the interpretations of the movements that came upon the high priest in the holy of holies to be given to his people in or from the door of the tabernacle...

In the present from that sojourn, those things pertaining to the mysteries of the temple, the mysteries of numbers, of figures, and things that have their hidden meaning, become as a portion of the entity.   987-2

Those then that are come into the new life, the new understanding, the new regeneration, there is then the new Jerusalem. For as has been given, the place is not as a place alone but as a condition, as an experience of the soul...those who have put away the earthly desires and become as the **new** purposes in their experience, become the new Jerusalem.   281-37

The Revelation study as this: Know, as there is given each emblem, each condition, it is representing or presenting to self a study of thine own body, with all of its emotions, all of its faculties. All of its physical centers represent experiences through which thine own mental and spiritual and physical being pass. For it is indeed the revelation of self. 1173-8

If you will read the Book of Revelation with the idea of the body as the interpretation, you will understand yourself and learn to really analyze, psychoanalyze, mentally analyze others. But you will have to learn to apply it in self first. 4083-1

The Revelation is a description of, a possibility of, thy own consciousness, and not as a historical fact, not as a fancy, but as that thy own soul has sought throughout its experiences. 1473-1

Q-Does Babylon symbolize self?
A-Babylon symbolizes self.
Q-Does the marriage of the Lamb symbolize the complete spiritualization of the body? Please explain.
A-As there has been given through the whole of Revelation; first how the symbols of the activity of the body mentally, spiritually, physically, are affected by influences in the earth--and as to how now the body has been raised to the realizations of the associations with the spirit and matter through mind, the builder, and comes now to that as represented by the Lamb--or the mind, spiritual--that has now so raised the body as to become as a new being; activity which motivates same within or as was given by Him--the body is the church, the Christ Consciousness is that activity which motivates same within the individual. 281-36

Q-What is meant by the "great city which is called Sodom and Egypt, where also our Lord was crucified"? (Revelation 11:8)
A-As has been so often given, all places--as Egypt or Sodom or the Crucifixion, or the Lord--are conditions, circumstances, experiences, as well as individual places. Then in the minds of those who would attempt or that would seek knowledge, they represent their own experiences. Thus these to the people represent--Egypt, the release from bondage, Gomorrah, as a reckoning with sin--as the Lord was crucified there. As has been given, there has never been an experience when His Christ-mass, His death, His birth, wasn't an experience of the age, the people.
Q-What is mean't by the war in heaven between Michael and the Devil?
A-...There is first--as is the spiritual concept--the spiritual rebellion, before it takes mental or physical form. This warring is illustrated there by the war between the Lord of the Way and the Lord of Darkness or Lord of rebellion. 281-33

The visions, the experiences, the names, the churches, the places, the dragons, the cities, all are but emblems of those forces that may war within the individual in its journey through the material, or from the entering into the material manifestation to the entering into the glory, or the awakening in the spirit, in the inter-between, in the borderland, in the shadow.

Hence we find, as the churches are named, they are as the forces that are known as the senses, that must be spiritualized by the will...

The great tribulation and periods of tribulation, as given, are the experiences of every soul, every entity. They arise from influences created by man through activity in the sphere of any sojourn. Man may become, with the people of the universe, ruler of any of the various spheres through which the soul passes in its experiences. Hence, as the cycles pass, as the cycles are passing, when there is come a time, a period of readjusting in the spheres (as well as in the little earth, the little soul)--seek, then, as known, to present self spotless before that throne; even as all are commanded to be.	281-16

Q-Are we correct in interpreting the seven churches as symbols of seven spiritual centers in the physical body?
A-Correct.

Q-Are we correct in interpreting the twenty-four elders as the twenty-four cranial nerves of the head especially related to the five senses?
A-Correct.

Q-Is the frequent reference to the throne indicating the head in which are found the higher gland centers?
A-Correct.

Q-Are we correct in interpreting the four beasts as the four fundamental physical natures (desires) of man which must be overcome?
A-Correct. In all of these, let this be understood: These are symbolized; they are as in these representing the elemental forces--as the body is of the earth, is of the elements.

Q-Are we correct in interpreting the 144,000 who were sealed as being spiritualized cellular structure of the twelve major divisions of the body?
A-Correct.	281-29

Q-What are the four angels that are bound in the river Euphrates?
A-As has been indicated, the four influences that are as the Air, the Earth, the Fire, the Water.	281-32

Q-Please explain the meaning of "Great star falls from heaven."
A-The star signifies simply the coming of the influence from without to the influences from within, as signified by "His Star have we seen." 281-31

Q-What is the correct meaning of the term "Essene"?

A-Expectancy.

Q-Was the main purpose of the Essenes to raise up people who would be fit channels for the birth of the Messiah who later would be sent out into the world to represent their Brotherhood?

A-The individual preparation was the first purpose...

Their purpose was of the first foundations of the prophets as established, or as understood from the school of prophets, by Elijah; and propagated and studied through the things begun by Samuel. The movement was **not** an Egyptian one, though **adopted** by those in another period--or an earlier period--and made a part of the whole movement.

They took Jews and Gentiles alike as members,--yes.

Q-Please describe the associate membership of the women in the Essene brotherhood, telling what privileges and restrictions they had, how they joined the Order, and what their life and work was.

A-This was the beginning of the period where women were considered as equals with the men in their activities, in their abilities to formulate, to live, to be, channels.

They joined by dedication--usually by their parents.

It was a free will thing all the way through, but they were restricted only in the matter of certain foods and certain associations in various periods--which referred to the sex, as well as to the food or drink.

Q-How did Mary and Joseph first come in contact with the Essenes and what was their preparation for the coming of Jesus?

A-As indicated, by being dedicated by their parents.

Q-Please describe the process of selection and training of those set aside as holy women such as Mary, Editha, and others as a possible mother for the Christ. How were they chosen, were they mated, and what was their life and work while they waited in the Temple?

A-They were first dedicated and then there was the choice of the individual through the growths, as to whether they would be merely channels for general services. For, these were chosen for special services at various times; as were the twelve chosen at the time, which may be used as an illustration. Remember, these came down from the periods when the school had begun, you see.

When there were the activities in which there were to be the cleansings through which bodies were to become channels for the new race, or the new preparation, these then were restricted--of course--as to certain associations, developments in associations, activities and the like. We are speaking here of the twelve women, you see--and all of the women from the very beginning who were dedicated as channels for the new race, see?

Hence the group we refer to here as the Essenes, which was the outgrowth of the periods of preparations from the teachings by Melchizedek, as propagated by Elijah and Elisha and Samuel. These were set aside for preserving themselves in direct line of choice for the offering of themselves as channels through which there might come the new divine origin, see?

Their life and work during such periods of preparation were given to alms, good deeds, missionary activities--as would be termed today. 254-109

Much might be given as to how or why and when there were the purposes that brought about the materialization of Jesus in the flesh.

In giving then the history: There were those in the faith of the fathers to whom the promises were given that these would be fulfilled as from the beginning of man's record.

Hence there was the continued preparation and dedication of those who might be the channels through which this chosen vessel might enter--through choice--into materiality.

Thus in Carmel--where there were the priests of this faith--there were the maidens chosen that were dedicated to this purpose, this office, this service.

Among them was Mary, the beloved, the chosen one; and she, as had been foretold, was chosen as the channel. Thus she was separated and kept in the closer associations with and in the care or charge of this office.

That was the beginning, that was the foundation of what ye term the church.   5749-7

In those days when there had been more and more of the leaders of the peoples in Carmel--the original place where the school of prophets was established during Elijah's time, Samuel--these were called then Essenes; and those that were students of what ye would call astrology, numerology, phrenology, and those phases of that study of the return of individuals--or incarnation...

Then there were again those soundings--that is, the approach of that which had been handed down and had been the experiences from the sages of old--that an angel was to speak. As this occurred when there was the choosing of the mate that had--as in only the thought of those so close--been immaculately conceived, these brought to the focal point the preparation of the mother...

Q-How were the maidens selected and by whom?

A-By all of those who chose to give those that were perfect in body and in mind for the service; and as Ann (mother of Mary)--or Anna--gave the same, and in the presentation could not be refused because of the perfectness of body, though many questioned and produced a division because she proclaimed it had been conceived without knowing a man.

Thus came the divisions, yet the others were chosen--each as a representative of the twelve in the various phases that had been or that had made up Israel--or man.

Q-How old was Mary at the time she was chosen?

A-Four; and, as ye would call, between twelve and thirteen when designated as the one chosen by the angel on the stair.

Q-Describe the training and preparation of the group of maidens.

A-Trained as to physical exercise first, trained as to mental exercises as related to chastity, purity, love, patience, endurance...

Q-Were they put on special diet?

A-No wine, no fermented drink ever given. Special foods, yes. These were kept balanced according to that which had been first set by Aran and Ra Ta.

Q-In what manner was Joseph informed of his part in the birth of Jesus?

A-First by Mathias or Judah. Then as this did not coincide with his own feelings, first in a dream and then the direct voice. And whenever the voice, this always is accompanied with odors as well as lights; and oft the description of the lights is the vision, see?

Q-How old was Joseph at the time of the marriage?

A-Thirty-six.

Q-How old was Mary at the time of the marriage?

A-Sixteen.

Q-At what time after the birth of Jesus did Mary and Joseph take up the normal life of a married couple, and bring forth the issue James?

A-Ten years. Then they came in succession: James, the daughter, Jude.

Q-Describe the choosing of Mary on the temple steps.

A-The temple steps--or those that led to the altar, these were called the temple steps. These were those upon which the sun shone as it arose of a morning when there were the first periods of the chosen maidens going to the altar for prayer; as well as for the burning of the incense.

On this day, as they mounted the steps all were bathed in the morning sun; which not only made a beautiful picture but clothed all as in purple and gold. As Mary reached the top step, then, there were the thunder and lightning, and the angel led the way, taking the child by the hand before the altar. This was the manner of choice, this was the showing of the way; for she led the others on **this** particular day.

Q-Was this the orthodox Jewish temple or the Essene temple?

A-The Essenes, to be sure.

Q-Where was the wedding performed? of Mary and Joseph?

A-In the temple there at Carmel.

Q-Who were the parents of Joseph?

A-That as recorded by Matthew, as is given, you see; one side recorded by Matthew, the other by Luke--these on various sides but of the house of David, as was also Mary of the house of David. 5749-8

The entity was of that sect or group known as the Essenes, and of those who were of the house of David, but of the kinship little to Joseph or Mary--and yet of those same groups.

The entity was among those (twelve chosen maidens) who saw the vision on the stairs, when the first choice of the maidens was made. The entity knew then of the voice of the unseen forces as were aroused within the groups, that made for the speaking with the unusual tongues; not unknown yet unusual tongues, or the ability to make known their wishes to many in many tongues.   2425-1

The entity was among those that were first chosen, among the twelve maidens that ascended and descended the stairs upon which Mary was chosen. To be sure, the entity was of the Essenes...a kinsman--in the correct (direct?) line of David.   1479-1

(The entity) sought--through the mysteries of the sages--to interpret time and place according to the stars and the numerological effects upon the period in which the entity found material expression...
(The entity) made the choices eventually of the twelve maidens who were to be chosen as channels that might know that truth so thoroughly as to be moved by the Holy Spirit.   2408-1

Q-Please describe the Essene wedding, in temple, of Mary and Joseph, giving the form of ceremony and customs at that time.
A-This followed very closely the forms outlined in Ruth...
Mary having been chosen as the channel by the activities indicated upon the stair, by the hovering of the angel, the enunciation to Anna and Judy and to the rest of those in charge of the preparations at that time,--then there was to be sought out the nearer of kin, though **not** kin in the blood relationships. Thus the lot fell upon Joseph, though he was a much older man compared to the age ordinarily attributed to Mary in the period. Thus there followed the regular ritual in the temple. For, remember, the Jews were not refrained from following their rituals. Those of the other groups, as the Egyptians or the Parthians, were not refrained from following the customs to which they had been trained; which were not carried on in the Jewish temple but rather in the general meeting place of the Essenes.   254-104

The Essenes were a group of individuals sincere in their purpose and not orthodox as to the rabbis of that particular period. 2067-11

The Essenes had the divisions, just as you will find that most churches have their groups and divisions, these were in opposite groups of the Essenes. One held to--that it can happen--the other that God makes it happen. Which comes first, the hen or the egg?   2072-15

Q-Explain the immaculate conception.

A-As flesh is the activity of the mental being (or the spiritual self and mental being) pushing itself into matter, and as spirit--as He gave --is neither male nor female, they are then both--or one.

And when man had reached that period of the full separation from Creative Forces in the spirit, then flesh as man knows it today became in the material plane a reality.

Then, the immaculate conception is the physical and mental so attuned to spirit as to be quickened by same.

Hence the spirit, the soul of the Master then was brought into being through the accord of the Mother in materiality that ye know in the earth as conception.

Q-Was Mary immaculately conceived?

A-Mary was immaculately conceived. 5749-7

Q-Is the teaching of the Roman Catholic Church that Mary was without original sin from the moment of her conception in the womb of Ann, correct?

A-It would be correct in **any** case. Correct more in this...In the beginning Mary was the twin-soul of the Master in the entrance into the earth!...There was no belief in the fact that Ann proclaimed that the child was without father. It's like many proclaiming today that the Master was immaculately conceived; they say "Impossible!" They say that it isn't in compliance with the natural law. It **is** a natural law, as has been indicated by the projection of mind into matter and thus making of itself a separation to become encased in same--as man did.

Then, that there has been an encasement was a beginning. Then there must be an end when this must be broken; and this began at that particular period. Not the only--this particular period with Ann and then the Master **as** the son; but the **only** begotten of the Father in the flesh **as** a son **of** an immaculately conceived daughter!

Q-Neither Mary nor Jesus, then, had a human father?

A-Neither Mary nor Jesus had a human father. They were one **soul** so far as the earth is concerned; because (otherwise) she would not be incarnated in flesh, you see. 5749-8

Q-Was Jesus the natural son of Joseph?

A-...A conception through the Holy Spirit. For the pouring out of the body thy (Ruth, sister of Jesus) **natural** mother, the natural daughter (Ruth, sister of Jesus) of Joseph the Carpenter...There were, there are, there can be such to those who **open** themselves into the Will of the Father-God, that **their** wills are one with His.

And in such even in the earth there comes the natural to be unnatural. For Nature proclaims God, as the unnatural in nature magnifies God...

Souls will evolve into the manner to be able to bring into the world souls, even as Mary did.

And these may come as the souls of men and women become more and more aware that these channels, these temples of the body are **indeed** the temple of the living God and may be used for those communications with God, the Father of souls of men.   1158-5

Q-Please give information concerning the immaculate conception.

A-As the spirit was made manifest in the body purified by consecration of purpose in the lives manifested in the earth, so might the spirit--with the brooding of the body itself--bring to the organs of flesh a body through which the spirit may itself manifest in the earth.

Remember those forms which have been given. First, He was created--brought into being from all that there was in the earth, as an encasement for the soul of the entity, a part of the Creator; knowing separation in death. Then He was made manifest in birth through the union of channels growing out of that thought of the Creator made manifest, but so expressed, so manifested as Enoch as to merit the escaping of death--which had been the result as the law of disobedience. He was made manifest in Melchizedek by desire alone, not knowing mind,--save its own; brought into being in materialization as of itself; passing from materialization in the same manner. Then there was perfected that period again in **body** when the other soul or portion of self was made manifest by the consecration of the mother; meeting then self by that same quickening power as had been made manifest in the beginning--or at first. Hence the cycle. Hence the circle. Hence the emblem of same becomes as the channel through which such takes its form, its expression, its symbol.   2072-4

As ye take hold of the thought of God, of the Christ-Consciousness, of the Way, it may be just as active and just as pregnant with life itself as may a body within thine own body.   2823-1

(The immaculate conception has) much more to do with the mental and spiritual aspects than the physical; though the body should be near to perfect coordination physically for such to be consummated in a body, and high mental and spiritual aspirations, desires and purposes. 2072-3

Mary had fulfilled all things that God had required of her and later fulfilled her physical karma by bearing three other children by Man. In bringing perfection by balancing the spiritual, mental and physical in her own activities she made it possible for all women to have that opportunity. The chains of transgression, slipped from all womenkind, and from that day forward they have been a guiding influence in the civilizations of the world.   1904-2

As the record is given, that is the common knowledge of most, there was born in Bethlehem of Judea that entity, that soul, Jesus...who becomes the Christ, the Master of Masters.   5749-7

The arrival was in the evening--not as counted from the Roman time, nor that declared to Moses by God when the Second Passover was to be kept, nor that same time which was in common usage even in that land, but what would **now** represent January sixth...

Under the hill, in the stable--above which the shepherds were gathering their flocks into the fold...the Savior, the Child was born; who, through the will and the life manifested, became the Savior of the world --that channel through which those of old had been told that the promise would be fulfilled that was made to **Eve**; the arising again of another like unto Moses; and as given to David, the promise was not to depart from that channel. But lower and lower man's concept of needs had fallen.

Then--when hope seemed gone--the herald angels sang. The star appeared, that made the wonderment to the shepherds, that caused the awe and consternation to all of those about the Inn...

All were in awe as the brightness of His star appeared and shone, as the music of the sphere brought that joyful choir, **"Peace on earth! Good will to men of good faith."** All felt the vibrations and saw a great light...

Just as the midnight hour came, there was the birth of the Master.   5749-15

Q-When was He born?
A-On the 19th day of what would now be termed March.
Q-And the year?
A-Dependent upon from what calendar or from what period ye would judge. From the Julian calendar, the year 4. From the Hebrew or the Mosaic calendar, the year 1899.   587-6

Q-In one Reading we are told Jesus' birthday was on March 19 according as we would reckon time now. In another Reading (5749-8) we were told that we keep Christmas about the right time, the 24th or 25th of December as we have our time now. Please explain seeming contradiction.

A-Both are correct according to the time from which same were reckoned. How many times have there been the reckonings? Take these in consideration, with the period of events being followed in the information indicated. Just as there was the reckoning from the various groups for their individual activity, so was the information given as to the records from that source with which those seeking were concerned.   2067-7

The entity had much to do in aiding those in the church, first in those about the Essene associations in Carmel, where such data began to be set--as from the birth. Hence A.D. and B.C. were begun...

And as we find there may be an activity of the entity in the present from those experiences, of judging not only as to relationships of groups or classes or masses but as to special character of data as related to the cycle of experiences as to the rise and fall not only of countries but of nations--and the activities as related one to another.   1486-1

(The entity was the Innkeeper) who was of the Essenes, though of Jewish descent, though a combination of Jewish and the Grecian.

For the entity then made a study of those peoples, knew of those things that had been foretold by the teachers of the Essenes, and made all preparations as near in keeping with what had been foretold as possible...

The entity did this (turned the Holy Family away) rather for protection, than because--as has been said--there was "no room in the Inn." 1196-2

Just before the sun in all its glory of the Palestine hills gave forth almost into the voice of nature, proclaiming the heralding of a new hope, a new birth to the earth, and the glorifying of man's hope in God--the spectre of His Star in the evening sky brought awe and wonder to all that beheld...

The brightness of His Star came nearer and nearer...The light as from His Star filled the place, the entity then first beheld the Babe.

Oft the entity in the stillness of the evening reviewed the happenings, and there was the seeking more and more as to what had become of His Star, His Light.

Q-How long did the holy family remain in Bethlehem?

A-Until the time of purification was passed. Twenty-nine days, as ye would count suns today.   1152-3

THE THREE WISE MEN

Q-Explain the relationship of the Wise Men and Jesus' birth?

A-As indicated by the travels of the Master during the periods of preparation, the whole earth, the whole world looked for, sought the closer understanding. Hence through the efforts of the students of the various phases of experiences of man in the earth, as may be literally interpreted from the first chapters of Genesis, ye find that those that subdued --not that were ruled by, but subdued the understandings of that in the earth--were considered, or were in the position of the wise, or the sages, or the ones that were holy; in body and mind, in accord with purposes.

Hence we find the Wise Men as those that were seekers for the truth, for this happening; and in and through the application of those forces

--as ye would termed today psychic--we find them coming to the place "where the child was"...

They represent in the metaphysical sense the three phases of man's experience in materiality; gold, the material; frankincense, the ether or ethereal; myrrh, the healing force as brought with same; or body, mind, soul.

These were the positions then of the Wise Men in their relationship, or to put into the parlance of the day--they were the encouragement needed for the Mother and those that had nourished, that had cherished this event in the experience of mankind.

They came during the days of purification, but to be sure only after she was purified were they presented to the Child.

Q-What relation did they have with the later travels of Jesus?

A-As has just been indicated, they represented then the three phases of man's experience as well as the three phases of the teacher from Egypt, from Persia, from India.   5749-7

In those periods that preceded the advent of the Prince of Peace in the earth, we find the entity was among those of the land that would now be called the Persian,--as a wise man, a counselor, a sage, that counseled with those peoples; using the mathematical activities of the ages old, as well as the teachings of the Persians from the days of Zend and Og and Uhjltd, bringing for those peoples a better interpretation of the astrological as well as the natural laws.

Hence we find the entity was associated oft with those who looked for the day, the hour when the **Great Purpose**, that event, was to be in the earth a literal experience.   1908-1

The entity was among those who were of the Wise Men coming into Jerusalem and to Bethlehem when the Master came into the earth...The entity gained through this period in pointing out that through the various forces necessary to keep the balance in the universal forces, the earth must bring forth that that would make man's balance of force with the Creative Energy as one, and the Son of Man appeared. The entity brought the frankincense and gave same to the Master at that period...

Become the astrologer for the Association's (of National Investigators, Inc.) membership! giving to these the weeks, the years, and that that influences without respect of will; or an **interpreter** with same of that information as to how an individual has or has not applied will's forces in the earth's experiences. Also the relationships of the sojourn in the various elements that have to do with the spheres as related to earth's sphere--the variations from one passing through Arcturus to other forces, or returned to Saturn!   256-1

This entity, Josie, was close to Mary when the selection was indicated by the shadow or the angel on the stair, at that period of consecration in the temple. This was not the temple in Jerusalem, but the temple where those who were consecrated worshiped, or a school--as it might be termed--for those who might be channels.

This was a part of that group of Essenes who, headed by Judy, made those interpretations of those activities from the Egyptian experience, --as the Temple Beautiful, and the service in the Temple of Sacrifice. Hence it was in this consecrated place where this selection took place.

Then, when there was the fulfilling of those periods when Mary was espoused to Joseph and was to give birth to the Savior, the Messiah, the Prince of Peace, the Way, the Truth, the Light,--soon after this birth there was the issuing of the orders first by Judy that there should be someone selected to be with the parents during their period of sojourn in Egypt. This was owing to the conditions which arose from the visit of the Wise Men and their not returning to Herod to report, when the decrees were issued that there should be the destruction of the children of that age from six months to two years, especially in that region from Bethany to Nazareth.

Thus this entity, Josie, was selected or chosen by those of the Brotherhood,--some times called White Brotherhood in the present,--as the handmaid or companion of Mary, Jesus and Joseph, in their flight into Egypt...

The care and attention to the Child and the Mother was greatly in the hands of this entity, Josie, through that journey.

The period of sojourn in Egypt was in and about, or close to, what was Alexandria.

Josie and Mary were not idle during that period of sojourn, but those records--that had been a part of those activities preserved in portions of the libraries there--were a part of the work that had been designated for this entity. And the interest in same was reported to the Brotherhood in the Judean country.

The sojourn there was a period of some four years,--four years, six months, three days.

When there were those beginnings of the journey back to the Promised Land, there were naturally--from some of the records that had been read by the entity Josie, as well as the parents--the desires to know whether there were those unusual powers indicated in this Child now,--that was in every manner a normal, developed body, ready for those activities of children of that particular period...

The return was made to Capernaum,--not Nazareth,--not only for political reasons owing to the death of Herod but the division that had been made with the kingdom after the death of Herod; and that there might be the ministry or teaching that was to be a part of the Brotherhood,--supervised in that period by Judy, as among the leaders of the Essenes in that particular period.

Hence much of the early education, the early activities, were those prompted or directed by that leader in that particular experience, but were administered by--or in the close associations by--Josie. Though from the idea of the Brotherhood the activities of the entity were no longer necessitated, the entity Josie preferred to remain--and did remain until those periods when there was the sending or the administering of the teachings to the young Master, first in Persia and later in India, and then in Egypt again--where there were the completions.

But the entity, Josie, following the return, was active in all the educational activities as well as in the care of the body and the attending to those things pertaining to the household duties with every developing child.

Q-What association with the entity who is now Cayce did I have in the Palestine experience?

A-The teacher of the Master knew only of Lucius through those activities in Laodicea,--for he came at the time of Pentecost, see?

Q-What was the nature of the records studied by Josie in Egypt?

A-Those same records from which the men of the East said and gave, "By those records we have seen his star." These pertained to astrological forecasts, as well as those records which had been compiled and gathered by all of those of that period pertaining to the coming of the Messiah. These had been part of the records from those in Carmel, in the early experiences, as of those given by Elijah,--who was the fore-runner, who was the cousin, who was the Baptist. All of these had been a part of the records--pertaining not only to the nature of work of the parents but as to their places of sojourn, and the very characteristics that would indicate these individuals; the nature and the character that would be a part of the experiences to those coming in contact with the young Child; as to how the garments worn by the Child would heal children. For the body being perfect radiated that which was health, life itself...

These records were destroyed, of course, in a much later period.

Q-Can any more details be given as to the training of the child?

A-Only those that covered the period from six years to about sixteen, which were in keeping with the tenets of the Brotherhood; as well as that training in the law,--which was the Jewish or Mosaic law...

Remember and keep in mind, He was normal, He developed normally. Those about Him saw those characteristics that may be anyone's who wholly puts the trust in God.   1010-17

Here we may give even portions of the records as scribed by the entity (1472) called Judy, as the teacher, as the healer, as the prophetess through that experience...

That the entity was a daughter, rather than being a male, brought some disturbance, some confusion in the minds of many.

Yet the life, the experiences of the parents had been such that still --fulfilling their promise--they brought the life of their child, Judy, and dedicated it to the study and the application of self to the study of those things that had been handed down as a part of the experiences of those who had received visitations from the unseen, the unknown--or that worshiped as the Divine Spirit moving into the activities of man...

There was the setting about to seek means and manners for the preservation, and for the making of records of that which had been handed down as word of mouth, as tradition...Eventually the manner was chosen in which records were being kept in Egypt rather than in Persia, from which much of the tradition arose--of course--because of the very indwelling of the peoples in that land...

The entity came in contact with the Medes, the Persians, the Indian influence of authority because of the commercial association as well as the influence that had been upon the world by those activities of Saneid and those that were known during the periods of Brahma and Buddha.

These brought to the experience of the entity the weighing of the counsels from the traditions of the Egyptians and of her own kind--and then the new understanding...

The entity, as would be termed, was hounded, yea was persecuted the more and more; yet remaining until what ye would call the sixty-seventh year **after** the Crucifixion; or until time itself began to be counted from same. For the records as were borne by the entity, it will be found, were **begun** by the activities of the entity during what ye would term a period sixty years **after** the Crucifixion.

And then they were reckoned first by the peoples of Carmel, and then by the brethren in Antioch, then a portion of Jerusalem, then to Smyrna, Philadelphia, and those places where these were becoming more active.

Q-How close was my association with Jesus in my Palestine sojourn?

A-A portion of the experience the entity was the teacher!

How close? So close that the very heart and purposes were proclaimed of those things that were traditions! For the entity sent Him to Persia, to Egypt, yea to India, that there might be completed the more perfect knowledge of the material ways in the activities of Him that became the Way, the Truth!   1472-3

Q-Why does so-called sacred history not give a record of me (1472)?

A-Ye were of the Essenes, not of the Jews not even the Samaritans. 1472-6

Q-You will please give at this time an outline of the life and activities of Jesus the Christ from the time of His birth until the beginning of His ministry in Palestine at approximately thirty years of age; giving birth place, training, travels, etc.

A-As seen from the records that were kept then regarding the promises and their fulfilments in many lands, "Thou Bethlehem of Juda (Matthew 2:6)--the birth place of the Great Initiate, the Holy One, the Son of man, the Accepted One of the Father."

During those periods in accordance with those laws and rulings, in the household of the father.

Then in the care and ministry from the period of the visit to Jerusalem, in first India, then Persia, then Egypt; for "My son shall be called from Egypt" (Matthew 2:15).

Then a portion of the sojourn with the forerunner that was first proclaimed in the region about Jordan; and then the return to Capernaum, the city of the beginning of the ministry. Then in Canaan and Galilee.

In the studies that were a portion of the preparation, these included first those that were the foundations of that given as law. Hence from law in the Great Initiate must come love, mercy, peace, that there may be the fulfilling wholly of that purpose to which, of which, He was called.

Q-From what period and how long did He remain in India?

A-From thirteen to sixteen. One year in travel and in Persia; the greater portion being in the Egyptian. In this, the greater part will be seen in the records that are set in the pyramids there; for **here** were the initiates taught.

Q-Outline the teachings which were received in India.

A-Those cleansings of the body as related to preparation for strength in the physical, as well as in the mental man. In the travels and in Persia, the unison of forces as related to those teachings of that given in those of Zu and Ra. In Egypt, that which had been the basis of all the teachings in those of the temple, and the after actions of the crucifying of self in relationships to ideals that make for the abilities of carrying on that called to be done.

Q-In which pyramid are the records of the Christ?

A-That yet to be uncovered.

Q-Are there written records which have not been found of the teachings?

A-More, rather, of those of the close associates, and those records that are yet to be found of the preparation of the man, of the Christ, in those of the tomb, or those yet to be uncovered in the pyramid.

Q-When will this chance be given for these to be uncovered?

A-When there has been sufficient of the reckoning through which the world is passing in the present. Thirty-six--thirty-eight--forty.   5749-2

Q-Please give facts about Jesus' education in Palestine, the schools He attended, how long, what He studied, under what name He was registered.

A-The periods of study in Palestine were only at the time of His sojourn in the temple, or in Jerusalem during those periods when He was quoted by Luke as being among the rabbi or teachers. His studies in Persia, India and Egypt covered much greater periods. He was always registered under the name Jeshua.

Q-Please describe Jesus' education in India, schools attended--did He attend the Essene school in Jagannath taught by Lamaas, and did He study in Benares also under the Hindu teacher Udraka?

A-He was there at least three years. Arcahia was the teacher...

These were not the true Essene doctrine as practiced by the Jewish and semi-Jewish associations in Carmel.

Q-Please describe Jesus' education in Egypt in Essene schools of Alexandria and Heliopolis.

A-Not in Alexandria,--rather in Heliopolis, for the periods of attaining to the priesthood, or the taking of the examinations there--as did John. One was in one class, one in the other.

Q-Please describe Jesus' contact with schools in Persia, and did He at Persepolis establish a method of entering the Silence as well as demonstrating healing Power?

A-Rather that was a portion of the activity in the "city in the hills and the plains."

Q-Name some of His outstanding teachers and subjects studied.

A-Not as teachers, but as being **examined** by these; passing the tests there. These, as they have been since their establishing, were tests through which ones attained to that place of being accepted or rejected by the influences of the mystics as well as of the various groups or schools in other lands. For, as indicated oft through this channel, the unifying of the teachings of many lands was brought together in Egypt; for that was the center from which there was to be the radial activity of influence in the earth,--as indicated by the first establishing of those tests, or the recording of time as it has been, was and is to be--until the new cycle is begun.

Q-Why does not the Bible tell of Jesus' education, or are there manuscripts now on earth that will give these missing details?

A-There are some that have been forged manuscripts. All of those that existed were destroyed,--that is, the originals--with the activities in Alexandria.

Q-When did the knowledge come to Jesus that he was to be the Savior of the world?

A-When he fell in Eden.

Q-Did Jesus study under Apollo and other Greek philosophers?

A-...Jesus, as Jesus, never appealed to the worldly-wise.

Q-Please describe Jesus' initiations in Egypt, telling if the Gospel reference to "three days and nights in the grave or tomb (Matthew 12:40)," possibly in the shape of a cross, indicated a special initiation.

A-This is a portion of the initiation,--it is a part of the passage through that to which each soul is to attain in its development, as has the world through each period of their incarnation in the earth. As is supposed, the record of the earth through the passage through the tomb, or the pyramid, is that through which each entity, each soul, as an initiate must pass for the attaining to the releasing of same,--as indicated by the empty tomb, which has **never** been filled, see? Only Jesus was able to break same, as it became that which indicated His fulfilment.

And there, as the initiate, He went out,--for the passing through the initiation, by fulfilling--as indicated in the baptism in the Jordan; not standing in it and being poured or sprinkled either! as He passed from that activity into the wilderness to meet that which had been His undoing in the beginning.

Q-Why do historians like Josephus ignore the massacre of the infants, and the history of Christ?

A-What was the purpose of Josephus' writing? For the Jews or for the Christians? This answers itself!   2067-7

John was more the Essene than Jesus. Jesus held rather to the spirit of the law and John to the letter of same...

Q-Tell about Judy teaching Jesus, where and what subjects she taught Him, and what subjects she planned to have Him study abroad.

A-The prophecies! Where? In her home. When? during those periods from his twelfth to his fifteenth-sixteenth year, when He went to Persia and then to India. In Persia, when His father died. In India when John went first to Egypt, where Jesus joined him and both became the initiates in the pyramid or temple there.

Q-What subjects did Judy plan to have Him study abroad?

A-What you would today call astrology.

Q-Was Judy present at the Crucifixion or the Resurrection?

A-No. In spirit--that is, in mind--present. For, remember, Judy's experience at that time was such that she might be present in many places without the physical body being there!   2067-11

There recently has been uncovered in the Ethiopian land the **records** made by this entity of the teachings of Philip and of Simon in that land. For, these are among the purest records; for they were written not only on the papyrus that is of the better character but in the Ethiopian land it still remains intact, this experience of the entity meeting Philip and as to what were the words and teaching of Jesus of Nazareth.

If the entity in this experience will hold these as the basis, as the standards, as the principles, with all the studies, all the delving into the mysteries of nature, the mysteries of how certain chants, incantations and intimations bring the arising of the influences in the experience of bodies of others as well as in self, if they are grounded in Him, greater may be the blessings and the material gains, and--most of all--the soul development in this experience. 315-4

THE LORD'S SUPPER AND JESUS' PHYSICAL LOOKS

The Lord's Supper--here with the Master--see what they had for supper --boiled fish, rice, with leeks, wine, and loaf. One of the pitchers in which it was served was broken. The handle was broken, as was the lip.

The whole robe of the Master was not white, but pearl gray--all combined into one--the gift of Nicodemus to the Lord.

The better looking of the twelve was Judas, while the younger was John --oval face, dark hair, smooth face--only one with the short hair. Peter, the rough and ready, always that of very short beard, rough, and not altogether clean; while Andrew's is just the opposite--very sparse, but inclined to be long more on the side and under the chin--long on the upper lip--his robe was always near gray or black, while his clouts or breeches were striped; while those of Philip and Bartholomew were red and brown.

The Master's hair is 'most red', inclined to be curly in portions, yet not feminine or weak--**strong**, with heavy piercing eyes that are blue or steel-gray

His weight would be at least a hundred and seventy pounds. Long tapering fingers, nails well kept. Long nail, though, on the left finger.

Merry--even in the hour of trial. Joke--even in the moment of betrayal.

The sack is empty. Judas departs.

The last is given of the wine and loaf, with which He gives the emblems that should be so dear to every follower of Him. Lays aside His robe, which is all of one piece--girds the towel about His waist, which is dressed with Linen that is blue and white. Rolls back the folds, kneels first before John, James, then to Peter--who refuses.

Then the dissertation as to "He that would be the greatest would be servant of all" (Luke 22:26).

The basin is taken as without handle, and is made of wood. The water is from the gherkins, that are in the wide-mouth shibboleths that stand in the house of John's father, Zebedee.

And now comes "It is finished" (John 19:30).

They sing the ninety-first Psalm--"He that dwelleth in the secret place of the Most High shall abide under the shadow of the Almighty. I will say of the Lord, He is my refuge and my fortress; my God; in Him will I trust."

He is the musician as well, for He uses the harp.

They leave the garden.   5749-1

A vision of the Master as might be put on canvas if the entity were to attempt to do so and be entirely different from all these which have been depicted of the face, the body, the eyes, the cut of the chin and the lack entirely of the Jewish or Aryan profile. For these were clear, clean, ruddy, hair almost like that of David, a golden brown, yellow-red, but blue eyes which were piercing; and the beard, not cut, but kept in the proportion at the contour of the face, and the head almost perfect.   5354-1

JESUS' BETRAYAL, TRIAL AND CRUCIFIXION

Q-Was Judas Iscariot's idea in betraying Jesus to force Him to assert Himself as a king and bring in His kingdom then?

A-Rather the desire of the man to force same, and the fulfilling of that as Jesus spoke of same at the Supper.   2067-7

When this man, this prophet, this master, was presented to those in authority for civil consideration; **claiming** by the ones in authority that there had been a neglect to pay tribute, or that there had been first that attempt upon the part of those that were as the followers of same to prevent the tax, the levies to be paid. **This** was the manner of presentation rather than much of that as ye have recorded even in Holy Writ. 1151-3

The trial--that was not with the pangs of pain, as oft indicated but rather glorying in the opportunity of taking upon self that which would **right** man's relationship to the Father--in that man, through his free will, had brought sin into the activities of the children of God. Here **His Son** was bringing redemption through the shedding of blood that they might be free.   5749-10

So that those who...beheld (the crucifixion), might know that they--themselves--must pass along that road, **crucifying** in their bodies that which would make for the gratifying of desires, that which would make for an exaltation of self rather than those tenets as He gave: "The new commandment I give, that ye love one another" (John 13:34).   897-1

How, why, was there the need for there to be a resurrection? Why came He into the earth to die the death, even on the Cross? Has it been then, the fulfilment of promise, the fulfilment of law, the fulfilment of man's estate? Else why did He put on flesh and come into the earth in the form of man, but to be one with the Father; to show to man **his** (man's) divinity, man's relationship to the Maker...

Then, though He were the first of man, the first of the sons of God in spirit, in flesh, it became necessary that he fulfil **all** those associations, those connections that were to wipe away in the experience of man that which separates him from his Maker.

Though man be far afield, then, though he may have erred, there is established that which makes for a closer, closer walk **with** Him, through that one who experienced all those turmoils, strifes, desires, urges that may be the lot of man in the earth...

Yea, as He gave his physical blood that doubt and fear might be banished, so He overcame death; not only in the physical body but in the **spirit** body--that it may become as **one** with Him, even as on that resurrection morn--that ye call thy Eastertide.

It is that breaking forth from the tomb, as exemplified in the bulb of the tree of nature itself breaking forth from the sleep that it may rise as He with healing in its very life, to bring all phases of man's experience to His Consciousness--that indeed became then the fulfilling of the law.

On what wise, then, ye ask, did this happen in materiality? Not only was He dead in body, but the soul was separated from that body. As all phases of man in the earth are made manifest, the physical body, the mental body, the soul body became as each dependent upon their own experience. Is it any wonder that the man cried, "My God, my God, **why** hast thou forsaken me?" (Matthew 27:46)   5749-6

Why did He (say), "Father, why hast thou forsaken me?" Even when the world was being overcome, the flesh continued to rebel.   281-3

When the Prince of Peace came into the earth for the completing of His **own** development in the earth, **He** overcame the flesh **and** temptation. So He became the first of those that overcame death in the body enabling Him to so illuminate, to so revivify that body as to take it up again, even when those fluids of the body had been drained away by the nail holes in His hand and by the spear piercing His side.

Yet this body, this entity, too, may do these things; through those promises that were so new yet so old, as given by Him. "Not of myself do I these things" (John 8:28), saith He, "but God, the Father that worketh in me; for I come from Him, I go to Him."

He came, the Master, in flesh and blood, even as thou didst come in flesh and blood. Yet as He proclaimed to thee, there is a cleansing of the body, of the flesh, of the blood, in such measures that it may become illumined with power from on high; that is **within** thine own body to **will!** "Thy will, O God; not mine, but Thine, be done in me, through me."

This was the message as He gave when He, too, overcame; surrendering all power unto Power itself, surrendering all will unto the will of the Father; making of self then a channel through which others taking hope through the knowledge that He hath perfected Himself, may bring to thee that grace, that mercy, that is eternity with Him and in Him.   1152-1

As in Adam all die, so in Christ all is made alive.

As to the conception of the resurrection, there are many presentations in the physical world of man's concept of same, for, as we find, to understand the resurrection, we must gain a concept of how the spirit force entered into the body and man became a living soul; for we begin first as this:

The earth and the universe, as related to man, came into being through the **Mind--Mind--**of the Maker...Man entered as man, through the **Mind** of the Maker, see? in the form of flesh **man**; that which carnally might die, decay, become dust, entering into material conditions. The Spirit the gift of God, that man might be One with Him, with the concept of man's creative forces throughout the physical world. Man, in Adam (as a group; not as an individual), entered into the world (for he entered in five places at once, we see--called Adam in one, see?), and as man's concept became to that point wherein man walked not after the ways of the Spirit but after the desires of the flesh **sin** entered--that is, away from the Face of the Maker, see? and death then became man's portion, **spiritually**, see? for the physical death existed from the beginning; for to create one must die, see?

In this, then, there is seen, as the body, in the flesh, of the Christ, became perfect in the flesh, in the world, and the body laid aside on the Cross, in the tomb, the **physical** body moved away, through that as **man** will know as dimensions, and the Spirit able then to take hold of that Being in the way as it enters again into the body, and as it presents itself to the world, to individuals at the time and to man at present.   900-227

Death hath no sting, no power over those that know the Resurrection... The Resurrection brought to the consciousness of man that power that God hath given to man, that may reconstruct, resuscitate, even every atom of a physically sick body, that may resurrect even every atom of a sin-sick soul, may resurrect the soul that it lives on and on in the glory of a resurrected, a regenerated Christ in the souls and hearts of men. 1158-5

Through that power, that ability, that love as manifested in Himself among His fellow men He broke the bonds of death; proclaiming in that act that **there is no death** when the individual, the soul, has and does put its trust in Him.   5749-13

Q-Explain what is meant by the first and second resurrection?
A-The first is of those who have not tasted death in the sense of the dread of same. The second is of those who have **gained** the understanding that in Him there **is** no death.   281-37

Q-What is meant by the resurrection of the body? What Body?
A-That body thou hast taken in thine individuality to draw upon, from matter itself, to give it shadow or form, see?...
Hence with what body shall ye be raised?
That same Body ye had from the beginning! or the same Body that has been thine throughout the ages! else how could it be individual?
The **physical**, the dust, dissolves; yes. But when it is condensed again, what is it? The **same** Body! It doesn't beget a different body!   262-86

For the law is, "In the day ye eat thereof, ye partake thereof, ye shall surely die" (Genesis 2:17)...
By one man sin came into God's creation. by one man death came. By that same man death was overcome.   2784-1

JESUS IS THE PATTERN, CHRIST IS THE POWER

The Christ Child was born into the earth as man; one born in due time, in man's spiritual evolution, that man might have a pattern of the personality of God Himself.   5758-1

Some individuals like to have their own way, irrespective of what anyone thinks. So does the mind if you train the body-mind to accept or reject certain conditions in your experience. These will never accept other suggestions unless the mental self is changed.
Thus it became necessary that God in His goodness give an example, a pattern, by which man might conduct his life, his ideals, his hopes, his fears, all of his idiosyncrasies.   5211-1

For as He, thy Master, thy Lord, thy Christ fulfilled the law by compliance with same, He became the law and thus thy Savior, thy Brother, thy Christ. For in Him ye find, ye see the example that is set before thee pertaining to the natural life, the mental life, the material life, the spiritual life. Not an extremist, and not a conservative--but one who met each experience in a manner in which there was **never** a question in His Consciousness as to its purpose, His desire and the ability to be one with the purpose of the Creative Force--God.   1662-1

An entity, then, is the pattern of divinity in materiality, or in the earth. As man found himself out of touch with that complete consciousness of the oneness of God, it became necessary that the will of God, the Father, be made manifested, that a pattern be introduced into man's consciousness. Thus the son of man came into the earth, made in the form, the likeness of man; with body, mind, soul. Yet the soul was the Son, the soul was the Light.   3357-2

Q-What is the significance and meaning of the words "Jesus" and "Christ" as they should be understood and applied?

A-...Jesus is the man--the activity, the mind, the relationships that He bore to others. Yea, He was mindful of friends, He was sociable, He was loving, He was kind, He was gentle, He grew faint, He grew weak--and yet gained that strength that He has promised, in becoming the Christ, by fulfilling and overcoming the world. Ye are made strong --in body, in mind, in soul and purpose--by the power in Christ. The **power** then, is the Christ. The **pattern** is in Jesus.   2533-7

All power in Heaven, in the earth, is given to Him who overcame. Hence He is of Himself in space, in the force that impels through faith, through belief, in the individual entity. As a Spirit Entity. Hence not in a body in the earth, but may come at will to him who **wills** to be one with, and acts in love to make same possible. 5749-4

All power hath been given unto Him. For He **alone** hath overcome.   954-5

Know that even as the Christ, even as the Jesus--had He withered the hands of those that smote Him because it was in His power, He could **not** be, He would **not** be, thy Christ, thy Savior, thy Lord!   1440-2

Christ (is) the universal consciousness of love that we see manifested in those who have forgotten self, **as** Jesus, give themselves that others may know the truth.   1376-1

There has also come a teacher who was bold enough to declare himself as the son of the Living God. he set no rules of appetite. He set no rules of ethics, other than, "As ye would that men should do to you, do ye even so to them" (Matthew 7:12), and to know "Inasmuch as ye do it unto the least of these, by brethren, ye do it unto thy Maker" (Matthew 25:40), He declared that the kingdom of heaven is within each individual entity's consciousness, to be attained, to be aware of--through meditating upon the fact that God is the Father of every soul.   357-13

In that the man, Jesus, became the example of the flesh, manifest in the world, and the will one with the Father, he became the first to manifest same in the material world. Thus, from man's viewpoint, becoming the only, the first, the begotten of the Father, and the example to the world, whether Jew, Gentile, or of any other religious forces. In this we find the true advocate with the Father, in that he, as man, manifest in the flesh the ability of flesh to make fleshly desires one with the will of the spirit...and in this we find he takes on all law, and a law unto himself, for with the compliance, of even an earthly or material law, such a person **is** the law, and in that Jesus lived as man, and died as man, and in that became the example to all who **would** approach the throne of God.   900-17

He came into the earth that we, as soul-entities, might know ourselves to be ourselves, and yet one with Him; as He, the Master, the Christ, knew Himself and yet one with the Father.   3003-1

In the life, then, of Jesus we find the oneness made manifest through the ability to overcome all of the temptations of the flesh, and the desires of same, through making the **will one with the Father**...Man, through the same channel, may reach that perfection, even higher than the angel, though he attend the God.   900-16

Unless each individual put away those selfish desires which arise and becomes as little children, one may never quite understand the simplicity of Christs faith; Christ-like faith, Christ-like simplicity, Christ-like forgiveness, Christ-like love, Christ-like helpfulness to others. 1223-9

For even in Elijah or John we find the faltering, the doubting. We find no faltering, no doubting, no putting aside of the purpose in the Master Jesus.   3054-4

As the sons of God came together and saw in the earth the unspeakable conditions becoming more and more for the self-indulgence, self glorification, the ability to procreate through the very forces of their activity, we find our Lord, our Brother **chose** to measure up, to earn, to **attain** that companionship for man with the Father through the overcoming of **self** in the physical plane.   262-115

It was not in the separation as John, not in the running away as Elijah, not as in sitting in high places as Isaiah, not as in that form of Jeremiah--morning; not in that lording as Moses--but **all things unto all men!** reaching them in their own plan of experience; and not with long-facedness.

For as He--He wined, He dined with the rich, He consorted with the poor, he entered the temple on state occasions; yea He slept in the field with the shepherds, yea He walked by the seashore with the throngs, He preached to those in the mount--**all things**; and yet ever ready to present the tenets, the truths, even in those forms of tales, yea parables, yea activities that took hold upon the **lives of men and women** in **every** walk of human experience.   1472-3

(Man) has an advocate **with** the Father through Him that gave Himself as a ransom. How? For, as the impulses in self arise, know those impulses have arisen in Him; yet through the ability to overcome death in the material world is His presence able to abide with thee.   524-2

In the beginning He was the Son--made the Son--those of the Sons that went astray; and through the varying activities overcame the world through the **experiences, bearing** the cross in each and every experience, reaching the **final** cross with **all** power, **all** knowledge in having overcome the world, and of Himself **accepted** the Cross. Hence doing away with that often termed karma, that must be met by all. The immutable law of cause and effect is, as evidenced in the world today, in the material, the mental and spiritual world; but He--in overcoming the world, the law--became the law. The law, then becomes as the school-master, or the school of training, and we who have **named** the Name then, are no longer **under** the law as law, but under mercy as in Him.   262-36

Q-What part did Jesus play in any of His reincarnations in the development of the basic teachings of Mohammedanism, Confucianism, Shintoism, Brahminism, Platonism, Judaism?
A-As has been indicated, the entity--as an entity--influenced either directly or indirectly all those forms of philosophy or religious thought that taught God was One..."Know, O Israel, the Lord thy god is **One!**" (Deuteronomy 6:4) whether this is directing one of the Confucian thought, Brahmin thought, Buddha thought, Mohammedan thought; these are as teachers or representatives...but it's **God** that gives the increase...
What are the commandments? "Thou shalt have no other **God** before me," and "Love thy neighbor as thyself." In this is builded the whole **law** and gospel of every age that has said, "There is **One** God."364-9

Q-Please explain how we may distinguish between the terms, especially pronouns, referring to the personality Jesus and God as used in this information, and how we may clarify this in terms we use in our lessons.
A-As their activities and personalities are one, in the activities of men often the pronoun used becomes confusing. Follow rather closely in that which has been given. It is used the same as **He** gave; Him refers to the Father, He to the Son...Those that would prefer good English, Him is rather inclusive while He is definite--or the one Son.   262-33

Q-Should the Christ Consciousness be described as the awareness within each soul, imprinted in pattern on the mind and waiting to be awakened by the will, of the soul's oneness with God?

A-Correct. That's the idea exactly.   5749-14

The Christ Consciousness is a Universal Consciousness of the Father Spirit. The Jesus Consciousness is that man builds as body worship.

In the Christ Consciousness, then, there is the oneness of self, self's desires, self's abilities made in at-onement with the forces that may bring to pass that which is sought by an individual entity.   5749-4

Q-Please explain clearly the difference between the Christ Consciousness, The Christ Spirit.

A-As the difference might be given in that which makes for the birth in the flower, and the flower. The consciousness of the Spirit and the abilities to apply same are the differences in the Christ Consciousness, the Christ Spirit...Those with the abilities to call upon, to be so unselfish as to allow the Spirit to operate in self's stead, are aware of the Spirit's activity, while those that may be conscious or aware of a truth may not wholly make it their own without that which has been given, "He that would have life must give life" (Matthew 10:39); for **He** thought it not robbery to be equal with the Father, yet of Himself did nothing, "but the Father that worketh in me, through me"...

The Christ Consciousness is the Holy Spirit, or that as the promise of His presence making aware of His activity in the earth. The Spirit is as the Christ in action with the Spirit of the Father.   262-29

It is ever those that draw nearer to the Universal Consciousness of the Christ that come closer to the perfect relationship to the Creative Forces or God, the Father--which the man Jesus attained when He gave of Himself to the World, that through Him, by and in Him, each entity might come to know the true relationship with the Father. 3357-2

Know that as ye are body, mind and soul, some portion of this Trinity evidently is a part of a Universal Consciousness; or is accustomed to being, or may be acquainted with being on speaking terms even with that which is a Universal Consciousness.   954-5

(Cosmic Consciousness is found) by the opening of those channels within the physical body through which the energies of the Infinite are attuned to the centers through which physical consciousness, mental activity, is attained,--or in deep meditation.   2109-2

One sees the infinite in the **Christ** life, one sees infinity in man's life.   1158-14

Q-With whose spirit, mentioned in the Apostles' Creed, would we commune; with ourselves or God's?

A-Within ourselves to God. For, as intimated elsewhere, "My spirit beareth witness with thy spirit" (Romans 8:16). Whose spirit? There is only **one** Spirit--of truth. there may be divisions, as there may be many drops of water in the ocean yet they are all of the ocean. Separated, they are named for those activities in various spheres of experiences that are sought to be expressed here. The communion of the spirit of the divine within self may be with the source of divinity. This is what is meant by the communion of saints, of those that are of one thought; for all thought for activity emanates from the same source and there is the natural communion of these who are in that thought.   262-87

The soul being a part or a shadow of the real spiritual self, it controls or rules the universe rather than being ruled by same. But, they that have entirely put on a consciousness are ruled by same. Hence, as each individual entity accepts and lives by this or that awareness, or consciousness, it gives power and spirit to same.

Thus is each soul, each entity, a co-creator with the Universal Consciousness ye call God.   2246-1

The greater soul development that may be for any soul is to be less and less self, less and less with any **material** desire, but more and more in accord with the Christ, the Holy One, the Life, the Manifestation of all those things that have been said to be so impractical as related to materiality; yet they are the **real**, the **true** things in the experiences of every soul.   410-2

Would that all would learn that He, the Christ Consciousness, is the Giver, the Maker, the Creator of the world and all that be therein...

He is at the right hand, **is** the right hand, **is** the intercessor for ye all. Hence thy destinies lie in Him...

He **IS**, He **WAS**, He **EVER WILL BE** the expression, the **concrete** expression of **LOVE** in the minds, the hearts, the souls of men.   696-3

Know that as the Mind is represented by the Christ Consciousness, it is the Builder, it is the Way, it is the Truth, it is the Light; that is, through the manner in which the Mind is held. Not that it denies, not that it rejects, but that it is **made** as one with the purposes He, thy Lord, thy Christ, thy God, thy holy self, would have it be.   1348-1

No influence without or within may be of a detrimental force to self; so long as self will surround self with the thought and the ability of the Christ Consciousness, and then practice same in its dealings with its fellow man.   2081-2

Q-Give meaning and pronunciation of the word J-A-H-H-E-V-A-H-E.
A-Java; meaning the ability within itself to know itself to be itself and yet one with, or one apart from, the infinite; to be a part of that realm of helpers; to know self as a part of and in the realm where the angels are, or in that realm of the individuals who have been, who are, with the Announcer, the Lord of the Way, and who have attained the consciousness of the Christ--within.   2533-8

(Hold) to the Law of One as manifested in the man Jesus, as signified in the Christ-Consciousness. (Please gain the difference of these!) 1010-12

He, that Christ Consciousness, is the first spoken of in the beginning when said, "Let there be light, and there was light" (Genesis 1:3). And that light manifested in the Christ. First it became physically conscious in Adam. And as in Adam we all die, so in the last Adam --Jesus, becoming the Christ--we are all made alive. Not unto that as of one, then. For we each meet our own selves, even as He; though this did not become possible, practical in a world experience, until He, Jesus became the Christ and made the way. Thus He became the first of those that within self arose to righteousness.   2879-1

In the beginning: God moved and said, "Let there be light," and there was light; not the light of the sun, but rather that of which, through which, in which, every soul had, has, and ever has its being. For in truth ye live and move and have thy being in Him (Acts 17:28).   5246-1

Do study creation, man's relationship to God. What is light, that came into the earth, as described in the third verse of Genesis one? Find that light in self. It isn't the light of the noon day sun, nor the moon, but rather of the Son of Man.   3491-1

The **Spirit** moved--or soul moved--and there was Light (Mind). The Light became the light of men--Mind made aware of conscious existence in spiritual aspects or relationships as one to another.   1947-3

In **Him** is the light, and the light came among men, showing men the way to find that consciousness in **self**--for the **kingdom** is of within, and when self is made one **with** those forces there may be the accord. 1741-1

"Let there be light," then was that consciousness that time began to be a factor in the experience of those creatures that had entangled themselves in matter; and became what we know as the influences in a material plane. And the moving force and the life in each, and the activities in each are the Spirit. Hence as we see, the divisions were given then for the day, the night; and then man knew that consciousness that made him aware that the morning and the evening were the first day.   262-115

Q-You will have before you Edgar Cayce, present in this room, and his enquiring mind in relation to the talk which he expects to give next Monday evening on the "Second Coming." You will give that he should present at this open meeting on this subject.

A-...Here today, in what ye call time, ye find them (discarnate entities that have preached concerning this Second Coming) gathering to **listen** to that as may be given them by one (Edgar Cayce?) who is to be forerunner of that influence in the earth known as the Christ Consciousness, the coming of that force or power into the earth that has been spoken of through the ages...

He has come in all ages when it has been necessary for the understanding to be centered in a **new** application of the same thought, "God **is** Spirit and seeks such to worship him in spirit and in truth!"

Then, as there is prepared the way by those that have made and do make the channels for the entering in, there may come into the earth those influences that will save, regenerate, resuscitate, **hold**--if you please--the earth in its continued activity toward the proper understanding and proper relationships to that which is the making for the closer relationships to that which is in Him **alone**. Ye have seen it in Adam; ye have heard it in Enoch, ye have had it made known in Melchizedek; Joshua, Joseph, David, and those that made the preparation then for him called Jesus. Ye have seen His Spirit in the leaders in all realms of activity, whether in the isles of the sea, the wilderness, the mountain, or in the various activities of every race, every color, every activity of that which has produced and does produce contention in the minds and hearts of those that dwell in the flesh.

For, what must be obliterated? Hate, prejudice, selfishness, backbiting, unkindness, anger, passion, and those things of the mire that are created in the activities of the sons of men.

Then again He may come in body to claim His own. Is He abroad today in the earth? Yea, in those that cry unto Him from every corner; for He, the Father, hath not suffered His soul to see corruption; neither hath it taken hold on those things that make the soul afraid. For, He is the Son of Light, of God, and is holy before Him. And He comes again in the hearts and souls and minds of those that seek to know His ways. 5749-5

Time never was when there was not a Christ and not a Christ mass...

(There) is in **every** birth--the possibilities, the glories, the actuating of that influence of that entrance again of god-man into the earth...

Know this had no beginning in the 1900 years ago, but again and Again and **Again!** And it may be today, He may be born into the consciousness; not as a physical birth--but each moment that a physical birth is experienced...is an **opportunity** for the Christ-entrance again. 262-103

He shall come as ye have seen Him go, in the **body** He occupied in Galilee. The Body that He formed, that was crucified on the Cross, that rose from the tomb, that walked by the sea, that appeared to Simon, that appeared to Philip, that appeared to "I, even John."

Q-When Jesus the Christ comes the second time, will He set up His kingdom on earth and will it be an everlasting kingdom?

A-Read His promises in that ye have written of His words, even as "I gave." He shall rule for a thousand years. Then shall Satan be loosed again for a season (Revelation 20:1-6).　　　　　5749-4

Having overcome He shall appear even **as** the Lord **and** Master. Not as one born, but as one that returneth to his own, for He will walk and talk with men of every clime, and those that are faithful and just in their reckoning shall be caught up with Him to rule and to do **judgement** for a thousand years.　　　　　364-7

Q-Please explain what is meant by "He will walk and talk with men of every clime." Does this mean he will appear to many at once or appear to various peoples during a long period?

A-As given, for a thousand years He will walk and talk with men of every clime. Then in groups, in masses, and then they shall reign of the first resurrection for a thousand years; for this will be when the changes materially come.

In the manner as He sat at the peace conference in Geneva, in the heart and soul of a man (President Woodrow Wilson?) not reckoned by many as an even unusually Godly man; yet raised for a purpose, and he chose rather to be a channel of His thought for the world. So, as there has been, so will it be until the time as set. As was given of Him, not given to man to know the time or the period of the end, nor to man--save by their constituting themselves a channel through which He may speak...

He walked with men as the Master among men, or when as Joseph in the kingdoms that were raised as the saving of his peoples that **sold** him into bondage, or as in the priest of Salem in the days when the call came that a peculiar peoples would proclaim His name, He has walked and talked with men. Or, as in those days as Asapha, or Affa, in those periods when those of that same Egyptian land were giving those counsels to the nations, when there would be those saving of the physical from that of their own making in the physical; or in the garden when those temptations came, or as the first begotten of the Father that came as Amilius in the Atlantean land and allowed himself to be led in ways of selfishness. Hence, as we see, all the various stages of developments that have come to man through the ages have been those periods when He walked and talked with man.

Q-In the Persian experience as San (or Zend) did Jesus give the basic teachings of what became Zoroastrianism?

A-In all those periods that the basic principle was the Oneness of the Father, He has walked with men.   364-8

Since His entry into the world, and His making it possible for man to find his way back to God, there has been and will continue to be an increase. For God has not willed that any soul should perish...For He will one day come again, and thou shalt see Him as He is, even as thou hast seen in thy early sojourns the glory of the day of the triumphal entry and the day of the Crucifixion, and as ye also heard the angels proclaim "As ye have seen Him go, so will ye see Him come again.".…

The entity was among the five hundred who beheld Him as He entered into glory, and saw the angels, heard their announcement of the event that must one day come to pass, and will only be to those who believe, and have faith, who look for and expect to see Him as He is. 3615-16

He will come again and again in the hearts, the minds, the experiences of those that **love** His coming. But those when they think on Him and know what His presence would mean and become fearful, He passeth by. 1152-1

Until there is again the seeking of such as ye not only proclaimed but manifested, He **cannot** come again.   1908-1

The Master has given, "As to the day, no man knoweth, not even the Son, but the Father" (Matt. 24:36) and they to whom the Father may reveal. The Son prepareth the way that all men may know the love of the Father. 262-58

Q-He said He would come again. What about His second coming?

A-The time no one knows. Even as He gave, not even the Son Himself. **Only** the Father. Not until his enemies--and the earth--are wholly in subjection to His will, His powers.

Q-Are we entering the period of preparation for His coming?

A-Entering the test period, rather.   5749-2

Q-What is meant by "the day of the Lord is near at hand"?

A-That has been promised through the prophets and the sages of old, the time--and half-time--has been and is being fulfilled in this day and generation, and that soon there will again appear in the earth that one through whom many will be called to meet those that are preparing the way for His day in the earth. The Lord, then, will come, "even as ye have seen him go" (Acts 1:11).

Q-How soon?

A-When those that are His have made the way clear, **passable**, for Him to come.   262-49

Q-What was meant by "As in the first Adam sin entered, so in the last Adam all shall be made alive"?

A-Adam's entry into the world in the beginning, then, must become the savior **of** the world, as it was committed to his care, "Be thou fruitful, multiple, and **subdue** the earth!" (Genesis 1:28) Hence Amilius, Adam the first Adam, the last Adam, becomes--then--that that is **given** the **power over** the earth, and--as in each soul the first to be conquered is self-- then **all things**, conditions and elements, are subject unto that self! that a universal law, as may be seen in that as may be demonstrated either in gases that destroy one another by becoming elements of the same, or that in the mineral or the animal kingdom as may be found that destroy, or **become** one **with** the other. Hence, as Adam given-- the Son of God--so he must become that that would be able to take the world, the earth, back to that source from which it came, and **all power** the grave even, become subservient unto Him **through** the con-quering of self in that made flesh; for, as in the beginning was the Word, the Word **was** with God, the Word **was** God, the same was **in** the beginning. The Word came and dwelt among men, the offspring of self in a material world, and the Word **overcame** the world--and hence the world **becomes**, then, as the servant of that that overcame the world.

Q-Please give the important reincarnations of Adam.

A-In the beginning as Amilius, as Adam, as Melchizedek, as Zend, as Ur, as Asaph, as Jeshua--Joseph--Jesus.   364-7

Man, in Adam (as a group; not as an individual), entered into the world (for he entered in five places at one, we see--called Adam in one, see?)   900-227

Then as we become more and more aware within ourselves of the answering of the experiences, we become aware of what He gave to those that were the first of **God's** projection--not man's but God's projection --into the earth; Adam and Eve.   262-115

The promises are true which have been made in that which is foolish-ness to the scientific or wise, the simple story of Jesus of Nazareth. But when or if the entity takes this as its study (and set this as its thought and then read, then study the Book which tells of Him, Jesus born in Bethlehem of the Virgin Mary), know this is the same soul-entity who reasoned with those who returned from captivity in those days when Nehemiah, Ezra, Zerubbabel were factors in the attempts of the reestab-lishing of the worship of God, and that Jeshua, the scribe, translated the rest of the books written up to that time. Then realize that is the same entity as mentioned who as Joshua was the mouthpiece of Moses, who gave the law, and was the same soul-entity who was born in Bethlehem, the same soul-entity who in those periods of the strength and yet the weakness of Jacob in his love for Rachael was their firstborn. This is the same entity, and this entity was that one who had manifested to father Abraham as the prince, as the priest of Salem, without father and without mother, without days or years, but a living human being in flesh made manifest in the earth from the desire of Father-God to prepare an escape for man, as was warned by the same entity as Enoch, and this was also the entity Adam. And this was the spirit of light. 5023-2

Q-Is Jesus the only begotten son of God, and what does this mean?
A-In this to give the full concept is to give the history then of all those who have entered into flesh **without** that act which man knows as copulation. For as those experiences Jesus, known as Jesus, the brother of this entity, came into the earth, the **first** that were of the sons of God to enter flesh, **there** the first and only begotten of God. Again, as names would say, Enoch walked with God, became aware of God in his movements--**still** that entity, that **soul** called Jesus--as Melchizedek, without father, without mother, came--**still** the soul of Jesus; the portion of God that manifests.

But each son, each daughter, through these very acts of the only begotten, of the son of Mary, of the first in the earth, of that without father and without mother, without days, without years--becomes then as the elder brother to all who are **born** in the earth, as the maker, as the creator, as the first, as the last; as the beginning, as the end of man's soul's experience through the earth and throughout the spheres of consciousness in and about the earth.

Thus is He the only begotten, the first-born, the first to know flesh, the first to purify it.   1158-5

Know that He--who was lifted up on the Cross in Calvary--was...also he that first walked among men at the beginning of man's advent into flesh! For He indeed was and is the first Adam, the last Adam.   2402-2

Q-Please list the names of the incarnations of the Christ, and of Jesus, indicating where the development of the man Jesus began.
A-First, in the beginning of course; and then as Enoch, Melchizedek, in the perfection. Then in the earth as Joseph, Joshua, Jeshua, Jesus. 5749-14

The entity was among those that aided in the establishing of that in the Persian land, which later became as the tenets of that people from whom--many ages later--Melchizedek came...the great-great grandson of the entity, who came as without days, as without father or mother.   884-1

Without Moses and his leader Joshua (that was bodily Jesus) there **is** no Christ. **CHRIST** is not a man! **Jesus** was the man; Christ the messenger; Christ in all ages, Jesus in one, Joshua in another, Melchizedek in another; **these** be those that led Judaism. These be they that came as that child of promise, as to the children of promise.   991-1

(Entities) were all together in Amilius. They were material bodies as came in Adam. They were as associated in body as came in Zan, or that that eventually became--through its incantations, incarnations, into the earth, those forces as the Savior in all periods.

Q-In this period, was I of the Jewish race?
A-No Jews then! That was years later! As Jews, as known today. 288-29

Q-What name was borne by Jesus in His reincarnations in France, England, America?
A-Rather these have been as the Spirit of the Christ, or the Master walked among men, than incarnated in these different countries; for whether among the priest, as it were, in France--or among the lowly monk in England, or the warrior bold in America, the **Spirit** that "God is **One!** Prefer thy neighbor, thy brother, before thyself!" These, as we find, took possession of--or rather labored with, until their own **personalities** were laid aside in individuals. Do thou likewise, would thou have Him walk with thee. "Not my will, O Lord, but thine, be done in me." 364-9

LUCIUS THE BISHOP OF CYRENE

Yes, we have the records of that entity now called Edgar Cayce; and those experiences in the earth's plane (when he was) known as Lucius of Cyrene--or known in the early portion of the experience as Lucius Ceptulus, of Grecian and Roman parentage, and of the city of Cyrene.

As a developing youth and young man, Lucius was known rather as a ne'er-do-well; or one that wandered from pillar to post; or became--as would be termed in the present day parlance--a soldier of fortune.

When there were those activities in and about Jerusalem and Galilee of the ministry of the man Jesus, Lucius came into those environs.

Being impelled by the experiences with the followers, and the great lessons as given by the Teacher, he became rather as one that was a hanger-on...

The entity was disregarded and questioned by those of the Jewish faith who were the close followers of the Master; yet it was among those that were sent **as** those who were to be as teachers--or among the Seventy.

With the arousing, and the demanding that there be more and more of the closer association with the Teacher, Lucius being of the foreign group was rejected as one of the Apostles...

In those activities then that followed the Crucifixion, and the days of the Pentecost, and the sermon or teachings--and when there was beheld by Lucius the outpouring of the Holy Spirit, when Peter spoke in tongues --or as he spoke in his **own** tongue, it, the message was **heard** by those of **every** nation in their **own** tongue--this so impressed Lucius that there came a rededicating, and the determination within self to become the closer associated, the closer affiliated with the Disciples or Apostles.

But when the persecutions arose, and there was the choice of those that were to act as those called the deacons--as Philip and Stephen and the others--again he was rejected because of his close associations with one later called Paul, or Saul; he being of Tarsus or of the country, and a Roman, and questioned as to his Jewish ancestry--though claimed by Paul (or Saul) that he was a Jew. His mother was indeed, and of the tribe of Benjamin, though his father was not.

Hence as we find the questions arose as to the advisability of putting those in position, either as teachers, ministers or those in active service, that were questioned as to their lineal descent.

And again the old question as to whether **any** were to receive the word by those of the household of faith, or of the Jews...

There is often the confusing of Lucius and Luke, for these were kinsmen (the mother of Lucius being the sister of Luke)...

In those latter portions of the experience he became the bishop or the director or the president of the Presbytery; or what ye would call the priest or the father or the high counsellor as given to those in the early periods of the Church; that is, the one to whom **all questions** were taken respecting what ye would term in the present as theology, or questions pertaining to the laws.

In such the entity as the bishop was the last word, other than that there might be the appeal from such a verdict to the church in Jerusalem--or the Apostles themselves.

Q-Please explain how all heard in their various tongues the message that was given by Peter in the one tongue (Acts 2:4).

A-This was the activity of the spirit, and what the spirit indeed meant and means in the experiences of the individuals during that period.

For one that was of Cyrene heard a mixture of the Greek and Aryan tongue; while--though Peter spoke in the Arabic--those that were of the Hebrew heard in the Hebrew language; those in Greek heard in Greek. 294-192

Luke was written by Lucius, rather than Luke, though a companion with Luke during those activities of Paul--and written, of course, unto those of the faith under the Roman **influence**. Not to the Roman peoples, but to the provinces **ruled** by the Romans. 1598-2

Q-Describe the psychic development of this entity Edgar Cayce in the Persian experience as Uhjltd and the direct influence on the present manner of giving or obtaining this information.

A-...In the first, we find that the entity Uhjltd was an incarnation of Asapha and also of the priest, both experiences being in Egypt--or Adonis and Asapha. In entering, then, we find, in the land then known as Iran, there were those that had held true to those teachings that had been propounded by the teachers in the Egyptian--or the land of the sun. With that coming together of those of Ur (pre-Abraham period?) interpretation, there had been set up in this land of Iran a group who sought again to establish those ideals that had been given from the land of the sun; and with the coming together of the daughters of Ra and of the son of Zu, there came into the physical experience that entity called in the physical Uhjltd, who in the youth rose then to be the nominal leader of the peoples of the plains...

And when joined with the companion--that later brought forth that leader (Zend?) who was to become the power that has ruled this portion of the land in some direction--then greater became the **power** of the abilities of that entity in that experience to manifest that in the various ways and manners as called psychic forces, psychic abilities. In that there was, then, the conscious **and** unconscious activities that gradually became the ability to become as one **well** endowed with the abilities to be the teacher of that one who became the world teacher and the Savior of men (Jesus). In the **spiritual** sense, the physical sense, Uhjltd was an excellent teacher--for were he not once the priest?...Much of that which later became as a portion of the archives (or what would be termed library) in Alexandria was of the teachings, and the lands of what later became the grandson (as known in the flesh) of Uhjltd, as the Zoroastrians, and those peoples that went into those that brought to the Carmanians, also the Pyrenees, also to Ararat, and those into the Caspians, and those of the later Huns, Gauls, and Norse--or Iddos.

In this development, then--these were through the things he suffered in body and mind, until these were cleansed and no hate, no ideas of the retrogression were in the active forces...of the entity Uhjltd. 294-142

The entity was in that land now known as the Persian or the Arabian land, during those periods when there were the gatherings of many from many lands to the "city in the hills and plains"; which arose not from its commercial valuation, nor yet from any cause other then the mental and spiritual good that arose from the activities of **that entity** who led in that period during the building of those experiences...during the first and second Croesus (Croesus kings in Persia); for this was among the **early** experiences, being some seven to ten thousand years B.C.   962-1

From those (Grecian subversion) attempts grew those differences of the entity (Uhjndt?) (Ujndt) with the associate or companion, or brother, Zend, as to the spiritual and the material activities..

One (Zend) held to the theory that only spiritual passiveness should be the activity of man; the other (Uhjndt?) held that there should be the practical application of spiritual, mental and material needs to meet the law of the nature of man--or natural sources.

These divisions gradually grew so that there became adherents to each group; not only in the city or land about the "city of the hills and the plains" but from other groups that were gradually fostered from the teachings in other lands,--the Egyptian, portions of Northern Persia, the Indian, the land of On or the Mongoloid, also Tau--as in the Indo-China land. All of these brought the undermining of those who held to the principles of the one, and to the purpose and principles of the other.

The entity then Uhjndt (?) (Ujndt), held to the belief that the spiritual influences were to be a practical application in the mental and material life, and that they were to be a part of **every** individual, as individuals, and in the same manner in principle applied to the associates of **any** individual, in the dealing with influences and forces from without,--that is, the **same** principles applied in the manner necessary to deal with influences from without; as in the attempted invasion, which later became--as would be termed--a military expedition from Greece.

(In Egypt in a previous incarnation) the entity was rather of the passive nature or influence, while in the Persian period...the entity was more active. The term would be,--progressive, determined, and for a purpose, for and ideal.

In the Egyptian experience the conditions were accepted. In the Persian period they were made daily applicable, practical.   2091-2

The entity was in the land now known as the Persian or Arabian, about the city builded in the "hills and the plains," about that **now** known as or called Shustar in Persia or Arabia...Hence those teachings that arose through the grandson of Uhjltd, or Zorastrianism, have a peculiar intent in the experiences of the entity.   991-1

The entity (Uldha in the Persian experience) then the **offspring** (daughter) in the flesh **of** the leader (Uhjltd).

Q-Have I in any experience through the earth plane been associated with Jesus Christ before he became the world teacher? If so, where?

A-In this same experience, that of the brother, the incarnation previous to the Master's entry into the earth's plane, for He became **then** the leader in those lands, and **much** is **still** gained in thought from those of the Persian efforts in this direction; or, as is termed in

the **present** day, the Persian philosophy.
Q-What was His name at that time?
A-San (?) (Zan) (sound rhymed with wan) (Zend).   993-3

Zan--that one who became the leader--trained in physical and mental much by the entity, and closely associated with the entity. Zan not in the earth's plane in the present. Came again as those that were the Sons of man, and--the Savior of the world...
(Ulda was) the sister of Zan, and a close associate.   538-32

The entity (Esdena was in) the Arabian and Persian land, during those periods when there were the comings of those to the city in the hills and the plains, to the leader in those experiences to many that brought a new hope, a new vision of brotherly love in the earth.   826-2

The entity's (Esdena) transition came at the age in years--as would be called in the present--of a hundred and seventy and eight.   826-4

Uhjltd was entombed, in the cave outside of the city that has recently been builded and termed Shushtar; this to the south and west of that city, in the cave there.   415-1

VIRGINIA BEACH

(Virginia Beach) is the center--and the only seaport and center--of the White Brotherhood.   1152-11

(Surrounding Virginia Beach is) that vibration as is a best predicated condition for the operation of psychic forces as may be manifested through this entity (Edgar Cayce), from associations in the earth's plane and desires as are manifested through earthly forces, see?...The conditions that surround the place, Virginia Beach...are such that through same the phenomena might receive greater force and expansion. The nearness to the various ones directly interested in the propagation of the phenomena, see? The nearness (at another season than present) to the nation's and world's Capitol, that through same many channels of the thinking peoples who study such phenomena may have direct access.   254-26

The sands (Virginia Beach) and the radiation upon same are such as to be most beneficial to the general nervous systems of **any**one. 2153-4

The radiation from the gold and radium in the proportions that you find in Virginia Beach, or Seabreeze Beach is the better for the conditions (colitis) of the body.   5237-1

(The Association for Research and Enlightenment) is to be first of all an educational factor in the lives of those that are contacted through the efforts of the Association. This pertaining to the physical, the mental, and the spiritual--for, as given, these and their relations to one another are the primary forces in the physical or material life. The greater understanding of the relationship of these factors, and that the whole is one, yet must be studied in their **individual**, and collective, and coordinating influence in the lives of individuals--and, as given, first to the individual, then to groups, to classes, to masses. This, then, is the work to be accomplished by the Association...

Hark! There comes the voice of one who would speak to those gathered here:

I AM MICHAEL, LORD OF THE WAY! BEND THY HEAD, O YE CHILDREN OF MEN! GIVE HEED UNTO THE WAY AS IS SET BEFORE YOU IN THAT SERMON ON THE MOUNT, IN THAT ON YON HILL THIS ENLIGHTENMENT MAY COME AMONG MEN! FOR EVEN AS THE VOICE OF THE ONE WHO STOOD BESIDE THE SEA AND CALLED ALL MEN UNTO THE WAY, THAT THOSE THAT WOULD HARKEN MIGHT KNOW THERE WAS AGAIN A STAFF IN DAVID, AND ROD OF JESSE HAS NOT FAILED: FOR IN ZION THY NAMES ARE WRITTEN, AND IN SERVICE WILL COME TRUTH!   254-42

The ideals and the purposes of the Association for Research and Enlightenment, Inc., are not to function as another cism or ism. Keep away from that. For these warnings have been given again and again. Less and less of personality, more and more of God and Christ in the dealings with the fellow man...

How did thy Master work? In the church, in the synagogue, in the field, in the lakes, upon the sands and the mountains, in the temple. And did He defy those? Did He set up anything different? Did He condemn the law even of the Romans, or the Jews, or the Essenes, or the Sadducees, or any of the cults or isms of the day? He gave, are as **One** --under the law. And grudges, cisms, isms, cults, must become as naught; that thy Guide, the Way, thy Master, yea, even Christ--as manifested in Jesus of Nazareth--may be made known to thy fellow man. 254-92

There is first the creation--in the universal forces--of the body-mind of such an organization; no matter of what nature, be it physical, material, or for spiritual purposes. It grows to be--with the activities of such a group, association, combination, body-mind...

Hence you speak of the spirit of America, of Germany, of the Nordic people, of the Mayan, of the Celtic, or what not. These are influences that have taken shape in the realms beyond matter, yet influence same, with as much a body as the mind (the builder) has builded.   254-95

242 ASSOCIATION FOR RESEARCH AND ENLIGHTENMENT

Let each be mindful of that place, that niche, that purport each is to fill, and **fill** that with **all** of the power, might, strength, that lies within that body. So cooperate with other individuals, working in their individual capacities, that the whole purport may be as one, "even as the Father and I are one in you. I speak not of myself, but that ye may know the truth, even as delivered in the day when I walked among men and became known as the **Son** of Man, and the savior of a benighted race." Here, my brethren, ye are come again to fulfill, in this place, a glorious principle, a glorious article of work among the sons of man.   254-50

Do not let any portion of that published be thrown at the public, or make claims that are not able to be verified, from **every** angle.   254-88

The organization is an ecclesiastical research, as well as a scientific research organization not of a sect or set--but as the **Law of One!**   254-89

We find the Association is organized, formed, for a definite purpose: To study psychic phenomena in all its phases.   257-20

Count it joy, then, even as He, that ye are called by Him in service-- in **loving** service--to thy fellow man; for through this lowly, weak, unworthy channel (Edgar Cayce) has He chosen to speak, for the purposes of this soul have been to do good unto his brethren.   254-76

The purpose, then, of the Association: the institution (is to be) builded around that of a place where the records of that accomplished through these sources are kept, and others of similar nature, or of the various philosophies that may be found that will coordinate--and combined in that oneness of purpose to bring the better understanding of the purpose **in** life, and thus enable man to realize the closer association with the Divine. In the lecture room and the library--members, then having access to such, gain better in the understanding of such, and the library may be made circulating, or a repository--as it will become --to all those who seek to see their **theory disseminated.**   254-37

There is much more spirituality needed in the life of the one (Edgar Cayce) through whom the information passes to the physical world, should this information be understood in the perfect physical manner...
The Forces through **themselves** would prepare that necessary for the propagation and expansion of the work itself. The information necessary has been given, in a manner then not wholly understood for this reason. 294-47

Never force an issue. Never attempt to show individuals, that they may be convinced. There is the necessity for each seeker to realize his need; and unless there is that realization, **how** can such find in that which is spiritual that which is true in his seeking.   254-97

Q-Please outline the course of study and reading that I should have, that will enable me to do well the work among study groups.

A-There has been a very thorough outline given for those that would be leaders, in those various approaches to kindred thought; as in Hudson's Law--Spiritual Law of Psychic Phenomena, Ouspensky's Tertium Organum, James' Varieties of Religious Experience, or the like. **These** approach the basis of thought of man in his varied environs, but **this** weighed with that which is the personal experience of those as they **lived** in preparing the lessons will make for the right kind of development. 307-4

Q-Outline or suggest material for study and reading.

A-With the study first, to be sure, of **His** words--as He gave, as is recorded. Those philosophical experiences of the writers--as James, as Ouspensky, as those who have followed in the lines of their studies-- as Swedenborg, or the like; but weigh these all with thine own.   256-4

Q-How may I better understand myself, time and space?

A-...The application brings consciousness to the individual and it must be of an **individual** application for an **entity** to gain the consciousness. Such lessons may be gained from reading **Tertium Organum**. 137-88

Q-Would a study of the Secret Doctrine be of benefit?

A-The study of any portion of same would be of benefit, but only in so far as it will enable the self to open for that which may be given in its meditation. Commence, and then we may aid.   470-10

Q-Is the revelation Oahspe, the Kosmon Bible, true in most particulars?

A-Individuals and individual instances, yes; some very far apart. 2067-2

Q-Is Rudolf Steiner's "Atlantis and Lemuria," and his "theosophy" true and correct in general?

A-In a trend; not as a toto--but a **vision of** an entity as reading a record **of** that as happened in space and time, and **given in** response **to** those seeking for their **own** understanding of inclinations with **their** own experience.   311-6

Q-What books should I read to bring out the divine within me?

A-None more beautiful than that found in the Scriptures, especially the latter portion of Genesis and the 14th, 15th, 16th, 17th chapters in that recorded by John in the Gospels, or those by the second John in his epistles; first, second and third John.

Then, in those that are more of the world, those that may make for the development in the experiences and the applications of same among men, read "The Lamplighter" (Charles Dickens)...

In others, there may be found such as in "The Roads to Yesterday" (B.M. Dix and E.J. Sutherland).   505-4

PART VII

THE CARE AND FUNCTION OF THE BODY

THE BODY IS A PATTERN OF THE SOUL

For, that we find in spirit taketh form in mind. Mind becomes the builder. The physical body is the result.   3359-1

The body is the **manifestation**, the movement of the mind, of the soul, through the mind that expresses itself in materiality. Not from materiality back, but up from soul **through** the **mental** processes of application in those things material.   262-95

The **body** is a pattern, it is an example of all the forces of the universe itself.   2153-6

Within the human body--living, not dead--**living** human forces--we find every element, every gas, every mineral, every influence that is outside of the organism itself. For indeed it is one with the whole.   470-22

When the earth was brought into existence or into time and space, all the elements that are **without** man may be found in the **living** human body. Hence these in coordination, as we see in nature, as we see in the air, as we see in the fire or in the earth, makes the soul, body and mind **one** coordinating factor with the universal creative energy we call God.   557-3

Each cell of its body is but a miniature of the universe without its body, its own cell of positive and negative force that applies to the material, the mental and the spiritual.   1776-1

The body finds that while spiritual thought and spiritual food values are essentially supplying elements to a physical body, in the material plane it is necessary also that material food values be taken for sustaining not only thy physical forces but the spiritual elements as well; to keep them in contact or as parallel one to another.   516-4

The body is made up of the physical, the mental, the spiritual. Each have their laws, which work one with another, and the whole is the physical man; yet do not treat physical conditions wholly through spiritual or mental laws and expect same to respond as one.   4580-1

The body--physically, mentally, spiritually--is one **body**; yet in the varied conditions as arise within a physical body, these must often be treated as a unit--that is, each element treated as a unit yet in the fullest application they are **one**.   2263-1

There is the body-physical, with all of its attributes--as related to **material** manifestation--as **growth** is from that assimilated in an organism one sets in motion by those influences for material manifestation of body, mind, soul.

Then there is the mental body, accredited oft with activity from reflexes or impulses of the nervous systems of the individual.

Then there is the **entity**, the soul body--that may find material manifestation or expression in the ability not only of **bodily** procreation but of every atom, every organ within itself to **reproduce** itself, its likeness, through the assimilation of that taken within--either physically **or** mentally.   2402-1

The body-physical becomes that which it assimilates from material nature. The body-mental becomes that which it assimilates from both the physical-mental and spiritual-mental. The soul is **all** of that the entity is, has been or may be.   2475-1

The physical body is that channel through which the mental and physical and spiritual of an entity **must** manifest. The nearer normal that reaction is, the more perfect may be the mental, physical and **spiritual** vibration of **that** body--for they are indeed one.   238-1

Let it be understood there is the pattern in the material or physical plane of every condition as exists in the cosmic or spiritual plane, for things spiritual and things material are but those same conditions raised to a different condition of the same element--for all force is as of one force...

In the make-up of the active forces of the physical body, it is constituted of many, many, cells--each with its individual world within itself, controlled by the spirit that is everlasting, and guided by that of the soul, which is a counterpart--or the breath that makes that body individual, and when the body is changed, and this is the soul body, the elements become the active particles, atoms, that make up that soul body.

When the soul passes, then, from the physical body it (the soul body) then constituted with those atoms of thought (that are mind) and are of the Creative Forces a part, and then we have the soul body, with the mind, the subconscious mind...which never forgets, and is then as the conscious mind of the soul body; the spirit or superconscious mind being that as the subconscious mind of the material body.   5756-4

Cosmic being the physical condition of the body, for that which the individual has **made** is its cosmic force, or cosmic body, with subconscious as the conscious mind, superconscious as the subconscious mind --viewed from the physical plane...

Cosmic forces are **THAT BUILDED by the entity in its passage through the physical planes...**

Immortality is of the Soul, that Body of the Cosmic Forces taking the form to which it has builded in its various experiences through physical world, or degraded, according to the lives, the Will Force, the manner as exercised in the physical plane.   900-147

Material sojourns are as the senses of the material body, just as the astrological sojourns are as the mental or dream body. Thus they find expression oft in **feelings** towards places, conditions, individuals, that in thine own inner self send out that radiation which (in mystical study) may be seen in the aura, or in the study of a part of numerology as to the number, or in the very emotions as may be expressed in lines of the hand, feet or face. For, remember the law--all carry the mark in their body; just as ye bear His mark in thy forehead. 2067-1

Each individual in its manifestations in the earth bears within its physical expression the marks of that which has been or may be termed as an expression of a development in the soul and spiritual forces.   1165-1

That portion of thy body which is of the earth-earthy remains with the earth, but that thou hast glorified, that thou has used as a channel for the manifestations of His Spirit--of thy soul in communion with Him, **that** body will be raised with Him in righteousness.   272-9

The body-physical with the emotions of same is physical and spiritual; the body-mental with its desires is both carnal and very spiritual. 1754-1

There is the body, the mind, the soul,--same as the Father, the Son, the Holy Spirit. Each is a pattern of the other,--they are one. 1947-1

The body-celestial or cosmic body has those attributes of the physical with the cosmic added to same; for all hearing, seeing, understanding, become as one...all odor as one odor, all feeling as one feeling--yet each being aware of that which it is and its relation to the whole.   900-348

There is nothing in nature so expressive of beauty--or God--as the body-beautiful; yet nothing so low--or loathsome--as that body made to be a vulgar expression.   2464-1

The body, physical, is of a circuit, in the form of an eight.   1800-6

The body is the whole the one.   3685-1

Q-You will give at this time a discourse on the endocrine glands of the human organism, discussing their functions in relation to the physical body and their relations to the mental and spiritual forces.

A-...This is the system whereby or in which dispositions, characters, natures and races all have their source...

There is an activity within the system produced by anger, fear, mirth, joy, or any of those active forces, that produces through the glandular, secretion those activities that flow into the whole of the system...

Most every organ of the body may be considered a gland, or at least there must be within the functioning activity of each portion--as the eye, the ear, the nose, the brain itself, the neck, the trachea, the bronchi, the lungs, the heart, the liver, the spleen, the pancreas that which enables it to perform its duty in taking **from** the system that which enables it to **reproduce** itself! That is the functioning of the glands!...

The glands are associated with reproduction, degeneration, regeneration; and this throughout--not only the physical forces of the body but the mental body and the soul body.

The glandular forces then are ever akin to the sources from which, through which, the soul dwells within the body...

Let us consider the race question. Why in the mixture of races is there in the third and then the tenth generation a reverting to first principles? (Remember, we are speaking only from the physical reaction.)

Because that period is required for the cycle of activity in the glandular force of reproduction to reassert itself. How is it given in our Word? That the sins of the fathers are visited unto the children of the third and fourth generation, even to the tenth. This is not saying that the results are seen only in the bodily functions of the descendants, as is ordinarily implied; but that the essence of the message is given to the individual respecting the activity of which he may or must eventually be well aware in his own being. That is, what effect does it have upon you to even get man, to laugh, to cry, to be sorrowful? All of these activities affect not only yourself, your relationships to your fellow man, but your next experience in the earth! 281-38

Glands are the creators of forces that make for the secondary (what may be called) the negative forces about a positive center that moves through the system in the form of a blood cell.   1065-1

(Occasionally take Atomidine) for the activity or cleansing of the glandular system...Small quantity, of course.   1158-21

Atomidine is a helpful stimulant to all glandular activity. If...taken for periods of two to three weeks, left off and then begun again... Periodical taking of anything...allows the body to react better. 920-11

There are centers, areas, conditions in which there evidently must be that contact between the physical, the mental and the spiritual.

The spiritual contact is through the glandular forces of Creative Energies, not encased only within the lyden gland of reproduction, for this is ever--so long as life exists--in contact with the brain cells through which there is the constant reaction through the pineal. 263-13

Lyden (Leydig) meaning sealed, that gland from which gestation takes place when a body is created through coition, or inception... Located in and above the gland called genital glands, see?   3997-1

The lyden, or 'closed gland', is the keeper--as it were--of the door, that would loose and let either passion or the miracle be loosed to enable those seeking to find the Open Door, or the Way to find expression in the imaginative forces in their manifestation in the sensory forces of a body; whether to fingertips that would write, to eyes that would see, to voice that would speak, to the whole of the system as would feel those impressions that are attuned with those of the infinite by their development and association or those inter-between or those passed over, or as to the unseen forces. For the world of unconsciousness is not in a material change from the physical world save as to its attributes or of its relationships with same. Whether the vision has been raised or lowered depends upon that height, depth, breadth or length, it has gone for its source of supply.   294-140

It (pituitary) is the door, as interpreted by some through which physically all of the reflex actions respond through the various forces of the nerve system. It is that to and through which the mental activities come that produce the influences in the imaginative system as well as the racial prejudices as termed the predominating influences --or the blood force itself. In the spiritual, it is that to which the singleness in the adult brings the awakening to its capabilities, its possibilities, its ultimate hope and desire.   281-58

The pituitary glands have more to do with the metabolism of the system, and thus effect the emotional forces.   357-7

Here we have information that will be of interest to all who study psychic experiences in the material plane, as to how such experiences of others may be given through an individual such as the source from which this information as may be given emanates. There must be in the physical or material world a channel through which psychic or spiritual forces may manifest...

In this particular body (Edgar Cayce) through which this at present is emanating, the gland with its thread known as the pineal gland is the channel along which same then operates, and with the subjugation of the consciousness--physical consciousness--there arises, as it were, a cell from the Creative Forces within the body to the entrance of the conscious mind, or brain, operating along, or traveling along, that of the thread or cord as when severed separates the physical, the soul, or the spiritual body. This uses, then, the senses of the body in an introspective manner, and they are not apparent in functioning in a physical normal manner as when awake. All faculties of the body become more alert.   288-29

Keep the pineal gland operating and you won't grow old.   294-141

The pineal has been and is the extenuation of the first cause.   281-47

In the body we find that which connects the pineal, the pituitary, the lyden, may be truly called the silver cord, or the golden cup that may be filled with a closer walk with that which is the creative essence in physical, mental and spiritual life; for the destruction wholly of either will make for the disintegration of the soul from its house of clay. To be purely material minded, were an anatomical or pathological study made for a period of seven years (which is a cycle of change in all the body elements) of one that is acted upon through the third eye alone, we will find one fed upon spiritual things becomes a light that may shine from and in the darkest corner. One fed upon the purely material will become a Frankenstein that is without a concept of any influence other than material or mental.   262-20

Q-What other glands, if any, besides the Leydigian, pineal, and glands of reproduction, are directly connected with psychic development?
A-...The generative organism is as the motor, and the Leydig as a sealed or open door, dependent upon the development or the use same has been put to by the entity in its mental, its spiritual, activity. The mental may have been misused, or used aright. The spiritual activity goes on just the same. It is as the electron that is Life itself; but raised in power and then misdirected may bring death itself, or--as in the activities of the glands as seen, or ducts--that used aright may bring serenity, hope, peace, faith, understanding, and the attributes of its source, as the experience of the entity; or, misdirected, may bring those doubts, fears, apprehensions, contentions, disorders, disruptions, in every portion of the body. Hence these may literally be termed, that the pineal and the Leydig are the **seat** of the soul of an entity...They are the **channels** through which the activities have their impulse! though the manifestations may be in sight, in sound, in speech, in vision, in writing, in dreams, in Urim or Thummim, or in any. For these represent Urim and Thummim in their essence, or in **any** of the **responding** forces in a body.   294-142

These (yoga breathing) exercises are excellent, yet it is necessary that special preparation be made--or that a perfect understanding be had by the body as to what takes place when such exercises are used...

In the body there is that center in which the soul is expressive, creative in its nature--Leydig center.

By this breathing, this may be made to expand...

As this life-force is expanded, it moves first from the Leydig center through the adrenals, in what may be termed an upward trend, to the pineal and to the centers in control of emotions--or reflexes through the nerve forces of the body.

Thus an entity puts itself, through such an activity, into association or conjunction with all it has **ever** been or may be. For, it loosens the physical consciousness to the universal consciousness.

To allow self in a universal state to be controlled, or to be dominated, may be harmful.

But to know, to feel, to comprehend as to **who** or to **what** is the directing influence when the self-consciousness has been released and the real ego allowed to rise to expression, is to be in that state of the universal consciousness--which is indicated in this body here, Edgar Cayce...

To be loosed without a governor, or director, may easily become harmful.

But as we would give, from here, let not such a director be that of an entity. Rather so surround self with the universal consciousness of the **Christ** as to be directed by that influence as may be committed to thee...

Make haste **slowly**! Prepare the mind, before ye attempt to loosen it in such measures, manners that it may be taken hold upon by those influences which constantly seek expressions of self rather than of a living, constructive influence of a **crucified** Savior.

Then, crucify desire in self; that ye may be awakened to the real abilities of helpfulness that lie within thy grasp...

This opening of the centers or the raising of the life force may be brought about by certain characters of breathing--for, as indicated, the breath is power in itself; and this power may be directed to certain portions of the body. But for what purpose? As yet it has been only to see what will happen!

Remember what curiosity did to the cat!

Remember what curiosity did to Galileo, and what it did to Watt-- but they used it in quite different directions in each case!   2475-1

In breathing, take into the right nostril, **strength**! Exhale through thy mouth. Intake in thy left nostril, exhaling through the right; opening the centers of thy body--if it is first prepared to thine **own** understanding, thine **own** concept of what ye would have if ye would have a visitor, if ye would have a companion, if ye would have thy bridegroom!

Then, as ye begin with the incantation of the Ar-ar-r-r--the e-e-e, the o-o-o, the m-m-m, **raise** these in thyself; and ye become close in the presence of thy Maker--as is **shown** in thyself! They that do such for selfish motives do so to their own undoing.   281-28

Q-How may I bring into activity my pineal and pituitary glands, as well as the kundalini and other chakras, that I may attain to higher mental and spiritual powers?

A-...**Fill** the mind with the ideal that it may vibrate throughout the whole of the **mental** being. Then close the desires of the fleshly self to conditions about same. **Meditate** upon "**Thy will with me.**" Feel same. 1861-4

These are the three centers (3d cervicle, 9th dorsal, 4th lumber) through which there is the activity of the kundalini forces, for distribution through the seven centers of the body.   3676-1

Q-Are the following statements true or false? Comment on each as I read it: The life force rises directly from the Leydig gland through the gonads thence to the pineal, and then to the other centers.

A-This is correct; though, to be sure, as it rises and is distributed through the other centers it returns to the solar plexus area for its impulse through the system...

One life force is the body-growth, as just described. The other is the impulse that arises, from the life center, in meditation.

Q-As the life force passes through the glands it illuminates them.

A-In meditation, yes. In the life growth, yes and no; it illuminates them to their own activity in life growth.

Q-The Leydig gland is the same as that we have called the lyden, and is located in the gonads.

A-It is in and above, or the activity passes through the gonads. Lyden is the meaning--or the seal, see? while Leydig is the name of the individual who indicated this was the activity.

Q-The life force crosses the solar plexus each time it passes to another center.

A-In growth, yes. In meditation, yes and no; if there remains the balance as of the attunement, yes.

Q-The solar plexus is the aerial gland.

A-No. By aerial we mean that impulse or activity that flows in an upward, lifting, raising or rising movement. It is an activity in itself, you see; not as a gland but as an activity **upon** glands as it flows... through the pineal, to and through all the centers. It aids the individual, or is an effective activity for the individual who may consciously attempt to attune, coordinate, or to bring about perfect accord, or to keep a balance in that attempting to be reached or attained. 281-53

Q-Is conception the physical activity?

A-Not necessarily. For, aerial activity produces conception. It is that movement by which the parts of the activity become one. **That** is conception...The sex is not determined at conception but is a development...

Within the nucleus at conception is the pattern of all that is possible. And remember, man--the soul of man, the body of man, the mind of man--is nearer to limitlessness than anything in creation...and it is not the same as an animal, insect or any of the rest of creation--which is limited.

Q-Can conception only take place when the spiritual ideal set by both (parents) is met?

A-True conception, **spiritual** conception, **mental** conception only takes place under such; but, as we have just stated above, physical conception may take place from purely carnal influences!   281-55

Conception may be wholly of the carnal or animal nature on the part of even one (parent), and yet conception may take place; and the end of that physical activity is written in that purpose and desire...

Thus the greater unison of purpose, of desire, at a period of conception brings the more universal consciousness--for a perfect or equalized vibration for that conception...

The cord that is eventually known or classified as the pineal is the first movement that takes place of a physical nature through the act of conception; determining eventually--as we shall see--not only the physical stature of the individual entity but the **mental** capacity also, and the spiritual attributes.   281-46

Then we have that illustration in the sons of Isaac, when there were those periods in which there was to be the fulfilling of the promise to Isaac and Rebekah. We find that their **minds** differed as to the nature or character of channel through which there would come this promise; when, as we understand, there must be the cooperation spiritually, mentally, in order for the physical result to be the same. **Here** we find a different situation taking place at the time of conception, for **both** attitudes found expression. Hence twins were found to be the result of this long preparation, and yet two minds, two opinions, two ideas, two ideals...

Hence we find, as indicated, there was **not** a union of purpose in those periods of conception. Hence we find both characteristics, or both purposes of the individuals, were made materially manifest...

The first cause--that purpose with which the individuals performed the act for conception to take place, or under which it did take place. **That** is the First Cause! And the growth of that conceived under the same environ, through the same circulation, through the same impulse, was such that--when gestation was finished--one was of the nature of characteristic of the mother, the other was of the nature of indifference with the determination of the father; one smooth as the mother, the other hairy, red, as the father in maturity; and their characteristics made manifest were just those examples of the variations. Though conceived at once, born together, they were far separated in their purposes, their aims, their hopes...

Do not think that one received a different instruction from the other?

One desired the chase, the hunt or the like, while the other chose rather the home, the mother, the environ about same...

What gland developed this characteristic in one and not in the other? The cranial and the thymus receiving the varied vibration, one brought harmony--not fear, but harmony--with caution; the other brought just the opposite, by this 'stepping up' in the rate of vibration. Or, if we were to study these by numbers, we would find one a three, the other a five; yet conceived together.

What do we mean here by the vibration of the number? One had the nucleus, the structure about same, three to one of its spiritual import; the other five to one of the material import, see?   281-48

Q-It is the spiritual activity within the body of the parents or the lack of it, that determines the influence predominant in their child.
A-This is correct.   281-54

Q-What mental attitude should I keep always before me during the coming months (of pregnancy)?
A-Depends upon what character of individual entity is desired. More beauty, music--if that is desired to be a part of the entity; art, and the like. Or is it to be purely mechanical? If purely mechanical, then think about mechanics--work with those things. And don't think that they won't have their effect, as the impressions give that opportunity.

Here is something that each and every mother should know. The manner in which the attitude is kept has much to do with the character of the soul that would choose to enter.   2803-6

Q-Is there an average period of time necessary between birth of one and conception of another?
A-Two years at least.   475-14

Q-Would the greater positivity of the woman attract a male child?
A-To be sure. These vary according to the number of the electrons about any center.

Q-Does intercourse while carrying child interfere with the physical or spiritual development of the child?
A-After three months, yes.   457-14

Ovulation is a law of nature. Conception is the law of God...

The sex of the child depends upon the attitudes of the individuals, and especially those held by the mother. As to whether it is the male or female oft may depend upon the discharge of the opposite sex. That of the mother brings the son; that of the father brings the daughter. They are opposites.

Q-Is the sex of a child determined at conception or developed later?

A-It may be determined at least six to ten years after birth.   457-11

Q-Why are the Y chromosomes found in some of the spermatozoa and are lacking in all ova and their polar bodies?

A-This is the variation in the very nature or character in the spermatozoa and the ovum activity itself. These are the natures of this. For, one was created first and the other came out **from** same.   281-63

THE SENSORY AND NERVOUS SYSTEMS

The soul's forces...(are) contained in the brain, in the nerve in the centers of the whole system. As to specific centers, nearer those centers of the sensory system, physically speaking.   900-17

The sense of speech is the highest developed vibration...for it partakes of vision, the hearing, the feeling, and all to combine same.   146-1

It is in the optic centers that all of those centers arise from the sensory system itself.   1861-17

The connection between spirit, mind and body are through the emunctory and the lymph flow in the body-force itself.   2946-4

The activity of the mental or soul force of the body may control entirely the whole physical through the action of the balance in the sympathetic system, for the sympathetic nerve system is to the soul and spirit forces as the cerebrospinal is to the physical forces. 4566-1

The nerve system is that channel through which the atomic energies --or electronic atomic energies--pass for activity.   907-1

In the nerve system, the brain is the head, and the active force through which all the conscious sensory consciousness is received. To see one eating produces that vibration--in the salivary gland that sets about the gastric juices of the stomach--one becomes hungry, see?

In the central brain (solar plexus) the knowledge of subconscious activity in the body is located.   1800-15

Hold to that **knowledge**--and don't think of it as just theory--that the body **can** the body **does** renew itself!   1548-3

For each cycle, every element, every condition must renew itself; else there becomes or is set up greater deterioration than creation. And each element, each organ, each functioning of the body throughout, is capable of reproducing itself. How?
Not merely from the ability of the glands to take from that assimilated those elements needed, but in each atom, in each corpuscle, is Life. Life is that ye worship as God. If God be with you, and you choose to use those elements in His creation that cause each atom, each corpuscle, to become more and more aware of that creative influence, there may then be brought resuscitation. May there not be created, then, health rather than disease, disorder, confusion?   2968-1

The human body is made up of electronic vibration, with each atom and element of the body, each organ and organism of same, having its electronic or unit of vibration necessary for the sustenance of, and equilibrium in, that particular organism. Each unit, then, being a cell or a unit of life in itself, with its capacity of reproducing itself by the first form or law as is known of reproduction, by division of same. When any force in any organ, any element of the body, becomes deficient in its ability to reproduce that equilibrium necessary for the sustenance of the physical existence and reproduction of same, that portion becomes deficient, deficient through electronic energy as is necessary. This may become by injury, by disease, received from external forces; received from internal forces by the lack of eliminations as are produced in the system, by the lack of other agencies. 1800-4

The body has in a seven-year cycle reproduced itself entirely. 257-249

He hath shown the way; not by some mysterious fluid, not by some unusual vibration, but by the simple method of **living** that which is **Life** itself. **Think** no evil; speak no evil; **hear** no evil. And as the Truth flows as a stream of life through the Mind in all its phases or aspects, and purifies same, so will it purify, revivify and rejuvenate the body. 294-249

How is the way shown by the Master? What is the promise in Him? The last to be overcome is death. Death of what? The **soul** cannot die; for it is of God. The body may be revivified, rejuvenated. And it is to that end it may, the body, **transcend** the earth and its influence. 262-85

The body renews itself according to the mental attitude it holds toward ideals, and in the light of the application of relationships to others. And this applies as well in the relationships of self.   2081-2

All building and replenishing for a physical body, is from within, and must be constructed by the mind of the entity; for **Mind** is the **Builder**; for each cell in the atomic force of the body is as a world of its own, and each one--each cell--being in perfect unison, may build to that necessary to reconstruct the forces of the body in all its needs.   93-1

(One) may remain in the physical as long as the ability lies within self to so apply the forces from without and within as to build or bring resuscitation to all forces from within, and, as desire is the father of **activity**, so is that brought **into** activity become life itself. Nothing grows, nothing remains alone unless dead. A mind, a body that sits alone and considers the outside and never turning that within to the out, nor that without from within, soon finds **drosses** setting up in the system; for development is change. Change is the activity of knowledge from within. Learn to **live**! Then there **is** no death, save the transition, when desired. See?...

Many live who have never died as yet!

Q-Then also it is true, one may preserve youth?

A-One may preserve youth, even as is desired, will they pay the price as is **necessary**.   900-456

(In Atlantis) the entity oft laid aside the physical body to become regenerated in its activities...From that sojourn (in Atlantis), there come the innate abilities to create the higher energies within self, as it were, that are stored up from the emotional forces of the body, those to find regenerations in the lower form of electrical vibrations. And if the body were to use for its own physical body the radio-active appliance in the lower force to the extremities, it may keep its body in almost **perfect** accord for many--many--many--many--**many** days.   823-1

The Father hath said "In the day ye eat or use the knowledge for thine own aggrandizement, ye shall die." But he that had persuaded the spirit, the souls that God had brought into being, to push into matter to gratify desire for self-expression, self-indulgence, self-satisfaction, said "ye shall not surely die," or what are then the activities of man--for as had been said, "A day is a thousand years, a thousand years as a day." What was the length of life then? Nearly a thousand years. What is your life today? May it not be just as He had given, just as He indicated to those peoples, just as He did to the lawgiver, just as He did to David--first a thousand years to a hundred and twenty, then to eighty? Why? Why? The sin of man is his desire for self-gratification.

What nations of the earth today vibrated to those things that they have and are creating in their own land their own environment? Look to the nations where the span of life has been extended from sixty to eighty-four years. You will judge who is serving God...These are the signs to those who seek to know, who will study the heavens, who will analyze the elements, who will know the heart of man.   3976-29

Q-How can one renew the body?
A-This depends upon the manner in which there has been the care of the body during those periods of the development. For there must be kept a balance in the activity of the glands through the body; through not only the period of development but the period of gestation--or of the normal activity, see? This may be done better, as we find, by foods, and activity in the bodily exercise in the open.
There is nothing more in order for the **renewing** of the activities of the glands of the body, as we find, than the use in the **proper** manner of the atomic iodine--Atomidine, especially if there is kept a proper balance in the diet as relating to same.   920-2

Would the assimilations and eliminations be kept nearer **normal** in the human family, the days might be extended to whatever period as was so desired; for the system is **builded** by the assimilations of that it takes within, and is able to bring resuscitation so long as the eliminations do not hinder.   311-4

Given properly silver and gold may almost lengthen life to its double, of its present endurance.   120-5

There may be obtained from the turtle egg those influences for longevity that may be created in certain cellular forces in the body.   659-1

The days upon the earth then (before the first destruction of Atlantis) were counted in the tens, the fifties and the hundreds, besides the days or weeks or years in the present. Or, the **life** existence of the entity, as compared to the present, would be years instead of weeks; or, in that experience, to live five to six to seven hundred years was no more than to live to the age of fifty, sixty or seventy years in the present. 1968-2

The life expectancy in those periods (Egypt at the time of Ra Ta) extended over a hundred, and hundreds of years; and...there were those groups that chose to lay aside the outer shell when the life expectancy--as would be termed in the present--was completed, as it had been laid out by those who gave the assignment, or the activity as was chosen by the individual. Or, there was chosen by the individual that period or particular part of the experience that was its contribution to the life of the period--and this was outlined or given. 2533-4

One is ever just as young as the heart and the purpose. Keep sweet. Keep friendly. Keep loving, if ye would keep young.   3420-1

All strength, all healing of every nature is the changing of the vibrations from within, the attuning of the divine within the living tissue of a body to Creative Energies. This alone is healing. Whether it is accomplished by the use of drugs, the knife or whatnot, it is the attuning of the atomic structure of the living force to its spiritual heritage.   1967-1

In every physical being, the whole body is made up of the atomic forces of the system, with the mind of each atom, as it is builded, supervised by the whole mental mind of the body, varied by its different phases and attributes, for, as is seen in its analyses, an atom of the body is a whole universe in itself, in the minutest state. The attitude, then, of all the attributes of the mind toward self, and the forces as manifest through same, become then paramount. As to any healing in a body, or **any application** of any source, nature, character, kind, or condition, is only to create that incentive **in** that same atomic force to create the better condition in a body.   137-81

Healing for the physical body, then, must be first the correct choice of the spiritual import held as the ideal of the individual. For it is returning, of course, to he First Cause, First Principles...
    Remember, healing--all healing--comes from within. Yet there is the healing of the physical, there is the healing of the mental, there is the correct direction from the spirit. Coordinate these and you'll be whole! But to attempt to do a physical healing through the mental conditions is the misdirection of the spirit that prompts same--the same that brings about accidents, the same that brings about the eventual separation. For it is **law**. But when the law is coordinated, in spirit, in mind, in **body**, the entity is capable of fulfilling the purpose for which it enters a material or physical experience. 2528-2

All phases of the body-physical must coordinate one with another as a unit, if it is to be healthy, well, strong.   2205-2

Remember the pattern in the mount, in self, in the physical body, in the mental body, in the spiritual body. **That** is the mount! So long as there is perfect coordination in the mount, all things work together for the good of the mount. When there is the rebellion in the mount, then there is disconnection, destruction, disconcerted effort, and the coordination--the cooperation of activity--is made awry. Hence death in the physical ensues.   262-36

In the physical body, as we have given, each atom is a whole universe in itself, and is a portion of the whole. When there is coordination within self, in the **inner** self--when the inner shrine receives the impulse, then healing is complete.   275-32

Disease arises from, first, dis-ease--as a normalcy that **is** existent and yet becomes unbalanced. Disease is, or dis-ease is, a state at-variance to the Ideal or First Cause or First Principle. Then, in its final analysis, disease might be called sin. It is necessary to keep a balance.   2533-3

The Christ Consciousness...is the **only** source of healing for a physical or mental body.   69-4

There are in truth, no incurable conditions...that which exists is and was produced from a first cause, and may be met or counteracted, or changed, for the condition is the breaking of a law.   3744-1

There is...in nature that is the counterpart of that in the mental and spiritual realms, and an antidote for **every** poison, for every ill.   2396-2

Q-What is the proper method or medicines to apply to correct or eliminate all of these conditions? (Arthritis and Poor Eliminations)
A-...First there must be a change in the mental attitude of the body. There must be eradicated that of any judgement or of condemnation on the part of self as respecting self or **any** associated with the body. 631-6

If in the atomic forces there becomes an overbalancing, an injury, a happening, an accident, there are certain atomic forces destroyed or others increased; that to the physical body become either such as to add to or take from the 'elan vitale'...
Then, in meeting these it becomes necessary for the creating of that influence within each individual body to bring a balance necessary for its continued activity about each of the atomic centers its own rotary or creative force, its own elements for the ability of resuscitating, revivifying, such influence or force in the body...
When a body, separate from that one ill, then, has so attuned or raised its own vibrations sufficiently, it may--by the motion of the spoken word--awaken the activity of the emotions to such an extent as to revivify, resuscitate or to change the rotary force or influence or the atomic forces in the activity of the structural portion, or the vitale forces of a body, in such a way and manner as to set it again in motion.
Thus does spiritual or psychic influence of body upon body bring healing to any individual; where another body may raise that necessary influence in the hormone of the circulatory forces as to take from that within itself to revivify or resuscitate diseased, disordered or distressed conditions within a body...
So may an individual effect a healing, through meditation, through attuning not just a side of the mind nor a portion of the body but the whole, to that at-oneness with the spiritual forces within, the gift of the life-force within each body.   281-24

Individuals may radiate, by their spiritual selves, health, life, that vibration which is destruction to disease. 1010-17

The physical body may be altered by the concerted activity of minds that are directed to the atomic forces of an individual, in raising their vibrations to a nominal or normal manner. Hence we have spiritual healing to a body. 5576-1

Q-If I have the power of healing, in what form will it express itself?
A-By the laying on of hands, when the **body** itself has been **purified by** the healing within its **own** self and the **vibrations** raised to that where the aura or vibratory force of self may accord or attune itself immediately with the vibrations of other individuals seeking aid. 516-4

(Laying on hands) takes vitality from a body. Rub hands thoroughly together, of course, before this is begun. Keep them very clean but let the vibrations from the body pass through the child's body. 2999-2

There must flow out of self Virtue (that is understanding) for healing to be accomplished in another. 281-10

Q-Please give a definition of vibration in relation to healing.
A-This would perhaps require several volumes to give a complete definition. Vibration is, in its simple essence or word, **raising** the Christ Consciousness in self to such an extent as it may flow **out** of self to him thou would direct it to. As, "Silver and gold I have none, but such as I have give I unto thee. In the **name** of Jesus Christ stand up and walk" (Acts 3:6). **That** is an illustration of vibration that heals, manifested in a material world. What flowed out of Peter or John? That as received by knowing self in its entirety, body, mind, soul, is one **with** that Creative Energy that is **Life** itself. 281-7

Q-Is there any treatment known today in the field of electromagnetic treatment that is superior to the physical treatments being used?
A-If physical electromagnetic treatments are given by those who have the ability to store within themselves those energies that may be transmitted to bodies, nothing surpasses. Where...individuals are not able, the low form of electro-vibration that emanate from the lowest form of electrical activity would produce similar and helpful conditions, and sometimes equal to and surpassing some electromagnetic treatments. 445-2

Q-Any specific (sound) compositions that can be used for healing?
A-...R and O and M are those combinations which vibrate to the center forces of the body itself. In any compositions of which these are a part there will be found that necessary for the individual. What might be healing for one might be distracting for another, to be sure. 1861-12

The stimuli that we would add for the body (insanity), then, would be the low form of electrical vibrations (Wet Cell Appliance).

As we may see in a functioning physical organism, electricity in its incipiency or lowest form is the nearest vibration in a physical sense to Life itself. 3950-1

The low electrical vibrations from the Wet Cell Appliance will be to recharge the body, as it were, furnishing the vibrations which are as Life itself in motivative active force in a material world. 1018-1

While life is an electrical energy...know that **constructive** are the **lowest** forms, destructive the higher forms. 1249-1

Bodily forces are electrical, and arise from the low forms of electrical vibration rather than from the higher that make for direct or alternating current. 1146-1

Q-What can I do to revitalize my nervous system?
A-Use that reionizer, the Radio-Active Appliance, as has been given.
This **revitalizes** the system throughout! For it coordinates impulses. As the cycle of impulse through the system flows through same, the Appliance, it is that which aids the vitality or vibratory forces of the body to be renewed or to coordinate and cooperate.
Hence at such periods that this Appliance is used, we would use the same periods for the deep meditation. And as the Mind is the Builder, we find that the revitalizing of the body will bring for the whole of the nervous system and also the whole regenerative system **new life** new energies awakened in same...
Restlessness, insomnia and irritation will disappear. 1472-2

The Radio-Active Appliance takes energies in portions of the body, builds up and discharges body electrical energies that revivify portions of the body where there is a lack of energies store. 3105-1

The Radio-Active Appliance is good for **anyone**, and especially for those that are tired or need an equalizing of the circulation; which is necessary for anyone that uses the brain a great deal--or that is unactive on the feet as much as is sufficient to keep proper circulation. 826-3

Vibrations from the Radio-Active Appliance properly given will make for rest that is both helpful and body, blood and nerve-building. 1278-7

In the Radio-Active Appliance we attune the Infinite within self to the Infinite without. 1211-2

The conditions here (throat cancer) may be best retarded by the use at times, about once a week, of a magnet--of sufficient strength to raise a railroad spike--this being passed over affected areas, see? This will aid in demagnetizing or producing a vibration that will destroy the active forces of the consuming of cells being enlivened by the infection. 3313-1

Many an individual that has had a brain wreck might be aided by electrical and music to a revivification of those cells, of those atomic forces that need their coercion and their regeneration by their absorbing one into another--rather than being separated and fighting its own self, or lack of proper coagulation of the cellular forces in the blood and brain forces; as in some forms of dementia, strained by great religious fervor or excitement.   933-2

The entity, with the very words or the blessings in planting even a nut, may insure the next generation a nut-bearing tree. The entity with its very abilities of the magnetic forces within self, may circle one with its hands and it'll bear no more fruit, though it may be bearing nuts in the present.   3657-1

EXERCISE

It's well that each body, everybody, take exercise to counteract the daily routine activity so as to produce rest.   416-1

Exercise of the body brings strength and resistance. Exercise of mental activity brings resistances, growth and expansion.   1206-13

To over exercise any portion (of the body) not in direct need of same, to the detriment of another, is to hinder rather than to assist. Exercise is wonderful, and necessary--and little or few take as much as is needed, in a systematic manner. Use common sense. Use discretion.   283-1

Walking is the best exercise, and in the **open** as much as possible. Not too great an amount, of course, but sufficient activities to prevent the settling of any of the drosses or used energies that are not elim-inated from settling in any portion of the system.   4633-1

Of morning the exercise for the upper portion of the body. Of evening, before retiring, exercise from the waist down, such as was used in setting up exercises of army...equalizing the circulation; remembering as of this: In the actions of the physical body, the blood, the blood forces are carried to the head in the day exercise, and must be equalized over the system by exercise in evening, would the body gain the physical rest that necessary to keep the body in perfect equilibrium.   257-8

Evening exercises for the blood flow away from head, and of mornings with the upper portion of body. Swinging, circular motion then of lower portion of body in evenings, and the circular motion of hands and upper portion of body of mornings, taking rub-downs of cold water on the spine after each exercise.   288-11

Golf, or riding, or rowing, or swimming requires the use of all the muscular forces of the system...Following such...the body should be rubbed down thoroughly, and a gentle massage--either **osteopathically or** neuropathically, or **Swedish** massage--given **all over** the body. 5602-1

Stretch the body as a cat would stretch. This is the best exercise to keep body in proportion.   5271-1

Q-What can I do for varicose veins, low blood pressure, fallen arches?
A-...No better exercises may be taken than the stretching exercise; as rising on toes--and this doesn't mean with shoes on!--on heels, rocking back and forth; stretching the arms upward, the bending exercises, what may literally termed--and is termed by some--the cat-stretching exercises, which includes, of course, being able--(put very coarsely)--to do the split, be able to put the head on the feet, to put the feet behind the head, to make the head and neck exercises and all of those activities that may be said to be of the feline or cat exercise.   681-2

Of morning, and upon arising especially (and don't sleep too late)--and before dressing, so that the clothing is loose or the fewer (worn) the better--standing erect before an open window, breathe deeply; gradually raising hands **above** the head, and then with the circular motion of the body from the hips bend forward; breathing **in** (and through the nostrils) as the body rises on the toes--breathing very deep: **exhaling** suddenly through the **mouth**; **not** through the nasal passages. Take these for five to six minutes.
Then as these progress, gradually **close** one of the nostrils (even if it's necessary to use the hand--but if it is closed with the left hand, raise the right hand; and when closing the right nostril with the right hand, then raise the left hand) as the breathing **in** is accomplished.
Rise, and (then have) the circular motion of the body from the hips, and (the) bending forward; **expelling** as the body reaches the lowest level in the bending towards the floor (expelling through the mouth, suddenly).
Then of an evening, just before retiring--with the (body prone, facing the floor and feet) braced against the wall, circle the torso by resting on the hands. Raise and lower the body not merely by the hands but more from the torso, and with more of a circular motion of the pelvic organs strengthen the muscular forces of the abdomen. Not such an

activity as to cause strain, but a gentle, circular motion to the right two to three times, and then to the left. 1523-2

Rise on the toes slowly and raise the arms easily at the same time directly above the head, pointing straight up. At the same time bend (the) head back just as far as you can. When (you) let down gently from this, you...give a better circulation through the whole area from the abdomen, through the diaphragm, through the lungs, head and neck.

Then let down, put the head forward just as far as it will come on the chest, then raise again at the top, bend the head to the right as far as it will go down. When rising again, bend the head to the left. Then, standing erect, hands on hips, circle the head, roll around to the right two or three times, then straighten self. Again, hands off the hip, down gently, rise again, down again, then circle to the opposite side. We will find we will change all of these disturbances through the mouth, head, eyes, and the activities of the whole body will be improved. Open your mouth as you go up and down, also. 470-37

Stretching of the abdomen as the exercise with feet against the wall; hands on the floor and raise and circle the body itself. This will keep the abdomen and the hips in correct position and keep body muscles through the hips and abdomen in such condition and positions as to make for much better activity in all organs of the pelvis, the abdominal area. 1206-16

The specific exercise (torpid liver and anemia) should be the turning or twisting of the body, as affect from the diaphragm up.

Q-Give some specific lower limb exercise for the evening. (27 year old amply endowed woman)

A-Those of the stooping with the feet together and those of the stooping with the feet, as the body raises--jumps up--and spread the feet apart--these are best--be well to pull down the shades though. 288-28

Q-How can I improve my vision?

A-...Each morning and each evening take this exercise regularly for six months and we will see a great deal of difference: sitting erect, bend the head forward three times, to the back three times, to the right side three times, to the left side three times, and then circle the head each way three times. Don't hurry through with it. 3549-1

A very helpful exercise (for hemorrhoids) would be the bending exercise with the hands raise high above the head, bending forward to bring the hands as close to the floor as possible. Do this for two or three minutes morning and evening. 4873-1

Don't work at golf, play at golf. 1154-1

Q-How can the body relax?

A-This is a **mental** as well as a physical process.

Concentration upon relaxation is the greater or better manner for **any** body to relax. That is, **SEE** the body **relaxing, CONSCIOUSLY!** Not concentrating so as to draw **in** the influence, but as to let all of the tension, all of the strain, flow **OUT** of self--and find the body giving--away.   404-6

Q-How can I overcome the nerve strain I'm under at times?

A-By closing the eyes and meditating from within, so that there arises --through that of the nerve system--that necessary element that makes along the **pineal** (don't forget that this runs from the toes to the crown of the head!), that will quiet the whole nerve forces, making for...the **true** bread, the true strength of life itself. Quiet, meditation, for a half to a minute, will bring strength--if the body will see **physically** this **flowing** out to quiet self, whether walking, standing, or resting.   311-4

Q-What should be done for fatigue and nervous exhaustion?

A-As given. The Fume Baths, sweats and rubs, and **especially** the Radio-Active Appliance for reionizing and revitalizing the system...

Restlessness, insomnia and irritation will disappear.   1472-2

Relax self more thoroughly. Not by sedatives, not by medicinal properties that would hinder some other functioning of the system. Rather by those of relaxations in the open, in the sunshine, in relaxation from mental worries, and of **exercise especially** of that that would cause the nearer equalizing of the circulation, both nerve and blood supply, between the head and the trunk and the lower limbs; exercising then in the open, as in horseback riding, swimming, walking--**any** of these are well, and after such an exercise be thoroughly rubbed down, after taking a hot bath--preferably shower and (be) rubbed down thoroughly--especially along the cerebrospinal system.   5616-1

Q-What is best way to relax my head, when I translate or read a lot?

A-Relax the body fully, just before attempting same, by repose. Then a little head and neck exercise. And after such experiences again a thorough relaxing, with plenty of water taken internally, and a little head and neck exercise; and we will find...quick recuperative forces. 1554-4

Dissolve a full teaspoonful of strained honey into a glass or tumbler of heated milk. Taking this about twenty to thirty minutes before retiring will be found to be most helpful. (Hypertension)   1539-1

Take time to work, to think, to make contacts for a social line and for recreation. This old adage might well apply: after breakfast, work a while, after lunch rest a while, after dinner walk a mile.   3624-1

As may be or should be worked upon or classified by man, there is the ability to make odors that will respond, and do respond, to certain individuals or groups; and many hundreds **are** responding to odors that **produce** the **effect** within their systems for activities that the psychoanalyst and the psychologist have long since discarded--much as they have the manner in which the Creative Forces or God **may** manifest...

What bringeth mace and allspice and the various peppers but that which would arouse within man that of vengeance...

Hast thou ever known the odor from a flesh body of a babe to be the same as the odor from a body that has been steeped in the sins of the world?...Look about thee; and thou may understand how that one of the canine or cat family may--through the very spoor of its master or one of its kind--determine not only the days of its passage but as to the state of its being, interpreted as to its ability for procreation within its own self.   274-10

Does the odor of an orris compound affect every individual alike? Or does the attar of roses or the essence of clover or of honeysuckle or crabapple or the life affect (everyone) the same way and manner? No. To some it would bring repellent influences; to others it would bring experiences that have been builded in the inner self...

There is no greater influence in a physical body (and this means animal or man; and man, presumptuously at times, is the higher order of same) than the effect of odors upon the olfactory nerves of the body...

How many of those that usually open an egg that's been buried for five to ten million years can, by its analysis, tell you what its composition is, or what the fowl or animal fed upon that laid it? This body can...

In opening a tomb wherein there had been the form of classifications or activities in a temple service, (the entity) would be able to tell whether there had been such sacrifices required as the destruction of animal life or of man, or whether there was used the odors of flowers, trees, buds, or a combination. How valuable would such an one as this body be to many engaged in such work?   274-7

Q-What should the entity study to develop mysticism?
A-The effect of odor, color, harmony, upon individuals.   1741-1

It will be found that the odors of henna, with tolu and myrrh, create an influence of ease.   1580-1

Lavender, odors that come from sandalwood have a peculiar influence upon the body in the present; for these bespeak of something innate within self that bespeaks of the abilities of the soul, mind and body to revivify and rejuvenate itself as to an ideal.   578-2

Some of it (migraine headaches) is due to allergy, but what is allergy? These are the effects of the imagination upon any influences that may react upon the olfactory or the sympathetic nerves. If we will cleanse the system (using colonics and Glyco-Thymoline), as we find, we should bring better conditions.   3400-2

Q-Am I allergic to any substance?
A-Did you ever consider what is meant by being allergic? Most of it is in your imagination. Do you imagine things? Then you are allergic to it. There are some pollens and odors (more odors with this body) that are offensive, and this the body is allergic to them. But these will also disappear if there is better circulation created and if the poisons are eliminated from the system.   3586-1

Q-What are all the things I am allergic to?
A-It would be a list from here to Egypt...especially dust.
Q-What is causing head troubles--ears, nose, throat and eyes?
A-Read just what has been indicated as to how the various centers in the body are affected by this discoordination of the sympathetic and cerebrospinal nerves, and as to how and why the careful massage should be given to coordinate the centers and set up direct coordination through the electrotherapy. And we will break up or, as it were, have direct connections and not short circuits through the body. But much of this has to do with the emotions.
This doesn't mean to imply that the body is mentally unbalanced, not at all. That's the trouble, it's too high-strung, it's too susceptible to suggestion.   3556-1

Q-Since the asthmatic attacks seem to occur every night between the hours of three and seven a.m. is there something in the room in which he sleeps that brings on these attacks?
A-It is not that sometimes called an allergy. It is more of the mental, but comes from the associations in the mind rather than physical things.
Q-Is there any particular thing to which he is allergic?
A-Mostly to himself and his family! But, as indicated, it is not **things** that he is allergic to--it's conditions!   2755-2

Q-Does coming in contact with flowers, feathers or furs have any effect on this body?
A-It does. For there are the radiations from every form of life, and as the plasms as have to do with coagulation are positive, and those of flowers or of any of the pollens that come from same, or vibrations, are negative--they produce irritation.   2884-1

Sufficiently strong odors are just as harmful to the body as dust. 3644-1

Colors affect the body, even as **pollen** does many another. 5511-1

Q-What causes the neuritis in my left side whenever I put on a pair of shoes, or brassiere, or glasses with plastic frames?
A-These are allergies through the sympathetic system.   3125-1

In another experience we find that the entity was a chemist, and she used many of those various things for the producing of itching in others. She finds it in herself in the present...In the presence of certain metals, certain plastics, certain odors, the body immediately is poisoned. Just as certain characters of leathers. If these are tanned with oak they do not harm the body. If they are tanned with those very same things the entity once used to hinder someone else, they hinder the entity. 3125-2

It is necessary that the body first, in its spiritual aspects, in its spiritual hopes and purposes set self aright. Then those things that pertain to wearing apparel as the brassiere, the glasses, the shoes, certain odors when it enters certain rooms, certain animals--will no longer have their effect upon the body; as the mind takes on those abilities to alleviate the disturbances produced by the resistance built up in the imaginative forces or mental-aptitudes of the body-mind. 3125-3

Q-In the present, why do I have the feeling of contamination when touching animals' hair, fur or feathers?
A-As in that experience in Atlantis, the thought forces brought into being were of the animal...and the **natural** tendency of abhorrence arose from seeing those things take form as menaces, or seeds of indiscretion of beings in the experience.   288-29

Q-Is this rash (eczema) an allergic case?
A-As indicated, there are certain foods, or properties in foods, to which the body has become allergic--which is those that are not assimilated through the regular digestive system. Hence the necessity of purifying the alimentary canal through the use of the properties indicated (Glyco-Thymoline), and the application of same externally.
Of course, keep the liver active. This may be best done through the use of massage or osteopathy.   274-17

Q-Is there any remedy for Poison Ivy which you could suggest?
A-The very tender shoots of same made into a mild tea and taken internally--as a tonic would prevent Poison Ivy being effective...
When it has been attracted, or is effective in the circulation, take small quantities of Atomidine internally--one to two drops in water for four to five days, and leave off. And bathe in a weakened solution of same, or bathe the portion thus effected.   1770-4

(For Hay Fever) before there is the blossoming of (ragweed) the body should take quantities of this weed. Brew same, prepare, take internally...This will enable the body to become immune because of the very action of this weed upon the digestive system...

Thus we would prepare the compound in this manner: Take a pint cup, gather the tender leaves of the weed, don't cram in but just fill level. Put this in an enamel or a glass container and then the same amount (after cleansing of course, don't put dirt and all in but put in same amount by measure) of distilled water, see? Reduce this to half the quantity by very slow boiling, not hard but slow boiling, strain and add sufficient grain alcohol as a preservative.

Begin and take it through the fifteen days of July and the whole of August, daily, half a teaspoonful each day...

Then, use through the latter portion of August and September, this as a combination: Prepare in the manner indicated, putting together the ingredients only in the order named. First we would prepare a bottle with a large-mouth, two vents through the cork and these vents capable of being corked themselves with a small cork. Neither of the vents is to enter the solution, so use a six ounce container. In this container put four ounces of grain alcohol (at least 90% proof), then add in the order named: Oil of Eucalyptus, 20 minims (drops); Rectified Oil of Turp, 5 minims; Compound Tincture of Benzoin, 15 minims; Oil of Pine Needles, 10 minims; Tolu in Solution, 10 minims.

When this is to be used, shake the solution together, remove the corks from the vent, inhale deep through the nostril so as to enter the nasal passages, also to the upper and back portions of throat, both passages. Shake between each deep inhalation.   5347-1

THE SCIENCE OF OSTEOPATHY

Through the sympathetic system (as it is called, or those centers not encased in cerebrospinal system) are the connections with the cerebrospinal system. Then, in each center--that is, of the segment where these connect--there are tiny bursa, or a plasm of nerve reaction. This becomes congested, or slow in its activity to each portion of the system. For, each organ, each gland of the system, receives impulses through this manner for its activity.

Hence we find there are reactions to every portion of the system by suggestion, mentally, and by the environment and surroundings.

Also we find that a reaction may be stimulated **internally** to the organs of the body, by injection of properties or foods...

We also find the reflex from these internally to the brain centers.

Then, the **science** of osteopathy is not merely the punching in a certain segment or the cracking of the bones, but it is the keeping of a **balance** --by the touch--between the sympathetic and cerebrospinal system. **That** is real osteopathy!   1158-24

Osteopathy is real work if done properly.   102-3

These adjustments are merely to attune the centers of the body with the coordinating forces of cerebrospinal and sympathetic systems. Thus the body is purified or attuned so that it in itself, and nature, do the healing.   3384-2

As a **system** of treating human ills, osteopathy--**we** would give--is more beneficial than most measures that may be given. Why? In any preventative or curative measure, that condition to be produced is to assist the system to gain its normal equilibrium. It is known that each organ receives impulses from other portions of the system by the suggestive forces (sympathetic nervous system) and by circulatory forces (the cerebrospinal system and the blood supply itself). These course through the system in very close parallel activity in **every** single portion of the body. Hence stimulating ganglia from which impulses arise--either sympathetically or functionally--must then be helpful in the body gaining an equilibrium.   902-1

There is every force in the body to recreate its own self--if the various portions of the system are coordinating and cooperating one with another. Hence the reason why, as we have so oft given from the sources here that mechanical adjustments as may be administered by a thorough or serious osteopathic manipulator may nearer adjust the system for its perfect unison of activity than most any other means--save under acute or specific conditions and even then more oft such becomes necessary.   1158-11

Set up better eliminations in the body this is why osteopathy and hydrotherapy come nearer to being the basis of all needed treatments for physical disabilities.   2524-5

Manipulative forces osteopathically given, unless there is necessity for corrections, only assist the body in breaking up congestion or congested areas or in assisting ganglia under stress or strain to be so adjusted that the eliminations or drainages in portions of the body are set up and stimulation to active functioning organs is produced.   1110-4

If mothers would only know that a good gynecologist of the osteopathic school would save more mothers from hard labor (during child birth).   457-14

At least one week out of each month should be spent in beautifying, preserving, rectifying the body--if the body would keep young, in mind, in body, in purpose. This doesn't mean that the entity should spend a whole week at nothing else, (but) choose three days out of some week in each month--not just three days in a month, but three days in some definite week each month--either the first, the second, the third or the fourth week of each month--and have the general hydrotherapy treatments, including massage, lights, and all the treatments that are in that nature of beautifying, and keeping the whole of the body-force young.   3420-1

Q-Epsom-salt baths were recommended in a variety of cases including arthritis, glandular disturbances, incoordination, injuries, lesions, lumbago, neuritis, paralysis, rheumatism, sciatica and toxemia.
The directions varied quite radically with different people.
A-We would have **every day** at least one bath with a good amount of Epsom Salts in it, following this with a good rubdown along the whole cerebrospinal system...The Epsom salts bath would be taken during the day. Put a pound of salts to about ten to twenty gallons of water; not too hot but rather a tepid bath, but remain in same so that the absorption and reaction to the whole nerve system is received. Add a little hot water to keep this warm, but so that the body may rest in same from 20 to 30 minutes. (Injuries)   349-12

Once a month or the like have a complete hydrotherapy administration; including a mild cabinet sweat, the sitz baths a full massage with an equal combination of Pine Oil and Peanut Oil; finishing, of course, with the alcohol rub. (Poor Eliminations and Incoordination)   1968-6

We would take systematically, a series of hydrotherapy. Each treatment should include a dry heat bath followed by the fumes with same of Witch Hazel; then the hot and cold shower, or needle shower; then the thorough rub-down--a massage of the body with Pine Oil (preferably for this body). (Anemia and Leukemia tendencies, and Poor Circulation)   3000-1

Steam or vapor baths--combining Witch Hazel and the Oil of Pine, or Oil of Pine Needles and Witch Hazel--will make for purifying, strengthening, cleansing of the body and skin. Such a bath would be taken once a week, or after a bit, once a month; with a thorough rub-down following same. (Pyorrhea and Obesity Tendencies)   1276-1

In the hydrotherapy treatment should be included a good sweat, not with dry heat but rather the fume bath cabinet sweat; for dry heat would be too draining on the body. For the fumes, use an equal combination of Witch Hazel and Rosewater, or a teaspoonful of each in a pint of water that would form vapor to settle over the body. (Incoordination)   2957-1

The why of the massage should be considered: Inactivity causes many of those portions along the spine from which impulses are received to the various organs to be lax, or taut, or to allow some to receive greater impulse than others. The massage aids the ganglia to receive impulse from nerve forces as it aids circulation.   1456-4

For this body (injuries), the hydrotherapy bath would be well; which would be to lie in great quantity or a tub of water for a long period-- this being kept a little above the temperature of the body; then followed by a thorough massage by a masseuse. This would be better than adjustments **or** deep treatments, though it will be found that with the massage along the spine, with the body prone upon the face, these would--with the knuckle on either side of the spinal column--tend to make many a segment come nearer to normalcy, by being so treated **after** having been thoroughly relaxed for twenty to thirty minutes **in** the warm or hot water, see?   635-9

The massage will keep the centers and ganglia along the spinal system in better coordination; and we will find the vision corrected, the taste and hearing and odors quite different, and the memory much bettered. 1965-2

Keep the liver active. This may be best done through the use of massage, or osteopathy, to stir the liver.   274-17

Q-Peanut oil rubs were recommended in a variety of cases including general debilitation, multiple sclerosis, neuritis, paralysis, Parkinson's disease, poor circulation, poor eliminations, stomach ulcers, toxemia.
A-About twice each week, almost bathe in Olive Oil or Peanut Oil; especially Peanut Oil--in the joints, the neck, across the clavicle, across all the areas of the spine, the rib and the frontal area to the pit of the stomach, across the stomach and especially in the diaphragm area; then across the hips and the lower portion of the back and across the sacral area and then the limbs themselves. Massage these by dipping the fingers in the oil. Do not sponge off immediately. Do this just before retiring, wipe off with tissue, and then bathe off in the morning, see? As we find, if these are kept consistently, we will not only build strength but supply the better circulation throughout the whole body ...Take from thirty minutes to an hour or an hour and a half to do it! (Ringing in Head and Ears)   1688-7

Those who would take a Peanut Oil rub each week need never fear arthritis.   1158-31

(Take Pure Peanut) Oil rubs once a week, and ye will never have rheumatism nor...stalemate in liver and kidney.   1206-13

Massage with Peanut Oil--yes, the lowly Peanut Oil has in its combination that which will aid in creating in the superficial circulation, and in the superficial structural forces, as well as in the skin and blood, those influences that make more pliable the skin, muscles, nerves and tendons, that go to make up the assistance to structural portions of the body. Its absorption and its radiation through the body will also strengthen the activities of the structural body itself.   2968-1

Q-Oil combinations containing Peanut Oil and Olive Oil were recommended in a variety of cases including arthritis, kidney disorders, multiple sclerosis, Parkinson's disease, prostatitis, rheumatism, and toxemia.
A-Each day when removing the (Wet Cell) Appliance from the body, massage the body thoroughly with this combination of oils:
Peanut Oil (2 ounces), Olive Oil (2 ounces), (liquefied) Lanolin (1 teaspoonful). Shake this solution and massage thoroughly into the lumber and sacral areas, and especially along limbs, the left limb that has the trouble and the right limb--under the knee, in the foot, especially in the bursa of the heel and the front under the toes or in the instep. (Multiple Sclerosis)   3232-1

Q-For varicose veins, tendinitis, strains, fractures, swelling in the feet and ankles, especially problems of the lower limbs.
A-Do use an equal combination of Olive Oil (heated) and Tincture of Myrrh to massage in knee, limbs and feet, right after these have been bathed in hot water. Massage these oils well into them. 3523-1

Q-For muscular sprains, strains, backache, and bruises.
A-To one ounce of Olive Oil, add: Russian White Oil (2 ounces), Witch Hazel (1/2 ounce), Tincture of Bensoin (1/2 ounce), Oil of Sassafras (20 minims), Coal Oil (6 ounces). It'll be necessary to shake this together, for it will tend to separate; but a small quantity massaged in the cerebrospinal system or over sprains, joints, swellings, bruises, will **take out** the inflammation or pain.   326-5

To 4 ounces of Russian White Oil add: Witch Hazel (2 ounces), Rub alcohol (not wood, but **rub** alcohol compound) (1 ounce), Oil of Sassafras (3 to 5 minims). Shake this together. Only use a small portion of same at the time. Begin with the hips and rub down (with upward pressure of the hands). This would be good for anyone that stands on the feet much, or whose feet pain.   555-5

Occasionally massage along the spine with Cocoa Butter; an ounce in which there has been put five grains of quinine, mix thoroughly. Massage this along the spine, under the arms and in the groin. Not only will the mosquito not bite, but there will be no malaria. 5188-1

Every one--everybody--should take an internal bath occasionally, as well as an external one. They would all be better off if they would.440-2

Have a good hydrotherapist give a thorough, but gentle colon cleansing; this possibly a week or two weeks apart. In the first waters, use salt and soda, in the proportions of a heaping teaspoonful of table salt and a level teaspoonful of baking soda (both) dissolved thoroughly--to each half gallon of water. In the last water use Glyco-Thymoline as an intestinal antiseptic to purify the system, in the proportions of a tablespoonful to the quart of water. (Anemia and Poor Eliminations)   1745-4

One colonic irrigation will be worth about four to six enemas. 3570-4

This does not mean that merely because there is the daily activity of the alimentary canal there is no need for flushing the system. But when ever there is the feeling of sluggishness, have the treatments (colonic irrigations). It'll pick the body up. For there is a need for such treatments when the condition of the body becomes drugged because of absorption of poisons through alimentary canal or colon, sluggishness of liver or kidneys, and there is lack of coordination with the cerebrospinal and sympathetic blood supply and nerves. For the hydrotherapy and massage are preventive as well as curative measures.   257-254

CAUSE OF SOME MIGRAINE HEADACHES

Most of these (migraine headaches), as in this case, begin from congestions in the colon. These cause toxic conditions to make pressures on the sympathetic nerve centers and on the cerebrospinal system. And these pressures cause the violent headaches and almost irrational activities at times. These, as we find, should respond to colonic irrigations.   3400-2

The headaches are the signs or warnings that eliminations are not being properly cared for. Most of this, in this body, comes from the alimentary canal, and from those conditions that exist in portions of the colon itself, as to produce a pressure upon those centers affected...Hence the suggestion for the osteopathic correction, which aid but which do not eliminate all of these conditions which are as accumulations through portions of the colon. Consequently, colonic irrigations are necessary occasionally, as well as general hydrotherapy and massage.   2602-2

Remove these pressures in the colon by high colonic irrigations. Keep these up, though it may bring on a mild attack during the first or second period. Keep these up until all of the mucus is entirely removed, for this is the source of the pressure--in a part of the caecum area. These colonics in the beginning should be given not more than fifteen days apart, until five or six have been given. And these must be scientifically given, not a 'slap dab' job. For, these are conditions where the special areas in the caecum center are to be purified. (Migraine Headaches) 3329-1

As in most conditions of the nature of migraine or so called headaches, the cause is in the colon--where there are patches of adhesions of fecal forces to the walls of the intestine, causing activities that come in general cycles. These may come at times regularly, almost so that you could set this by your clock at times; for it is as the regularity of the system itself. 3630-1

GLYCO-THYMOLINE AS AN INTESTINAL ANTISEPTIC

To purify the alimentary canal, give every day about three drops of Glyco-Thymoline or Lavoris; and keep this up until such may be detected as an odor in the stool. 2015-8

Use an alkalizer for the alimentary canal...each day take three to four drops of Glyco-Thymoline internally in a little water. Take this for sufficient period until the **odor** (of Glyco-Thymoline) may be detected from the stool. This will purify the whole of the alimentary canal and create an alkaline reaction **through** the lower portion of the alimentary canal. 1807-3

Q-How can I get rid of bad breath?
A-By making for better conditions in (the) eliminations. Take Glyco-Thymoline as an intestinal antiseptic. Two, three times a day. Put six drops of Glyco-Thymoline in the drinking water. 5198-1

We would use the Glyco-Thymoline packs over the nasal passages, or sinus passages. Saturate three to four thicknesses of cotton cloth, or gauze, in warm Glyco-Thymoline, and apply over the passages, allowing such a pack to remain on for 15 to 20 minutes at the time-- and keep up until the passages are clear. Apply such packs whenever there is any distress--either in the sinus or in the digestive system. Such packs may also be applied over the abdominal area to advantage as well as over the face, see?
Also we would take Glyco-Thymoline internally, 2 to 3 drops in 1/2 a glass of water about twice a day (and drink a glass of water afterwards) until the system has been purified. (Sinusitis) 2794-2

For making or keeping a good complexion--this for the skin, the hands, arms and body as well--we would prepare a compound to use as a massage (by self) at least once or twice each week. To six ounces of Peanut Oil, add: Olive Oil, two ounces; Rose Water, two ounces; Lanolin, dissolved, one tablespoonful. This would be used after a tepid bath, in which the body has remained for at least fifteen to twenty minutes; giving the body then (during the bath) a thorough rub with any good soap--to stimulate the body-forces. As we find, Sweetheart or any good Castile soap, or Ivory, may be used for such.

Afterwards, massage (with) this solution, after shaking it well.   1968-7

Q-What soap, manner of cleansing, creams and make up would be least harmful and most helpful in correcting and beautifying the skin?

A-Pure Castile soap is the better as a cleanser. As a cleansing cream ...the Genuine Black and White products are nearer normal. 2072-6

(Use soap) prepared with Olive Oil, or Cocoanut Oil rather than other characters of fats.   3051-3

Génuine Black and White preparations...are preferable to most compounds that carry leads or poisonous conditions for the skin. 2154-2

About twice a month...have the Mud Packs; face and neck, and across the shoulders and upper portion about the neck; especially extending over the area of the thyroids--as an astringent and as a stimulation for a better circulation throughout the system.   1968-3

Q-Should one use a deodorant under the arms to stop perspiration?
A-The **best** to use--the safest--is soap and water!
Q-Give a good skin freshener.
A-To one half pint of Olive Oil add one ounce of Rose Water, a few drops of Glycerine and one ounce of a 10% solution of Alcohol, and shake these well together. This is a skin invigorator.   404-8

To one tablespoon of melted Cocoa Butter add, while it is liquid: Rose Water, 1 tablespoonful; Compound tincture of Benzoin, 1 tablespoon...This would be a very, very good skin cleanser for anyone!1016-1

As to the face lotion, we find that a cream that is...wholly alkaline and non-acid is preferable. (Face Rash)   275-37

If there is the desire for that which will be almost a perfect skin lotion, use on same a compound prepared in this manner: Rose Water, 2 ounces; Usoline, 1/2 ounce; Lanolin, dissolved, 1/2 teaspoonful. Rubbing this on the hands, in the palms and on the feet will heal, and prevent burning--or the roughness or those tendencies for rash. 2769-1

(Dry and scaly skin) may be aided by the rubbing with a combination of Rose Water and Olive Oil--equal parts. This is to soothe the skin, but the general applications should be from within.   274-9

By massaging it (birthmark) with an equal mixture of Olive Oil and Castor Oil--it will be prevented from increasing. Marks on bodies, as on this one, are for a purpose--and if a life reading would be given it would be seen that it (the child) has a purpose to perform in the affairs of those in its surroundings and in many others. A mark!   573-1

Q-Is it well to remove matter from the pimples and blackheads?
A-This is very well, provided the areas are rubbed soon afterward with this combination of oils: Peanut Oil, 2 ounces; Olive Oil, 2 ounces; Lanolin, liquified, 1/4 ounce.   2072-13

Q-What is the correct treatment for frostbite?
A-The better, as we find, is Petrol--or Coal Oil--massaged, and taken in very small quantities (taken internally and rubbed on too!)   276-7

It will require patience, persistence, if we would eliminate this character of acidity (herpes simplex) from the system...
Drink about six or eight glasses of water daily, but in at least three of these, put five drops of Glyco-Thymoline.
Also we would have colonic irrigations...
Use over the abdominal area, as well as the area along the right side, Glyco-Thymoline packs. These we would do regularly. Do this about two days in succession and rest a period of two days between each series. These would be taken for at least an hour. Saturate a cotton cloth, three to four thicknesses with Glyco-Thymoline. Do this and keep the diet towards those things that produce eliminations. This application should include a thorough massage given twice a week.   5152-1

Q-Since diet has not caused hair on lips to diminish, is there anything which will prevent this that can be used externally? Will cutting or bleaching increase growth?
A-Do not shave off, do not attempt to bleach or dye, but use this mixture:
Cocoa butter, 3 drams; Calomel, 2 grains; Epsom salts, 20 grains. Mix these thoroughly, as with (mortar) and pestle. Massage this ointment gently in the areas where there are the disturbances from superfluous hair, and after leaving on for 15 to 20 minutes, rub off. This, used as an ointment will remove hair without injury to the body. To be sure, mercury is in the Calomel, and this is a poison, but with this combination and in this quantity there is not sufficient for a body to absorb enough to become detrimental...After this is used, as the base for a better skin condition use the Genuine Black and White cream.   2582-4

The sun during the period between eleven or eleven-thirty and two o'clock carries to **great** a quantity of the actinic rays that make for destructive force to the superficial circulation.   934-2

Sun baths are of benefit to **most** bodies; would be helpful to this (body) if not too **much** is given.   5455-1

It is the absorption of the ultra-violet which give strength and vitality to the nerves and muscular forces.   3172-2

Better that the ultra-violet rays (from the sun) be absorbed...than to have mechanical applications or other measures.   1861-16

Q-What is the best formula that will make my skin brown from the sun?
A-...(If the body is insistent that it desires the tan) use vinegar and Olive Oil (not vinegar made from acetic acid, or synthetic vinegar, but the use of Apple Vinegar) combined with coffee made from resteaming or revaporing used coffee grounds. The tannin in each of these and acids combined,--would become very effective. But it will wear off, of course, in a very short time.   276-7

Any good lotion would be well for the sunburn; such as Soda Water, or any application that would act as a balm, in the forms of some characters of oils...such as Glyco-Thymoline.   3051-1

As for the acute conditions (sunburn) we would daub or apply Spirits of Camphor by using tufts of cotton. Then in an hour or two hours afterward have a tepid bath, and then apply Peanut Oil.   303-33

CAMPHORATED OIL COULD REDUCE SCAR TISSUE

Camphorated Oil (which is, of course, Camphor added to Olive Oil) will make for an opening to the pores of the body, you see.   566-3

The use of Camphorated Oil twice each day is best application for removing scar or scar tissue on any portion of the body.   1566-4

Camphorated Oil will aid same (scars from the abscesses (boils) that have been lanced), of course, more than anything else.   3167-1

Camphorated Oil, with occasionally Carbolated Vaseline. This should be put on (scar from burn) before the oil is rubbed in.   1567-4

To relieve much of the scar tissue (after effects of severe burns) on the left limb, we would use Sweet Oil (Olive Oil) combined with

Camphorated Oil (equal parts). Massage this each day for three to six months and we would reduce the most of this...

Any scar tissue detracts from the general physical health of a body, for it requires a changing in the circulation continually.   487-15

These (scars) may be aided in being removed by sufficient time, precaution and persistence in the activity; by the massage over those portions of small quantities at a time of Tincture of Myrrh and Olive Oil, and Camphorated Oil. These would be massaged at different times to be sure; one, one day and the other the second day from same--see? In preparing the Olive Oil and Tincture of Myrrh, heat the oil and add the Myrrh--equal portions, only preparing such a quantity as would be used at each application. The Camphorated Oil may be obtained in quantity. Only massage such quantities as the cuticle and epidermis will absorb. This will require, to be sure, a long period but remember the whole surface may be entirely changed if this is done persistently and consistently. In the massaging, do not massage so roughly as to produce irritation. The properties are to be absorbed. Do not merely pat the solution on, and do not use tufts of cotton or other properties to dab it on--dip the finger tips into the solution, and it won't hurt the fingers either--it'll be good for them! and massage into affected portions...

The therapeutic value of the properties given to the skin itself is as follows: As given, as known and held by the ancients more than the present modes of medication, Olive Oil--properly prepared (hence pure Olive Oil should always be used)--is one of the most effective agents for stimulating muscular activity, or mucous membrane activity, that may be applied to a body. Olive Oil combined with Tincture of Myrrh will be very effective...The Camphorated Oil is merely the same basic force (Olive Oil) to which has been added properties of Camphor in more or less its raw or original state, rather than the Spirits of same. Such activity in the epidermis is not only to produce soothing to affected areas but to stimulate the circulation in such effectual ways and manners as to combine with the other properties in bringing what will be determined, in the course of two to two and a half years, a new skin.   440-3

While the (burns) appear very serious in the present, because of the blister or the water...we would cleanse and use the Tannic Acid; followed with...Unguentine, and the Sweet Oil and Camphorated Oil (which) are to take away scar tissue, see? These are to follow with ten days to two weeks, see?   2015-6

(The combination of oils): Camphorated Oil, 2 ounces; Lanolin, dissolved, 1/2 teaspoonful; Peanut Oil, 1 ounce will quickly remove this tendency of the scar. (Severe burn two years earlier) 2015-10

Q-Castor Oil Packs were recommended, often in conjunction with colonics, for adhesions, appendicitis, arthritis, cancer, cholecystitis, cirrhosis of the liver, colitis, constipation, cysts, epilepsy, gallstones, gastritis, hepatitis, hernia, Hodgkin's disease, hookworm, incoordination, intestinal impaction, lesions, lumbago, lymphitis, migraine, multiple sclerosis, neuritis, Parkinson's disease, pelvic cellulitis, poor eliminations, scleroderma, sluggish liver, sterility, strangulation of the kidneys, structure of the duodenum, toxemia, tumors, ulcers, uremia.

A-There are those forms of gravel or sand in the gall duct itself, not so much in the gall bladder, but the activity of these not coordinating.

We would apply the Castor Oil Packs regularly; that is, about 3 days a week for an hour each day for 3 or 4 weeks. Thus we may eliminate the sources of this disturbance (acne), eliminating the bad taste, the tendency for bad breath, the tendency for tired achey feelings, things not tasting just right.

For an hour each day that these packs are to be taken, use about 3 thicknesses of heavy old flannel saturated, with Castor Oil. Apply over the liver and gall duct area. It is well if this extends to the caecum area on the right side, to be sure. As this is applied to the body, cover with oilcloth so as to prevent soiling of linens. Then apply the electric pad. Let this keep very warm for an hour, sponge off with a weak soda water solution, a teaspoonful of baking soda in a pint or water well dissolved. Then after each 3-day series of the packs, take 2 table-spoonfuls of Olive Oil internally.

The second day after the first series, do have a colonic irrigation, so as to cleanse the entire alimentary canal or the colon, this will aid in cleansing the condition. We will find conditions may disappear.5092-1

The effect of these Oil Packs is to enliven, through the activity of the absorption through the perspiratory system, the activities in such natures and measures as to produce a greater quantity (than at present) and a superficial activity of the lymph circulation; hence setting up drainages to such measures that the poisons will be eliminated from the system. (Arthritis)   631-4

For one hour each day, for three days in succession, apply hot Castor Oil Packs over the liver. Apply the packs warm, sufficient to make for that radiation of activity to the body, and then apply the electric pad--that throughout the whole body there may be that radiation which brings the eliminations of poisons from the body.

On the evening of the third day take internally half a teacup of Olive Oil. Then rest from these five days, and then repeat for three days--again taking the Olive Oil. Do this for at least three series, after you have found yourself and your relationship to the Creator. Without finding that, apply it not.

Then begin with the careful massage daily of the whole sacral area, the hips, across the hips and the limbs, to the points of the pelvic bones and down through the area of the sciatic centers; using Cocoa Butter--all that will be absorbed...

If these are applied spiritually, mentally, materially the body will walk again--it will have the use of the limbs--it will be rid of those disturbances through the alimentary canal and the liver disturbance. A healing will come for the liver activities, and the kidneys and prostate disturbances will be eliminated from the body. (Impaired Locomotion)   3492-1

Have at least three to four thicknesses of old flannel saturated thoroughly with Castor Oil, then apply an electric heating pad. Let this get just about as warm as the body can well stand--cover with oilcloth to prevent soiling of linens. Keep this on every afternoon or evening for an hour. Then sponge off (the oil on the body) with soda water. Do this for at least seven days without breaking. One hour each day, same hour each day. After and during those periods take small doses of Olive Oil two, three times each day. These (small doses of Olive Oil) should not be so severe as to cause strain, but be careful after about the 3rd or 4th day to observe the stool, and there should be indications of the gall ducts being emptied, and should be gravel, and there should be some stones. This can be eliminated. If there are none indicated, rest one day, then repeat for another 7 days, and we will find changes come about, unless there is undue exercise.

Q-Where do the packs go?

A-Over the gall duct area and extend to the caecum down the right side, and across the abdomen. (Gallstones)   5186-1

Take these (Castor Oil Packs) each evening for three days in succession, and then the large dose of **Olive Oil**. Leave off three to four days, then take another series. Continue in this manner until the conditions has entirely cleared. Then leave off three to four weeks; then these should be taken again--regularly--in series--even though there is not the severe pain. (Cholecystitis with resulting Gastroduodentitis)   294-199

Begin with the use of Castor Oil Packs an hour each day for three days. Use at least three thicknesses of flannel, lightly wrung out of the Castor Oil, as hot as the body can stand it and applied over the liver and the whole of the abdomen, especially upon the right side. Keep the packs warm by using an electric pad. After the third day of using the packs, take a high enema to relieve the tensions throughout the colon and lower portions of jejunum, using a colon tube. (Poor Eliminations) 2434-1

Q-What causes the warts on the hand and how may they be removed?
A-This happens to most every individual in those periods of the change that comes about for glandular reaction...They may be removed by touching same with a (20%) solution of Hydrochloric Acid. 487-22

Equal portions of Castor Oil and Soda on the finger tip, massage this, it'll make it (wart on knee) sore but it'll take it away also. 308-13

Q-There are two growths that appear to be warts on the ball of my left foot; what is the best way to dissolve them or remove them?
A-Apply each evening a small amount of Baking Soda wet thoroughly with Spirits of Camphor or, just sufficient to cover same--and bind on so as to keep over the night. This will cause some little sharp pain, and a little soreness for a few days, but it will dissolve and prevent any irritation following same; for these are as but those eliminations in system being thrown in improper directions. 1101-3

Massage with Castor Oil twice each day; not rubbing hard, but **gentle** massage around and over the place. And it (mole) will be removed. **573-1**

STRENGTHENING YOUR FINGERNAILS

Q-What causes the deep ridges in thumbnail and what treatment?
A-...Take often chicken neck, chew it. Cook this well, the feet and those portions of the fowl, and we will find it will add calcium to the body. Also eat bones of fish, as in canned fish. Also parsnips and oyster plant (salsify); all of these, of course, in their regular season. Wild game of any kind, but chew the bones of same. 5192-1

(Splitting and breaking fingernails) is a lack of the glandular forces, especially in the thyroid, which will be materially aided by the addition of A and D vitamin forces as combined with the B complex. 667-14

Q-What can I do to keep my fingernails from splitting?
A-Add the vitamins necessary so that the glandular forces, and especially the thyroid, are improved...(Also) once a month, just before the (menstrual) period, take one drop of Atomidine in half a glass of water before the morning meal, for three to five days. Also massage the fingernails with Atomidine. 2448-1

Q-What will strengthen the fingernails against peeling and breaking?
A-The orange juice, the stimulation to the glandular circulation, and especially the diets of the potato peels. 1102-2

A massage with Baking Soda which has been dampened with Spirits of Camphor will be good for anyone having calloused places or any attendant growths on feet; for it will remove them entirely.   276-4

For five to ten days, use (massage thoroughly) Common Baking Soda wet or saturated with Spirits of Camphor. Then, after this has been used until the soreness is removed, use equal parts of Olive Oil and Tincture of Myrrh, and it'll (callous or bunion) be like a baby's foot.   574-1

Misfitting of shoes is usually the cause of corns. The best treatment is to use Camphor and Soda. Wet plain Baking Soda with Spirits of Camphor and apply nightly until corn is removed.   1309-7

Q-How can I remove the knot on my right second finger?
A-Massage with Castor Oil and Soda mixed.   303-32

This (excessive cracking in the bones of the feet) comes from a lack of proper circulation. A gentle but thorough massage of the limbs **downward**, with Cocoa Butter, especially through the feet and bursa of the heel and the ball of the foot, and across the toes, will aid--this done once or twice a week.   1158-21

Q-What causes the aching and burning of the feet?
A-Poor circulation, and acid in the system.   779-21

Use occasionally Witchhazel in its full strength to reduce this (Athlete's foot)...Bathe them often in **Salt** Water.   903-16

Local application of any solution with alcohol, or the Pure Grain Alcohol--weakened--will remove (crustiness between the toes).   480-45

Once each week we would use the Atomidine as a massage for the soles of the feet, and as a dressing for the toenails...this will change the disturbance with ingrowing nails. Lift up the nail and put small parts of cotton saturated with Atomidine under the edge of the toenail.   2988-1

These (ingrown toenails) as we find would respond to the dampening of Baking Soda with Spirits of Camphor and putting a small quantity of same on cotton, or alone under the tip of the nail, close to the irritated place. This will remove the condition if used daily or nightly.   1770-4

Q-Should the right hand or the left hand be developed?
A-Right. While the body is tended to be in the nature of both-handed, or super-dexterous, yet in the developing of the body--with the positions of the muscular forces and the position of the heart itself in the body --the **right** would be much better. Notice the positions when individuals are left-handed: it is more often the position of their heart!   758-27

To man hair in the head is as strength--to woman is as beauty. 636-1

Q-What foods or treatments are especially good for bringing more of the luster--reds, coppers and golds--back into the hair?
A-Nothing better than peelings of Irish potatoes or juices from same. Don't put the peelings in water and cook them, because most of the necessary properties will go out, but put them in Patapar to cook. 2072-14

If the juice of potato peelings is taken regularly (two to three times a week) it will keep the hair nearer to its normal color than all other forms of chemical preparations. 3051-3

If you desire to prevent gray hair, drink at least once each week half a pint of juice prepared from Irish potato peelings. 3900-1

Q-What causes dandruff? Can you give a formula for curing it?
A-It's poor circulation--and, of course, a germicidal condition, which arises from the poor circulation. Use alternately as a shampoo Listerine once a week, then the next week a Pure Tar Soap as a wash or shampoo...
(Gray hair) arises from many, many causes--but it is a general condition of the stimulation to the scalp pores or of the hair itself. It may be worry, it may come from anxiety, it may come from fear or fright, or lack of elements in the superficial circulation. 1947-4

Q-What treatment should be used to rid hair of dandruff?
A-Any of those preparations that are a good scalp cleansing tone; as Lavoris or Glyco-Thymoline. 1523-3

Q-Will you give a prescription for a solution that will make straight hair wave, if possible without heat?
A-If the pits of the lowly persimmon--with the bark of the roots of the tree--are distilled, adding only the preservatives as necessary for the keeping of same, and used as a massage for a period into the scalp it will make the hair wave--even kinky, if so desired. 276-7

The massaging of the scalp with old coffee grounds would be effective. Of course this would keep the hair colored, but it would be effective to make same grow. 2301-5

For this particular body, use Olive Oil shampoo, for there is needed the oil for the scalp and the opening of same. Cleanse the scalp with some good cleanser, preferable Tar Soap, and then apply the Olive Oil shampoo. 3379-1

Take at least five to ten minutes to massage the scalp with the White Petroleum Jelly. Afterwards take an Olive Oil shampoo. Do this **each** day during the ten days when the Atomidine is taken. (Baldness) 970-1

Q-What oil should be used on scalp before washing

A-...The Crude Oils are the most satisfactory for stimulating the scalp, to prevent falling hair, to add lustre, and to stimulate the growth. Following the oil shampoo there should be the cleansing with alcohol; that is, one to twenty, but this should be preferably of the pure **grain**, for any of the ingredients such as in pyro or those that make for the denaturing produce breaking and burning of the hair.

Q-What soap should be used on hair for washing?

A-Preferably that carrying the tar content as its base, or Packer's Tar, or any that have a tar and glycerine content; or Pear Soap.   276-4

A scalp treatment would be given in this manner: About once each month have a Crude Oil Shampoo, preferably done by self--it is messy, but it is necessary for the stimulation from the Pure Crude Oil. Then cleanse same with twenty percent **Grain** Alcohol--not wood alcohol... although some of the oil will have struck in sufficient to stimulate the circulation to the growth of the roots of the hair itself. Then use occasionally a little White Vaseline. The **massage** is more important for it.

Q-How long should the Crude Oil stay on before cleansing with the alcohol solution?

A-This depends, of course, upon the circumstances. For half to three quarters of an hour, if possible.   816-1

If the scalp were massaged at least every week with the Crude Oil and then cleansed with a weak solution of Grain Alcohol, and then followed by the White Vaseline rub, this will restore color, will thicken hair and make it more brilliant in its lustre.   982-5

Q-Please give me a better and sure treatment for bald heads.

A-There has never been a better than the Crude Oil treatment... This will grow on **most** bald heads, unless it is of the germ nature that has destroyed the bulbs that **grow** hair. But this will prevent four-fifths of all types of disorder, and will be especially efficient with such a diet as outlined (seafood and skins of Irish potatoes); and occasionally specific gland treatment.   636-1

Use Crude Oil, cleansing with a twenty percent solution of Grain Alcohol. Then massage just a small portion or quantity of White Vaseline into the scalp. This will cure **any** dandruff, unless it is produced--of course--by acne or some skin disorder.   850-2

Use a cleansing of Crude Oil for the scalp; clear same with Grain Alcohol--not wood or denatured (alcohol)...The condition (oily hair) arises from the poor circulation, or the poor coordination between the superficial and deeper circulation, by poisons in the system.   276-10

Q-What is a good tooth cream and mouth wash that will keep the teeth and gums in good condition?

A-That which is **best** as a mouth wash for the gums may be found in that of Ipsab. That which is best for the teeth is a combination of Salt and Soda, which is better than all the concoctions that have been sold in tubes or pastes.   1131-1

Q-What is the best cleanser for teeth?

A-Equal combinations of Salt and Soda...nothing better.   276-7

Q-Give care of teeth so I will have less decaying.

A-Use as a massage for the gums and teeth an equal combination of Common Salt and Baking Soda; about once a month, add one drop only of Chlorine to a pint of water and rinse the mouth with this. Do not swallow it, but rinse the mouth and then brush the teeth. This will preserve them, even aid in filling cavities.   2981-2

(Ipsab) is a universally beneficial property or compound for the teeth and gums. And the combination is such as to offer particular benefits for any condition where there is the tendency towards irritation in this portion of the body.   275-31

To 6 ounces of distilled water, add 2 ounces of Prickly Ash Bark. Reduce by simmerings (not boiling) to 2 ounces. Strain and add powdered Common Salt until we have a very thin paste. (Ipsab Formula)   4436-2

The receding gums and tendencies towards pyorrhea would be allayed by consistent use of Ipsab as a massage for the teeth and gums. 3696-1

Q-What causes the gray film on teeth?

A-...Discharge from breath in the lungs...Keeping such cleansed with an equal combination of Soda and Salt at least three to four times a week will cleanse these (teeth) of this disturbance. The use of Ipsab as a wash for mouth and gums will further aid in keeping these conditions cleansed; and use any good dentifrice once or twice a day. 457-11

Q-Suggest diet beneficial to preserving teeth.

A-Eggs, potato peelings, seafood.   1523-3

Q-What can I do to prevent the teeth from wearing down?

A-Use more of an alkaline-reacting diet; as quantities of orange juice with a little lemon in same, as four parts orange juice to one part lemon; (also) grapefruit, raw vegetables, potato peelings. 365-4

Q-Does gold in the mouth help to cause bitterness?

A-It does! No teeth should ever be filled with heavy metals, (such) as gold.   325-55

Q-Is it true that the intake of certain form and percentage of fluorine in drinking water causes mottled enamel of the teeth?

A-This, to be sure, is true; but this is also untrue unless there is considered the other properties with which such is associated in the drinking water.

If there are certain percents of fluorine with free limestone, we will find it is beneficial. If there are certain percents with indications of magnesium, sulphur and the like, we will have one motley, another decaying at the gum...It depends upon the combinations, more than it does upon the quantity of fluorine itself. But, to be sure, too much fluorine in the water...may contribute to the condition.

But, where there is iron or sulphur or magnesium, be careful...

In some portions of Texas, portions in Arizona, others in Wyoming --where the teeth are seldom ever decayed. Study the water there, the quantity of fluorine there, the lack of iron or sulphur or the proportions of sulphur; that is in the regular water.

There are many sections, of course, where fluorine added to the water, with many other chemicals would be most beneficial. There are others where, even a small quantity added would be very detrimental...

There's scarcely an individual place in Ohio that it (fluorine) wouldn't be helpful, for it will...cause a better activity in the thyroid glands; while, for a general use, in such a district as Illinois (say in the extreme northern portions) it would be harmful.   3211-1

Be careful of the water as is taken in system. Let that be pure. Not too much lime, not too little, but carrying much silica, lithia, magnesia and soda. That is nearer **pure** waters.   3762-1

Water in motion over stone or those various forces in natural forces purifies itself in twenty feet of space.   364-12

ELM AND SAFFRON WATER FOR ULCERS AND PSORIASIS

The water to be used should not be the well water, as has been used, because it caused too much calcium. the water this body uses should be thoroughly boiled and cooled, and to each glass should be added either a stick of Slippery Elm, or a pinch of the Ground Elm Bark; and keep the water cold that is given to this system. (Stomach Ulcers) 5421-2

(Have Slippery Elm Bark) to supply that coating alone the walls of the intestine themselves, as to prevent the strains from which blood has appeared. (Periodic Intestinal Hemorrhaging)   257-215

To the normal water that may be had in the surroundings, we would add to each gallon (to be kept for drinking water, you see) a five-grain lithia tablet. Dissolve this and it would make about the proper proportion, and it would be added and dissolved in same preferably after the ordinary water had been boiled--or had come to a boil and strained or filtered off before used. Then when this is to be taken, once or twice a day we would have just a pinch of the Elm Bark (between the thumb and forefinger) in a glass of water--the Ground Elm Bark. If it is more preferable, it may be used with a small piece of ice in same; this would be all the better, but stir same and let it stand for a minute or two before it is taken. We would also from the same type of water, have the Yellow Saffron--the American Saffron is correct, or may be used if so desired. This would be (in) the proportions of about a heaping teaspoonful to a gallon of water. This preferable we would make in an enamel container or in a glass container, preferable to the aluminum. This would be allowed to steep as would tea. Then it may be drawn off and kept as a portion of the drinking water to be taken at the regular intervals when the body desires water. Not that there would never be any of the regular routine or drinking of water outside, but let the most--and as much as possible all--that is taken either carry one or the other of those properties as indicated. This would be the first precaution, for--while it is, of course, slow acting--it will make for a cleansing of the kidneys, a better activity through the alimentary canal, clear those tendencies for the poisons to accumulate through the lymph and emunctory circulation, and overcome these tendencies for toxic forces to arise in the body that affects the body throughout. (Dermatitis and Psoriasis) 840-1

Q-Please give me the cause and cure for my so-called psoriasis.
A-The cause is the thinning of the walls of the intestinal system, which allows the escaping of poisons--or the absorption of same by the mucous membranes which surround same, and become effective in the irritation through the lymph and emunctory reactions in the body...
In the system we would use Elm Water and Saffron Water.   289-1

(Have) **quantities** of water! All the body would drink. Take water rather as medicine! Well that occasionally those properties in the Elm or the Saffron be given as an easing for the conditions in stomach proper. (Stomach Adhesions)   2190-1

Do not take any water unless it carries in same either the Elm or the Saffron. The Elm would be made just a few minutes before it is taken. The Saffron may be made and kept. A gallon or so may be made at a time, provided it is kept where it is cool or sufficient to prevent the bringing about of fermentation. (Stomach Lacerations)   843-1

A body is more susceptible to cold with an excess of acidity **or** alkalinity, but **more** susceptible in case of excess acidity. For, an alkalizing effect is destructive, to the cold germ...

This leaves many questions that might be asked:

Does draft cause a cold? Does unusual change in dress? Does change in temperature? Does getting the clothes or the feet damp? etc.

All of these, to be sure, **affect** the **circulation** by the depletion of the body-balance, the body-temperature, or body equilibrium. Then at such times if the body is tired, worn, overacid or overalkaline, it is more susceptible to cold--even by the very changes produced through the sudden unbalancing of circulation, as from a warm room overheated. Naturally when overheated there is less oxygen, which weakens the circulation in the life-giving forces that are destructive to **any** germ...

The use of an **abundant** supply of vitamins is beneficial, of **all** characters; A, B, B-1, D, E, G, and K.

When once, the cold has attacked the body...do not attempt to go on, but **rest**!...(and) generally the liquid diet is best.   902-1

It would require volumes to give that which would prevent any one from having colds! for all those conditions that produce colds would have to be considered; diet, eliminations, drafts, changes of temperature, and everything of the kind. But if a body is sufficiently balanced as to make for resistance, there will be sufficient leucocytes in the blood supply to choke a cold to death immediately! But to keep such a resistance is to keep a body normally balanced...For, colds are plasms that find their reaction in the blood supply itself, and **feed** upon the white more than upon the red blood, until they have become some form of the strept nature. Then they work through the organs of the system. 386-3

Bolting food or swallowing it by the use of liquids produces more colds than **any one** activity of a diet.   808-3

CLEARING FOGGY THROATS

(For speakers or teachers with sore or foggy throats) beat the white of an egg very stiff, add a little sugar (very little), and the juice of half a lemon. Stir this, and take about half the quantity just before there is to be the lecture. After such a lecture, take the rest. This should create a clearing influence for the mucous membranes of throat, larynx and also contribute to betterment of purifying all the passages through which there are the activities of air as well as foods. 3011-2

Sedatives and hypnotics are destructive forces to brain and nerve reflexes. 3431-1

Hypnotics or narcotics...produce a reaction to the whole eliminating system that clogs rather than clears. 1082-2

A bromide of any nature **must** eventually become destructive. 1264-1

Keep as far from these (sleeping power) as possible...But be sure whenever such **is** taken that there is taken afterwards...something to increase the eliminations through the system. 808-3

Q-Were hay fever shots in any way responsible for this trouble?
A-Any shots are responsible for most anything. 3629-1

THE USE AND ABUSE OF TOBACCO

Q-Would smoking be detrimental to me or beneficial?
A-This depends very much on self. In moderation, smoking is not harmful; but to a body that holds such as being out of line with its best mental or spiritual unfoldment, do not smoke. 2981-2

Q-Is the moderate use of liquor, tobacco and meat a bar to spiritual growth?
A-For this entity, yes. For some, no. 2981-1

What is your ideal? Would you prepare these (tobacco and alcohol) for that you would worship as your Maker? If you would, use them: If you wouldn't they are harmful. 3100-1

There is a relaxation from nicotine for the system that is **not** harmful to anyone, **if** taken moderately. 5545-1

Tobacco in moderation, as all stimulants, is not so harmful. However, overacidity or overalkalinity causes same to become detrimental.
Q-What brands of tobacco are best?
A-Just tobacco, and not brand, is best! In its **natural** state it is preferable to any...ordinarily put on the market in package tobacco. 462-6

The best brands, we would find, are those that are of the purer tobacco that are not either toasted or mixed with foreign conditions. 1131-2

Pure tobacco is always better than any concoction of the compilation of other things with same. If it's to be used at all, use the natural leaf. Then you won't use much of it either! 462-4

PART VIII

SELECTING AND PREPARING FOODS

OWN ENOUGH LAND TO BE SELF-SUSTAINING

Every individual should own sufficient of the earth to be self-sustaining. For the earth is the mother of all: just as God is the father in the spiritual, the earth is the mother in the material.

Q-May information be given through this channel on the proper methods of farming which would insure the production of products of the best possible food value and balanced content?

A-If there is to be insured the producing of the character of fertilization needed, or the making of the proper fertilizer--none exceeds, of course, the value of chicken fertilizer, especially for some vegetables. Hence this should be used in rather an abundance, not excessively but in large measures; as well as that produced by the methods of adding such as lime and potash with portions of the soil, or portions of vegetable matter or refuse of vines or grasses in certain characters of vegetation--but always mixed with the droppings of the chicken,-- for this is the better of **any** that may be had for vegetables...

There is a great deal in the theories that are propagated by some groups, that what is in the vegetables and fruits has much to do with the character. If the man who raises and cares for them does it with love, it makes all the difference.   470-35

Anyone who can buy a farm is fortunate, and buy it if you want to grow something and don't want to grow hungry in some days to come.   3620-1

Hold the acreage; for that may be the basis for the extreme periods through which all portions of the country must pass.   416-17

Q-Should farming supplement present occupation or supplant it?

A-Supplement, **not** supplant. The character of farming should be, not so much the **main** activity, but sufficient to meet the needs of its own household, and **in** same more than supply the needs for **maintaining** same, see? and the products that are to be preserved, canned, or made into such as to supply not merely for the moment but through season to season. Fruits, small fruits, vegetables, meats, fish and the like.   2301-2

Q-What foods are acid-forming for this body?

A-All of those that are combining fats with sugars. Starches naturally are inclined for acid reaction. But a normal diet is about twenty percent acid to eighty percent alkaline-producing. 1523-3

Keep a tendency toward alkalinity in the diet. This does not mean there should **never** be any acid-forming foods in the diet--for over-alkalinity is much more harmful than a little tendency toward acidity occasionally. But remember that there are tendencies in this system toward cold and congestion...and cold **cannot, does not** exist in alkalines. 808-3

In all bodies, the less activities there are in physical exercise or manual activity, the greater should be the alkaline-reacting foods taken. **Energies** or activities may burn acids; but those who lead the sedentary life or the non-active life can't go on sweets or too much starches. 798-1

The body should not take things that produce acid. We have things that are not acid themselves, but change into acid when taken into the mouth. Normally there are glands in the throat which produce lactic fluid or pepsin, this body is not producing sufficient lactic fluid, so that whatever is taken is carried into acid. There are properties that are not acid themselves but are turned into acids when taken into the mouth; and properties that are acids that are not acids when taken into the mouth. Should be careful about diet, eat wild game which eats from nature, tame game eats what it is fed. Pear, which is acid, forms into iron and loses its acid, certain apples are acid, others are not. 4834-1

There are foods that require (as meats) acids for their proper fermentation; while most...vegetable forces, especially of the leafy nature, require more of the slow combination of the lacteals' reaction or the greater quantity of the combination of acid and alkaline. Then if foods are taken in quantities that require an alkaline for their digestion and an acid is in the system--this produces improper fermentation. 1259-2

The diet should be more body-building; that is, less acid foods and more of the alkaline-reacting (foods)...Milk and all its products should be a portion of the bodies diet now; also those food values carrying an easy assimilation of iron, silicon, and those elements or chemicals--as all forms of berries, most all forms of vegetables that grow under the ground, most vegetables of a leafy nature. Fruit and vegetables, nuts.

Q-Can immunization against (contagious diseases) be set up in any other manner than by inoculations?

A-As indicated, if an alkalinity is maintained in the system--especially with lettuce, carrots and celery, these in the blood supply will maintain such a condition as to immunize a person. 480-19

Q-What diet should be taken?

A-There might be one diet given today and then next week you would have another. That which keeps the spittle or salivary reaction alkaline. That which keeps the blood reaction, by test, negative. That which keeps the urine eliminations as a balance at twenty-four without albumin, without sediment, and with an alkaline tendency, but not too great a tendency. That which makes for the proper eliminations.   681-2

Test the alkalinity or acidity of the body through the salivary glands or through the salivary gland membranes, or by taking the litmus paper in the mouth. This also may be indicated through the urine.   540-11

Be mindful that the foods taken are those of the non-acid producing in the system. Beware, then, of meats to any great extent--and especially of those vegetables of the tuberous nature. Then, the leaves or those of the pod nature will be found the better for the body, as will be those of the citrus fruits or those that grow from the vine. Beware, though, of those that carry too much of the seed itself. 4172-1

Oranges, lemons, limes, grapefruit are well and are alkaline in their reaction--**unless** starches, as especially form cereals, are taken at the same meal. Then they become acid-producing for this body and in ninety-nine cases out of a hundred become so for any body!   1334-2

Sugars are, in the **main** combined with starches, acid-producing.   877-28

Keep those foods that are the more alkaline; that is, do not take red meats--such as roast beef or heavy roasts that carry a great deal of grease and fats. No fried foods.   710-1

The tomato is...**non**-acid forming.   584-5

Whenever there is a great anxiety or stress, do not eat especially apples raw nor bananas, rather use the easily assimilated foods. Not too much white bread, not too much of meats--and never fried foods.   1724-1

Do not take in the system any foods that produce an over acidity in the lower end of the stomach--such as pickles, or any food carrying over amount of acid or vinegar, or acetic acid, and never any canned goods having benzoate of soda. This includes relishes.   340-5

We would keep an alkaline-reacting diet; only using the whole wheat and barley at times as a body-building, you see?   865-1

Eno Salts has a fruit reaction and is thus alkalizing as well as forming better eliminations.   1688-5

(Lemon) juice is a good alkalizer.   1709-10

Q-What foods should I avoid?

A-Rather it is the combinations of foods that makes for disturbance with most physical bodies...

Those tending towards the greater alkaline reaction are preferable. Hence avoid combinations where corn, potatoes, rice, spaghetti or the like are taken all at the same meal. Some combinations of these at the meal are very good, but all of these tend to make for too great a quantity of starch--especially if any meat is taken at such a meal. If no meat is taken, these make quite a difference. For the activities of the gastric flow of the digestive system are the requirements of one reaction in the gastro flow for starch and another for proteins...Then, in the combination, do not eat great quantities of starch with proteins or meats. If sweets and meats are taken at the same meal, these are preferable to starches. Of course, small quantities of breads with sweets are alright.

Then, do not combine also the (alkaline) reacting acid fruits with starches, other than **whole wheat bread**! that is citrus fruits, oranges, apples, grapefruit, limes or lemons or even tomato juices. And do not have cereals (which contain the greater quantity of starch than most) at the same meal with citrus fruits.   416-9

Avoid too much combinations of starches. Do not take a combinations of potatoes, meat, white bread, macaroni or cheese, at the same meal; no two of these at any one meal...Do not take onions and radishes at the same meal with celery and lettuce.   2732-1

Have 80 percent alkaline-producing to 20 percent acid-producing foods in the diet...Do not take citrus fruit juices and cereals at the same meal. Do not take milk or cream in coffee or tea.   1568-2

When cereals or starches are taken, do not have citrus fruit at the same meal--or even the same day; for such a combination in the system at the same time becomes **acid**-producing!   1484-1

Sugars are in the **main** combined with starches, acid-producing...It is the combinations of these that become rather the hindrances than the **individual** properties themselves, see?   877-28

Starches and sweets should not be taken at the same meal, or so much together (That's why that ice cream is so much better than pie, for the body!). Meats or the like should not be taken with starches that grow above the ground...Hence potatoes or the peelings of same with meats are preferable to eating bread with meats see?   340-32

Orange juice and milk are helpful, but these should be taken at opposite ends of the day; not together.   274-9

It will be much better if you add a little lime (juice) with the orange juice, and a little lemon (juice) with the grapefruit (juice). Not too much, but a little...For many of these are hybrids, you see. 3525-1

Do not add lemon or lime to grapefruit, not to the pineapple or grape juices; but add same to the orange juice. 1593-1

(Tomatoes) should not be eaten with meats, sugars or vinegars. 379-10

Q-Are tomatoes good?
A-This depends, too, upon what combination. If they are taken with a great deal of starch, no. If taken with vinegar or acetic acids, or such combination, no. If they are taken with lettuce as a salad, as a part of the meal, very good. If taken alone with a little salt, **very** good. 257-210

Carrots, beets, watercress...should never be combined with any vinegar or acetic acid. 3316-1

Oysters should never be taken with whiskey. 2853-1

Beware of some combinations--especially of shellfish of **any** nature with alcoholic influences for the system near the same time. 1293-2

COFFEE AND TEA

(Caffeine) is not digestible in the system, and must necessarily then be eliminated. When such are allowed to remain in the colon there is thrown off from same poisons. Eliminated..coffee is a food value, and is preferable to many stimulants that might be taken, see? 294-86

Coffee is a food if it is taken without cream or sugar, and especially without cream; and if taken without the caffeine--as Kafa Hag. 816-3

Tea is more harmful than coffee. Any nerve reaction is more susceptible to the character of tea that is usually found in this country. 303-2

Tea is rather hard on most bodies. If it is taken with lemon it is preferable. 850-2

Do not have those combinations that produce great acid. Do not take coffee or tea with milk in same. A little sugar is not as bad. 1512-2

Coffee old or stale, or overdone, is bad for **any**body! 271-4

Q-What breakfast drink besides Ovaltine would be well?
A-...Citrus fruit juices...(and) Sanka Coffee is very good. 340-30

Do use only the health salt or kelp salt or deep sea salt. All of these are of the same characters. But they are better than just that which has been purified, for the general health of many.   2084-16

Q-Is salt harmful?
A-In excess, harmful.   404-6

The sea salt should be preferably used from the kelp rather than that from sea water.   658-15

Table salt--acts only as a condiment, or making palatable for those of the gastric juices of the ducts that produce the saliva while the Veg-Sal (Nu-Veg-Sal) acts with the gastric juices of the stomach itself, and makes it more savory through the stomach digestion. 404-2

Beware of stimuli, especially of an alcohol nature. No condiments, either should be taken; no highly seasoned foods--or spices or peppers of any nature. No pickle nor kraut, or such. (Duodenal Ulcer) 719-1

Not **ever** any acetic acid or vinegar or the like with same (raw vegetables)--but oils, olive or vegetable oils, may be used.   275-45

Olive oil in **small** quantities is **always** good for the whole of the intestinal system. Quantities are not advisable, unless taken as an emit...(and then) the dosage should be about half a teaspoonful two to three to four hours apart, just as much as the body will assimilate.
Q-How much olive oil on a salad at a meal?
A-Teaspoonful.   846-1

(Olive oil) acts as an irritant to the gastric and to the juices of the intestines and digestion, when not assimilated.   4874-3

AVOID CARBONATED DRINKS

Q-Are soft drinks alright for this body?
A-No; for very few bodies.   2157-2

Do not take any form of drinks that carry carbonated waters. The gases of these, as well as all such, are detrimental.   1013-3

Take Coca-Cola occasionally as a drink...but do not take it with carbonated water. Buy or have a syrup prepared and add plain water to this. Take about one half ounce or one ounce of the syrup and add plain water. This to be taken about every other day, with or without ice. This will aid in purifying the kidney activity and bladder. 5097-1

Do not have large quantities of any fruits, vegetables, meats that are not grown in or come to the area where the body is at the time it partakes of such foods. This will be found to be a good rule to be followed by all. This prepares the system to acclimate itself to any given territory.   3542-1

Have vegetables that are fresh and especially those grown in the vicinity where the body resides. Shipped vegetables are never very good.   2-14

Coffee loses its value in fifteen to twenty to twenty-five days after being roasted, so do foods or vegetables lose their food values after being gathered in the same proportion in hours as coffee does in days. 340-31

Do have plenty of vegetables above the ground; at least three of these to one below the ground. Have at least one leafy vegetable to every one of the pod vegetables taken.   2602-1

(Have) fruits **and** vegetables, not those that have been frozen but those that are preserved either in their own syrup or in the regular cane syrup and **not** those prepared with benzoate or any preservative. 826-14

Beware of fats of any kind, and greases. No meats save fish, fowl or lamb. No fried foods. No white bread. Not too much of pastries. 2415-2

Not great quantities ever of white bread, but rather use rye or whole wheat or the like--these are the more preferable.   540-11

Supply vitamins B-1, as well as A, B, and G--through the cereals... The cracked whole wheat at one time, the steel cut oats at another time, and wheat and barley at another time. These would be taken with cream or milk, and **not too much sugar!**   849-47

Use honey as the sweetening for most things.   2276-3

Milk, whether it is the dry or the pasteurized or raw, is near to the perfect combination of forces for human consumption.   1703-2

Do not take any form of drinks that carry carbonated waters. 1013-3

Eggs may be taken, but use more of the yolk than of the white.   924-1

Of all the vegetables, tomatoes carry most of the vitamins in a well balanced assimilative manner...Yet...they may become very destructive to a physical organism if they ripen after being pulled.   584-5

Use fruits that are **not** artificially ripened, even though it is necessary to use those that are canned.   509-2

Apples should only be eaten when cooked; preferable roasted. 935-1

Filberts and almonds are preferable in the nuts.   1151-2

Never take food, meat or drink, when worried in mind, physically tired, or mad. 4124-1

Especially to this body there should not be food taken when the body is overwrought in any manner, whether of high-strung conditions or that of wrath, or of depressions of any nature...Take water, or buttermilk--**never** sweet milk under such conditions. 243-7

Bolting food or swallowing it by the use of liquids produces more colds than **any one** activity of a diet. Even milk or water should be **chewed** two to three times before taken into the stomach. 808-3

Drink **always plenty** of water, before meals and after meals--as has oft been given, when any food value **enters** the stomach **immediately** the stomach becomes a storehouse, or a medicine chest, that may create all the elements necessary for proper digestion...If this **first** is acted upon by aqua pura, the reactions are more near normal. Well, then, each morning upon first arising, to take a half to three quarters of a glass of **warm** water...this will clarify the system of poisons. 311-4

Q-How much water should the body drink daily?
A-Six to eight tumblers or glasses full. 1131-2

That thou eatest, **see** it **doing** that **thou** would **have** it do...Give one a dose of clear **water**, with the impression that it will act as salts--how often will it act in that manner?...

Do not eat like a canary and expect to do **manual** labor. Do not eat like a rail splitter and expect to do the work of a mind reader or a university professor...

Just as great a sin to **over** eat as to over drink; to over **think** as to over act! 341-31

WINE, LIQUOR AND BEER

Alcohol in moderation is well for **most** bodies. But not too great a quantity taken as to cause a slow congestion in the liver area. But alcohols taken evenings--very well. 877-13

Wine is good for all, if taken alone or with black or brown bread. Not with meals so much as with just bread. This may be taken between meals, or as a meal; but not too much--and just once a day. Red wine only. 462-6

Wine taken in excess--of course--is harmful; wine taken with bread alone is body, blood and nerve and brain building. 821-1

When taken as a **food**, not as a drink. An ounce and a half to two ounces of red wine in the afternoon, after the body has **worn** itself out...Not beer or ale, nor any of the hard drinks--but **red wine**! 578-5

Q-What is meant by red wine?
A-Means **red** wine! Not white wine, not sour wine; not that that is too sweet but any of those that are in the nature of adding to the body the effect of grape sugar...The addition of red wine is carrying more of a tartaric effect upon the active forces of the body, is correct; while those that are sour or draw out from the system a reaction upon the hydrochlorics become detrimental. 437-7

Red wine in the late afternoon with black or brown bread is helpful, **not** taken, however, at mealtimes. This, as we find, brings a stimulation that is laxative in its **reaction**; only the **red** wine, not the white wine. If the sauterne or the light wines are taken, these should always be **with** meals, not separate. (Neurasthenia) 1192-6

The light wines or the champagnes or the like are for stimulation, while the red wines are strengthening. 325-68

Foods produce that **within** the system that is the same fermentation that is called wines, or beer, or liquor, or ales, or such **for** the digestion to be proper in a body! 275-21

Be mindful especially of raw or new beer. 1005-18

Do not drink beer or those things that are of malt fermentation, unless taken **as** medicine. Beer that would be prepared--one glass each day with a raw egg in same--the yolk of the egg put into it--would be very well--but not alone. (Anemia) 2277-1

It would be well that there be taken Malted Milk with the yolk of an egg, and a little bit of spirits frumenti or pure apple brandy... about a spoonful to the yolk of one egg; this beaten well together, then added to the malted milk...but this, too, would be taken in sips --a glassful taken during a whole day. (Asthenia) 2631-2

Cook the yolk of a raw egg by dropping the whiskey over it, and then adding milk. This will aid materially in giving strength and vitality. For one egg use a teaspoonful or more of the spirits frumenti, with about half a glass of milk--and this quantity taken during a whole day, but keep on ice when not being taken, of course. 1553-15

Spirits frumenti with the eggnog and milk would be very stimulating in the evening, or afternoon when first attempting to rest. Not too much, not too strong--but this will assimilate well. 303-27

Beware of all fried foods. No fried potatoes, fried meats, fried steaks, fried fish or anything of that nature. 926-1

No fried foods of any kind. Baked, broiled or boiled, or preferably the vegetables cooked in their own juices--as in Patapar paper (vegetable parchment paper) or **steamed** in a manner as to retain their own salts, their own vitamins, and not combining them together. All seasoning should be done with butter and salt or paprika (or whatever may be used as the seasoning) **after** the foods have been cooked! The cooking of condiments, even salt, **destroys** much of the vitamins of foods. 906-1

(Have) vegetables that are cooked in their **own** juices, not combined with others--each cooked alone. 3823-3

The salts and juices of these (vegetables cooked in Patapar paper) are to be taken as much or more than the **body** of the vegetables themselves. (Poor Assimilation) 849-27

Do not cook the vegetables with meats to season them; only use a little butter, with pepper or salt or such. And preferable use the sea salt entirely, or iodized salt--this is preferable. 1586-1

Prepare such (vegetable) juices...in the Patapar paper or in a steam steamer, so that the juices from the vegetables may be obtained and no water added in the cooking at all...
A little later the body may begin with stewed chicken, or broiled chicken or broiled fish...The chicken or fish would be better cooked in the Patapar paper or a steam cooker. (Rheumatism, and Colitis) 133-4

Q-Does cooking destroy the calcium in foods?
A-To be sure. At times, but if the cooking is done in Patapar paper, so that all the juices are saved with same, then these are just as well--and, as indicated--at times more preferable, or they are more easily assimilated, and especially so during pregnancy. 457-9

(Have) fruits **and** vegetables, not those that have been frozen but those that are preserved either in their own syrup or in the regular cane syrup and **not** those prepared with benzoate or any preservative. 826-14

Q-Considering the frozen foods, especially vegetables and fruits that are on the market today (1942)--has the freezing in any way killed certain vitamins and how do they compare with the fresh?
A-...Some are affected more than others. So far as fruits are concerned, these do not lose much of the vitamin content. Yet some of these are affected by the freezing. Vegetables--much of the vitamin content of these is taken unless there is the re-enforcement in same when

these are either prepared for food or when frozen.

Q-Consider also the steam pressure for cooking foods quickly. Does it destroy any of the precious vitamins of the vegetables and fruits?

A-Rather preserves than destroys. 462-14

Keep away from too much greases or to much of any foods cooked in quantities of grease--whether it be the fat of hog, sheep, beef, or fowl. But rather use the **lean** portions and those (meats) that will make for body-building forces throughout. Fish and fowl are the preferable meats. No raw meat, and very little ever of hog meat. Only bacon. Do not use bacon or fats in cooking the vegetables. 303-11

Fats are the most detrimental to **all** infants in this developing stage. And **anger**! Keep from **anger**! (Male 5 days old) 1208-2

The oyster or clam should be taken raw as much as possible; while the others (shrimp, lobster), prepared through roasting or boiling with the butter, would be better than prepared in other manners. 275-24

The juices from these (beets and carrots) are to be prepared fresh each day. Do not attempt to keep them from one day to the next--it would be injurious rather than helpful. (Arthritis Tendency) 462-13

For many who are effected by nervous digestion or an overactivity of the nerve forces during the state of digestion taking place, the body should be warned about using or having foods cooked in aluminum. 843-7

Do not eat foods prepared in aluminum at all...especially tomatoes or greens of any character or kind. 2423-1

Some foods are effected in their activity by aluminum, especially in the preparation of certain fruits, or tomatoes, or cabbage. 1852-1

(Foods) which are acid will take particles of aluminum into body. 5211-1

Cook in granite (enameled ironware), or better in Patapar paper. 1196-7

This (stainless steel) is the best, except enamel. 379-10

Egg white, unless it is prepared in the form of a coddled egg, makes for a formation of acid. 567-8

Let the water come to a hard boil, then drop an egg in and immediately set the water off the heat; and when it is possible to take the egg out with the hand (without a spoon), then it is ready to give to the child (five months old)--but **only** the yolk...This is the manner of preparation, and is what we would call a **coddled** egg. 1788-6

Cauliflower is very well when prepared, but not creamed. 3642-1

Wheat...should be the greater portion of that which is to supply not only body-heat but body-development for an equal balance in the mental influences upon the physical forces of man.   826-5

Not too large a quantity of starches, no white bread. The dark breads ...pumpernickel or rye or whole wheat are well.   5374-1

We would use only such as Ry-Krisp as bread or **always** using toasted whole wheat bread. Preferably the Ry-Krisp, though. (Obesity)   1657-2

Q-Would it be well to alternate Soy Bean bread with Whole Wheat?
A-Soy Bean bread is wholesome for certain characters and conditions; provided the body is to be out in the open, very active, fiery or dictatorial, then eat Soy Bean bread! But if it is to remain indoors, with more of the normal **temperamental** reactions, leave it off.   340-31

The cereals should carry an over amount of vitamins E, D, A, and B; E and D especially...
Have cereals that carry the heart of the grain.   1131-2

Supply vitamins B-1, as well as A, B, and G--through the cereals...These should be cooked cereals. The cracked whole wheat at one time, the steel cut oats at another time, and wheat and barley at another time. These should be taken with cream or milk, and **not too much sugar!**   849-47

When cooked cereal is used, preferably use only the whole wheat. This may be merely rolled, crushed or ground--but the **whole** of the grain is to be taken...and cook for at least three hours--but do not cook same in an **open** kettle nor in an aluminum kettle. Use either glass **or** enamelware with the top on at all times.   1703-1

(Take) oatmeal that is cooked a long time, not the oats cooked only a few minutes--that isn't good for anyone. These are much better if they are of the whole grain and not rolled or so treated chemically as to cause them to cook easily.   3326-1

Give the strained oatmeal, but use the steel cut oats, not rolled oats; and cook a **long** time, in a double boiler, of course. When it is strained the husks of course will be out, but it will retain much of the vitamin B and thiamine that will be most helpful in the developing of the nerves, as well as resistance against cold. (Baby Care)   1788-6

Mornings--use oatmeal, but the steel cut oats--not the rolled oats. The rolled oats make for too much acidity.   1419-5

Steel cut oats well cooked, and dry cereals that carry the vitamin in same, with plenty of milk and malted milks. (Duodenal Ulcers)   481-4

(Have) whole wheat, pressed, cleansed and pressed, and this formed into a well prepared gruel, with the milk as would be used, with this only beet sugar, and sufficient milk to make such palatable to the body. Do not take large quantities of this, but take it more often. Graham crackers may be used, Junket may be used. (Stomach Ulcers)   4709-5

Morning--should be of **gruels**, with those of oaten or corn or rice, or such. Little of the citrus fruits may be taken. (Stomach Ulcers)   5641-2

(Have) rice, provided it is of the brown rice or the uncut rice or unpolished rice.   844-1

NUTS AND THE MIGHTY ALMOND

An almond a day is much more in accord with keeping the doctor away ...than apples. For the apple was the fall, not the almond--for the almond blossomed when everything else died. Remember this is life!   3180-3

The almond carries more phosphorus **and** iron in a combination easily assimilated than any other nut.   1131-2

Those who would eat two to three almonds each day need never fear cancer. Those who would take a peanut oil rub each week need never fear arthritis.   1158-31

If ye would take each day, through thy experience, two almonds, ye will never have skin blemishes, ye will never be tempted even in body toward cancer.   1206-13

Not so much those that carry too much grease or oils in same as Brazilian nuts; but particularly almonds and filberts will be helpful.   1140-2

Use the fruit and vegetable diet. The fats should be more from nuts than meats; for these, as we find, would be most helpful and especially cashew nuts, almonds, filberts. (Cancer Tendency)   1000-11

(Have) those foods that have a tendency towards an alkaline reaction, but let the proteins be taken rather in the form of nuts and fruits--for the fats and oils, you see.   741-1

Nuts are good, but do not combine same with meats. Let them take the place of same. Filberts and almonds are preferable in the nuts.   1151-2

There should be one meal almost entirely of nuts, and the oils of nuts. (Arthritis)   951-1

Q-Suggest best sugars for the body.
A-Beet sugars are the better for **all**, or the cane sugars that are not clarified. (Turbinado Sugar?)   1131-2

Saccharin may be used. Brown sugar is not harmful. The **better** would be to use beet sugar for sweetening.   307-6

(Have) **sufficient** of sweets to form sufficient alcohol for the system ...Chocolates that are **plain**, not those of any brand that carry corn starches should be taken--or those that carry too much of the cane sugar. Grape sugar, or beet sugars, or of that nature may be taken.   487-11

Should there be the desire for the sugar, use the **brown** or maple sugars--in small quantities, to be sure.   340-31

Do not combine **any** of starches with any quantities of sweets. 1125-2

Have more of the natural sweets, as from fruits--or the salts from vegetables supplying the carbohydrates. (Anemia)   1023-1

Proteins are made more harmful when they are taken oftentimes with sweets.   404-4

Let the sweets be taken in such forms as of honey, corn or Karo syrup. These are body building, also supply energies that are well for a growing, developing body.   1188-10

Use honey as the sweetening for most things, whether this be with the cereals or upon cakes or in whatever pastry is prepared--make same partially with honey.   2276-3

Q-What sweets may be taken, or are best for the body?
A-Honey, or those made with honey. Not cane sugars, **not** cakes, **not** pies! These should be taken very, **very** seldom. (Arthritis)   849-54

Q-How much honey may be taken each day?
A-Half an ounce to two ounces would not be too great a quantity. But only that in the honeycomb, **with** the honeycomb.   440-17

Small quantities (honey) may be taken with impunity, yet the greater portion...**should** be **comb** from clover and buckwheat. (Diabetes) 953-21

Occasionally there may be taken rice cakes, with honey--but the honey should **not** be other than that **with** the honeycomb. Not strained honey. (Stomach Lacerations)   5545-1

Dissolve a full teaspoonful of strained honey into a glass or tumbler of heated milk. Taking this about twenty to thirty minutes before retiring will be found to be most helpful. (Hypertension)   1539-1

(Chocolate) should be very, very seldom given. But after these conditions (anemia) are improved, or removed, this will be helpful in the form of a chocolate drink, rather than in candy. 2004-2

Q-Is chocolate or bittersweet chocolate hard for me to digest?
A-Any of the chocolates are hard to digest at the present. These may be taken in moderation as conditions progress. (General Debilitation) 2426-1

Ices, fruit ices, are very good for the system, especially pineapple and orange ices, see? (Malaria Tendency) 4281-6

Not very much ice cream should be taken; but **ices**--as fruit ices or sherbet--may be taken. (Obesity) 2315-1

In the matter of the diet, be very mindful that in the beginning this consists much of pre-digested foods. Junket, and things of such nature would be the first characters of food. (Asthenia) 895-1

THE JERUSALEM ARTICHOKE AND DIABETES

Instead of using so much insulin; this can be gradually diminished and eventually eliminated entirely if there is used in the diet one Jerusalem artichoke every other day. This should be cooked only in Patapar paper, preserving the juices and mixing with the bulk of the artichoke, seasoning this to suit the taste. The taking of the insulin is habit forming. The artichoke is not habit forming, not sedative-producing in the body as to cause accumulations of poisons as do sedatives; though it will be necessary to take a sedative when there are the attacks, but take a hypnotic rather than a narcotic--only under the direction, however, of a physician. 4023-1

The oyster plant, the Jerusalem artichoke occasionally--once a week sufficient for this; this adds adrenalin and is that which will keep down accumulations and prepare the activity of the glands--especially the spleen, the liver, the pancreas--and work well with the balancing of the sugar content for the system. (Diabetes) 1490-1

Eat a Jerusalem artichoke once each week, about the size of a hen egg. Cook this in Patapar paper, preserving all the juices to mix with the bulk of the artichoke. Season to taste. This will also aid in the disorder in the circulation between liver and kidneys, pancreas and kidneys, and will relieve those tensions from the desire for sweets. (Diabetes) 3386-2

Keep these Jerusalem artichokes fresh, not by (their) being put in the refrigerator, but by keeping them in the ground. 2472-1

Milk, whether it is the dry or the pasteurized or raw, is near to the perfect combination of forces for human consumption.   1703-2

Q-How did the trouble of pinworms originate, or what caused it?
A-Milk! You see, in every individual there is within the intestinal tract that matter which produces a form of intestinal worm. This is in everyone. But with a particular diet where the milk has any bacillus, it will gradually cause these to increase, and they oftentimes develop or multiply rapidly; and then they may disappear, **if** there is taken raw, green food.   2015-10

So few milks are free from tubercle; so few are free from those influences that cause a great deal more irritation than help--unless irradiated or dried milk is used. These as a whole are much more healthful to most individuals than raw milk.   480-42

This should be goat's milk or mare's milk and if this **cannot** be obtained--**we** would prefer those of Dryco or malted milk--these would be much preferable to those of the raw milk. (General Debilitation)4320-3

Be very mindful that in the beginning this (diet) consists much of pre-digested foods; as malted milks with a little stimuli of brandy (preferably apple brandy)--a few drops. (Asthenia)   895-1

Especially to this body there should not be food taken when the body is overwrought in any manner...Preferably take water, or butter-milk--**never** sweet milk under such conditions.   243-7

Q-Is it advisable for the body to drink soybean milk?
A-...If there is sufficient of the energies used for physical activities to make same more easily assimilated it is well. If these energies are used for activities which are more mental than physical, it would not be so well.   1158-18

YOGURT, BUTTERMILK AND BUTTER

Add yogurt in the diet as an active cleanser through the colon and intestinal system. This would be most beneficial, not only purifying the alimentary canal but adding the vital forces necessary to enable those portions of the system to function in the nearer normal manner. 1542-1

Milk--this in some manners is taboo for the body, yet in others is excellent. Those of the Bulgarian milk (yogurt?), or of the buttermilk would be the **better** for the system. This is acid in the reaction, to be sure, in **some** cases. Not so here! For the bacilli as is created in system through same will produce effects such that we will have a cleansed colon by the use of the same. 5525-1

Then for the strengthening of the body, for the gradual building up of the vitality, use yogurt. 5210-1

Begin with an almost wholly Bulgarian milk diet. (Stomach Ulcers) 556-2

No greases, no fats should be taken. Of course, butter may be taken. And the vegetables should be prepared preferably with butter if any seasoning is to be used. 3033-1

A great deal of fats will be hard on the body...Butter fats and cheeses and such are well to be taken in moderation. 1409-9

EGGS AND EGGNOG

Q-Why does she have severe attacks of indigestion after eating eggs? **A**-The tendency for the nervous reaction to those elements especially that are found more prevalent in eggs; as phosphorus and the natures that make for the gluten. This trouble will not be experienced if only the yolk of the egg is prepared--coddled. 607-1

Use more of the yolk than of the white and they should be prepared either in the form of soft-scrambled or coddled. 924-1

Egg in milk if the white is taken in same produces acid; if only the yolk is taken it is good. 340-20

It is best that they (eggs) **not** be taken raw. If taken raw, take them **with** something else; as in orange juice or beer or the like. 1158-31

Keep away from any drinks that have malt in same. However, malted milk is very well. If the raw egg yolk is taken in malted milk once a day it will be most beneficial. (Duodenal Ulcers) 481-4

Well that the yolk of one or two eggs be beaten either in milk or malt and drunk as the morning meal, **with** whole wheat gruel or oaten gruel-- but either or both should be well cooked before taken. (Anemia) 501-1

We would find it well to use every character of food that is body and blood-building. Milk, but preferably the malted with an egg and a little spirits frumenti in same; taken once to twice a day rather than solid foods. (General Debilitation) 1278-7

Do eat quantities of sea foods, not fresh water fish, but sea foods, including salt water fish, oysters clams, lobster and the like. 3687-1

Keep the diets body-building. Plenty of vitamins A and D; plenty of B-1 and the B-complex; or plenty of fish and fowl. Plenty of carrots, of squash. 2947-1

Do have oft for the body those properties that carry a great deal of iodine and calcium; or sea foods often. 3056-1

(Have) body-building foods. Not too much of fats, but foods that are easily assimilated; plenty of fish both canned and fresh. 3267-1

(Seafoods) are good, whether in the dried or in the fresh. The fresh carry more of that vitamin as makes for stamina in the vital forces of reproduction of **every** form **of** life...Remember, this is for good and bad influences or bacilli as may be in (the) body. Hence, these should be carefully selected, and be **very** fresh and not from polluted waters. 501-1

Fish would be very well to supply more calcium; as well as those boney portions of same that are cooked to such an extent that these may be masticated also--that is, the heavy bones, not the small ones. Hence these boiled or broiled or roasted would be preferable for the body, and of the larger varieties. 1973-1

Eat bones of fish, as in canned fish. 5192-1

The vitamins necessary in the system, and especially vitamin E-- whose activity in the system is for reproduction of the activity through every **gland** of the body itself, or those forces that are from silicon, iron, gold, or the activities for phosphorus--as of shellfish. Especially clams, oysters, more than any of the others--unless it is lobster. These are well to be taken two to three times each week; but these should be boiled. (Anemia Tendencies) 1048-4

There is nothing better for anemia than phosphorus with these conditions. Conch soup would be the **more** effective. **Nothing** more effective in the blood supply than gold, that we obtain from the seafoods; such as oysters, clams--but not crabs, not such natures as these. Certain elements as we would find in the **lobster** would be well, but not the Maine Lobster; preferably those of the southern waters. 698-1

In the diet; keep those that are blood and nerve and body-building. Once or twice a week have shellfish, or those that are of the conch nature--as conch soups...The broth of the conch is the most excellent for any body! for it carries the greater quantity of phosphorus than any food that may be assimilated by man--the conch! (Anemia) 1065-1

The meats taken would be preferably fish, fowl and lamb; others **not** often. Breakfast bacon, crisp, may be taken occasionally. 1710-4

Meats should be preferably fowl, fish, lamb, rather than beef or other meats. Wild fowl are, of course, the better.   1158-1

Meats should be wild game, nothing that has been killed with blood in it...Eat wild game which eats from nature, tame game eats what it is fed. (Anemia)   4834-1

Any, wild game is preferable even to other meats if these are prepared properly. Rabbit--be sure the tendon in both legs is removed, or that as might cause a fever.   2514-4

Have squirrels, rabbit or any wild game. Any of these are good for the body. Chew the bones when masticating same, as this will add to the strength, blood-building and resistance of the body. (Tuberculosis) 5053-1

Fish, fowl and lamb are those that supply elements needed for brain, muscle and nerve-building.   4008-1

Have plenty of sea foods, fowl and occasionally lamb. These would be the only characters of meats. Do not change wholly to the vegetable diet, for this would be too weakening for the body conditions. 4031-1

No raw meat, and very little ever of hog meat. Only bacon. 303-11

For that we think on, as that we assimilate in our bodies, that we gradually grow to be. Can anyone fill his body with swine and not eventually become pigish or hoggish in his relationships with others. 1562-1

Have especially those foods that carry more of the calcium and vitamins A, D, B-1 and other B complexes. Hence we would have plenty of fish, fowl, lamb and liver.   2679-1

For this body there should be little or no animal fat or animal matter. For the form of the activity of the infection (arthritis) is that which is created by, or lives upon, the animal matter.   5402-1

No meats, if any are taken, only the broths of fowl; especially those portions of the neck, the feet, the back or the like, cooked for a long period and broths made from same. From the portions we find calcium in an assimilated form, would aid in strengthening the blood stream.   1885-1

With roasts, do not eat the fat of the lamb or the fowl. Of the fowl preferably eat plenty of the body portions, as the thigh, the wing, the neck, the head. Chew these so that the juice from same may be swallowed ...the calcium from same will be beneficial. (Arthritis Tendency) 1888-1

When there is weakness indicated (as the body tends towards anemia)...give the body plenty of beef juice. This should be taken as medicine. Give a teaspoonful at the time, but let the body be at least two minutes in sipping that quantity. Let it rather be absorbed than swallowed. Let it just flow with the salivary glands and be absorbed through the body force by the gentle swallowing. There will be little or none to digest, but will be absorbed.   3316-1

Q-How should the beef juices be prepared?

A-Take a pound to a pound and a half of beef--**lean** beef, not fat! Dice it into small pieces, about the size of a good sized marble--or the thumb. Put in a glass jar. Seal the jar, no water in same. Put this in water, with a cloth or something in to prevent from breaking or cracking the jar. Let it boil for two to three hours. Extract the juice. Throw the meat away. Season the juice and take it as directed. There will be enough in a pound to last for two or three days. Keep in a cool place. Not beef broth, but beef **juice**! (Anemia)   461-1

Be sure it (beef juice) is kept rather fresh; or make it fresh each day. Sip it two, three, four, five, six times a day. A teaspoonful of this is worth much more than a quarter pound steak. This is worth much more than five pounds of potatoes. It is worth much more than a whole head of cabbage, unless the cabbage is eaten raw. (Anemia)   667-8

There is more strength and body-building in one spoonful of beef juice than a pound of the raw meat or rare meat or cooked!   1259-2

The **juices** contain iron. The meats contain little.   488-3

(To make beef juice) preferably use round steak or rump steak.1045-6

Juices from beef, without bulk, works directly with the duodenum and the active forces in the pancreas and spleen, giving new blood.   1377-3

Beef juice assimilates if taken in small quantities, taken in quantities as to act upon or by gastric juices it becomes an astringent.   379-6

Liver juice is made in the same way and manner as the beef juice. 623-3

Use those (foods) which are body-building as beef juice, beef broth, liver, fish, lamb...Include butter and milk. Also raw vegetables and then prepared with gelatin. Only the yolk of eggs, leafy vegetables, raw cabbage, cooked red cabbage, spinach, string beans.   5269-1

Blood building foods; as the whole wheat, beef juices, broiled liver, pig's feet and the like. These carry the hormones and the gluten that supplies in the assimilating system the better body building. 1519-4

Let the diet be that as is nerve and blood building. Let it be composed of--at least once each week--tripe, liver, codliver, fish liver, hog liver, pig liver, calf liver--any of those--at least once or twice each week, see? and vegetables and fruits, as plenty of celery and the leafy vegetables. If cabbage is taken let it be raw, rather than cooked. Lentils, beans, peas, spinach, celery, lettuce, and the like. Fruits--pears; no apples; cherries, **berries**--provided they grow off of ground, not **on** the ground. (Anemia, General Debilitation and Neurasthenia) 3842-1

Q-What should the body eat to increase blood supply?
A-Liver, blood pudding, those of pig knuckles, souse, eggs (yolk of same) milk, dry milk, and the like. Plenty of prunes.   340-17

(Take) a little tripe or pig's feet...for the gelatin in same that is active in making for coagulations in the body-building.   908-1

Do keep up more of those foods that tend to make muscle, tendon, nerve tissue and the like--in gelatin, see.   849-73

Eat liver--calve's liver--not fried--it may be broiled or parbroiled--at least three times each week. Use eggs, not with the white, stirred well into the malt, as one of the meals; with those of the whole wheat gluten...At least twice a week, were beef tripe or hog tripe taken as a diet, this will be of real value in blood building.   2335-1

The larger varieties (of fish) carry a great quantity of those properties for body and blood-building.   1973-1

Vegetables will build gray matter faster than meat or sweets. 900-386

(Have) especially nerve building forces in blood. Meats only that of wild game or fish. Vegetable matter that grows above the ground and cereals with fruits, especially pears.   4120-1

(Avocado pears) are good for anemia. They contain most iron. Pears are helpful to **anyone**, especially where body and blood building influences are needed; for they will be absorbed. These are best to be taken morning and evening; not through the active portions of the day. 501-4

Those that will build for new blood--as of the liver, the tripe, pig knuckles, or the like, or those that are of the blood building in the vegetables--as of cooked carrots, peas, beans, lentils, lettuce, asparagus, salsify, and the like. Those of the cabbage.   5518-1

Fish, fowl and lamb are those that supply elements needed for brain, muscle and nerve building...Carrots, celery and lettuce are especially nerve building and supply the vitamins called B and B complex. 4008-1

Have at least one meal each day that includes a quantity of raw vegetables, such as cabbage, lettuce, celery, carrots, onions and the like.
Tomatoes may be used in their season. **Do** have plenty of vegetables
above the ground; at least three of these to one below the ground. Have
at least one leafy vegetable to every one of the pod vegetables.   2602-1

Have at least three of the leafy vegetables to one below the ground, or
with the leafy vegetables there may be one or two of the bulbous nature
--as squash, beans, peas, etc., and (well cooked) onions. (Acidity) 703-1

(Have) **green, fresh, crisp** (vegetables); never any of the wilted or
withered, but used more **outside** leaves than inside.   932-1

(Have) two of the leafy vegetables to one of the pod, and three of
the leafy to one of the tuberous.   1183-2

(Have) well cooked vegetables that grow **above** the ground; none that
grow below the ground--none! Those that are of the activity as to make
for tuberous forces and heavy starches (as all of these are) make for
heaviness that is hard to eliminate. (Poor Eliminations)   4293-1

Leafy vegetables will make for the better eliminations.   480-24

In the evening meals, those of the well cooked vegetables, but only
those of the leafy nature--or that grow in pods; not the bulb nature.
No potatoes, no carrots, no beets, no turnips, nothing of that nature.
The **tops** of these may be taken...but not the bulb nature. (Stomach
Ulcers)   482-3

Plenty of lettuce should always be eaten by most **every**body; this supplies an effluvium in the bloodstream that is a destructive force to **most**
of those influences that attack the blood stream. It's a purifier.   404-6

The (pinworms) will be eliminated if there will be taken rather
regularly some lettuce and some of such nature of green raw vegetables,
raw carrots, raw fruits...eat lettuce and celery and carrots--even a small
amount. One leaf of lettuce will destroy a thousand worms. 2015-10

(Have) lots of lettuce, lots of celery, lots of asparagus, and such...
green vegetables; especially of the lettuce that **does not** head. 102-2

Have a great deal of the leafy and green vegetables, such as carrots,
celery, lettuce, and preferable that that does not head--for this body,
more soporiferous than that of the iceberg (variety).   5557-1

When the celery is selected, use the green portion rather than that
which has been bleached. These portions have from twenty to forty
percent more of the vitamins.   920-13

Q-What can be done for extreme nervousness?
A-Taking or having in the diet plenty of celery juices, celery soups, celery raw, celery cooked. 2501-12

Use whole wheat bread and vegetables that carry a high percentage of carbons such as asparagus, celery, salsify. (Anemia) 4439-1

(Have) plenty of cabbage in slaw, thoroughly grated, and used with whatever character of dressing is desired. (Duodenal Ulcers) 481-4

Quite a dissertation might be given as to the effect of tomatoes upon the human system. Of all the vegetables, tomatoes carry most of the vitamins in a well balanced assimilative manner for the activities of the system. Yet if these are not cared for properly they may become very destructive to a physical organism; that is, if they ripen after being pulled, or if there is the contamination with other influences...
The tomato is one vegetable that in most instances (because of the greater uniform activity) is preferable to be eaten after being canned, for it is then much more uniform. 584-5

(Give foods) that are of easy digestion. Tomato juice--especially that of canned tomatoes, that are canned good. Tomato juice as soups that are with beans, peas, tomatoes, potatoes...Well for the body to cut teeth on carrots, or parsnips (raw, see?). (Baby one year old) 608-1

The salts that are in same (Irish potatoes) close to the peel will supply starch **and** carbohydrates in a manner that the activities of the vitamins A and D are in such proportions as to build strength and vitality...an not build fat. (Obesity Tendencies) 1073-1

Keep white potatoes **away from this body!** Sweet potatoes or yams may be taken occasionally. (Toxemia) 1593-1

(Have potato) jackets and the small portion that adheres to the jacket--for this portion of the potato carries properties that are **not** acid-producing and not too great an amount of starch; but do not eat the bulk of the potato. 632-6

Roasted yams or sweet potatoes are very good if plenty of butter is taken with same. 1342-1

(Green peppers) are better in combinations than by themselves...with green cabbage, lettuce, are very good for this body in moderation. 404-6

Q-What is the best source of nicotinic acid?
A-Of course, squash, pumpkin, and especially in what is called the oyster plant (salsify). 1158-31

(Have) vegetables that have a direct bearing upon the optic forces... such as carrots, green peas, green beans, onions, beets. (Glaucoma) 3552-1

That portion especially close to the top (of the carrot)...carries the vital energies, stimulating the optic reactions.   3051-6

This to be sure, is not an attempt to tell the body (a vegetarian) to go back to eating meat. But do supply then, through the body forces, supplements, either in vitamins or in meat substitutes. This is necessary for those who hold to these vegetarian influences. 5401-1

Let the diet be only vegetables forces, do not lower the plane of development by animal vibrations.   1010-1

Once or twice a week take vegetables juices that would be prepared by a vegetable juicer, but only using the vegetables for same that would combine well. They may be combined or taken separately; the juices from such as lettuce, celery, beets, spinach, mustard, carrots, radishes, and a tiny bit of leek or onion--not more than one very small onion. 1968-3

There are periods when they (carrots) are better assimilated cooked than raw, but the juices are the source of the vitamin--and that, of course, close to the skin.   457-9

VEGETABLE AND GELATIN COMBINATIONS

(Have) a great deal of raw vegetables, especially mixed with gelatin. Even vegetable juices taken with gelatin would be well; not set, however, but taken as soon as the gelatin is stirred in same.   5031-1

Raw vegetables as watercress, celery, lettuce, tomatoes and carrots... may be prepared rather often with gelatin, such as lime or lemon gelatin, or Jello. These will not only taste good but be good for you.   3429-1

Each day take half a teaspoonful of Knox gelatin stirred in two ounces of water, drinking this before it begins to jell. (Anemia) 3070-1

(Have) any of the gelatin products, though they may carry sugar at times, these are to be had oft in the diet. (Anemia)   2520-2

Q-Please explain the vitamin content of gelatin.
A-It isn't the vitamin content but it is ability to work with the activities of the glands, causing the glands to take from that absorbed or digested the vitamins that would not be active if there is not sufficient gelatin in the body.   849-75

Q-Is raw fruit harmful?

A-Apples but not other fruits. Pears and all citrus fruits are **good**. Grapes without the seeds, well. Figs are very beneficial, whether the ripe or those packed. (Indigestion and Neurasthenia)   5622-3

Be sure that all (fruits) taken are fresh, firm, and not that that is **overly** ripe; that is, fermentation not already begun.   2261-1

(Have foods) that are easily assimilated; less acid-producing, though plenty of orange juices and **fruits** of all kinds. (Diabetes Tendency)   454-8

Every character of fruit tend to aid eliminations, also carrying the correct character of sugars.   1188-10

Oranges, pineapple, grapefruit...are **not** acid-**producing**. They are alkaline-reacting.   1484-1

Mornings--citrus fruit or stewed fruits (as figs, apples, peaches or the like), but do not serve the stewed fruits with the citrus fruit juices; neither serve the citrus fruits with a dry cereal.   623-1

Cooked apples, if they are of the jenneting (Jonathan?) variety, may be given. None of those of the more woody variety, as those of Ben Davis or Winesap or of the fall or wood variety. These should **not** be given to this body in **any** manner. (20 month old baby--indigestion)   142-5

Apples should only be eaten when cooked; preferable roasted and with butter or hard sauce on same, with cinnamon and spice.   935-1

Fruits, especially apples, contain iron.   4841-1

(Avocado pears) are good for anemia. They contain most iron. Pears are helpful to **anyone**.   501-4

Build up the body with more of iron, as maybe had from dried fruits, dates and the like.   849-23

Do not overtax the system with bananas, unless these are ripened in their natural state...or that have been gathered or prepared when they were fully matured may be taken in moderation.   658-15

Have a diet...mostly of grapes--or grape juice...(Seeds) should never be eaten--not in the juice taken. The Concord grapes are the best, if it is possible to obtain them. If not, use the purple grapes...as the California grapes, but **not** the white grapes. (Colitis Tendency)   324-7

Especially use the garden blueberry. (This is a property which someone, some day, will use in its proper place!) These should be stewed, but with their own juices, little sugar. (Anemia and Multiple Sclerosis)   3118-1

(Have) vegetables or fruits that are especially **yellow** in color; as squash (only the yellow character), yellow peaches--not white.   2277-1

Q-What type of fruits particularly would aid in eliminations?
A-Figs, prunes, pears, oranges, dates and such. Figs that would be dried and then stewed, you see--both black and the regular fig.   849-55

(For) better eliminations--figs, raisins, grapes, pears.   69-4

The basic of the food of the Atlanteans and the Egyptians--corn meals with figs and dates prepared together with goat's milk.   5257-1

For this particular body equal portions of black figs or Assyrian figs and Assyrian dates--these ground together or cut very fine--and to a pint of such a combination put half a handful of corn meal, or crushed wheat. These cooked together--well, it's food for such a spiritually developed body as this.   275-45

No meats or too much sweets, but of vegetables and fruits--no tomatoes or strawberries--any other fruits of the acid taste. (Cancer)   3751-6

In the diet--do live mostly, for a while, on watermelon. The watermelon is for the activity of the liver and the kidney. (Cancer)   3121-1

THE THREE DAY RAW APPLE DIET

No raw apples; or if raw apples are taken, take them and **nothing** else --three days of raw apples only, and then olive oil, and we will cleanse **all** toxic forces from any system! Raw apples are not well unless they are the jenneting variety. Apples cooked, apples roasted, are good. 820-2

Occasionally--not too often--take the periods for the cleansing of the system with the use of the **apple diet**; that is: At least for three days-- two days or three days--take **nothing** except **apples--raw apples!** Of course, coffee may be taken if so desired, but no other foods but the raw apples. And after the last meal of apples of the third day, or upon retiring on that evening following the last meal of apples, drink half a cup of olive oil. This will tend to cleanse the system.   543-26

(The apple diet) would remove fecal matter that hasn't been removed for some time! But it will certainly indicate there is no tapeworm. 567-7

(For the apple diet use) the Jonathan variety...or the jenneting; the Black Arkansas, the Oregon Red...the Sheepnose, the Delicious, the Arkansas Russet; any of those that are of the jenneting variety. 294-182

Q-How can I reduce weight to feel better?

A-Such massages and sweats the more often, as indicated, will tend to reduce. Also for this body we find that the grape juice and grapefruit diets would be beneficial. Take two ounces of grape juice (Welch's preferably, unless fresh grapes are used) stirred in one ounce of plain water (not carbonated water), half an hour before each meal and at bedtimes. The grapefruit juice should be a drink taken once or twice each day, about two or three ounces.   619-10

Take grape juice four times each day; one ounce of plain water and three ounces of grape juice, taken half an hour before each meal and upon retiring. Then in the matter of the diet, it will almost take care of itself, and take those things the appetite calls for, save sweets, chocolate or the like; not great quantities of sugars, nor of pastries; but all other foods, vegetables or meats, provided they are not fats, may be taken according to the appetite; but we will find the appetite will change a great deal. (Obesity)   1309-2

Q-Is the Welch grape juice prepared without benzoate of soda? (1937)

A-Prepared without benzoate of soda. Pure grape juice...

If the grape juice is taken it supplies a sugar, the kind of sugar though that works with the system--that which is necessary, see? and then that prevents the system's desire for starches and sweets in excess.   470-19

Q-Any special kind of grape juice?

A-Pure grape juice; not that that's fermented.   1339-1

THE FUNCTION OF VITAMINS

Q-What relation do the vitamins bear to the glands? Give specific vitamins affecting specific glands.

A-You want a book written on these! They (vitamins) are food for same. Vitamins are that from which the glands take those necessary influences to supply the energies to enable the varied organs of the body to reproduce themselves. Would it ever be considered that our toenails would be reproduced by the same (gland) as would supply the breast, the head, or the face? or that the cuticle would be supplied from the same (source) as would supply the organ of the heart itself? These (building substances) are taken from **glands** that control the assimilated foods, and hence (require) the necessary elements of vitamins in same to supply the various forces for enabling each organ, each functioning of the body, to carry on in its creative or generative forces, see?

These will begin with A--that supplies portions to the nerves, to bone, to the brain force itself; not (being) all of (the supply to) this (area), but this is a part of (the function of) A.

B and B-1 supply the ability of the energies, or the moving forces of the nerve and of the white blood supply, as well as the white nerve energy in the nerve force itself, the brain (force) itself, and (supply) the ability of the sympathetic or involuntary reflexes through the body. Now this includes all (such energy), whether you are wiggling your toes or your ears or batting your eye or what! In these (B vitamins) we (also) have that (which is) supplying to the chyle that ability for it to control the influence of fats, which is necessary (and this body has never had enough of it!) to carry on the reproducing of the oils that prevent the tenseness in the joints, or that prevent the joints from becoming atrophied or dry, or (from seeming) to creak. And at times the body has some creaks!

In C we find that which supplies the necessary influences to the flexes of every nature throughout the body, whether of a muscular or tendon nature, or a heart reaction, or a kidney contraction, or the liver contraction, or the opening or the shutting of your mouth the batting of the eye, or the supplying of the saliva and the muscular forces in (the) face. These are all supplied by C--not that it is the only supply, or a part of the same. It is that from which the (necessary supply for) structural portions of the body are (taken and) stored, and drawn upon when it is necessary...

G supplies the general energies, or the sympathetic forces of the body itself. These are the principles.   2072-9

Have ye not read that in Him ye live and move and have thy being (Acts 17:28)? What are those elements in food or drink that give growth or strength to the body? Vitamins? What are vitamins? The Creative Forces working with body-energies for the renewing of the body. 3511-1

NATURAL VITAMIN SOURCES

(Vitamins) are better assimilated...if taken in the food values. No synthetic principle is as good as the real thing...Vitamins may best be taken through the vegetable forces that are yellow in color; as carrots, squash, yellow corn and yellow corn meal; peaches; oats.   257-224

Most of this (vitamin taking) is fad, save as to what may be necessary to create a balance (in the diet).   2778-6

(Vitamins) are more efficacious if they are given for periods, left off for periods and began again. For if the system comes to rely upon such influences wholly, it ceases to produce the vitamins even though the food values may be kept normally balanced. And it's much better that these be produced in the body from the normal development than supplied mechanically, for nature is much better yet than science! 759-12

If they (vitamins) are not put to work by the activities of the system --either physical or mental--they become destructive tissue. 341-31

Q-What foods are the best sources of vitamin B?
A-And B-1. All of those that are of the yellow variety, in fruits and vegetables...This is a vitamin that is not stored as is A, D, C, or G but needs to be supplied each day. 1158-31

Keep an excess of foods that carry especially Vitamin B, iron and such. Not the concentrated form, you see, but oft obtain these from the foods. These would include all fruits, all vegetables that are yellow in their nature. Thus,--lemon and orange juice combined, all citrus fruit juices; pineapples as well as grapefruit...
Squash,--especially the yellow; carrots cooked and raw; yellow peaches; yellow apples (preferably the apples cooked, however)...
Yellow corn, yellow corn meal, buckwheat. 1968-7

(B-1 is found) in **all** cereals, and in bread; and especially the **green** leaves of lettuce--not so much in the beautiful white pieces. 257-236

Supply vitamins B-1, A, B, and G through the cereals. 849-47

(Have) B-1 especially, the exercise or energy vitamin. These are found in the breads, of course, the reinforced cereals, all yellow foods, and especially sunshine. 849-62

B and B-1, with also G and M (are in yellow vegetables). 2287-1

B, B-1, A, C, and D...(are in) citrus juices, plenty of raw vegetables --as carrots, spinach, celery, lettuce. 2153-1

Have especially those foods that carry more of the calcium and the vitamins A, D, B-1 and other B complexes. Hence we would have plenty of fish, fowl, lamb and liver..whole wheat grain,--as cracked wheat, crushed or steel cut oats, and plenty of citrus fruits. 2679-1

Keep the diets body building. Plenty of vitamins A and D; plenty of B-1 and the B-complex or plenty of fish, fowl...carrots, (raw) spinach. 2947-1

As we find, we would use oft in the diet the supplementary vitamins especially of the E or the wheat germ oil, see? 5170-1

Little of minerals should ever be the properties within the system, save as may be taken through the vegetables forces, save where individuals have so laxed themselves as to require or need that which will make for an even balance of same.   364-11

Q-What foods contain gold, silicon and phosphorus?
A-...These are contained more in those of the vegetable, of the fish ...cabbage, carrots, lettuce, celery--all such. Fish, oysters, eggplants at times...much of these depend upon where the vegetation is grown... Yolks of eggs...Raw cabbage at times carry those properties--especially the red cabbage. Those of the fruits and the nuts.   1000-2

(Have) much of that which will add more phosphorus and gold to the system; as we will find in certain of the vegetables--as carrots, salsify, squash, the rind of Irish potatoes (not the pulp), okra. (Anemia) 698-1

The phosphorus-forming foods are principally carrots, lettuce (rather the leaf lettuce, which has more soporific activity than the head lettuce), shellfish, salsify, the **peelings** of Irish potatoes (if they are not to large)...fresh milk that is warm with the animal heat.   560-2

The yolk of egg, none of the white. Those in carrots, celery, turnips, **all** carry a form of phosphorus that are additions, and solubles to the system. Milk also, if warm with the animal heat. That which has been pasteurized does not carry same.   255-3

Carrots, salsify, turnips, parsnips (carry phosphorus).   2214-1

The broth of the conch...carries the greater quantity of phosphorus that any food that may be assimilated by man.   1065-1

Add all of the foods that carry silicon and the salts...as foods of the tuberous nature of every character--the oyster plant (salsify), every form of turnip or potatoes or yams or the ground artichoke. 3694-1

Silicon, lime, salts--**these**, as we find, will be in the **green** vegetables ...including plenty celery.   1225-1

Take as food values much that carries iron, silicon...as we find in certain vegetables, as beets, celery, radishes; all of those natures that give the cleansing forces to the system. Spinach and eggs.   257-11

Leafy vegetable juices or leafy vegetables may be taken; as lentils, broccoli, and such that carry sufficient iron and silicon.   257-28

(Have) all of those that carry a great deal of iron and silicon...that is turnips, turnip greens, all of those that grow under the ground through the winter--as parsnips, carrots , beets and oyster plant. 538-66

Two or three pears each day will be **most** helpful in the manner of furnishing iron, silicon.   1049-1

Iron may be had from dried fruits and dates.   849-23

Fruits, especially apples, contain iron.   4841-1

Q-Please give foods that supply iron, calcium and phosphorus.
A-Cereals that carry the heart of the grain; vegetables of the leafy kind, fruits and nuts. The almond carries more phosphorus and iron in a combination easily assimilated than any other nut.   1131-2

We would find (calcium) especially in raw carrots, cooked turnips, and turnip greens, all characters of salads--especially as of water-cress, mustard, and the like. These are especially helpful taken raw, though turnips should be cooked--but cooked in their own juices. 1968-6

Q-What are the best sources of calcium in foods?
A-The ends of boney pieces of fowl or the like, gristle, pig's feet, souse (pickled pig's heads, ears and feet). Vegetables such as turnips, parsnips, and all of those that grow under the ground.   1158-31

Prepare such pieces (of fowl) as the neck, the head, the wing, the feet, and the boney pieces, so that the small bones may be very well masticated by the body, or the juice chewed out of these. For, the juices from these carry more of the calcium that is needed. This the calcium, may not be supplied as well in other ways as it may be by taking extra quantities of seafoods (which carry a great deal of the iodines as well as calcium) and boney pieces of fowl or chicken. 3076-1

Especially the larger bone in the back of the fish--baked--should be **eaten** for the calcium that is in same.   1560-1

Calcium is needed (crippled with arthritis), in a manner that may be assimilated...This we would add in the form which we have indicated as the **best**--the chewing of bones or ends of bones of the fowl (boney pieces of fowl, well stewed, until soft). If this is abhorrent or disagreeable, then take **calcios** (pulverized chicken bones), about three times each week, just what would cover a Premium Cracker as butter. 849-53

The addition of those foods which carry large quantities of calcium will make for bettered conditions in this direction (deep ridges in thumbnail). Take often chicken neck, chew it. Cook this well, the feet and those portions of the fowl, and we will find it will add calcium to the body. Also eat bones of fish, as in canned fish. Also parsnips and oyster plant; all of these, of course in their regular season. Wild game of any kind, but chew the bones of same.   5192-1

PART IX

ATTITUDES AND EMOTIONS

IT'S A RECIPROCAL WORLD

It has ever been and is, even in materiality, a reciprocal world. "If ye will be my people, I will be thy God" (Jeremiah 32:38), If ye would know **Good**, do Good. If ye would have life, give life. If ye would know Jesus, the Christ then be like him..."There is no life without death, there is no **renewal** without the dying of the old."   1158-9

What ye do to others, ye are doing to thyself.   3198-3

"As ye would that others should do to you, do ye even so to them" is not...merely a saying that has found ready utterance on the tongues of those who would have their way here and there. They are principles. 584-4

If ye would have love, ye must show thyself lovely. If ye would have friends, ye must show thyself friendly. If ye would have peace and harmony, forget self and make for harmony and peace in thy associations.
So oft is the ego so enrapt in self that it feels it will lose its importance, its place, its freedom. Yet to have freedom in self, give it. To have peace in self, make it--give it!...
"In the manner ye do it unto the least of these ye meet day by day, so ye do it unto thy God" (Matthew 25:40)...
In giving out ye receive...In helping the discouraged ye found courage; in helping the weak ye became strong.   1650-1

As ye condemn, so **are** ye condemned. As ye forgive, so may ye be forgiven. As ye do unto the least of thy brethren, so ye do unto thy Maker. These as laws, as truths, are unfailing. And because He may oft appear slow in meting out the results of such activity does not alter or change the law...Any error, or a fault, or a failure, **must** be met...each entity, each soul--**as Himself**--must pay to the last jot or tittle!   2449-1

As we seek, we find. As we knock, we are heard. If we are timid, if we are fearful, if we are overcautious in our giving out that hope which has sustained our own selves, then we grow weaker and more fearful ourself. This is a spiritual law.   877-7

For they that would have life, love, hope, faith, brotherly love, kindness, gentleness, mercy, must **show** these things in their relationships to those they meet in every walk of life. 694-2

If ye would be happy (it is the law), ye must make others happy. Ye cannot know happiness unless ye experience that ye have brought happiness, hope, joy, into the experience of another. 412-9

As you give, so is it given. Only what you have given away do you possess. What you lose was never yours. What you gain is an opportunity. What you possess is not yours except as you use it in relationships to others, to your Maker, to your purpose, to your fellow man. 1387-1

As ye forgive, ye are forgiven. As ye love, so are ye loved. As ye resent, so are ye resented. This is **law**, physical, mental, **spiritual.** 2600-2

If you would create confidence in thyself, **find** and **have** confidence in others; see in thy fellow man, though he may be thy enemy, the **motivating** force or power or spirit ye would worship in thy Maker. 2419-1

If ye would be antagonized, then be antagonistic. 969-1

Yes, in healing others one heals self. 281-16

Minimize the faults of others, if ye would have others minimize thy faults in thee. Magnify the virtues if ye would have thy Father, thy God, magnify thy blessings, thy virtues in thy dealings with others. 2791-1

"He that would be the greatest among you will be the servant of all" (Luke 22:26). He that will humble himself shall be exalted. 294-155

Know that ye **cannot** expect others to be any more sincere with **thee** than thou art with thyself or others. 934-6

As ye would have mercy shown thee, ye show mercy to those that even despitefully use thee. 987-4

Quit finding fault with others and others will quit finding fault with you. 3544-1

What ye sow, ye reap. Remember others will never mistreat you if you never mistreat someone else...for like begets like. 5354-1

They that would have cooperation **must** cooperate by the **giving** of self **to** that as is to be accomplished. 262-3

Only that as ye have taught to others do ye come to comprehend thyself ...It blossoms and grows to fruition in the lives of others. 1992-1

If you criticize then you may expect to be criticized yourself. 4035-1

Q-What is the law of love?

A-Giving. As is given in this injunction, "Love thy Neighbor as Thyself." As is given in the injunction, "Love the Lord Thy God with all Thine Heart, Thine Soul and Thine Body" (Luke 10:27)...**That is the Law of Love.** Giving in action, without the force felt, expressed, manifested, shown, desired or reward for that given.   3744-4

In love all life is given, in love all things move. In giving one attains. In giving one acquires. In giving love comes as the fulfillment of desire, guided, directed in the ways that bring the more perfect knowledge of application of self as related to the universal, all powerful, all guiding all divine influence in life--or it **is** life.   345-1

Love is giving...love grows; love endures; love forgiveth; love understands; love keeps those things rather as opportunities that to others would become hardships.   939-1

Do not confuse affection with love. Do not confuse passion with love. Love is of God, it is Creative; it is all-giving.   3545-1

When duty, love and reason are one, then such consciousness approaches near that of the universal love that gave all that man might be one with that universal love.   31-1

Let love be without dissimulation--that is, without **possession**, but as in the manner as He gave, "Love one another, even as I have loved you"; willing to give the life, the self, for the purpose, for an ideal. 413-11

The reverse of love, is suffering, hate, malice, injustice.   281-51

Which is more real, the love manifested in the Son the Savior, for His brethren, or the essence of love that may be seen even in the vilest of passion? They are one. But that they bring into being in a materialized form is what elements of the One Source have been combined to produce a materialization. Beautiful, isn't it?   254-68

To **live** love is to be love. To be one with the Father is to be equal **with** the Father.   900-331

Love healeth the wounded; it binds up the broken hearted; it makes understandings where differences have arisen. For **God is** love!   688-4

Love thine enemies, or those who would despitefully use you. 1900-1

(Loving indifference is) acting as if it had not been; disregarding as if it were not. Not animosity, for this only breeds strife.   1402-2

Greatest thought that comes to the mind to man 'someone cares'. 3365-1

Q-Why was the entity a man or horseman in the Arabian incarnation?

A-That would depend upon those desires as were made by the entity from its appearance in the **previous** incarnation, see? and finding, as it were, the opportunity in this particular period to enter in that capacity as had been desired, so the entity entered in as one who could fill, **fulfill** that desire; for, as should be gained by all: Desire brought the earth and the heavens into being from the All-Wise Creator. So man, by his heritage to that creation, may bring through desire, whether of earthly, heavenly, spiritual, those things that they, the individual, the entity, must meet, by creating, making, **being**, that desire! Hence, as we find, all the various phases of changes as may be wrought in man's, or woman's activities; for by taking **thought** no man may add one cubit nor can--by taking thought--the head be changed one whit; yet desire, and the fathering and mothering of desire, may change a whole universe! for, from the desires of the heart do the activities of the brain, of the physical being shape that as would be created by same, See?   276-3

He has given, "as the man thinketh in his heart, so is he" (Proverbs 23:7). Not that thinking takes place in the heart. For thinking is of the mind. Yet the flow, the impulse, the emotions in material things are activative through impulse of nature, of character, of purpose, of will. 585-9

Desire is that impulse which makes for the activity of the mental body, whether the impulse is from that desire or the desire is produced by the environs that affect a physical organism--or that which arouses or attunes the spiritual or soul body to an activity.   276-7

In the creating first of thought is the creating of the idea. In the creating of desire is the creating then of action. Now combine action, combine thought, and these become a reality in the physical plane and subject to the laws of physical existence. Yet the beginning, the conception, the inherent forces as are gained are **not** subject to finite or to material law, until those have become in a form where they become subject to same. When do they become subject to same? The same as in the seed of the pollen of a flower, of an atomic force, of a force as is seen manifested in the material world of the sex germ of male and female--the desire of each for each, and the thought transference of each--when this becomes in association one with another, there takes place that which in its growth becomes the manifested conception of material forces, remaining in the ethereal or cosmic forces until such does take place, see? Then we see how the physical law applies to the spiritual laws, and how spiritual laws apply to the physical conditions. One within another, each bearing its relation one with another--as the conception of idea, of desire, of will's forces--then beginning of the material law. 136-37

Truly is there found that the desire must precede the action and that directed thought becomes action in the concrete manner through each force that the spiritual elements manifest through.   106-9

Biologically, man makes himself as an animal of the physical; with the desires that are as the instinct in animal for the preservation of life, for the development of species, and for food. These three are those forces that are instinct in the animal and in man. If by that force of will man uses these within self for the aggrandizement of such elements in his nature, these then become the material desires--or are the basis of carnal influences, and belittle the spiritual or soul body...

Then, what is the basis of mental desire? The mental as an attribute is also of the animal, yet in man--with his intellect--the ability to make comparisons, to reason, to have the reactions through the senses; that are raised to the forces of activity such that they create for man the environs about him and make for change in hereditary influences in the experience of each soul. These are the gifts with that free-will agent, or attributes of same; or mind is a development of the application of will respecting desire that has become--in its essence--used as a grace, the gift to give praise for that which it has applied in its experience.   262-63

The heart is ordinarily considered the seat of life in the physical, while the will a motivative factor in the mental and spiritual realm. To be sure, these may be made one. But how? In that the will of self and the desire of the heart are selfless in the Christ Consciousness. Even as He gave in the shadow of the day when the Cross loomed before Him on Calvary, when the desire of the heart and the will of self were made one...

Desire, as first given, was in the motivating force that may separate or make the soul one with or separate from the Whole, through the manifestations in the will. And it builds in that the spirit moves in the direction in which it is motivated by will and desire.

Q-Is it necessary to give up physical desires for spiritual development?

A-Rather spiritualize physical desires as He did in the Garden (Gethsemane)...offering Himself for the world--then thou must pass through same, making physical desire and the will of the Father as one. 262-64

What separated spirit from its first cause, or causes good and evil? Desire! **Desire!**

Hence desire is the opposite of will. Will and desire, one with the Creative Forces of Good, brings all its influence in the realm of activity that makes for that which is constructive.   5752-3

Q-Where does desire originate?

A-Will   262-62

That which is carnal and that which is mental and that which is spiritual may be found--in **desire**. For, it builds--and is that which is the basis of evolution, and of life, and of truth. It also takes hold on hell and paves the way for many that find themselves oft therein. 262-60

Will and desire are spiritual as well as carnal, as well as mental. 315-3

The entity has in itself **will**, that knowledge, that understanding, with which the entity exercises its choice, to which it adds either for the satisfying or gratifying of self's emotions or self's desires or for the magnifying and glorifying of the spiritual sources or help.
These may be one, if the entity makes the hope, the desire of the body, the mind, the soul, in accord. Yet the soul ever seeks to magnify or glorify the divine. Hence the constant warring that one finds in members --body, mind, soul. Those are as the real of the shadows of appetites, of desires, of those things that are habits of body and that takehold as a habit. Yet who ever saw a habit? For it is a mental thing. 3420-1

Habit and desires are akin. Habit is a physical reaction to the senses of the body, while desire is both mental, physical **and** spiritual. 486-1

Q-To what development must the soul reach before it may first find lodgement in the flesh?
A-Desire for flesh. 900-70

As man's concept came to the point wherein he walked not after the ways of the Spirit, but after the desires of the flesh, **sin** entered--that is, away from the Face of the Maker, see? and death then became man's portion, **spiritually**, see? for the physical death existed from the beginning; for to create one must die, see? 900-227

As has been given of old, when the children of Israel stood with the sons of the heathen (Daniel 1:5-8) and all ate at the King's table, that which was taken that only exercised the imagination of the body as physical desires--as strong drink, strong meats, condiments. 341-31

From what may **anyone** be saved? Only from themselves! That is, their individual hell; they dig it with their own desires! 262-40

Nothing may separate the soul of man from its Maker but desires and lusts. 1293-1

That which a conscious mind does with pleasure becomes a part of the entity's personality. 378-14

For, while the woman is ordinarily changeable in mind, the real desire and purpose remains truer in woman than in man. 3051-4

As creative activities are applied, what ye desire becomes law. 5265-1

The spirituality of each soul is such that--the purpose, the design, the desire, the application of self in any direction changes the urges and builds or lessens the emotions in the physical.   2279-1

The mind in the entity becomes aware of longings, innate in the inner self; also the arousing of emotions in the physical attributes of the body,--as indicated as to how these came into **being**; as self is a part of Creative Forces or God, Spirit, the Son. These are one. The body, mind and soul are one. Their desires must be one; their purposes, their aim must be one--then--to be ideal....

The body was first a cell by the union of desire...Then of itself at birth into materiality the consciousness gradually awoke to the influences about same of body, mind, and soul, until it reached the consciousness of the ability for the reproduction within itself of desire, hope, fear. And the whole of creation, then, is bound in the consciousness of self. That influence, that force is the psychic self.   1947-3

SEX

In the experience of Amilius and I (Ai? or Ay?), Adam and Eve, the knowledge of their position, or that as is known in the material world today as desires and physical bodily charms, the understanding of sex, sex relationships, came into the experience. With these came the natural fear of that as had been forbidden, that they know themselves to be a part of, but not **of**, that as partook of **earthly**, or the desires in the manner as were **about** them, in that as had been their heritage.

Were this turned to that period when this desire, then, becomes consecrated in that accomplished again in the virgin body of the mother of the **Son** of man, we see this then crystallized into that, that even that of the flesh may be--with the proper desire in all its purity--consecrated to the living forces as manifest by the ability in that body so brought into being, as to make a way of escape for the erring man. Hence we have found throughout the ages, so oft the times when conception of truth became rampant with free-love, with the desecration of those things that brought to these in the beginning that of the **knowledge** of their existence, as to that that may be termed--and betimes became--the **moral**, or morality **of** a peoples. Yet this same exaltation that comes from association of kindred bodies--that have their lives consecrated in a purposefulness, that makes for the ability of retaining those of the essence or creation in every virile body--can be made to become the fires that light truth, love, hope, patience, peace, harmony; for they are **ever** the key to those influences that fire the imaginations of those that are gifted in **any** form of depicting the high emotions of human experience, whether it be in the one or the other fields, and hence is judged by those that may not be able, or through desire submit themselves--as did Amilius and I (?) to those **elements**, through the forces in the life as about them. 364-6

(Sex relations are) of the highest vibrations that are experienced in a material world...and are the basis of that which is termed the original sin; and hence may be easily misunderstood, misconstrued, misinterpreted, in the experience of **every** individual, but these would be known--that the control of such, rather than being controlled by such gives that which makes for the awareness of **spiritual** intent and purpose. 911-5

(The sex organs are) the centers through which all creative energies-- whether mental or spiritual--find their inception in a material world for an expression. As has been given, when this force in sex is raised, or rated, in its inception through the mental forces of the body, this finds expression in that of giving love influence in the life or lives of the individual, as well as that which may be brought into being as a gratification of a physical desire...For there is no soul but what the sex life becomes the greater influence in the life. Not as always in gratification in the physical act, but rather that that finds expression in the creative forces and creative abilities of the body itself. 911-2

(Sexual activities) turned into the channel more for spiritual insight may raise one to a high **mental** expression, as well as to a plane of judgment that may bring greater understanding and advancement. 2054-2

The abstinence of or from relationship with the opposite sex is well when the Creative Force is put to creative activity in the mental, but when these are at variance with other conditions these may become just as harmful to the imaginative system or to the central nervous system, from breaking off activities with the sympathetic and cerebrospinal, and thus become harmful. 5162-1

Q-How should love and the sexual life properly function?

A-...(Sexual relations) should be the outcome--not the purpose of, but the outcome of the answering of soul to soul in their associations...

Know that Love and God are One; that relations in the sexual life are the manifestations in the mental attributes of each...

For, unless such associations become on such a basis, they become vile in the experience of those who join in such relations. 272-7

Q-Through my meditation, has the kundalini fire risen to the head or top of spine at the base of the skull?

A-...When this has arisen--and is disseminated properly through the seven centers of the body, it has purified the body from all desire of sex relationships. For **this is** an outlet through which one may attain celibacy.   2329-1

There **are** those for whom it is best that they keep a life of celibacy, owing to their circumstance and their activities.   2588-2

Not that these (sexual) desires are not to be gratified to the extent that makes for the developments in a normal manner, but to gratify **any** desire in the carnal forces **of** the body--rather than in the satisfying of the spiritual life that comes of creation itself in such emotions as to become such an one as to make for the pricks that are to be kicked against time and time again...Cultivate the **spiritual**, the mental and physical desire, rather than those carnal desires.   911-7

Q-Is masturbation or self-abuse injurious?

A-Ever injurious, unless it is the activity that comes with the natural raising of the vibrations in the system to meet the needs or the excess of those impulses in a body.   268-2

Q-Is the destiny of woman's body to return to the rib of man, out of which it was created? If so, how; and what is meant by "the rib"?

A-With this ye touch upon delicate subjects, upon which **much** might be said respecting the necessity of that union of influences or forces that are divided in the earth in sex, in which all must become what? as He gave in answer to the question, "Whose wife will she be?" (Luke 20:33) In the heavenly kingdom ye are neither married nor given in marriage; neither is there any thing as sex; ye become as **one**, in the union of that from which, **of** which, ye have been the portion from the beginning. 262-86

Here again we find an entity every whit a woman, not having changed its sex in its experiences in the earth. No wonder the entity doesn't understand men, nor men understand the entity. They cannot think in the same channel, not having experienced that which is the prompting urge from the first cause and the twig or a rib out of the first cause.   3379-2

Q-What causes changes in sex and why do some change, others not?

A-That is from the **spiritual** desire. Now--**desire** may begin in a varied form or manner, and in some conditions appear only as wish, or as an expression of a **sensing** from within...

In the same **sphere**--that is, in other planets there may be an entirely different sex, by the desire or that builded, see?   311-3

The (sex) urge is inborn, to be sure; but if the purpose of those who bring individuals into being is only for expressing the beauty and love of the Creative Forces or God, the urge is different with such individuals. Why? It's the law; it's the **Law!**   5747-3

If such forces (sex) are turned to those channels for the aggrandizement of selfish motives, or for the satisfying of that within the urge for the gratification of **emotions**, they become destructive; not only in the manner of the offspring but also in the very **physical body** of the offspring, as well as in the energies of the bodies so producing same...

Relationships in the sex are the exercising of the highest emotions in which a physical body may indulge. And **only** in man is there found that such are used as that of **destruction** to the body-offspring!

Q-Is monogamy the best form of home relationship?

A-Let the teachings be rather toward the spiritual intent. Whether it's monogamy, polygamy, or what not, let it be the answering of the spiritual **within** the individual!

But monogamy is the best, of course as indicated from the Scripture itself--One--**ONE!** For the union of one should ever be **One...**

Life is of, and is, the Creative Force; it is that ye worship as God.

Those then that besmirch same by over-indulgence besmirch that which is best within themselves. And that should be the key to birth control or sex relations, or every phase of the relationships between the sons and daughters of men--that would becomes the sons and daughters of God.

Q-Is continence in marriage advisable except when mating to produce offspring?

A-...For some yes; in other cases it would be **very** bad on the part of each, while in others it would be bad on one or the other, see?

Q-Should men or women who do not have the opportunity to marry have sex relationships outside of marriage?

A-This again is a matter of principle within the individual. The sex organs, the sex demands of every individual, must be gratified in **some** manner as a portion of the biological urge within the individual. These begin in the present (child) with curiosity. For it is as natural for there to be sexual relations between man and women, when drawn together in their regular relations or activities, as it is for the flowers to bloom in the spring, or for the snows to come in the winter. 826-6

There should be agreement between those individuals in such (sex) relationships and only when there is such should there be the relationships. For the lack of such agreements brings more discordant notes between individuals than any portion of relationships with the opposite sex. The disagreements may be very slight at times, but they grow.   4082-1

Q-Is sex outside of marriage injurious morally or spiritually?

A-This must ever be answered from one's own inner self. Those attributes of procreation, of the pro-activity in individuals, are from the God-Force itself. The promptings of the inner man must ever be the guide; not from **any** source may there be given other than, "Study to show thyself approved unto the God that thou would worship"...In the light of thine own understanding keep the body pure...For thy body is the temple of the living God. Do not desecrate same in thine own consciousness.   826-2

Q-Since my husband has been impotent these many years, would sexual relationship with some trusted friend (a bachelor) help me so I can function positively and rhythmically in carrying on the normal business of home life and work? Please advise me in regard to such.

A-Such questions as these can only be answered in what is thy ideal. Do not have an ideal and not attempt to reach same. There is no condemnation in those who **do** such for helpful forces, but if for personal selfish gratification, it is sin.   2329-1

As given by the Master that it has been written that man shall not commit adultery, "yet I say unto thee that he that looketh on a woman to lust after her has committed adultery already" (Matthew 5:28). 900-347

Q-When one partner in a marriage loses desire for sexual relation and to the other it is still necessary, how may this problem be met?

A-Only in a united effort on the part of each to fill that which **is** the need of each.   2035-1

All boys should be (circumcised).   161-1

GIVE SEX EDUCATION BEFORE PUBERTY

Q-You will have before you the question of sex and sex relations as related to delinquency of the teens and younger ages.

A-...It is given in thy writings of Scripture (although in a hidden manner, ye may observe if ye will look) how Adam named those that were brought before him in creation. Their **name** indicates to the carnal mind their relationships in the sex condition or question. Hence the question ye seek is as old as or older than man.

This has been the problem throughout man's experience or man's sojourn in the earth; since taking bodily form, with the attributes of the animal in which he had **projected** himself as a portion of, that he might through the self gain that activity which was visualized to him in those relationships in the earth. Hence slow has been the progress through the ages...

This is ever, and will ever be, a question, a problem, until there is the greater spiritual awakening within man's experience that this phase biologically, sociologically, or even from the analogical experience, must be as a stepping-stone for the greater awakening; and as the exercising of an influence in man's experience in the Creative Forces for the reproduction of species, rather than for the satisfying or gratifying of a biological urge within the individual that partakes or has partaken of the first causes of man's encasement in body in the earth...

For these that would be of a help must of necessity take the conditions as they **exist**, and not as they would **like** to have them...

So, then, give ye unto men as this: train ye the child when he is young, and when he is old he will not depart from the Lord. Train **him**, train **her**, train **them** rather in the sacredness of that which has come to them as a privilege, which has come to them as a heritage; from a falling away, to be sure, but through the purifying of the body in thought, in act, in certainty it may make for a peoples, a state, a nation that may indeed herald the coming of the Lord...

Every child born into the earth, from the age of 2.5 to 3 years begins to find there is something that takes place within its **body**, and that it is **different**; not as animals, though the **animal** instinct is there, of the biological urge, that is a law! For that is the source of man's undoing. But ye who set yourselves as examples in the order of society, education, Christian principles, religious thought, religious ideals, hold rather than to anything else to that **love** which is **unsexed**! For He hath given that in the heavenly state, in the higher forces, there is neither marriage; for they are as **one**! Yet ye say ye are in the earth, ye are born with the urge!...**Purify** same in service to Him, in expressions of love; in expressions of the fruits of the spirit, which are: Gentleness, kindness, brotherly love, long-suffering.

Q-Are there any sex practices that should be abolished?

A-(Interrupting) There are many sex **practices** in the various portions of this land, as in other lands, that should be--**must** be abolished. **How**? Only through the education of the **young**! Not in their teen age, for **then** they are set! 5747-3

Even in the **formative** years...even as the child studies its letters, let a portion of the instructions be in the care of the body, and more and more the stress upon the care in relation to the sex of the body...

Do not begin after there has been already begun the practice of the conditions that make for destructive forces, or for the issue of the body itself--to become as a burning within the very elements of the body itself--and to find expression in the gratifying of the emotions. 826-6

Those changes wrought in the earth expression are ever done when man is just beginning. It is not in old men or old women, or even when they are just beginning to form their ideas, but when the body, mind and spirit are at an at-onement with one another that changes are wrought in the earth purpose--through the first six to twelve years of the entity's experience. This, man is just beginning to learn. After that, as termed by the psychologist--psychoanalysts and the like, they reach the stage of puberty when there is the altering of all the impressions. And many cannot, do not outgrow those first impressions received from three to six years. Their character is builded.   3379-2

The greater numbers of the changes (of the young) are during the first, second and third year of experience in an earthly plane.   2390-2

True, each and every entity should be allowed to live their own life-- but, as has been given, "Train the child in the way, and when he is old he will not depart from same" (Proverbs 22:6), but to force issues when in the formative period is to break the will, or to build resentment that makes for the breaking of other wills as the development comes.
Training in the way of an ideal, and the purposes of the ideal--as it may enfold and unfold in the life of an individual--is to give such an one the basis upon which they will build their lives...Train such an one to depend upon the divine that lies within.   276-2

The greater aid is to counsel as respecting his purpose, his ideal. For each soul enters the material plane for the manifesting of its individual application of an ideal in respect to the Creative Forces or Energies.
Each soul is then endowed by its Maker with that of choice, with that birthright. And to live another's life, and to direct or counsel even-- other than that which is in accord with that of choice, is to become rather a hindrance than an aid...For to subjugate an individual soul to the will of another is to break that which is the greater power, the greater influence in the experience of the soul for its advancement. 830-2

(An entity) is more often trained or convinced **away** from its natural spiritual import. For, is it not for spiritual development that each soul enters? and not merely for mental **or** material or physical? 1521-2

For the more oft are the girls or boys in their teens, in their younger years, misdirected when they are only attempting to give **soul**-expression of that which **moves** them! Those that are ground in their **own** subtle selves to **their** idea, without an ideal, **misconstrue** the individual's or child's intent and purpose.   5747-2

Teach the entity discipline...but in love, in patience.   1976-1

Break not the will of an entity, rather guide guard and direct same in those channels through the development, for we all must pay the price necessary for development of self. Hence, never give to an entity a dictum, for the entity. Rather outline that as found in self, and let others apply same to self. For the mind partakes of memory and thought of its own and takes that necessary for its own development.   900-23

Do not make so many **corrections!** Make it once and then let it pay the price for same. Not in punishments as in bodily punishments, but rather the denial of things that are liked.   608-10

Give the entity a reason, ever, for corrections given; not only because you say so but because of its moral influence upon the entity. Take the time to explain such to the entity when corrections are made. Indeed it may be said, while the entity may be spoiled, they that spoil the child and spare the rod will eventually regret same. Not that this means the corrections are to be made by force alone, but those tendencies, those temperaments must be guided in the direction in which the strong mind, the indomitable temper, the determinations, may be guided correctly. Reason with the entity oft; especially in the stories, the tales told, let them have something of the spiritual nature also.   2148-7

As the developing mind is reaching that with its studies, its readings, towards hero-worship--unless self (the father or the mother) can **remain** the hero, you fail in meeting the full needs of the developing mind...
Remember, the mind and the body is a growing thing. **Grow** with same!
Unless that growth is apparent, then the parent becomes to the growing mind a 'back number', and out of date...
To deny the daily activities, the daily instructions in school as being passe' or forward is to create a barrier between the child and parent...
To deny or to build a barrier between one parent and another in its correction, then this again builds a barrier. And they (the children) cannot love two masters. They (the parents) must be **one!**...
Forbidding, in the life of **this** entity, as in most others, becomes--
what temptation!   759-12

Do not answer the entity, especially in the early teen years, by saying "Because I said so," or "Because it is right," but explaining **why** you said so, and **why** it is right.   1401-1

Q-How is the best way to explain God to a child under twelve years?
A-In nature?   5747-1

Q-What can I do to help my son physically and materially?
A-By precept, by example.   1493-1

In the choice of a companion, an associate, those relationships as may bring about the state, the ability of becoming co-creators or channels for soul's expression in the earth--there should be the assurance that they be of one mind, of that of the spirit of truth; that the ideals, the purposes, the hopes are one.   2464-2

Individuals should, as this couple, work towards a oneness of purpose...Two manifesting as one in their hopes, in their fears, in their desires, in their aspirations.   2072-15

There must be the **answering** within each that their **spiritual** and **mental** desires are **one**. For the Lord thy God is One.   1173-11

If it (marriage) is to be a success--it must be considered not from merely the outward appearance, a physical attraction; for these soon fade. Rather it should be considered from the angle of spiritual ideals, mental aspirations, and physical agreements...
These relationships are representative of the purpose of propagation of the species, as well as those ideals that arise from spiritual and mental relationships.   1776-2

Where the planning of recreation, of activity, of thought or study, or interest, is separate, ye grow apart. Where the interest may be together --whether in a hobby, in a recreation, in a study, in a visitation, in an association--ye grow in purpose as one...
So live, then, that each activity is to the **glory** of God and to the **honor** of thy conscience!   263-18

Each (marital partner) then becomes as a stay one for the other; becoming as a prop, as a brace, as a helpmeet.   688-4

Love is giving; it is a growth. It may be cultivated or it may be seared. That of selflessness on the part of each is necessary...
This does not mean **either giving up**; but they each should express themselves as a complement to the best that is in each.   939-1

Q-What attitude should she take toward her husband?
A-Not merely of duty's tolerance, but that of helpfulness; for one is as **necessary** to the other as is that of **any** condition where there are two poles. **Remembering** that, even in the atom its polarization is necessary, or the energy is soon expended. So in that union of body in the mental being, in the physical being--for the resuscitation of life elements--that they become as necessary for one another. Such conditions do arise at times when these **do not** need to be as polarizations, but for the better, the bigger, the **broader**, the greater **development** of each, these are **necessary** one to another.   5439-1

The home is the nearest pattern in the earth (where there is unity of purpose in the companionship) to man's relationship to his Maker. For it is ever Creative in purpose from personalities and individualities coordinated for a cause, an ideal. 3577-1

Making an artistic home, making a home that is the expression of beauty in **all** its phases, is the greater career of **any** individual soul. 2571-1

The greater of all the abilities of an entity is the ability to build an ideal in the home. Rather than so much the ideal home, the ideal in the home; that there may be the seed of the spirit of truth. 1947-1

To few it is given to have a career and a home, but the greatest of all careers is the home, and those who shun it shall have much yet to answer for. For this is the nearest emblem of what each soul hopes eventually to obtain, a heavenly home. 5070-1

He that makes material gains at the expense of home or opportunities and obligations with his own family does so to his own undoing. 1901-1

It is a very hard problem to have a home and a career and both be a success. 1125-3

MARRIAGE AND SEPARATION

Before God and man there was the promise taken "Until death do us part." This is not idle; these were brought together because there are those conditions wherein each can be a complement to the other. Are these to be denied?...
For a period of six months, never leave the home, either of you, without offering a prayer together; "Thy will, O God, be done in me this day." This is not sissy; this is not weak; this is strong. 2811-3

True, an individual, a soul, must become less and less of self--or thoughts of self; yet when those activities of others in **relationships** to the mental, the spiritual, the **soul** developments, are such that the own soul development and own soul expression becomes in jeopardy, then--as he hath given, "I came not to bring peace but a sword. I came to give peace, not as the world counts peace" (Matt.10:34), but as that which makes for those experiences wherein the soul, the entity, is to **fulfill** those purposes, those activities, for which it--the soul-entity--came into being...
But when there have been all of those experiences, all of those attempts, and there is still **naught**, then the jeopardy of self, of

self-expression, of self-activity, as related with Creative Forces becomes as He hath given--a division.

Q-Would a separation of any sort be of help?

A-This must be a choice within self. Self's own development is in jeopardy. Choose thou.

As **we** would find, it would be helpful for a separation. 845-4

Q-What can I do to make our marriage happier and harmonious?

A-Act toward the wife, or thine own activities, as ye would like her or others to act toward thee. Ask no more than ye give. Demand no more than ye allowed, or allow, to be demanded of thee. Marriage, such an association, is a oneness of purpose. Unless there is the oneness of purpose, there can be no harmony. This can be accomplished not of self alone--for remember, you made a mighty mess in the experience before this--ye suffered for it! Better make it up now or it'll be ten times worse the next time! 5001-1

When the periods come in the experience of each soul that the associations are unbearable, as to become hindrances to their keeping their **own** ideal, then to awaken or to attune or to change, or to alter those associations becomes necessary.

But each should look into their **own** consciousnesses...

In prayerful meditation counsel within self as to the approach; not stern, not just forgiving without a purposefulness, but in love, in simplicity, state, give thine own feelings, thine own desires, and see if they coordinate with the purposes and desires that may be stated by him.

If these are so far apart then that they may not be drawn sufficiently together for a purposeful life, well that changes be. 1192-7

The entity and its associate or companion should realize that there are obligations and duties that each one owes to those for whom they have been responsible, for the development and training of lives, of life itself and the part it has to play in contributing to the better welfare of those minds and bodies.

Then, though there may be conditions not conducive to the better fulfilling of personal desires, these should be forgone in the face of obligations to others. 1449-2

Q-What suggestion and advice may be given me at this time regarding the advisability of another marriage?

A-This as we find may come about in a year or two, but remember-- as has been given--with the present companion it has not been finished yet. There **must** be the more perfect understanding, before there is the full release. 2786-1

Know, the soul is rather the soul-mate of the Universal Consciousness than of an individual entity.   2988-2

As ye begin to show forth in thy relationships with thy fellow man the love that the Father hath shown to the sons of men, by not being willing that any soul should be separated from Him, ye must--by the very manifestations--at **some** experience come to be a separation or a fusion or union with the Creative Forces; with the abilities--by will itself--to **know** thyself yet one with thy Maker.   816-10

Such as have in an experience found an ideal may be said to be soul-mates, and no marriages (are) made in heaven nor by the Father save as such do His biddings. for His sons, His daughters, His mothers, His fathers, are they that do his will in the earth.   275-38

Q-Please explain for me what is meant by soul-mate.
A-Those of any sect or group where there is the answering of one to another; as would be the tongue to the groove, the tenon to the mortise; or in any such where they are a complement one of another --that is what is meant by soul-mate. Not that as from physical attraction, but from the mental and spiritual help.   1556-2

Necessary, then, becomes the **proper** mating of those souls that may be **answers** one to another, of that that may bring, through that association, that companionship, into being that that may be more helpful, more sustaining, more the well-rounded life or experience of those that are a **portion** one of another. Do not misinterpret, but knowing that all are **of** one--yet there are those divisions that make for a **closer** union, when there are the proper relationships brought about.   364-7

Q-Is this girl the type best suited to this man for a successful life?
A-May be made so in each. No one is suited in the beginning, unless it has been foreordained through the ages of the mating of each.   257-15

Q-I am interested in the theory of twin souls. Is this true?
A-It depends upon what is the purpose, as to the application. That there are identical souls, no. No two leaves of a tree, no two blades of grass are the same. They are the complement one to another, yes; but these are dependent upon the purpose. Rather study that as we have indicated regarding what takes place in conception.   3285-2

That the soul--a portion, an expression of God's desire for companionship--might find expression, the souls of men and women came into being; that there might be that which would make each soul, then as a fit companion for that realm. There is the necessity of fitting itself through the experiences of all phases and realms of existence, then; that it, the soul, may not cause disruption in the realm of beauty, harmony, strength of divinity in its companionships with the Creative Force. 805-4

(Edgar Cayce and entity 288) as in the present earth's plane, have had many experiences together, and their soul and spirit are well knit, and must of necessity present each that they may be one. For we find in the beginning that they, these two (which we shall speak of as they until separated), were as one in mind, soul, spirit, body; and in the first earth's plane as the voice over many waters, when the glory of the Father's giving of the earth's indwelling of man was both male and female in one.

In flesh form in earth's plane we find the first in that of the Poseidian forces, when both were confined in the body of the female; for this being the stronger in the then expressed or applied forces found manifestations for each in that form. Yet with the experiences as have been brought in that plane and period, we find then the separation of the body. For the desire of the flesh being to give of self in bodily form to the other, it brought the separating of the spirit and soul from the carnal forces when next brought to earth's plane. The experiences there were as these:

These two were the giving of the spiritual development in the land (Atlantis), and the giving of the uplift to the peoples of the day and age. The desire came for the bodily connection of coition with one of lower estate, and through this treachery of one not capable of understanding it brought physical defects in the limbs (see 288-38 and 288-2) of these then contained in the one body in physical form. Hence in the coma (?), and karma exercised in coma (?), there was brought the separation, as given in the injunction from the Maker: "I have this day set before you good and evil. Choose the light or the darkness" (Deut. 30:15).

With this desire of self's aggrandizement there was brought separation in the next plane, yet bound together in physical affections one for the other. In that of the Egyptian rule, in the first of the pharaohs do we fine this connection as separated brought to the earth's plane. There we find again the priest and the lawgiver in they, though separated now in male and female. In 12,800 B.C. we find together. The desires then coming from the sex desire between the two for the developing, and in that we find it counted as righteousness in both, for--though in the priestcraft in the one, and given to sexual desires in more than in one--the desire remained in the One (God), for which the Oneness was created...

In these we give one of the illustrations of the history of these associations, of which there were many...and for which both suffered physically, and they each bear in the body at present a mark designating these conditions. On the female body, just below the left breast, to the side and on the edge of breast itself, the mark, and an answering one on the body of the male, in the opposite proximity of the breast.   288-6

Keep a normal balance, not being an extremist in any direction,--whether in diet, exercise, spirituality or morality,--but in all let there be a coordinant influence. For, every phase of the physical, mental and spiritual life is dependent upon the other. They are one. 2533-3

To be well-balanced is only to be well equipped and doesn't mean movement or activity has begun. The knowledge of self, the knowledge of the various influences in the experience of self is only valuable or constructive when applied in the experience of self.   440-11

One day must be kept in that way that will feed the mental and **spiritual** life of a body. All work and no play will destroy the best abilities. Yet these have been set in the manner as is outlined in the **spirit** of "Remember to keep the day holy." The life must be well-balanced life, not lopsided in any manner, to bring contentment--not necessarily be satisfied, for that is to become stagnant; but to find self in whatever position self occupies, force self to be **content** but **not** satisfied, knowing that the applications of the spiritual, mental, and physical laws are but the pattern one of another, and in so setting self in the direction all must be working in coordination and cooperation.   349-6

As has been indicated so oft, those that live rather what to many is rather the mediocre but never the extremes make life and its associations in the world better.

There is in a normal healthy individual (alive) **every element** that is known--or may be known--outside of that body. Hence for these to live in harmony it becomes necessary that an even balance be kept within and without. Just as when there are the atmospheric pressures upon a body, the body finds itself adjusting itself to the various changes... And this should be the same activity throughout the diets of a body...

Do not be excessive in anything! Do not be **abnormal! Let's be normal in everything!**   340-29

The body should be mindful of the physical forces of the body, that the body may keep a well-rounded, even balance. Do not allow anxiety, nor those conditions that bring success or distraughtness, to force the physical activities to such an extent as to **bring** an **unbalanced** condition in the physical system; for a body (physical) to function under stress is to break down either the mental or the physical **result.** 257-60

When the wheel of life, that is given to each soul, becomes lopsided or heavy through carnal or too great seeking into those things that are not to be used other than in the will and desire of the Creator, it makes for the lack of that called in the earth poise, or temperament, such as to be the better for an inner or soul development.   315-4

In the mental attributes--take those of the physical, mental and spiritual, and keep the well-rounded forces for a fourfold life. Do not allow the **material** things to outweigh the mental or the spiritual life--for to become lopsided in **any** direction is to make for discontent, and discouraging conditions as must sooner or later arise in each one's experience. Do not allow any discouraging forces and disorders in the lives of others, or loss of confidence in others, to disturb the equilibrium.   4406-1

While one must think highly of self do not be over-democratic; neither too self-sufficient. There is the medium ground on which all may meet. For God is not a respecter of persons.   3474-1

Through diet and exercise the greater portion of all disturbances may be equalized and overcome, if the right mental attitude is kept. 288-38

Some use the theory that if it is good for a little, more would be better. Usually, more is worse--in most anything. The best is that individual or soul-entity that keeps well balanced, never the extremist --but all things to all men.   1861-16

It is true that one rarely succeeds who has many diversified interests, yet thy activities and the dividing of thy time should be diversified according to a definite undertaking in a specific direction,--that the choice of thy dealings with thy fellow man may be the more thoroughly understood from **every** direction; and not merely diversified in the attempt to be a piddler in many undertakings.   1901-1

Q-How can he prepare himself to render a great service to God and know what is expected of him?
A-Keeping well-balanced and not becoming lopsided or self-centered in any manner.   759-22

He that contributes only to his own welfare soon finds little to work for. He that contributes only to the welfare of others soon finds to much of others and lost the appreciation of self, or of its ideals. 3478-2

Do not become a crank on any subject.   342-1

All work and no play is as bad as all play with no work.   2597-2

Q-Please explain to me what is meant by being passive.
A-Passive, as the word itself indicated; not being one-sided. As indicated, not in a mood or manner where a hard feeling, a resentment is held or grudge, but rather as being used--a channel, a door, an outlet. 262-39

Keep all the forces well-rounded in that straight and narrow way that leads to the perfect understanding.   2801-1

Q-Please advise and guide me in my attempt to bring the physical body to a point where it may be a better channel for the manifestation of the spiritual forces.

A-...So conduct, so arrange the activities of the body as to be better **balanced** as to the mental and the physical attributes of the body. Take more outdoor exercise...It isn't that the mental should be numbed, or should be cut off from their operations or their activities--but make for a more evenly balanced body--physical **and** mental. Know how to apply the rules of **metaphysical** operations to a corncob, or to fence rail, or to a hammer, an axe, a walking cane, as well as the **theories** of this, that, or other mind, that in nine cases in ten is seen to become a storehouse for mental deficiencies of **physical** energies! Now get the difference! It is not mental unbalance, but a mental body may be so **over**-used as to allow physical energies to become **detrimental** forces **in a physical body**; for each energy **must** expend itself in some direction, even as a thought takes form brings into being a mental image. Is that image in the position of being a **building** force cooperative with the energies of the physical body? Or do they **destroy** some motive force in the physical without allowing an outlet for its activity?

Then, be a well-rounded body. Take specific **definite** exercises morning and evening. Make the body **physically**, as well as mentally, tired and those things that have been producing those conditions where sleep, inertia, poisons in system from non-eliminations, will disappear...

There is the lack of vitamins as B and C, in this body. One, the C, stamina for mental energies that are carried in the white tissue in nerve energy and plexus. B, as is of calcium, of silicon, of iron. These would be well-balanced, will those...of the food values that carry same be taken, but **unless** the activities-physical for the body are such as to put same into **activity** they become drosses and set **themselves** to become operative, irrespective of **other** conditions...Now, when these are taken into the system, if they are not put to work by the activities of the system--either physical or mental--they become destructive tissue...

That thou eatest, see it doing that thou would have it do. Now there is often considered as to why do those of either the vegetable, mineral, or combination compounds, have different effects under different conditions? It is the consciousness of the individual body! Give one a dose of clear water, with the impression that it will act as salts--how often will it act in that manner?

Just as the impressions to the whole of the organism, for each cell of the blood stream, each corpuscle, is a whole **universe** in itself...In the layers of one is dependent upon the activity of another. One that fills the mind, the very being, with an expectancy of God will see His movement, His manifestation, in the wind, the sun, the earth, the flowers, the inhabitants of the earth...

Just as great a sin to **over** eat as to over drink; to over **think** as to over act!   341-31

Remember that overenthusiasm is as bad as dilatory activity. Great movements, great forces, move slowly.   1151-21

Make haste slowly. Be not overanxious. Be intense, yes. Be consistent, sure. Be ye perfect, yes--even as ye desire that others be. But leave much of the results with Him.   2441-2

Let the attitudes be--everything that is eaten, as well as every activity --purposeful in conception, constructive in nature. Analyze that! 1183-2

To do good is to think constructively, to think creatively. What is creative, what is constructive, ye may ask? that which never hinders, which never makes for the bringing of any harm to others. 1206-13

The **physical** is to use cooperative natures; cooperating with nature, cooperating with spirit, cooperating with mind, to make that which will be the **Whole!**

For what is the first law? "The Lord thy God is **One!**" (Mark 12:29) 1527-3

Take time to be holy...For, holiness is oneness of the mental, spiritual **and** the material body.   303-32

For, as the physical body is but a temple, each portion must coordinate one with another for a perfect union or perfect unison of service or activity, so must the mental mind, the physical mind, the spiritual mind, coordinate as one with another.   1123-1

To do good is to **live** good, and **not** to **appear** good. **Be** good--not just **appear** good. To **live** love is to be love.   900-331

It is not all just to live--not all just to be good, but good **for** something; that ye may fulfill that purpose for which ye have entered this experience.   2030-1

(There are) no short cuts in metaphysics, no matter what those say who would force by visualization, by application of numbers, or stars, or bars, or any phase of the astrological aspects. These are urges. Life is lived within self. You live it; you don't profess it--you live it.   5392-1

What is it all about then? "Thou shalt love the Lord thy God with all thine heart, thine soul, thine mind, thine body, and thy neighbor as thyself" (Luke 10:27). The rest of all the theories that may be concocted by man are nothing, if those are just lived.   3976-29

Know, as the Teacher of teachers gave, there is one proof for all--"By their fruits ye shall know them" (Matthew 7:20).   2067-1

As the understanding comes more and more, never, **NEVER** does it make the...entity other than the more humble, the more meek, the more long-suffering, the more patient. Of this ye may be sure.   281-31

Q-In what form does the anti-Christ come, spoken of in Revelation?
A-In the spirit of that opposed to the spirit of truth. The fruits of the spirit of the Christ are love, joy, obedience, long-suffering brotherly love, kindness. Against such there is no law. The spirit of hate, the anti-Christ, is contention, strife, fault-finding, lovers of praise.   281-16

Let thy patience, thy tolerance, thy activity be of such a positive nature that it **fits** thee--as a glove...to minister to those that are sick, to those that are afflicted, to sit with those that are shut-in, to read with those that are losing their perception, to reason with those that are wary of the turmoils; showing brotherly love, patience, persistence in the Lord, and the love that overcometh all things.   518-2

What is righteousness? Just being kind, just being noble, just being self-sacrificing, just being willing to be the hands for the blind, the feet for the lame--these are constructive experiences.   5753-2

Being holy is just being kind, gentle, patient, long-suffering. 1387-1

Live those that are the fruits of the spirit; namely: peace, harmony, long-suffering, brotherly love, patience. **These**, if ye show them forth in thy life, in thy dealings with thy fellow man, grow to be what? **Truth!** In Truth ye are **free**, from what? **earthly** toil, **earthly** cares!
These then are not just axioms, not just sayings, but **living** truths!...
For it has not entered the heart of man all the glories that have been prepared, nor all the beauties that may be experienced by those that seek His face...
Showing mercy, showing grace, showing peace, long-suffering, brotherly love, kindness--even under the most trying circumstances.
For what is the gain if ye love those **only** that love thee? But to bring hope, to bring cheer, to bring joy, yea to bring a smile again to those whose face and heart are bathed in tears and in woe, is but making that divine love **shine--shine--**in thy own soul!
Then **smile**, be joyous, be glad! For the day of the Lord is at hand. 987-4

Those who would teach--whether the teaching be that of shoveling dirt, raising cabbage, extracting square root, or making drinks, be done with that purpose "That I **may make manifest** My Love, **My** Concept, of the God that I trust with my soul."   2087-1

Not in some great deed of heroism; not in some great speech or act that may be pointed to with pride--but rather in the little kindnesses from day to day.   3795-1

Dare to speak gently when thou art even berated by those from whom, in the material sense, ye have every right to expect or to even demand honor, and hope and faith.   649-2

Remember, the soft word turns away wrath.   5098-1

Only those things that are just, those things that are beautiful, those things that are harmonious, that arises from brotherly kindness, brotherly love, patience, hope and graciousness, **live**. These are the fruits of those **unseen** forces that ye recognize as being the powers that rule this universe--yea, this heterogeneous mass of human emotions and human souls; that power which arises from **good**--not from hate nor malice nor greed nor covetousness. For these take hold upon the gates of hell and are the torments to man's soul!   1776-1

According to the true law of spirit, like begets like. Thus as harmony and beauty and grace reign within the consciousness of an entity, it gives that to others--and others wonder what moved them to feel different, when no one spoke, no one appeared to be anxious. This is the manner in which the spirit of truth operates among the children of men. 3098-2

He is in His temple in thee, and will meet thee in thine search for Him; not from without but rather from within may each soul know Him, through patience with self, with others; seeing in those that would speak evil of thee, those that would despitefully use thee, those even who would take advantage of thine gentleness, thine kindness, only the good; knowing that none may do such save that the power be given them through the Giver of all power, all life, that thou--through thine own experience--may know that the Father suffereth with each child He hath purged, that it may be a companion with Him. For it was in seeking for such companionship that thy soul was brought into being; and would those lose that birthright in Him? For He will guard, sustain thee in thine seeking. 695-1

Merely living a life that does not bring an incentive to someone else to glorify God is sin and just as vile in His eyes as one who in lack of thought or of judgment would err.   5294-1

Faith, hope, patience, long-suffering, kindness, gentleness, brotherly love--these be those over which so many stumble; yet they are the very voices, yea the very morning sun's light in which the entity has caught that vision of the **New Age**, the new understanding, the new seeking for the relationships of a Creative Force to the sons of men.   1436-1

Who is the greatest among you? He that is the servant of all. He that has not merely the material but the **whole** of an association, a corporation, in mind--as to whom it serves, as to what it serves, and how.   1470-2

The greatest service to God is service to his creatures.   254-17

As the Teacher of teachers has given, he that is the greatest in the earth is he that ministers the most to others.

Great indeed are they that build in the consciousness of each soul they meet,--greater than they that build a city.   2823-1

In service alone may any soul find advancement or development.   721-1

Service is asked of all men, rather than sacrifice. In sacrifice there is penance, but grace doth more greatly abound to him who sheds the love of the Father upon those that the body may contact from day to day.

Q-How can I use my abilities to best serve humanity?

A-By filling to the best possible purpose **and** ability that place, that niche the body, mind **and** soul occupies; being the **best** husband, the **best** neighbor, the **best** friend to each and every individual the body meets...He that is willing to become as naught that they may **serve** the better in whatever capacity--as a merchant, be the **best** merchant, as a neighbor, the **best** neighbor; as a friend, the **best** friend.   99-8

Don't be weary of well-doing. If it requires years, give years.   3684-1

You'll not be in heaven if you're not leaning on the arm of someone you have helped.   3352-1

Helping others is best way to rid yourself of your own troubles.   5081-1

Talk is well. Action is wise. Deeds are golden.   254-35

The manner in which an individual, a community, a state or nation treats those less fortunate, those ill, those aged and infirm, those mentally possessed, is the manner in which such an individual, community, state or nation serves its Maker.   3615-1

The **joy**, the peace, the happiness, that may be ours is in **doing** for the **other** fellow.   262-3

While position, power, wealth, is to be sought, to be sure--but let these conditions be rather from service given in the little things, service rendered to the fellow man.   1720-1

Few people are worth anything until someone is dependent on them.   758-31

He that marrieth doth well; he that marrieth not--that has gone into service--doeth better.   1249-1

All that ye may ever keep is just what you give away, and that you give away is advice, councel, manner of life you live yourself. The manner in which you treat your fellow man, your patience, your brotherly love, your kindness, your gentleness. That you give away, that is all that ye may possess in those other realms of consciousness. 5259-1

To help one to help himself is greater than giving, giving, without the ability of the one receiving to see.   1770-2

What is to be given in this (donations) or that direction for any purpose shall be prompted by the real heart of the individual, and not by even a suggestion from others.   3663-1

What said the Master to those that saw the poor widow cast in three pence? "She has given more than them all" (Mark 12:43).   254-92

Q-How much should she give of her earning capacity to charity?
A-Ten percent, as all should.   451-1

The earth is the Lord's and the fullness thereof, and they that hoard same--whether it be bread, wood, gold or what--are only cheating themselves in cheating the Lord. For thy brethren are thy obligation. For thou art thy brother's keeper.   3409-1

The basic principle of that love manifested by the Son was ever, "Others, Lord, others."   1206-13

That which we give enriches us, rather than that which we receive.4208-12

KNOWLEDGE MUST BE APPLIED

It is not what the mind knows but what the mind applies about that it knows, that makes for soul, mental or material advancements.   444-1

There are no shortcuts to knowledge, to wisdom, to understanding--these must be lived, must be experienced by each and every soul. 830-2

Know--the Lord thy God is One. And all that ye may know of good must first be within self. All ye may know of God must be manifested through thyself. To hear of Him is not to know. To apply and live and be **is** to know!   2936-2

Communion with Him means **doing**; not shutting self away from thine brother, from thine neighbor, even from thine self--rather **applying** self to the duties material, mental **and** spiritual, as **is** known.   99-8

Knowledge is well, but knowledge without the works or without the application is worse than useless. 1510-1

Knowledge of God is a growing thing, for ye grow in grace, in knowledge, in understanding **as** ye apply that ye **know**. But remember, as given by Him, to know to do good and do it not is sin. 281-30

Knowledge without the practical ability to apply same may become sin. For, it is knowledge misapplied that was the fall--or the confusion --in Eve. 281-63

As ye **use** that as is **known**, there is given the more and more light to know from whence ye came and whither ye go! 364-4

Put into practice day by day that as **is** known. Not some great deed or act, or speech, but line upon line, precept upon precept, here a little, there a little. 257-78

As ye use that thou hast in hand day by day the next step may be given thee. Not all at once, for these become rather overpowering if more is gained than may be used in the present. 1695-1

It is not the knowledge, not the power or might, but the simplicity of application that is the wisdom of the sages, the understanding of Creative Forces. 1318-1

Knowledge may not be put on as a cloak, but must be an internal growth toward that which has been determined as an ideal. 256-5

Life is earnest, life is work, life is **doing**; not having it poured out, not having it given--but work! 1235-1

The Spirit does not call on anyone to live that it does not already know and understand. In the doing does there come the knowledge, the understanding for the next step. 262-25

Do not gain knowledge only to thine own undoing. Remember Adam.
Do not obtain that which you cannot make constructive in thine own experiences and in the experience of those whom ye contact day by day.
Do not attempt to force, impel or to even try to impress thy knowledge upon another. Remember what the serpent did to Eve. 5753-2

Unless one is good for something, unless it is to make the experience of another appreciate the opportunity of the blessing of the spirit of truth in their activities, it must eventually come to naught. Hence not religion, not even goodness, but rather the practical application of not tenets but the acts and the soul of the Christ-Consciousness in the material world is to be sought. 276-6

All knowledge is to be used in the manner that will give help and assistance to others, and the desire is that the laws of the Creator be manifested in the physical world...All power is given through knowledge and understanding. Do not abuse that power lest it turns and rends the perpetrator...And who seek knowledge is seeking the greatest gifts of the gods of the universe, and in using such knowledge to worship God renders a service to the fellow man.   254-17

Knowledge without judgment may easily become sin. Understanding without spirituality may too soon become egotism.   3268-1

He that hath **great** knowledge, understanding and experience, **of** him **much** is required.   2708-1

The more knowledge, the more responsibility. The more love, the more ability.   281-23

Wisdom, then, is fear to misapply knowledge in thy dealings with thyself, thy fellow man.   281-28

Many individuals have knowledge and little wisdom. Many have wisdom without knowledge.   1206-13

Few get understanding that have mere knowledge.   262-19

Without knowledge there is not the comprehension; and without understanding it does not become practical.   518-1

Wisdom is indeed to be willing to be led by the Spirit of **God** rather than to be guided by thine own concept **of** paralleling or classifying or reasoning.   1158-5

And what is knowledge? To know the Lord, to do good, to cast out fear; for partaking of knowledge symbolizes the bringing of fear.   1246-2

The beginning of knowledge is to know self and self's relationship to **God! Then** the relationship to the fellow man; then material knowledge to any entity, any soul, may **become** valuable, worthwhile, aggressive advancing--success!   1249-1

Thou art conscious in a living world, aware of suffering, of sorrow, of joy, of pleasure. These, to be sure, are the price one pays for having will, knowledge.   3581-1

All knowledge,--then (prehistoric Egypt), now, or in the future,--is latent within self,--would man but begin to understand. The stamp, the image of the Creator is a part of the heritage of each soul.   2533-4

No soul gains knowledge or understanding save through experience.   2608-1

Q-Please define spiritual faith.
A-The application of that that is awakened by the spirit within. 262-18

As self is lost in doing **His** biddings does the **faith** grow; for growth is made through the exercising of, the **losing** of, self in Him. 262-17

What is faith? Evidence. What is evidence? Assurance.   3051-2

Thoughts are things and...**as** the mental dwells upon these thoughts, so does it give strength, power to things that do not appear. And thus does indeed there come that as is so oft given, that faith **is** the evidence of things not seen.   906-3

In Him, by faith and works, are ye made every whit whole. 3395-2

Faith without works is dead.   254-73

As has been given, "By faith are ye healed and that not of yourself." Again as it hath been given, "Show me thy faith by thy works." 264-50

What one believes alone is not sufficient; but what one does about that one believes either makes for advancement, growth, or retardment. 262-55

If ye would have healing for this body, not merely by saying, "Yes, I believe Jesus was the Son of God--yes, I believe He died that I might have an advocate with the Father."
Yes, this also--but what are ye doing about it? Are ye living like that? Do ye treat thy brother, thy neighbor, thy friend, thy foe, as though this were true? For no matter what ye say, the manner in which ye treat thy fellow man is the answer to what ye really believe. 3684-1

Hope and faith are living--**Living**--things.   1504-1

(One) may never put into words nor tell another by words--or acts even --as to what that consciousness of faith is. Yet we may see the shadows of same in what faith has prompted in the experiences of others, as it is so well expressed in the seventh of Hebrews, or as given in that God so had faith in man as to give His Son, **Himself,** to die--**in** the flesh...Or, even as a man, Abraham, the son of faith, the author of faith, offered-- or was willing to offer--his only son, his physical heir; knowing that there **must** be a purpose from that inner voice as to that command. 2174-2

Honest skepticism is a seeker.   254-95

Doubt creates fear, as does insincerity create abhorrence.   2897-2

Honest doubt is not a sin.   2519-8

Faith is an attribute of the soul and spiritual body.   281-10

Expect much, you will obtain much. Expect little, you will obtain little. Expect nothing, you will obtain nothing.   5325-1

Unless the body looks upon the experiences day by day as necessary influences and forces, and uses them as a stepping-stone, soon does life become a pessimistic outlook. If each and every disappointment, each and every condition that arises, is used as a stepping-stone for better things and looking for it and expecting it, then there will still be continued the optimism. Or the looking for and expecting of. If an individual doesn't expect great things of God, he has a very poor God hasn't he?   462-10

JUST TRY YOUR VERY BEST

It is the 'try' that is the more often counted as righteousness, and **not** the success or failure.   931-1

You only fail if you quit trying.   3292-1

To not know, but do the best as is known, felt, experienced in self, to him it is counted as righteousness.   1728-2

Each individual may have the try counted as righteousness; not as an excuse, neither as justification. For ye have been justified once for all, through the Christ Consciousness that ye seek.   5758-1

Man may make **all** efforts, all activity, but only the Spirit of Truth, only God may give the increase, the result...For remember ever, the little leavening that ye do day by day leavens the whole lot. 254-87

Man looks upon the outward appearances and judges success by material standards. God looks on the heart and judges rather by the sincerity of the individuals' 'try'.
For, remember, though he walked in many ways contrary to God's edicts and laws, Abram's try was counted to him for righteousness. 3129-1

Do not lose faith in self, for if faith is lost in self and self's abilities to accomplish, then there is already defeat staring thee in the face. This would be true for every individual. Becoming discouraged only lessens the capacities of individuals to become aware of that consciousness of the divine forces and divine rights that may be sought by each individual, if it is doing that which enables it to look its Savior, its guide, its Lord in the face and say, "I have done my best." 257-131

The Lord abhorreth the quitter.   518-2

Sincerity is the keynote of every individual soul. Who is sincere? One in a million.   5249-1

Only thine own self may one be sincere with. Then the sincerity to another must follow, as the night does the day. False actions, false activities, do not bring truth; do not make for any good thing that may come from same. Only in truth, only in sincerity, may truth--or that upon which growth, or development for which one enters into this life, or any phase of life--will this **bring** a development for anyone. 5534-1

"The judgements my son, of thy sincerity are ever according to thy **spiritual** life."   294-185

We find in Jupiter the universal consciousness, the sincerity of the entity. For, when the entity gives expression of its feelings, one may be sure that it is the entity speaking. For, as indicated the entity is deep, sincere. Though the entity may be called by others the plodder, it may arrive, it may attain to that peace, that understanding which comes only from true sincerity.   2571-1

Ye have made promises to self, to thy Maker, to thy friends. Remember --what thou hast vowed, keep. For the Lord hath need of those who are honest with themselves.   3085-2

Half a truth is worse than a whole lie, it deceiveth even the soul.   366-1

JOY AND HAPPINESS

Happiness is a state of mind attained by giving same to others. 2772-2

The **joy**, the peace, the happiness, that may be ours is in **doing** for the **other** fellow.   262-3

Happiness is love of something outside of self. It may never be obtained, may never be known by loving only things within self. 281-30

Few are willing to pay the price for happiness--which is tolerance, patience, and **selflessness** in the expressions to its associates, its fellow man, its activities in the earth.   852-12

Do all in the joyous manner, for **His** gospel is the **glad** gospel, the **joyous** life, the happy life.   397-1

The Lord loveth those who expect much of Him, in giving much of themselves--**joyously**!   2401-1

"Know, O Israel, the Lord thy god is **One**" (Mark 12:29). And while each soul seeks to manifest in a material world, the purpose, the idea--yea, the ideal is that all are to work in unison for the good of all. 3976-23

If the world will ever know its best, it must learn cooperation. 759-12

When the earth was brought into existence or into time and space, all the elements that are **without** man may be found in the **living** human body. Hence these in coordination, as we see in nature, as we see in the air, as we see in the fire or in the earth, makes the soul, body and mind **one** coordinating factor with the Universal Creative Energy we call God...Coordinate thyself, then, **with** nature, **with** the environs thou art in, **through** thine inner self.   557-3

The whole of the experience of an individual entity in a material plane is the coordinating and cooperation of Creative Forces from without to the Divine within as to keeping an activity that may bring into manifestations health and happiness.   1158-8

When one looks in nature of every character, the first law is harmony, and is of divine origin, even as life, and when same is not in accord **with** that of the Creative Energy, or God, discord is the result.   4733-1

INNER PEACE

Patience, love, kindness, gentleness, long-suffering, brotherly love ...of themselves bring peace.   3175-1

For He **is** peace; not as men count peace, not as men count happiness, but in that harmonious manner in which life, the expression of the Father in the earth, **is One**--even as He is **ONE**.   849-11

As He gave: "That peace I give you; that ye may know that thy spirit, ye thy soul, beareth witness with me that ye are mine--I am thine," even as the Father, the Son, the Holy Spirit.   987-4

Ye will find that peace, that harmony, that comes only from loving thy neighbor as thyself.   1493-1

Only that which enables the individual also to bear the cross, even as He, will enable that individual to know that peace which encompassed Him in such a measure that He broke the bonds of death, overcame hell and the grave, and rose in a newness of life; that ye--here--and now-- might know that peace in these troubled periods.   3976-27

Content**ment** is the greatest boon in man's whole experience. 1925-1

While storms and trials are necessary in every soul, as we see manifested in nature, only in contentment does growth make manifest. Not contentment to that point of satisfaction, for a satisfied mind or soul ceases to seek. But only in contentment may it receive and give out. In **giving** does a soul grow. 699-1

With **His** peace there comes contentment, no matter what may be the vicissitudes of life. 451-2

The greater an individual, the more content the individual may be. Not as an animal that is satisfied with the body filled, but rather that contentment which is seen in the acts of those that bring joy with the expression of themselves; as a bird in song, a bird in flight, an animal in the care of its young. **That** is contentment; the other lethargy. 347-2

If the ideal is prompted by Truth...it will bring contentment, peace, harmony and the like.
And unless it does bring that, know that error lies at the door. 1470-2

TIME, SPACE AND PATIENCE

Time, space, and patience, then, are those channels through which man as a finite mind may become aware of the infinite.
For each phase of time, each phase of space is dependent as one atom upon another. And there is no vacuum, for this, as may be indicated in the Universe, is an impossibility with God. Then there is no time, there is no space, when patience becomes manifested in love. 3161-1

In the consciousness of eternity, time is not, neither is space. In man's consciousness there appears so much mercy, so much love that these have been called time and space. 3660-1

God **is** in the material experience of man--**Time, Space, Patience!** 262-114

Man's concept of the Godhead is three-dimensional--Father, Son and Holy Spirit. The communication or the activity or the motivating force we find is three-dimensional--time, space and patience. Neither of these exists in fact, except in the concept of the individual as it may apply to time or space or patience. 4035-1

Time and space are the elements of man's own concept of the infinite and are not realities...as a tree, a rose, a bird, an animal. 2533-8

We define for this entity what we mean by the entity having patience --in an active, positive manner and not merely as a passive thing.

Taking or enduring hardships, or censure, or idiosyncrasies of others, is not necessarily patience at all. It may become merely that of being a drudge not only to self but an outlet of expression from others that may never be quite satisfying because there is no resistance.

Passive patience, to be sure, has its place; but consider patience rather from the precepts of God's relationship to man: Love unbounded is patience. Love manifested is patience. Endurance at times is patience, consistence ever is patience.   3161-1

Patience the most beautiful of all virtues and the least understood! Remember, it is one of the phases or dimensions through which thy soul may catch the greatest and more beautiful glimpse of the Creator.   2448-2

As the teacher of old has given--"In patience possess ye your souls." This does not mean in bearing with individuals that willfully disobey but rather being strong and steadfast and humble in the sight of higher forces, yet active in that known to be not only duty in the spiritual sense but duty in the mental and material sense.   517-1

Patience, long-suffering and endurance...cease to be a virtue when the entity allows self merely to be imposed upon, and to take second place merely because someone else of a more aggressive nature imposes. 3029-1

Long-suffering does not mean suffering of self and not grumbling about it. Rather, though you be persecuted, unkindly spoken of, taken advantage of by others, you do not attempt to fight back or to do spiteful things; that you be patient--first with self, then with others. 3121-1

If one smite thee on the one cheek, did he say withdraw? No! Rather, turn the other! Be active in thy patience; be active in thy relationships with thy fellow man!   815-2

Not a tolerance that becomes timid--this would make rebellion in self. Not a patience that is not positive. Not humbleness that becomes morbid or lacking in beauty. For as orderliness is a part of thy being, so let consistency--as persistency--be a part of thy being.   1402-1

Persistency is very well; but **consistency**...is indeed a jewel. 257-186

(Patience) doesn't mean patience in the sense of just submissiveness, or just being quiet--but an **active** patience, **conscious** of being patient with self and with others. Force self to do some unpleasant things that it hasn't wanted to do once in a while, and like it!   911-3

Patience is meekness in action, pureness in heart.   262-25

While the body is subject to all the influences of materiality, it may be controlled--the emotions thereof--by the mind. And the mind may be directed by the spirit. 2533-1

The conquering of self is truly greater than were one to conquer **many** worlds. 115-1

Be consistent in all thou doest, and when thou hast conquered self thou mayest be able to govern another. 257-53

In the accomplishment of good, self must first be conquered and put in submission to the Will of the Giver, the Omnipotent Force as is manifested through the various phases of those experiences...in which the Oneness in Him is made One with Him, the **All**. 5618-8

This is what was meant by the command to the individual soul to be fruitful, to multiply, to subdue the earth. Too oft does the individual apply this only to secular or sexual associations, when it has nothing whatsoever to do with such in the spiritual or mental self, but has to do with the spiritual and mental in controlling, in governing self, self's appetites, self's desires, self's impatience, self's wilfulness. Thus does one multiply. Thus does one **subdue** the influences of materiality. 1056-2

FORGIVING AND FORGETTING

The soul that holds resentment owes the soul to whom it is held, much! Hast thou forgiven the wrong done thee? Then thou owest naught! 1298-1

Who gains by being forgiven and by forgiving? The one that forgives is lord even of him that he forgives. 585-2

When individuals hold a grudge they are fighting the God within themselves against the God within the individual or soul for whom or towards whom such is held. 1304-1

To not forgive would be giving way to self in such a manner as to become even worse then those that in a moment of self-delusionment gave way...or bring this disturbance. 2293-3

Only as ye forgive those who blamed thee without a cause, who have spoken vilely of thee without reason, can the giver of life and light forgive thee. 3660-1

Then how forgiving art thou? Answer this, and ye will know just how ye have been forgiven. It is the law, it is the Lord, it is love. 3376-2

Though ye may be reviled, revile not again. Though ye may be spoken of harshly, smile--**smile**! For it is upon the river of life that smiles are made. Not grins!...but the smile of understanding cheers on the hearts of those who are discouraged, who are disheartened. It costs so little. It does so much good, and lifts the burdens of so many.   281-30

It is by thy smile and not a word spoken, that the day may be brighter for many a soul and in making the day brighter, even for the moment, ye have contributed to the whole world of affairs.   2794-3

Know that a smile will rally many to thy cause, while a frown would drive all away.   2448-2

Smile and the world smiles with you--frown and it turns its back on you.   1261-1

A smile gains entrance into the confidences of individuals when reprimands bring little but resentments.   5230-1

Smile even though it takes the hide off, even when you are cross. 1005-17

Be happy and glad. Smile though the heavens fall. And though the best friend deceive thee, and though thine own loved ones forsake thee.   272-8

THE ABILITY TO LAUGH

Know that thy Lord, thy God, **laughed**--even at the Cross...
Man alone in God's creation is given the ability to laugh.   2995-1

Don't think a grouchy man can ever raise a headed cabbage or a tomato that will agree as well as those raised by a man who laughs and tells a good joke, though it may be smutty.   470-35

If ye lose the ability to laugh, ye lose that ability to be joyous. And the religion, the principle of the Christ-life is joyous! For remember-- He laughed even on the way to Calvary; not as pictured so oft, but laughed even at those that tormented Him. This is what angered them most. 3003-1

See the funny side--don't be too serious. Remember, He even made a joke as He walked to the Garden to be betrayed. Remember, He looked with love upon His disciple that denied Him, even as He stood alone. 2448-2

Laugh under the most straining circumstance.   1823-1

(See) the ridiculous side of every question--the humor in same. Remember that a good laugh...is good for the body, physically, mentally.   2647-1

See not only the sublime things in life, but the humor, the wit, yes, the ridiculous also--that may be drawn from the cynic as well as the pessimist, as in cartoons and the like. 3636-1

See the humor in any experience, whether it is the most sacred, the most cherished experience, or that which comes as a trial. 2560-1

Q-Should I keep going to the same doctors?
A-If you want to die. 5051-1

Q-How much better am I?
A-37.3%. 567-4

Q-Which shoulder should be taped?
A-The one that's hurt. 1710-5

Q-Would it be better for the body to remain in bed without moving about?
A-It'll move when you give it the Castor Oil. 348-18

Q-Have I ever contacted my husband in any other experience?
A-He bought you! Doesn't he act like it at times? 1222-1

Hide not skeletons in thine own closet, for they will rattle when ye least expect them. 3246-1

COMPANIONSHIP AND LONELINESS

Remember, the ability to attain to good companionship is to be capable of being interested in and to acquaint self with all phases of experiences of those with whom ye come in contact. 1206-13

Few individual souls really enjoy the companionship of themselves. Not merely because they love themselves the less or that they despise themselves the more. But their thoughts and things, and the emotions of the body, are seldom in accord one with the other--or their individuality and personality don't reflect the same shadow in the mirror of life. 3351-1

Fortunate indeed is the entity who has applied or may so apply self as to find self good company. 1664-2

Loneliness is destructive, yet in **Him** ye may find companionship. 845-4

Q-How can the entity best overcome loneliness?
A-Fill the life with the interests of others. 295-2

Creation is God's desire for companionship and expression. 5749-14

Sentiment and friendship are indeed different. One desires; the other fulfills.   1467-10

Friendships are only the **renewing** of former purposes, ideals.   2946-2

Count thy friends as the greatest of thy opportunities. No soul may have so many friends that it can afford to lose a single one. Yet there are obligations, there are duties that are combined with such associations. These **never** neglect in thy thought or thy activities.   1709-3

Friendships beget friendships, love begets love. Making self beautiful is to be beautiful in the lives of others.   1206-13

TORMENTS, TRIALS AND TEMPTATIONS

Only in disillusion and suffering, in time, space, and patience, does he come to the wisdom that his real will is the will of God, and in its practice is happiness and heaven.   2537-1

The spirit is continually at war with the flesh...and when an individual so attunes the mental, the spiritual life, as **not** to be in accord with that element within self that demands as much recognition as the purely material body, then one must know that there must be the price paid in that of discontent, of disruption.   5469-1

Q-Will we be punished by fire and brimstone?
A-...Each entity's heaven or hell must, through **some** experience, be that which it has builded for itself.
Is thy hell one that is filled with fire or brimstone? But know, each and every soul is tried so as by fire; purified, purged; for He, though He were the Son, learned obedience through the things He suffered. 281-16

All are tried as in the fires of self. For He has not willed that any soul should perish, but has with every temptation, every trial, prepared a way of escape. And they that are His, He will not allow to be tempted beyond that they are able to bear.   3292-1

Through error, through rebellion, through contempt, through hatred, through strife, it became necessary then that all pass under the rod; tempted in the fires of flesh; purified, that they may be fit companions for the **glory** that may be thine.   262-89

From what may anyone be saved? Only from themselves. That is, their individual hell; they dig it with their own desires.   262-40

Doubts and fears and desires and disturbances burn and burn, yet all must be tried so as by fire. And the fires of the flesh in their activity in material associations must be purified in the love.   294-174

As He struggled alone with His own Cross; so ye--as ye struggle--**have** the assurance that His presence abideth...Keep ye the faith in not the Cross as sacrifice but as the Cross as the **Way**, as the **Light**, the **Life**.
For without the Cross there is not the Crown!   1472-1

Without the cross there is no crown. Without the bitter there is no sweet. Without love, ye are lost indeed.   254-78

The way of the Cross is not easy, yet it is the tuneful, the rhythmic, the beautiful, the lovely way.   1089-6

If these (hardships) are held continually as crosses, or as things to overcome, then they will remain as crosses. But if they are to be met with the spirit of truth and right in their own selves, they should create **joy**; for that is what will be built.   552-2

They who would gain the greater will suffer the more.   5242-1

In suffering **strength** is gained.   5528-1

His love faileth not to sustain those that put their trust in Him. And though He slay thee, though He break thee as flax upon the wheel, though He bestir thee to the depths of despair, know thy Redeemer liveth--and thou shalt see Him, and He shall purify thee in those things that thou doest that are lovely unto thy fellow man.   378-18

The weaknesses in the **flesh** are the scars of the soul.   275-19

The entity has in itself **will**, that knowledge, that understanding, with which the entity exercises its choice, to which it adds either for the satisfying or gratifying of self's emotions or self's desires, or for the magnifying and glorifying of the spiritual sources or help.
These may be one, if the entity makes the hope, the desire of the body, the mind, the soul, in accord. Yet the soul ever seeks to magnify or glorify the divine. Hence the constant warring that one finds in members--body, mind, soul. Those are as the real of the shadows of appetites, of desires, of those things that are habits of body and that take hold as a habit. Yet who ever saw a habit? For it is a mental thing and is personal. Its individuality may be of the creative forces or of the destructive forces.   3420-1

Through trials, trouble, tribulations, one arrives at the best things in life and the trials are forgotten.   288-1

So long as there remains within self's own mind that of indecision, or that "anything will do," then--necessarily--will the body put up with "anything will do" and nothing becoming definite! But making the definite decision, the definite choice as to what direction this activity is to be given, will make for opening of channels...

First there must be a determination within self as to what **is** to be the activities; whether sweeping streets, running engines, motors, flying machines, digging ditches, or what! But **choose!** and then stick to that! Its the only way that those abilities that are latent may be developed in **any** entity.   419-3

Know that there are those realms wherein there is as much confusion as there is in the material world, unless the ideal that is ever creative in its purpose is the directing influence.   3617-1

Only that which is temporal causes confusion. For that which is eternal is the straight way.   954-6

Self-indulgence, or self-aggrandizement, can only bring confusion-- whether it be in the spiritual, mental or physical self.   589-4

But if ye are attempting to have thy physical doing just as it pleases, thy mental body controlled by "What will other people say?" And the spiritual body and mind shelved only for good occasions and for the good impressions that you may make occasionally, there **cannot** be other than confusion.   1537-1

FEW DOES POWER NOT DESTROY

Few does power not destroy.   3976-13

Man's answer to everything has been **Power**--Power of money, Power of position, Power of wealth, Power of this, that or the other. 3976-8

When Alexander sought to conquer the world the tenets of the ideal were forgotten in the desires of the flesh, and while the principles as set forth in the mind and heart of the man as the student under Plato and Archimedes, and Aurelius and others, the man became so gorged by the greed of power as to become the loathsome body--as it passed to its reward for the use of the power as given into the hands. 3976-4

For as given, be faithful and subdue the world. All power is given through knowledge and understanding. Do not abuse that power lest it turns again and rends the perpetrator of such conditions.   254-17

Being afraid is the first consciousness of sin's entering in, for he that is made afraid hast lost consciousness of self's own heritage with the Son; for we are heirs through Him to that Kingdom that is beyond all of that that would make afraid or that would cause a doubt. 243-10

Self awareness, **selfishness**, is that that makes men afraid. The awareness of the necessities of the carnal forces in a material world seeking their gratification...Peace **is** with thee, contentment is in thine hand, who becomes not afraid but trusts rather in Him.   262-29

Self-awareness, self-consciousness brings fear and doubt.   3357-2

Fear is the root of most of the ills of mankind whether of self, or of what others think of self, or how self will appear to others. To overcome fear is to fill the mental, spiritual being with that which wholly casts out fear: the love manifest in the world through Him. 5459-3

Perfect love casteth out fear. Where fear enters, there sin lieth at the door.   136-18

For he, or she, that is without fear is free indeed.   5439-1

It is the **fear** of the unknown that first makes fear.   1776-1

Fear is as the fruit of indecisions respecting that which is lived and that which is held as the ideal. Doubt is as the father of fear...
Fear is as the beginning of faltering. Faltering is as that which makes for dis-ease throughout the soul and mental body.   538-33

As he gave, "That which I feared has come upon me" (Job 3:25). 4047-2

In nature and in the animal instincts we find only the expressions of a universal consciousness of hope, and never of fear--save created by man in his indulging in the gratification of material appetites. 2067-1

Worry in its last analysis--is that of fear.   2502-1

Do not burden self with that as is unnecessary to be met until the time arises, for **worry** killeth. Labor strengthens.   900-345

Never worry as long as you can pray. When you can't pray--you'd better begin to worry. For then you have something to worry about.   3569-1

The fear of the Lord is the beginning of wisdom; but the fear of man is the indication of weakness in the body-man.   531-9

Worry and fear being the greatest foes to **normal** healthy physical body, turning the assimilated forces in the system into poisons that must be eliminated, rather than into life-giving vital forces. 5497-1

Be mad and sin not. Righteous anger is a virtue. He that has no temper is very weak; but he who controls not his temper is much worse. 3416-1

One that may control self in anger is beginning the first lessons or laws of experience...Disliking that which would produce such a feeling within self, yet able to love the soul of one that causes or produces such a state of feeling. This is patience, and love.   262-25

When little petty disturbances call for the quick retort, find rather the fault in self, if there be one; then, if there is not, according to thy standard that is set in thine ideal, open not thy mouth--even as He did not when railed upon...
Be angry, but sin not. Means there has been lost rather the desire of exaltation.   262-24

When anger hath beset thee, hast thou stopped and considered what the fruit of rash words would bring.   793-2

Anger can destroy the brain as well as any disease. For it is itself a disease of the mind.   3510-1

No one can be jealous and allow the anger of same and not have upset digestion or heart disorder.   4021-1

While, to be sure, one without some fire, some determination, some exercising of self's will is worth little, but one unable to control self, or to control temper, is worse than one that has none, or becomes as an individual pushed hither and thither by every circumstance, every condition that may contact, becoming gradually as one with no stability; but controlling same, one may build that as will be a revolution, or evolution, of self's own abilities.   4405-1

Not that the entity in its meekness is not capable of being fired by emotions even to madness or anger. These are well. For they that are not cable of becoming emotional over their own ideas and ideals are very lax, but those who may not control same are in a sad plight indeed! 1129-2

No man is **bigger** than that which makes him lose his temper. 254-55

The entity is one, then, who has learned to **hold** the temper, and yet not entirely suppressed in doing so--or by the needs of such; rather being able to gain from same, through the very virtue of patience and long-suffering.   1857-2

Often those who flare-up quickly, also forgive quickly--if they remain as little children asking, seeking, living "Guide thou me, O God, in the steps I take and in the words I say day by day."   3645-1

The spirit of hate, the anti-Christ, is contention, strife, fault-finding, lovers of self, lovers of praise.   281-16

Just as hate and animosity and hard sayings create poisons in the body, so do they weaken and wreck the mind.   1315-10

Attitudes oft influence the physical conditions of the body. No one can hate his neighbor and not have stomach or liver trouble.   4021-1

That ye dwell upon, that ye become;--just as that ye hate suddenly befalls thee. This is natural law.   2034-1

"Vengeance is mine, saith the Lord" (Romans 12:19).
Hence those who attempt to "get even" or who would stand for their rights irrespective of what may be brought for others will find disturbing forces in their experience in the material sojourns.   1539-2

He who swears vengeance pays even unto the last farthing...for when there is jealousy, hate, things that do not make the soul of man free, these bring retardments to an individual.   5177-1

JUDGING AND FAULT-FINDING

See only the pure, the **good**! For until ye are able to see within the life and activities of those ye have come to hate the most, **something** ye would worship in thy Creator, ye haven't begun to think straight.
Look for good and ye will find it. Search for it, for it is as a pearl of great price. For there is so much good in the **worst**, that ye may never judge another by thine own short standards.   1776-1

There is so much good in the worst of us, and so much bad in the best of us, it doesn't behoove any of us to speak evil of the rest of us. 3063-1

"Judge not lest ye be judged" (Luke 6:37). Who are ye to judge what the other would do? Hast thou been in the same position, in the same place? Are thine own purposes and desires pure?   3976-14

In wisdom thou wilt not find fault. In wisdom thou wilt not condemn any In wisdom thou wilt not cherish grudges. In wisdom thou wilt love those, even those that despitefully use thee.   262-105

Speak gently, speak kindly to those who falter. Ye know not **their** own temptations, nor the littleness of their understanding. Judge not as to this or that activity of another; rather pray that the light may shine even in **their** lives as it **has** in thine.   2112-2

Ye have the ability to judge things. It is well to judge things--it is bad to judge yourself or your fellow man.　　3544-1

When we see rather Him that we worship even in the faults of others, **then** we are at the **beginning** of patience.　　262-24

In patience condemn not, neither find fault; not condoning, not agreeing, but let thine own life so shine that others, seeing thy patience, knowing thy understanding, comprehending thy peace, may take hope. 3459-1

Anyone can find fault. It is the wise person who finds that which encourages another in the turmoils and strifes of the day.　　1449-2

Learn the lesson well of the spiritual truth: Criticize not unless ye wish to be criticized. For, with what measure ye mete it is measured to thee again. It may not be in the same way, but ye cannot even **think** bad of another without it affecting thee in a manner of a destructive nature. Think **well** of others, and if ye cannot speak well of them don't speak! but don't think it either! Try to see self in the other's place.　　2936-2

The magnifying of virtues in others and the minimizing of faults is the beginning of wisdom in dealing with others. **Not** that the evil influence is denied, rather that force within self is stressed which when called upon is so powerful that those influences about self may never hinder. 2630-1

The kind word turneth away wrath, even as the haughty look or the unkind word stireth up and maketh for troubles.　　2096-1

Know this, and never forget it, that: It is the spirit with which a thing is said that carries the force or power.　　1497-5

That one cannot endure within itself it finds as a fault in others. That thou findest as a fault in others is thine own greatest fault, ever.　815-2

As given of old, each soul shall give an account of every idle word spoken. It shall pay every whit.　　3124-1

Think twice before you speak once.　　341-31

Hold thy tongue from gossip, then, oft, and think what you would like to have said about thee if circumstances were reversed. 2798-1

"Of the abundance of the heart the **mouth** speaketh" (Matthew 12:34), and all nature hath been tamed but the tongue hath no man tamed. It may be **stilled** in the earth, but that it has spoken goes on--and on. 275-22

The attitude in (the home) should be rather in loving action and word that the differences be pointed out, rather than by contention, abuse, or any word or act that condemns anyone for their activity.　　585-1

Those that find fault with others will find fault in themselves; for they are writing their own record. 487-17

Condemning of self is as much of an error as condemning others. 3292-1

While selflessness is the law, to belittle self is a form of selfishness and not selfless. 2803-2

Think not more highly of thyself than ye ought to think, yet no one will think more of you than you do yourself. 3420-1

The entity pities self. And an individual soul that begins to pity self soon finds fault with others and forgets the real freedom. 2706-1

The entity is more tolerant with others than with self; the usual, of course, is to excuse self and blame others. 1744-1

It is error to sit still. As we have oft indicated, **do something**: but never find fault,--and **no not** condemn self for being this or that. Just **do with thy might what thy hands find to do!** 2437-1

Learn to live with self and you will learn to live with others. 5392-1

Fear not--for fear brings that of contempt first from those that **bring** same, and then the seed is the dissatisfaction in self, and condemnation of self's position. 2686-1

Q-How can I overcome the terrible timidity in speaking with people?
A-Do not attempt to overcome. Rather let the speaking come as from the heart in a service to others. 2559-1

VAINGLORY

Self-exaltation damns more souls than anything save vainglory and selfishness. 317-7

Selflessness is the greater tolerance. For when self seeks exaltation beware. 1298-1

Ye that seek self-glory know its hardships. Ye that seek the glory of the Father know its beauties. 254-95

Humbleness does not mean degrading nor becoming discouraged when self has been refused that which according to the principles of self is defaced by those that **should** be, are in the position to be, helpful experiences in the affairs of the entity. 1466-3

Q-Why is the thought always with me to kill myself?

A-Self-condemnation. For, not enough of that seeking to manifest God's will has been manifested. When this thought occurs, let thy prayer be as indicated: "**Lord, here am I--thine! Use me in those ways and manners as THOU seest, that I may ever glorify thee.**"   2540-1

Q-Why is suicide considered wrong?

A-So long as there are those that depend upon the body! And how hath it been given? No man liveth to himself, no man dieth to himself. No man hath been so low that **some** soul hath not depended upon, relied upon same for strength.

Thus we find while there may be those experiences, these are rather of a selfish nature.   1175-1

Q-When I desire death more than life, how can I use my will?

A-When desire for death and desire for life is presented, what is it that makes the life go on? The will! The spiritual life, the essence of God itself! Would the body be so weak as to crucify that it worships, rather than that which is only tagged on--in desires?

Make thy life **one with** His love! When such desires, such thoughts, even, find lodgement, look about self and see the struggle so many souls are making to keep body and soul together. How hast thou in **any** manner ministered to making **their** burden lighter?

In lightening the burden of another thine own is lightened twofold. In lightening the burdens of another the whole of will's power is strengthened manyfold.   911-70

She lost in soul development, for she took her own life to satisfy self, not in defence of principle, self, country, or position.   369-3

THINK ON THESE THINGS

An individual that may be...termed more spiritual minded, than material minded, and this is the nicest one can say of an entity. 1717-1

Let him that is weak of mind or heart not take the handle, for he that ploweth and looketh back is worse than the infidel.   3976-4

Weakness is only strength misapplied or used in vain ways. 436-2

Only those who seek become aware of that which **is** the motivative force of any condition, phase or stage of development in the spiritual, the mental or the material.   2012-1

Even the toad is as beautiful in the sight of the Creator as the lily, and he that heedeth not the little things may not be master of the great things, for he that was capable of using the talents in the little way was made ruler over **great** cities.   257-53

One had best be active and in error than not doing anything. 262-126

There is progress whether ye are going forward or backward! The thing is--to move!   3027-2

Take things, conditions and circumstances where they are,--not merely where you wishfully think, hope or desire that they are!   459-12

Keep the heart singing! Keep the mind clear! Keep the face toward the light! The shadows then are behind.   39-4

Do ever in self that thou knowest to be right, though it may make of self even an outcast to thine neighbor.   373-2

It is never right to do that which is evil that good may come. 254-7

Know that in whatever state ye find thyself, **that**--at the moment--is best for thee.   369-16

Better to trust one heart and that deceiving, than doubt one heart which if believing would bless thy life with **true** understanding. 2448-2

Remember, that which would be ideal for self must also be that which would be ideal for others.
Then, self must become selfless, and not in any form or manner desire those things that would be advantageous over others in that others would have to suffer for that is selfishness, and not selflessness.
And selflessness is that to which each entity, each soul, must attain through the varied experiences in the material plane.   2185-1

One who has a soul has a psychic power; but remember...there are no shortcuts to God! You are there--but self must be eliminated. 5392-1

We correct habits by forming others! That's everybody.   475-1

Know that each soul constantly meets its own self. No problem may be run away from. **Meet** it **now!**   1204-3

No fault, no hurt comes to self save that thou hast created in thine consciousness, in thine inner self, the cause. For only those that ye love may hurt you.   262-83

No nation...no individual is stronger than the weakest habit. 3976-17

Make life, make God, a **practical** thing.   912-1

Do not attempt to be good, but rather good **for something!** 830-3

Ever be a worker, as the bee, yes--but in that way in which it is ever a contribution to making thy portion of the earth a more beautiful place for men to live in. 3374-1

You never lose anything that really belongs to you, and you can't keep that which belongs to someone else. No matter if this spiritual, mental or material, the law is the same. 3654-1

Know that what is **truly** thine **cannot** be taken away from thee; nor is any character ever lost. 2448-2

Know, the earth and all therein is the Lord's. All thine **own** is lent thee, not thine but **lent** thee. Keep it inviolate. 2622-1

Don't preach one thing and practice another. For this is inconsistent, and inconsistency is sin. 5275-1

Make concessions only to the weak.
Defy the strong if thy are in the wrong. 1336-1

Arguments will seldom change the aspects or views of any. And truth itself needs no champion for it is of itself champion of champions...
It is much easier to refrain from error--in speech or in activity-- than to seek forgiveness for the word quickly spoken. 1669-1

Think no evil; speak no evil; **hear** no evil. 294-183

It is the spirit with which ye do a thing, the purpose that brings weal or woe in its effect in the experience. 3285-2

Most of us think we need a great deal more than we do. 262-89

An entity should comprehend and **know**, and **never** forget, that life and its experiences are only what one puts into same! 1537-1

It is the little things in the association one with another that build those that prove to be the real experiences of the life. A word, a look, a sign, may undo, all of the thoughts of many. 2154-1

To fulfill that purpose for which an entity, a being, has manifested in matter is the greater service that can possibly be rendered.
Is the oak lord over the vine? Is the Jimson (weed) beset before the tomato? Are the grassy roots ashamed of their flower beside the rose?
All those forces in nature are fulfilling rather those purposes to which their Maker, their Creator, has called them into being...reflecting --as each soul, as each man and each should do in their particular sphere--**their** concept of their Maker! 1391-1

PART X

PAST AND FUTURE WORLD CONDITIONS

ATLANTIS AT THE TIME OF AMILIUS

Atlantis as a continent is a legendary tale. Whether or not that which has been received through psychic sources has for its basis those few lines given by Plato, or the references made in Holy Writ that the earth was divided, depends upon the trend of individual minds...

There has been considerable given respecting such a lost continent by those channels such as the writer of Two Planets, or Atlantis--or Poseidia and Lemuria--that has been published through some Theosophical literature. As to whether this information is true or not, depends upon the credence individuals give to this class of information.   364-1

The first (Atlanteans) became dwellers in the rocks, in the caves, and those also that made their homes or nests, as it were, in the trees. 364-12

The position as the continent Atlantis occupied, is that as between the Gulf of Mexico on the one hand--and the Mediterranean upon the other. Evidences of this lost civilization are to be found in the Pyrenees and Morocco on the one hand, British Honduras, Yucatan and America upon the other. There are some protruding portions within this that must have at one time or another been a portion of this great continent. The British West Indies or the Bahamas, and a portion of same that may be seen in the present--if the geological survey would be made in some of these--especially, or notably, in Bimini and in the Gulf Stream through this vicinity, these may be even yet determined.

What, then, are the character of the peoples? To give any proper conception, may we follow the line of a group, or an individual line, through this continent's existence--and gain from same something of their character, their physiognomy, and their spiritual and physical development.

In the period, then--some hundred, some ninety-eight thousand years before the entry of Ram into India--there lived in this land of Atlantis one Amilius, who had first noted that of the separations of the beings as inhabited that portion of the earth's sphere or plane of those peoples into male and female as separate entities, or individuals. As to their forms in the physical sense, these were much rather of the nature of thought forms, or able to push out of themselves in that direction in which its development took shape in thought--much in the way and manner as the amoeba would in the waters of a stagnant bay, or lake in the present. As these took form, by the gratifying of their own desire for that as builded or added to the material conditions, they became hardened or set --much in the form of the existent human body of the day, with that of color as partook of its surroundings much in the manner as the chameleon in the present. Hence coming into that form as the red, or the mixture peoples--or colors; known then later by the associations as the red race. These, then, able to use in their gradual development all the forces as were manifest in their individual surroundings, passing through those periods of developments as has been followed more closely in that of the yellow, the black, or the white races, in other portions of the world; yet with their immediate surroundings, with the facilities for the developments, these became much speedier in this particular portion of the globe than in others--and while the destruction of this continent and the peoples are far beyond any of that as has been kept as an absolute record, that record in the rocks still remains--as has that influence of those peoples in that life of those peoples to whom those did escape during the periods of destruction make or influence the lives of those peoples to whom they came. As they may in the present, either through the direct influence of being regenerated, or re-incarnated into the earth, or through that of the mental application on through the influences as may be had upon thought of individuals or groups by speaking from that environ.

In the manner of living, in the manner of the moral, of the social, of the religious life of these peoples: there, classes existed much in the same order as existed among others; yet the like of the warlike influence did not exist in the peoples--as a people--as it did in the other portions of the universe.   364-3

As to the supplying of that as necessary to sustain physical life as known today, in apparel, or supplying of the bodily needs, these were supplied through the natural elements; and the **developments** came rather in the forms--as would be termed in the **present** day--of preparing for those things that would pertain to what would be termed the aerial age, or the electrical age, and supplying then the modes and manners of transposition of those materials about same that did not pertain to themselves bodily; for of themselves this was transposed, rather by that ability lying within each to be transposed in thought as in body.

In these things, then, did Amilius see the beginning of, and the abilities of, those of his own age, era, or period, not only able to build that as able to transpose or build up the elements about them but to transpose them bodily from one portion of the universe to the other, **through** the uses of not only those **recently** re-discovered gases, and those of the electrical and aeriatic formation in the breaking up of the atomic forces to produce impelling force to those means and modes of transposition, or of travel, or of lifting large weights, or of changing the faces or forces of nature itself, but with these transpositions, with these changes that came in as personalities, we find these as the Sons of the Creative Forces as manifest in their experience looking upon those changed forms, or the daughters of men, and there crept in those pollutions, of polluting themselves with those mixtures that brought contempt, hatred, bloodshed, and those that build for desires of self **without** respect of **others'** freedom others' wishes, and there began then, in the latter portion of this period of development, that that brought about those of dissenting and divisions among the peoples in the lands. With the attempts of those still in power, through those lineages of the pure, that had kept themselves intact as of the abilities of forces as were manifest **in** their activities, these **builded** rather those things that **attempted** to draw **back** those peoples; through first the various changes or seasons that came about, and in the latter portion of the experience of Amilius was the first establishing of the altars upon which the sacrifices of the fields and the forest, and those that were of that that **satisfied** the desires of the physical body were builded.

Then, with the coming in or the raising up of Esai, with the change that had come about, began that period when there were the invasions of this continent by those of the animal kingdoms, that brought about that meeting of the nations of the globe to **prepare** a way and manner of disposing of, else they be disposed of themselves. With this coming in, there came then the first of the destructive forces as could be set and then meted out in its force or power. Hence that as is termed, or its first beginning of, **explosives** that might be carried about, came with this reign, or this period, when **man**--or **men**, then--began to cope with those of the beast form that **overran** the earth in many places. Then, with these destructive forces, we find the first turning of the altar fires into that of sacrifice of those that were taken in the various ways, and human sacrifice began. With this also came the first egress of peoples to that of the Pyrenees first, **of** which later we find that peoples who enter into the black or the mixed peoples, in what later became the Egyptian dynasty. We also find that entering into the Og, or those peoples that later became the beginning of the Inca, or Ohum, that builded the walls across the mountains in this period, through those same usages of that as had been taken on by those peoples; and with the same, those that made for that in the other land, became first those of the mound dwellers, or peoples in the land. With the continued disregard of those that were keeping the pure race and the pure peoples, of those that were to bring all these laws as applicable to the Sons of God, man brought in the destructive forces as used for the peoples that were to be the rule, that combined with those natural resources of the gases, of the electrical forces, made in nature and natural form the first of the eruptions that awoke from the depth of the slow-cooling earth, and that portion now near what would be termed the Sargasso Sea first went into the depths. With this there again came that egress of peoples that aided, or attempted to assume control, yet carrying with them **all** those forms of Amilius that he gained through that as for signs, for seasons, for days, for years. Hence we find in those various portions of the world even in the present day, some of that as **was** presented by those peoples in **that** great **development** in this, the Eden of the world.

In the latter portion of same we find as **cities** were builded more and more rare became those abilities to call upon rather the forces in nature to supply the needs for those of bodily adornment, or those of the needs to supply the replenishing of the wasting away of the physical being; or hunger arose, and with the determinations to set again in motion, we find there--then Ani, in those latter periods, ten thousand seven hundred years before the Prince of Peace came--again was the bringing into forces that to **tempt**, as it were, nature--in its storehouse--of replenishing the things--that of the **wasting** away in the mountains, then into the valleys, then into the sea itself, and the fast disintegration of the lands, as well as of the peoples--save those that had escaped into those distant lands.

How, then, may this be applicable to our present day understanding? As we see the effects as builded in that about the sacred fires, as through those of Hermes, those of Arart, those of the Aztec, those of Ohum, each in their respective sphere **carrying** some portion of these blessings--when they are kept in accord and **pure** with those through which the channels of blessings, of the Creative Forces, may manifest.

Q-Please give a description of the earth's surface as it existed at the time of Atlantis' highest civilization, using the names of continents, oceans and sections of same as we know them today?

A-As to the highest point of civilization, this would first have to be determined according to the standard as to which it would be judged--as to whether the highest point was when Amilius ruled with those understandings, as the one that understood the variations, or whether they became man made, would depend upon whether we are viewing from a spiritual standpoint or upon that as a purely material or commercial standpoint; for the variations, as we find, extend over a period of some two hundred thousand years--that is, as light years--as known in the present--and that there were many changes in the surface of what is now called the earth. In the first, or greater portion, we find that **now** known as the southern portions of South America and the Arctic or North Arctic regions, while those in what is **now** as Siberia--or that as of Hudson Bay --was rather in that region of the tropics, or that position now occupied by near what would be as the same **line** would run, of the southern Pacific, or central Pacific regions--and about the same way. Then we find, with this change that came first in that portion when the first of those peoples used that as prepared **for** the changes in the earth, we stood near the same position as the earth occupies in the present--as to Capricorn, or the equator, or the poles. Then, with that portion, **then** the South Pacific, or Lemuria, began its disappearance--even, before Atlantis, for the changes were brought about in the latter portion of that period, or what would be termed ten thousand seven hundred light years, or earth years, or present setting of those, as set by Amilius--or Adam.   364-4

Q-How large was Atlantis during the time of Amilius?

A-Comparison, that of Europe including Asia in Europe--not Asia, but Asia in Europe--see? This composed, as seen, in or after the first of the destructions, that which would be termed now--with the present position --the southernmost portion of same--islands as created by those of the first (as man would call) volcanic or eruptive forces brought into play in the destruction of same.

Q-Was Atlantis one large continent, or a group of large islands?

A-Would it not be well to read just that given? Why confuse in the questionings? As has been given, what would be considered one large continent, until the first eruptions brought those changes--from what would now, with the present position of the earth in its rotation, or movements about its sun, through space, about Arcturus, about the Pleiades, that of a whole or one continent. Then with the breaking up, producing more of the nature of large islands, with the intervening canals or ravines, gulfs, bays or streams, as came from the various **elemental** forces that were set in motion by this **charging**--as it were--**of** the forces that were collected as the basis for those elements that would produce destructive forces, as might be placed in various quarters or gathering places of those beasts, or the periods when the larger animals roved the earth--**with** that period of man's indwelling. Let it be remembered, or not confused, that the **earth** was peopled by **animals** before peopled by man!

Q-Describe one of the ships of the air that was used during the highest period of mechanical development in Atlantis.

A-Much of the nature, in the **earlier** portion, as would be were the hide of **many** of the pachyderm, or elephants, made into the **containers** for the gases that were used as both lifting and for the impelling of the crafts about the various portions of the continent, and even abroad. These, as may be seen, took on those abilities not only to pass through that called air, or that heavier, but through that of water--when they received the impetus from the **necessities** of the peoples in that particular period, for the safety of self. The shape and form, then, in the earlier portion, depended upon which or what skins were used for the containers. The metals that were used as the braces, these were the **combinations** then of what is **now** a lost art--the **tempered** brass, the temperament of that as becomes between aluminum (as now called) and that of uranium, with those fluxes that are from those of the **combined** elements of the iron, that is carbonized with those of other fluxes--see? These made for lightness of structure, non-conductor or conductors of the electrical forces-- that were used for the **impelling** of same, rather than the gases--which were used as the lifting--see? For that as in the **nature's** forces may be turned into even the forces **of** that that makes life, as given, from the sun's rays to those elements that make for, or find **corresponding** reaction in their **application** of same, or reflection of same, **to** the rays itself--or a different or changed form of storage of **force**, as called electrical.   364-6

In the beginning (occult or psychic science) were the natural expressions of an entity. As there developed more of the individual association with material conditions, and they partook of same in such a manner as to become wholly or in part a portion **of** same, farther--or more hidden, more unseen--has become occult or psychic manifestations. First there were the occasional harking back. Later by dream. Again we find individuals raised in certain sections for specific purposes. As the cycle has gone about, time and again has there arisen in the earth those that **manifested** these forces in a more magnificent, more beneficent, way and manner. And, as has been given, again the time draws near when there shall be seen and known among men, in many places, the manifestations of such forces in the material world; for "As ye have seen him go, so will He return again" (Acts 1:11)...With the use of those sources of information, the abilities to become a portion of those elements that were the creative forces **of** the compounds or elements within the universal forces, at that period brought about those forces that made for destruction of the land itself, in the attempt to draw that as was in man then back **to** the knowledge; and these brought about those destructive forces (that are known today) in gases, with that called the death ray, that brought from the bowels of the earth itself --when turned into the sources of supply--those destructions to portions of the land. Man has ever (even as then) when in distress, either mental, spiritual **or** physical, sought to know his association, his connection, with the divine forces that brought the worlds into being...

This is what psychic force, and so called occult science, **did** mean, **has** meant, **does** mean in the world today.

Q-Describe in more detail the causes and effects of the destruction of the part of Atlantis now the Sargasso sea.

A-As there were those individuals that attempted to bring again to the mind of man more of those forces that are manifest by the closer association of the mental and spiritual, or the soul forces that were more and more as individual and personal forms in the world, the use of these elements--as for the building up, or the passage of individuals through space--brought the uses of the gases then (in the existent forces), and the individuals being able to become the elements, and the elementals themselves, added to that used in the form of what is at present known as the raising of the powers from the sun itself, to the ray that makes for disintegration of the atom, in the gaseous forces formed, and brought about the destruction in that portion of the land now presented, or represented, or called, Sargasso Sea.

Q-What was the date of this first destruction, estimating in our present day system of counting time in years B.C.?

A-Seven thousand five hundred years before the final destruction, which came as has been given.

Q-Please give a few details regarding the physiognomy, habits customs and costumes of the people of Atlantis during the period just before this first destruction.

A-...First there were those as projections from that about the animal kingdom; for the **thought** bodies gradually took form, and the various **combinations** (as may be called) of the various forces that called or classified themselves as gods, or rulers over--whether herds, or fowls, or fishes, etc.--in **part** that kingdom and part of that as gradually evolved in a physiognomy much in the form of the present day man (were one chosen of those that were, or are, the nearest representative of the race of peoples that existed in this first period as the first destructions came about). These took on **many** sizes as to stature, from that as may be called the midget to the giants--for there were giants in the earth in those days, men as tall as (what would be termed today) ten to twelve feet in stature, and in proportion--well proportioned throughout.

The ones that became the most **useful** were those as would be classified (or called in the present) as the **ideal** stature, that was of both male and female (as those separations had been begun); and the most ideal (as would be called) was Adam, who was in that period when he (Adam) appeared as five in one--See?

In this the physiognomy was that of a full head, with an extra **eye**--

as it were--in those portions that became what is known as the **eye**. In the beginning these appeared in **whatever** portion was desired by the body for it use!

As for the dress, those in the beginnings were (and the Lord made them coats) of the skins of the animals. These covered the parts of their person that had become, then, as those portions of their physiognomy that brought much of the desires that made for destructive forces in their own experience; and these then were of those about them that were given as meat, or used as same--that partook of the herbs. These were those same herbs that the seed were to have been for good for the man in self, and only those that partook of same may be called even **clean**--in the present day. 364-11

Before the first destruction of the land...the entity lived to be 1000 years old, in years as termed today, and saw great changes come about, not only in the earth but in those ways in which preparations were made for the advent of the souls of men to be brought to their relationship with the Creative Forces or God. 3579-1

In the Atlantean period, when at that time before the first of the destructive forces, and the usages of the influences as were gathered by the peoples to the lands about, when the entity builded those that make for the carrying of those machines of destruction that sailed both through the air and under the water. 1735-2

CHILDREN OF THE LAW OF ONE

For in giving the experience of an entity's sojourn in a period as remote as the early destructive influences in that land called Atlantis, or in Poseidia, there is oft a confusion in the interpretations of the records--as to whether Poseidia was the land or Atlantis was the land.

There were also other centers that were developing. For in the projections they began as many, and in creating influences they began as five--or in those centers where crystallization or projection had taken on such form as to become what was called man.

Hardly could it be said that they were in the exact form as in the present. For there were more of the influences that might be used when necessary; such as arms or limbs or feet or whatnot.

So, in following or interpreting the Poseidian period--or in Atlantis --let it be understood that this was only **one** of the groups; and the highest or the greater advancement in the earthly sojourning of individual entities or souls at that particular period--or the highest that had been save that which had been a part of the Lemurian age.

Hence we find there had been the separating into groups (as we would call them) for this or that phase of activity; and those that were against that **manner** of development.

The Sons of Belial were of one group, or those that sought more the gratifying, the satisfying, the use of material things for self, **without** thought or consideration as to the sources of such nor the hardships in the experiences of others. Or, in other words, as we would term it today, they were those without a standard of morality.

The other group--those who followed the Law of One--had a standard. The Sons of Belial had no standard, save of self, self-aggrandizement.

Those entities that were then the producers (as we would term today), or the laborers, the farmers or the artisans, or those who were in the positions of what we would call in the present just machines, were those that were projections of the individual activity of the group.

And it was over these then, and the relationships that they bore to those that were in authority, that the differences arose.

Then we find the entity, now known as or called 877, was among the children of the Law of One; entering through the natural sources that had been considered in the period as the means of establishing a family. However, they were rather as a group than as an individual family.

For those who were of the ruling forces were able by choice to create or bring about, or make the channel for the entrance or the projection of an entity or soul, as the period of necessity arose.

Then such were not as households or as families, like we have today, but rather as groups.

Their **standard** was that the soul was given by the Creator or entered from outside sources **into** the projection of the **mental** and spiritual self at the given periods. **That** was the standard of the Law of One, but was **rejected** by the Sons of Belial...

That was among the first entrances, or the second entrance of the entity **from** the without, into that form which became encased as an entity, an **individual** body, see?

The name then, as we would term in the present, was Deui (pronounced Dar, or D-R); and the entity was active in the recording of the messages, the directing of those forces that came with the use of the light that formed the rays upon which the influence from without was crystallized into what would become as the sound from the outer realm to the static or individual realm.

These were not only the rays from the sun, set by the facets of the stones as crystallized from the heat from within the elements of the earth itself, but were as the combination of these.

For it was these gases, these influences that were used for what we call today the conveniences as for light, heat, motivative forces, or radial activity, electrical combinations; the motivative forces of steam, gas and the like for the conveniences...

The use of these influences by the Sons of Belial brought, then, the first of the upheavals; or the turning of the etheric rays' influences **from** the Sun--as used by the Sons of the Law of One--into the facet for the activities of same--produced what we would call a volcanic upheaval; and the separating of the land into **several** islands--five in number.

Poseidia, the place, or the settlement of that particular sojourning of the entity--Deui--at the time, then became **one** of these islands.

This sojourn was nearer to fifty or five hundred thousand years before we even have the beginning of the **Law as** the Law of One manifested.   877-26

The first disturbing forces brought the first destruction in the continent, through the application of spiritual things for self-indulgences of material peoples. Those were the periods as termed in thy Scripture when "The sons of God looked on the daughters of men, and saw them as being fair" (Genesis 6:2).   1406-1

The entity was in that land now known as or called the Atlantean, during those periods when there were the destructions or separations of the land during the period of the first destruction. The entity was among those who aided in the preparation of the explosives, or those things that set in motion the fires of the inner portions of the earth that were turned into destructive forces (unawares to many of those, yet)--as was experienced by those that followed in the Law of One, and those that followed the law of Baal, the laws of nature are used by the spiritual laws for the completing of what are as destined forces in the lives and experiences of those that journey through this mundane sphere.   621-1

The entity was enjoined with the sons of the Law of One, yet made for those associations with--and saw the divine and spiritual laws become destructive in the lands and the activities of--the sons of Belial.

For when those facets were prepared for the motivative forces from the rays of the sun to be effective upon the activities of those ships and the electrical forces then, these turned upon the elements of the earth caused the first upheavals.   1297-1

The entity was in the Atlantean experience when there was the breaking up of the land itself (first destruction?) through the use of spiritual truths for the material gains of physical power.

Yet the entity was among those that were of the children of the

Law of One, in the name Aian.

In the experience the entity was among those that ministered in the Temple of the Sun, from which all power was used for the aid of those in material things. Yet the entity was among those that understood how that the spirit of those that are given charge concerning the affairs among men came again and again, and gave the power to those that remained true in and among the sons of men!

When those periods came for dissolution of the earth's surface...the entity aided in giving those instructions for the preservation of the lives of many of the faithful, to go into other lands.   1152-1

The entity was in the Atlantean land, in those periods when there were first begun the with-drawings from the Law of One, those establishings of the sons--or of the **son** Belial in that experience.

The entity...through the activities of Belial became the priestess in the temple that was built in opposition to the ones--or the sons of **One**. And in this the entity lost. When there were those destructive forces brought through the creating of the high influences of the radial activity from the rays of the sun, that were turned upon the crystals into the pits that made for the connections with the internal influences of the earth, the entity through turmoil again joined with those of the Law of One. 263-4

ATLANTEAN COMMUNICATION WITH THE SAINT REALM

In **Atlantis**, the children of the Law of One--including this entity, Rhea, as the high priestess--were giving periods to the concentration of thought for the use of the universal forces, through the guidance or direction of the saints (as would be termed today).

There are few terms in the present that would indicated the state of consciousness; save that, through the concentration of the group mind of the children of the Law of One, they entered into a fourth-dimensional consciousness--or were absent from the body.

Thus they were able to have that experience of crystallizing, through the Light, the speech from what might well be termed the saint realm, to impart understanding and knowledge to the group thus gathered.

To be sure, there were those influences apparent in which the children or sons of Belial sought more and more the use, or the interpreting of that spiritual unity into individuals or material things for self-aggrandizement or indulgences without due consideration for the freedom of choice or decision by those who were then, in a physical experience, in that state of evolution developing their mental abilities for single or separate activity...

Among those of the entity's own group that division had come in which there had arisen the separation of the sexes. There were those who had listened, and who were inclined to listen to the tempting applications made by the sons of Belial.

Those individuals who had through their sojourns in the earth as souls pushed into matter as to become separate entities, without the consideration of principle or the ability of self-control, might be compared to the domestic pets of today,--as the present development of the horse, the mule, the dog, the cat.

This is not intended to indicate that there is transmigration or transmutation of the soul from animal to human; but the comparison is made as to trait, as to mind, and as to how those so domesticated in the present are dependent upon their masters for that consideration of their material as well as mental welfare,--yet in each there is still the instinct, the predominant nature of that class or group-soul impregnation into which it has pushed itself for self-expression.

Hence those interpretations are implied by the characteristics indicated in the name itself, as to the relationships to its group and its dealing in sexual relationships. Hence the term,--as docile as the horse, as catty as the cat, as stubborn as the mule...

The entity then was the high priestess in authority, or the interpreter to the groups of the messages attained or gained from the periodical meetings with those from the universal realm, for instruction, for direction, for understanding in those periods of activity.

Being influenced by the groups or individuals about same, there were those disputations with them as to the purposes of the children of Belial; that these were to be exploited rather than to be equals with those thus endowed with the spiritual understanding...

Q-Describe in detail the entity's work with the White Stone.

A-...The entity was the interpreter of the messages received through the concentration of the group upon the stone from which the oracle spoke from the realm of the saints.   2464-2

In Atlantis, a priestess, and aid to an Es-Se-Ne (?), and the keeper of the White Stone or that through which many of the peoples, before the first destructions in Atlantis kept their accord with the universal consciousness, through speaking to and through those activities. 5037-2

The stones that are circular, that were of the magnetized influence upon which the Spirit of the One spoke to those people as they gathered in the service, are of the earliest Atlantean activities in religious service, as would be called today.   5750-1

The entity was in those experiences in the Atlantean land, before those periods of the second upheavals or before the lands were divided into the isles.

The entity was among those of the household of the leaders of the One, and aided in the attempts to establish for those that were developing or incoming from the thought forces into physical manifestations to gain the concept of what their activities should be to develop towards a perfection in physical body, losing many of those appurtenances.   444-1

The entity is one that has never changed sex; thus it is every whit a woman--dependent, and yet free from the needs of the companionship as many. These emotions the entity in others oft never comprehends...

The entity was in the Atlantean land, when there were those periods of activity in which there was the changing of individuals from the double sex, or the ability of the progeneration of activities from self.

The entity was a priestess in that experience just before there were the activities of the sons of Belial that brought about the period of the second destruction of the land.   2390-1

The entity was in the Atlantean land in those periods when there were the second divisions, or when there was the destruction of the lands which made Poseidia the remaining portion in which there was the greater activity of the sons of the Law of One.

Those were the periods in which there was the application of much of that being discovered or rediscovered today, in the application of power to modes of transit as well as the use of nature's means for a helpful force in giving greater crops for individual consumption. Also they were periods when a great deal of thought was given as to conveniences of every nature.   2562-1

Q-In relation to the history of Atlantis as presented, at what period did the flood as recorded in the Bible in which Noah took part, occur?

A-In the second of the eruptions, or--as is seen--two **thousand**--two-- two thousand and six--before the Prince of Peace, as time is counted now, or light years--day and night years. Not light years as the akashic records, or as the esoteric records, or as counted by astrology or astronomy, in the speed or the reflection of a ray of light.   364-6

In that land known as Atlantis, the entity was...among those destroyed (second destruction?) in the overflow of the land.   105-2

The entity was in Atlantis when there was the second period of disturbance--which would be some twenty-two thousand, five hundred before the periods of the Egyptian activity covered by the Exodus; or it was some twenty-eight thousand before Christ, see?   470-22

In Atlantean land just after second breaking up of the land owing to misapplication of divine laws upon those things of nature or of the earth; when there were the eruptions from the second using of those influences that were for man's own development, yet becoming destructive forces to flesh when misapplied.   1298-1

These (power from the firestone), not intentionally, were **tuned** too high--and brought the second period of destructive forces to the peoples in the land, and broke up the land into the isles.   440-5

Before there were the second upheavals, when there was the dividing of islands, when the temptations were begun in the activities of the sons of Belial and the children of the Law of One, the entity was among those that interpreted the messages that were received through the crystals and the fires that were to be the eternal forces of nature, and made for helpful forces in the experience of groups during the period.
New developments in air, in water travel...were the beginning of the developments at that period for the escape.   3004-1

The entity was in Atlantis, during those periods just before the second breaking up of the land.
The entity was among the sons of Belial who used the divine forces for the gratifying of selfish appetites.   3633-1

ATLANTIS AT THE TIME OF THE THIRD DESTRUCTION

In the Atlantean land before the third destruction--assisted Alta, the scribe, in preparing a history of the land.   339-1

The Atlanteans are all **exceptional**. They either wield woe or great development. And their influences are felt, whether the **individual** recognizes it in himself or not...
This entity as we find, as in most of the Atlanteans' experiences, requires a great deal of mental and oft physical activity to satisfy, or to fill the self. For it is a very **active** mind...
The entity was in the Atlantean land during those periods between the second and the last upheavals; when there were the great antagonistic feelings between the sons of Belial and the children of the Law of One.
The entity was among the children of the Law of One who made the greater overtures to those peoples for the acknowledging of the laborers, and to make their experience easier--those laborers that were considered by many as merely **things** rather than individuals souls.   1744-1

The entity was in the Atlantean land, during those periods when there were those activities that brought about the last destruction of same through the warrings between the children of the Law of One and the sons of Belial or Baal.

There the entity was among those who waned between the children of faith or the Law of One and those who sought the use of the spiritual forces for their own self-indulgences, self-aggrandizements.   1599-1

The entity was in the Atlantean land when there were those periods of the last upheavals or the disappearance of the isles of Poseidia.

The entity was among those groups that went into what later became known as the Inca...in the Peruvian land.   3611-1

Q-What were the principal islands called at the time of the final destruction?
A-Poseidia and Aryan, and Og.   364-6

EXODUS FROM ATLANTIS

In the Atlantean land the entity was...the keeper of the portals as well as the messages that were received from the visitations of those from the outer spheres...for it was the entity that received the message as to the needs for the dividing of the children of the Law of One for the preservation of the truths of same in other lands.

Hence we find the entity was among those who were as the directors of those expeditions, or the leaving for the many varied lands just before the breaking up of the Atlantean land.

Hence the entity outlined in the most part, it might be said, the expedition guided by Ax-Tell and the ones to the Pyrenees and to the Yucatan and to the land of Og...

Later, with the revivifying of the Priest in Egypt, the entity was among those who set about the unifying of the teachings of the Atlanteans, the Egyptians (as they would be called today), the Indian, the Indo-Chinan, the Mongoloid and the Aryan peoples.   1681-1

The entity was in Atlantis during those periods when there were the separations, just before the breaking up of Poseidia. The entity then controlled those activities where communications had been established with other lands, and the flying boats that moved through the air or water were the means by which the entity carried many of those to the Iberian land, as well as later those groups in the Egyptian land when there had been determined that the records should be kept there.   3184-1

Q-Describe briefly one of the large cities of Atlantis at the height of its commercial and material prosperity, giving name and location.

A-This we find in that as called Poseida, or the city that was built upon the hill that overlooked the waters of Parfa (?), and in the vicinity also of the egress and entrance to the waters from which, through which, many of the peoples passed in their association with, or connection with, those of the outside walls or countries. This we find not an altogether walled city, but a portion of same built so that the waters of these rivers became as the pools about which both sacrifice and sport, and those necessities for the cleansing of body, home and all, were obtained, and these--as we find--were brought by large ducts or canals into these portions for the preservations, and yet kept constantly in motion so that it purified itself in its course; for, as we find, as is seen, water in motion over stone or those various forces in the natural forces purifies itself in twenty feet of space.

In the type of the buildings, these were much in that of tiers--one upon another; save principally in the temples--that were about the sacred fires where these were offered, the sacrifices that were gradually builded by the people in their attempt to appease those forces in nature, and from which we find there came all those forms in the various portions of the earth in which these were carried in their necessary channels, to make for the variations in its surroundings and the conditions thereunto. In this temple, we find these of large or semi-circular columns of onyx, topaz, and inlaid with beryl, amethyst, and stones that made the variations in catching the rays of the sun. Hence a portion of same became as the sun worshipers in other portions, from which there were an egress of the peoples.

In this the sacred fires burned, and there were the rising of the intermittent fires that came and went, that were later worshiped by some that brought on much of the destruction, because they waited long at the period before the destructions came. These were those places where there became eventually the necessity of offering human sacrifices, which when put into fires became the ashes that were cast upon the waters for the drinking of same by those that were made prisoners from portions of other lands.

In the setting up of same, these in the temple ruled--rather than those who held official positions in carrying out the orders of those in these positions.

These, as to the manner of the buildings, were of the outer court--or where groups or masses might collect. The inner, those that were of a select group, or those of the second chambers. Those of the inner court, or shrine about the altar, were only for the elect, or the chosen few.   364-12

Q-Going back to the Atlantean incarnation--what was the Tuaoi stone? Of what shape or form was it?

A-It was in the form of a six-sided figure, in which the light appeared as the means of communication between infinity and the finite; or the means whereby there were the communications with those forces from the outside. Later this came to mean that from which the energies radiated, as of the center from which there were the radial activities guiding the various forms of transition or travel through those periods of activity of the Atlanteans.

It was set as a crystal, though in quite a different form from that used there. Do not confuse these two, then, for there were many generations of difference. It was in those periods when there was the directing of aeroplanes, or means of travel; though these in that time would travel in the air, or on the water, or under the water, just the same. Yet the force from which these were directed was in this central power station, or Tuaoi stone; which was as the beam upon which it acted.

In the beginning it was the source from which there was the spiritual and mental contact.

Understanding, these are the following of laws--if there would be the understanding or comprehension of these. For, as has been given, the basis, the beginning of law carries all the way through. And that which comes or begins first is conceived in spirit, grows in the mental, manifests in the material, as was this central force in the Atlantean experience. First it was the means and source or manner by which the powers that be made the centralization for making known to the children of men, and children of God, the directing forces or powers. Man eventually turned this into that channel for destructive forces,--and it is growing towards this in the present.   2072-10

Q-Give an account of the electrical and mechanical knowledge of the entity as Asal-Sine in Atlantis.

A-...In the center of a building, that today would be said to have been lined with non-conductive metals, or non-conductive stone--something akin to asbestos, with the combined forces of bakerite (bakelite?) or other non-conductors that are now being manufactured in England under a name that is known well to many of those that deal in such things.

The building above the stone was oval, or a dome wherein there could be or was the rolling back, so that the activity of the stone was received from the sun's rays, or from the stars; the concentrating of the energies that emanate from bodies that are on fire themselves-- with the elements that are found and that are not found in the earth's atmosphere. The concentration through the prisms or glass, as would be called in the present, was in such a manner that it acted upon the instruments that were connected with the various modes of travel, through induction methods--that made much the character of control as the remote control through radio vibrations or directions would be in the present day; though the manner of the force that was impelled from the stone acted upon the motivating forces in the crafts themselves...

The preparation of this stone was in the hands only of the initiates at the time, and the entity was among those that directed the influences of the radiation that arose in the form of the rays that were invisible to the eye but that acted upon the stones themselves as set in the motivating forces--whether the aircraft that were lifted by the gases in the period of whether guiding the more pleasure vehicles that might pass along close to the earth, or what would be termed the crafts on the water or under the water.

These, then, were impelled by the concentrating of the rays from the stone that was centered in the middle of the power station, or power house (that would be termed in the present).

In the active forces of these the entity brought destructive forces, by the setting up--in various portions of the land--the character that was to act as producing the powers in the various forms of the people's activities in the cities, the towns, the countries surrounding same. These, not intentionally, were **tuned** to high--and brought the second period of destructive forces to the peoples in the land, and broke up the land into the isles that later became the periods when the further destructive forces were brought in the land.

Through the same form of fire the bodies of individuals were regenerated, by the burning--through the application of the rays from the stone, the influences that brought destructive forces to an animal organism. Hence the body rejuvenated itself often, and remained in that land until the eventual destruction, joining with the peoples that made for the breaking up of the land--or joining with Baalilal (Baal? Belial?) at the final destruction of the land. In this the entity lost. At first, it was not the intention nor desire for destructive forces. Later it was for the ascension of power itself.

As to describing the manner of construction of the stone, we find it was a large cylindrical glass (as would be termed today), cut with facets in such a manner that the capstone on top of same made for the centralizing of the power or force that concentrated between the end of the cylinder and the capstone itself.

As indicated, the records of the manners of construction of same are in three places in the earth, as it stands today: In the sunken portions of Atlantis, or Poseidia, where a portion of the temples may yet be discovered, under the slime of ages of sea water--near what is known as Bimini, off the coast of Florida. And in the temple records that were in Egypt, where the entity later acted in cooperation with others in preserving the records that came from the land where these had been kept. Also the records that were carried to what is now Yucatan in America, where these stones (that they know so little about) are now (1933)--during the last few months--**being** uncovered.

Q-Is it for this entity to again learn the use of these stones?

A-When there have come those individuals who will purify themselves in the manner necessary for the gaining of the knowledge and the entering into the chambers where these may be found; yes--if the body will purify itself. In '38 it should come about, should the entity --or others may--be raised.

In Yucatan there is the emblem of same. Let's clarify this, for it may be more easily found--for they will be brought to this America, these United States. A portion is to be carried, as we find, to the Pennsylvania State Museum. A portion is to be carried to the Washington preservations of such finds, or to Chicago.

The stones that are set in the front of the temple, between the service temple and the outer court temple--or the priest activity, for later there arose (which may give a better idea of what is meant) the activities of the Hebrews from this--in the altar that stood before the door of the tabernacle. This altar or stone, then, in Yucatan, stands between the activities of the priest (for, of course, this is degenerated from the original use and purpose, but is the nearest and closest one to being found).

As to the use of same, and as to how it's to be applied, one must prepare self--and it may not wholly be given through any channel, until an individual has so purified his purposes and desires.   440-5

In Poseidia the entity dwelt among those where there was the storage, as it were, of the motivative forces in nature from the great crystals that so condensed the lights, the forms, the activities, as to guide not only the ship upon the bosom of the sea but in the air and in many of those now known conveniences for man as in the transmission of the body, as in the transmission of the voice, as in the recording of those activities in what is soon to become a practical thing in so creating the vibrations, as to make for television.   813-1

(There was) what may be known in the present as the photographing from a distance, or the...ability for reading inscriptions through walls-- even at distances...(and) there was the over-coming of (termed today) the forces of nature or gravity itself; and the preparations through the crystal, the mighty, the terrible crystal.   519-1

Q-What is the best substance for induction, conduction, transmission of etheronic energy?

A-This is as raised power that would be produced from a combination of crystals...It is very much like that used by the body in destructive forces in the Atlantean sojourn. Not that which caused the cosmic ray, or the death ray, or the healing ray--but the ray that came from setting of the prismatic influences from high heating--it may be from Arcturus or it may be from the Sun; though Arcturus would be nearer proper. The sun may be induced to make for destructive or constructive forces.   440-3

Q-Is etheronic energy amenable to mental control?
A-It **is** mental control.   443-5

Q-Describe some of the mental abilities that were developed by the Atlanteans at the time of their greatest spiritual development.

A-Impossible to describe achievements physical in their spiritual development. The use of **material** conditions and spiritual attributes in a material world would, and do, become that as are the miracles of the Son in the material world; for even as with Him in--and as He walked, whether in Galilee, in Egypt, in India, in France, in England, or America --there were those periods when the activities of the physical were as was what would be termed the everyday life of the Sons of God in the Atlantean or Eden experience; for as those brought the various changes from the highest of the **spiritual** development to the highest of the mental, then of the **material** or physical developments, then the fall--see? 364-7

WORLD GATHERING TO COMBAT ANIMAL MENACE

Q-Please advise me regarding the preparation and presentation of the article I am preparing (1933) on the Great Congress held during the age of the destruction of the enormous animals that once roamed the earth.

A-...As to the manner in which these gathered, it was very much as would be were the Graf (Graf Zeppelin?) to start to the various portions for those that represented, or were to gather those that were to counsel, or were to cooperate in that effort. And, as this, then, was in that particular plane or sphere that then was in the land which has long since lost its identity, except in the inner thought or visions of those that have returned or are returning in the present sphere, the ways and means devised were as those that would alter or change the environs for which those beasts were needed, or that necessary for their sustenance in the particular portions of the sphere, or earth, that they occupied at the time. And this was administered much in the same way or manner as were there sent out from various central plants that which is termed in the present the Death Ray, or the super-cosmic ray, that which many are seeking into which will give their lives much, from the stratosphere, or cosmic rays, that will be found in the next twenty-five years.

Q-What was the date B.C. of this gathering?
A-50,722.   262-39

The entity was in the Indian land or in those periods of Saad as the leader the ruler...

The entity then was among those who were of the group who gathered to rid the earth of the enormous animals which overran the earth, but ice, the entity found, nature, God, changed the poles and the animals were destroyed.   5249-1

In that land when there were gathering of nations to combat forces of animal world and kingdom, that made men's and man's life miserable. The entity then among those that stood for the use of elements in the air, the elements in the ocean, the elements in the lands as applied **to** forces to meet and to **combat** those of the animal kingdom. Oft has the entity from this experience been able to **almost** conceive wherein the disappearance of those known as prehistoric animals came about.   2893-1

During those periods when there were the first of the activities of peoples in the lands which now represent a portion of Arizona, New Mexico, Colorado and Utah, the entity was among those who made for the associations with those activities when the great powers, or nations--through those influences as brought by the activities in Egypt, the Gobi, the Og--cooperated in one great cause. The entity then as a leader among those peoples for the alleviating of man's influence upon that created by man in the enormous animals that had lost control by the influences of the powers of suggestion in the associations of the spirit--or sons of men--upon the animal world.   1211-1

In the days when the peoples of the nations were gathered as one to defend self against the fowls of air and beasts of the field. The entity among those as would be called an envoy to such gatherings, and came to that gathering in what would **now**--this period--present, be called lighter than air machines.   2749-1

In Egypt (this before the mountains rose in the south, and when the waters called the Nile then emptied into what is **now** the Atlantic Ocean) the entity was among those peoples who gathered in places to establish various groups, or families, or sects, to prevent the inroads upon the peoples from the beasts from without.   276-2

Q-In several readings the second ruler in Egypt gave the first laws concerning man's relation to the Higher Forces. You will give me an outline of this teaching and how same was given to the people.

A-Yes, we have the work here and that phase concerning the indwelling in the earth's plane of those who first gave laws concerning indwelling of Higher Forces in man. In giving such in an understandable manner to man of today, (it is) necessary that the conditions of the earth's surface and the position of man in the earth's plane be understood, for the change has come often since this period, era, age of man's earthly indwelling, for then at that period, only the lands now known as the Sahara and the Nile region appeared on the now African shores; that in Tibet, Mongolia, Caucasia and Norway in Asia and Europe; that in the southern cordilleras and Peru in the south-western hemisphere and the plain of now Utah, Arizona, Mexico of the north-western hemisphere and the spheres were then in the latitudes much as are presented at the present time.

The man's indwelling was then in the Sahara and the upper Nile regions, the waters then entering the now Atlantic from the Nile region rather than flowing northward; the waters in the Tibet and Caucasian entering the North Sea; those in Mongolia entering the South Seas; those in the Cordilleras entering the Pacific; those in the plateau entering the Northern Seas.

When the earth brought forth the seed in her season, and man came in the earth plane as the lord of that in that sphere, man appeared in five places then at once--the five senses, the five reasons, the five spheres, the five developments, the five nations.

In this now then as we receive, we find many peoples, or man became the union against the invasion from the now Tibetan and Caucasian forces. The separating of the peoples in their castes was only the beginning then of group understandings, and the first ruler of groups set self in that place in the upper Nile, near what is now known as the Valley of Tombs.

In the second rule there came peace and quietude to the peoples, through the manner of the ruler's power over the then known world forces. At that period, man exchanged with the forces in each sphere that necessary for the propagation of the peoples of the sphere then occupied. In each of the spheres given was the rule set under some individual by this second ruler in now Egyptian country, and the period when the mind of that ruler brought to self, through the compliance with those Universal Laws ever existent, then that ruler set about to gather those wise men from the various groups to compile those as that ruler felt necessary understanding to all peoples for the indwelling of the Divine Forces to become understood and to break away from the fear of the animal kingdom then overrunning the earth.   5748-1

Q-Continue with reading 5748-1.

A-Now, as we see, as given, how and what the classifications were of the physical in the earth's plane at that period, the numbers then of human souls in the earth plane being a hundred and thirty and three million souls. The beginning then of the understanding of laws as applied from man's viewpoint being in this second rule in the country now Egypt. The rule covering the period of a hundred and ninety and nine years, and the entity giving the chance to the peoples, for the study being in the twenty and eighth year, when he began to gather the peoples together for this and surrounding himself with those of that land and of the various lands wherein the human life dwelled at that period. The numbers of the people that came together for the purpose then numbering some forty and four.

The Courts as were made were in the tents and the caves of the dwellers of the then chosen priest from the Arabian or Tibetan country, who came as one among those to assist with the astrologer and the soothsayers of the desert of the now eastern and western world, and with this the conclave was held for many, many moons. The period of the world's existence from the present time being ten and one-half million years, and the changes that have come in the earth's plane many have risen in the lands. Many lands have disappeared, many have appeared and disappeared again and again during these periods, gradually changing as the condition became to the relative position of the earth with the other spheres through which man passes in this solar system.

The first laws, then, partook of that of the study of self, the division of mind, the division of the solar system, the division of man in the various spheres of existence through the earth plane and through the earth's solar system. The **Book of the Dead**, then, being the first of those that were written as the inscribed conditions necessary for the development in earth or in spirit planes. These, as we see, covered many various phases. About these were set many different ones to give the interpretation of same to the peoples in the various spheres that the individuals dwelled in that came together. Hence the difference in the manner of approaching the same sacrificial conditions in the various spheres, yet all using the Sun, the Moon, the Stars, as the emblems of the conditions necessary for the knowledge of those elements as enter in; same as the fish representing the water from which all were drawn out, as we would see from the various changes.

The beginnings then of this in a systematic manner beginning with this second rule, in this manner, in this land.   5748-2

Q-Continue with reading 5748-2.

A-...In that land (Egypt) we find the peoples comparatively free from the invasion of the beasts of the field, save those as were being used for man's development and for the use of man as servant or as man's beasts of burden. While we find in the now Tibetan country, then the land of the many waters, the indwelling of those of many beasts whom man had to defend self against. Again in the Mongoloid region many others of the species and nature that were destructive to man's indwelling in many ways. Also those in Caucasia, or the lighter or whiter peoples. Also in the land of the plains in the Northern spheres in the Western portion of the earth's plane, many beasts and many conditions, and man then was in the way of having a different understanding, for different conditions were to be met as were also in the Southern portion.

Then, as these were gathered from the five nations, we find the subjects of those pertaining to manifestation of the development of man and man's ability to cope with the conditions, and the forces wherein men were given their supremacy over the other conditions in the earth plane. And the first as was given by the ruler was, then, that the force that gives man, in his weak state, as it were, the ability to subdue and overcome the great beasts that inhabit the plane of man's existence must come from a higher source. Hence the first law of self-preservation in the physical plane attributed to Divine or Higher Forces. Just as the elements adding to the betterment of man's condition in the earth plane, we have then the rudiments of that as was taught. Hence began, as given, the study of the indwelling of that other than man's physical prowess, yet there were many men of giant stature to meet the conditions as seen yet the approach of that same force to some was reached through the power, heat, significance of Sun's force, of Moon's wane, of waters bringing forth all manners of organisms necessary for developments in the plane.

Then, we have the gathering then of this group, from the farthest places--forty and four. As we see, this number will run through many numbers, for, as we find, there is the law pertaining to each and every element significant to man's existence considered and given in one manner or form by the groups as gathered at this meeting.   5748-3

Q-Continue with reading 5748-3.

A-Yes, we have these here and the conditions surrounding same. As these were gathered in their tents and caves, each were given the portion of the fact as related to each group's conception regarding man's supremacy over the animal world, and how same was reached. As these were given, we find that each gave that conception in the way that was in relation to man's surroundings in the earth plane, so in this manner were the first laws as relating to the indwelling of the Higher Forces given to man. With the absence of the communications as is given, this was written on tables of stone and slate, with the characters of same. In the first of the pyramids built in the Valley of the Shadow, there still may be found unto this day portions of data as was preserved with the ruler, who afterward was worshiped as the representative of God made manifest in earth. These will be found in the northwest corner or chamber of this mound.

As to the peoples as gathered there, we find there are many in the plane today, many that have become associated one with the other, and there comes then the urge for the return of man's more perfect understanding of the Divine laws as have been made manifest through the various ages of the evolution of man in the plane from that day.   5748-4

In the Egyptian forces, the greater laws were being given, and during the reign or the second of that rule, wherein the greater civilization of earth's people were being given, and the greater civilization of earth's people were being exhibited and the first temples being built.   760-4

(The Book of the Dead) was rather the Book of Life; or it represents that which is the experience of a soul in its sojourn not only in the land of Nirvana, the land of Nod, or the land of night, but rather those things that make for the cleansing of a physical body for the aptitudes of expression through the senses or the emotions in the physical forces to the spiritual truths.   706-1

In that land known as Egypt, when there were the peoples coming in from the north, the entity then that one whom the people overran, and in the name Raai, and the entity was of those peoples who first brought to that land the study of the relationships of man to the Creative Energy, and attempted to **establish** this relation with the peoples in the gathering and calling of same together, and neglected to countenance those that called on the entity for the defence against the hordes that came in from the North country, in the name of Arart, and the entity fought **little** with the peoples, subjecting self rather than making bloodshed for the peoples of the land, and through the application of self in the period--while condemned by others, condemned by (his) own peoples for the time--the entity gained **most** in **all** its experiences through that period.

Not in merely submission, but in that the **principle** as was given **by** the entity **during** that period became the basis for the studies of the Prince of Peace, and the establishing **of** those schools as began in the land by those that overran the land.   1734-3

In the Egyptian forces, when the first rule was given to the people as regarding relations of individuals to a higher being, and those orders and those rules as were being set...The entity then occupying that position as the councillor to the ruler at that time, coming as he did from the plains country of now the Arabian to the rule of the Egyptian forces as were first set in Gizeh.   953-13

Q-You will have before you the soul-body and the mind of Edgar Cayce, present in this room. You will give a detailed life history of this entity's appearance in Egypt as Ra Ta, and his associations with those of that period with whom he is closely associated in the present.

A-Yes, we have the entity and those conditions or records that are apparent in the inner self of the entity or body in the present, from that as seen and recorded as Ra Ta the priest.

In giving this interpretation we must find there are many peoples, even nations, that were influenced by the material activities of the entity in that experience.

That the entity came into the land Egypt with others that had come for a purpose is evidenced by that which has been given. He came with that people from what was to be later the earthly sojourn of the entity as a leader, and as a man then of unusual abilities as well as appearance and manners of conduct.

The entity chose rather the peoples that were to enter in the land, and was the son of a daughter of Zu that was **not** begotten of man. In the entrance, then, he came rather as one that was rejected by those peoples about him; for ever has there been that question where such has been the experience among peoples who had formed any associations of home.

Home, as has been remembered, began with a peoples in an entirely different land, and was then projected in thought by those various leaders in those places where man, as man, had come into being through that crystallization of thought that had been given by those Sons of the Most High.

In this entity's appearance, then, in this particular experience, there was brought to those peoples of Zu's the condemnation of those of Ararat, who had established what would now be called a **community** home in the land later known as Ararat, or where the flood later brought those peoples who again joined with many in peopling the earth after that destruction which was caused by those changes in the land known as Og.

The entity then grew in grace with the peoples by the manner of conduct, though with the action of those peoples of Ararat these brought hardships for the mother of the entity in that experience, until there had been a change in the environs and brought among a new surrounding.

In this period, then, there was the prophecy by Ra Ta that the **son** (Arart) of Ararat was to journey into this land (Egypt) where there was then the higher state of developments as to the necessities, and those abilities to enjoy and enjoin the activities of the mental and material bodies in their associated actions. These brought, then, those things that are classed in the present as pleasures that gratify the senses of man's own development, for much that is now as the developments that are necessities as well as luxuries were **then** commonplace as the most common necessities in the present. Hence to those peoples, while Ra Ta was one that was still looked on askant, with the removal of the peoples into the Egyptian land, during that age of Ra Ta as would be called today one score and one, then the entity gave much in the way of aiding those peoples, children of Arart and the families of same, in making the easy, even control of a land that might be said to be supplying then all the luxuries of the earth in that particular period.

With the peaceful arrangements that were brought about, then, after the period of dissension with the young natives and the changing of the natives's name to that of the king, Aarat, then the priest was in the position of gradually gathering those that would harken to those words as pertaining to there being any relations with an outside world, or of there being those divisions in the body that were represented by those divisions of the intermission, or the body of intermission of an entity, from an experience to an experience. The natives held more strongly to the necessity of materialization for the enjoyment, as may be surmised from the conditions that were surrounded and evidenced in those particular conditions of this period.

With Ra Ta then beginning with the natives and those that listened to the uncovering of the records (in what would be termed archaeological research in the present), gradually more and more adherence was made to those words of this peculiar leader that had come into this land leading or guiding the conquerors, who were seeking for the expression of various thoughts that were coming through in those entities entering that group in that particular period. This being at that period (as would be called, in the study of such) of the change of the race to become--and is now--the white. Hence, as Ra Ta means and indicates, among--or the first **pure** white in the experience then of the earth...

With the subsiding, then, of contentions with the natives and those that rose against them, and those that had come in the raising to that of what was to be the experimentation (as would be called in the present) of those that were given to Ra Ta by the king and that native who was to be counseled or judged by those who had been chosen in the positions as the group called (that as would be expressed in the present) the material minded, the spiritual minded the business minded, the political minded.

These in their divisions, then, made for what may be seen as a **real** representative of the conditions that are arisen in the earth in the present period, when there is the drawing near to that period of a change again, which is as a cycle that has brought about that period when there must be the establishing of that which is in the present the representation of that experimentation for the advancement of those various groups in that particular period.   294-147

Following the conquering of the Egyptian country by the peoples of the north or hill country, the entity (Aarat?) then among those who were the learned of the conquered people. The people coming in, or the hills people, using the ways of warfare in that of the sling, and of those projections as were fastened to beasts and turning beasts loose on the people, who were **trained** animals to destroy the foes or enemies of the invaders--and, as is later seen, there becomes much of this same training, in the Egyptian hill country, in which animals--bulls, bear, and the leopard, and the hawk, are trained to give warfare against peoples...

These were then, when conquered, not a warlike people--one not prepared for defense or of a way of defending self. Weapons only used in agriculture and in building...

Archeology, was to these people of that period as much of a science as it is today--1926, see? and the buildings and the various conditions represented more of the national life than these represent today.   900-277

The Egyptian period may be considered one of the most momentous occasions or periods in the world's history...

We find the entity then as the scribe (Aarat), in the position as would be termed today as the teacher, or the interpreter to the peoples of the laws as applying in the physical sense to the peoples. The tenets of the priests and Christian peoples in the sense to the same peoples...

We find the scribe (Aarat) among those of the Egyptians that were of the old rule, conquered by the peoples as came in from the hill country and set up the rule. When the young king came into power, Araaraart (son of Arart), the king set about to gather those of the learned to prepare those tenets for those peoples, to make same secure, and to give the proper rule and order. The priest (Ra Ta) being chosen, the scribe and the councillors being chosen, the scribe set about to give those interpretations in the combination as Jefferson gave that of liberty to peoples, the scribe gives same to the peoples, the rules, in the separation of those truths as pertaining to man's relation with the higher creative energy and forces, and those first tenets as were presented were of no time, no space, all force one force, man the representative of the higher creative energy in the earth, and through same gave to the peoples, and that subdued that conception of that creative force, see?

Q-What was the date, as man knows time, of this battle?

A-Ten thousand and fifty-six years before the Prince of Peace came. The records of much of the scribe may yet be found--many of the tenets were the lessons that the five nations, that gathered later, studied. Many are the temples builded later in the plains that are yet to be uncovered, near the Sphinx, as seen at present, which represents a portion of contemporary forces and contemporaries during the period, see?   900-275

The Priest (Ra Ta) was an individual who had received inspiration from within. And, realizing that such an influence or force might be given to others in their search for **why** and **what** were their purposes in material life. He then sought out one who might foster such a study in materiality.

Thus, from those places that were a portion of what is now called the Carpathias, he came with a great horde, or a great number (as to individual souls, numbering nine hundred), into the land now called Egypt.

Why Egypt? This had been determined by that leader or teacher (not physical leader, but spiritual interpreter or guide) as the center of the universal activities of nature, as well as the spiritual forces, and where there might be the least disturbance by the convulsive movements which came about in the earth through the destruction of Lemuria, Atlantis, and--in later periods--the flood.

What were the factors, ye ask, which determined this in his mind? or from what concept did the entity gain that knowledge? Was it just a concept, just a revelation, just a physical analysis, or what?

When the lines about the earth are considered from the mathematical precisions, it will be found that the center is nigh unto where the Great Pyramid, which was begun then, is still located.

Then, there were the mathematical, the astrological and the numerological indications, as well as the individual urge.

Ye say, then, such an entity was a god! No. No,--ye only say that because there is the misunderstanding of what were the characters or types of spiritual evolution as related to **physical** evolution in the earth at that period.

As an illustration (this merely illustrating, now): It is hard for an individual, no matter how learned he may be, to conceive of the activities that exist only three miles above the earth. Why? Because there are no faculties within the individual entity in the present **capable** of conceiving that which is not represented within his individual self.

Yea,--but the individual of that period was not so closely knit in matter. Thus the activities of the realms of relativity of force, relativity of attraction in the universe, **were** an experience of the souls manifesting in the earth at that period, see?

Thus we find that the experiences of individuals of the period, seeking for the understanding as to the evolution of the souls of men, might be compared to the minds of individuals in the present who are seeking an understanding as to man's use of physical or atomical structure in his own relationships.   281-42

With Arart as the king and Ra Ta as the prophet or seer, there began a period that may well be called a division of interests of the peoples. Ra Ta attempted to induce the king to have only those natives that were tried and true in their acceptance of those attempts that would bring closer relationship, according to those visions and experiences of Ra Ta in line with those being established as customs, rules and regulations. These conditions naturally made for some disturbance among the natives, that would be called the upper class..

With the political situation, then, the king--the young king, then only thirty--gathered about him many that were to act in the capacity of council...the departments being much in that day as they are in the present; for remember, there is nothing in the present that hasn't existed from the first. Only the **form** or the manner of its use being changed, and many an element then used that the art of its use has been lost, as we will see the reason why, and many being re-discovered by those called scientists in the present when in that day it was the common knowledge of the most illiterate...

There were the necessities of matching the abilities of the king's council, or king's people, with the facilities of the natives--as it were-- in the various phases of what would be termed in the present as progress. Hence the opening by Araaraart (son and heir of Arart) of mines in Ophir, in what was later known as Kadesh, or in the land now called Persia. Also in the land now known as Abyssinia, and those portions yet undiscovered or used in the upper lands of the river Nile there were those mines of the precious stones--onyx, beryl, sardis, diamond, amethyst, opal, and the pearls that came from the sea near what is now called Madagascar. In the northern (or then the southern) land of Egypt, those mines that produced quantities--and quantities-- and quantities--of gold, silver, iron, lead, zinc, copper, tin...

The physical attributes were worshiped much more in many ways in this period than the religious are in the present period, and rightly so--though there were the preparations for the spiritual worship that comprised not only the sacrificial altars, which were not as for the offering of sacrifice in the slaying of animal or bird, or beast, or reptile, or man; rather that upon which individuals put their faults and blotted them out with the fires of those forces that were set in motion by Ra Ta, in the ability to give to each that for which his or her activity were best adapted in the developing of themselves, when they had chosen to give themselves in service in that particular position in which their activity was necessary. See the difference?

There were also established storehouses, that would be called banks in the present, or places of exchange, that there might be the communications with the individuals in varied lands; for even in this period (though much had been lost even by these peoples) was there the exchange of ideas with other lands, as of the Poseidian and Og, as well as the

Pyreneen and Sicilian, and those that would now be known as Norway, China, India, Peru and American. These were not their names in that particular period, but from whence there were being gathered a portion of the recreations of the peoples; for the understandings were of one tongue! There had not been as yet the divisions of tongues in this particular land. This was yet only in the Atlantean or Poseidian land.

With the gathering of these people and places, there began the erecting of the edifices that were to house not only the peoples, but the temple of sacrifice, the temple of beauty--that **glorified** the activities of individuals, groups or masses, who had **cleansed** themselves for service. Also the storehouses for the commodities of exchange, as well as that gathered by the peoples to match--as it were, still--one against the other. Hence we find the activities of the priest, or seer, as really a busy life--yet much time was given in keeping self in communion with those that brought the knowledge of that progress made in the spiritual sense in other lands, especially so from Poseidia and Og.

In these visitations that were caused, or that necessitated the absenting of the priest from these places, there arose more and more a dissension with those peoples...and there arose at that time the first--as may be said--of that saying, "When the devil can't get a man any other way, he sends a women for him."

Among those, then, of the priests' daughters, was one (Isris) of the king's favorites--that made for the entertaining of the king and his council, and his visitors--who was more beautiful than the rest, and she was induced to gain the favor of the priest through the activities of herself in body, and in the manners that would induce some fault to be found. This was not by her own volition, but rather by the counsel of those that made for the persecutions of her own peoples that were being protected by the activities of the body, and divisions arose that were even unknown then to Ra Ta, for he being among those that trusted all, believed all, and--as it were--for the time the gods laughed at his weakness! 294-148

Q-What did this High Priest (Ra Ta) do to cause disfavor?

A-It being permissible for the Priest to have only one wife, and this High Priest taking of the daughters (Isris) of the second sacrificial priest and a favorite to the King, as the Concubine to the Priest. 341-10

When the priest (Ra Ta) broke the law that was set by him concerning the number of wives accorded or given to the priest. And this brought first the political uprising. Then the religious war. And the priest with the princess (Isris) was banished, with all those that adhered to the priest's activity, including the aid to the priest (Hept-supht of Atlantis) to the Libyan land.   275-38

During that experience of man's advent into materiality, and to the entity individually, there was the losing of appendages, of attachments arising from the injection of the souls of individuals into animal influences--or partially of animal bodies...

This entity was born of those that were among the rulers of the land (Egypt) that took unto self the beings that were part human (as we would know today) and part of other beings--or animals, see? 264-50

The body was worshiped in this period as sincerely as most of the physical or spiritual worship that may be seen today, for the bodies were changing in their forms as their developments or purifications were effective in those temples, where the consecrations and changes were taking place by the activities of the individual in their abilities to turn themselves towards (in the mental) the **spiritual** things of an existence. They gradually lost, then, many feathers from their legs. Many of them lost the hairs from the body, that were gradually taken away. Many gradually began to lose their tails, or their protuberances in their various forms. Many of them gradually lost those forms of the hand and foot, as they were changed from claws--or paws--to those that might be more symmetrical with the body. Hence the activities or the uses of the body, as they became more erect and more active, more shaped to them in their various activities. These were, to be sure, considered as the body beautiful. Beauty as divine; for the Divine has brought--and does bring--those various beauties of form or figure to the body, and should be **considered** as it was given so; for "the body is the temple of the living God"...

In the Temple Beautiful then, we find here the altars where various forms of desire were sacrificed, that brought to the individuals, or persons, or bodies, the gradual falling away of those things that made for the **animal** activity in the bodies of those that were attempting to so consecrate, so concentrate themselves and consecrate their bodies, their lives, their activities, in this service. Let's don't forget the thesis, or the key for which all of this understanding had come: That there might be a closer relationship of man to the Creator, and of man to man.   294-149

In that particular experience there were still those who were physically entangled in the animal kingdom with appendages, with cloven hoofs, with four legs, with portions of trees, with tails, with scales, with those various things that thought forms (or evil) had so indulged in as to separate the purpose of God's creation of man, as man--not as animal but as man. And the animal seeks only gratifying of self, the preservation of life, the satisfying of appetites. With infinity injected in same brought the many confused activities or thoughts that we know now as appetites. Yes, a dog may learn to smoke! Yes, a horse may learn to eat sugar! But these are not natural inclinations--rather man's influences upon these activities by associations.

All these forms, then, took those activities in the physical beings of individuals. This priest, this Ra Ta attempted to eradicate same; in that manner as might be compared to the hospitalization in the present, where individuals--through the lack of the proper application of the physical laws--have allowed growths, tumors, cancers, those things or conditions in the body,--stones in various portions of the organism; and the necessity--as considered in the present--of operative measures to remove growths of various characters throughout the system. 2072-8

The loss of the animal appendages was through operative forces in the Temple of Sacrifice, not in the Temple Beautiful. There was also the preparation of individuals through reading and through the application of the law of diet, as to make such appendages be gradually released entirely from certain types of individuals. Only those who had mixed with the thought forms had same (appendages), you see.

Q-How much transformation from the animal to the human could be completed in a life-time?

A-Little, save in the offspring--by the change of thought, diet, and the operative forces. In third or fourth generation it was completed. 2067-6

There was the Temple of Sacrifice; or that wherein the body was shed of the animal representations through the sacrificing of the desires of the appetite, through the **changing** of self in the temple service.

There was also the Temple Beautiful, wherein those labored who were released gradually of those appurtenances that would hinder; as the feathers fell away, the hair was removed here or there, the claws and the bill and the hoofs--and the like--began to disappear...

As an individual attunes itself to that which it has attained, even at a **moment** of time, there is aroused the abilities to **know** even that which **was** known through the experience.   275-33

The viola tuned to the vibrations of the fires of nature may be destructive or smothering or aflaming same. So in that Temple of Sacrifice...those that offered themselves in those manners of purifying; that burned away not only the desires of the flesh but the appendages of same that marred their bodies. And thus through much of thine effort came forth man as he walks upright today; no longer with the feet as of the cloven ox; or the horns as of the roe, the goat; nor the hog; nor those that would make themselves as a tree, nor those whose bodies were alive with the serpents of wisdom. But rather in the godly sons of the Sons of God that wasted not their wanton selves in the mire of despair with the sons of men but kept the faith. 275-43

The entity found greater disturbances with the Atlantean peoples because of their color, because of their odor. These became very repulsive to the entity until--through those purifications in the Temple-- there was the changing of those vibrations of the body forces through the electrical charges that were a part of the application that becomes a part of man's experience in the present...When such are used in various forms, they may not only destroy disorders or diseases in a body but may also change entirely the attitude of an individual. 585-12

The entity was among those purified in the Temple of Sacrifice for the bringing into the world of a purer, a better race.   1223-4

Being purified in the Temple of Sacrifice for the propagation of a new race...that entity, Tek-Le-On, was among the offspring of those who were entangled in matter, yet with a spiritual import; yet having blemishes in the body that kept them--as individuals--from their associations with those of the race represented by the Priest in that experience...
The entity was among the first of the individuals to be offered in the Temple, called the Temple of Sacrifice, as ones who might be dedicated to the activities according to the theory or idea of the Priest as to how individuals might be prepared for the incoming of a different type, or a more perfect stature of man...
The entity lived to be quite an elderly person--as it was two hundred and ninety-eight years.   1223-6

The entity was among those from the lands that were later called the Parthenian lands, or what ye know as the Persian land from which the conquerors then of Egypt had come. As a Princess from that land the entity came to study the mysteries for the service it might give to those of her own land, the Carpathians. The entity was among the first of the pure white from that land to seek from the Priest and those activities in the Temple Beautiful for the purifying of self. 1472-1

The Temple of Sacrifice was a physical experience, while the Temple Beautiful was rather of the mental,--in which there was the spiritual- ization--not idolizing, but crystallizing of activities or services to a special purpose,--or specializing in preparation for given offices. 281-43

The teachings and education through the Temple Beautiful would be the same as represented in today's universal school or college. 2533-4

That as written over the door of the Temple Beautiful: PARCOI (?) SO (?) SUNO (?) CUM (?). LORD, LEAD THOU THE WAY. I COMMIT MY BODY, MY MIND, TO BE ONE WITH THEE...
Do not, my children, confuse thine bodies of today with those attributes

of same, with the conditions existent in the Temple Beautiful.

In structure, this:...The materials outwardly were of the mountains nigh unto the upper waters of the Nile.

It was in the form of the pyramid, within which was the globe--which represented to those who served there a service to the world.

The furnishings maybe surmised from the fact that the most beautiful things from each land were gathered there; gold, silver, onyx, iron, brass, silk, satins, linen.

As to the manner of the service there: The individuals having cleansed themselves of those appendages that hindered, came not merely for the symbolic understanding. For these, to be sure, were all symbolized--the faults, the virtues of man, in all his seven stages of development--in the light or the lamp borne by those who served as the Light Bearers to be that as given by the teachers--even Ra Ta.

There were first the songs, the music, as we have indicated that ye sing Ar-r-r--Ou-u--Ur-r; which makes for the losing of even the association of the body with that save the vibrations of which the body was then composed; yea now is, though encased in a much more hardened matter, as to materiality; which made for the vibrating of same with light, that **becomes** color, that becomes tone, that becomes activity.

Seek then **in** tone--all of you Ar-r-r-r-AR that ye may know how the emanations, that are termed as the colors of the body, make for the expression then given. With the music came the dance, that enabled those with the disturbing forces and influences to become more erect, upright in body, in thought, in activity.

Then there was the giving by the Prophetess of the seal of life that was set upon each and every one who passed through these experiences, how or in what field of activity the relationships were of an individual to its fellow man in maintaining material existence; being in the world yet not **of** the world...

Ye ask, where is this now? Disintegrated and in that sphere ye may enter, and some have entered, where these are sealed as with the seven seals of the law...

Here it may be well that there be given a concept of what is meant by the journey (about the Temple Beautiful), or what journey is meant. As indicated, it, the globe within the pyramid without, was four forty and four cubits (twenty-seven and one-half inches was a cubit then, or a mir then--myr?). The height was four and twenty and forty and four mir, making then that in the form of the ova, or the egg in its ovate form.

From station to station in the seven phases or seals or stands or places of the activities, they were such as to make each station lead from one to another by ever crossing the one; making the continued web. 281-25

The priest and the companion were banished into the land that lies to the south and east of this land, or the Nubian Land.

Here all became changed...Still some remained faithful to the priests who remained in the land, and troublesome times arose for many, many suns, or until at least nine seasons had passed before there was even the **semblance** of the beginning of a quieting, and that not until there had been definite arrangements made that the priest **would** return and all would be submissive to his mandates; and he became, then, as may be termed in the present, a dictator--or a monarch in his own right...

In the land to which these were banished, not only were there the two but a **number**; some two hundred and thirty-one souls. 294-149

There came the banishment of the Priest, with the companion, as well as the many numbers of those who chose to be banished into the Abyssinian land, who were attracted by the natural intent and purpose of the Priest,--not only those of his own peoples but many of the Natives.

There then followed the nine years in banishment; as well as the periods of the King's own household in the Ibex; as well as the entrance into Egypt of the peoples from the Atlantean land, which had begun the breaking up--as had been told by that entity, the Priest. 281-42

As the priest in this period (exile) entered more and more into the closer relationships with the Creative Forces, greater were the abilities for the entity or body Ra Ta to be able to make or bring about the **material** manifestations of that relationship...

There were begun some memorials in the Nubian land which still may be seen, even in this period, in the mountains of the land. Whole mountains were honeycombed, and were dug into sufficient to where the perpetual fires are **still** in activity in these various periods, when the priest then began to show the manifestations of those periods of reckoning the longitude (as termed now), latitude, and the activities of the planets and stars, and the various groups of stars, constellations, and the various influences that are held in place, or that **hold** in place those about this particular solar system. Hence in the Nubian land there first begun the reckoning of those periods when the Sun has its influence upon human life, and let's remember that it is in this period when the **present race** has been called into being--and the **influence** is reckoned from all experiences of Ra Ta, as the effect upon the body physical, the body mental, the body spiritual, or soul body; and these are the reckonings and the effects that were reckoned with, and about, and of, and concerning, in their various phases and effects. These all were set, not by Ra Ta--but **expressed** in the **development** of Ra Ta, that these **do** effect--by the forces as set upon all--not only the inhabitant of a given sphere or planet, but the effect all has upon every form of expression in that sphere of the Creative Energies in action in that given sphere, and this particular sphere or earth--was the **reckoning** in that period. Hence arose what some termed those idiosyncrasies of planting in the moon, or in the phases of the moon, or of the tides and their effect, or of the calling of an animal in certain phases of the moon or vegetable kingdom, animal kingdom, in various periods, were **first** discovered--or first given, not discovered--first **conscious** of--by Ra Ta, in his first giving to the peoples of the Nubian land...

The priest, who--under the **strain**--in a very short period had, to the apparent eye of those about him, become aged, decrepid, and not able physically to carry on; and **fear** began to be felt that there would not be the sustaining strength sufficient that there might be given to the peoples that which had been begun by the entity in the Egyptian land, and that which was being manifested in this land (of banishment).   294-150

THE MARK OF RA TA

Eventually came the period when there was to be the attempt, that there was to be the return of the priest to the land. Then did this priest of himself, and of the Creative Forces, **edict** that those who were in close association with this entity--that had meant an extenuation or savior of a peoples, into a regeneration of same--would have marks set in their bodies that would remain throughout their appearance in the earth's plane, that they might be known to one another, would they seek to know the closer relationships of the self to the Creative Forces and the **source--physical**--of **their** activity **with** that source. To some in the eye, to some in the body, to some the marks upon the body, in those ways and manners that may only be known to those that are in that physical and spiritual attunement with the entity as they pass through the material or earth's sphere together. They are drawn, then, by what? that same element that was being accentuated in the earth's plane, as also the other laws that were discovered--or were given, or were conscious of--by the entity in that particular period. The purpose of such, then, that there may be known, that with such an association there may come an awakening to that which was accomplished by those of the select--not elect, but **select**--in that particular endeavor.

These are, then, in that position wherein their relationships may be of the best, the **closest** relationships of the mental, the material, the **spiritual** developments of all that aided in that particular experience, for the good of the group, the nation, the world--and hence the activities in whatever direction must **influence** the **whole** of the human race. 294-150

Q-What is meant by marks being placed upon the body, in those ways and manners that may only be known to those who are in that physical and spiritual attunement with Ra Ta as they pass through the material or earth's sphere together?

A-As has been indicated, their names as set, their titles as given to each.   275-38

The type of mark--this indicated the manner, the channel in which the entity would become aware of that union or united effort, or of being a member of that group--as of a sign or a symbol to any great body...

Thus to those individuals who find their relationship and become aware of same in the present experience, this naturally becomes that channel through which the great awakening may come to those individuals...

Ra Ta was not a lord, not a god, but a teacher, an instructor, an interpreter; and an individual entity that would still hold to an ideal. 2072-10

Q-Why do I have a mark on my physical body?

A-As given, there is set a mark in those that they--themselves--may know that they have been called; that they may understand that they have been called. For it has been given, "I will set my mark upon my own, and they shall hear my voice, and answer--**within.**"   540-3

Q-What is the significance of the birthmark on my head?

A-As everyone in Atlantis, as well as the Egyptian period, the entity carries the experience of being marked. This has been and will be with thee throughout thy experience. **Use thy head**--or judgment! Be not too rash, but do see the ridiculous as well as the sublime.   2746-1

Q-Was I given a mark in Egypt; if so, please explain what it was and the significance?

A-That close to the left eye; indicated the far-seeing eye of the entity in the searching out and the interpreting of not only the material, but the purpose in the preparation of bodies for the new race.   2464-2

Q-Was I given a mark by Ra Ta? If so, where is it, and what is the meaning of it?

A-The upper portion of the lip, or between the nasal passages and the corner of the lip--which exists at times--especially a feeling of twitching there: the messenger, the speaker to those that need counsel. 1100-26

The entity, as a soldier and warrior (in a previous incarnation) lost a portion of the hand, see? Watch marks as seen on the left hand below the fourth finger and thumb that appear at times, see?   341-16

When the (emigrating) Atlanteans in that experience began to influence the spiritual and moral life of the Egyptians, under those turmoils which had arisen through the Rebellions as indicated, there came that desire, that purpose--especially on the part of the Natives, as well as those who had been adherents partly to the tenets of the Priest--that the Priest be returned that there might be a better understanding. For the Native leaders, especially, realized that their own activities or representation in the spiritual moral and religious life would be destroyed if there was the adhering to the tenets being presented by the Atlanteans.

And, as might be termed in the present, some indicated that the Priest alone would be a match for those activities of some of the stronger or more forward Atlanteans. For they had brought with them (as had the Priest) many **things**, or individuals, or entities, that were without purpose,--or merely automatons, to labor or act for the leaders in the various spheres of activity.

And, as the Natives found, such beings were classified or judged to be such as many of the Natives of the land.   281-43

As to the dress of the day, whether in the temple service or otherwise, this was always of linen--and in the manner as indicated, in the color as indicated, white and purple. The men and women were not much different in the manner of dress, save as in the Atlanteans who wore trousers when they came and coats, though much shorter or longer according to their class or distinction of their class.

Q-In what kind of vehicles did the priest and his retinue return to Egypt after the banishment?

A-In what would be called chariots driven by the gases; for the Atlanteans prepared those that brought these back. The followers were on the camels and the animals that were used in the service during that period. The camel, the donkey, the horse were later in this land, and introduced by the Arabians.

Q-What was the climatic condition of the country at this time?

A-More fertile than even in the present with the overflow as occurs, for only about a third of the present Sahara was there, though it was sandy loam with silt--in the use of the agriculture portions.   275-38

After the return of the Priest to the land there were the beginnings of the correlating of the tenets from Mongolia, Caucasia, India, Oz and Mu --or that now known as the American land, or the Zu of the Oz. 980-1

With the return of the Priest from banishment, with the establishing of the tenets that were as a united influence in the experience of the then known world, the entity became one who carried to those of many lands the correlating influence from those teachers; as Ra Ta in Egypt,

Ajax the teacher from Atlantis, Saneid from India, Yak from Carpathia, Tao from Mongolia. The teachings of these were combined.   991-1

The entity was in the land now known as the Indian and Egyptian, during those periods when there were the gatherings of those from many of the lands for the correlating of the truths that were presented by Saneid in the Indian land, by Ra Ta in the Egyptian land, by Ajax from the Atlantean land, by those from the Carpathian land, by those from the Pyrenees, by those from the Incal and those from the Oz lands, and by those from that activity which will again be uncovered in the Gobi land...

The entity became first as the representative of the Temple Beautiful, in the Indian land; and later--and during the period of its greatest height--in the land of the Gobi, or the Mongoloid. **There** the entity was as the Priestess in the Temple of Gold, which is still intact there. 987-2

The entity was in that now known as or called the Egyptian land, during those periods when there were those journeying hither from the Atlantean land.

The entity then was the princess of fire, or that one of the Law of One who acted in the capacity oft of the interpreter from and to the masters, the sons of the Most High, that would communicate with those in the earth.

Then the entity, as Princess Ilax, made for the establishing of the material activities in the sun god worship, that were later set up by Isis, Ra, Hermes, Ra Ta and those who became the teachers. 966-1

The entity was in the land that has been called the Atlantean, during those periods when there was the breaking up of the land there had been the edict that the land must be changed.

The entity was among those that set sail for the Egyptian land, but entered rather into the Pyrenees and what is now the Portuguese, French and Spanish land. And there **still** may be seen in the chalk cliffs there in Calais the activities, where the marks of the entity's followers were made, as the attempts were set with those to create an activity to the follower of the Law of One...

The entity may be said to have been the first to begin the establishment of the library of knowledge in Alexandria; ten thousand three hundred before the Prince of Peace entered Egypt for His first initiation there. For, read ye, "He was crucified also in Egypt" (Rev. 11:8). 315-4

The entity then among those, or that **one** given charge of that land **then** known as Deosho--now Alexandria--that founded that making for the greatest collection of manuscripts, of writings, of the various forces, that has ever been known in the **world**.   412-5

During that period a great deal of the time of Asphar and Ajax-ol was devoted to the use of the electrical forces maintained from the use of static forces, as called today...for the fusion of copper and brass with the alloy that comes from gold impregnated with arsenic, with the casting of electrical forces through same. This brought those abilities of sharpening or using such metals as these for cutting instruments.

Also there were those activities and abilities of the entity to use the electrical devices...for operative measures; wherein the electrical knife was in such a shape, with the use of the metals, as to be used as the means for bloodless surgery, as would be termed today,--by the very staying forces used which formed coagulating forces in bodies where larger arteries or veins were to be entered or cut.   470-33

With the return then of the Priest to the Temple Beautiful, there first began the Priest to withdraw himself from the whole that regeneration in body might become manifest, and the body lay down the material weaknesses--and from those sources of regeneration **recreated** the body in its **elemental** forces for the carrying on of that which these material positions gave the opportunity for; leaving first the records of the world from that day until there is the change in the race.   294-150

Q-Describe the physical appearance of Ra Ta at the height of his spiritual development.

A-The priest in body, as has been given, in the height of the development was at the regeneration, or when over a hundred years (or light years) in the earth. Six feet one inch tall, weighing--what in the present would be called--a hundred and eighty-one pounds. Fair of face, not to much hair on the head nor too much on the face or body. In color nearly white, only sun or air tanned.   275-38

With the regeneration, more and more became noised abroad that which had been and was being accomplished in this land of plenty, in foods, in ornaments, in the recreation, in the needs of the inner man, in the necessities for the satisfying of desires for the material mind, in the aiding or setting up of the various conditions that are called sciences...

Then began what may be truly termed the first national or nation **spirit** of a peoples; for with the divisions, rather than this causing a dispersing of ideals or a dividing up of interests, it **centralized** the interests; for these were being guided by a ruler or king whose authority was not questioned any more, nor were the advisings of the Priest questioned, who was acting in rather the capacity of preparing for this very spirit to manifest itself in the way of the national emblems, the national ideas, that stood for the varied activities of not only individuals or groups, but for the general masses.

Hence there began the first preparation for what has later become that called the Great Pyramid, that was to be the presentation of that which had been gained by these peoples through the activities of Ra Ta, who **now** was known as Ra.

For with the entering in of Hermes **with** Ra--who came as one of the peoples from the mount to which these peoples had been banished--and the raising of that one (Isris?) who had been condemned with the Priest in banishment to one that was to be without question the queen, or the advisor to all of her own peoples, there was brought the idea of the preservation of these, not only for those in the present but for the generations that were to come in the experiences and experiences throughout that period, until the changes were to come again in the earth's position that would make for, as it had in this inundation that brought about Ra Ta's coming in the experience from the gods in the Caspian and the Caucasian mountains, that had brought this change in the peoples. Hence under the authority of Ra, and Hermes as the guide, or the actual (as would be termed in the present) constructing architect with the Priest or Ra, giving the directions--and those of Isis in the form of the advisor--for the laying in of those things that would present to those peoples the **advancement** of the portion of man, or woman, to her position in the activities of the human race or human experience, these changed the position or attitude of these particular peoples as to the position that was held by woman in her relations to the developing of the conditions that either were to be national, local, or individual...

This, then, made for an **endowing** of this body Iso, Isis, to the position of the first goddess that was so crowned, and there was given then that place that was to be sought by others that would gain counsel and advice even from the Priest, gained access through that of Isis to the throne itself. Not that it rose above the authority of the king, but for that developing necessary for the activities of the woman in those spheres of activities in this particular development.

Then began the laying out of the pyramid and the building of same, the using of those forces that made for the activity of bringing then from those very mountains where there had been those places of refuge that which had been begun to establish these, not only into that which would remain as the place for receiving that which had been offered in the Temple Beautiful on the various altars of the activities of an individual's innate self, but to be the place of initiation of the initiates that were to act in the capacity of leaders in the various activities through this period. This building, as we find, lasted for a period of what is termed now as one hundred years. It was formed according to that which had been worked out by Ra Ta in the mount as related to the position of the various stars, that acted in the place about which this particular solar system circles in its activity, going towards what? That same name as to which the priest was banished--the constellation of Libra, or to Libya were these people sent. Is it not fitting, then that these must return? as this priest may develop himself to be in that position, to be in the capacity of a **liberator** of the world in its relationships to individuals in those periods to come; for he must enter again at that period, or in 1998...

In and with these became the preparing of the Temple Beautiful for a more perfect place of preservation of those things that were to make known later in the minds of peoples, as the changes came about in the earth, the rise and fall of the nations were to be depicted in this same temple that was to act as an interpreter for that which had been that which is, and that which is to be, in the material plane.   294-151

Q-You will please give at this time detailed information regarding the origin, purpose and prophecies of the Great Pyramid of Gizeh near Cairo, Egypt. Please answer the questions asked.

A-Yes. In the information as respecting the pyramids, their purpose in the experience of the peoples, in the period when there was the rebuilding of the priest during the return in the land, some 10,500 before the coming of the Christ into the land, there was first that attempt to restore and add to that which had been begun on what is called the Sphinx, and the treasure or storehouse facing same, between this and the Nile, in which those records were kept by Arart and Araaraart in the period.

Then, with Hermes and Ra (those that assumed or took up the work of Araaraart) there began the building of that now called Gizeh, with which those prophecies that had been in the Temple of Records and the Temple Beautiful were builded, in the building of this that was to be the Hall of Initiates of that sometimes referred to as the White Brotherhood.

This, then, receives all the records from the beginnings of that given by the priest, Arart, Araaraart and Ra, to that period when there is to be the change in the earth's position and the return of the Great Initiate to that and other lands for the folding up of those prophecies that are depicted there. All changes that came in the religious thought in the world are shown there, in the variations in which the passage through same is reached, from the base to the top--or to the open tomb **and** the top. These are signified by both the layer and the color in what direction the turn is made.

This, then, is the purpose for the record and the meaning to be interpreted by those that have come and do come as the teachers of the various periods, in the experience of this present position, of the activity of the spheres, of the earth.

In the period that is to come, this ends--as to that point which is between what is termed in chronological time in present--between 1950 and 1958, but there have been portions that have been removed by those that desecrated many of those other records in the same land. This was rejected by that Pharaoh who hindered in the peoples leaving the land.

Q-Are the deductions and conclusions arrived at by D. Davidson and H. Aldersmith in their book on The Great Pyramid correct?

A-Many of these that have been taken as deductions are correct. Many are far overdrawn. Only an initiate may understand.

Q-What corrections for the period of the 20th Century?

A-Only those that there will be an upheaval in '36.

Q-Do you mean there will be an upheaval in '36 as recorded in the pyramid?

A-As recorded in the pyramid, though this is set for a correction which, as has been given, is between '32 **and** '38--the correction would be, for this--as seen--is '36--for it is in many--these run from specific days; for, as has been seen, there are periods when even the hour, day, year, place, country, nation, town, and individuals are pointed out. That's how correct are many of those prophecies as made.

Oft may there be changes that bring periods, as seen in that period when there was an alteration in that initiate in the land of Zu and Ra that **brought** a change, but at a different point because of being driven by those that were set as the guides or guards of same.

In this same pyramid did the Great Initiate, the Master, take those last of the Brotherhood degrees with John, the forerunner of Him, at that place. As is indicated in that period where the entrance is shown to be in that land that was set apart, as that promised to that peculiar peoples, as were rejected--as is shown in that portion when there is the turning back from the raising up of Xerxes as the deliverer from an unknown tongue or land, and again is there seen that this occurs in the entrance of the Messiah in this period--1998.   5748-5

Q-Continue with reading 5748-5.

A-Much as been written respecting that represented in the Great Pyramid, and the record that may be read by those who would seek to know more concerning the relationships that have existed, that may exist, that do exist, between those of the Creative Forces that are manifest in the material world. As indicated, there were periods when a much closer relationship existed, or rather should it be said, there was a much better understanding **of** the relationship that **exist** between the creature and the Creator.

In those conditions that are signified in the way through the pyramid, as of periods through which the world has passed and is passing, as related to the religious or the spiritual experiences of man--the period of the present is represented by the low passage or depression showing a downward tendency, as indicted by the variations in the character of stone used. This might be termed in the present as the crucitarian (crucigerian?) age, or that in which preparations are being made for the beginning of a new sub-race, or a change, which--as indicated from the astronomical or numerical conditions--dates from the latter portion or middle portion of the present fall (1932). In October there will be a period in which the benevolent influences of Jupiter and Uranus will be stronger, which--from an astrological viewpoint--will bring a greater interest in occult or mystic influences.

At the correct time accurate imaginary lines can be drawn from the opening of the Great Pyramid to the second star in the Great Dipper, called Polaris or the North Star. This indicated it is the system toward which the soul takes its flight after having completed its sojourn through this solar system. In October there will be seen the first variation in the position of the polar star in relation to the lines from the Great Pyramid. The dipper is gradually changing, and when this change becomes noticeable--as might be calculated from the Pyramid--there will be the beginning of the change in the races. There will come a greater influx of souls from the Atlantean, Lemurian, La, Ur or Da civilizations. These conditions are indicated in this turn in the journey through the pyramid.

How was this begun? Who was given that this should be a record of man's experiences in this root race? for that is the period covered by the prophecies in the pyramid. This was given to Ra and Hermes in that period during the reign of Araaraart when there were many who sought to bring to man a better understanding of the close relationship between the Creative Forces and that created, between man and man, and man and his Maker.

Only those who have been called may truly understand. Who then has been called? Whosoever will make himself a channel may be raised to that of a blessing that is all that entity-body is able to comprehend. Who, having his whole measure full, would desire more so to his own undoing.

Q-What are the correct interpretations of the indications in the Great Pyramid regarding the time when the present depression will end?

A-The changes as indicated and outlined are for the latter part of the present year (1932). As far as depression is concerned, this is not --as in the minds of many--because fear has arisen, but rather that, when fear has arisen in the hearts of the created, **sin** lieth at the door. Then, the change will occur--or that seeking will make the definite change--in the latter portion of the present year. Not that times financially will be better, but the minds of the peoples will be fitted to the conditions better.

Q-What was the date of the actual beginning and ending of the construction of the Great Pyramid?

A-Was one hundred years in construction. Begun and completed in the period of Araaraart's time, with Hermes and Ra.

Q-What was the date B.C. of that period?

A-10,490 to 10,390 before the Prince entered into Egypt.

Q-What definite details are indicated as to what will happen after we enter the period of the King's Chamber?

A-When the bridegroom is at hand, all do rejoice. When we enter that understanding of being in the King's presence, with that of the mental seeking, the joy, the buoyancy, the new understanding, the new life, through that period.

Q-What is the significance of the empty Sarcophagi?

A-That there will be no more death. Don't misunderstand or misinterpret! but the **interpretation** of death will be made plain.

Q-If the Armageddon is foretold in the Great Pyramid, please give a description of it and the date of its beginning and ending.

A-Not in what is left there. It will be as a thousand years, with the fighting in the air, and--as has been--between those returning to and those leaving the earth.

Q-What will be the type and extent of the upheaval in '36?

A-The wars, the upheavals in the interior of the earth, and the shifting of same by the differentiation in the axis as respecting the positions from the Polaris center.

Q-Is there not a verse of scripture in Isaiah mentioning the rock on which the Great Pyramid is builded?

A-Not as we find; rather the rock on which John **viewed** the New Jerusalem--that is, as of the entering in the King's Chamber in the Pyramid.

Q-What is the date, as recorded by the Pyramid, of entering in the King's Chamber?

A-'38 to '58.

Q-If the Passion of Jesus is recorded in the Great Pyramid, please give the date according to our present system of recording time?

A-This has already been presented in a fair and suitable manner through those students of same, and these descriptions have been presented as to their authenticity.

Q-How was this particular Great Pyramid of Gizeh built?

A-By the use of those forces in nature as make for iron to swim. Stone floats in the air in same manner. This will be discovered in '58. 5748-6

Q-What connection did the entity have at that time with the building of the Great Pyramid?

A-A great deal in various experiences of same; that is, in the interpreting of periods of those activities which preceded that period in which the building was begun there. For, remember, this was not an interpretation only from that period **forward** but as to the very **place** and experience in which there is to be the change in the activities in the earth!

Those periods especially having to do with the influences which followed, **especially** during and after the periods of the sojourn of Truth, as manifested in man, in Him in the earth.

Q-What was the color of the Native Egyptian race, to which the entity belonged?

A-Near to the color of the true Chinese in the present,--though the physiognomy of the face was entirely different, see?   849-45

THE SECOND DYNASTY OF ARAARAART

As to that accomplished (by Araaraart), we find this in one of the highest civilizations of this country in its present position, for we find this same country had been submerged for nearly a quarter of a million years since the civilization had been in this portion of the country, and the peoples as had overrun the country in the various changes by invasions from the east and north, and this ruler, Araaraart, being then the second of the northern kings, and followed in the rule of the father, Arart, and began the rule, or took the position as the leader in his sixteenth year and ruled over these peoples for ninety-eight years. The country, as we find, was brought to a higher state of understanding with the surrounding nations, and there was much of the religious ceremonies practiced in this time, much of this being brought in from the northern country and of the religions a existed in this same country through the religion of that of the one taken as the companion, for there were many taken, and with the unearthing of the tribal rites and ceremonies, the coalition of these truths we find were correlated with these peoples as were gathered about this ruler, and much of the architectural forces were set in motion. As we see, the first foundations of the emblematical condition as is set in the sphinx was begun in this rule, for this, as we see, has remained the mystery of the ages.

In the accomplishments then, we have as these in Araaraart. This: Much of the sealing of the peoples' abilities in being drawn together for benefits of the masses rather than classes, for we find, though this ruler was worshiped by man, yet remaining much in that same spirit as is found in the better classes of the ones serving Higher Forces than self, which is service to fellowman. The monuments as were unearthed and added to from time to time, we find some are still existent, though many buried beneath shifting sands. Others underneath sands that became the bed of the sea that overflowed this country.

Q-Did this ruler have any other names or titles?

A-There were many titles given in the various dialects of the peoples. This is one as will be found as recorded with that of the other rulers. Araaraart, known as one of the household of rulers in the Egyptian forces.

Q-Was this entity, as history gives it, one of the Pharaohs, or Rameses?

A-As one of the Pharaohs of which there were more than three thousand. This coming, as given, in the eleven thousand and thirteen to sixteen years before the Prince of Peace came into this country--coming in during the second year, see?   341-9

Q-Was this ruler, Araaraart, a native of this country (Egypt)?

A-A native of this country, though the father (Arart) the native of the North country, for this is how the second rule came in this country under this line of rulers, and remained same until the insurging forces from the Eastern hills came in, many, many, many years later.   341-10

There are many in the present earth's plane that experienced many of the changes--pro and con--during the Egyptian sojourn, that meant so much to the history of the human race from that period to the present ...and the activities of the entity (Araaraart), being the root or the beginning of that as became the tenet of the lessons given by Him who made Himself One with the Creative Energy in the earth's plane.

In the entity that we are to deal with there come many things that may be given as being **set**. Set in this sense: that conditions--by the application of correlation of entities, their urges, experiences--are in the earth's plane. That as the fact. The urge to accomplish certain ends toward the reestablishment, as it were, of the tenet that would draw man closer in his relationships to the Creative Energy is set forth. As to what the individual entity will do toward that condition set is the activity of the **will** of the entity...

Araaraart being the leader, or one in power--as man would classify such exalted position--yet being servant of all he became **master** of all through the ability to serve and to give others the opportunity to express, manifest, and give--in active action--their expression of laud and praise to the faith as founded through the example of the entity in and during that sojourn. The position as that of ruler coming in the youth--ruling, or leading and guiding those peoples for **many** years, correlating the activities of thought--and through thought the mind, and physical activity of leaders--toward **one concept** of truth toward relationship of man to the Maker, and the Maker's relationship to man. 341-24

Q-What is the significance of the character of the figure of the Sphinx?

A-In this particular period of Araaraart and of the priest (that began those understandings--and passed through those of the hell in the misinterpretation of same), there was even then the seeking through those channels that are today called archaeological research. In those periods when the first change had come in the position of the land, there had been an egress of peoples--or **things**, as would be called today--from the Atlantean land, when the Nile (or Nole, then) emptied into what is now the Atlantic Ocean, on the Congo end of the country. What is now the Sahara was a fertile land, a city that was builded in the edge of the land, a city of those that worshipped the sun--for the use of its rays were used for supplying from the elements that which is required in the present to be grown through a season; or the abilities to use both those of introgression and retrogression--and mostly retrograded, as we are in the present. The beginnings of these mounds were as an interpretation of that which was crustating in the land. (See, most of the people had tails then!) In these beginnings these were left.

When there was the entrance of Arart and Araaraart, they begin to build upon those mounds which were discovered through research. With the storehouse (where the records are still to be uncovered), there is a chamber, or passage from the right forepaw to this entrance of the record chamber, or record tomb. This may not be entered without an understanding, for those that were left as guards may not be passed until after a period of their regeneration in the Mount, or the fifth root race begins.

In the building of the pyramid, and that which is now called the Mystery of Mysteries, this was intended to be a **memorial**--as would be termed today--to that counsellor who ruled or governed, or who acted in the capacity of the director in the **material** things in the land. With the return of the Priest (as it had been stopped), this was later--by Isis, the queen, or the daughter of Ra--turned so as to present to those peoples in that land the relationships of man and the animal or carnal world with those changes that fade or fall away in their various effect. These may be seen in a different manner presented in many of the various sphinxes, as called, in other portions of the land--as the lion with the man, the various forms of wing, or characterizations in their various developments. These were as presentations of those projections that had been handed down in their various developments of that which becomes man--as in the present.   5748-6

(The entity was the) chief councillor, during the reign of the first conqueror (Arart) of this people, but is retained as the councillor to that ruler. When the second ruler (Araaraart) rises to position, still retained as chief councillor, and at the time of the divisions among the peoples, on account of conditions arising between the high priest (Ra Ta), or the head of the religious study, as would be termed today, the councillor persuaded, ruled, as it were, with the king for the banishment of the ruler priest, for, as is set, the law **above** that of the maker, and is, as has been seen and given, a factor in the entity's life to-day...

During this period was the completion of the memorial standing as the mystery of the ages today, and this (the Sphinx), as is seen, represents this councillor to the kings, for, as is seen in the figure itself, not as one of the kings made in beast form, yet overseeing, supervising giving council, giving strength, to the kings before and the kings since. The face, even as was given then, is the representation of this councillor to this great people. These, and many findings, as given, may be found in the base of the left forearm, or leg, of the prostate beast, in the base of the foundation. Not in the underground **channel** (as was opened by the ruler many years, centuries, later), but in the real base, or that as would be termed in the present parlance as the cornerstone. The council of the entity in that day brought much good to the peoples, not only of that land, but of many others.   953-24

The entity then was in the name of Arsrha and was the stone and the precious stone designer and carver for that entity, the ruler, Araaraart. The entity also gave the geometrical forces to the people, being then the mathematician, and an assistant to the astrologer and soothsayer of the day. He arranged then the first monuments that were being restored and builded in those places, being then the founder of now that mystery of mysteries, the Sphinx.

Q-In what capacity did this entity act regarding the building of the sphinx?

A-As the monuments were being rebuilt in the plains of that now called the pyramid of Gizeh, this entity builded, laid, the foundations; that is, superintended same, figured out the geometrical position of same in relation to those buildings as were put up of that connecting the sphinx. And the data concerning same may be found in the vaults in the base of the sphinx. We see this sphinx was builded as this:

The excavations were made for same in the plains above where the temple of Isis had stood during the deluge, occurring some centuries before, when this people (and this entity among them) came in from the north country and took possession of the rule of this country, setting up the first dynasty. The entity was with that dynasty, also in the second dynasty of Araaraart, when those buildings were begun. The base of the sphinx was laid out in channels, and in the corner facing the Gizeh may be found the wording of how this was founded, giving the history of the first invading ruler and the ascension of Araaraart.   195-14

With the reestablishing of the Priest and those in order for the regeneration of the peoples for the new race--which was a part of the experience of the entity in Poseidia, the entity became the supervisor of the excavations,--in studying the old records and in preparing and in building the house of records for the Atlanteans, as well as a part of the house initiate--or the Great Pyramid.

These colors, that presented or represented the various periods, as well as the interpretations of On, Ra Ta and Hermes, and the wise men of the period, were placed by the orders of the entity then--as Ajax-ol...

The pyramids, the house of records as well as the chamber in which the records are built in stone,--were put together by song.   2462-2

As there was the entering of the priest from the land Egypt to Poseidia, that there might be gained more of an understanding of the law of One (or God), that there might be the interpretations and the records of same carried to the Egyptian land, the **entity** returned--or **journeyed**, soon after the priest's return from Atlantis, to Egypt.

Hence, as there continued to be the rebellions and the exodus of the peoples in Atlantis before the final destruction...and when there was the putting of the young king against the royal native Aarat, the entity then took counsel--as it were--with self, and made Egypt the home...

Hence, of particular interest to the entity is the manner in which a record is kept of the activities of **every** branch of man's mental or spiritual activity...not only of the period but as to how the varied activities were to be in the land pertaining to the records of that which was to be, as well as that which had been, and the records in that monument or tomb or pyramid yet to be opened. Records also of those that were transferred from the destruction of the Atlantean land. For, the entity (Hept-supht) was still in charge of these records when the last of the peoples of Atlantis journeyed to the various quarters of the globe.   378-13

Q-Who was the individual that climbed to the top (of that tomb or first cone pyramid not yet uncovered, and the tomb of so many that were associated at that time) and clang the big sheet of metal of some kind?

A-The entity has not yet (January 25, 1932) approached for information. When he does, it will be given. It was the one who later became as the leader of those peoples that had **followed** the priest **back** from the Nubian or Abyssinian country.   294-131

Q-Was the entity (Hept-supht) the entity that, at the completion of the pyramid, clanged the sheet of metal? (This reading was given September 26, 1933. See reading 294-131 above.)

A-Clanged the sheet of metal at the completion of Gizeh, that **sealed** the records in the tomb yet to be discovered.

Q-Please describe incident and ceremony.

A-This is rather unreasonable, and may be best given with the entity present; for it would prolong much at the sitting here.

The apex (that has been long since removed by the sons of Heth) (Genesis 10:15), the crown or apex, was of metal; that was to be indestructible, being of copper, brass and gold with other alloys that were prepared by those of the period.

And, as this was to be (Gizeh we are speaking of) the place for the initiates and their gaining by personal application, and by the journey or journeys **through** the various activities--as in the ceremonial actions of those that became initiates, it became very fitting (to those as in Ra, and those of Ra Ta Ra) that there should be the crowning or placing of this symbol of the record, and of the initiates' place of activity, by one who represented both the old and the new; one representing then the sons of the law in Atlantis, Lemuria, Oz and Og. So, he that keeps the record, that keeps shut, or Hept-supht, was made or chosen as the one to **seal** that in the tomb.

The ceremony was long; the clanging of the apex by the gavel that was used in the sounding of the placing. Hence there has arisen from this ceremony many of those things that may be seen in the present; as the call to prayer, the church bell in the present, may be termed a descendant; the sounding of the trumpet the call to arms, or that as revelry; the sound as of those that make for mourning, in the putting away of the body; the sounding as of ringing in the new year, the sounding as of the coming of the bridegroom; **all** have their inception from the sound that was made that kept the earth's record of the earth's building, as to that from the change. The old record in Gizeh is from that as recorded from the journey to Pyrenees; and to 1998 from the death of the Son of man (as a man).   378-14

Much might be given respecting the activities of the entity who sealed with the seal of the Alta and Atlanteans, and the aid given in the completion of the pyramid of initiation as well as in the records that are to be uncovered.

At the completion of that called Gizeh, there was the mounting of that which completed the top, composed of a combination or fluxes of brass, copper, gold, that was to be sounded when all the initiates were gathered about the altar or the pyramid...

The Priest, with those gathered in and about the passage that led from the varied ascents through the pyramid, then offered there incense to the gods that dwelt among those in their activities in the period of developments of the peoples.

In the record chambers there were more ceremonies than in calling the peoples at the finishing of that called the pyramid. For, here those that were trained in the Temple of Sacrifice as well as in the Temple Beautiful were about the sealing of the record chambers. For, these were to be kept as had been given by the priests in Atlantis or Poseidia (Temple), when these records of the race of the developments of the laws pertaining to one were put in their chambers and to be opened only when there was the returning of those into materiality, or to earth's experience, when the change was imminent in the earth; which change, we see, begins in '58 and ends with the changes wrought in the upheavals and the shifting of the poles, as begins then the reign in '98 (as time is counted in the present) of those influences that have been given by many in the records that have been kept by those sojourners in this land of the Semitic peoples.

Then, the **sealings** were the activities of Hept-supht with Ra Ta and Isi-so and the king Araaraart...in the period, as given, of 10,500 years before the entering of the Prince of Peace in the land to study to become an initiate in or through those same activities that were set by Hept-supht in this dedicating ceremony.

Q-If the King's Chamber is on the 50'th course, on what course is this sealed room?

A-The sealed room of records is in a different place; not in this pyramid.

Q-Give in detail what the sealed room contains.

A-A record of Atlantis from the beginnings of those periods when the Spirit took form or began the encasements in that land, and the developments of the peoples throughout their sojourn, with the record of the first destruction and the changes that took place in the land, with the record of the **sojournings** of the peoples to the varied activities in other lands, and a record of the meetings of all the nations or lands for the activities in the destructions that became necessary with the final destruction of Atlantis and the buildings of the pyramid of initiation, with who, what, where, would come the opening of the records that are as copies from the sunken Atlantis; for with the change it must rise (the temple) again.

This in position lies, as the sun rises from the waters, the line of the shadow (or light) falls between the paws of the Sphinx, that was later set as the sentinel or guard, and which may not be entered from the connecting chambers from the Sphinx's paw (right paw) until the time has been fulfilled when the changes must be active in this sphere of man's experience.

Between, then, the Sphinx and the river.

Q-Were there any musical instruments sealed in that room?

A-Many...The lyre, the harp, the flute, the viola.   378-16

The entity...was the first to set the records that are yet to be discovered, or yet to be had of those activities in the Atlantean land, and for the preservation of the data, that as yet to be found from the chambers of the way between the sphinx and the pyramid of records.

Hence is it a wonder in the present that the entity is in this experience under the symbol and sign of both the sphinx and the pyramid, when there is to be given a new awakening in many portions of the earth?   1486-1

The temples of records lie just beyond that enigma that still is the mystery of mysteries to those who seek to know what were the manners of thought of the ancient sons who made man--a beast--as a part of the consciousness.   2402-2

Q-Where are those records or tablets made of that Egyptian experience?
A-In the Tomb of Records, as indicated. For the entity's tomb then was a part of the Hall of Records, which has not yet been uncovered. It lies between--or along that entrance from the Sphinx to the temple --or the pyramid; in a pyramid, of course, of its own...
For remember there are 32 of these plates.
Q-Is it indicated as to when, approximately, these tablets may be discovered, or uncovered?
A-By fifty-eight...
As for the physical records--it will be necessary to wait until the full time has come for the breaking up of much of that has been in the nature of selfish motives in the world. For, remember, these records were made from the angle of **world** movements. So must thy activities be in the present of the universal approach, but as applied to the individual. 2329-3

During the entity's sojourn; when there was begun the pyramid of understanding, or Gizeh--and only to the king's chamber was the pathway built. But the entity will see in the present the empty tomb period pass; hence rise to heights of activity in the present experience.
The entity's harps--and the entity's **menus**, as they would be termed in the present--are among those things preserved in the pyramid of unknown origin, as yet, but in the storehouse of records.   275-33

The entity persuaded many of those to make for the activities that would preserve to the peoples what would be in the present termed recipes or placards, and the like, that were the first of such intents brought to the Egyptian peoples (to be sure, not to the Atlanteans, but to the natives and those who had joined there to preserve such records) and the first attempt to make for a **written** language.   516-2

Q-In which pyramid are the records of the Christ?
A-That yet to be uncovered.   5749-2

Seek either of the three phases of the ways and means in which those records of the activities of individuals were preserved--the one in the Atlantean land, that sank, which will rise and is rising again; another in the place of the records that leadeth from the Sphinx to the hall of records, in the Egyptian land; and another in the Aryan or Yucatan land, where the temple there is overshadowing same. 2012-1

There was not only the adding to the monuments, but the Atlanteans aided in their activities with the creating of that called the Pyramid, with its records of events of the earth through its activity in all of the ages to that in which the new dispensation is to come. 281-43

The entity then builded the first of the pyramids that are yet not uncovered, and gave to the peoples that first concept of the square, the compass, and its meaning to those peoples as a mode of leaving for those that would study same, **history** in its making, history as has been builded.

Q-In referring to the uncovered pyramids in the Egyptian land, near what present place are those pyramids?

A-Between that known as the Mystery of the Ages and the river. 2124-3

Q-Was I a man at the time when among those that put up the first of the pyramids?

A-Then there was rather that as a woman, the entity was the ruler **over** those of man--and had many men as husbands, then.

Q-Which of the pyramids were these, and where are they now located?

A-As has been given, during this upheaval sojourn, as was in the beginning here, much were those sought after. These, as we find, are not as **now** in the Valley of the Kings; rather in that portion **farther** toward the head of what is now head of the Nile, though in the **hill** region--see? for the later pyramids, or those yet not uncovered, that has been spoken of, are between the Sphinx (or the Mystery) **and** the Nile, or the river, while these the **entity then** began building were **closer**--as it were--to the source of supply of material **from** which, **of** which, many of the later and the present were constructed. 993-3

Q-Who will uncover the history of the past in record form which are said to be near the sphinx in Egypt?

A-As was set in those records of the Law of One in Atlantis, that there would come three that would make of the perfect way of life. And as there is found those that have made, in their experience from their sojourn in the earth, a balance in their spiritual, their mental, their material experiences or existences, so may they become those channels through which there may be proclaimed to a seeking, a waiting, a desirous body, those things that proclaim how there has been preserved in the earth (that as is a shadow of the mental and the spiritual reservation of God to His children) those truths that have been so long proclaimed.   3976-15

With the periods of reconstruction after the return of the Priest, the entity joined with those who were active in putting the records in forms that were partially of the old characters of the ancient or early Egyptian, and part in the newer form of the Atlanteans.
These may be found, especially when the house or tomb of records is opened, in a few years from now.   2537-1

We might say that the whole of the records are in hieroglyphics; that might be interpreted in the form of both Egyptian and Persian. 1809-1

The interpretations of the records as we find here of the entity through the Egyptian experience (at the time of Ra Ta) in that age or period five thousand five hundred before the Prince of Peace entered Egypt, ten thousand five hundred in the experience as Aidol-Isisao...is not from English,--neither is it from the Egyptian language of the present day, but rather from the language that the entity's people brought into the land,--not Sanskrit, not the early Persian; though the peoples came from that land which is now a part of Iran or Carpathia...
The entity's experience in the life was that of many, many, **many** years, if it would be counted by the years of today,--it being more than six hundred years,--yes, season years,--that is, the seasons from winter to winter, or spring to spring, or summer to summer.   1100-26

There are found even to this day many of the plastic forms in that country (Egypt) of the entity (Isris, who was banished with Ra Ta), though this was 10,996 earth years before the Prince of Peace came. 538-9

Q-How can the Egyptian history be completed?
A-...The Egyptian history should be especially correlated for the benefit of those attempting to carry on the work at the present time; for with these correlated influences, much is being attempted at this time, even as during that experience. Time is used here only figuratively. Or again the cycle has rolled to that period when the individual entities again in the earth's experience gather for a definite work, with their various experiences as cause and effect through the various forms of the effect upon the environmental and hereditary conditions; yet these studied aright, any given fact may be worked out, even mathematically, as to what will be the response of an individual towards any portion of same.   254-47

There came then that period when all the pyramid or memorial was completed, that he, Ra, ascended into the mount and was borne away. 294-152

Astrologically we find little influences in the experience of this entity. For, the activities in the earth have so outweighed, outnumbered those. And no individual entity save the Master Himself has given greater material demonstration of the activities of the spiritual forces in the earth of **every** nature...

As to the appearances in the earth, then--these have been few.

Before this the entity was in the Scotch land. The entity began its activity as a prodigy, as one already versed in its association with the unseen--or the elemental forces; the fairies and those of every form that do not give expression in a material way and are only seen by those who are attuned to the infinite.

Then the entity in the developing was in the name Thomas Campbell, the reformer in the land of the present nativity; which, as combined later with Barton Stone, brought into activity that known as a denomination.

The intent and purpose was to **unify** all Protestant thought, speaking where the Book spoke, keeping silent where it kept silent...

Before that the entity was that one (Elisha) upon whom the mantle of Elijah fell--who in his material activity performed more unusual acts, or miracles, that are only comparable with the Master Himself...

Before **that** the entity was that one to whom was entrusted man's advent into the world--Noah.

From this we find those weaknesses. Then, not as one refraining from those, but beware ever of any strong drink or fruit of the vine passing the lips of **this** entity. 2547-1

The deluge was not a myth (as many would have you believe) but a period when man had so belittled himself with the cares of the world, with the deceitfulness of his own knowledge and power, as to require that there be a return to his dependence wholly--physically and mentally--upon the Creative Forces.

Will this entity see such again occur in the earth? Will it be among those who may be given those directions as to how, where, the elect may be preserved for the replenishing again of the earth?

Remember, not by water--for it is the mother of life in the earth-- but rather by the elements, fire. 3653-1

All thought forms in matter were put away--through the experience of Noah. 257-201

Q-In the relation to the history of Atlantis as presented, at what period did the flood as recorded in the Bible in which Noah took part, occur?

A-In the second of the eruptions, or--as is seen--two **thousand**--two-- two thousand and six--before the Prince of Peace, as time is counted now, or light years--day and night years. 364-6

The entity was in that land known now as the Peruvian, during the period of the Ohums, before the Incals and the peoples of the Poseidian land entered.   1916-5

The entity was among those that were the leaders of the Ohums when there was the breaking up of the deeps, and the land disappeared and reappeared.   2365-2

Before this (second rule in Egypt), we find in the now Peruvian country the peoples were destroyed in the submerging of the land. 2903-1

Before this (second rule in Egypt) we find in the days of the peoples coming from the waters in the submerged areas of the Southern portion as is now of Peru, when the earth was divided, and the people began to inhabit the earth again. The entity among those who succeeded in gaining the higher grounds.   470-2

Before this (second rule in Egypt) we find in that land known now as the Peruvian, and when there was the end of the Ohums (Aymaras) and their rule over the land. The entity was among those that came from the Atlantean lands and gave to the peoples much of the impulse of the added forces in a practical building up of **material** things of life, as pertaining to court hangings, ritualistic forces, the adding-to by the entity then of the worship to the sun and the solar forces, even to that of the offering of human sacrifice.   2887-1

THE DESTRUCTION OF MU

The entity was in that land now known as the American, during the periods when the Lemurian, or the lands of Mu and Zu, were being in their turmoils for destruction.

And the entity was among those that--in what is now not far from that land in which the entity in this sojourn first saw the light, that must in the near future fade again into those joinings with the land of Mu--established a temple of worship for those that escaped from the turmoils of the shifting of the earth at that particular period.

The entity, in the name of Oeueou, established near what is now Santa Barbara, the temple to the sun and the moon, for the satellite of the moon had not faded then.   509-1

The entity was in that land that has been termed Zu, or Lemuria, or Mu. This was before the sojourn of peoples in perfect body form; rather when they may be said to have been able to--through those developments of the period--be in the body or out of the body and act upon materiality. In the spirit or in flesh these made those things, those influences, that brought destruction; for the atmospheric pressure in the earth in the period was quite different from that experienced today.   436-2

The entity was in the Mongolian land, or in the land of Zu. 774-5

Before that (Ra Ta period of ancient Egypt) we find the entity was in that land now known as Mu, or the vanished land of the Pacific, the Peaceful during those periods when many of those had risen to power when there were being those banishments and preparations for the preserving; for they had known that the land must be soon broken up.

The entity was among those that journeyed from Mu to what is **now** Oregon, and there may **still** be seen **something** of the worship as set up, in what was the development **from** that set up by the entity's associates, as the totem, or the family tree...

Then the women **ruled**--rather than men.   630-2

In a strange land, now unknown in the world's experience; that lying westward from what is **now** southern California and Mexico. In this land the entity ruled as with an iron hand, for--from and through this land--many were the escapes from the various upheavals that occurred in those olden periods when there were the divisions of water and the divisions of land, an dry land appeared.   2669-1

The full consciousness of the ability to communicate with or to be aware of the relationships to the Creative Forces and the uses of same in material environs. This awareness during the era or age in the age of Atlantis and Lemuria or Mu brought what? Destruction to man. 1602-3

The entity was in the land of the long ago, in the Lemurian land, when there were the many changes coming about in the surface of the earth; even when there were those interpretations between the sons and the daughters of men and the sons of (and?) the daughters of God.

For they partook rather of those things when those expressions or periods of the injection of thought form and forces took their activity in the earth, and produced then in other portions of the earth's surface the monsters that would destroy, the periods when it is given "and in those days there were giants in the earth" (Genesis 6:4).

The entity then was among those that were of the daughters of the sons of God, those that with their physical bodies presented those influences and forces that made for that period of regeneration when not only the bodies must be presented as a living sacrifice, holy and acceptable unto Him, but that through these the soul and the mind... being a portion of the Universal Forces...express themselves.   1183-1

The entity was in the...Atlantean land, during those periods in which it was breaking up, and when the children of the Law of One...journeyed from the land into portions of what is now the Yucatan land.

The entity then was a Princess in the Temple of the Sun, or the Temple of Light; though others have interpreted it as the Sun.   2073-2

Before the periods of the final destruction (of Atlantis)...the entity came into that land now known as the Central America land, where the people built many of the temples that are being uncovered today...

The entity may answer much that has been questioned in the minds of those that have sought to know **why** there are no remains of the settlements or peoples that left the land without showing any **burial grounds**. For the entity was one who began the cremations, the ashes of much of which may be found in one of those temples.   914-1

The entity was in the Atlantean land, during those periods when there were the beginnings of the exodus...with the keepings of records...

Hence we find the entity making for the establishments in the Yucatan, in the Luzon, in what became the Inca, in the North American land, and in what later became the land of the Mound Builders in Ohio.   1215-4

The mounds (in Ohio) were called the replica or representative of the Yucatan experience, as well as the Atlantean and the Gobi land.   3004-1

The sons of the Atlanteans had settled and later became the Mound Builders, when joined with the peoples that had crossed the Pacific.   500-1

The entity was among those of the second generation of Atlanteans who struggled northward from Yucatan, settling in what is now a portion of Kentucky, Indiana, Ohio; being among those of the earlier period known as Mound Builders.   3528-1

Before that (period of the Temple of Sacrifice in Egypt) the entity was in...what is now Ohio, the entity was a sun worshipper, but one who worked with cloth, weaving of camels' hair and those things having to do with creating of clothes from the long-haired animals.   2780-3

The entity during the first of the appearances of man in the earth's plane, during that period when the five appeared. The entity then was in that now of the Nevada and Utah.   195-14

The entity was then among the peoples, the Indians, of the Iroquois; those of noble birth those that were the pure descendants of the Atlanteans, those that held to the ritualistic influences from nature itself.

Hence **all nature**, all experiences of nature, all natural forces become as a part of the entity's experience.   1219-1

(In Atlantis during) second disturbance--among those persuaded to go to land of Mayra or what is now Nevada and Colorado.   497-1

In the one before the (first Incal period in Peru) we find the entity was among those first in that country now known as the South-west, and among those who became the first cliff dwellers...The earthenware, that pieces of same may still be seen, though in earth's years thousands and thousands of years ago.   4805-1

In the one before this (in the days when the change was being made from the Atlantean countries to the northern portions of now Spanish forces) we find in the land of now the Utah and Nevada forces, when the first peoples were separated into groups as families...
In the ruins as are found that have arisen in the mounds and caves in the northwestern portion of New Mexico, may be seen some of the drawings the entity made some ten million years ago.   2665-2

In the one before the (Ra Ta period in ancient Egypt) we find (the entity) in that land known as the land of Og, now known as the American plateaus, or in north portion of now new Mexico and such...
In the one before this we find again in that land now known as Egypt. The entity then among those that set up the first of the pyramids. 993-1

In the city of Poseidon...(the entity) acted as the priestess in the Temple of Light...who oversaw the activities of the communications between the various lands--as from Om, Mu, the hierarchy land in that **now** known as the United States, in that particular portion of Arizona and Nevada, that are as a portion of the Brotherhood of those people from Mu.   812-1

From what was left of Lemuria, or Mu--in what is now lower California, portions of the valleys of death (an Atlantean priestess) journeyed there to see, to know.
And during those experiences much was set up that may be of interest to the entity, that will be a part of the discoveries of natures or natural formations in what is now the Canyon Island.
For **this** was the entity's place of the temple.   1473-1

The entity was in the Norse land, and among those who were the daring, as the sailors; and the entity was Eric (Ericsson the Great), as called through that experience; journeying to or settling in (America).
Q-How often and in what years did I cross the ocean?
A-In 1552, 1509 and 1502...
In this country there were the settlements in the northwestern lands; portions even of Montana were reached by the entity--because the entrance then was through the St.Lawrence, through the Lakes. 2157-1

Q-You will give an historical treatise on the origin and development of the Mayan civilization, answering questions.

A-Yes. In giving a record of the civilization in this particular portion of the world, it should be remembered that more than one has been and will be found as research progresses.

That which we find would be of particular interest would be that which superseded the Aztec civilization, that was so ruthlessly destroyed or interrupted by Cortez.

In that preceding this we had rather a combination of sources, or a high civilization that was influenced by injection of forces from other channels, other sources, as will be seen or may be determined by that which may be given.

From time as counted in the present we would turn back to 10,600 years before the Prince of Peace came into the land of promise, and find a civilization being disturbed by corruption from within to such measures that the elements join in bringing devastation to a stiffnecked and adulterous people.

With the second and third upheaval in Atlantis, there were individuals who left those lands and came to this particular portion then visible.

But, understand, the surface was quite different from that which would be viewed in the present. For, rather than being a tropical area it was more of the temperate, and quite varied in the conditions and positions of the face of the areas themselves.

In following such a civilization as a historical presentation, it may be better understood by taking into consideration the activities of an individual or group--or their contribution to such civilization. This of necessity, then, would not make for a complete historical fact, but rather the activities of an individual and the followers, or those that chose one of their own as leader.

Then, with the leavings of the civilization in Atlantis (in Poseidia, more specific), Iltar--with a group of followers that had been of the household of Atlan, the followers of the worship of the One--with some ten individuals--left this land Poseidia, and came westward entering what would now be a portion of Yucatan. And there began, with the activities of the peoples there, the development into a civilization that arose much in the same manner as that which had been in the Atlantean land. Others had left the land later. Others had left earlier. There had been the upheavals also from the land of Mu, or Lemuria, and these had their part in the changing, or there was the injection of their tenets in the varied portions of the land--which was much greater in extent until the final upheaval of Atlantis, or the islands that were later upheaved, when much of the contour of the land in Central America was changed to that similar in outline to that which may be seen in the present.

The first temples that were erected by Iltar and his followers were destroyed at the period of change physically in the contours of the land. That now being found, and a portion already discovered that has laid in waste for many centuries, was then a combination of those peoples from Mu, Oz and Atlantis.

Hence, these places partook of the earlier portions of that peoples called the Incal; though the Incals were themselves the successors of those of Oz, or Og, in the Peruvian land, and Mu in the southern portions of that now called California and Mexico and southern New Mexico in the United States.

This again found a change when there were the injections from those peoples that came with the divisions of those peoples in that called the promised land. Hence we may find in these ruins that which partakes of the Egyptian, Lemurian and Oz civilizations, and the later activities partaking even of the Mosaic activities.

Hence each would ask, what specific thing is there that we designate as being a portion of the varied civilizations that formed the earlier civilization of this particular land?

The stones that are circular, that were of the magnetized influence upon which the Spirit of the One spoke to those peoples as they gathered in their service, are of the earliest Atlantean activities in religious service, as would be called today.

The altars upon which there would be the cleansings of the bodies of individuals (not human sacrifice; for this came much later with the injection of the Mosaic, and these activities of the area), these were later the altars upon which individual activities--that would today be termed hate, malice, selfishness, self-indulgence--were cleansed from the body through the ceremony, through the rise of initiates from the source of light, that came from the stones upon which the angels of light during the periods gave their expression to the peoples.

The pyramid, the altars before the doors of the varied temple activities, was an injection from the people of Oz and Mu; and will be found to be separate portions, and that referred to in the Scripture as high places of family altars, family gods, that in many portions of the world became again the injection into the activities of groups in various portions, as gradually there were the turnings of the people to the satisfying and gratifying of self's desires, or as the Baal or Baalilal activities again entered the peoples respecting their associations with those truths of light that came from the gods to the peoples, to mankind, in the earth.

With the injection of those of greater power in their activity in the land, during that period as would be called 3,000 years before the Prince of Peace came, those peoples that were of the Lost Tribes, a portion came into the land; infusing their activities upon the peoples from Mu in the southernmost portion of that called America or United States, and then moved on to the activities in Mexico, Yucatan, centralizing that now about the spots where the central of Mexico now stands, or Mexico City. Hence there arose through the age a different civilization, a **mixture** again.

Those in Yucatan, those in the adjoining lands as begun by Iltar, gradually lost in their activities; and came to be that people termed, in other portions of America, the Mound Builders.

Ready for questions.

Q-How did the Lost Tribe reach this country?

A-In boats.

Q-Have the most important temples and pyramids been discovered?

A-Those of the first civilization have been discovered, and have not all been opened; but their associations, their connections, are being replaced--or attempting to be rebuilt. Many of the second and third civilization may **never** be discovered, for these would destroy the present civilization in Mexico to uncover same.

Q-By what power or powers were these early pyramids and temples constructed?

A-By the lifting forces of those gases that are being used gradually in the present civilization, and by the fine work or activities of those versed in that pertaining to the source from which all power comes.

For, as long as there remains those pure in body, in mind, in activity, to the law of the One God, there is the continued resource for meeting the needs, or for commanding the elements and their activities in the supply of that necessary in such relations.

Q-In which pyramid or temple are the records mentioned in the readings (364 series) given through this channel on Atlantis, in April, 1932?

A-As given, that temple was destroyed at the time there was the last destruction in Atlantis.

Yet, as time draws nigh when changes are to come about, there may be the opening of those three places where the records are one, to those that are the initiates in the knowledge of the One God:

The temple by Iltar will then rise again. Also there will be the opening of the temple or hall of records in Egypt, and those records that were put into the heart of the Atlantean land may also be found there --that have been kept, for those that are of that group.

The **records** are **One**.

We are through for the present.   5750-1

We have the records here of that entity now known as 877, in the experience as Muzuen, the son of Mu, in that experience as the Prince in the Gobi land...

The land was among those in which there was the first appearance of those that were as separate entities or souls disentangling themselves from material or that we know as animal associations. For the projections of these had come from those influences that were termed Lemure, or Lemuria, or the land of Mu.

These then we find as the period when there was the choice of that soul that became in its final earthly experience the Savior, the Son in the earth indwellings, or of those as man sees or comprehends as the children of men.

The land under those influences of Mu became as what would be termed in the present as among or the highest state of advancement in material accomplishments for the benefit or conveniences for man's indwelling, or the less combative influence of the elemental or of that man knows as nature--in the raw.

These activities included those things known as colonies or groups that were gathered for a common purpose, and submitting themselves to an order as might be proclaimed by one of their own number. Or Mu, the ruler, the prophet, the sage, the lawgiver, was of this particular group.

This influence or force covered something like what would be termed now a hundred and two thousand square miles of domain. This land or domain then was at that stage or period of advancement when there were those things from which clothing and leather were made, and materials for building. And here, as may be discovered when these are excavated, the greater use of timbers or wood as a building material was exercised just prior to the entrance of this entity, Muzuen, into this environ.

Flax, cotton, ramie, silk and such properties were in active use; as were workers in the metals--gold, silver, lead, radium.

All these had been and were in use by those peoples under these environs, when the entity entered into the experience--a period that collaborated or made for what would be called collaboration of the teachings of Saneid, Ra Ta, Og, and the remnants of the Atlantean experience...

There was the beginning of the building of the temple of gold, or overlaid--its beams, its walls, its panelings with many colored, polished woods...

Muzuen was five feet eleven inches. Blue of eye. Hair dark gold. Six-fingered; five-toed.

In dress; leather, linen, cotton, silk--in their varied seasons...

And during the entity's experience when the greater warning was through the destruction of the mighty forests of the north, upon what are now the mountains of lime, salt and sodas, the entity in these combinations saw the development of what are now called explosives for defense. Armors were not of this people, though later became a part of same.

Ornaments, adornments; the finer works in laces, fabrics, spun gold, silver, carved ivory and the like--these were the portions.   877-10

Q-Continue with reading 877-10.

A-...As to the manner of defense and offense, as has been indicated, much that is yet to be found again was a part of those preparations in those periods. For these that had to do with the setting of long-period drums for defense in which there might be any attempts by other's to interfere to cause their **own** undoing...

As to the manner of locomotions in the experience, the entity injected much of that which--when there is the discovery of the Temple of Gold --will be found; lifts or elevators, the one-line electrical car, the very fast aerial locomotion...

The entity lived to a hundred and eighty and six years.

Q-What was the basic philosophy of that day?

A-He who eats must produce same; that was the material relationship. The spiritual philosophy was that the relationships of the Father **through** the soul forces manifest themselves in given periods or **messages** to those that were called to act in the capacity of the priests.

Q-Was there a relationship then between myself and Ra Ta of Egypt? If so, how were the two countries connected or akin in their civilization?

A-Emissary, and by those activities as has been indicated; as it was with Saneid, On, and those in Carpathia, the Pyrenees and Atlantis.   877-11

Q-Continue with reading 877-11.

A-...The entity was among the first to establish an exchange between other lands, owing to those associations that were begun with the lands now known as or called India, Egypt, Caucasia, Pyrenees and those of the latter portions of the Atlantean land--in those periods, or this particular period in the Gobi land--as in most of the others save the Atlantean; or these groups, or this people of Mu, or--as indicated-- Muzuen, the son of Mu that had first builded this particular city or group that became or was the City of Gold--or Golden; as we have indicated should be later discovered...

Those very **old**, as would be termed today, were **mercifully** put away.

In those activities with the associations with other groups, other nations, this group or this nation or this people--headed by the entity-- first made what would today be called coin, which was of gold. It was almost square but with a hole in same, smooth but edged that it might be known from other groups that gradually used the same--and was changed to this when it was found that the Atlanteans' were almost the same. Holes in same and strung to be worn about the waist or about the neck. These--as the exchange then--were as so much daily labor or exercise. There were **no** individuals that did not labor if they were above twelve years of age, unless they were ill, lame or blind or with child--others **all** labored! There were **no** individuals that did nothing!...

As for the groups in its own land, as has been indicated, the worshipfulness was in a temple where those gathered that made for speechmaking. There were no priests as in many other lands. They were **all** those that spoke and would be called a forum, or more as a group known in thine own land as the Quakers--who spoke when they were moved by not anxiety, not wrath, but by the spirit of **thoughtfulness**--or the recognizing of Mind, the Builder. But the laborer was heard as well as those that were of **every** trade as would be termed in the present.

In the exchange between those of other lands, when these associations were established, there were the spices from India, linens and cut stones from Egypt. These were especially for the women.

There was equality between the sexes during that experience. There was only, as has been indicated, monogamy; not polygamy **ever** practiced among these peoples. The rights of each were the rights of the other. When by injury, wrath, accident the mate was destroyed or killed, or by death, then the **choice** was made by the individual and seconded by those that were in the authority as to judgements. But those that judged were **as** the common people, as those in authority. For only the Prince, only those of the household of the Prince were the last word-- but they never as lords, priests, presidents or dictators, but as **interpreters of** the law between man and men: And **all** interpreters were moved to speech, or moved by the spirit in that ye call religion.

Q-What was the system of taxation?

A-There was **no** taxation. **All labored**; hence not necessary for taxation. For they were **all** the Government, for all were as one. A common storehouse, a common bank, a common activity throughout in each; each giving as it were the day for that of a piece of gold. A piece of gold then was a day's labor. Not as dollars, not as cents, not as shillings, not as pence, not as livres, not as any of those used at present; but each piece represented a day's **labor**, and the women and the children were the same as the men--for each represented **their** ability to give that they could in their respective activity, and each--for it was all for the one, and one for the all.   877-12

The entity was in what is now known as the Mongoloid or the Gobi land, when there were those interpretations by the Carpathians, those of the land of On, those by Saneid, those by Ra Ta; and those studies first from the earlier portions of the Zoroasters, as termed today.

The entity then was a princess in the Golden Temple...

Hence we may find the entity's interests in many of the various thoughts that have grown to seed in the varied groups and the varied traditions of groups in their activity or a social order, or a worship-fulness order. Yet to the entity they all lead from the one, the source, the sun--with its **inner** meaning.   1219-1

The entity was in what is now called the Gobi land, with the children of the Sun. Then in the name Taoi, the entity was a priestess in the Temple of Gold, that is yet to be unearthed, that there may be more known of those things that are as old as the earth itself.   2402-2

For with the City of Gold there will be found--well, there is not so much now even in the treasury or vaults of the U.S.A.   1554-6

A whole city--yes, a temple--will be uncovered; as will be the City of Gold in the Gobi land.   1554-3

The entity there (Peru) made use of the metal known as iron, or the combinations of iron and copper--which have long since been removed from use in the present; or copper so tempered by the use of same with a little of the iron, or in its formation in such a way and manner as to be hardened to the abilities for same to be used much in the way that many of those combinations have been found in the Egyptian, the Peruvian and portions of the Chaldean lands--and **more** will be found in the Indo-China city yet to be uncovered...

From the direct current passing through the activity of the fusing of metals and the transmutation that forms from same, and the active forces as turned into that which it makes for the clearing of the refuse forces of the ore in such a manner that the very fuse itself becomes the source of an alternating current to which there is added then a stepped-up activity in which the direct current then becomes the source of the energy to produce this fusing of metals or ores.

Again we find in the activities of same the entity made a soon return to the Egyptian land, when the entity made preparations for a part of the armor, or part of the defense...

All of these activities then became a part of the use of electrical forces for metals and their activity upon same to be used as carbon-izing them, or directing them in manners in which they became as magnetic forces for the applications to portions of the body for transmuting or changing the **effect** of activities upon the physical energies and forces of the body; able to use same as re-ionizing or re-generating the bodily forces themselves.   470-22

Each nation, each people have builded--by the very spirit of the peoples themselves--a purposeful position in the skein, the affairs not only of the earth but of the universe.   1554-3

When man began to defy God in the earth and the confusion arose which is represented in the Tower of Babel--these are representations of what was then the basis, the beginnings of nations. Nations were set up then in various portions of the land, and each group, one stronger than another, set about to seek their gratifications...
What is the spirit of America? Most individuals proudly boast "freedom." Freedom of what? When ye bind men's hearts and minds through various ways and manners, does it give them freedom of speech? Freedom of worship? Freedom from want?...
What then of nations? In Russia there comes the hope of the world, not as that sometimes termed of the Communistic, or the Bolshevistic; no. But freedom, freedom! that each man will live for his fellow man! The principle has been born. It will take years for it to be crystallized, but out of Russia comes again the hope of the world. Guided by what? That friendship with the nation that hath even set on its present (1944) monetary unit "In God We Trust"...
That principle (is) being forgotten--when such is the case, and that is the sin of America.
So in England, from whence have come the ideas--not ideals--ideas of being just a little better than the other fellow. Ye must **grow** to that in which ye will deserve to be known, deserve to receive. That has been, that is, the sin of England.
As in France, to which this principle first appealed, to which then came that which was the gratifying of the desire of the body--that is the sin of France...
The sin of China? Yea, there is the quietude that will not be turned aside, saving itself by the slow growth. There has been a growth, a stream through the land in ages which asks to be left alone to be just satisfied with that within itself. It awoke one day and cut its hair off! And it began to think and to do something with its thinking! This, here, will be one day the cradle of Christianity, as applied in the lives of men. Yea, it is far off as man counts time...
As in India, the cradle of knowledge not applied, except within self. What is the sin of India? **Self**, and left the 'ish' off--just self. 3976-29

Changes are coming, this may be sure--an evolution, or revolution, in the ideas of religious thought. The basis of it for the world will eventually come out of Russia; not Communism, no!--but rather that which is the basis of same, as Christ taught--His kind of Communism.   452-5

Those who are in power must know that they **are** their brother's keeper, and give expression to that..."Thou shalt love the Lord with all thy heart and mind and body, and thy neighbor as thyself" (Luke 10:27)...

It is true that in some of those factions in Russia this is an attempt, yet there **are** those who have applied and do apply same in not only the economic life but attempt to in the mental and spiritual life. And this brings or works hardships where it should **not** be.

Q-Make such comment as may be presented on the following affairs, as I name them: The unemployment situation in America.

A-...There must be more and more return to the toil upon the land, and not so much of the makeshift of labor in specific or definite fields. For unless this comes, there must and will come disruption, turmoils strife.

Q-Labor and capital in America.

A-Unless there is the give and the take, and the considerations of those that produce--so that they have as much of the use and the division of the excess and profits of the labors--there must be brought greater turmoils in the land. (Reading given in 1938)   3976-19

Ye are to have turmoils--ye are to have strifes between capital and labor. Ye are to have a division in thine own land before there is the second of the presidents that next will not live through his office--a mob rule!...

Unless there is, then, a more universal oneness of purpose on the part of all, this will one day bring--here--in America--revolution.

Q-Is the Fascist movement a danger to this country?

A- Any **movement** that is other than that of the brotherhood of man, the Fatherhood of God is dangerous...

Raise not democracy nor any other name above the brotherhood of man, the Fatherhood of God. (Reading given in 1939)   3976-24

What right has any man to set state or nation above that principle of brotherly love?   3976-27

Those principles of self-government have gone to the best rule through many many ages.   2801-5

Q-Will prohibition be lost in America and about when?

A-No one may ever **legislate goodness** into the heart or the soul of anyone.   3976-8

The entity's activities would be with the granaries, as it were, of the world. Learn to deal, then, with those portions of Saskatchewan as well as in the Pampas area of the Argentine, as well as in portions of South Africa. For these rich areas, with some portions of Montana and Nevada, must feed the world.   3651-1

The world, as a world--that makes for the disruption, for the discontent--has lost its ideal. Man may not have the same **idea**. Man-- **all** men--may have the same **ideal**..."Thou shalt love the Lord thy God with all thine heart, thy neighbor as thyself!" This is the whole law, this is the answer to the world, to each and every soul. That is the answer to the world conditions as they exist today.   3976-8

Let that rather be thy watchword, "I am my brother's keeper." Who is thy brother? Whoever, wherever he is that bears the imprint of the Maker in the earth, be he black, white, gray or grizzled, be he young, be he Hottentot, or on the throne or in the president's chair. 2780-3

If those in position to give of their means, their wealth, their education, their position, **do not** take these things into consideration, there must be that leveling that will come.

For unless these are considered, there must eventually become a revolution...things as crime, riots, and every nature of disturbance.   3976-19

Differences of opinions in the different religious groups, as well as the economic conditions in the varied land, will be those things that will cause greater disputations.

Q-Will it be possible to maintain a fair standard of living for our own people while helping to raise economic standards elsewhere in world?

A-Not only **must** it be possible, it **must** be **done**! if there will be **any** lasting peace. It must begin in the hearts, minds of individuals.

Q-Would it be feasible to work out an international currency, or an international stabilization of exchange values?

A-This, too, will be worked toward. It will be a long, long time before established. There may indeed be another war over just such conditions, but it'll be a step in the right direction--in the attempts in bringing peace at this time (1943).   3976-28

Without (the brotherhood of the world) there will again come the Armageddon, and in the same there will be seen that the Christian forces will **again** move westward.   900-272

In love the world was saved and made; in hate and indifference the world may be destroyed.   903-3

More wars, more bloodshed have been shed over the racial and religious differences than over any other problem!   3976-27

In England, during the Crusades, the entity learned much, that they who fight, they who war against their brethren find themselves warring as against the spirit of truth. For that as is sown in dread, must be reaped in turmoil and in strife.   1226-1

Q-We seek at this time such information as will be of value and interest to those present, regarding the spiritual, mental and physical changes which are coming to the earth. (Reading given in 1934)

A-...First, then: There is soon to come into the world a body; one of our own number here that to many has been a representative of a sect, of a thought, of a philosophy, of a group, yet one beloved of all men in all places where the universality of God in the earth has been proclaimed, where oneness of the Father as God is known and is consciously magnified in the activities of individuals that proclaim the acceptable day of the Lord. Hence that one John, the beloved in the earth--his name shall be John, and also at the place where he met face to face (Genesis 32:30?). He comes as a messenger, not as a forerunner, but as a messenger; for these are periods when mental, material, are to be so altered in the affairs of men as to be even bringing turmoil to those that have not seen that the **Spirit** is moving in His ways to bring the knowledge of the Father in the hearts and lives of men.

When, where, is to be this one? In the hearts and minds of those that have set themselves in that position that they be come a channel through which spiritual, mental and material things become one in the purpose and desires of that physical body!

As to the material changes that are to be as an omen, as a sign to those that this is shortly to come to pass--as has been given of old, the sun will be darkened (Joel 2:10) and the earth shall be broken up in divers places--and **then** shall be **proclaimed**--through the spiritual interception in the hearts and minds and souls of those that have sought His way--that **his** star has appeared, and will point (pause) the way for those that enter into the holy of holies in themselves. For, God the Father, God the teacher, God the director, in the minds and hearts of men, must ever be **in** those that come to know Him as first and foremost in the seeking of those souls; for He is first the **God** to the individual and as He is exemplified, as He is manifested in the heart and in the acts of the body, of the individual, He becomes manifested before men. And those that seek in the latter portion of the year of our Lord (as ye have counted in and among men) '36, he will appear!

As to the changes physical again: The earth will be broken up in the western portion of America. The greater portion of Japan must go into the sea. The upper portion of Europe will be changed as in the twinkling of an eye. Land will appear off the east coast of America. There will be the upheavals in the Arctic and in the Antarctic that will make for the eruption of volcanoes in the Torrid areas, and there will be the shifting then of the poles--so that where there has been those of a frigid or the semi-tropical will become the more tropical, and moss and fern will grow. And these will begin in those periods in '58 to '98, when these will be proclaimed as the periods when His light will be seen again in the clouds. As to times, as to seasons, as to places, **alone** is it given to those who have named the name--and who bear the mark of those of His calling and His election in their bodies. To them it shall be given.

As to those things that deal with the mental of the earth, these shall call upon the mountains to cover many. As ye have seen those in lowly places raised to those of power in the political, in the machinery of nations' activities, so shall ye see those in high places reduced and calling on the waters of darkness to cover them. And those that in the inmost recesses of theirselves awaken to the spiritual truths that are to be given, and those places that have acted in the capacity of teachers among men, the rottenness of those that have ministered in places will be brought to light and turmoils and strifes shall enter. And, as there is the wavering of those that would enter as emissaries, as teachers, from the throne of life, the throne of light, the throne of immortality, and wage war in the air with those of darkness, then know ye the Armageddon is at hand. For with the great numbers of the gathering of the hosts of those that have hindered and would make for man and his weaknesses stumbling blocks, they shall wage war with the spirits of light that come into the earth for this awakening; that have been and are being called by those of the sons of men into the service of the living God. For He, as ye have been told, is not the God of the dead, not the God of those that have forsaken Him, but those that love His coming, that love His associations among men--the God of the **living**, the God of **Life**! For, He **IS** Life!

Who shall proclaim the acceptable year of the Lord in Him that has been born in the earth in America? Those from that land where there has been the regeneration, not only of the body but the mind and the spirit of men, **they** shall come and declare that John Peniel is giving to the world the new **order** of things. Not that these that have been proclaimed have been refused, but that they are made **plain** in the minds of men, that they may know the truth and the truth, the life, the light will make them free.

"I have declared this" (John 17:26?), that has been delivered unto me to give unto you, ye that sit here and that hear and that see a light breaking in the east, and have heard, have seen thine weaknesses and thine faultfindings, and know that He will make thy paths straight if ye will but live that **ye know** this day--then may the next step, the next word, be declared unto thee. For ye in your weakness (pause) have known the way, through that as ye have made manifest of the **spirit** of truth and light that has been proclaimed into this earth...The weakling, the unsteady, must enter into the crucible and become as naught, even as He, that they may know the way. I, Halaliel, have spoken.

Q-What are the world changes to come this year (1934) physically.

A-The earth will be broken up in many places. The early portion will see a change in the physical aspect of the west coast of America. There will be open waters appear in the northern portions of Greenland. There will be new lands seen off the Caribbean Sea, and **dry** land will appear. There will be the falling away in India of much of the material suffering that has been brought on a troubled people. There will be the reduction of one risen to power in central Europe to naught. The young king son will soon reign. In America in the political forces we see a re-stabilization of the powers of the peoples in their own hands a breaking up of the rings, the cliques in many places. South America shall be shaken from the uppermost portion to the end, and in the Antarctic off of Tierra Del Fuego **land**, and a strait with rushing waters.

Q-To what country is the reference made regarding the young king.

A-In Germany.

Q-Is America fulfilling her destiny?

A-...If there is not the acceptance in America of the closer brother-hood of man, the love of the neighbor as self, civilization must wend its way westward--and again must Mongolia, must a hated people, be raised.

Is it filling its destiny?...Yea, here and there...for, as given, His messenger shall appear there.   3976-15

Q-Three hundred years ago Jacob Boehme decreed Atlantis would rise again at this crisis time when we cross from this Piscean Era into the Aquarian. Is Atlantis rising now? Will it cause a sudden convolution and about what year?

A-In 1998 we may find a great deal of the activities as have been wrought by the gradual changes that are coming about. These are at the periods when the cycle of the solar activity, or the years as related to the sun's passage through the various spheres of activity become paramount or catamount (?) (tantamount?) to the change between the Piscean and Aquarian age. This is a gradual, not a cata-clysmic activity in the experience of the earth in this period.   1602-3

The entity was in Atlantis when there were the periods of the first upheavals and destruction that came to the land, as must in the next generation come to other lands.   3209-2

Poseidia will be among the first portions of Atlantis to rise again. Expect it in sixty-eight and sixty-nine. Not so far away.   958-3

There will be found much more gold in the lands under the sea than there is in the world circulation today...And as may be known, when the changes begin, these portions (Bimini) will rise among the first.   587-4

The first highest civilization will be uncovered in some of the adjacent lands to the west and south of the isles (Bimini), see?

Q-Is this the continent known as Alta or Poseidia?

A-A temple of the Poseidians was in a portion of this land.996-12

As to conditions in the geography of the world, of the country--changes here are gradually coming about.

No wonder, then, that the entity feels the need, the necessity for change of central location. For, many portions of the east coast will be disturbed, as well as many portions of the west coast, as well as the central portion of the U.S.

In the next few years lands will appear in the Atlantic as well as in the Pacific. And what is the coast line now of many a land will be the bed of the ocean. Even many of the battle fields of the present, will be ocean, will be the seas, the bays, the lands over which the **new** order will carry on their trade as one with another.

Portions of the now east coast of New York, or New York City itself, will in the main disappear. This will be another generation, though, here; while the southern portions of Carolina, Georgia--these will disappear. This will be much sooner.

The waters of the lakes will empty into the Gulf, rather than the waterways over which such discussions have been recently made. It would be well if the waterway were prepared, but not for that purpose for which it is at present being considered.

Then the area where the entity is now located (Virginia Beach for reading) will be among the safety lands, as will be portions of what is now Ohio, Indiana and Illinois, and much of the southern portion of Canada and the eastern portion of Canada; while the western land--much of that is to be disturbed--in this land--as, of course, much in other lands...

Q-Will Los Angeles be safe?

A-Los Angeles, San Francisco, most all of these will be among those that will be destroyed before New York even.

Q-Is Virginia Beach to be safe?

A-It is the center--and the only seaport and center--of the White Brotherhood.   1152-11

Q-Will the earth upheavals during 1936 affect San Francisco as it did in 1906?

A-This'll be a baby beside what it'll be in '36!   270-30

Q-Are details of the earth's eruptions in 1936 so fixed that you can give me an outline of the Pacific Coast area to be affected?

A-...That some are **due** and **will** occur is **written,** as it were...as to specific date or time in the present this may not be given.   270-32

Q-What is the primary cause of earth quakes?

A-The cause of these, of course, are the movements about the earth; that is, internally--and the cosmic activity or influence of other planetary forces and stars and their relationships produce or bring about the activities of the elementals of the earth; that is, the Earth, the Air, the Fire, the Water--and those combinations make for the replacement in the various activities.

If there are the greater activities in the Vesuvius, or Pelee, then the southern coast of California--and the areas between Salt Lake and the southern portions of Nevada--may expect, within the three months following same, an inundation by the earthquakes.

But these, as we find, are to be more in the southern than in the northern hemisphere.   270-35

Q-How soon will changes in the earth's activity begin to be apparent?

A-When there is the first breaking up of some conditions in the South Sea (that's South Pacific, to be sure), and those as apparent in the sinking or rising of that that's almost opposite same, or in the Mediterranean, and the Aetna area, then we may know it has begun.

Q-How long before this will begin?

A-The indications are that some of these have already begun, yet others would say these are only temporary. We would say they have begun. '36 will see the greater changes apparent, to be sure.

Q-Will there be any physical changes in the earth's surface in North America? If so, what sections will be affected, and how?

A-All over the country we will find many physical changes of a minor or greater degree. The greater change, as we find, in America, will be the North Atlantic Seaboard. Watch New York! Connecticut, and the like.

Q-When will this be?

A-In this period. As to just when--

Q-What, if any, changes will take place around Norfolk area, Va?

A-No **material**, that would be effective to the area, other than would eventually become more beneficial--in a port, and the like.

Q-Is the Rosicrucian Order, Amorc, fully aware of the impending changes in the earth's activities, and is it taking proper steps to meet these conditions?

A-This, to be sure, would involve many of those that are secrets, or for many of only initiates for this particular order. There is being a concerted effort to warn those of that particular trend of thought in the direction, though the period as is mostly given, as we find, **begins** then and goes on--rather than being the period of the greater change, as is being taught by these--see? Some of these, it's best not to give, for we would involve others; for some here are not initiates!   311-8

Q-Are there to be physical changes in the earth's surface in Alabama?
A-Not for some period yet.
Q-When will the changes begin?
A-Thirty-six to thirty-eight.
Q-What part of the State will be affected?
A-The northwestern part, and the extreme southwestern part. 311-9

Q-Are the physical changes in Alabama predicted for 1936-38 to be gradual or sudden changes?
A-Gradual.
Q-What form will they take?
A-To be sure, that may depend much that deals with the metaphysical, as well as to that people called actual or in truth! for as understood--or should be by the entity--there are those conditions that in the activity of individuals, in line of thought and endeavor, keep oft many a city and many a land intact through their application of the spiritual laws in their associations with individuals. This will take more of the form here in the change, as we find, through the sinking of portions with the following up of the inundations by this overflow.
Q-When will the physical changes start in Norfolk and vicinity?
A-This would be nearer to '58 than to '38 or '36, as we find. 311-10

Q-In view of the uncertainty of existing conditions, did I act wisely in establishing my home in Norfolk?
A-It's a mighty good place, and a safe place when turmoils are to arise, though it may appear that it may be in the line of those areas to rise, while many a higher land will sink. This is a good area to stick to. 2746-2

As to those experiences paralleling the cycle of astrological activity now (April 28, 1941),--beginning on the morrow,--there will be the Sun, the Moon, Jupiter, Uranus and Venus all in the one sign.
When last this occurred, as indicated, the earth throughout was in turmoil, in strife...
The powers of light and darkness, as then, as sixteen hundred years before. As in those periods, so today,--we find nation against nation; the powers of death, destruction...
Strifes will arise through the period. Watch for them near Davis Strait in the attempts there for the keeping of the life line to a land open. Watch for them in Libya and in Egypt, in Ankara and in Syria, through the straits about those areas above Australia, in the Indian Ocean and the Persian Gulf.
Ye say that these are of the sea; yes,--for there shall the breaking up be, until there are those in every land that shall say that this or that shows the hand of divine interference. 3976-26

Q-What great change or the beginning of what change, if any, is to take place in the earth in the year 2000 to 2001 A.D.?
A-When there is a shifting of the poles. Or a new cycle begins. 826-8

(The records are) to be opened only when there was the returning of those into materiality, or to earth's experience, when the change was imminent in the earth; which change we see, begins in '58 and ends with the changes wrought in the upheavals and the shifting of the poles, as begins then the reign in '98 (as time is counted in the present). 378-16

The catastrophes of outside forces to the earth in '36 will come from the shifting of the equilibrium of the earth itself in space, with those consequential effects upon the various portions of the country--or world --affected by same.   3976-10

Q-What will be the type and extent of the upheavals in '36?
A-The wars, the upheavals in the interior of the earth, and the shifting of same by the differentiation in the axis as respecting the positions from the Polaris center.   5748-6

The entity then was among those who...gathered to rid the earth of the enormous animals which overran the earth, but ice the entity found, nature, God, changed the poles and the animals were destroyed. 5249-1

(In Atlantis) when there were the attempts of those to bring quiet, to bring order out of chaos by the destructive forces that has made for the eruptions in the land that had divided the lands and had changed not only the temperature but to a more torrid region by the shifting of the activities of the earth itself.   884-1

The extreme northern portions were then (at the time of the Five Projections) the southern portions, or the polar regions were then turned to where they occupied more of the tropical and semi-tropical regions; hence it would be hard to discern or disseminate the change...
When there came the uprisings in the Atlantean land, and the sojourning southward--with the turning of the axis--the white and yellow races came more into that portion of Egypt, India, Persia and Arabia. 364-13

The entity was in the Gobi land, yes--one of the great places to which the Five Nations or Five Peoples came...(and) there were the shiftings of those lands into that near unto their present positions.   1580-1

There will be the shifting then of the poles--so that where there has been those of a frigid or the semi-tropical will become the more tropical, and moss and fern will grow. And these will begin in those periods in '58 to '98.   3976-15

These changes in the earth will come to pass, for the time and times and half times are at an end and there begin those periods for the re-adjustments. For how hath He given? "The righteous shall inherit the earth" (Psalms 37:29).   294-185

Q-In Revelation 21--What is the meaning of "a new heaven and a new earth: for the first heaven and the first earth were passed away; and there was no more sea"?
A-When the foundations of the earth are broken up by those very disturbances. Can the mind of man comprehend no desire to sin, no purpose but that the glory of the Son may be manifested in his life? Is this not a new heaven, a new earth?   281-37

Q-What is meant by Matthew 24:34, "This generation shall not pass till all these things be fulfilled"?
A-Those individual that were in hearing and in keeping with those things presented by the Master in that experience would be in the manifested form in the earth during the periods of fulfillment in the earth of the prophecies spoken of. Not in what is termed as three-score-and-ten years, but the experiences of those souls in the earth during those periods when there must come the completing or ful-filling of those things spoken of.   262-60

As has been oft given, Jupiter and Uranus influences in the affairs of the world appear strongest on or about October 15th to 20th--when there may be expected in the minds, the actions--not only of individuals but various quarters of the globe, destructive conditions as well as building. In the affairs of man many conditions will arise that will be, very, very strange to the world at present (1926)--in religion, in politics, in moral conditions, and in the attempt to curb or change such, see?   195-32

With those changes that will be wrought, Americanism--the ism--with the universal thought that is expressed and manifested in the brother-hood of man into group thought, as expressed by the Masonic Order, will be the eventual rule in the settlement of affairs in the world.
Not that the world is to become a Masonic Order, but the principles that are embraced in same will be the basis upon which the new order of peace is to be established in '44 and '45.   1152-11

When the day of the earth as earthy, is fulfilled in Him, this body--Edgar Cayce--**shall be** rejuvenated, shall be purged, shall be made free! **Then** they that in their earthly manners work, labor, here, there, will be --and **are**--directed, guided, as to the means, the manners, the ways that they may as individuals, as souls, be as a helpmeet, as an aid to **their** portion of the service towards the great brotherhood of man. 254-83

INDEX OF NAMES, SUBJECTS AND IDEAS

of a group mind, 381-382

Conception, 195, 339:
mental, physical and spiritual, 252-254
See Immaculate conception

Concubine, 401

Condemning:
others, 322, 365-366
self, 93, 99, 259, 367-368

Condiments, 296, 327:
See spices

Confucian thought, 227

Confusion, 45, 112-113, 146, 155, 255, 349, 362, 402, 439:
in other realms, 362

Conscience, 61, 65, 113-114, 140, 336:
is the judge, 114

Consciousness, 3, 12-13, 21, 39, 82, 110, 118, 120-121, 126, 128, 140, 158, 161-162, 180, 203, 222, 229, 328, 369, 424:
Cosmic, 16, 96, 126, 157-158, 166, 178, 228
first consciousness as an entity's begin-
-ning, 174, 230
multi-dimensional, 46, 143-144, 167, 381
other realms of, 120, 128, 139-141, 143-145, 157-159, 235, 348
permanent, 18
physical, 6, 11, 22, 94, 96-97, 112, 126-127, 157, 164, 180, 250
planes, steps, cycles or places of, 162
self-consciousness, 94, 250, 363
sensuous, 15-16, 102, 178, 254
subconsciousness, 15, 22, 80-82, 86, 93-94, 96, 99, 101-102, 127-128, 142, 178
subjugation of, 3, 5-7, 16, 80, 82, 249-250
superconsciousness, 7, 80-82, 85, 98, 101, 127, 141, 246
Universal, 19, 43, 57, 73, 116-117, 122, 128, 144, 152, 166, 225, 228-229, 250, 252, 339, 353, 363, 382
See Christ Consciousness
See Mind: subconscious
See Mind: superconscious

Consistency, 344, 356-357, 370

Constellations, 156, 176, 406:
See specific constellations

Constipation, 280

Constructiveness, 18, 28, 32, 39, 43, 45, 64, 88-89, 119, 166-167, 250, 261, 341, 344-

345, 349:
purposefulness, 9, 44, 65, 146, 162, 167, 328, 338, 344, 439

Contentment, 33, 48, 341-342, 355, 363:
discontent, 360

Cooking methods, 300-302:
baking, 300, 321
boiling, 220, 300-301, 308
broiling, 300, 308, 311
cooking in Patapar paper, 284, 300-301, 305
frying not advised, 293, 297, 300
roasting, 301, 308
steaming, 300-301

Cooking pots made of:
aluminum not advised, 288, 301-302
enameled ironware, 288, 301-302
glass, 288, 302
stainless steel, 301

Cooperation, spirit of, 120, 168, 252, 323, 344, 354

Coordinating:
bodily forces, 244, 261, 270, 344
self with God, 11, 119, 354
the literal, spiritual and metaphysical interpretation of scripture, 193
the triune entity, 21, 83, 119, 258, 341, 344

Copper, 56, 60, 400, 411, 422, 438

Cordilleras, 392

Corns, 283

Cornstarch, 304

Corn syrup, 304

Cortez, 432

Cotton, 435

Covetousness, 152, 346

Crank, 342

Creation, 185-187, 230, 359:
beginning of an entity's existence, 119, 174
in six days, 176
in the inner self, 105
last, 185
next, 175
of man, 50, 166, 175-178, 183, 193, 210, 402
of the soul, 165, 170, 178-179, 183, 195, 339, 346
of the universe, 175-176, 180
three creations, 177
See First Cause: in the beginning

Creative Force or Energy, 1, 9, 11, 13, 17, 25, 28, 53, 64-65, 84, 104, 172, 185, 249, 329,

apples (cooked), 297, 315-316, 319
artificially ripened, 297
avocados, 311
bananas, 293, 315
berries, 292, 311
blueberries, 315
cherries, 311
citrus, 293-294, 303, 315, 319
dates and figs, 315-316
dried, 315
grapefruit, 286, 293-294, 319
grapes, 315-316
lemons and limes, 293-295
oranges, 293-294, 315-316
peaches, 315-316, 318-319
pears, 292, 311, 316, 321
pineapples, 315, 319
prunes, 311, 316
raisins, 316
strawberries, 316
Fruit juices:
grape, 295, 315, 317
grapefruit, 295, 315, 317, 319
lemon, 286, 289, 293, 295, 319
lime, 295
orange, 282, 286, 295, 307, 315, 319
pineapple, 295, 319

Galilee, 217, 232, 390
Galileo, 250
Gallstones, 280-281
Ganglia, 270, 272
Gas(es), 1-2, 26, 52, 146, 175, 186, 234:
See Atlantean use of gases
Gastric juices, 254, 296, 310
Gastritis, 280
Gastroduodentitis, 281
Gauls, 238
Gelatin, 310, 314:
importance of, 311, 314
Knox gelatin and Jello, 314
Gemini, 74, 76, 156, 158-159
Gems, 59-60:
See specific gems
Genealogy, 141
Geniuses, 91, 141, 182:
gifted, 109, 152, 182, 329
talents, 369
Gentiles, 205, 226

Gentleness, 146, 225, 333, 345-346, 348, 354, 365:
speak gently, 346, 365
Geocentric, 143
Geological survey, 176, 371
Germany, 241, 444
Gestation, 248, 252, 257
Giants, 377, 394, 429
Gizeh, 395, 420-424:
ceremony at completion, 422-423
date regarding, 423
place for the initiates, 422
rebuilding of monuments, 420
See Great Pyramid
Glands, 58, 103-104, 201, 247-251, 255, 257, 269, 271, 282, 285, 292, 305, 308, 310, 314, 317:
endocrine, 247
food for, 317
glandular circulation, 282
glandular system, 151
higher gland centers, 204
seven centers, 70, 73, 163, 204, 251, 330
See specific glands
Glaucoma, 314
Globe, 405
Gluten, 307, 310-311
Gluttonousness, 128, 298
Glycerine, 276, 285
Glyco-Thymoline, 267-268, 274-275, 277-278, 284
Gnomes, 9, 14
Gnosticism, 192
Gobi, ancient, 182, 190, 391, 410, 435-438, 448:
advanced transportation, 436
ancient civilization, 435-438
basic philosophy, 436
City of Gold will be found, 436, 438
destruction of mighty forests, 235
euthanasia practiced, 436
explosives, 436
square gold coins used, 436-437
temple of gold, 410, 435, 438
God, 11, 13, 27-28, 39, 42, 51, 65, 85, 99, 111, 113, 159, 179, 231, 335, 354-355, 391:
as Love and Law, 30, 128, 194, 324, 329
as the Active Principle, 29, 51, 176
as the First Movement, 17, 25-27, 35, 51,